Palgrave Companions

Martin A. Coleman • Glenn Tiller
Editors

The Palgrave Companion to George Santayana's Scepticism and Animal Faith

palgrave
macmillan

Editors
Martin A. Coleman
Indiana University Indianapolis
Indianapolis, IN, USA

Glenn Tiller
Department of Philosophy
Texas A&M University – Corpus Christi
Corpus Christi, TX, USA

ISSN 3004-9172   ISSN 3004-9180   (electronic)
Palgrave Companions
ISBN 978-3-031-46366-2   ISBN 978-3-031-46367-9   (eBook)
https://doi.org/10.1007/978-3-031-46367-9

© The Editor(s) (if applicable) and The Author(s), under exclusive licence to Springer Nature Switzerland AG 2024

This work is subject to copyright. All rights are solely and exclusively licensed by the Publisher, whether the whole or part of the material is concerned, specifically the rights of translation, reprinting, reuse of illustrations, recitation, broadcasting, reproduction on microfilms or in any other physical way, and transmission or information storage and retrieval, electronic adaptation, computer software, or by similar or dissimilar methodology now known or hereafter developed.

The use of general descriptive names, registered names, trademarks, service marks, etc. in this publication does not imply, even in the absence of a specific statement, that such names are exempt from the relevant protective laws and regulations and therefore free for general use.

The publisher, the authors, and the editors are safe to assume that the advice and information in this book are believed to be true and accurate at the date of publication. Neither the publisher nor the authors or the editors give a warranty, expressed or implied, with respect to the material contained herein or for any errors or omissions that may have been made. The publisher remains neutral with regard to jurisdictional claims in published maps and institutional affiliations.

This Palgrave Macmillan imprint is published by the registered company Springer Nature Switzerland AG.
The registered company address is: Gewerbestrasse 11, 6330 Cham, Switzerland

Paper in this product is recyclable.

Standard Reference Bibliography

The following is a list of abbreviations and bibliographical references to Santayana's works and secondary source materials.

Primary Sources

BR — *The Birth of Reason & Other Essays*. Edited by Daniel Cory. New York and London: Columbia University Press, 1968.

COUS — *Character and Opinion in the United States: With Reminiscences of William James and Josiah Royce and Academic Life in America.* New York: Charles Scribner's Sons; London: Constable and Co. Ltd.; Toronto: McLeod, 1920. Volume XI of the critical edition of *The Works of George Santayana* (WGS).

CP — *The Complete Poems of George Santayana: A Critical Edition.* Edited by William G. Holzberger. Lewisburg, PA: Bucknell University Press; London: Associated University Presses, 1979.

DL — *Dialogues in Limbo*. London: Constable and Co. Ltd., 1925; New York: Charles Scribner's Sons, 1926. Volume XIV of the critical edition (WGS).

DP — *Dominations and Powers: Reflections on Liberty, Society, and Government*. New York: Charles Scribner's Sons; London: Constable and Co. Ltd., 1951. Volume XIX of the critical edition (WGS).

EGP — *Egotism in German Philosophy*. New York: Charles Scribner's Sons; London and Toronto: J. M. Dent & Sons Ltd., 1916. Volume X of the critical edition (WGS).

GTB — *The Genteel Tradition at Bay*. New York: Charles Scribner's Sons; London: "The Adelphi," 1931. Volume XVII of the critical edition (WGS).

HC — *A Hermit of Carmel and Other Poems*. New York: Charles Scribner's Sons, 1901; London: R. Brimley Johnson, 1902.

ICG	*The Idea of Christ in the Gospels; or, God in Man: A Critical Essay.* New York: Charles Scribner's Sons; Toronto: Saunders, 1946. Volume XVIII of the critical edition (WGS).
IPR	*Interpretations of Poetry and Religion.* New York: Charles Scribner's Sons; London: Black, 1900. Volume III of the critical edition (WGS), edited by William G. Holzberger and Herman J. Saatkamp Jr. Cambridge, MA: The MIT Press, 1989.
LP	*The Last Puritan: A Memoir in the Form of a Novel.* London: Constable and Co. Ltd., 1935; New York: Charles Scribner's Sons, 1936. Volume IV of the critical edition (WGS), edited by William G. Holzberger and Herman J. Saatkamp Jr. Cambridge, MA: The MIT Press, 1994.
LGS	*The Letters of George Santayana.* Volume V (in eight books) of the critical edition (WGS), edited by William G. Holzberger, Herman J. Saatkamp Jr., and Marianne S. Wokeck. Cambridge, MA: The MIT Press, 2000–2008. (Citations in the notes refer to book and page number; i.e., LGS, 8:150 is page 150 of Book Eight.)
LR	*The Life of Reason: or, the Phases of Human Progress.* Five volumes. New York: Charles Scribner's Sons; London: Constable and Co. Ltd., 1905–6. Volume VII of the critical edition (WGS), edited by Martin Coleman and Marianne Wokeck. Cambridge, MA: The MIT Press.
LR1	*Introduction and Reason in Common Sense.* Book 1, 1905 (2011).
LR2	*Reason in Society.* Book 2, 1905 (2013).
LR3	*Reason in Religion.* Book 3, 1905 (2014).
LR4	*Reason in Art.* Book 4, 1905 (2015).
LR5	*Reason in Science.* Book 5, 1906 (2016).
LE	*Little Essays: Drawn From the Writings of George Santayana by Logan Pearsall Smith, With the Collaboration of the Author.* New York: Charles Scribner's Sons; London: Constable and Co. Ltd., 1920.
LUC	*Lucifer: A Theological Tragedy.* Chicago and New York: Herbert S. Stone, 1899.
LHT	Revised second edition published as *Lucifer, or the Heavenly Truce: A Theological Tragedy.* Cambridge, MA: Dunster House, 1924.
MARG	*George Santayana's Marginalia: A Critical Selection.* Volume VI (in two books) of the critical edition (WGS), edited by John McCormick. Cambridge, MA: The MIT Press, 2011.
OB	*Obiter Scripta: Lectures, Essays and Reviews.* Edited by Justus Buchler and Benjamin Schwartz. New York: Charles Scribner's Sons; London: Constable and Co. Ltd., 1936.
PP	*Persons and Places: Fragments of Autobiography.* Volume I of the critical edition (WGS), edited by William G. Holzberger and Herman J. Saatkamp Jr. Cambridge, MA: The MIT Press, 1986.
PP1	*Persons and Places: The Background of My Life.* New York: Charles Scribner's Sons; London: Constable and Co. Ltd., 1944.

PP2	*The Middle Span.* New York: Charles Scribner's Sons, 1945; London: Constable and Co. Ltd., 1947.
PP3	*My Host the World.* New York: Charles Scribner's Sons; London: Cresset Press, 1953.
POML	*Physical Order and Moral Liberty.* Edited by John Lachs. Nashville, TN: Vanderbilt University Press, 1969.
PSL	*Platonism and the Spiritual Life.* New York: Charles Scribner's Sons; London: Constable and Co. Ltd., 1927. Volume XV of the critical edition (WGS).
PSA	*Poems: Selected by the Author and Revised.* London: Constable and Co. Ltd., 1922; New York: Charles Scribner's Sons, 1923.
PT	*The Poet's Testament: Poems and Two Plays.* New York: Charles Scribner's Sons, 1953.
RB	*Realms of Being.* Four volumes. New York: Charles Scribner's Sons; London: Constable and Co. Ltd., 1927–40. Volume XVI of the critical edition (WGS).
RE	*The Realm of Essence: Book First of Realms of Being,* 1927.
RM	*The Realm of Matter: Book Second of Realms of Being,* 1930.
RT	*The Realm of Truth: Book Third of Realms of Being,* 1938.
RS	*The Realm of Spirit: Book Fourth of Realms of Being,* 1940.
RB1	*Realms of Being.* One-volume edition, with a new introduction by the author. New York: Charles Scribner's Sons, 1942.
SAF	*Scepticism and Animal Faith: Introduction to a System of Philosophy.* New York: Charles Scribner's Sons; London: Constable and Co. Ltd., 1923. Facsimile reprint, New York: Dover, 1955. Forthcoming volume XIII of the critical edition (WGS).
SB	*The Sense of Beauty: Being the Outlines of Aesthetic Theory.* New York: Charles Scribner's Sons; London: A. and C. Black, 1896. Volume II of the critical edition (WGS), edited by William G. Holzberger and Herman J. Saatkamp Jr. Cambridge, MA: The MIT Press, 1988.
SE	*Soliloquies in England and Later Soliloquies.* New York: Charles Scribner's Sons; London: Constable and Co. Ltd., 1922. Volume XII of the critical edition (WGS).
SOV	*Sonnets and Other Verses.* Cambridge and Chicago: Stone and Kimball, 1894.
STTMP	*Some Turns of Thought in Modern Philosophy: Five Essays.* New York: Charles Scribner's Sons; Cambridge: Cambridge University Press, 1933. Volume XVII of the critical edition (WGS).
TPP	*Three Philosophical Poets: Lucretius, Dante, and Goethe.* Cambridge, MA: Harvard University Press; London: Oxford University Press, 1910. Volume VIII of the critical edition (WGS), edited by Kellie Dawson and David E. Spiech. Cambridge, MA: The MIT Press, 2019.

WD   *Winds of Doctrine: Studies in Contemporary Opinion.* New York: Charles Scribner's Sons; London: J. M. Dent & Sons Ltd., 1913. Volume IX of the critical edition (WGS), edited by David E. Spiech, Martin A. Coleman, and Faedra Lazar Weiss. Cambridge, MA: The MIT Press, 2023.

SECONDARY SOURCES

WAGS   Arnett, Willard. *George Santayana.* New York: Washington Square Press, 1968.
LY   Cory, Daniel. *Santayana: The Later Years: A Portrait with Letters.* New York: George Braziller, 1963.
UAS   Flamm, Matthew Caleb, and Krzysztof Piotr Skowroński, eds. *Under Any Sky: Contemporary Readings of George Santayana.* Newcastle upon Tyne, United Kingdom: Cambridge Scholars Publishing, 2007.
AFSL   Lachs, John, ed. *Animal Faith and Spiritual Life.* New York: Appleton-Century-Crofts, 1967.
JLGS   Lachs, John. *George Santayana.* Boston: Twayne Publishers, 1988.
OnS   Lachs, John. *On Santayana.* Belmont, CA; London: Wadsworth, 2001.
SPSL   Levinson, Henry S. *Santayana, Pragmatism, and the Spiritual Life.* Chapel Hill: University of North Carolina Press, 1992.
GSB   McCormick, John. *George Santayana: A Biography.* New York: Alfred A. Knopf, 1987.
OIS   *Overheard in Seville: Bulletin of the Santayana Society.* Edited by The George Santayana Society. https://www.ulib.iupui.edu/digitalcollections/Santayana.
PGS   Schilpp, Paul Arthur, ed. *The Philosophy of George Santayana.* Volume II of *The Library of Living Philosophers.* Evanston: Northwestern University Press, 1940; second edition, New York: Tudor, 1951.
TRS   Singer, Beth. *The Rational Society: A Critical Study of Santayana's Thought.* Cleveland, OH: Press of Case Western Reserve University, 1970.
SAEP   Sprigge, Timothy L. *S. Santayana.* London and Boston: Routledge, 1995.
LITE   Woodward, Anthony. *Living in the Eternal: A Study of George Santayana.* Nashville, TN: Vanderbilt University Press, 1988.

Acknowledgments and Dedication

We would like to thank David E. Spiech, assistant editor and textual editor of the Santayana Edition at Indiana University, Indianapolis, for his invaluable editorial work on this project; and Faedra Weiss, assistant editor of the Santayana Edition at Indiana University, Indianapolis, for editorial assistance in preparation of this book and, in particular, her historical research into the composition and publication of *Scepticism and Animal Faith*, which greatly enhanced the introduction to this book.

This book is dedicated to the memory of Kris Frost, who began with the Santayana Edition as an editorial assistant in 1986 and retired in 2016 as associate editor and assistant director. Her conscientious editing was extraordinary, and her commitment to *The Works of George Santayana* ensured organizational continuity and enduring personal relationships with Santayana scholars.

Contents

Introduction   1
Martin A. Coleman and Glenn Tiller

Part I   Scepticism and Animal Faith   9

Santayana: Philosopher for the Twenty-First Century   11
Herman J. Saatkamp Jr

The Last Sceptic: Santayana, Descartes, and the External World   33
Douglas McDermid

Laying Siege to the Truth: Santayana's Discourse on Method   57
Diana B. Heney

Scepticism, Anti-scepticism, and Santayana's Singularity   73
Daniel Pinkas

Knowledge as a Leap of Faith   95
Jessica Wahman

Animal Faith and Its Object   109
John J. Stuhr

Natural Knowledge and Transcendental Criticism in *Scepticism and Animal Faith*   125
Paul Forster

Santayana's Naturalism at the Junction of Epistemology and
Ontology   149
Ángel M. Faerna

Reconstruction from Ultimate Scepticism   163
Angus Kerr-Lawson

Part II   Ontology and Spirit   175

The Centrality of the Imagination in *Scepticism and Animal Faith* 177
Richard Marc Rubin

Spiritual Exercises and Animal Faith   193
Martin A. Coleman

The Cries of Spirit: Santayana in Dialogue with Andrey Platonov   219
Matthew Caleb Flamm

Fumbling Toward the Animal in "Animal Faith"   241
Charles Padrón

A Tension at the Center of Santayana's Philosophy   257
Michael Hodges

Truth and Ontology   273
Glenn Tiller

Part III   Philosophical Relations   291

On Gnats and Barnacles, or Some Similarities Between
Santayana's Idea of Change and Ancient Greek Thought   293
Andrés Tutor de Ureta

The Ideal of a Philosophic Redemption: Baruch Spinoza's Place
in Western Philosophy and in Santayana's Thought   309
Lydia Amir

G. Santayana (*Scepticism and Animal Faith*, 1923) and E. Husserl
(*Cartesianische Meditationen*, 1929), Readers of R. Descartes   325
Daniel Moreno

Hermes as an Interpreter and the Guide to Hades: Re-reading "The Lord Chandos Letter" with Reference to Santayana's *Scepticism and Animal Faith*   341
Katarzyna Kremplewska

The Conservative Disposition in Santayana's Philosophy   373
Michael Brodrick

Index   389

Notes on Contributors

Lydia Amir is a French-Israeli Associate Professor of Philosophy, visiting professor in the Department of Philosophy at Tufts University, Boston, USA. She has published articles and essays in ethics and the practice of philosophy, authored *Humor and the Good Life in Modern Philosophy: Shaftesbury, Hamann, Kierkegaard*, and co-edited *Practicing Philosophy*.

Michael Brodrick is a philosopher with the Institute for Humane Studies at George Mason University. Previously, he taught philosophy at Vanderbilt University, Indiana University Purdue University Indianapolis, Miami University of Ohio, and Arkansas Tech University. He is the author of *The Ethics of Detachment in Santayana's Philosophy*.

Martin A. Coleman is director and editor of the Santayana Edition. He is Associate Professor of Philosophy and Adjunct Associate Professor of American Studies at Indiana University, Indianapolis. He has edited books on or by George Santayana and published articles on figures in American philosophy and literature.

Andrés Tutor de Ureta is assistant professor at the University of Tsukuba, Japan, where he teaches Spanish language and culture and coordinates the Department of Publicity. A former lecturer in Spain and Indonesia, he has carried out research stays in Germany and the United States. His research interests lie within contemporary political thought, where he deals with notions such as freedom, value pluralism, and rationality.

Ángel M. Faerna is Professor of Philosophy at the Universidad de Castilla-La Mancha (Spain). His research and publications focus on pragmatism, American philosophy, and epistemology. He translated into Spanish *Scepticism and Animal Faith* and Dewey's *Logic: The Theory of Inquiry*.

Matthew Caleb Flamm is Professor of Philosophy at Rockford University. He has written on the thought of Santayana in relation to a variety of topics, including Santayana's critique of select German philosophers (Schopenhauer,

Hegel, and Nietzsche) and select American contemporaries of Santayana (Dewey and Royce).

Paul Forster is Professor of Philosophy at the University of Ottawa, Canada. He is the author of *Peirce and the Threat of Nominalism*. He has published papers on pragmatism, analytic philosophy and their interconnections and is currently writing a book about Dewey and Russell. He is also author of "Why Santayana and Dewey Cannot Agree About Philosophy," "What Grounds the Categories? Peirce and Santayana," and the introduction to the critical edition of *Winds of Doctrine*.

Diana B. Heney is Assistant Professor of Philosophy at Vanderbilt University. She first read *Scepticism and Animal Faith* in 2004, which sparked an enduring interest in Santayana. Her broader research interests are in ethics, well-being, and American pragmatism.

Michael Hodges is Professor of Philosophy at Vanderbilt, where he has taught for over 50 years. He works in the areas of American Philosophy with special emphasis on James and Santayana. In 2000 he coauthored *Thinking in the Ruins—Wittgenstein and Santayana on Contingency* with John Lachs. He has also published a number of papers on Santayana, including "The Realm of Truth in Santayana" in *Santayana at 150: International Interpretations*.

Angus Kerr-Lawson (1932–2011) was professor in the Department of Pure Mathematics at the University of Waterloo (Canada), where he taught from 1956 to 1998. Along with Herman J. Saatkamp Jr., he was co-editor of *Overheard in Seville* (1983–1997) and he was the journal's general editor from 1998 to 2010.

Katarzyna Kremplewska is assistant professor in the Institute of Philosophy and Sociology, Polish Academy of Sciences. She has authored articles in English and Polish, as well as two monographs: *Life as Insinuation: George Santayana's Hermeneutics of Finite Life and Human Self* and *George Santayana's Political Hermeneutics*.

Douglas McDermid is Professor of Philosophy at Trent University (Canada), where he has taught since 2002. He is the author of two books: *The Varieties of Pragmatism* and *The Rise and Fall of Scottish Common Sense Realism*.

Daniel Moreno teaches philosophy at the IES Miguel Servet (Zaragoza, Spain) and belongs, together with José Beltrán, to the staff for *Limbo: Boletín internacional de estudios sobre Santayana*. He has published numerous articles on Santayana both in Spain and the USA. He has edited *El egotismo en la filosofía alemana*, and, together with José Beltrán, *Pequeños ensayos sobre religión*, and has translated into Spanish *Platonism and the Spiritual Life*, *Soliloquies in England*, *Essays on History of Philosophy*, and *Ensayos filosóficos*. His book *Santayana filósofo: La filosofía como forma de vida* has been translated into

English by Charles Padrón and published as *Santayana the Philosopher: Philosophy as a Form of Life*.

Charles Padrón is a scholar in Gran Canaria, Spain. He has published articles and essays on Santayana and edited and translated books related to Santayana's life and thought.

Daniel Pinkas is honorary professor at Haute École d'Art et de Design de Genève (HEAD–Geneva). He has taught and written on the philosophy of mind, the philosophy of art, visual perception, digital art and design, and the philosophy of George Santayana. He is the author of *La Matérialité de l'esprit*, and *Santayana et l'Amérique du bon ton,* and the editor of *Recently Discovered Letters of George Santayana*. He has published numerous articles, particularly on Santayana, the philosophy of mind, and the aesthetics of digital art forms.

Richard Marc Rubin is in his sixth year as president of the George Santayana Society and editor of its bulletin, *Overheard in Seville*. He has published numerous philosophic articles, many on Santayana. He has taught at Washington University in St Louis, where he received his PhD. He also has an MA (Drama) from New York University and an AB (Humanities) from the University of Chicago.

Herman J. Saatkamp Jr is retired. His scholarship focuses on Santayana, American philosophy, and medical genetics. He was the founding editor of *The Works of George Santayana*, and he established the George Santayana Society and *Overheard in Seville: Bulletin of the Santayana Society*. He has edited 48 books and authored 59 articles. He is the author of *A Life of Scholarship with Santayana*, edited by Charles Padrón and Krzysztof Piotr Skowroński.

John J. Stuhr is Arts and Sciences Distinguished Professor of Philosophy and American Studies at Emory University. He received his BA from Carleton College and his MA and PhD from Vanderbilt University. In addition to many scholarly articles and book chapters, he is the author or editor of over a dozen books, including: *Pragmatic Fashions: Pluralism, Democracy, Relativism, and the Absurd*; *Philosophy and Human Flourishing*; *100 Years of Pragmatism: William James's Revolutionary Philosophy*; *Pragmatism and Postmodernism*; *Genealogical Pragmatism: Philosophy, Experience, and Community*; and *John Dewey*. He is the founding director of the American Philosophies Forum, editor of the *Journal of Speculative Philosophy*, general editor of the *American Philosophy* series at Indiana University Press, and past president of the Society for the Advancement of American Philosophy.

Glenn Tiller is Professor of Philosophy at Texas A&M University-Corpus Christi. His research and publications focus on American Philosophy, especially the philosophies of Charles Peirce and George Santayana. He is past president of the George Santayana Society and past editor of *Overheard in Seville: Bulletin of the Santayana Society*.

Jessica Wahman is Senior Lecturer and Director of Undergraduate Studies at Emory University. She is the author of *Narrative Naturalism: An Alternative Framework for Philosophy of Mind*. She is also co-editor of and contributor to *Cosmopolitanism and Place*. She has published several essays on Santayana's work, particularly with regard to his concept of the psyche, truth, the radicality of pragmatism, and theater as a kind of philosophical expression.

Introduction

Martin A. Coleman and Glenn Tiller

George Santayana (1863–1952) believed that a philosophy of orthodox common sense exists beneath all major systems of philosophy and religion. This philosophy is a form of naturalism. It begins with the assumption that we are animals generated by and sustained for a time within a vast impersonal physical cosmos that is the sole source of power. Although rational argumentation cannot justify this assumption, our actions repeatedly confirm it, and we could not live without it. Another central feature of Santayana's philosophy of naturalism is that we are conscious as well as active animals. The inner light of awareness, or what he calls "spirit," arises by the activities of the physical body but is itself powerless. Our experience of the world is rendered in the morally charged signs of human cognition, and these may be aesthetically appreciated for their own sake in imagination, granting us the possibility of contemplative respite from the exigencies of life. Santayana's philosophy is atheistic and holds out no religious hope of redemption. Still, it is celebratory of the life of consciousness and offers a path toward naturalistic spirituality.

Santayana articulated his system of philosophy in his four-volume magnum opus *Realms of Being* (*RB*), comprising *The Realm of Essence* (1927), *The Realm of Matter* (1930), *The Realm of Truth* (1938), and *The Realm of Spirit*

M. A. Coleman (✉)
Indiana University Indianapolis, Indianapolis, IN, USA
e-mail: martcole@iupui.edu

G. Tiller
Department of Philosophy, Texas A&M University-Corpus Christi, Corpus Christi, TX, USA
e-mail: glenn.tiller@tamucc.edu

© The Author(s), under exclusive license to Springer Nature Switzerland AG 2024
M. A. Coleman, G. Tiller (eds.), *The Palgrave Companion to George Santayana's Scepticism and Animal Faith*, Palgrave Companions,
https://doi.org/10.1007/978-3-031-46367-9_1

(1940). According to him, *Scepticism and Animal Faith* (*SAF*), published in 1923, is "a critical introduction" (*SAF*, v) to his system. Ostensibly a work in foundationalist epistemology, he described *SAF* as a "*reductio ad absurdum* of modern paradoxes" (*RB*, xxv) intended to reconstruct, on a foundation of scepticism[1] and natural reason, the fundamental convictions of common sense. One of his main motivations for writing *SAF* was his belief that we live in an age of "intellectual insurrection" (*PGS*, 534) so that a "philosopher to-day would be ridiculous and negligible who had not strained his dogmas through the utmost rigours of scepticism" (*SAF*, 9). He undertook this task by adopting Descartes's method of doubt and driving scepticism to its logical conclusion, which, in his analysis, is the suspension of all belief. Since scepticism demonstrates that belief and knowledge rest on ungrounded presuppositions, they are restored only through an instinctive act of animal faith. For Santayana, scepticism liberates spirit from unnecessary entanglements and thereby prepares the way for a forthright statement of the tenets of animal faith.

Santayana stated his initial plan for what would become *Scepticism and Animal Faith* in a May 1911 letter to his sister Susana: "I am writing a brand new system of philosophy to be called 'Three realms of Being'—not the mineral vegetable and animal, but something far more metaphysical, namely Essence, Matter, and Consciousness. It will not be a long book, but very technical" (*LGS*, 2:37). He reported progress on the book over the next few years. In September 1913, he wrote to B. A. G. Fuller that since arriving in Oxford, England, in August, he had "been very industrious. The three realms of being have increased to four [with the addition of the realm of truth], and the work of composition and revision has advanced greatly" (*LGS*, 2:142). The next month, he expressed the hope of finishing the book that winter (*LGS*, 2:146). But, in fact, much would happen before the work was completed: the First World War (28 July 1914–11 November 1918) would enforce Santayana's residence in England, he would publish six other books before *SAF*, and his plan of work on the realms would expand beyond one book.

This long interval between initial work and publication of *SAF* was not without substantial work on the book, and Santayana published two essays of great significance for *SAF*. In August 1918, Santayana published the article "Literal and Symbolic Knowledge" (Santayana 1918), which presented "a more mature version of our theory" (*LGS*, 2:281); and in 1920, after several drafts and many delays, he published "Three Proofs of Realism" (Santayana 1920). Santayana revised or copied text from both essays as he worked on what would become *SAF*.

More than ten years after sharing plans with Susana for *Realms of Being*, Santayana wrote to Constable, his UK publisher, in September 1922 that he had completed a manuscript that "is the first volume of my system of

---

[1] Santayana habitually used the British spellings of "sceptic" and "scepticism," for example, in the title of his book. To be consistent with Santayana's preferences, the British spellings of "sceptic" and "scepticism" are used throughout the volume.

philosophy, which I have had in hand for many years. I propose that it be published separately under the title Scepticism and Animal Faith. A second volume, entitled Realms of Being will complete the work, and I hope to have it ready in a year or two" (*LGS*, 3:86–87). Over the next two decades, the proposed second volume would become four books.

In October 1922, Santayana sent the manuscript to Constable, providing three different titles and asking for the publisher's preference (*LGS*, 3:88):

1. *Scepticism and Animal Faith: An Introduction to Realms of Being*
2. *A System of Philosophy; Part First: Scepticism and Animal Faith*
3. *Scepticism and Animal Faith: Part First of a System of Philosophy*

When Santayana submitted a signed contract to Constable in November 1922, they had agreed that the title would be *Scepticism and Animal Faith*. For a subtitle Santayana suggested "Introduction to a System of Philosophy" (*LGS*, 3:92), which the publisher confirmed the following week (*LGS*, 3:95). Santayana reviewed page proofs in January 1923 and completed an index for the book by the end of the month (*LGS*, 3: 118, 122). He saw final proofs in February (*LGS*, 3:125), but there was some further back-and-forth in March about final corrections. On 27 May 1923, Santayana received, while in Paris, six copies of *SAF*.

The book was published in the United States by Charles Scribner's Sons using pages printed by Constable. The first edition was printed four times: 1923, 1924, 1929, and 1936. Scribner's sold the book for $3.50, which at the time would have purchased at least five popular novels.

In 1936, Scribner's began publishing a limited-edition, multi-volume set of Santayana's works known as the Triton Edition.[2] *SAF* appeared in Volume XIII, published in 1937. The book was reset and included the corrections made in the 1936 printing of the first edition and a few additional corrections.

In 1941, Scribner's proposed a one-volume edition of the four books of *Realms of Being*. There was a question about including *SAF* in this omnibus edition, and Santayana reasoned that the four books of *Realms* "would be … more in one key" than if *SAF* were included (*LGS*, 7:6). He wrote, "Better leave the Realms to speak for themselves, like some entirely independent or ancient work, and leave Scepticism and the Apologia[3] to serve as technical introductions, to be studied separately, by those who wish to criticize my philosophical position as a whole" (*LGS*, 7:7). The 900-page *Realms of Being*

---

[2] In a letter to his publisher, Santayana explained that "what suggested the word to me is that my windows in Rome look down on the Fontana del Tritone and Via del Tritone. The Triton, by Bernini, is well known, and might be reproduced for a frontispiece or paper-cover. Then there is the association with Wordsworth's sonnet: 'a pagan suckled in a creed outworn' and 'hear old Triton blow his wreathèd horn'" (*LGS*, 5:351).

[3] George Santayana. 1940. "Apologia Pro Mente Sua." In *The Philosophy of George Santayana*, vol. II of *The Library of Living Philosophers*, ed. Paul Arthur Schilpp. Evanston and Chicago: Northwestern University, 495–605.

appeared in 1942 with a new introduction that described *SAF* as "expressly written to introduce *Realms of Being*," adding that the "earlier book was essentially more sophisticated than the later volumes" (*RB*, xxv).

Santayana was not a philosopher who longed for literary fame or professional influence. In 1950, he wrote in a letter to the editor of an anthology of his work, "I never wished to be a professional or public man. Nor do I want disciples: I want only a few sympathetic friends, and I have them" (*LGS*, 8:265). It is in this spirit we present this collection of chapters. The authors are sympathetic friends and inquirers into the rich intricacies of Santayana's philosophy rather than upholders of a unitary doctrine. While they are all intimately familiar with his work and find it enormously rewarding for its many philosophical insights and literary power of expression, there is neither pretension of complete agreement with Santayana's philosophy nor one accepted interpretation of its significance.

For Santayana, fundamental interpretive disagreements and criticisms are expected in philosophy. The critic must inevitably make assumptions and admit principles, even if tacitly, which are the basis for criticism. These assumptions and principles will vary with natural disposition, personal interest, and individual experience. Insofar as different interpretations and criticisms are sincere and not based on misunderstanding, they are valid, not in the sense of refutation, but by making explicit the assumptions and principles to which the critic is committed.

Santayana's pluralism about final philosophies makes the notion of a "companion"—knowledgeable, sympathetic, and encouraging of further inquiry—especially pertinent to his work. The chapters in this volume do not address all the philosophical ideas of *SAF*, nor do they address all the elements of Santayana's philosophy expressed in *SAF*. They aim to cast light on some of the central ideas of *SAF* and offer interpretations—sometimes rival interpretations—that help elucidate his philosophy. Ideally, these companion chapters will assist the reader in more fully reflecting on Santayana's philosophy.

The chapters in the volume are organized under three general sections. The chapters in the first section, "Scepticism and Animal Faith," discuss Santayana's radical scepticism and his reconstruction of knowledge. *Herman J. Saatkamp Jr.* contextualizes Santayana biographically and culturally and gives an account of his philosophical development leading to *SAF* and his mature philosophy of the realms of being. Saatkamp then explores the significance of Santayana's philosophy for the twenty-first century and in particular for philosophical understanding of developments in neuroscience and for the relation of philosophy and literature. *Douglas McDermid*'s contribution clarifies the nature of Santayana's scepticism by examining his response to the traditional sceptical problem of the external world. McDermid explains in what sense we can regard Santayana as a sceptic and in what sense Santayana is a critic of the sceptical method promulgated by Descartes. *Diana B. Heney*'s chapter considers *SAF* alongside the work of Descartes, first in terms of structure, style, and substance and then in terms of method and purpose. She contrasts Cartesian and

Santayanan scepticism, concluding that Descartes is not a foil but an inspiration for Santayana in attempting to order his mind as a sort of personal improvement. *Daniel Pinkas* discusses Santayana's treatment of scepticism in relation to Descartes and Hume, as well as twentieth-century philosophers, such as Wittgenstein, Moore, and Strawson. He argues for the singularity of Santayana's approach to scepticism while showing some of the commonalities he shares with other sceptical philosophers. *Jessica Wahman* argues that Santayana's account of knowledge as a leap of faith is a unique, important, and underappreciated contribution to epistemology. She explains that Santayana's account of animal faith does not so much express a limitation of knowledge as a characterization of what it actually achieves: a faithful and practical transition of the mind from thoughts to the natural things that undergird them. *John J. Stuhr* challenges Santayana's claim that animal life inevitably requires the "posit" of an external and independent environment and shows this claim is both mistaken and a move from empirical science to metaphysics. Stuhr concludes by suggesting this move originates in both a quest for permanence and a plea for humility. *Paul Forster* explains how Santayana squares his commitment to naturalism with his reliance on methods of transcendental criticism. Rather than view naturalism and transcendental criticism as antagonistic, Santayana reconciles them in an account of human knowledge that he considers more comprehensive than either is alone. *Ángel M. Faerna* inquires into the ways in which Santayana's philosophy is part of the tradition of philosophical naturalism. He finds two strains of naturalism at play in Santayana's system, namely, epistemological naturalism and ontological naturalism, and he helps illuminate Santayana's philosophy by probing some of the tensions between these two strains. In a posthumous chapter, *Angus Kerr-Lawson* discusses the reconstruction of knowledge Santayana undertakes in the second half of *SAF*. Kerr-Lawson explains Santayana's general approach to the reconstruction, his treatment of *a priori* knowledge, factual knowledge, and the traditional definition of knowledge as justified true belief.

The chapters in the second section, "Ontology and Spirit," take up a variety of themes pertaining to Santayana's categorial ontology, his naturalism, and the various roles of spirit in his philosophy. *Richard Marc Rubin* examines the central role of the imagination in Santayana's life and works. He shows how the imagination is fundamental to Santayana's sceptical inquiry in *SAF* and a necessary condition for knowledge about the material world. *Martin A. Coleman* reads *SAF*, following Levinson, as a book of spiritual exercises in the service of abnormal sanity. He examines three distinct exercises in *SAF*—scepticism, pure intuition, and an inquiry into self that relies on animal faith—and different possible ways for practicing these exercises. The spiritual life is a dominant theme in Santayana's philosophy. Putting Santayana's philosophy in dialogue with the novella *Soul (Dzhan)* by Andrey Platonov, *Matthew Caleb Flamm* examines the various ways Santayana associates crying with a materialist conception of the spiritual life. *Charles Padrón*'s chapter focuses our attention on the *animality* in *SAF*. He shows how the fact that we are descended from other animals with similar capacities is central to both Santayana's earlier and later philosophy and how our animality plays a pivotal role in Santayana's treatment of scepticism. *Michael Hodges* explores Santayana's doctrine of matter. Interpreting the realm of matter as the irrational, ineffable counterpart to the realm of essence, he elucidates the function and profound moral significance of materialism in Santayana's system of philosophy. Truth is one of Santayana's realms of being introduced in *SAF*. *Glenn Tiller* considers how the realm of truth is situated in Santayana's ontology. He notes some of the defining features of ontological truth and differentiates it from Santayana's account of true judgment.

Throughout his career, Santayana never abandoned the ideals of being a student of philosophy, and he drew much inspiration from philosophy's history and his contemporaries. The chapters in the third and final section of the book, "Philosophical Relations," discuss how many of the leading ideas of *SAF* connect and contrast with the ideas of some major historical philosophical and literary figures. *Andrés Tutor de Ureta* regards Santayana's realm of matter— which is in flux, as Heraclitus claimed—and his realm of essence—which is unchanging, as Parmenides maintained—as resolving problems for knowledge presented by change and permanence. Zeno's paradox of Achilles and the tortoise, in demonstrating how a finite continuum can be infinitely divided into discrete parts, suggests how ever-changing matter can be known symbolically by intuition of essences. With the benefit of long and close acquaintance with Spinoza's work, *Lydia Amir* investigates Santayana's explicit statements on Spinoza in *SAF*. The chapter answers the question of how Santayana can acknowledge Spinoza as "his master" and "hero" while systematically rejecting Spinoza's philosophy. Santayana believed he had found an ally regarding his doctrine of essence in the philosophy of Husserl; and *Daniel Moreno* reveals the parallels and differences between Santayana's and Husserl's philosophies, instructively bringing each thinker's ideas into sharper relief. *Katarzyna Kremplewska* discusses how Santayana's engagement with radical scepticism has a cross-disciplinary import and can be seen as a response to some of the intellectual and moral concerns prominent in the literature of the first half of the twentieth century. In particular, she employs Santayana's analysis of scepticism as the basis for an interpretive philosophical re-reading of Hugo von Hofmannsthal's "The Lord Chandos Letter." *Michael Brodrick* portrays Santayana as a conservative in behavior, thinking, and feeling, if not in creed. With his close reading of *SAF* and bearing in mind the ontology of *RB*, Brodrick demonstrates how *SAF* provides a philosophy of human imperfection and limits, yet supports a conservative vision of human flourishing.

References

Santayana, George. 1918. Literal and Symbolic Knowledge. *The Journal of Philosophy, Psychology and Scientific Methods* 15 (16): 421–444.

———. 1920. Three Proofs of Realism. In *Essays in Critical Realism: A Co-Operative Study of the Problem of Knowledge*, 163–186. London: Macmillan.

———. 1940. Apologia Pro Mente Sua. In *The Philosophy of George Santayana*, The Library of Living Philosophers, ed. Paul Arthur Schilpp, vol. II, 495–605. Evanston and Chicago: Northwestern University.

———. 2001–2008. *The Letters of George Santayana*, Books 1–8, The Works of George Santayana, eds. William G. Holzberger and Herman J. Saatkamp, Jr., vol. V. Cambridge, MA: The MIT Press. Cited as "*LGS*, n:m"—to book n, page m.

PART I

Scepticism and Animal Faith

Santayana: Philosopher for the Twenty-First Century

Herman J. Saatkamp Jr

On the critical edition dust jacket of *Persons and Places*, Hilary Putnam writes:

> Santayana was a towering figure in the great period of American philosophy, the period of the great department at Harvard, with William James, Santayana, and Royce. If there has been less attention paid to Santayana's philosophy than to that of Royce or Peirce, this is in large part because his philosophical mood and philosophical intuitions were actually ahead of his time. In many ways he anticipated some of the dominant trends in American philosophy of the present period. (*PP* [1986], dust jacket)

How is it possible for a person to foresee major trends in philosophy a century ahead of their time? Even more interesting, how is it possible for a philosopher to anticipate trends outside of philosophy, particularly in the neurosciences, that a century later confirm his views on consciousness, its objects, and its relationship with our brain? Santayana did just that. And now there is a revival of interest in his mature philosophical work, beginning with *Scepticism and Animal Faith: An Introduction to a System of Philosophy* (1923; cited as *SAF*) and its prelude to his four books on realms of being: essence, matter, truth, and spirit (*RE, RM, RT, RS*). To understand how this came about, one needs to have a sense of Santayana's stature in philosophy in the first half of the twentieth century, his Spanish heritage and his decision to leave

H. J. Saatkamp Jr (✉)
Santayana Edition, Indianapolis, IN, USA

© The Author(s), under exclusive license to Springer Nature Switzerland AG 2024
M. A. Coleman, G. Tiller (eds.), *The Palgrave Companion to George Santayana's Scepticism and Animal Faith*, Palgrave Companions, https://doi.org/10.1007/978-3-031-46367-9_2

his professorship at Harvard in 1912 at the age of forty-eight, and his philosophical transformation that led to his being a naturalist.

Santayana's Stature in the Twentieth Century

Santayana's prominence in the first half of the twentieth century began with his publications as a faculty member at Harvard. These included his poetry and a book on aesthetics in 1896, *The Sense of Beauty* (SB 1896, 1988). He gained recognition in 1905–1906 with his five-volume *The Life of Reason* (LR 1905a, 1905b, 1905c, 1905d, 1905e) (LR 2011, 2013, 2014, 2015, 2016). But his reputation and stature grew considerably after he retired from Harvard at the age of forty-eight. Through his publications after 1912, he became a renowned figure in philosophy and literature. Harvard tried to bring him back as early as 1918. In 1927 he was awarded the Gold Medal of the Royal Society of Literature in London, and in 1929 he was offered one of Harvard's most distinguished chairs, the Norton Chair of Poetry. In April 1931, he was offered a position at Brown University, and at the end of that year he received another invitation from Harvard to occupy for a term a new honorary post as the William James Lecturer in Philosophy, in which Dewey had preceded him as the first lecturer. He declined all offers (McCormick 1987, 301–302). Santayana appeared on the cover of *Time* (3 February 1936) in conjunction with his novel *The Last Puritan* (LP 1936, 1994) which, along with his autobiography *Persons and Places* (PP 1944, 1986), was a Book-of-the-Month Club bestseller in the U.S. These books were translated into many languages in Europe and Asia, as were many of his major philosophical works.

Neither popularity nor a return to the U.S. were sought by Santayana, and he was pleasantly surprised by the successes of his publications and European lectures. During his previous stay in England, he had begun to write using British spellings, such as "scepticism" (McCormick 1987, 360), and this seemed to foreshadow his later abandonment of America. Largely leading a life of travel and conscious delight, he eventually settled in Rome in 1924 (McCormick 1987, 263), and throughout the remainder of his life he fostered and cherished many enduring friendships and wrote his most significant mature philosophy independent of the American focus on progress and pragmatic outcomes. He found it amusing and somewhat amazing that many people, mostly charming strangers, came to see him in Rome after the Allied forces liberated the city on 4 June 1944. Then there was considerable support and sometimes pressure for him to complete his work on the remaining two volumes of his autobiography, *The Middle Span* (MS 1945; critical edition 1986) and *My Host the World* (MHW 1953; critical edition 1986) as well as *The Idea of Christ in the Gospels* (ICG 1946), *Dominations and Powers* (DP 1951), and a one-volume publication of *The Life of Reason* (LR 1953) edited by Daniel Cory, his long-standing friend and literary executor.

Following his death, philosophy took a dramatic turn toward analytic and phenomenological studies that led to a significant decline in attention being paid to Santayana's works. That trend is now being reversed.

Spanish Heritage and Departure from Harvard

Born in Spain (16 December 1863) and raised in a Catholic tradition, Santayana came to the U.S. in 1872. He learned English in a kindergarten with children younger than him. He became a student at the Boston Latin School and then Harvard College. As an undergraduate and graduate student, he was active in many clubs and student activities, and he also drew cartoons and published in the student newspaper. He participated in Boston society, often joining in Mrs. Isabella Gardner's gatherings and discussions at her home and her residence on Cape Cod. He was not thinking of becoming a professor and considered a career in architecture. But he was an excellent student and went on to complete his graduate work in philosophy under the direction of Josiah Royce. Santayana indicated he wanted to write his dissertation on Schopenhauer or Hegel, but Royce assigned Santayana a dissertation on Rudolph Hermann Lotze. When offered a temporary teaching position at Harvard, he accepted the offer because it provided an income as well as the freedom to travel and to meet individuals and students whose views were not solely influenced by American capitalism and its view of success. Having accepted the position, he quickly became a prominent teacher and eventually was offered a more permanent position without tenure and with modest pay. His view of Harvard life is captured by his chance meeting with President Eliot in the Harvard Yard. Eliot asks how Santayana's classes are going. Santayana begins to explain how well his students are learning and the difficulties they encounter. Eliot quickly interrupts saying, "No, no Santayana, what I mean by my enquiry is, *how many* students have enrolled in your lectures" (*COUS* 1920, 186). In Santayana's view the leadership at Harvard was focused on numbers, financial gains, and preparing students for political and business leadership, not on learning. During these early years at Harvard, he published poetry and his book on aesthetics. These works were well received and recognized as significant. Even so, it was not clear that he was an appropriate candidate for a full professorship at Harvard because he was quite different from the other faculty. He spoke only Spanish at home, was sceptical of the American focus on progress and consumption, and his friendships included individuals not widely accepted at Harvard, including Jews (who lived in separate dorms at the time), socialists, and homosexuals. However, that changed with *The Life of Reason*. Following its publication and positive reviews, he became a full professor, and his career as a professional philosopher was launched. The book was even advertised by Scribner's as a work in pragmatism. Santayana understood this was done as a way of attracting readers and for financial gains, but he objected to the classification and asked that it be corrected (*LGS*, 1:361). Scribner's abided by the request sometime after the success of the publication.

Notably, Santayana began planning for his retirement in the mid-1890s, calling it his *metanoia*, a change in one's life. The term "metanoia" reflects Santayana's family background in the Catholic church, in which metanoia means a change in one's life through penitence or a spiritual conversion. This change occurred over a somewhat lengthy period ending with his official retirement in 1912. Earlier he indicated he was leaving Harvard around 1909–1910, but the new president, A. Lawrence Lowell, asked him not to leave and agreed that Santayana would teach only in the fall term and take a full year's leave in 1912–1913. Santayana agreed but indicated he was not sure how long he would honor the agreement. In 1910, he gave lectures at Columbia University and the University of Wisconsin, and in 1911 he lectured at the University of California for six weeks. He wrote to his half-sister Susana in December 1911, "I am very sick of America and of professors and professoresses" (*LGS*, 2:110). His mother was ill with dementia (perhaps Alzheimer's), and in 1911 he visited her weekly and then daily before he left on his usual trip to Europe in January 1912. His half-sister Josefina was caring for their mother and the doctors did not think she was close to death. Sadly, she died while he was on board ship to England. Santayana's savings from his publications plus the $10,000 he and each of his siblings inherited from their mother made retirement possible. Even so, he did not fully decide to retire until June, when he sent his official resignation to President Lowell. He asked his half-brother, Robert Sturgis, to manage all his financial affairs and to provide him enough to live on, establishing that after Santayana's death the Sturgis family would inherit what remained. Robert died in 1921 and his son, George Sturgis, took over the management of the estate. For the most part, Santayana was able to live off the royalties from his publications, leaving his capital to grow primarily through George's wise investments.

After many trips between England and mainland Europe in 1912–1913, Santayana decided Paris was where he wanted to live. However, WWI broke out while he was in England, and there he would remain until the end of the war. The return of veterans, widows, and orphaned children made it impossible for Santayana to maintain a naturalistic neutrality to war. He wrote an article for the *New Republic*, "The Logic of Fanaticism" (Santayana 1914) and published *Egotism in German Philosophy* (EGP 1915). He turned from writing on animal faith and the realms of being, as well as his work on dominations and powers, and instead he wrote some of his best poetry. Calling himself "almost a poet" (*SAF*, ix), he had abandoned poetry in the early 1900s. However, during WWI he wrote "The Undergraduate Killed in Battle," that was included in Edith Wharton's *The Book of the Homeless* (Wharton 1916), which raised money for American Hostels and the Children of Flanders Rescue Committee. Another poem, "To a Pacifist Friend," was likely written for Bertrand Russell in 1916 when Russell was removed from his academic position at Trinity College, Cambridge, because of his pacifism.

When the war ended, Santayana returned to traveling extensively, though never to the U.S. He was free of financial concerns, never owned a home or property, and lived in hotels or in the residences of friends. Finally, in 1924, he settled in Rome at the Bristol Hotel at the Piazza Barberini. During Rome's summers, he would retreat to the Cortina d'Ampezzo in the Dolomites. He attempted to leave Mussolini's Italy in 1939, but the Swiss authorities would not accept his papers when he arrived at their border. Following his efforts to leave Rome, he changed hotels several times and lived for a month at the Danieli Hotel in Venice. On 14 October 1941, he entered the Clinica della Piccola Compagna di Maria (Clinic of the Little Company of Mary), a hospital-clinic in Rome administered by a community of nuns known as the Blue Nuns for the color of their habits. At that time, it was not unusual for hospitals to care for well-known individuals in their later years. Because of the war, his funds from the U.S. and England eventually were cut off, and the Blue Nuns agreed to care for him until he could compensate them after the war. After the war was over, there were further delays due to the death in 1945 of his nephew, George Sturgis, who had been managing Santayana's finances. Santayana never knew why there was considerable delay in his receiving funds after George's death. The cause was complex. George Sturgis had divorced his first wife, Rosamond, by moving to a state where divorce was permitted. He then married another woman but died on their honeymoon. Both the divorce and the second marriage were contested in court because they were not recognized as legal in Massachusetts. The court proceedings and the appearance of an illegitimate son caused the delay in Santayana's funds coming to Rome through much of 1946, but he was finally able to compensate the Blue Nuns for their care.

As Santayana's health worsened and he contemplated the end of his life, he asked not to be buried in the U.S. nor in consecrated ground. Daniel Cory discovered that the only non-consecrated ground in Roman cemeteries was for criminals and unknown persons. Finding a suitable neutral burial ground seemed impossible. The Spanish Embassy came to the rescue and suggested Santayana be buried in the Pantheon of the Obra Pía Española in the Campo Verano cemetery in Rome. This burial site is officially the property of Spain, and Cory thought Santayana would have approved of being buried in Spanish soil, even if consecrated. The embassy would later turn the site into a significant tribute to Santayana. At the burial ceremony Daniel Cory chose a remarkably appropriate poem of Santayana's to read, "The Poet's Testament." A portion of the poem reads: "I give back to the earth what the earth gave, All to the furrow, none to the grave, The candle's out, the spirit's vigil spent" (*CP* 1979, 268).

Philosophical Transformation

Santayana's dramatic change in lifestyle after leaving Harvard also involved a dramatic philosophical transformation. In many ways he was best known in the U.S. for his *Life of Reason*, but since its publication he had navigated away from its views and turned wholeheartedly toward a naturalistic outlook. Throughout his life after Harvard, he cast doubts on the *Life of Reason* being a valid approach to understanding his work. He did note that there are some good things in the work and he emphasized this in 1948 when he was trying to help his friend Daniel Cory publish a heavily edited one-volume edition of the *Life of Reason* (LR, 1954). He wrote to Cory: "How I wish I could erase all that cheap work! Yet there are sentences and even paragraphs in the Life of Reason that are good, and I like them when I find them quoted" (*LGS*, 8:100). He was particularly positive when writing to his publisher. Daniel Cory's financial situation was not the best at the time, and as literary executor he expected he could live off Santayana's royalties without further income. This proved very hard to do after Santayana's death. Santayana had tried to assist Cory, for example, with a letter to John Hall Wheelock of Charles Scribner's Sons in February 1952:

> By the way, Cory and I have both been surprised to find "The Life of Reason" so much like my latest views. The difficulty will be the choose [sic] the out-of-date passages. He is very much interested in the work and has already revised it all in a cursory way. I have stopped before the last volume, having fallen a victim of influenza on top of my double catarrh. But he will be able and happy to do everything himself. (*LGS*, 8:421)

His later letter in April 1952 to Rosamond Sturgis Little was less enthusiastic about the book:

> The revision of my old "Life of Reason" is finished as far as my help is concerned and Cory will take the responsibility of deciding what to keep and what to leave out. He is strangely interested in the work, and we both have found the text less positivistic and philistine than we had expected. (*LGS*, 8:434)

Santayana's more consistent view of *The Life of Reason* may be represented in two letters. In 1928 he writes to Otto Kyllmann, his contact at his UK publisher Constable and Company:

> I have never heard of Mr Boris Takovenko before, but his proposal does seem to me worth accepting, at least in part. If you are willing, I should send him "Scepticism" "The Realm of Essence", and "Platonism": and in doing so I should ask him whether he had already read my "Character & Opinion in the U.S", "Soliloquies in England" and "Dialogues in Limbo": because if not, these seem to me much better for his purpose (especially "Character & Opinion in the U.S", than the "Life of Reason", which I regard as more of biographical than doctrinal interest, for a person wishing to understand my opinions. I should therefore prefer that he should judge me by the later books mentioned above, rather than by the "Life of Reason," which I shouldn't send to him, unless he already knows the other books and wishes to complete his study of my work. (*LGS*, 4:49)

And in 1933 he writes to Charles Davis:

The Life of Reason, which they prefer at Columbia, is not so well written, is more professorial and lecture-like, and is philosophically less fundamental than my later books; but it was largely written in America, and when I was teaching, so that it moves in a moralistic, humanistic, atmosphere which they can appreciate. I think it is sensible, and contains some good passages and sayings, such as Erskine quotes. But neither as a writer nor as a philosopher can I be judged by it. (*LGS*, 5:45)

Even before he left Harvard, Santayana was focusing on developing his naturalism, but WWI interrupted. Once the war was over, he again turned to writing about naturalism, but turning to scepticism as a way of establishing a naturalistic philosophy was a surprise to many. Of course, rationalists like Descartes and others developed a sceptical approach to establish the certainty of their beliefs, claiming that their system of philosophy was founded on undeniable rational certainty. Santayana took quite a different approach, using sceptical arguments to show there are no rational foundations for knowledge or belief. Instead of building a metaphysical base for knowledge, Santayana bases knowledge on common sense and natural beliefs shared by human beings and other animals. He frequently uses the terms "materialism" and "naturalism" interchangeably. And in the Preface to *Scepticism and Animal Faith* he makes his non-metaphysical approach clear.

> Now in natural philosophy I am a decided materialist—apparently the only one living; and I am well aware that idealists are fond of calling materialism, too, metaphysics, in rather an angry tone, so as to cast discredit upon it by assimilating it to their own systems. But my materialism, for all that, is not metaphysical. I do not profess to know what matter is in itself, and feel no confidence in the divination of those *esprits forts* who, leading a life of vice, thought the universe must be composed of nothing but dice and billiard-balls. (*SAF*, vii–viii)

One should never forget that in reading Santayana his ironic humor often comes through as he is making important points. He writes:

> But whatever matter may be, I call it matter boldly, as I call my acquaintances Smith and Jones without knowing their secrets: whatever it may be, it must present the aspects and undergo the motions of the gross objects that fill the world: and if belief in the existence of hidden parts and movements in nature be metaphysics, then the kitchen-maid is a metaphysician whenever she peels a potato. (*SAF*, viii)

The principal aim of philosophy for Santayana is not to improve human practices but to articulate a clear account of human life and actions based on commonly held beliefs that do not have a rational foundation. Some mistakenly classified him as a closet pragmatist, perhaps because of his focus on action and his test of truth (which I will turn to later). But these attempts to argue that he is a closet pragmatist run into trouble, especially because he directly rejects the label. As he writes in a letter to Horace Kallen, "... in spite of your better opinion of me, I am no pragmatist" (*LGS*, 2:363). Earlier he had noted pragmatism's confusion "between the test and the meaning of truth" (*LGS*, 1:325). The main task of philosophy, he thinks, is an inventory of kinds or categories of things "worth distinguishing" (*SAF*, vi). He begins his Preface with humor: "Here is one more system of philosophy. If the reader is tempted to smile, I can assure him that I smile with him ..." And then he clearly notes:

> My system, accordingly, is no system of the universe. The Realms of Being of which I speak are not parts of a cosmos, nor one great cosmos together: they are only kinds or categories of things which I find conspicuously different and worth distinguishing, at least in my own thoughts. (*SAF*, vi)

As he introduces his notion of animal faith and the realms of being (essence, matter, truth, and spirit), he is clear that he is not developing a metaphysics. He notes that metaphysics is "an attempt to determine matters of fact by means of logical or moral or rhetorical constructions" (*SAF*, vii). It is a confusion between our reflective thoughts and the realm of matter, as if our thoughts somehow shaped reality rather than being an aftereffect of our physical interactions with the material world.

> Metaphysics, in the proper sense of the word, is dialectical physics, or an attempt to determine matters of fact by means of logical or moral or rhetorical constructions. It arises by a confusion of those Realms of Being which it is my special care to distinguish. It is neither physical speculation nor pure logic nor honest literature, but (as in the treatise of Aristotle first called by that name) a hybrid of the three, materializing ideal entities, turning harmonies into forces, and dissolving natural things into terms of discourse. (*SAF*, vii)

To put it simply, metaphysics is a category mistake. Rather than turning natural objects into terms of discourse, Santayana develops a naturalistic philosophy that describes the beliefs of animals, including humans, based on the conditions in their physical environments. He notes that he waits for the "men of science to tell me what matter is, in so far as they can discover it, and [I] am not at all surprised or troubled at the abstractness and vagueness of their ultimate conception: how should our notions of things so remote from the scale and scope of our sense be anything but schematic?" (*SAF*, viii).

Then why does he begin with scepticism, reducing knowledge and beliefs to that which is indubitable? For some, including me, his ironic smile hovers over significant parts of *Scepticism and Animal Faith*. Searching for that which cannot be doubted, he uses the Cartesian method to reject all accounts of rational certitude and determines all claims of rational certitude are counterfeits. Santayana accomplishes this with his account of a sceptical attack on belief. Cartesian scepticism is halfhearted, finding a fully developed person with an image of God inscribed upon his soul is not the foundation of rational belief but only raises the question of what the basis for such a belief is. The first eight chapters of *Scepticism* are a careful analysis that discredits any first principles of rational certitude, as he focuses on dogma and doubt, wayward scepticism, self-consciousness, and finally arrives at the ultimate scepticism of "nothing given exists" (*SAF*, 42–48), leading to Chapter VIII, "Some Authorities for this Conclusion."

That which cannot be doubted cannot be the rational foundation for belief or knowledge. For Santayana only the immediate object of consciousness (spirit, as he calls it) cannot be doubted as it is given in instances, but if one attempts to identify that object (essence) of consciousness, one immediately enters the area of doubt and uncertainty. Even if one maintains that one is seeing a simple essence and calls it blue, that takes time and the essence may have changed over the course of time, and one's physical interaction that causes the intuiting of blue takes time as well. And, of course, our physiologies may differ, causing others to see a different color or shade or no color at all. That our consciousness of the world is an aftereffect of our physical being (psyche, as he calls it) interacting with the world, means that what we are conscious of is mediated by our material being interacting with our physical environment. Hence, there is no certainty to be found in the awareness of mental phenomena. Nothing given in consciousness exists; what is given is a universal and not a particular. Hence, no idea promising self-evidence can withstand the sustained questioning of the sceptic. This is a thoroughgoing scepticism, not a halfhearted one, and it is a dead end leading nowhere. The rationalists' efforts to base knowledge on certainty are reduced to a momentary consciousness of a single essence providing no basis for knowledge.

Some, including myself, have taken Santayana's approach to consciousness as an epiphenomenalist's view, since spirit or consciousness is an aftereffect of the psyche's generating a non-causal spirit. But Santayana clearly denies being an epiphenomenalist, although he does maintain the impotence of spirit and its being a non-causal aftereffect of the psyche. Santayana's denial rests on his account of consciousness not being a separate entity from the psyche. Epiphenomenalism is defined as one entity generating another entity, the second entity being epiphenomenal. This is an account of one phenomenon generating an epiphenomenon. But Santayana does not characterize thought as being a separate entity from the psyche, and he emphasizes that consciousness is not emitted from a phenomenon but from a substance, the psyche. Consciousness or awareness would have to be a separate entity generated by our psyche to be an epiphenomenon, but for Santayana, our consciousness or spirit is not a separate entity existing independent from our physical being. He made this clear as early as 1913 in a letter to his former graduate student, Horace Kallen, even before he established spirit as the term for consciousness or mind:

> And this leads me to make a slight complaint against you for having said that I am an "epiphenomenalist"—I don't complain of your calling me a "pragmatist"

because I know that it is mere piety on your part. But the title of epiphenomenalist is better deserved, and I have only this objection to it: that it is based (like the new realism) on idealistic prejudices and presuppositions. An epiphenomenon must have some other phenomenon under it: but what underlies the mind, according to my view, is not a phenomenon but a substance—the body, or nature at large. To call this is [sic] a phenomenon is to presuppose another thing in itself, which is chimerical. Therefore I am no epiphenomenalist, but a naturalist pure and simple, recognizing a material world, not a phenomenon but a substance, and a mental life struck off from it in its operation, like a spark from the flint and steel, having no other substance than that material world, but having a distinct existence of its own (as it is emitted continually out of bodily life as music is emitted from an instrument) and having a very different kind of being, since it is immaterial and moral and cognitive. This mental life may be called a phenomenon if you like, either in the platonic sense of being an instance of an essence (in which sense every fact, even substance, is a phenomenon) or in the modern sense of being an observable effect of latent forces; but it cannot be called an epiphenomenon, unless you use the word phenomenon in the one sense for substance and in the other sense for consciousness. (*LGS*, 2:127)

Having reduced the quest for a rational foundation of knowledge to the indubitable "nothing given exists," one might expect Santayana to follow the rationalist tradition and establish the basis for natural belief by starting with our consciousness of essences and then step by step leading to our knowledge of the natural world. For some, his not doing this seems an omission in the projected outline of his hypothesis. But it is not. Since there is no rational foundation for knowledge, one cannot conceptually outline how we move from the intuition of essences to beliefs and actions in the natural world. Instead, it is animal faith, without a rational foundation, that leads us naturally to take the essences we intuit as indicative of the physical world. So, there is no step-by-step approach to building up a knowledge base from that which cannot be doubted. He then spends considerable time developing his notion of essences in four chapters on "The Discovery of Essence," "Some Uses of this Discovery," "The Watershed of Criticism," and "Identity and Duration attributed to Essences" (*SAF*, Chapters IX, X, XI, and XII).

Santayana then turns to his naturalism and animal faith. The use of the term "faith" may suggest a religious origin, but not for Santayana, who is an atheist: "It has nothing to do with religion: by 'animal faith' I mean the confidence one has for instance, that there will be a future, that you will find things where you have hidden them, etc." (*LGS*, 3:150); "Dogmas are instances of intellectual faith: animal faith is only the confident unspoken assurance that action implies" (*LGS*, 4:30). Hume's "natural belief" and Russell's "animal inference" (*LGS*, 8:150) are contrasted with animal faith, a term unique to Santayana (*LGS*, 4:30). Both "belief" and "inference" indicate concepts and mental actions, but for Santayana animal faith does not: "animal faith, as I use the words, involves no intellectual belief whatsoever ... The object of animal faith is always substance, as that of intuition is always essence. Neither asserts propositions. That is why I call it faith and not opinion or judgement" (*LGS*, 4:30–31) And to Curt John Ducasse he writes in 1928:

> There was a point in your letter which I meant to have spoken of, viz., about "animal faith" extending to propositions. This shows that you don't feel at all the force of this word which I use, and perhaps, abuse—<u>animal</u>. The animal organism is wound up, and has certain potentialities which it discharges upon occasion: the sentiment which accompanies this discharge, when it is conscious, is a <u>vague, wordless</u> confidence or premonition. It is not a proposition to be verified, because it has no terms. That is why I call it faith, not belief. (*LGS*, 4:40)

Transitioning to his naturalism he writes, "I have now reached the culminating point of my survey of evidence, and the entanglements I have left behind me and the habitable regions I am looking for lie spread out before me like opposite valleys" (*SAF*, 99). Indeed, animal faith does not provide a rational basis for belief; it only clarifies why we take objects of consciousness as indicative of our physical world, and it is experience that enables us to determine as best we can whether these essences describe the world adequately enough for us to act upon these beliefs. We know that the facts of the world are quite different from the essences we intuit because science has shown us the dramatic difference between the objects we perceive and their atomic structures' interaction with our physiology, and science will likely show us even more as its technologies and methodologies develop. The real nature of the world is like an opposite valley from the perspective of essences and spirit. "To take the leap from one intuition to another, and assert that they view the same essence, or have the same intent, I must take my life in my hands and trust to animal faith. Otherwise all dialectic would be arrested" (*SAF*, 117). How is it that one takes one's life in hand? If one were immersed only in the momentary intuition of essences, there would be no basis for action, no need for nourishment, company, or engagement in the world. Such total immersion would be possible only for a disembodied spirit without the natural inclination to act. So long as that immersion involved only the delight of essences, conscious life would be a joyful fascination of the immediate. But we are not disembodied, nor is any living being. Indeed, theologians and philosophers have wrestled with the notion of a disembodied spirit, mostly concerned with how one could identify such beings without physical characteristics, an issue Aquinas spent considerable time trying to resolve. Santayana moves in a different direction, noting that a disembodied spirit seeing all things under the form of eternity would be a very unusual being who could not be all-knowing because: "This would be a very special kind of spirit, and many an essence would be excluded from its intuition; for instance, the essence of surprise" (*SAF*, 276). All existing beings are embodied, and spirit is generated from their embodiment's interaction with its material environment. "The spirit that actually breathes in man is an animal spirit, transitive like the material endeavours which it expresses; it has a material station and accidental point of view, and a fevered preference for one alternative issue over another" (*SAF*, 125). No being is free of the passage of time and the demands of the external world. Action based on faith and common sense is found in all animals.

> Knowledge accordingly is belief: belief in a world of events, and especially of those parts of it which are near the self, tempting or threatening it. This belief is native to animals, and precedes all deliberate use of intuitions as signs or descriptions of things; as I turn my head to see who is there, before I see who it is. Furthermore, knowledge is true belief. It is such an enlightening of the self by intuitions arising there, that what the self imagines and asserts of the collateral thing, with which it wrestles in action, is actually true of that thing. Truth in such presumptions or conceptions does not imply adequacy, nor a pictorial identity between the essence in intuition and the constitution of the object. Discourse is a language, not a mirror. The images in sense are parts of discourse, not parts of nature: they are the babble of our innocent organs under the stimulus of things; but these spontaneous images, like the sounds of the voice, may acquire the function of names; they may become signs, if discourse is intelligent and can recapitulate its phases, for the things sought or encountered in the world. The truth which discourse can achieve is truth in its own terms, appropriate description: it is no incorporation or reproduction of the object in the mind. (*SAF*, 179)

Intuition and essence are different realms. Essences do not exercise "a non-natural control over nature" (*SAF*, 78):

> Not the data of intuition, but the objects of animal faith, are the particulars perceived: they alone are the existing things or events to which the animal is reacting and to which he is attributing the essences which arise, as he does so, before his fancy. These data of intuition are universals; they form the elements of such a description of the object as is at that time possible; they are never that object itself, nor any part of it. Essences are not drawn out or abstracted from things; they are given before the thing can be clearly perceived, since they are the terms used in perception; but they are not given until attention is stretched upon the thing, which is posited blindly in action; and they come as revelations, or oracles delivered by that thing to the mind, and symbolizing it there. (*SAF*, 93–94)

The intuition of essences may be captivating, as when one is speechless and fully absorbed in seeing a sunset or hearing a symphony; collective instances when there is no sense of time, only the immediate, only the present, and the captivating delight of the moment. So, why should we not spend our life "cultivating congenial intuitions" (*SAF*, 104) and not be bothered by everyday demands? It is exactly the external demands of the material world that startle one's attention, withdrawing one from the beauty of the essence and toward the significance of what the event expresses or foreshadows (*SAF*, 104). We are animals embodied in a particular physiology, in a particular material environment, in a particular time. And if we are to survive, we need to act, to eat, to find shelter, to gather in communities, organize, and structure a life that is the best we can make it. As much as we may delight in the momentary intuition of an essence, we must move forward with our lives, keeping separate our momentary delight while maintaining our practical judgments of living a well-balanced and sane life that meets the challenges facing us daily. For Santayana, we may delight in the intuition of essences, but we cannot yield to the illusion that they are identical to material objects, nor can we plan our lives only on this delight. There is an equilibrium we must establish. He turns to the practical example of simply finding our way home to highlight the importance of animal faith and the illusion of essences.

> It is precisely by *not* yielding to opinion and illusion, and by *not* delegating any favourite essences to be the substance of things, that I aspire to keep my cognitive conscience pure and my practical judgement sane; because in order to find my way home I am by no means compelled to yield ignominiously to any animal illusion; what guides me there is not illusion but habit; and the intuitions which accompany habit are normal signs for the circle of objects and forces by which that habit is sustained. The images of sense and science will not delude me if instead of hypostatising them, as those philosophers did the terms of their dialectic, I regard them as graphic symbols for home and for the way there. That such external things exist, that I exist myself, and live more or less prosperously in the midst of them, is a faith not founded on reason but precipitated in action, and in that intent, which is virtual action, involved in perception. (*SAF*, 105–106)

Although not fully explicated in *Scepticism*, Santayana's account of spirit lays the foundation for his more fully developed notion of the spiritual dimension of life. This aspect of life is usually embedded in religious belief, and for some philosophers, such as Royce, it is central to their outlook. Unlike Santayana, they give substance to spirit, enabling religious spirituality to assure life after death. In contrast, Santayana reconceives spirit as the momentary light of animal existence, always precarious and easily snuffed out. It is against this background that our moral and aesthetic victories must be measured. If one is careful in maintaining a balance between the necessities of existence and the intuition of essences that bring delight, then a spiritual life is possible, as momentary or extended as it may be.

If animal faith enables us to take intuited essences as indicative of the material world, our knowledge is pictorial, and not identical to the material objects, leaving an "insecurity inseparable from animal faith, and from life itself" (*SAF*, 107). Santayana suggests that the relationship of essences to the physical world is like different languages noting particular objects. "These signs are miscellaneous essences—sights, sounds, smells, contacts, tears, provocations—and they are alternative or supplementary to one another, like words in different languages" (*SAF*, 175).[1] There are different words in different languages that indicate an object in the world such as a tree. But no one supposes any of the different words resemble a real tree even though we do believe that the words indicate something existing in the world.

How then do we establish the correctness of our knowledge? First, error tells us our interpretation of essences is incorrect whether it be something as

---

[1] See page 206, note 28.

simple as mistaking a sunset for a sunrise, or something far more complex when after years of belief and apparent evidence that the earth is flat and the center of the universe, we find it is not. Or after years of a seemingly close friendship, we discover that person never was our friend. To establish that our claims to knowledge are reliable, we need not only error to correct our ways but also demonstration through successful action. So how do we come to believe in events, in material things, and in truths we hold? In the remaining chapters of *Scepticism* Santayana advances his explanations of how we come to rely on animal faith and an evidentiary base rooted in action to live well and to maintain an equilibrium with our momentary delight in the intuition of essences. Even so, he is careful to note that his reasons "are but prejudices and human" founded in animal faith. Animal faith precedes intuitions; it is a "sort of expectation and open-mouthedness" (*SAF*, 107) that enables us to move forward in the world even when we are not focusing on the immediacy of intuition but rather on maintaining and advancing our material existence, as fragile and temporary as it may be.

In "Identity and Duration Attributed to Essences" (Chapter XII), Santayana examines how human beliefs can be arranged in three series or orders: genesis, discovery, and evidence. He notes all origins lie in the realm of matter. "It is accordingly in the realm of matter, in the order of events in animal life, that I must distribute human beliefs and ideas if I wish to arrange them in the order of their genesis" (*SAF*, 109). What comes first in the order of discovery is most likely goods and evils discovered in one's interactions with others and the material environment (*SAF*, 110). He is quick to note that the order of evidence is the only method he is concerned with in *Scepticism* (*SAF*, 110). He has shown that once one finds that which cannot be doubted, it leads nowhere because any attempt to identify the given essence takes time and therefore an openness to doubt and error. Hence, belief that the essence is indicative of the world is an "arbitrary belief or interpretation added by my animal impulse" (*SAF*, 110). Essences are universals and not particular material entities. Essences are not only universals, but they are infinite in number. Even value predicates are essences, but no intuition of an essence is causal or confers authority in the world. Some may find Santayana's use of Plato's term "essence" an unhappy choice of words. Platonic forms are generic and value laden. Santayana's essences, by contrast, encompass every feature and every shade of determinateness displayed by the world. But Santayana does not stop there: every quality that never matured beyond the stage of possibility is also an essence. Even the impossible is an essence or else we could not determine its logical status. Essences provide the terms of awareness, even as we act, but neither intuition nor essences are causally interacting with the world; they are generated by the psyche's interaction in a physical environment. One may capture this by using the image of a costumer's gallery. What clothes are to be worn, how are they chosen, and in what order? The intuition of essences as indicative of the natural world and the order they appear in are determined by one's natural makeup embodied in one's psyche.

"Material categories such as existence, substance, and change, none of which are applicable to pure data, are thus insinuated by the animal intellect into contemplation" (*SAF*, 114). How does one maintain a sane approach to life when all our knowledge is pictorial; how does one maintain beliefs about the world and the sense that they are true? Santayana holds a correspondence theory of truth. If I say that the earth is the center of the universe, to be true that must correspond with the exact location of the earth. But given that our beliefs are mediated by symbols our knowledge is loose or partial (*SAF*, 114–115). But this is the normal pattern for belief and knowledge in all animals. With that in mind, one may enjoy reading the chapter, "Normal Madness," in *Dialogues in Limbo* (*DL*, 36–57).

Santayana masterfully turns to beliefs that result from animal faith; they are mediated by symbols (*SAF*, 164). These include belief in demonstration, experience, self, substance, nature, and the implied belief in truth. He ends his volume with the chapter "Comparison with Other Criticisms of Knowledge" and with an introduction to his upcoming volumes on the realms of being:

> This natural faith opens to me various Realms of Being, having very different kinds of reality in themselves and a different status in respect to my knowledge of them. I hope soon to invite the friendly reader to accompany me in a further excursion through those tempting fields. (*SAF*, 309)

Scepticism was clearly written as an introduction to Santayana's later books on the realms of being, but when Scribner's published the four books in *Realms of Being* as a single volume (RB 1942), *Scepticism* was not included. Why not? In his correspondence with John Wheelock at Scribner's (Santayana's American publisher), Santayana writes:

> In previous letters I have expressed my satisfaction at your project of publishing Realms of Being in a single volume. Now, in your letter of Dec. 6, 1940 you broach the question of including Scepticism & Animal Faith in that volume. Certainly, if the purpose is to supply a single text-book for college classes studying my philosophy as a system, Scepticism should not be left out; it is the link between Realms and the history of modern philosophy, which such students might be supposed to have some notion of to begin with. But your proposed volume might have another use. It might be a work for general or desultory reading, for the general public, especially for ladies; and then it would be a positive advantage to omit Scepticism. Such readers look only for separate thoughts, to compare them with their own feelings; and the author's further opinions do not concern them. As a work of belles lettres, The Realms would be complete enough, and more in one key than if Scepticism, with its paradoxes, were interposed. It might be read as people read Montaigne or Nietzsche or Chekov, as a pleasant stimulus. (*LGS*, 7:6)

Santayana sees *Scepticism* as a technical, philosophical volume to be used by students and professors. He highlights the paradoxes in the book based on its use of technical terms in uncustomary ways. He seems to hope that the one-volume *The Realms of Being* will be more accessible to a larger public (while making an unseemly comment about "ladies"), perhaps like his novel and autobiography. In some ways this is puzzling, since the discussions of essence, matter, truth, and spirit are not easy to read nor accessible to a wide range of the public. He also notes there is a shorter introduction to his system, without the technical language and philosophical paradoxes, in the Schilpp volume on Santayana in The Library of Living Philosophers (Schilpp 1940), "Apologia pro Mente Sua," and that this work is likely to be found in every college library. Then both his honesty and sense of humor come into play:

> I had no intention, in writing all these books, to become a subject in college classes. That is not a sympathetic way of approaching those books. I was only thinking aloud, with presuppositions of which I was not always quite conscious, and which in any case I should not impose on anyone else without his consent. But America is looking for things to do, and turning me into a "subject" may momentarily be one of them. It is in one sense an immense honour, but also in another sense a misunderstanding. Do, then, whatever seems to you best about the proposed volume. (*LGS*, 7:7)

Wheelock decided to publish the *Realms of Being* in one volume without *Scepticism*.

Philosopher for the Twenty-First Century

In many ways Santayana's accounts of consciousness, essences, and animal faith were a century ahead of his time. It is somewhat startling that his views of spirit and its objects are now being explored by neurosciences, and many of the conclusions are consistent with Santayana's unorthodox views put forward in the first half of the twentieth century. We know that the objects of consciousness vary depending on an animal's makeup and physical environment. For example, the use of reflective sounds by whales and other sea animals enables them to navigate underwater and to communicate over long distances. No one imagines that these reflective sounds are identical to the characteristics of the objects in the sea, but they produce a knowledge that is based on faith and successful action that demonstrates their usefulness leading to belief and action. Humans do not have such physical abilities but can build technologies that mimic the abilities of sea animals and enable us to move about below the surface of the sea. Indeed, many animals have conscious abilities not available in human physiology. For example, human vision cannot distinguish between male and female mockingbirds, but there is a level of color perception in mockingbirds that enables them to see a color difference between male and female. Even in navigating the world, humans move in the direction of a place in front of them because the visual field of their eyes is located on the front of their heads. However, birds' eyes are located on the sides of their heads and they fly through their environment with an experience different from that of humans—though now many automobiles have a mode showing a 360-degree view of your car's close surroundings. Hence, we have affirmation of Santayana's claim that there is an infinity of essences potentially available to animals. What is generated depends on an animal's physical nature, its psyche, and its interactions with the physical environment. For Santayana the psyche provides order, direction, and the habits of life. He writes: "The self-maintaining and reproducing pattern or structure of an organism, conceived as a power, is called a psyche. The psyche, in its moral unity, is a poetic or mythological notion, but needed to mark the hereditary vehement motion in organisms towards specific forms and functions" (*RB* 1942, 569–570). But we also know that this discourse with nature may be misleading. Dementia causes one to no longer be able to rely on one's habits and assumptions. Psychiatric wards reveal faulty beliefs that may result in human beings not able to live outside of confinement, and they also reveal that sometimes medical treatments may correct or reduce such behavior, enabling a person to live a more suitable life. Animals in confinement, even in zoos, sometimes lose their sense of place and habits and must be removed to different habitats or be euthanized.

There is importance in Santayana leaving to the sciences any explanation regarding the causes of human action. Spirit reflects the psyche's interactions with the physical environment, but spirit is an aftereffect with no causal efficacy because it is not a material entity. Santayana's philosophical or literary account of consciousness seems to be confirmed in recent neuroscience research indicating our awareness of decisions comes after the material causes in our physiology. Several researchers continue these studies indicating that by studying brain activities one can predict decisions a person is making before the person is aware of making the decision. Stephen Hawking, for example, emphasized this view. He cites neurologist Ben Libet of the University of California, San Francisco, who found that there are brain processes that occur nearly half a second before a person is aware of the decision to act (Burton 2016) and an earlier account in Smith (Smith 2008). More recent studies have found that neuroscientists can read brain activity and predict decisions 11 seconds before a person acts (Goldhill 2019; Van Praet 2020). In other words, there are action-specific electrical activities in the brain that precede any awareness of a decision being made to act. This seems consistent with Santayana's non-scientific view that consciousness, thought, and reason are aftereffects of physical activities that precede them. Indeed, it is becoming more apparent that Santayana's common sense, non-scientific naturalism surprisingly aligns with some of current neuroscience research findings regarding concepts as well as processes of consciousness, rationality, intelligence, agency, ethics, knowledge, and truth. Of course, there is much more to be done regarding these concepts as well as the notions of reflection, inference, and hypothesis testing. We have yet to see how this research will enhance, alter, or discount philosophical accounts of reasoning, societal structures, sensations, habits, emotion, culture, responsibility, freedom, blame, art, music, and more.

Historically, many philosophers held that one's mental activities were always somehow private, not public like objects in the physical world. This privacy enabled them to maintain the uniqueness of the mental, interpreting it as if it were a non-physical entity and calling it a mind or soul. Santayana's account is quite counter to such interpretations. If one's conscious activities are the aftereffects of one's psyche, then one could conjecture that one may be able to know what another is thinking simply by examining the physical causes generating consciousness. For many philosophers and others, this seems impossible. However, now there is research that on a limited basis enables us to know what a person is seeing or thinking by examining parts of the brain (Choi 2013; Lanese 2022). Jack Gallant's suggestion goes further (Gallant 2011). He projects something called the "Google Cap" that one may be able to place on someone's head and know what the person is thinking, perhaps even if the person is not aware of it (see Velasquez-Manoff 2020). Dr. Rafael Yuste, Professor of Biological Sciences and Director of Neurotechnology Center at Columbia University, and twenty-four other signatories have called for "neurorights" as a protection against threats posed by machines that can read our brains and our thoughts. He led a small group of scientists that inspired the US BRAIN Initiative, announced by President Barack Obama in 2013, and helped form the International Brain Initiative (IBI) in 2017. This led to the establishment of the NeuroRights Foundation chaired by Yuste. On their website one finds the following:

> Any technology that records or interferes with brain activity is defined as Neurotechnology. Neurotechnology, especially brain-computer interfaces, has the potential to foundationally alter society. In the coming years, it will be possible to decode thought from neural activity or enhance cognitive ability by linking the brain directly to digital networks. Such innovations could challenge the very notion of what it means to be human. (Yuste 2019)

One can imagine the issues such an approach may bring for court cases, personal relations, child rearing, education, and more. And this research continues and is reported on in various settings.

The implications of such research for our understanding of consciousness and thought are extraordinary, with so many of the historic accounts of mental life now challenged by scientific research relating to the causes of human action and of human thought. A new generation of scholars has much to look forward to in collaborating with natural scientists regarding human nature, the causes of our actions, and the role of consciousness in human activity. Santayana, if he were still living, would smile at such developments.

The future of any discipline in the academic world is difficult to predict and perhaps especially so for philosophy. One controversial area that Santayana ventured into is the relationship between philosophy and literature. Richard Rorty and a few others have taken an approach that suggests philosophy is a form of literature, not a means of discovering the nature of human reality or realities in our world: philosophy is seen as more of a literary expression of one's point of view. There are numerous places in which Santayana notes that he is only giving voice to distinctions and categories that he finds worthwhile "at least in my own thoughts" (*SAF*, vi). In some ways, Santayana's work fits in with a view that philosophy may best be understood as literature. Some already find his style of writing non-philosophical, and in many ways they are right. From a literary perspective his writing often is more like that of the best literary styles, portraying colorful thoughts in a flowing language. Wallace Stevens wrote: "The exquisite and memorable way in which [Santayana] has always said things has given so much delight that we accept what he says as we accept our own civilization. His pages are a part of the *douceur de vivre* and do not offer themselves for sensational summary" (Stevens 1957, 187). And in some ways Santayana's Epilogue to *The Last Puritan* may capture his sense of philosophical literature. In a conversation with his fictional character, Mario, Santayana asks whether he should publish the novel. Mario concludes by saying, yes, because it is better than the usual philosophical writings. When Santayana asks how that can be, Mario replies: "Because now you're not arguing or proving or criticizing anything, but painting a picture. The trouble with you philosophers is that you misunderstand your vocation. You ought to be poets, but you insist on laying down the law for the universe, physical and moral, and are vexed with one another because your inspirations are not identical" (*LP*, 572).

Conclusion

Estimating the importance of *Scepticism and Animal Faith*, one may note that after Santayana's death in 1952 his readership suffered a significant decline. A century later there is a noticeable revival occurring, recognizing the significance and implications of Santayana's naturalism as explicated in this book. Santayana scholar Norman V. Henfrey writes in the *Encyclopædia Britannica*: "*Scepticism and Animal Faith* conveys better than any other volume the essential import of Santayana's philosophy. It formulates his theory of immediately apprehended essences and describes the role played by 'animal faith' in various forms of knowledge" (Henfrey 2022). The resurgence of interest in Santayana resulted from the critical edition publications of *The Works of George Santayana* by The MIT Press, as well as the founding of the Santayana Society and two international journals, *Overheard in Seville: The Bulletin of the Santayana* Society and *Limbo: boletin de estudios sobre Santayana*.

Given the increasing interest in Santayana and his works, one can be optimistic about the future of such scholarship and recognition. But whether Santayana's work continues to be read, scientific research will continue in the areas of consciousness, its objects, and the relationship between our mental activities and our physical realities opening the doors for philosophers to learn from such research. I had appointments in medical schools for over two decades, principally in medical genetics, molecular biology, and ethics. When I worked with geneticists and neurologists, they found it interesting that

Santayana had anticipated some of their findings, but they always noted that reading him or any other philosopher would not shape the results of their research. I was quick to note that their research would shape my understanding of human activity. Some readers find Santayana's literary style of writing too dense and pictorial to count as contemporary philosophical work. Regardless of what the future brings to Santayana scholarship, it is clear that his naturalistic approach to describing human and animal behavior is embedded in our physical natures. His account of animal faith will continue to be central to human behavior so long as humans exist.

References

Burton, Robert A. 2016. The Life of Meaning (Reason not Required). *New York Times*, 5 September.

Choi, Charles Q. 2013. Brain Researchers Can Detect Who We Are Thinking About. *Scientific American*, 14 March. https://www.scientificamerican.com/article/brain-researchers-can-detect-who-we-are-thinking-about/.

Gallant, Jack L. 2011. Reconstructing Visual Experiences from Brain Activity Evoked by Natural Movies. *Current Biology*: 1641–1646.

Goldhill, Olivia. 2019. Neuroscientists Can Read Brain Activity to Predict Decisions 11 Seconds Before People Act. *Quartz*, March 9. https://qz.com/1569158/neuroscientists-read-unconscious-brain-activity-to-predict-decisions

Henfrey, Norman V. 2022. George Santayana: Spanish-American Philosopher. *Encyclopædia Britannica*, 12 December. https://www.britannica.com/biography/George-Santayana#ref257854.

Lanese, Nicoletta. 2022. Scientist Design Algorithm That 'Reads' People's Thoughts from Brain Scans. *LiveScience*, 24 October. https://www.livescience.com/algorithm-mind-reading-from-fmri.

McCormick, John. 1987. *George Santayana: A Biography*. New York: Alfred A. Knopf.

Santayana, George. 1896. *The Sense of Beauty: Being the Outlines of Aesthetic Theory*. New York: Scribner's; London: A. and C. Black.

———. 1905a. *The Life of Reason: Or the Phases of Human Progress*. New York: Scribner's; London: Constable.

———. 1905b. *Reason in Common Sense*. New York: Scribner's; London: A. and C. Black.

———. 1905c. *Reason in Society*. New York: Scribner's; London: A. and C. Black.

———. 1905d. *Reason in Religion*. New York: Scribner's; London: A. and C. Black.

———. 1905e. *Reason in Art*. New York: Scribner's; London: A. and C. Black.

———. 1914. The Logic of Fanaticism. *New Republic*, 28 November, pp. 18–19.

———. 1915. *Egotism in German Philosophy*. New York: Scribner's.

———. 1920. *Character and Opinion in the United States, with Reminiscences of William James and Josiah Royce and Academic Life in America*. New York: Charles Scribner's Sons.

———. 1923. *Scepticism and Animal Faith: Introduction to a System of Philosophy*. In New York: Scribner's. London: Constable.

———. 1925. *Dialogues in Limbo*. New York: Charles Scribner's Sons.

———. 1927. *The Realm of Essence: Book First*. New York: Scribner's; London: Constable.

———. 1930. *The Realm of Matter: Book Second*. New York: Scribner's; London: Constable.

———. 1935. *The Last Puritan: A Memoir in the Form of a Novel*. London: Constable; New York: Scribner's (1936).

———. 1938. *The Realm of Truth: Book Third*. New York: Scribner's; London: Constable.

———. 1940. *The Realm of Spirit: Book Fourth*. New York: Scribner's; London: Constable.

———. 1942. *Realms of Being*. One-Volume Edition, with a New Introduction by the Author. New York: Scribner's.

———. 1944. *Persons and Places: The Background of My Life*. New York: Scribner's; London: Constable.

———. 1945. *The Middle Span*. New York: Scribner's; London: Constable (1947).

———. 1946. *The Idea of Christ in the Gospels, or God in Man: A Critical Essay*. New York: Scribner's; Toronto: Saunders.

———. 1951. *Dominations and Powers: Reflections on Liberty, Society, and Government*. New York: Scribner's; London: Constable.

———. 1953. *My Host the World*. New York: Scribner's; London: Cresset Press.

———. 1954, *The Life of Reason, or The Phases of Human Progress*. One-Volume Edition. Revised by the Author in Collaboration with Daniel Cory. New York: Charles Scribner's Sons.

———. 1979. *The Complete Poems of George Santayana: A Critical Edition*. Ed. William G. Holzberger. Lewisburg: Bucknell University Press.

———. 1986. Persons and Places: Fragments of an Autobiography. In *The Works of George Santayana, Volume I*, ed. William G. Holzberger and Herman J. Saatkamp Jr. Cambridge, MA; London: MIT Press.

———. 1988. The Sense of Beauty: Being the Outlines of Aesthetic Theory. In *The Works of George Santayana, Volume II*, ed. William G. Holzberger and Herman J. Saatkamp Jr. Cambridge, MA; London: MIT Press.

———. 1994. The Last Puritan: A Memoir in the Form of a Novel. In *The Works of George Santayana, Volume IV*, ed. William G. Holzberger and Herman J. Saatkamp Jr. Cambridge, MA; London: The MIT Press.

———. 2001. The Letters of George Santayana, Book One, 1868–1909. In *The Works of George Santayana, Volume V*, ed. William G. Holzberger and Herman J. Saatkamp Jr. Cambridge, MA; London: MIT Press.

———. 2002a. The Letters of George Santayana, Book Two, 1910–1920. In *The Works of George Santayana, Volume V*, ed. William G. Holzberger and Herman J. Saatkamp Jr. Cambridge, MA; London: MIT Press.

———. 2002b. The Letters of George Santayana, Book Three, 1921–1927. In *The Works of George Santayana, Volume V*, ed. William G. Holzberger and Herman J. Saatkamp Jr. Cambridge, MA; London: MIT Press.

———. 2003a. The Letters of George Santayana, Book Four, 1928–1932. In *The Works of George Santayana, Volume V*, ed. William G. Holzberger and Herman J. Saatkamp Jr. Cambridge, MA; London: MIT Press.

———. 2003b. The Letters of George Santayana, Book Five, 1933–1936. In *The Works of George Santayana, Volume V*, ed. William G. Holzberger and Herman J. Saatkamp Jr. Cambridge, MA; London: MIT Press.

———. 2006. The Letters of George Santayana, Book Seven, 1941–1947. In *The Works of George Santayana, Volume V*, ed. William G. Holzberger and Herman J. Saatkamp Jr. Cambridge, MA; London: MIT Press.

———. 2008. The Letters of George Santayana, Book Eight, 1910–1920. In *The Works of George Santayana, Volume V*, ed. William G. Holzberger and Herman J. Saatkamp Jr. Cambridge, MA; London: MIT Press.

———. 2011. Book One: Reason in Common Sense. In *The Works of George Santayana*, ed. Marianne W. Wokeck and Martin A. Coleman. Cambridge, MA; London: The MIT Press.

———. 2013. Book Two: Reason in Society. In *The Works of George Santayana*, ed. Marianne W. Wokeck and Martin A. Coleman. Cambridge, MA; London: The MIT Press.

———. 2014. Book Three: Reason in Religion. In *The Works of George Santayana*, ed. Marianne W. Wokeck and Martin A. Coleman. Cambridge, MA; London: The MIT Press.

———. 2015. Book Four: Reason in Art. In *The Works of George Santayana*, ed. Marianne W. Wokeck and Martin A. Coleman. Cambridge, MA; London: The MIT Press.

———. 2016. Book Five: Reason in Science. In *The Works of George Santayana*, ed. Marianne W. Wokeck and Martin A. Coleman. Cambridge, MA; London: The MIT Press.

Schilpp, Paul Arthur, ed. 1940. *The Philosophy of George Santayana*. Evanston, IL: Northwestern University Press.

Smith, Kerri. 2008. Brain Makes Decisions Before You Even Know It. *Nature*, 11 April. https://www.nature.com/articles/news.2008.751.

Stevens, Wallace. 1957. *Opus Posthumous*. New York: Knopf.

Van Praet, Douglas. 2020. Our Brains Make Up Our Minds Before We Know It. *Psychology Today*, 21 December. https://www.psychologytoday.com/us/blog/unconscious-branding/202012/our-brains-make-our-minds-we-know-it?amp.

Velasquez-Manoff, Moises. 2020. The Brain Implants That Could Change Humanity: Brains Are Talking to Computers, and Computers to Brains. Are Our Daydreams Safe? *New York Times*, 28 August. https://www.nytimes.com/2020/08/28/opinion/sunday/brain-machine-artificial-intelligence.html.

Wharton, Edith. 1916. *The Book of the Homeless*. New York: Charles Scribner.

Yuste, Rafael. 2019. The NeuroRights Foundation. https://neurorightsfoundation.org/.

The Last Sceptic: Santayana, Descartes, and the External World

Douglas McDermid

> *There is but one indefectibly certain truth, and that is the truth that pyrrhonistic scepticism itself leaves standing,—that the present phenomenon of consciousness exists. That, however, is the bare starting-point of knowledge, the mere admission of a stuff to be philosophized about.*
> —William James *(1897, 14–15)*

> *All direct data are internal facts; and in the strictest sense all data are direct. Suppose a merely passive acceptance of what is in consciousness, and you have no belief in an external world. An addition to the data of consciousness, a more or less clearly voluntary reaction, is involved in your idea of external reality.*
> —Josiah Royce *(1885, 300–301)*

> *It is only because we are active beings that our world is bigger than the content of our actual experience ... [F]or the passive being the whole of reality would collapse into the actual procession of the given; indeed it must collapse into the specious present, since the objectivity of memory and anticipation is a complex interpretation put upon presented imagery.*
> —C. I. Lewis *(1929, 140–141)*

D. McDermid (✉)
Department of Philosophy, Trent University, Peterborough, ON, Canada
e-mail: dmcdermi@trentu.ca

© The Author(s), under exclusive license to Springer Nature Switzerland AG 2024
M. A. Coleman, G. Tiller (eds.), *The Palgrave Companion to George Santayana's Scepticism and Animal Faith*, Palgrave Companions, https://doi.org/10.1007/978-3-031-46367-9_3

I

In what sense is Santayana a sceptic, and in what sense is he a critic of scepticism? The purpose of this chapter is to shed some light on this question by examining Santayana's approach to the problem of the external world in *Scepticism and Animal Faith* and related writings.[1] That problem can be formulated very simply: assuming I have immediate knowledge of nothing but appearances, have I any reason to think that the way things appear to me is the way they really are? To put it another way, how can I know that the contents of my mind—ideas, impressions, perceptions, experiences—faithfully represent a mind-independent world?

II

Depending on your point of view, Descartes either invented or discovered the problem of the external world. Here is how he formulates it in Meditation I:

1. Knowledge of Nature is possible if and only if my beliefs about external things ultimately rest on something indubitable or absolutely trustworthy: "Reason ... convinces us that we should withhold assent just as carefully from whatever is not completely certain and indubitable as from what is clearly false" (Descartes 2000, 18).
2. Our pre-philosophical or "folk" theory of knowledge is naively empiricist. That is, we naturally think that our beliefs about external things are based on sensory appearances: "Everything I have accepted as being most true up to now I acquired from the senses or through the senses" (Descartes 2000, 19).
3. If our folk theory of knowledge is correct, we can have knowledge of Nature only if sensory appearances can guarantee the truth of at least some of our beliefs about external things. [From 1, 2]
4. In theory, however, I can doubt the existence of anything and everything I perceive (or seem to perceive) by means of my senses.
5. Either external world scepticism is true, or our pre-philosophical understanding of knowledge is false. [From 3, 4]

There is much one could say about the first and second premises of this argument. For the time being, however, let us confine our attention to its fourth premise. Why does Descartes think our ordinary perceptual judgments are not indubitable? He presents no fewer than five arguments in support of this contention.

a. *Fallibility.* Like everyone else, I have learned from experience that it is possible for an object to appear F when the object is not F (e.g., a square tower

---

[1] John McCormick, Santayana's biographer, describes *Scepticism and Animal Faith* as "[w]ithout any question, the single most distinctive work of Santayana's productive postwar period, or any in his life" (McCormick 1987, 256).

may look round when seen from a great distance). To make this discovery is to lose one's epistemological innocence; for once I know that things are not necessarily as they appear, I can no longer take sensory appearances at face value. Trusting my senses thus gives me a reason not to trust them implicitly.

b. *Delusions:* Why does yonder madman believe he is a purple-clad king surrounded by genteel, adoring courtiers? Answer: because that is the way things appear to him. For my part, I believe he is a poor naked patient in a mental asylum, watched over by sullen and brutal warders. And why do I believe this? Answer: because that is the way things appear to me. Well and good; but why am I entitled to assume that the way things really are is how they appear to me, and not the way they appear to the Man Who Would Be King?

c. *Dreams:* If it is possible that I am merely dreaming that I perceive external things, it is not certain that I really perceive them. However, it is always possible that I am only dreaming that I perceive external things, because any sensory or perceptual experience I can imagine having while awake has a subjectively indistinguishable dream counterpart. Sensory appearances, I now realize, can never guarantee the truth of any belief about trees and rocks. Yet sensory appearances seem to be the only evidence I have for the existence of external things. It follows, or seems to follow, that I can doubt the existence of anything which I perceive (or seem to perceive), even under the most favorable epistemic conditions I can imagine: "When I think about this more carefully, I see so clearly that I can never distinguish, by reliable signs, being awake from being asleep, that I am confused and this feeling of confusion almost confirms me in believing that I am asleep" (Descartes 2000, 19; cf. 61, 70).

d. *The Demon:* If it is possible that a fiendish arch-deceiver, hell-bent on deceiving me, has woven a web of invincible illusions, it is possible that all my perceptual judgments are false. Hence, I cannot be certain that things are as they appear unless I can conclusively rule out the possibility that "some evil mind, who is all powerful and cunning, has devoted all their energies to deceiving me" (Descartes 2000, 22). Much to my chagrin, this evil demon can never be exorcised; any attempt I make to rule out the possibility that I am his dupe will rely on something which I cannot know unless I have already ruled out the possibility that I am his dupe. Consequently, I cannot be certain that I am seated by the fire; I can only be certain that it seems to me as if I were so seated. That is to say, I can doubt the existence of everything except my mind and its contents: perceptions, ideas, impressions, appearances, experiences, representations, and the like.

e. *Experience and Causation:* The logical thrust of the previous two arguments can be presented in a slightly more formal way. If we suppose that your experience of a tree cannot constitute evidence for the tree's existence unless your experience of the tree is caused by the tree, you cannot be certain that your experience of the tree is evidence for the tree's existence unless you are certain that your experience of the tree is caused by the tree. However, you cannot be certain that your experience is caused by the tree unless you are certain that the tree exists, and you cannot be certain that the tree exists unless you are certain that your experience constitutes evidence for the tree's existence. Yet this was the very thing we set out to prove. It follows that you can never be certain that your experiences of trees are evidence that trees exist, that your experiences of rocks are evidence that rocks exist, and so on.

III

The conclusion of the Cartesian argument, the reader will recall, is not that external world scepticism is true; it is that scepticism is an inescapable consequence of our pre-philosophical or "folk" theory of knowledge (according to which our beliefs about external things ultimately rest on sensory appearances). In other words, Descartes's conclusion is a conditional: if we accept naive empiricism, scepticism is a foregone conclusion. For his part, Descartes is convinced that neither naive empiricism nor scepticism is correct. Knowledge of Nature is indeed possible, he contends, but only because there is something deeper and greater than Nature—something which our senses cannot grasp, but from which they derive whatever authority they may possess. How does Descartes arrive at this conclusion? His argument has four main steps.

a. *Self*: Although I can always doubt that things are as they appear, I cannot doubt anything unless I myself am something. To be more precise, I cannot doubt (or be dreaming, deluded, or deceived) unless I think: *cogito, ergo sum*. So, the first thing I know without any doubt is that I exist as a mind or a thing that thinks: "[T]his proposition 'I am, I exist' is necessarily true whenever it is stated by me or conceived by my mind" (Descartes 2000, 24). Although I have no idea yet how my mind is related to my body (assuming I have a body), I know this much: the existence of my mind is known immediately and with perfect certainty, whereas the existence of my body (if I have one) is not.

b. *God*: Having freed my thinking from its slavish dependence on the senses, I turn my gaze inward, only to find an idea of a supremely perfect being stamped upon my mind. Since I can prove that this idea must be more than a mere idea, I cannot doubt that a supremely perfect being or God exists. I also cannot doubt that this being will never deceive me, because "[a]ll deception or fraud involves some imperfection" (Descartes 2000, 44). It follows that my God-given faculties must be attuned to the truth and that whatever I can clearly and distinctly conceive cannot be false or impossible.

c. *Nature*: Since God's veracity ensures that I cannot make mistakes which I could never detect or correct, God would surely be a deceiver if external world scepticism were true: "I cannot see how he can be understood as not being a deceiver if they [ideas of physical things] originated from anything except physical things" (Descartes 2000, 63). Why is this? If my ideas of trees and rocks were not caused by mind-independent trees and rocks, (i) I would still believe such objects existed (because my God-given constitution naturally inclines me to believe in them); and (ii) I could never know I was mistaken (because God has not given me any faculty which would enable me to figure this out). But God is no deceiver. Therefore, most of our experiences must be caused by mind-independent objects, and those objects must be basically as they appear to us under favorable epistemic conditions.

d. *Science*: The key word here is "basically," because God's veracity only guarantees the independent reality of qualities which I can clearly and distinct conceive. Accordingly, I am not entitled to believe that secondary qualities of bodies (such as color, taste, or smell) are woven into the very fabric of the world. However, I can know that the primary qualities of bodies (such as shape and extension) are fully objective and mind-independent, because I can form clear and distinct conceptions of them. Since primary qualities can be quantified and measured, proof of their independent reality lays a sceptic-proof foundation for the scientific study of Nature. But if the underlying structure of Nature can only be fathomed by mathematics, reason has more authority than sense-perception. Hence, naive empiricism and scepticism have both been refuted.

IV

What does Santayana make of all this? To answer this question properly, we need to introduce a simple distinction. According to what we may call *certainty scepticism*, no beliefs in a given domain can be reckoned indubitable. According to what we may call *knowledge scepticism*, no beliefs in a given domain can constitute knowledge. Armed with this distinction, I shall now try to convince the reader of three things. First, that Santayana is a certainty sceptic—a much more radical and consistent one than Descartes. Second, that Santayana is not a knowledge sceptic about the external world; that is, he does not deny that we can and do know truths about mind-independent things. Third, that Santayana rejects knowledge scepticism *because* he accepts certainty scepticism (instead of defending knowledge scepticism on the basis of certainty scepticism *à la* Descartes).

V

According to Santayana, Descartes is a poor excuse for a certainty sceptic. So what, exactly, did the author of the *Meditations* fail to doubt? Santayana identifies four main issues.

Thesis 1: Descartes Fails to Doubt Metaphysical Principles Whose Truth Is Uncertain

a. *No Doubt without Dogma*: It can be doubted whether I see a real tree, Descartes argues, because it can be doubted whether a tree is the cause of my experience. However, this doubt rests on an invisible dogma: the premise that my experience must have a cause, an explanation, or a sufficient reason. Santayana is baffled by Descartes's willingness to rely on this assumption: "He thus assumed the principle of sufficient reason, a principle for which there is no reason at all" (*SAF*, 289). If we can doubt the testimony of our senses, Santayana asks, why can't we doubt the principle of sufficient reason?

b. *Insufficient Reason*: The rationalist's reply—"The principle of sufficient reason, unlike the contingent facts to which perception attests, is a necessary truth known independently of experience"—will not satisfy any certainty sceptic worth her salt, because we can doubt the rationalist's assumption that all things, seen and unseen, must obey the so-called truths of reason. Why on earth should we suppose that an objective world (assuming there is one) must meekly submit to the municipal laws of human subjectivity? To believe that Nature has a duty to conform to our minds is as presumptuous as it is implausible: "If any idea or axiom were really *a priori* and spontaneous in the human mind, it would be infinitely improbable that it should apply to the facts of nature" (*SAF*, 289).

c. *Facts and Principles*: Santayana draws two conclusions. In the first place, Descartes is much better at doubting facts (or classes of facts) than he is at doubting principles: "He could doubt any particular fact easily, with the shrewdness of a man of science who was also a man of the world" (*SAF*, 289). In the second place, Descartes's doubts about facts are made possible by his refusal to doubt principles (such as the principle of sufficient reason): "Descartes ... never doubted his principles of explanation" (*SAF*, 289). Scepticism in one domain thus depends on dogmatism in another.

Thesis 2: In theory, It Can Be Doubted Whether I Exist, Because the Existence of a Mind, Soul, or Self Is Not Self-evident

a. *The Cogito and Circularity*: If the cogito is supposed to be an argument, knowledge of the conclusion is presupposed by knowledge of the premise: "'I think, therefore I am,' if taken as an inference is sound because analytical, only repeating in the conclusion, for the sake of emphasis, something assumed in the premise" (*SAF*, 290). However, an argument is vitiated by circularity if we cannot know that its premises are true unless we already know that its conclusion is true. Hence the cogito, if construed as an argument, is question-begging.

b. *The Cogito and Uncertainty*: What if the cogito is understood not as an argument but as a direct statement of fact? The problem with this interpretation is straightforward: only the content of the present moment is indubitable but belief in the existence of anything requires one to go beyond the present moment. Existence, then, is never a given: "No fact is self-evident; and what sort of fact is this 'I,' and in what sense do I 'exist'?" (*SAF*, 290). Consequently, one's own existence is not indubitable.

c. *Solipsism*: Santayana thus agrees with F. H. Bradley that romantic solipsism is indefensible not because the self is immediately given in experience but precisely because it isn't: "Existence does not belong to a mere datum; nor am I a datum to myself; I am a somewhat remote and extremely obscure object of belief" (*SAF*, 290). Since doubting everything that can be doubted leaves the principled doubter without a self to call her own, any metaphysician seduced by solipsism is either (1) an inept certainty sceptic (because she already believes in the existence of something which is not immediately given) or (2) an inept knowledge sceptic (because if she knows that she exists, there is no reason to suppose she cannot know more than this). The first kind of sceptic is inconsistent because she believes too much; the second kind is inconsistent because she believes too little.[2]

    d. *The Humean Dissolution of the Self*: Santayana's doubts about the cogito are more radical than Hume's. The latter, it will be recalled, maintained that what we call the self is a mere bundle of perceptions. From Santayana's point of view, this supposedly sceptical analysis still takes far too much for granted. Pace Hume, perceptions themselves are merely posits; they are not self-certifying data or the immediate objects of human knowledge. Hence, a truly rigorous sceptic, determined to judge everything by the gold standard of certainty, will refuse to recognize their existence.

    e. *Hume's Dogma*: To put it another way, Hume must think that he knows there are impressions and ideas; otherwise, he could hardly espouse the bundle theory of the self. Yet if Santayana is right about the status of perceptions, no one can know that there are impressions and ideas unless posits are knowable. It follows that Hume's position requires him to acknowledge the epistemic respectability of posits. Yet this acknowledgment compromises Hume's scepticism. For if we are free to believe in entities which are not immediately given, why stop with impressions and ideas?[3]

Thesis 3: In Theory, It Can Be Doubted Whether Any Datum Is an Appearance. Hence, Knowledge of Your Own Ideas (Perceptions, Experiences, Impressions, Sense-data) Is Not Immediate and Certain

    a. *Certainty and Interpretation*: Certainty means that error is impossible. Since error is always possible when I interpret what is given, I can be wrong about everything except what is given exactly as it is given. Yet nothing is ever given to me as an appearance, because appearances always point beyond themselves: "In order to reach existence, intent must transcend intuition, and take data for what they mean, not for what they are" (*SAF*, 65). Consequently, it can be doubted whether any datum is an appearance.

    b. *Appearances as Signs*: Taken in itself, a datum is an essence; it is not a sign of anything. Yet appearances are signs, because appearances (whether veridical or non-veridical) are always appearances *of* something. It follows that data per se are not appearances; data become appearances when interpreted as such. However, interpretation introduces the possibility of error. It can therefore be doubted that any datum has the status of an appearance: "I have absolute

---

[2] In Bradley's words, "[w]e always have too much or too little" (Bradley 1930, 219).
[3] For more on Santayana's objections to Hume's philosophy, see Wahman (2007).

assurance of nothing save of the character of some given essence; the rest is arbitrary belief or interpretation added by animal impulse" (*SAF*, 110).

  c. *Appearances and Interpretation*: Since signs refer to what is not given, I cannot think of anything as an appearance without thinking of it as related to something which is not a datum: "If I hypostatise an essence into a fact, instinctively placing it in relations which are not given within it, I am putting my trust in animal faith" (*SAF*, 99–100). However, it cannot be the case that the datum is given as an appearance if I must think of more than the datum in order to think of it as an appearance. Hence it can be doubted whether any datum is an appearance.

  d. *Interpretation and Animal Faith*: Just as there can be no appearances or signs without interpretation, there can be no interpretation without *animal faith*: "This assurance of the not-given is involved in action, in expectation, in fear, hope, or want; I call it animal faith" (*BH*, 255; cf. *PP*, 171, 443).[4] To be more precise, Santayana uses the term "animal faith" to refer to a shared framework of principles and categories which are psychologically irresistible (we cannot help accepting them or suspend our natural credulity for long), theoretically groundless (they are not the products of reason), and practically indispensable (we cannot engage with the world or one another unless we take them for granted). In short, the principles of animal faith are practical postulates; they are what every agent qua agent believes spontaneously and without proof.[5]

  e. *Interpretation and Agency*: Since appearances presuppose animal faith, and animal faith presupposes action, there can only be appearances for striving, self-assertive beings with practical interests. Agency is thus a condition of knowledge; without a will, I would have no world or self to call my own.

> In reality none of the facts which the sturdy Briton feels that he knows—and they are the true facts of nature and of moral life—would be known to him if he were without tentative intelligence and instinctive animal faith; indeed, without these the senses would have no virtue and would inform us of nothing.... (*SE*, 193–194)

Perfectly passive and receptive spirits, having no preferences to satisfy and no aims to pursue, could know nothing; for they would only be acquainted with data per se, not with data as signs. Knowledge is thus the natural child of need, not the legitimate offspring of logic. In short, our way of relating to the world in thought as well as in action depends in the end on will. This truth was intuited by Fichte and Schopenhauer, however imperfectly they articulated it.

  f. *Fair Harvard Holds Sway*: From what we have seen, it is clear that Santayana agrees with William James, Josiah Royce, and C. I. Lewis about two

---

[4] McCormick's elucidation of "animal faith" is succinct and concrete: "Animal faith is what makes action possible; it is his version of common sense. It is the athlete's certainty that the ball he hits with his bat is a substantial ball and not the idea, or essence, of a ball; it is the rabbit's unthinking zigzag when pursued by the hound" (McCormick 1987, 257–258).

[5] Compare this with Royce's definition of postulates: "Postulates ... are not blind faith. Postulates are voluntary assumptions of a risk for the sake of a higher end" (Royce 1885, 298).

things of considerable importance. (1) *The Dualism of Scheme and Content*: Because data per se are not objects of knowledge, something must be added to them; otherwise, knowledge would be impossible. Hence, interpretation is a condition of knowledge: concepts and categories must be applied to whatever is immediately given. (2) *The Primacy of Practice*: Because human beings are primarily practical creatures, not placid Platonic contemplatives, human knowledge cannot be understood apart from human agency.[6] Far from being passive or unbiased, the human mind is selective; far from being disinterested, our interpretations are expressions of purpose and will.

VI

Santayana's next complaint is that Descartes refuses to doubt the testimony of memory. Why is this sin of omission so serious? Simple: "Belief in memory is implicit in the very rudiments of mind; mind and memory are indeed names for almost the same thing" (*SAF*, 150).

Thesis 4: In Theory, It Can Be Doubted Whether Memory Is Trustworthy, Whether Any Datum Is a Memory, and Whether Time Is Real

a. *Memory and Perception*: Memory depends on perception, because we cannot identify past events without referring to a public world apprehended by sense: "Memory itself must report facts or events in the natural world, if it is to be knowledge and deserve the name of memory" (*SAF*, 13; cf. 158–159, 242). It follows that I cannot be certain that memory can be trusted unless I can be certain that perception can be trusted. However, Descartes showed us that we can never be certain that our perceptions are veridical: "Perception *is* faith; more perception may extend this faith or reform it, but can never recant it except by sophistry" (*SAF*, 69). Therefore, we can never be certain that our memories of facts or events are veridical.

b. *No Memories without Appearances*: If memory is beholden to perception, I can be certain that some datum is a memory only if I can be certain that some datum is a perception or an appearance: "Memory records moral events in terms of their physical occasions; and if the latter are merely imaginary, the former must be doubly so, like the thoughts of a personage in a novel" (*SAF*, 13; cf. 150, 242). However, it can be doubted whether any datum is a perception or appearance. It can therefore be doubted whether any datum is a memory.

c. *Memory and Interpretation*: Since "in memory ... there is a tacit assumption of things removed, threatening, eventual, as yet unknown" (*RE*, 47), memories are signs (just as appearances and perceptions are signs). Hence, I

---

[6] No-one has stated this more clearly than John Lachs: "The standards of knowledge must ... grow naturally out of the demands imposed upon us by the need for intelligent action" (Lachs 1988, 18).

cannot think of a datum as a memory unless I relate that datum to something which is not a datum: "In remembering I believe that I am taking cognisance not of a given essence but of a remote existence" (*SAF*, 164). However, it cannot be the case that the datum is given as a memory if I must think of more than the datum in order to think of it as a memory. Consequently, it can be doubted whether any datum is a memory (just as it can be doubted whether any datum is an appearance or a perception).

d. *The Reality of Change*: In order to perceive a ball rolling down an inclined plane, I must knit or weave my perceptions together in a certain order, connecting what I see now with what I saw a moment ago. Similarly, I cannot dream that I am seated by the fire unless I am conscious of a sequence of appearances, a private parade of phantasms. The point is that awareness of change is impossible unless there is awareness of succession—of one thing following another in time. Yet this kind of awareness is impossible without apperception, and apperception is impossible without memory. Since apperception and memory both depend on animal faith, the latter is a condition of our awareness of succession. It follows that the reality of actual change can be doubted, as can the reality of causal relations: "Events, and the reality of change they involve, may therefore be always illusions. The sceptic can ultimately penetrate to the vision of a reality from which they should be excluded" (*SAF*, 30; cf. p. 26).[7]

e. *The Past is Another Country*: So far, we have taken it for granted that something happened yesterday, a week ago, a month ago, a century ago, and so on. However, a thoroughgoing certainty sceptic will remind us that the reality of the past can be doubted (just as the existence of Nature can be doubted).

> As the whole world might collapse and cease at any moment, nullifying all expectations, so it might at any moment have sprung out of nothing, and have begun today, with this degree of complexity and illusive memory, as well as long ago, with whatever energy and momentum it was first endowed with. (*SAF*, 36)

Since nothing can be certain but what is given, and nothing is given but the present moment, everything can be doubted except the content of the present moment. Hence the past, no less than the future, is a posit; memory, no less than hope, is "an act of faith" (*SAF*, 154).

f. *The Reality of Time*: Because it is essentially a member of a temporal series, a moment can only be experienced as such in relation to other moments. Similarly, a moment can only be experienced as present (as "Now") in relation to a remembered past and an anticipated future. It is at this point that Santayana poses his overwhelming question: What if nothing given is given to you but the present moment?[8] The answer is paradoxical. If nothing but the present

---

[7] Santayana's views on causation are clarified by Kerr-Lawson (2005).

[8] "[W]hat would experience of the present be if the veracity of primary memory were denied, and if I no longer believed that anything had just happened, or that I had ever been in the state from which I suppose myself to have passed into this my present condition?" (*SAF*, 36; cf. 39).

moment is given, what is given cannot be given as the present moment; and if what is given is not given as the present moment, we cannot be certain that any temporal predicates apply to what is given. However, we cannot be certain that temporal predicates apply to anything if we cannot be certain that they apply to what is given. Time is thus "an immense postulate" (*SAF*, 112) whose reality can be doubted.

g. *Santayana and Royce*: Santayana's reasoning here is the mirror-image of an argument advanced by Royce thirty years earlier.[9] The major premise of Royce's argument is the following conditional: if I can know the present moment, I must know more than the present moment. Affirming the antecedent, Royce arrives at his idealist-friendly conclusion: there must be more to the self that knows the present moment than can be given in the present moment.[10] The major premise of Santayana's argument is a conditional similar (though not identical) to Royce's: if it is certain that I am aware of the present moment as the present moment, it is certain that I am aware of more than the present moment. Unlike Royce, Santayana does not affirm the antecedent; instead, he audaciously denies the consequent. Since the present moment is not given to me as the present moment, Santayana reasons, what is immediately given must be stripped or divested of its temporal character.

VII

Nature, events, substance, space, time, duration, identity, change, causation, perceptions, memories, minds, selves: our worldview is peopled with posits from top to bottom. So, what remains when the meaning added to data by animal faith is subtracted? To answer this question is to know what is truly indubitable.

Thesis 5: *In Theory, It Can Be Doubted Whether Anything Exists or Has Ever Existed. For Nothing Is Indubitable Except Essences, and Essences Do Not Exist*

a. *The Given De-mythologized*: What is the nature of the immediately given? It is much easier to say what it isn't. (i) No spatial or temporal predicates can be applied to what is immediately given. (ii) Unlike contingent things, what is immediately given is neither fleeting nor enduring; it can neither change nor remain the same. (iii) What is immediately given is not a part of any whole nor a member of any series. (iv) What is immediately given has no external

---

[9] In "The Implications of Self-Consciousness" (1892), reprinted in Royce (1898).

[10] "The Self is never *merely* the self of this moment, since the self of this moment never fully knows who he even now is. It is of his very essence to appeal beyond the moment to a justly reflective Self who shall discover and so reflectively determine who he is, and so who I am. For I am he" (Royce 1898, 154).

relations; it is an ontological island, entire unto itself. (v) There is no more to the pure datum than what we intuit; here seeming and being necessarily coincide.

b. *Ultimate Scepticism*: Since Santayana maintains that anything whose being is defined by this litany of negations cannot be said to exist except in a Pickwickian sense, he concludes that "nothing given exists" (*SAF*, 49).[11] Yet if nothing given exists, it cannot be certain that anything does: "For all an ultimate scepticism can see, therefore, there may be no facts at all, and perhaps nothing has ever existed" (*SAF*, 40; cf. 35). Does it follow that what is immediately given is nothing? No, because existence is not the only mode of being: "[P]eople suppose that whatever is non-existent is nothing—a stupid positivism, like that of saying that the past is nothing, or the future nothing" (*SAF*, 129).

c. *The Pure Datum*: When data are not viewed through the turbulent medium of our needs or forced to serve as signs, they show us what they are in themselves, without reference to anything else: "The datum ceases to be an appearance, in the proper and pregnant sense of this word, since it ceases to imply any substance that appears or any mind to which it appears" (*SAF*, 39; cf. *DP*, 21). Stripped of its practical and human meaning, the pure datum has no implications or relations, no location or duration; it is simply what it is, neither mental nor physical, insubstantial yet eternal.

d. *The Realm of Essence*: Uninterpreted data are "ideal and definite forms of being" (*DP*, 12), or what Santayana calls essences. Since the distinction between appearance and reality does not apply to essences, we cannot be mistaken about them. Nevertheless, essences cannot be known, because they do not exist; they can only be intuited or contemplated.[12] Hence our quest for certainty has yielded certainty but not *knowledge*.

> My scepticism at last has touched bottom ... Whatever essence I find and note, that essence and no other is established before me. I cannot be mistaken about it, since I now have no object of intent other than the object of intuition. (*SAF*, 74)

What have we discovered? According to Santayana, the doubts of the certainty sceptic have freed us from the flux and contingency of existence; the suspension of animal faith has revealed a realm of immutable being; and our

---

[11] Some readers might object that it is Santayana's notion of existence which is hopelessly artificial or Pickwickian. Lachs disagrees: "Santayana's concept of existence ... is not far removed from our ordinary notion. When we say that something exists, we mean at least that it can be found as an item separate from others, that it endures for a while, and that it can do a variety of things to affect its neighbours. This is the notion we have in mind when we say that the Atlantic Ocean exists but that Socrates does not any more, that snakes exist but the square root of seven never did" (Lachs 1988, 36–37).

[12] Timothy Sprigge's re-statement of Santayana's conclusion is helpful: "[O]ne who really succeeds in giving up every belief not established as true by immediate experience, will not believe in the existence even of that which, in fact, he does immediately experience, still less of his immediate experience of it" (Sprigge 1995, 41).

scrupulous refusal to interpret data has uncovered a form of cognition—intuition of essence—more fundamental than belief or knowledge of fact.

VIII

Given that Santayana endorses a form of certainty scepticism than which no greater can be conceived, why doesn't he deny that knowledge of the external world is possible? Here are three reasons.

Thesis 6: The Distinction Between Appearance and Reality Cannot Be Exploited by Realism's Opponents: External World Sceptics, Idealists, Phenomenalists, and the Like

a. *A Dualism and a Dilemma*: Santayana observes that we cannot distinguish appearances from real things unless we have epistemic access to both: "Were it not for what we know of the outer world and of our place in it, we should be incapable of attaching any meaning to subjectivity" (*LR*5, 185). Hence, one of two things must be true: either we cannot know there are appearances (because we lack epistemic access to real things), or external world scepticism must be false (because we have such access). Sceptical doubts about appearances must thus be based on common sense and science.[13] To put it another way, no-one who denies that Nature is knowable can rely on the distinction between appearance and reality, because that distinction is part of a scientific theory:

> [H]ow are we supposed to know that what we call facts are mere appearances and what we call objects mere creations of thought? We know this by physics. It is physiology, a part of physics, that assures us that our senses and brains are conditions of our experience. (*LR*5, 185)

If external world scepticism were true, Santayana reasons, we could not contrast perceptions with objects, ideas with things, or appearances with reality.[14] Therefore, philosophers who employ these dualisms to defend scepticism have contradicted themselves.

b. *Taking Leave of our Senses*: You cannot have senses unless you have a body, and your body is an object in space and time. Therefore, you cannot believe that you have senses unless you believe that Nature is not wholly unknowable. It follows (or seems to follow) that we cannot assume that our beliefs about Nature depend on the testimony of our senses without assuming that Nature is knowable. Since the external world sceptic happily endorses the

---

[13] Santayana thus anticipates one of Quine's key claims about scepticism: "Doubt prompts the theory of knowledge, yes; but knowledge, also, was what prompted the doubt. Scepticism is an offshoot of science. The basis for scepticism is the awareness of illusion, the discovery that we must not always believe our eyes. ... Illusions are illusions only relative to a prior acceptance of genuine bodies with which to contrast them" (Quine 1975, 67–68).

[14] A version of this argument can be found in Royce (1897), Sections IV–VI.

first assumption while rudely rejecting the second, her premise is logically cancelled by her conclusion: "The contradiction would be curious if a man should declare that his ideas were worthless, being due to his organs of sense, and that therefore these organs (since he had an idea of them) did not exist" (*LR5*, 186). Scepticism about the veracity of our senses thus effectively subverts itself; for if it were true, no-one could defend it.[15]

c. *Self-knowledge and Interpretation*: Knowledge of my own mind is no more immediate or indubitable than knowledge of Nature, Santayana maintains, because neither sort of knowledge is possible without interpretation and animal faith: "Belief in the existence of anything, including myself, is something radically incapable of proof, and resting, like all belief, on some irrational persuasion or prompting of life" (*SAF*, 35). Since I cannot believe that I have experiences but stubbornly refuse to believe in trees and rocks, the invidious Cartesian distinction between the knowledge each of us has of our own minds (as immediate and indubitable) and the knowledge we have of Nature (as mediate and problematic) must be given up. The bad news, at least for devout Cartesians, is that our subjectivity is no sanctuary for world-weary doubters. The good news is that Nature is not hidden behind a veil of perception or an iron curtain of representations:

> There is certainly a vehicle in the perception and conception of natural objects, a sensuous and logical vehicle quite unlike the efficacious thing; and often the symbol is the more faithful in effect, the more succinct and alien it is in quality. But there is no screen of ideas; there is no arrest of cognition upon them. The "idea" is not an object. ... (*LSK*, 437–438)

Since knowledge of ideas is neither immediate nor immaculate, Mind is not epistemically prior to Nature. But if Mind is not epistemically prior to Nature, the Cartesian mind is a myth; there is no self-intimating inner world, no sceptic-proof sphere of pure subjectivity. Santayana arrives in this way at the same conclusion as his fellow naturalist John Dewey: philosophers must set aside the dogmatic subjectivism and representationalism which have dominated their discipline since the seventeenth century.[16]

d. *Animal Faith and Parity*. To say that appearances are not data is to say, inter alia, that we believe in appearances because animal faith compels us to posit them. However, animal faith also compels us to posit mind-independent things or substances: "The belief [in substance] must always remain an assumption, but one without which an active and intelligent creature cannot honestly act or think" (*RM*, 8). Consequently, it is no less natural or reasonable to

---

[15] Santayana echoes Epicurus: "If you fight against all sensations, you will have no standard by which to judge even those of them which you say are false" (*Principal Doctrines*, XXIII; cf. Bailey 1926, 101).

[16] "Since the seventeenth century this conception of experience as the equivalent of subjective private consciousness set over against nature, which consists wholly of physical objects, has wrought havoc in philosophy" (Dewey 1929, 11).

believe that objects exist apart from our perceptual experiences than it is to believe that we have perceptual experiences. Unfortunately, sceptics and idealists have failed to see this; that is why they insist that human knowledge is confined to appearances or ideas. Accordingly, veil-of-ideas scepticism is internally inconsistent, as is the kind of idealism developed in response to it: "I see here how halting is the scepticism of those modern philosophers who have supposed that to exist is to be an idea in the mind, or an object of consciousness, or a fact of experience" (*SAF*, 45; cf. 57–58, 65).[17]

e. *Either-Or*: Santayana's objection can be re-formulated as a dilemma. *First horn*: If we know there are appearances, knowledge cannot require certainty, because it is not certain that any datum is an appearance. But if appearances are knowable, why aren't mind-independent objects? The sceptic's taste in posits seems utterly capricious and unprincipled.[18] *Second horn*: If we do not know there are appearances, they are in the same boat, epistemically speaking, as mind-independent objects. But the external world sceptic assumes that appearances are better known to us than trees and rocks. *Conclusion*: Either certainty is not a condition of knowledge, or the problem of the external world is ill-posed.

f. *Against Things-In-Themselves*: Santayana rejects the Kantian claim that there is a realm of things-in-themselves lurking, Polonius-like, behind the arras of appearances. Why? Since we cannot say anything about the nature or attributes of a wholly unknowable reality, we cannot distinguish it from anything—or, for that matter, from nothing.[19] The thing-in-itself thus has no content; it is a vacuous and idle abstraction.

> Nothing can be intrinsically unknowable; for if any one was tempted to imagine a substance such that it should antecedently defy description, inasmuch as that substance had no assignable character, he would be attributing existence to a nonentity. (*USL*, 8; cf. *USL*, 16, *LSK*, 425)

To put it another way, we cannot think or speak meaningfully about things-in-themselves unless we can form some conception of them. However, we cannot form any conception of what lies permanently beyond our ken. Consequently, sceptics have attempted to do the impossible; where one should remain silent, they chatter and babble with abandon. One needn't be a Hegelian to endorse

---

[17] Jessica Wahman highlights Santayana's exposure of this inconsistency: "Santayana's philosophy of animal faith aims to correct modern philosophy's dogmatic scepticism by asserting that we should be both more sceptical about our knowledge of ideas and less sceptical about our knowledge of fact" (Wahman 2007, 7).

[18] As Glenn Tiller has observed, one of Santayana's targets in *Scepticism and Animal Faith* is traditional empiricism: "A thorough and consistent empiricism, he argued, necessarily terminates in a stultifying scepticism where every belief is renounced as unwarranted. ... In Santayana's analysis, the empiricist only retains the belief in appearances because he is not sufficiently sceptical" (Tiller 2006, 212–213).

[19] For more on Santayana and the varieties of unknowability, see Tiller (2006).

Bradley's terse verdict: "The assertion of a reality falling outside knowledge, is quite nonsensical" (Bradley 1930, 114).

g. *Appearances and Relativity*. Because our awareness of the world is conditioned by our peculiar faculties and interests, we can only know things as they appear to us: "The ideas we have of things are not fair portraits; they are political caricatures made in the human interest" (*SAF*, 104). Does this admission of relativity open the door to scepticism, idealism, or phenomenalism? No, because knowledge of things as they appear to us is still knowledge of *things*; it is not knowledge of Kantian phenomena or mere appearances: "Knowledge ... is not knowledge of appearance, but appearances are knowledge of substance when they are taken for signs of it" (*USL*, 25). As Santayana points out, the fact that we know things by means of our senses does not mean that the things we know are sense-data or ideas:

> Even if ideas intervene between us and things, it does not follow that the ideas must become the object of knowledge and keep the things from being known. Words often intervene between us and ideas, but they do not necessarily prevent us from gathering what those ideas are. So ideas themselves may be an instrument or vehicle for knowing things ... (*LSK*, 422)

In short, appearances are not *what* we know (the immediate objects of knowledge); they are *how* we know (the vehicles or medium of knowledge). Here Santayana is much closer to Aquinas (who held that the intelligible species is that by which our intellect knows and understands things) than he is to Locke (who held that ideas or subjective representations are the immediate objects of perception and knowledge).[20]

h. *Literal and Symbolic Truth*. Old-fashioned empiricism assumed that our ideas must resemble things in order to represent them. Like James and Dewey, Santayana repudiates the copy conception of knowledge and mind:

> The discouragement we may feel in science does not come from failure; it comes from a false conception of what would be success. Our worst difficulties arise from the assumption that knowledge of existences ought to be literal, whereas knowledge of existences has no need, no propensity, and no fitness to be literal. (*SAF*, 101)

According to Santayana, perceivers do not copy the given; they interpret it: "Perception is a stretching forth of intent beyond intuition; it is an exercise of intelligence" (*SAF*, 282). Truth in this domain is not literal, because perceptions and appearances are signs; at once poetical and practical, they point beyond themselves with the assistance of animal faith, directing our attention to what is not given. Since there need be no qualitative similitude between a sign and what it signifies, an object can be known by means of appearances or

---

[20] For more on the contrast between Thomistic realism and modern representative realism, see Gilson (1939).

perceptions which do not resemble it. Accordingly, "knowledge is, and ought to be, symbolic" (*SAF*, 101; cf. 103; cf. *PP*, 443).

i. *The Vindication of Realism*: Once we have seen through scepticism and idealism, we have no choice but to endorse some form of metaphysical realism. Is this because we can prove that mind-independent objects exist? No, replies Santayana; it is because we can prove that no proof of this was ever needed. Since it is evident to any honest observer that human beings cannot act without positing an independent world in which we live and move and have our being, the idea that Nature exists in its own right is unquestionably an article of animal faith.[21] However, the articles of animal faith are our ultimate presuppositions; and ultimate presuppositions can neither be demonstrated nor doubted. Consequently, no proof of an external world is necessary or possible:

> You cannot prove realism to a complete sceptic or idealist; but you can show an honest man that he is not a complete sceptic or idealist, but a realist at heart. So long as he is alive his sincere philosophy must fulfil the assumptions of his life ... (*TPR*, 184)

> What presuppositions do we make in pursuing knowledge of anything? And I reply: We presuppose that there is some real object or event to be known or reported, prior or subsequent to the report that reaches us ... To assert this principle of realism is no more than honesty. (*RS*, 277; cf. *SAF*, 8, 172)

If Santayana is right, Descartes was doubly deceived: first, because he thought he could prove the existence of an external world; second, because he thought he needed to prove it. As far as Santayana is concerned, the realist only needs to show that there is no reason for us to doubt what all of us must believe without reason: that there exists a comprehensive whole, spread out in space and time, whose parts (seen and unseen) exist in their own right and are systematically interconnected.

Thesis 7: *Knowledge Is Compatible with the Possibility of Error; It Does Not Require Absolute Certainty*

a. *By Their Fruits*. If certainty is necessary for knowledge, no-one can know whether anything exists (or has ever existed). Now, one would be hard pressed to find a more counterintuitive and incredible claim than this. So we must choose: will we reject that claim, or will we reject Aristotle's view that philosophy must give endoxa their due? Santayana, it is plain, sides with the Stagirite:

> I am not concerned about make-believe philosophies, but about my actual beliefs ... Scepticism, if it could be sincere, would be the best of philosophies. But I suspect that other sceptics, as well as I, always believe in substance, and that

---

[21] Indeed, Lachs describes realism as "the first great tenet of animal faith ... the central commitment of animal faith" (Lachs 1988, 47).

their denial of it is sheer sophistry and the weaving of verbal arguments in which their most familiar and massive convictions are ignored. (*SAF*, 186; cf. *DP*, 6–8)

Since the preposterous conclusion that no-one can know whether anything exists is a logical consequence of the certainty requirement, the latter must be rejected along with the former. Certainty, then, cannot be a necessary condition of knowledge or of warranted belief.[22]

b. *The Logical Limits of Self-criticism*: It is one thing to say we know less than we think we know; quite another to say that no-one can know anything at all. The first assertion is admirably Socratic; the second is impudent misology disguised as modesty. Not coincidentally, this second view is also self-defeating: "[T]he critical attitude, when it refuses to rest at some point on vulgar faith, inhibits all belief, denies all claims to knowledge, and becomes dishonest; because it itself claims to know" (*SAF*, 187). Since our faculties cannot be regarded as trustworthy if scepticism is true, sceptics can have no reason to believe anything (including the thesis of scepticism) or to doubt anything (including our common-sense beliefs).[23] What can we infer from this? Santayana reaches the same conclusion as Reid and Hegel: our cognitive faculties cannot sit in judgment on themselves, so they must be regarded as basically trustworthy (though not infallible). All inquirers must thus take it for granted "that intelligence is by nature veridical, and that its ambition to reach the truth is sane and capable of satisfaction" (*SAF*, 9).

c. *The Priority of Common Sense*: Nothing is more credible or evident than the soothing truisms of common sense: "[C]ommon sense, in a rough dogged way, is technically sounder than the special schools of philosophy, each of which squints and overlooks half the facts and half the difficulties" (*SAF*, v). However, the premises of a sceptical argument must be more evident to us than the proposition against which the argument is directed; otherwise, the objection will be self-subverting. So Reid and Peirce were right: we can never think of ourselves as having good reason to doubt the truth of our instinctive convictions, even though these convictions are not logically certain.[24] The metaphilosophical moral, Santayana contends, couldn't be clearer: since nothing

---

[22] It would be hard to improve on Sprigge's characterization of Santayana's anti-sceptical strategy: "On the whole Santayana's explorations of scepticism are designed to show the hopelessness of a certain conception of knowledge, that for which knowledge must be based on indubitable foundations, not to show the impossibility of knowledge on a more sensible interpretation of the term" (Sprigge 1995, 47).

[23] Herman Saatkamp, I believe, is absolutely right: "Santayana is using reason to undermine rationality itself. Sceptical doubts taken to the extreme remove the foundation for reason; and, in so doing, undermine the basis of scepticism itself" (Saatkamp Jr. 2017, 12).

[24] Recall Peirce's indignant critique of the feigned or paper doubts of the Cartesian sceptic: "Do you call it doubting to write down on a piece of paper that you doubt? If so, doubt has nothing to do with any serious business. But do not make-believe; if pedantry has not eaten all reality out of you, recognize, as you must, that there is much that you do not doubt, in the least" (Peirce 1931–1935, 5.416; cf. 5.265). For more on Santayana's relation to Peirce, see Lachs (1980) and Tiller (2008).

has more authority for us than these humble yet tenacious beliefs, "any pretensions which criticism might set up to being more profound than common sense would be false pretensions" (*SAF*, 187). Reason cannot contradict Nature, we must conclude, because Reason derives its authority from Nature.

d. *Sola Fide*: Because there can be no knowledge without interpretation, there can be no knowledge without animal faith. However, the principles of animal faith are mere postulates; they are not clear and distinct ideas (Descartes), divinely revealed truths (Malebranche), first principles of common sense (Reid), or synthetic *a priori* judgments (Kant).[25] If this is so, our beliefs and our doubts depend in the end on things for which there is no theoretical justification. It follows that even the most tough-minded souls among us live by faith and not by sight: "[A]ll alleged knowledge of matters of fact is faith only ... an existing world, whatever form it may choose to wear, is intrinsically a questionable thing" (*SAF*, 49). To put it another way, knowledge cannot be understood apart from agency, and agency is inconceivable without faith or unreasoned commitments. Since none of us can survive without believing in things which none of us can prove, knowledge must be compatible with the possibility of error.

e. *Animal Faith and Truth*: Truth means that our signs agree with the things they are intended to signify. However, a sign refers to something which is not immediately given, and anything which is not immediately given can be doubted in theory. Strictly speaking, therefore, it is not certain that there is such a thing as truth, at least in the sense of true belief or judgment.[26] But can we doubt it? No, because doubting makes sense only if you recognize some objective and independent standard to which opinions and descriptions ought to conform: "Scepticism is a suspicion of error about facts, and to suspect error about facts is to share in the enterprise of knowledge, in which facts are presupposed and error is possible" (*SAF*, 8; cf. *IPR*, 12–14). We can see well enough where this leads: if there is no doubt without a belief in truth, and no belief in truth without animal faith, the framework of animal faith is a condition of the possibility of doubt. Therefore, scepticism cannot attack animal faith without destroying itself.

f. *The Analysis of Knowledge*: According to Santayana, S knows that p if and only if (i) S believes that p; (ii) p is true; and (iii) S believes p because p is true, and S would not believe p if p were not true:

---

[25] Compare Santayana's "animal faith" with James's "postulates of rationality" (James 1890 II, 670).

[26] This claim had already been defended by James in a passage which deserves more attention than it has received: "Our belief in truth itself, for instance, that there is a truth, and that our minds and it are made for each other,—what is it but a passionate affirmation of desire, in which our social system backs us up? We want to have a truth, we want to believe that our experiments and studies and discussions must put us in a continually better and better position towards it; and on this line we agree to fight out our thinking lives. But if a pyrrhonistic sceptic asks us *how we know* all this, can our logic find a reply? No! certainly it cannot. It is just one volition against another" (James 1897, 9–10; cf. 12, 17, 23).

[K]nowledge is true belief grounded in experience, I mean, controlled by outer facts. It is not true by accident; it is not shot into the air on the chance that there may be something it may hit. It arises by a movement of the self sympathetic or responsive to surrounding beings ... (*SAF*, 180; cf. 164, 178)

If Santayana is right about this, warrant (or whatever converts a true belief into knowledge) does not need to be something to which the believer has epistemic access. Hence, Descartes was wrong: in order to know that I am seated by the fire, I do not need to exclude the possibility that I am dreaming. Nevertheless, Descartes was right about this much: I cannot be certain that I am seated by the fire unless I can rule out the possibility that I am dreaming. Hence, knowledge cannot require certainty if Santayana's analysis is sound.

g. *The Tables Turned*: Am I certain that the certainty requirement is false? No, but I do not need to be certain of this unless the certainty requirement is true, which is the very point at issue. Furthermore, philosophers who think the certainty requirement is true cannot claim to know that it is true, because they cannot be certain that it is true. Consequently, knowledge sceptics who measure our beliefs by the standard of certainty cannot accuse us of dogmatism without being guilty of it themselves.

Scepticism is accordingly a form of belief. Dogma cannot be abandoned; it can only be revised in view of some more elementary dogma which it has not yet occurred to the sceptic to doubt; and he may be right in every point of his criticism, except in fancying that his criticism is radical and that he is altogether a sceptic. (*SAF*, 8–9)

Think of it this way: since doubt requires grounds or reasons, nothing can be doubted unless something is not doubted. Hence if nothing is certain, the certainty-besotted Cartesian cannot doubt anything. What this shows, Santayana thinks, is that doubt is possible only if we do not doubt everything that can be doubted: "Scepticism is always possible while it is partial" (*LR1*, 55).

Thesis 8: Not Only Is Knowledge Compatible with the Possibility of Error; Knowledge Is Impossible Without that Possibility

a. *Knowledge and Data*: Data per se are essences, and essences cannot be known; they can only be intuited. Consequently, knowledge must be concerned with something over and above what is immediately given. Yet nothing is certain except what is immediately given: "For all an ultimate scepticism can see, therefore, there may be no facts at all, and perhaps nothing has ever existed" (*SAF*, 40; cf. 35). Hence, knowledge by its very nature cannot be certain, any more than a triangle can have four sides.

b. *Certainty without Truth*: The point can be made in another way. Nothing interpreted can be certain; everything except what is immediately given can be doubted. However, what is immediately given is neither true nor false; it simply *is*: "That which is certain and given ... is something of which existence cannot be predicated, and which, until it is used as a description, cannot be either false or true" (*SAF*, 45; cf. *LSK*, 432). Hence, certainty and knowledge must be mutually exclusive, because there is no possibility of knowledge where there is no possibility of truth. Doubt thus leads not to the denial of knowledge but to a deeper understanding of knowledge's nature.

c. *Belief and Interpretation*: Since belief in the existence of anything is impossible without interpretation, our beliefs must go beyond what is immediately given; otherwise, they would not be beliefs. Yet anything can be doubted which goes beyond what is immediately given. Since "the belief in existence, in the nature of the case, can be a belief only" (*SAF*, 35) because it is a hypothesis, beliefs can never be certain: "Belief in the existence of anything ... is something radically incapable of proof" (*SAF*, 35). Hence, the Cartesian idea of indubitable knowledge with respect to matters of fact is a contradiction in terms.

d. *Belief and Expectation*: There can be no knowledge without belief, and no belief without expectation or anticipation. However, there can be no expectation without the possibility of disappointment or frustration:

> [E]xpectation is like hunger; it opens its mouth, and something probably drops into it, more or less, very often, the sort of thing it expected; but sometimes a surprise comes, and something nothing. Life involves expectation, but does not prevent death. (*SAF*, 36)

Because beliefs are essentially forward-looking and predictive, there is no guarantee that future experience will not falsify them. Accordingly, we cannot be perfectly certain of their truth; it is always possible to doubt them, at least in theory. It follows that Cartesian-style epistemology depends on a catastrophic category mistake, because the possibility of error is built into the concept of knowledge.

e. *A Salutation, not an Embrace*: Knowledge is not the incorporation or possession of what is present; it is the acknowledgment or recognition of what is absent: "Knowledge ... is a salutation, not an embrace" (*LR1*, 48; cf. *LSK*, 424; *RT*, 29, 90; *USL*, 16, 28). But if knowledge is a species of acknowledgment, nothing can be known which cannot exist apart from our knowledge: "Knowledge is knowledge because it has compulsory objects which pre-exist" (*SAF*, 172). Hence, nothing can be an object of knowledge unless we can be wrong about it.

f. *From Santayana to Hegel*: Near the beginning of the *Phenomenology*, Hegel asks himself the following question: "If I subtract everything which my thinking has superimposed on the given, what remains?" Because I have removed all conceptual filters which could distort or falsify my apprehension of things, won't I be left with pure and perfect knowledge—a secure and immediate grasp of the truth in its full concreteness? Not so, replies Hegel. Knowledge is impossible without judgment, and judgment is impossible without concepts.

Hence, what was supposed to purify and perfect my knowledge—the elimination of everything contributed or projected by my mind—actually destroys it.

g. *From Hegel to Santayana*: At bottom, Santayana's argument against indubitable knowledge is the same as Hegel's argument against immediate knowledge. Since there is no possibility of knowledge without interpretation or theory, and since there is no interpretation or theory without the possibility of error, Santayana concludes that knowledge and certainty are incompatible; we can have one only at the expense of the other. If we seek certainty, only the contemplation of essence will do; if we seek knowledge, the rights of animal faith must be respected. In short, Santayana's view is that we can have certainty, and we can have knowledge; but we cannot have certain knowledge.

IX

Having worked through the details of Santayana's defense of certainty scepticism and his critique of knowledge scepticism, let us return to the question with which we began: In what sense is Santayana a sceptic, and in what sense is he a critic of scepticism? The short answer has two parts. (1) Santayana agrees with the sceptic that no theoretical justification of our conceptual scheme is possible. Because the premises of any justificatory argument must be drawn from the very scheme we have been asked to justify, any attempted justification of our scheme will be question-begging. Descartes, alas, is not the only celebrated philosopher who has failed to perceive this. (2) Unlike the Cartesian sceptic, Santayana denies that any theoretical justification of our scheme is necessary. Since everything we call justification presupposes our conceptual scheme and must occur within it, there is no standard outside our framework by which our framework can be judged.[27] Hence, the sceptic's demand—that we justify the very thing which makes justification possible—is a piece of impudent nonsense. Our task as theorists of knowledge is not to damn or bless our conceptual scheme from without but to study and describe its structure from within.[28],[29]

REFERENCES

WORKS BY SANTAYANA

Santayana. 1900. *Interpretations of Poetry and Religion*. Ed. William G. Holzberger, and Herman J. Saatkamp Jr. Cambridge, MA: MIT Press, 1989. Cited as *IPR*.
———. 1905. *The Life of Reason: Introduction and Reason in Common Sense*. Ed. Martin Coleman, and Marianne Wokeck. Cambridge, MA: MIT Press, 2011. Cited as *LR1*.

---

[27] Lewis agreed: "There can be no Archimedean point for the philosopher" (Lewis 1929, 23).
[28] I have explored the central themes of this chapter at greater length in other publications. See McDermid (2006, 2008, 2009, 2018).
[29] My thanks to the editors for their helpful suggestions.

———. 1906. *The Life of Reason: Reason in Science.* Ed. Martin Coleman, and Marianne Wokeck. Cambridge, MA: MIT Press, 2016. Cited as *LR5*.

———. 1918. Literal and Symbolic Knowledge. *Journal of Philosophy* 15: 421–444. Cited as *LSK*.

———. 1920. Three Proofs of Realism. In *Essays in Critical Realism: A Co-operative Study of the Problem of Knowledge*, ed. Drake Durant, 163–184. London: Macmillan. Cited as *TPR*.

———. 1922. *Soliloquies in England and Later Soliloquies.* London: Constable and Company. Cited as *SE*.

———. 1923a. *The Unknowable: The Herbert Spencer Lecture.* Oxford: Clarendon Press. Cited as *USL*.

———. 1923b. *Scepticism and Animal Faith: Introduction to a System of Philosophy.* New York: Dover Publications. (1955 Reprint). Cited as *SAF*.

———. 1927. *The Realm of Essence: Book First of Realms of Being.* New York: Charles Scribner's Sons. Cited as *RE*.

———. 1930a. A Brief History of My Opinions. In *Contemporary American Philosophy: Personal Statements*, ed. George P. Adams and William Pepperell Montague, 237–257. New York: Macmillan. Cited as *BH*.

———. 1930b. *The Realm of Matter: Book Second of Realms of Being.* New York: Charles Scribner's Sons. Cited as *RM*.

———. 1938. *The Realm of Truth: Book Third of Realms of Being.* New York: Charles Scribner's Sons. Cited as *RT*.

———. 1940. *The Realm of Spirit: Book Fourth of Realms of Being.* New York: Charles Scribner's Sons. Cited as *RS*.

———. 1951. *Dominations and Powers: Reflections on Liberty, Society and Government.* New York: Charles Scribner's Sons. Cited as *DP*.

———. 1953. *Persons and Places: Fragments of Autobiography.* Ed. William G. Holzberger, and Herman J. Saatkamp Jr. Cambridge, MA: MIT Press, 1986. Cited as *PP*.

WORKS BY OTHERS

Bailey, Cyril. 1926. *Epicurus: The Extant Remains.* Oxford: Clarendon Press.
Bradley, F.H. 1930. *Appearance and Reality.* 2nd ed. Oxford: Clarendon Press.
Descartes, René. 2000. *Meditations and Other Metaphysical Writings.* Trans. Desmond Clarke. London: Penguin.
Dewey, John. 1929. *Experience and Nature.* London: George Allen and Unwin.
Gilson, Etienne. 1939. *Thomist Realism and the Critique of Knowledge.* Trans. Philip Trower. San Francisco: Ignatius Press.
James, William. 1890. *The Principles of Psychology.* New York: Dover Publications.
———. 1897. *The Will to Believe and Other Essays on Popular Philosophy.* New York: Dover Publications.
Kerr-Lawson, Angus. 2005. Santayana on Causation. *Overheard in Seville: Bulletin of the Santayana Society* 23: 28–32.
Lachs, John. 1980. Peirce, Santayana and The Large Facts. *Transactions of the C. S. Peirce Society* 16: 3–13.
———. 1988. *George Santayana.* Boston: Twayne. Cited as *JLGS*.

Lewis, C.I. 1929. *Mind and the World Order: A Theory of Knowledge*. New York: Dover Publications.

McCormick, John. 1987. *George Santayana: A Biography*. New York: Alfred A. Knopf. Cited as *GSB*.

McDermid, Douglas. 2006. *The Varieties of Pragmatism: Truth, Realism, and Knowledge from James to Rorty*. London and New York: Bloomsbury.

———. 2008. Platonists, Poets, and the God's-Eye View: Reading Santayana's "On the Death of a Metaphysician". *The Pluralist* 3: 132–153.

———. 2009. Santayana or Descartes: Meditations on *Scepticism and Animal Faith*. *Overheard in Seville: Bulletin of the Santayana Society* 27: 1–8.

———. 2018. *The Rise and Fall of Scottish Common Sense Realism*. Oxford: Oxford University Press.

Peirce, C.S. 1931–1935. *Selected Papers of Charles Sanders Peirce*. Ed. Charles Hartshorne, and Paul Weiss. Cambridge, MA: Harvard University Press.

Quine, W.V.O. 1975. The Nature of Natural Knowledge. In *Mind and Language*, ed. Samuel Guttenplan, 67–81. Oxford: Clarendon Press.

Royce, Josiah. 1885. *The Religious Aspect of Philosophy*. Boston and New York: Houghton, Mifflin and Company.

———. 1897. *The Conception of God*. New York: Macmillan.

———. 1898. *Studies of Good and Evil*. New York: D. Appleton and Company.

Saatkamp, Herman J., Jr. 2017. Is Animal Faith the End of Philosophy? *Overheard in Seville: Bulletin of the Santayana Society* 35: 11–20.

Sprigge, T.L.S. 1995. *Santayana: An Examination of His Philosophy*. Boston and London: Routledge and Kegan Paul. Cited as *SAEP*.

Tiller, Glenn. 2006. The Unknowable: The Pragmatist Critique of Matter. *Transactions of the C. S. Peirce Society* 42: 206–228.

———. 2008. Counting Categories with Peirce and Santayana. *Overheard in Seville: Bulletin of the Santayana Society* 26: 1–7.

Wahman, Jessica. 2007. Corpulent or a Train of Ideas? Santayana's Critique of Hume. *Overheard in Seville: Bulletin of the Santayana Society* 25: 1–9.

Laying Siege to the Truth: Santayana's Discourse on Method

Diana B. Heney

George Santayana's *Scepticism and Animal Faith* (*SAF*) is the introduction to his systematic philosophy, developed in the *Realms of Being*. It may seem like an odd introduction to an odd system: a system which Santayana says is not his, not new, and not "of the universe." It may also seem like an odd engagement with scepticism. Santayana describes Descartes's scepticism as a "not very serious shipwreck," and sets out to cause a more spectacular wreckage—one which turns out to have a large crew of survivors, in the form of his categories and the four-volume ontology that follows.

It is perhaps not surprising that Santayana has been described as a "latter-day Janus,"[1] as he appears to pivot smoothly from a deliberately radical scepticism to a rather sumptuous ontology. In this chapter, I explore that apparent pivot: the movement from scepticism to animal faith. I begin by considering parallels between *SAF* and Descartes's *Meditations*, which have been a subject of interest to numerous Santayana scholars. I then argue that despite its structural similarity to the *Meditations*, *SAF* can be interpreted as a discourse on method—one which has broader ramifications than Santayana's often ecumenical tone suggests. Drawing comparisons with a different work by Descartes—

---

[1] Edward L. Shaughnessy (1975), "Santayana: Latter-Day Janus," *The Journal of Aesthetics and Art Criticism*, 33(3):309–319.

D. B. Heney (✉)
Department of Philosophy, Vanderbilt University, Nashville, TN, USA
e-mail: diana.b.heney@vanderbilt.edu

© The Author(s), under exclusive license to Springer Nature Switzerland AG 2024
M. A. Coleman, G. Tiller (eds.), *The Palgrave Companion to George Santayana's Scepticism and Animal Faith*, Palgrave Companions, https://doi.org/10.1007/978-3-031-46367-9_4

the *Discourse on Method*—helps to draw out those ramifications. In concrete terms, *SAF* offers generalizable lessons for the "discipline of daily thoughts" (*SAF*, 305), that discipline which makes laying siege to the truth possible.

Structure, Style, and Substance: *SAF* and the *Meditations*

We are marking the centenary of a work that has been variably received. Douglas McDermid recalls his first encounter with *SAF* as on a par with an art-lover's rhapsodic and disoriented reaction to a "surfeit of beauty"—his philosophical equivalent of which involved being "dazzled, vexed, shaken and stirred by turns." McDermid describes *SAF* itself as "philosophical without ceasing to be poetic, and conservative without ceasing to be creative" (2009, 1). Not all readers were stirred in the same way. In a nuanced engagement with *SAF* thirty years after its publication, Frederick Olafson sums up a then "common view": that "Santayana's way of doing philosophy was loose, literary, and more or less irresponsible and that its destructive criticism of science and human knowledge, generally, was a malicious one" (1954, 43). Olafson himself offers a more favorable take on the work, describing *SAF* as a "notable achievement," with particular praise for Santayana's remaining "faithful throughout to the sceptical method" (1954, 44).

One way that scholars have sought to situate the import of *SAF* is by placing it against philosophy's most famous sceptical treatise, Descartes's *Meditations*. It is a significant interpretive challenge to determine how *SAF* as a whole relates to Cartesian scepticism. Because Santayana says relatively little in direct reference to Descartes,[2] interpretations have varied widely. Given the content of the actual engagement in the text, perhaps *SAF* is patterned after the *Meditations* in the way that Voltaire's *Candide* is patterned after Leibniz's *Monadology:* an engagement for the sake of revealing absurdity. Herman Saatkamp seems to offer a version of this conclusion: "That both skepticism and proofs against skepticism lead nowhere is precisely Santayana's point" (2020). Others try to locate Santayana in primarily either a sceptical or anti-sceptical mode. For example, John Michelson claims that the crucial affinity in Santayana's philosophy as a whole is with Pyrrhonian scepticism, attributing to him "a modern and far more thorough and adequate version of the scepticism developed by Pyrrho in the 3rd century B. C." (1993, 32).[3] By contrast, Paul Kuntz declares that "like a pragmatist, Santayana is far from wholly sceptical and consequently arbitrary about the real and the good" (1971, 99). Douglas Greenlee seems willing

---

[2] The index entry for "Descartes" in the original version of *SAF* appears as follows: "Descartes, 17; doubts facts only, 289; *cogito ergo sum*, 290–293" (*SAF*, 311).

[3] Interestingly, Michelsen claims that this is an affinity and not an actual intellectual debt because he thinks that Santayana had not read accounts of Pyrrho's philosophy carefully, and that he had instead more or less independently generated a twentieth-century version consonant with his own wider philosophy (1993, 32ff).

to attribute to Santayana both stark scepticism and its implicit rejection for the sake of naturalism, going so far as to call his position "philosophical schizophrenia" (1978, 55). In more subtle treatments, Beth Singer and Angus Kerr-Lawson allow that Santayana takes scepticism seriously, but argue that his final relation to scepticism is that it is supportable only when "limited" (Singer 1978; Kerr-Lawson 1980).

A curious feature of much of the scholarly work on Santayana and Descartes as a pair is the tendency to cite Santayana directly and merely refer to Descartes.[4] Perhaps—and perhaps, fairly—the working presumption is that we all understand Descartes well enough that we may simply refer to his views without explicit textual anchoring. I'm not so sure. In any case, in what follows, I engage with both philosophers on a textual basis. I proceed by considering structure and then style; reflecting on each offers opportunities to think anew about the content.

To begin with structure, it is clear that in *some* sense, *SAF* is patterned after the *Meditations*. Chapter XXVII, "Comparison with Other Criticisms of Knowledge," makes this evident: "In adopting the method of Descartes," Santayana says, "I have sought to carry it further, suspending all conventional categories as well as all conventional beliefs; so that not only the material world but all facts and all existences have lost their status, and become simply the themes or topics which intrinsically they are" (*SAF*, 292). As Saatkamp frames the work, Santayana "structures his argument after Descartes' *Meditations* but arrives at an anti-foundationalist conclusion" (2020/2002).[5]

But just how congruent is the structure of *SAF* meant to be to the *Meditations*? Descartes traces his descent into a state bereft of knowledge in the opening of the text, at rock bottom discovers his "Archimedean point" in the form of the proof offered in the *cogito*, and then makes an ascent back to the recovery of knowledge about pretty much everything. The descent is accomplished by finding in all opinions "some reason for doubt," a procedure intending to systematically "[undermine] the foundations" (*Med* I, 19). In seeking a place to stand to begin anew, Descartes invokes Archimedes, whom he casts as having "sought but one firm and immovable point in order to move the entire earth from one place to another" (*Med* II, 24). The grandness of the movement offered as an analogy for Descartes's own attempt to move from one place to another—from the nadir of nothing-knowing to laying foundations for the sciences—is noteworthy. Descartes declares that he is in pursuit of "great things," not merely muddling through (*Med* II, 24). The place to stand is discovered in the form of the *cogito* argument, which invokes a separation of

---

[4] McDermid's (2009) is a case in point. He offers an excellent comparative consideration of Santayana and Descartes "*qua* epistemologist[s]" (2009, 1), noting nine similarities between *SAF* and the *Meditations*, as well as six notable differences. Throughout the comparison, all the citations are to Santayana.

[5] See Saatkamp's entry, "George Santayana," in *The Stanford Encyclopedia of Philosophy* (Fall 2020 Edition) for further helpful discussion of the structure of *SAF*. (The entry is now maintained by Martin Coleman.)

cases. Two possibilities arise in response to the thought, "I am; I exist"—either I am seeing the matter clearly, or I am deceived. But I must exist in order to be deceived. So my existence is in either case assured; the pronouncement "is necessarily true every time I utter it or conceived it in my mind" (*Med* II, 25). The ascent to well-founded knowledge is accomplished throughout the remainder of the *Meditations*; by its close, Descartes's positive project of identifying both the source and substance of knowledge is well underway.

The structure of *SAF* is less linear. After considering dogma and doubt, which turn out to be closer companions than one might have imagined, Santayana works through the varieties of scepticism that he describes as "wayward." A scepticism is wayward when it is muddied with "religious and psychological motives that are foreign to its essence"; to maintain an honest trajectory, we must be prepared to lose not just our knowledge of the world but "to lose our own personal histories and identities with it" (Olafson 1954, 44). Santayana begins his own journey with Chapter IV, "Doubts about Self-Consciousness," and the sceptical trip to nowhere (while being no-one) is accomplished by Chapter VI, "Ultimate Scepticism." There, Santayana observes that "for all an ultimate scepticism can see [...] there may be no facts at all, and perhaps nothing has ever existed." This is as far as scepticism can go: the ultimate sceptic may deny "change and memory, and reality of all facts."

Santayana wryly observes that such a denial "would have to be entertained, and that event would be a fact and an existence." In fact, the ultimate sceptic "exist[s] with a vengeance," even while holding to the tenability of the sceptical dogma (*SAF*, 40). While he treats the ultimate sceptic with relative gentleness, it is clear that Santayana does not share his attachments. Scepticism is work, not doctrine—"an exercise, not a life" (*SAF*, 69). This is at least in part because Santayana does not model the sceptical exercise as a descent but an ascent—to an "apex," where all vistas stretch out before us and allegiance is given to none (*SAF*, 108; Tiller 2008, 135). We cannot stay there, just as mountaineers do not linger too long at the summit. No matter how intoxicating and freeing the climb, we must return to our daily lives, to those facts and existences in which we cannot help but believe. From those great heights, we return to our practical purpose: "to map the land and choose a habitation" (*SAF*, 108).[6]

On the sketch I have just drawn, it would be fair to ask: why *Scepticism* and *Animal Faith*, rather than *Scepticism* to *Animal Faith*? As Kerr-Lawson reminds us, "Santayana insists that scepticism is a permanent part of his philosophy," a position which "is not easy to reconcile [...] with the Cartesian motif of *SAF*" (1980, 178).[7] What the insistence suggests is that what occurs in the later portions of the text is not a repudiation of scepticism but a working-with.

---

[6] The summit of scepticism is opposed to life, while "the vanishing point of scepticism [...] is also the acme of life" (*SAF*, 126).

[7] John Lachs has also made the argument that we should not try to read the latter portions of *SAF* as an attempt to offer a logical proof; see Lachs (1972).

Kerr-Lawson points out that in presenting the "ascent" portion of *SAF* as a "marshalling of beliefs," Santayana shows himself "prepared to accept dogmas of animal faith with no other assurance than the fact that he finds he must believe them" (1980, 179). Kerr-Lawson does frame this as "reconstructive," but in that reconstruction, Santayana "considers what objects animal faith requires him to posit, based only on an instinctive assurance of their existence" (Kerr-Lawson 2009, 29; *SAF*, 106).[8] The structure of *SAF* cannot be a symmetrical journey—an ascent to the great heights of sceptical clarity and a triumphant descent to a secure system of knowledge—because some form of scepticism remains a companion on the return journey. Instead of a step-wise recovery from one indubitable truth to a system of knowledge, the structure of *SAF* reflects the way in which an enduring scepticism is the expression of a responsible sense of one's own limits—limits that nonetheless do not render us unable to go on.

Having considered structure, let us move on to style: both works are presented as personal reflections. In the *Meditations*, Descartes begins not with a grand question or a programmatic announcement but with a self-audit. He declares his intention: to "converse with myself alone and look more deeply into myself" in order to "render myself gradually better known and more familiar to myself" (*Med* III, 35). In approaching the text, the reader may feel inclined to take the role of spectator, watching the meditator attempt his proofs as an audience watches a magician working an elaborate escape act.

But the careful reader cannot help but notice that by the end of the show, she, too, has been implicated. Even as he celebrates his own release from doubt, Descartes generalizes the importance of the project of the *Meditations*. No longer speaking as an "I" but now for a "we," he concludes that "because the need to get things done does not always permit us the leisure for [...] careful inquiry, we must confess that the life of man is apt to commit errors regarding particular things, and we must acknowledge the infirmity of our nature" (*Med* 6, 90). It is *our* nature as knowers that is at issue. Security from infirmity in the form of the logical separation of cases offered by the *cogito* is meant to bolster us toward firmity—perhaps not *perfectly* firm ground but at least a reliable mechanism to test its firmness at any point before moving ahead in an inquiry. That method is the test of clear and distinct perceptions: "if I hold off from making a judgment when I do not perceive what is true with sufficient clarity and distinctness, it is clear that I am acting properly and am not committing an error" (*Med* 4, 60).[9] Descartes's proof begins as first-personal and ascends to the level of generality: not just his own judgments but all those judgments made in conformity with the criteria of clarity and distinctness are proper. So long as we remain judicious, the world is ours once more.

---

[8] We shall return to this "instinctive assurance" in our discussion of animal faith.

[9] This mechanism articulated in *Meditation Four* is reliant on the proof of the existence of God offered in *Meditation Three*, which I shall not rehearse here. It is perhaps merely worth remarking that the strength of the proof is such that Descartes himself opted to offer a second proof in *Meditation Five*.

Santayana is also ruminating in the first-person voice.[10] He asks himself at the beginning of Chapter IV, "Doubts About Self-Consciousness," "Do I know, can I know, anything? Would not knowledge be an impossible inclusion of what lies outside? May I not rather renounce all beliefs? If only I could, what peace would descend into my perturbed conscience!" (*SAF*, 21). While also first-personal, this is quite different from the way Descartes portrays the sceptic who has achieved the demolition of all his previous beliefs, who feels as if they had "suddenly fallen into a deep whirlpool," "tossed about," and unable to gain their bearings (*Med II*, 24). Although their temperamental responses to the specter of scepticism differ, the matter is nonetheless personal for Santayana. In presenting the possibility of a thoroughgoing scepticism as a respite, he gives us a window into a different perspective—the one from which he is operating in seeking to build toward the positive ontology of the *Realms of Being*. His goal is not unshakeable foundations but supportive conceptual architecture. As he puts it, the project is to describe "categories of things I find conspicuously different and worth distinguishing," those kinds that emerge as important "in my personal observation of the world" (*SAF*, vi).

As we have already seen, *SAF*'s engagement with scepticism begins with the "wayward" varieties.[11] In discussing whether solipsism or scepticism could be durable, he invites us to imagine an "ephemeral creature," capable of staying serenely and undirectedly in the present moment. Such a creature would "not suppose, as Descartes did, that in thinking anything his own existence was involved" (*SAF*, 17). We, however, are not ephemeral; we are "long-lived and teachable animals." As such, we have a tendency to "dwell in [our] expectations" (*SAF*, 68). To attempt to shake loose of such expectations altogether is a "violent posture," and one where we tend to cheat and compensate in order to hold the pose (*SAF*, 17).

Though some scepticisms are wayward, some might be sincere—sincere, at least, in the sense of being deeply and personally felt. Much depends on what exactly the sceptic is up to. Consider that the sceptic engaged in an "honest retreat knows nothing of a future, and has no need of such an unwarrantable idea" (*SAF*, 14). What is an honest retreat a retreat *from*? I am in agreement with Singer, who diagnoses it as a retreat from infallibilism, foundationalism, *and* a (purely) representationalist realism (Singer 1978, 415). As Singer

---

[10] Douglas Anderson has argued that Santayana's entire outlook should be understood as a "philosophy of the personal" (2009, 579). Citing *Obiter Scripta*, Anderson reminds us of Santayana's remark that "Viewed from a sufficient distance all systems of philosophy are seen to be personal, temperamental, accidental, and premature" (*OB*, 94). The timing of this remark is notable—the essays of *OB* were published in 1936 in the midst of the writing of *Realms of Being*, with *The Realm of Essence* (1927) and *The Realm of Matter* (1930) already published, and *The Realm of Truth* (1938) and *The Realm of Spirit* (1940) yet to come. Even while expending tremendous philosophical energy in the construction of a system—recall, not his and not new—Santayana reminds the reader that systems spring from somewhere and from someone.

[11] This is, however, not where the text begins—it begins with the system-launching "Preface" and with Chapter I, "There is No First Principle of Criticism." I return to *SAF*'s beginnings in the next section.

helpfully articulates the movement through scepticisms in *SAF*, Santayana makes the effort to engage in the rigorous ultimate scepticism that turns out to be unstable, though "philosophically hygienic" (Singer 1978, 415). The honest retreat is not from the possibility of knowledge *simpliciter* but from the idea that knowledge could be "certain, infallible, 'literal' knowledge of fact or existence, of self or substance" (Singer 1978, 416). Singer aptly quotes from Santayana's "Apologia Pro Mente Sua": "Only the demand for literal knowledge makes knowledge impossible" (*PGS* 518; Singer 1978, 416).

What, then, is the nature of proof on offer in *SAF*? We know what it is *not*: Santayana argues that we cannot arrive at the conclusion, first-personally, that one "lives and thinks." One cannot simply find a loose thread inside the sweater of scepticism and unravel it from within. One must "appeal to animal faith," which allows us to see belief for what it is: adventurous (*SAF*, 41, 45).[12] Indeed, belief is necessary for the adventures of life, and animal faith paves the way for belief to be honored in knowledge claims that are not literal and that never had any reason to be: "knowledge of existences has no need, no propensity, and no fitness to be literal" (*SAF*, 101). That we must make such an appeal is not a logical requirement but a practical one.[13] Thus, this "proof" does not dispel scepticism but shows that we can make peace with it.[14] It opens up new prospects for us by freeing us from the expectation that knowledge should be literal and complete (*SAF*, 101).

We are now speaking, as well, in terms of "we." Insofar as what is true of Santayana is true of his readers, we are invited to share this shift in thinking about the pursuit of knowledge. What we gained from attempting to think in a consistently sceptical mode is the realization that we cannot have a particular type of knowledge: literal, absolute, or certain. We have knowledge all the same, a knowledge which Santayana describes as "faith mediated by symbols" or "beliefs mediated by symbols, in the region of animal faith" (*SAF*, 164, 115). On this definition, "knowledge lies in thinking aptly about things," a

---

[12] Readers sometimes seem to have an allergic reaction to this term. Pragmatists in particular, accustomed to broadly empirical approaches, may shy away. Here I simply place alongside Santayana's notion a remark from John Dewey: "There is a kind of music of ideas which appeals, apart from any question of verification, to the mind of thinkers!" Sidney Hook seemed to be particularly fond of this remark, citing it on a number of occasions, including his Presidential Address to the American Philosophical Association (Hook 1959–1960). Hook also cites it in his 1970 "Philosophy and Public Policy," where he ends with a quote by Santayana—prefaced with the claim that he regards Santayana's "soaring thought" as "much more impressive than his petty and uneventful life."

[13] This should be more familiar to readers of pragmatism, as the appeal to regulative assumptions of inquiry is a typical maneuver. For more on how such assumptions are deployed by Peirce, James, Dewey, and Lewis, see Heney (2016).

[14] As we shall see in sections "How to Lay Siege to the Truth" and "Conclusions", Santayana might well have said that we *must* make peace with it.

process which turns on the fact that our knowledge claims express "faith in the existence of an external thing or event" (*SAF*, 95; Kerr-Lawson 1980, 180).[15]

If we accept the limit that taking scepticism seriously reveals, we are not thereby cut off from all our dealings with the material world. It is just that we recognize them for what they are: our dealings, for our purposes, with instinctive belief as an inevitable compensation for the firm foundations that scepticism could not deliver. Nor are we particularly hampered, so long as we do not overreach. As Santayana puts it in the "Preface," "whatever matter may be, I call it matter boldly, as I call my acquaintances Smith and Jones without knowing their secrets" (*SAF*, viii). By the end of *SAF*, we have not regained the world in the way that Descartes sought to do. Rather, we have situated ourselves, moving through that world, whatever it may be. As McDermid aptly puts it, "coping, not copying, is what counts" (2009, 7).

To summarize: we have seen that Santayana scholars have disagreed about whether we should read him as any sort of sceptic at all. I have argued, following Singer and Kerr-Lawson, that we should—though scepticism in its proper place turns out to be conducive to, rather than contrary to, the knowledge that we can obtain as the kind of animals that we are. Clearly, others have disagreed and may continue to do so.[16] We could treat this as the end of an entertaining but not especially edifying discussion. After all, the actual references to Descartes in *SAF* are thin and make meager connection with the content of Descartes's writings, and the same is often true in the secondary literature reflecting on points of contrast and contact between the two philosophers. However, I suggest that a different—and potentially fruitful—comparison between Santayana's system-launching work and Descartes's philosophy can still be drawn. This is because there are interesting parallels yet to be explored between *SAF* and the *Discourse on Method*.

METHOD AND PURPOSE: *SAF* AND THE DISCOURSE ON METHOD

The primary objectives of *SAF* are methodological. Santayana is engaging in window-cleaning, not yet peering through the windows to what lies inside or flinging them open to admit the world—that work comes later, in the *Realms of Being*. In *SAF*, the "endeavour is to think straight in such terms as are offered to me, to clear my mind of cant and free it from the cramp of artificial traditions." But Santayana does not set out to proselytize. He goes on to add, "I do not ask any one to think in my terms if he prefers others. Let him clean better, if he can, the windows of his soul, that the variety and beauty of the prospect

---

[15] Kerr-Lawson nicely fleshes out the parameters of a knowledge claim in Santayana's sense of symbolic knowledge: "it is always a claim of existence," "uncertain and as well imprecise," "an instinctive claim with unseen biological roots," "confirmed by successful action, not by similarity between image and object" (1980, 180).

[16] It is not too difficult to find expressions along Greenlee's "philosophical schizophrenia" lines. I was once informed by a (still-living and hence not here named) philosopher that *SAF* was the only book of philosophy that he had ever thrown in the trash.

may spread more brightly before him" (*SAF*, vi–vii). While the work is substantial, it is preparatory all the same. For before Santayana can begin to offer what Glenn Tiller has termed his "common sense ontology," we must consider how such a project is possible.[17]

The work in which we find Descartes similarly engaged in a preparatory spirit is the 1637 *Discourse on the Method for Conducting One's Reason Well and Seeking Truth in the Sciences*. Consider how Descartes begins the *Discourse*: "my purpose here is not to teach the method that everyone ought to follow in order to conduct his reason well, but merely to show how I have tried to conduct my own." He adds that he is "putting forward this essay merely as a story or, if you prefer, as a fable in which, among some examples one can imitate, one will perhaps also find many others which one which have reason not to follow" (*DM*, 4). Descartes is clear that his purpose—like Santayana's—is cleaning intellectual house. "My plan," he insists, "has never gone beyond trying to reform my own thoughts and building upon a foundation which is completely my own." This purpose is generalizable, even if the means of achieving it is not. Others ought to embark upon it, even if they may accomplish it by conducting their reason well by some other regimen. In a tone of exhortation, Descartes enjoins the reader, "it is not enough to have a good mind; the main thing is to apply it well" (*DM*, 2). Santayana's opening remarks are strikingly similar. In concluding the "Preface" to *SAF*, he invites the reader into the work to come with the advisement that "no great wit is requisite [...] only (what is rarer than wit) candour and courage" (*SAF*, x).

It might be thought that *which* guiding ideal is fit for applying one's mind well should be a point of deep disagreement. After all, Santayana does not orient himself toward the sciences in the way that Descartes explicitly does. And it is true that elements of the *Discourse* appear somewhat specialized; perhaps relatively few readers of philosophy are much animated by the question of whether or not the venous artery was ill-named (*DM* 5, 48). Yet naming, in the mode of categorizing, *is* at the heart of Santayana's attempt at systematicity. Further, while he clearly operates as both a scientist and a philosopher,[18] Descartes's encouragement to take up the challenge of applying one's mind well need not be construed so narrowly as to confine us all to the study of the venous artery. Indeed, all that he proposes is, from his own perspective, "to advance further in the investigation of nature" (*DM*, 1). Santayana makes no pretense at "exact science" but cares all the same about "the hang of the world," including its stars, seasons, and swarms of animals (*SAF*, x).

Descartes and Santayana are both commonly misinterpreted as simply arguing in favor of scepticism. But as their overtly methodological remarks clearly

---

[17] Tiller (2008) offers a detailed and instructive overview of how Santayana takes on the seemingly paradoxical project of making common sense systematic.

[18] Ironically, Descartes's sincere dual habitations—philosophy and science—make his closest parallel in the pragmatist tradition the person who is also likely his least charitable interpreter, Charles S. Peirce.

show, neither is interested in scepticism for its own sake. Each is interested in what must first be done before a systematic engagement can be properly pursued. Descartes frames his pursuits in the language of scientific endeavor, while Santayana describes his as an "old-fashioned" materialism, but both are in pursuit of those forms of knowledge they believe we can honestly earn.

In sum, one crux of disagreement between Descartes and Santayana is whether scepticism can be fully repelled or whether some form of it must be retained. Descartes believes that he has solved scepticism, finding through the *cogito* a truth "so firm and so assured that all the most extravagant suppositions of the skeptics were incapable of shaking it" (*DM* 4, 32). Santayana, by contrast, believes that it is possible to get on friendly terms with scepticism and retain both its intellectual benefits and its company in our engagements with the material world. That key difference bears out in their considered view about the nature and possibilities of human knowledge, which shows that this is not a small disagreement or a minor quibble. Still, to treat it as exhausting the interesting points of comparison between two systematic, ambitious, nature-oriented philosophers would be to miss opportunities for reflection on the challenges they both take themselves to be tackling and the ways forward that they offer. Reminding ourselves of the program and purpose of Descartes's *Discourse* shows that there is more common cause between these two philosophers than previously appreciated.

There are, I suggest, two major implications to be drawn from this reading of *SAF*. The first is that Santayana scholars should not be too swift to ridicule Descartes. The second is that Santayana's writings may be more hortatory than their author lets on.[19]

Considering the parallels drawn here, perhaps the first point is already made: the resonances between Santayana's system-launching work and Descartes's treatise on philosophical methodology are intriguing and potential fruitful points for reflection. The fun of reading *SAF* as an ironic send-up of the *Meditations* is undeniable, but it sells short both the substantive content of *SAF* and the richness of Descartes's considered remarks on method, which we are in a position to draw from if we add the *Discourse* to the conversation.

As such, I devote what space remains to me here to the second implication: in *SAF*, Santayana comes suspiciously close to telling us what to do. The suspicion—surely he wouldn't be giving us actual advice?—arises because the idea of melioristic recommendation sits cross-ways with many readings of Santayana and perhaps of his own self-understanding—including the ironic, detached, critical-familial stance that marks his mature presentation of his philosophical purposes.[20] Henry Levinson describes a prevalent attitude toward Santayana's place in the pragmatist pantheon aptly: "his apparently solitary career—or bet-

---

[19] For a similar suggestion couched in an investigation of the relevance of Santayana's writings to education, see Martin Coleman, "'It doesn't matter where you begin. ...': Pound and Santayana on Education," *The Journal of Aesthetic Education*, 44(4):1–17, 2010.

[20] See, for example, his "Apologia" (*PGS*).

ter, career in solitude—does not adhere to the tendency of twentieth-century American intellectuals to construe philosophy—or intellectual discourse at large—as a cooperative enterprise best placed at the center of culture, where it can have a realistic effect on social policy formation" (1987, 289).[21] We now part ways with Descartes to consider how, in *SAF*, Santayana actually does offer solutions—through equipping himself and his reader to lay siege to the truth.

How to Lay Siege to the Truth

In describing the project of *SAF*, Greenlee claims that Santayana "set out with a program to push scepticism to its limits" (1978, 52). While this is true, it captures the purpose of *SAF* only incompletely. *SAF* is Santayana's discourse on method, a preparatory work for the *Realms* to follow. It is a meditation and a demonstration. I suggested above that Santayana did not set out to proselytize, but there is nonetheless a kind of guidance offered. Here, I emphasize three aspects of *SAF* that have consequences for what Santayana terms "the discipline of my daily thoughts" (*SAF*, 305). These are: how to begin, how to proceed, and how to come to terms with who we are.

I have already cited Santayana's remark that scepticism is "an exercise, not a life." Yet it is where we must begin if we are to be rigorous. This is not just because scepticism is fit to "purify the mind"—though it is—but because we must be rigorous about scepticism itself (*SAF*, 69). We should distrust both "proofs and disproofs" (*PGS*, 604), which we have seen take us "wayward" by inviting us to think that we have achieved more than we have. This is where the sceptical exercise of *SAF* is meant to be helpful. What one can gain from the sceptical exercise is two related results: the awareness from the first-person perspective that indubitable, foundational knowledge is not to be found from that vantage point, and the realization that such a knowledge was never what we needed in the first place. Recall that the scepticism Santayana maintains is limited, but it also *sets* a limit.

It is certainly true, as Levinson allows, that *SAF* and the *Realms* are unlikely to have major effects on social policy—nor are they, really, a cooperative enterprise. We are invited along with Santayana, given the tour, but always with the understanding that we may leave any time we like. Indeed, he sometimes seems to want to remind us where the exits are. If we stray from his system, all to the good—so long as we build our own in similarly honest ways. When Santayana declares that "I stand in philosophy exactly where I stand in daily life; I should not be honest otherwise" (*SAF*, vi), he is not commanding us to follow along. He is demonstrating what honest philosophy looks like for him, and the

---

[21] It is common for "big books" on American pragmatism to bear this kind of view of Santayana out. The 2023 *Routledge Companion to Pragmatism* has no chapter on Santayana; indeed, there are a scant two references to his work in the volume as a whole. The *Oxford Handbook of American Philosophy* casts a wider net—beyond just the pragmatists to American philosophy in general—and there Santayana's work does receive a chapter-length treatment, Glenn Tiller's "George Santayana: Ordinary Reflection Systematized" (2008, 125–143).

invitation is left implicit: "you could be honest, too." Levinson frames Santayana as attempting "to show, by example, how philosophical meditation functioned to restore individuals to life at first hand, to an acknowledgment of what they did avow and believe as distinguished from what they thought they should avow and believe" (1987, 293). This theme is made explicit in *Realms*, where he calls back to *SAF*, describing the system to follow as "not an exercise in controversy but in meditation." Such meditation is meant to speak to "reflective moments and speculative honesty" open to all alike (*RB*, xvv).

Thus, in order to proceed, we must above all be honest. This means keeping both our limits and our aspirations in view. We can "lay siege to the truth only as animal exploration and fancy may do," "first from one quarter and then from another" (*SAF*, vi). Despite our limitations, it *is* truth that is at stake. Getting at it requires "clear eyes and honest reflection" so that we may "distinguish the edge of truth from the might of imagination" (*SAF*, x). Crucially, Santayana does think that we can make this distinction. He does not think that admitting the impossibility of literal knowledge undermines our ability to aim at the truth. "Certainly truth is there, if the thing pursued is such as the animal presumes it to be; and in searching for it in the right quarter and finding it, he enacts a true belief and a true perception" (*SAF*, 264). Truth is in fact so much there that it comprises one of Santayana's realms, one that he describes as "impersonal and super-existential" (*RB*, 485). We lay siege to it all the same, "from all sides" (*SAF*, 106).

It is worth considering this second siege plan at some length, as it shows both the approach and the result that Santayana offers for the inquirer willing to balance scepticism about literal knowledge with animal faith in symbolic knowledge:

> The aspect [a] thing wears, as it first catches my attention, though it may deceive me in some particulars, can hardly fail to be, in some respects, a telling indication of its nature in relation to me. Signs identify their objects for discourse, and show us where to look for their undiscovered qualities. Further signs, catching other aspects of the same object, may help me lay siege to it from all sides; but signs will never lead me into the citadel. (*SAF*, 106)

We do not need to breach the citadel. As Tiller reminds us, Santayana is inviting us to reflection on what a system can be without being a scam: "a conceptual scheme of extreme generality" (2008, 130).[22] Our symbolic knowledge—which Santayana describes as "knowledge of existence, without ceasing to be instinctive faith"—is adequate to the task (*SAF*, 107).

We have now considered Santayana's demonstration of how to begin and how to proceed in philosophical reflection. The pursuit of knowledge is work and reward together. Such knowledge as we are capable of requires humility and honesty. So perhaps it comes as no surprise that as we negotiate the work,

---

[22] "For me," Santayana says, "it will simply be a question of good sense and circumstantial evidence how many substances I admit, and of what sort" (*SAF*, 183). For further discussion of what is admitted, see Forster (2008), Tiller (2009).

we come to terms with who we are. Coming to an understanding with scepticism offers the potential for "a massive moral experience," when the person so engaged is willing to accept that the wisdom gained from the experience would truly be "negative or merely liberating" (*SAF*, 297). I have suggested that Santayana is not proselytizing in *SAF*, and he isn't moralizing either. He does not tell the reader: have a massive moral experience! Only that we could.[23]

What does this "moral experience" consist in? It is not a discovery of duties or obligations but a discovery of what wisdom requires of the one who seeks it. Only humility and honesty can offer us a chance at harmony. As Santayana frames this connection in an oft-quoted passage from *Egotism in German Philosophy*:

> Happiness is impossible, and even inconceivable, to a mind without scope and without pause. To be happy, you must be reasonable, or you must be tamed. You must have taken the measure of your powers, tasted the fruits of your passion, and learned your place in the world and what things in it can really serve you. To be happy, you must be wise. (*EGP*, 152)

The meditation of *SAF* offers what happiness requires. It forces the pause, a step back from piling up "fabulous dogmas" in our luxuriant "mental jungle[s]" (*SAF*, 8, 53). It offers scope by redirecting us away from what cannot be known to what can. To adopt the discipline of daily thoughts is a kind of "taming" of more grandiose tendencies to seek first principles. With our place in the world understood, we can seek our greatest possible harmony within it.[24]

Conclusions

We can conclude that it is true that Santayana is a latter-day Janus, but not in the sense that Shaughnessy suggests. The key to resisting Shaughnessy's representation, along with Greenlee's diagnosis of philosophical schizophrenia, is attention to the way in which Santayana moves *through* scepticisms. His philosophy is not "two-faced" in the sense of promising one thing and delivering another. Rather, we should consider what Janus is the God of: doorways, gates, and all those places of transition that are meaningful because we pass through them. What *SAF* offers us is passage. It is not safe passage, as we must be prepared to take scepticism seriously, to push it to the point of "intellectual suicide" (*SAF*, 10). But once we have, we are free—free "to map the land and choose a habitation," and to do so in harmony with our natures and our interests.

---

[23] Olafson also highlights this aspect of *SAF*, framing "the great issue separating Santayana and his critics [as] a moral one" (1954, 45).

[24] For a contemporary account of well-being as harmony between mind and world, see von Kriegstein (2020). For a discussion of how this ideal of harmony fits into Santayana's ethical thought, see Heney (2012). Colapietro also takes up the work Santayana sets before us as the "task of reconciling ourselves with the conditions of our existence" (2009, 563).

REFERENCES

Anderson, Douglas. 2009. Santayana's Provocative Conception of the Philosophical Life. *Transactions of the Charles S. Peirce Society* 45 (4): 579–595.

Colapietro, Vincent. 2009. A Poet's Philosopher. *Transactions of the Charles S. Peirce Society* 45 (4): 551–578.

Coleman, Martin. 2010. 'It doesn't matter where you begin...': Pound and Santayana on Education. *The Journal of Aesthetic Education* 44 (4): 1–17.

Descartes, René. 1998a. *Discourse on Method*. Reprinted in *Discourse on Method and Meditations on First Philosophy*. Trans. Donald A. Cress, 4th ed. Hackett Publishing Company. Citations are listed as *DM* plus the paragraph number.

———. 1998b. *Meditations on First Philosophy*. Reprinted in *Discourse on Method and Meditations on First Philosophy*. Trans. Donald A. Cress, 4th ed. Hackett Publishing Company. Citations are given as *Med* # plus the paragraph number.

Forster, Paul. 2008. What Grounds the Categories? Peirce and Santayana. *Overheard in Seville: Bulletin of the Santayana Society* 26: 8–18.

Greenlee, Douglas. 1978. The Incoherence of Santayana's Scepticism. *Southern Journal of Philosophy* 16: 51–60.

Heney, Diana B. 2012. Santayana on Value: Expressivism, Self-Knowledge, and Happiness. *Overheard in Seville: Bulletin of the Santayana Society* 30: 4–13.

———. 2016. *Toward a Pragmatist Metaethics*. New York: Routledge.

Hook, Sidney. 1959–1960. Pragmatism and the Tragic Sense of Life. *Proceedings and Addresses of the American Philosophical Association* 33: 5–26.

———. 1970. Philosophy and Public Policy. *Journal of Philosophy* 67 (14): 461–470.

Kerr-Lawson, Angus. 1980. Santayana's Limited Scepticism. *Southern Journal of Philosophy* 18: 177–185.

———. 2009. On the Absence of Argument in Santayana. *Overheard in Seville: Bulletin of the Santayana Society* 22: 29–35.

Kuntz, Paul Grimley. 1971. Introduction. In *Santayana's Lotze's System of Philosophy*, ed. Paul Kuntz. Bloomington: Indiana University Press.

Lachs, John. 1972. Belief, Confidence and Faith. *The Southern Journal of Philosophy* 10 (2): 277–285.

Levinson, Henry. 1987. Meditation at the Margins: Santayana's *Scepticism and Animal Faith*. *The Journal of Religion* 67 (3): 289–303.

McDermid, Douglas. 2009. Santayana or Descartes?: Meditations on Scepticism and Animal Faith. *Overheard in Seville: Bulletin of the Santayana Society* 27: 1–8. https://doi.org/10.5840/200927273.

Michelsen, John M. 1993. George Santayana: A Pyrrhonian Sceptic of Our Time. *Overheard in Seville: Bulletin of the Santayana Society* 11: 33–43.

Olafson, Frederick A. 1954. Skepticism and Animal Faith. *The Journal of Philosophy* 52 (2): 42–46.

Saatkamp, Herman. 2020/2002. George Santayana. *The Stanford Encyclopedia of Philosophy*, Edward N. Zalta (ed.). https://plato.stanford.edu/archives/fall2020/entries/santayana/. (Moving forward, the entry is now maintained by Martin Coleman).

Santayana, George. 1916. *Egotism in German Philosophy*. New York: Charles Scribner's Sons; London and Toronto: J. M. Dent & Sons Ltd. Citations are given as *EGP*.

———. 1923. *Scepticism and Animal Faith: Introduction to a System of Philosophy.* New York: Charles Scribner's Sons; London: Constable and Co. Ltd. Citations are given as *SAF*.

———. 1936. *Obiter Scripta: Lectures, Essays and Reviews.* Ed. Justus Buchler and Benjamin Schwartz. New York: Charles Scribner's Sons; London: Constable and Co. Ltd. Citations are given as *OB*.

———. 1940. Apologia Pro Mente Sua. In *The Philosophy of George Santayana*, ed. Paul Arthur Schilpp, 2nd ed. LaSalle, IL: The Open Court Publishing Company. Citations are given as *PGS*.

Shaughnessy, Edward L. 1975. Santayana: Latter-Day Janus. *The Journal of Aesthetics and Art Criticism* 33 (3): 309–319.

Singer, Beth. 1978. Signs of Existence. *Southern Journal of Philosophy* XVI (4): 415–427.

Tiller, Glenn. 2008. George Santayana: Ordinary Reflection Systematized. In *Oxford Handbook of American Philosophy*, ed. Cheryl Misak, 125–143. Oxford: Oxford University Press.

———. 2009. Commonsense Ontology. *Transactions of the Charles S. Peirce Society* 45 (4): 506–515.

von Kriegstein, Hasko. 2020. Well-Being as Harmony. In *Explorations in Ethics*, ed. David Kaspar, 117–140. Palgrave Macmillan.

Scepticism, Anti-scepticism, and Santayana's Singularity

Daniel Pinkas

THE SIGNIFICANCE OF SCEPTICISM

As Barry Stroud writes in *The Significance of Philosophical Scepticism*,

> [S]cepticism in philosophy has been found uninteresting, perhaps even a waste of time, in recent years. The attempt to meet, or even to understand, the sceptical challenge to our knowledge of the world is regarded in some circles as an idle academic exercise, a wilful refusal to abandon outmoded forms of thinking in this new post-Cartesian age. When this attitude is not based on ignorance or a philistine impatience with abstract thought it often rests on the belief that we already understand quite well just how and why traditional philosophical scepticism goes wrong. […]. There are those on the other hand who take no interest in scepticism because they think it is so obviously true as not to bear repeating. (Stroud 1984, viii–ix)

One can find examples of the first attitude among those who, essentially in the English-speaking philosophical world, suppose that the arguments of Moore, Carnap, Wittgenstein, or Austin have sealed once and for all the fate of scepticism; as for the second attitude, perhaps one can see it at work among certain "post-modernists" whose positions amount, more or less explicitly, to a particularly virulent form of radical scepticism.

D. Pinkas (✉)
Department of Media Design, Haute École d'Art et de Design de Genève, Geneva, Switzerland
e-mail: dpinkas@worldcom.ch

© The Author(s), under exclusive license to Springer Nature Switzerland AG 2024
M. A. Coleman, G. Tiller (eds.), *The Palgrave Companion to George Santayana's Scepticism and Animal Faith*, Palgrave Companions, https://doi.org/10.1007/978-3-031-46367-9_5

The general theme of Stroud's book is that scepticism has at least a conditional validity, in the sense that it would be the more or less inevitable result of the kind of general evaluation of human knowledge that philosophy has traditionally claimed as its specific task. Without going so far as to consider, with Kant, that scepticism is "a benefactor of human reason," Stroud is convinced, as the title of his book suggests, that it has real philosophical relevance and importance. Several contemporary English-speaking philosophers share this view. Thus, Thomas Nagel considers that scepticism is inseparable from the project of understanding our situation in the world from a fully objective point of view; the problem raised by scepticism "has [...] no solution; but to recognize that is to come as near as we can to living in the light of truth" (Nagel 1986, 231). Stanley Cavell, for his part, emphasizes that even if scepticism proves to be, in the end, incoherent, it nevertheless possesses a kind of residual but profoundly revealing truth about the human condition, "what I might call the moral of skepticism, namely, that the human creature's basis in the world as a whole, its relation to the world as such, is not that of knowing, anyway not what we think of as knowing" (Cavell 1979, 241). Peter Strawson, finally, explicitly advocates, in *Skepticism and Naturalism*, a return to Hume's "naturalistic solution" according to which there are certainties so fundamental that they can neither be undermined nor supported by arguments, which is a way of granting a form of theoretical invulnerability to scepticism (cf. Strawson 1985).

These convergences suggest the emergence of a current in contemporary philosophy, in reaction to the post-Wittgensteinian and Neo-pragmatic tendency to consider that, given the "unreality" of philosophical problems, the best one can do is to *dissolve* or *diffuse* them. Michael Williams, in *Unnatural Doubts*, a very thorough study of modern scepticism, proposes to call the above-mentioned authors, and a few others, "The New Sceptics" or "The New Humeans" (Williams 1996, 10). The latter label seems appropriate given that for Hume, the hallmark of sceptical arguments is that they "admit of no answer and produce no conviction" (Hume 1975 [1748, 1751], 155). For Hume this curious combination of irrefutability and non-credibility reveals something important about the human condition. On the one hand, Hume sees scepticism as a perfectly natural endpoint for anyone gifted (or afflicted) with a "reflective turn of mind." In his view, there is no hope of attaining a satisfactory theoretical account of human knowledge that could surpass in intuitive plausibility the arguments of the sceptic: the condition of human beings is such that they must "act and reason and believe; though they are not able, by their most diligent enquiry, to satisfy themselves concerning the foundation of these operations, or to remove the objections, which may be raised against them" (Ibid., 159–60), so much so that "the understanding, when it acts alone, and according to its most general principles, entirely subverts itself, and leaves not the lowest degree of evidence in any proposition, either in philosophy or common life" (Hume 1888 [1739], 267–8). But on the other hand—and this is what thwarts the presumed consequences of this epistemological pessimism— "Nature, by an absolute and uncontroulable necessity has determin'd us to judge as well as to breathe and feel" (Ibid., 183). Thus, "whoever has taken the pains to refute the cavils of this *total* scepticism, has really disputed without an antagonist, and endeavour'd by arguments to establish a faculty, which nature has antecedently implanted in the mind, and render'd unavoidable" (Ibid.). We *cannot help* believing in the existence of physical objects any more than we can help forming beliefs in general agreement with the canons of induction. One might think that this iron law of Nature relegates scepticism to the level of a frivolous amusement for the mind. But this is not the case: by displaying "the arguments of that fantastic sect," Hume intends "to make the reader sensible of the truth of [his] hypothesis, [...] that belief is more properly an act of the sensitive, than of the cogitative part of our natures" (Ibid.).

The central motif of Hume's philosophy is that of a tension, not to say a conflict, between two perspectives: that of critical philosophical reflection in which we are unable to see our certainties, inferences, and everyday practices as anything other than unfounded certainties, inferences, and practices, and that of ordinary life and thought, in which sceptical doubts appear to us as "[...] cold, and strain'd, and ridiculous" (Ibid., 269). On this point Cavell remains close to Hume when he explains that scepticism presents itself both as a shocking *discovery* that brings to light something "deeper than our everyday, average ideas" but also as a notoriously *unstable* conclusion whose convincingness "will not detach from the context of investigation itself" (Cavell 1979, 165).

Santayana is another thinker whose proximity to Hume on these matters seems undeniable. The author of *Scepticism and Animal Faith*, however, is reluctant to acknowledge this debt explicitly; he states that of Locke, Berkeley, and Hume, the latter "was the one that [he] least appreciated" (Santayana 1986, 238). And yet, as George Herbert Palmer, the professor who introduced Santayana to the theories of the English moralists, once told him: "[you] have Hume in your bones." Professor Palmer's insight was, to a large extent, perfectly accurate, as we will see.[1] Beforehand, however, I shall devote several groundwork pages, first, to the emergence of the problem of scepticism in Descartes, and, second, to three (canonical) philosophical responses to Descartes' sceptical discovery. These preliminaries are intended to provide a background that should help bring out the singularity of Santayana's approach to scepticism as well as certain similarities and differences with Wittgenstein's approach.

Descartes' Discovery

All the above-mentioned authors refer to Descartes' First Meditation, where Descartes tells how, having reached a moment in his life when he wanted to "step back" or "take stock" (as one would say today), the philosophical problem of our knowledge of the external world arose for him:

---

[1] For a thorough analysis of Santayana's ambivalence toward Hume, see Wahman (2007).

It is now some years since I detected how many were the false beliefs that I had from my earliest youth admitted as true, and how doubtful was everything I had since constructed on this basis; and from that time I was convinced that I must once for all seriously undertake to rid myself of all the opinions which I had formerly accepted. [...]

But inasmuch as reason already persuades me that I ought no less carefully to withhold my assent from matters which are not entirely certain and indubitable than from those which appear to me manifestly to be false, if I am able to find in each one some reason to doubt, this will suffice to justify my rejecting the whole. (Descartes 1911 [1641], 6)

Affirming that "the destruction of the foundations of necessity brings with it the downfall of the rest of the edifice" (Ibid., 6–7), Descartes ties at once his "methodological" scepticism to a *strict foundationalism*, a position that can be characterized as the conjunction of three theses:

1. All knowledge is either mediate or immediate, and all mediate knowledge stands at the end of a chain of justifications whose starting point is immediate knowledge.
2. Immediate knowledge is indubitable and infallible.
3. When immediate knowledge has been discovered, one can proceed to the reconstruction of the edifice of knowledge from its foundations. (Saatkamp 1980, 135)[2]

At the very moment when Descartes launches into the investigation that is the main subject of the *Meditations*, he is sitting in a room, by the fire, attired in a dressing gown, holding a sheet of paper in his hands. And he chooses this present belief ("For example, [...] that I am here, seated by the fire, attired in a dressing gown, having this paper in my hands") as representative of an optimal epistemic situation, in the sense that if, in this situation, he were unable to know that he is sitting by the fire, holding this paper, etc., then he would also be unable to know anything about the surrounding world in any other situation. But how could he, in his situation, doubt that he is sitting by the fire, holding a paper? This case is not comparable to that of the square tower which appears round at a distance. The fire and the paper are there, in front of his eyes, neither too small nor too far away. Besides, says Descartes, "how could I deny that these hands and this body are mine, were it not perhaps that I compare myself to certain persons, devoid of sense, whose cerebella are so troubled and clouded by the violent vapours of black bile?" (Ibid., 7).

It is then that Descartes is "astonished" to discover that "there are no certain indications by which we may clearly distinguish wakefulness from sleep"

---

[2] Strict foundationalism should be distinguished from moderate foundationalism in which the basic beliefs grounding the epidemic edifice are neither indubitable nor infallible, but only provide a scalar and revisable justification. Glenn Tiller has argued convincingly that Santayana's position excludes both types of foundationalism (Tiller 2000, 43–45).

(Ibid.); to discover, therefore, that the reliability of the chosen belief can be reasonably doubted.

The consequences of this discovery are described by Stroud as follows:

> With this thought, if he is right, Descartes has lost the whole world. He knows what he is experiencing, he knows how things appear to him, but he does not know whether he is in fact sitting by the fire with a piece of paper in his hand. It is, for him, exactly as if he were sitting by the fire with a piece of paper in his hand, but he does not know whether there really is a fire or a piece of paper there or not. [...] He realizes that if everything he can ever learn about what is happening in the world around him comes to him through the senses, but he cannot tell by means of the senses whether or not he is dreaming, then all the sensory experiences he is having are compatible with his merely dreaming of a world around him while in fact the world is very different from the way he takes it to be. That is why he thinks he must find some way to tell that he is not dreaming. (Stroud 1984, 12)

In other words, in order to *know* that he is sitting by the fire, Descartes must know whether he is not dreaming that he is sitting by the fire. He sees this as a necessary condition for knowing something about the external world. And he discovers that this condition—which could be called the "condition of non-oneirism"—cannot be met.

The Cartesian problem of the knowledge of the external world can thus be formulated as follows: how can we know by means of the senses something about the external world if the information provided by the senses is compatible with a state of affairs in which we are dreaming a number of things about the physical world but know nothing about this world? In Strawson's terms: "At its most general, the skeptical point concerning the external world seems to be that subjective experience could, logically, be just the way it is without it being the case that physical or material things actually existed" (Strawson 1985, 5).

Why can't the condition of non-oneirism, *if* it is a necessary condition of knowledge, be satisfied? Because any attempt to satisfy it leads into a regression. Descartes must try to make sure that he is not dreaming; this is a condition that must be met if he is to *know* that he is sitting by the fire, holding this paper in his hands. But he has just discovered that the fact of seeing his hand and the paper, of feeling the heat of the fire, of experiencing certain proprioceptive sensations is not enough to satisfy the condition of non-oneirism. All this could take place, exactly in this way, during a dream. Therefore, one would have to look for a "non-oneirism test" outside the currently available sensory information. But how could any test make him *know* that he is not dreaming, if the condition of non-oneirism is a necessary condition of *all* knowledge? How could Descartes obtain the information necessary to set up and apply the test? He would, *per impossibile*, need to *already* have at his disposal a test (i.e., to have been at some point in time in a state of knowing that he was not dreaming) in order to be able to apply later the test that is supposed to allow him to know whether he is dreaming or awake.

Even assuming Descartes is supplied with a test for non-oneirism, the problem remains. How can he exclude that he is dreaming when he applies the test? To find out if he is sitting by the fire holding a paper in his hands, he must apply the test. But to know that the test has been applied, Descartes must first establish that he did not simply dream that he was applying the test. And how would he know that? The test cannot guarantee its own authenticity. So, a third test would be needed, and so on. To satisfy the condition of non-oneirism, one would need to have knowledge which itself is only possible if the condition is already satisfied, in one way or another.[3]

Moore's "Proof"

An example of an attempt at a "direct" refutation of this type of scepticism is provided by the famous "proof" that G. E. Moore presents in "Proof of an External World" (Moore 1959 [1939]). Moore begins with a well-known quotation from Kant, taken from the Preface to the second edition of the *Critique of Pure Reason*: "it always remains a scandal of philosophy and universal human reason that the existence of things outside us (…) should have to be assumed merely *on faith*, and that if it occurs to anyone to doubt it, we should be unable to answer him with a satisfactory proof" (Kant 1998 [1787], 121). Moore shares Kant's sentiment: it ought to be possible to put an end to the tormenting situation that the absence of justifying evidence for particularly obvious truths constitutes. As he had explained a decade earlier, in another famous article, "A Defence of Common Sense": "We are all, I think, in this strange position that we do *know* many things, with regard to which we *know* further that we must have had evidence for them, and yet we do not know *how* we know them, i.e. we do not know what the evidence was" (Moore 1959 [1925], 44). Thus, Moore intends to take up Kant's challenge and he devotes a few paragraphs to explain in detail what would be the necessary conditions to succeed in demonstrating the existence of external things. Moore distinguishes external things (such as sheets of paper, shoes and socks, human hands, soap bubbles) from "internal" entities (pains, consecutive images, etc.); the existence of the latter implies that someone experiences them or has experienced them, whereas the former do not allow any such inference: from the fact that an external thing exists one cannot conclude that someone perceives or has perceived this thing. If the existence of at least two things of this kind could be proved, the existence of external things would have been proved.

The proof itself is very brief: Moore raises both hands, makes a pointing gesture with his right hand, saying "Here is a hand" and a similar pointing gesture with his left hand saying "And here is another." And since he has just

---

[3] A contemporary version of the Cartesian condition of non-oneirism arises for the "brain in the vat" *Gedankenexperiment* (cf. Putnam 1981, chapter 1).

explained that this would be sufficient to demonstrate that external objects exist, Moore argues that his demonstration "prove[s] *ipso facto* the existence of external things" (Moore 1959 (1939), 146). According to him, this is a "perfectly rigorous" demonstration, since he *knows* that the premises ("Here is a hand," "Here is another hand") are true and that the conclusion follows validly from the premises, so much so that it is probably impossible to provide a better or more rigorous proof of anything (Ibid.).

It is well known that this opinion is far from being universally shared. Indeed, there is a widespread feeling that Moore's "proof" misses the point, although it is not always easy to say exactly why. Thus, Thomas Nagel mocks Moore's reaction to scepticism by saying that it consists in "turn[ing] one's back on the abyss and announc[ing] that one is now on the other side" (Nagel 1986, fn. 1, 69). What is hardly debatable is that we routinely accept similar proofs in everyday life: when it comes to proving that a certain printed text contains at least three typos, one would not go about it any differently: "here's a typo, here's another, and here's a third!" Yet, as Stroud points out, "[o]nce we are familiar with the philosophical problem of our knowledge of the external world [...] we immediately feel that Moore's proof is inadequate" (Stroud 1984, 86). This feeling can be expressed by saying, with Strawson, that "Moore [...] either misses the point of the sceptical challenge or has recourse to an unacceptable dogmatic claim to knowledge" (Strawson 1985, 5).

In a sense, the existence of external objects trivially follows from the existence of two human hands. But this is obviously not how the sceptic understands the question of the existence of external things. The question he poses requires, in Stroud's terms, a certain withdrawal or detachment from the whole body of our knowledge of the world. When the philosophical question of the existence of external objects is raised in this "detached" mode, we are not supposed to resort to what we think we know about external things in order to settle the question. As Stroud explains, "[a]ll my knowledge of the external world is supposed to have been brought into question at one fell swoop; no particular piece of it is to be available as unquestioned knowledge to help me decide whether or not another particular candidate is true" (Stroud 1984, 118). The sceptical question is, so to speak, "external" to the field of knowledge, whereas Moore reacts as if it could be answered "internally," from inside the body of our present knowledge. But in the "external" perspective, Moore's certainties are not available anymore.

It would obviously be very interesting, but rather long, to examine here the objections that Wittgenstein addresses to Moore's proof in *On Certainty*. We can perhaps be content to mention one of his simplest and most incisive:

> If a blind man were to ask me "Have you got two hands?" I should not make sure by looking. If I were to have any doubt of it, then I don't know why I should trust my eyes. For why shouldn't I test my eyes by looking to find out whether I see my two hands? What is to be tested by what? (Wittgenstein 1969, §125)

Jacques Bouveresse summarizes Wittgenstein's critique of Moore as follows: "it is a mistake to answer someone who says 'I don't know' by affirming that one knows. For we must not forget that one can 'believe that one knows.' What should be established in such a case is that one is really in a position to know" (Bouveresse 1976, 563). Furthermore, as Norman Malcolm remarks, a sentence like "I know that here is a human hand" cannot be intelligibly uttered in just any situation; there are conditions for the proper use of the verb "know": Normally, (a) there must be a question to be settled or a doubt to be removed, (b) the person who says she knows something must be able to explain her assertion by citing some reason, and (c) there must be a method or procedure which, if applied, would settle the question. Moore's proof, according to Malcolm, violates these conditions (cf. Malcolm 1949, 203 ff). A last point worth noting at this juncture is that no ostensive definition (i.e., referring to something by pointing) can fulfill the role Moore would have it play. Normally, by pointing, one wants to draw attention to something that has certain properties that distinguish it from other things. But one cannot distinguish in this way, by pointing, "an external thing" for the good reason that it is impossible to point at something which is not also an "external thing"!

Carnap's Anti-sceptical Strategy

A second "canonical" anti-sceptical strategy in which the internal/external couple plays a central role is the one devised by Carnap in "Empiricism, Semantics and Ontology" (Carnap 1950).

Carnap distinguishes two possible interpretations of the sentence "There are or exist physical or external objects." According to the first interpretation, the proposition is simply the trivial consequence of a host of empirically verified propositions, such as, for example, "here are two hands," which Moore's sensory experience empirically validates for him. If one understands it in this way, Moore's proof seems impeccable. But, as we have seen, philosophers do not generally understand it in this way. According to the other interpretation, which is the *philosophical* one, the sentence in question is neither an empirically verifiable proposition nor a trivial consequence of propositions that are empirically verifiable. As Strawson explains:

> Carnap accepts the point that, as the sceptic understands [...] the words "There exist physical things," Moore's experience, or any experience, could be just the way it is without these words expressing a truth; and hence that no course of experience could establish the proposition these words are taken by the sceptic to express; that it is in principle unverifiable in experience. (Strawson 1985, 5)

Now, since Carnap accepts the verification criterion of meaning, the conclusion he draws from the compatibility of any experience with the falsity of the sentence "there are physical objects" (taken philosophically), cannot be the sceptical conclusion. He concludes, rather, that these words, in the intended sense, do not express any proposition at all, that they are meaningless, and that, consequently, the question of whether the proposition they are supposed to express is true or false cannot arise.

Thus, for Carnap, within the "linguistic framework" in which we speak of physical objects, it is an analytic truth that there are physical objects (this is the first interpretation). But the sceptic is trying to ask an "external" question, about the empirical adequacy of the linguistic framework itself, or about the correspondence between reality and the linguistic framework. But there is no verifiable answer to this question, because the notion of truth is intra-theoretical and therefore the "external" question is devoid of cognitive meaning. One can ask empirical questions *within* a linguistic framework, but not *about* a linguistic framework. The only theoretical questions about a given linguistic framework are those about the rules and principles that constitute it; other "external" questions about the framework itself (e.g., "should we adopt the linguistic framework of physical objects or that of sense-data?") are matters of decision or convention and are therefore resolved by invoking pragmatic rather than factual considerations. In other words: although the philosophical question does not *seem* meaningless, it actually *is*. What are we to make of this?

Nagel's objection to any "technical" attempt to refute or "diagnose" scepticism could be applied to Carnap: the obvious intelligibility of the sceptic's words will inevitably call into question the more or less abstruse theories of language that have to be deployed in support of the accusation of incoherence or nonsense. A few "Nagelian" rhetorical questions would be in order here: isn't our certainty of understanding the sceptic's discourse always greater than the confidence we can place in Carnap's theoretical distinctions and verificationism? Aren't we convinced, before any theorizing, that talking about objects reflects much more than a convention or a decision? Do we not honestly believe that a material world really exists and that it is not absurd to affirm that it does? (cf. Nagel 1986, Chapter V).

These rhetorical questions point to a major difficulty: Carnap removes our belief in the reality of the external world from the realm of factual beliefs; but then he seems to have reached, by a roundabout route, a fairly fundamental agreement with the sceptic! What a concession! Carnap begins by disputing that the sceptic's statements make sense, but he ends up questioning the conception of objectivity that prevents us from altogether identifying *what is true* with *what we think is true*. The conclusion we can draw with Stroud is that "there appears to be no verificationist short-cut to a dismissal of philosophical scepticism" (Stroud 1984, 207), and the fundamental rationale for this conclusion is that "for anyone who finds the sceptical argument at all persuasive its very persuasiveness provides just as strong an argument against accepting the verifiability principle as that principle can provide against the meaningfulness of the sceptical conclusion" (Ibid., 205).

We can see similarities between the Carnapian approach to the problem of scepticism and the Wittgensteinian idea that Hacker and Baker have called "the autonomy of grammar" (Baker & Hacker 1985, 164). According to this idea, the rules of grammar cannot be justified by reality, nor can they conflict with it; grammar is not beholden to any pre-existing meanings, since it is grammar that constitutes meanings. The crucial difference between the two approaches lies, of course, in the fact that Wittgenstein never talks of *deciding to adopt* one linguistic framework (e.g., that of physical objects) rather than another. For Wittgenstein we "see the world," and distinguish what is true from what is false, against an "inherited background," and not by choosing from a range of alternative frames: "[…] I did not get my picture of the world by satisfying myself of its correctness; nor do I have it because I am satisfied of its correctness. No: it is the inherited background against which I distinguish between true and false" (Wittgenstein 1969, §94); "This doubt isn't one of the doubts in our game. (But not as if we *chose* this game!)" (Ibid., §317). In any case, Carnap, for his part, verges on the paradoxical: in what frame do we think when we choose one frame over the others? To which framework belong the concepts that allow us to formulate the thesis that no statement about external things is true or false independently of the adoption of the language of physical objects?

The Ordinary Language Court of Appeal

A third "canonical" reaction to radical scepticism is to examine its arguments and conclusions with reference to "ordinary language," in the light of what we say and mean ordinarily, that is, when we are not engaged in philosophizing. By resorting to the testimony of ordinary language against scepticism, "ordinary language" philosophers, and in particular Austin, intend to draw attention to the strangeness of the use of words in the Cartesian context. They accuse the sceptic of having changed the meaning of words or altered the normal criteria for their correct use. (Of course, Malcolm's objection to Moore, mentioned at the end of section "Moore's "Proof"", clearly belongs to this brand of criticism).

Prima facie, ordinary language considerations are hardly favorable to the sceptical enterprise: the condition of non-oneirism is not normally a condition of knowledge; we do not, in everyday life, require people to know that they are not dreaming before we grant them that they are in a position to know this or that, any more than we expect to find, at the end of a scientific experiment protocol, the statement "and when the experimenter took these measurements, he knew that he was not dreaming." Thus, it might seem that Descartes only reaches his sceptical conclusion by way of a violation (or perhaps more accurately a pushing to the limit) of our epistemological and semantic norms.

Moreover (and this is perhaps the most general form of the anti-sceptical argument drawn from ordinary language), the ultimate semantic court of appeal that ordinary usage is supposed to represent would rule that a scepticism so radical as to consider, even temporarily, that there is no knowledge, would be inconsistent. To doubt the truth of a judgment or the veracity of a perception presupposes that one knows what it would be, for a judgment, or for a perception, to be veridical. It is only on the basis of knowledge and certainty that sceptical doubt can be exercised. Truth and error are like legal tender and counterfeit money: if the former did not exist, how could the latter? As Strawson paraphrases the ordinary language philosopher's contention: "[the sceptic] pretends to accept a conceptual scheme, but at the same time quietly rejects one of the conditions of its employment. Thus, his doubts are unreal" (Strawson 1959, 35).

The ordinary language philosopher proceeds by singling out an expression used by the sceptic and then asking, "In what concrete circumstances would we use such an expression?" or "In what real-world context could we imagine that a question similar to the one posed by the sceptic would need to be taken seriously?" Here is a somewhat cartoonish example of this procedure. Suppose that someone were to declare that there are no doctors in Geneva. This is a very surprising statement which certainly contradicts a certain number of things that we thought we knew. When we inquire further about the astonishing discovery of this unfortunate state of affairs, it is explained to us that this is true because by "doctor" we mean a person who has a degree in medicine and is capable of curing any illness in less than two minutes. Our surprise subsides. We are well aware that (unfortunately) no one in Geneva (or elsewhere) meets the exorbitant criteria of this strange redefinition. The sceptical conclusion seems to be cut from the same cloth: at first, the idea that nobody can know anything about the outside world seems surprising. But when we learn that the "knowledge" in question is subject to extraordinary conditions (such as that of non-oneirism), which are not those of ordinary or scientific knowledge, our surprise subsides: the sceptic has merely redefined the notion of knowledge.

Austin's approach is of course less cartoonish, but, as Cavell notes, it is not entirely without analogies with the foregoing.[4] Let us take the statement: "here is a table." In the spirit of Descartes, I ask myself: "How do I know that there is a table here?" I could answer: "I see it." But the Cartesian reasons for doubt assail me: what I perceive through the senses is, in general, unreliable; I do not see the *whole* table, but only a table profile or a table surface; I might be hallucinating or dreaming, etc. Therefore, I don't *know* that there is a table here.

The philosopher of ordinary language (Austin in this case) proposes as an object of comparison an analogous case. Someone says that there is a goldfinch in the garden. He is asked: "How do you know it's a goldfinch?" And his answer could be: "By its red head." But a doubt is still possible: "How do you know it isn't a woodpecker? Woodpeckers have red heads too." In this example, a doubt is certainly reasonable, but does not, according to Austin, support any far-reaching conclusions: "I don't by any means always know whether it's [a goldfinch] or not. It may fly away before I have a chance of testing it, or of inspecting it thoroughly enough. This is simple enough: yet some are prone to argue that because I sometimes don't know or can't discover, I never can" (Austin 1961, 67). Austin considers that what prompts the sceptical conclusion

---

[4] Cf. Cavell (1979, Chapter III).

is simply the adoption of exorbitant or unusual criteria for the application of words: for example, the fact that I cannot see the whole table cannot be cited in support of a generalized doubt, because what we normally call "seeing" is a vision of surfaces and profiles: our view is neither radiographic nor holographic. For him, the sceptic sets the bar of certitude norms so high that all knowledge will necessarily seem deficient in comparison.

The sceptic will retort that doubts that seem out of place in ornithology are appropriate in a general epistemological investigation. She recognizes that the norms of truth that she has imposed on herself in the course of her investigation are stricter than those with which we are normally satisfied in everyday life or in more particular scientific research. But, she insists, they are the same standards, simply freed from practical limitations.

Thompson Clarke offers a good example to illustrate how the sceptic understands the relation between philosophical and ordinary or scientific contexts (Clarke 1972, 759–60). He asks us to imagine wartime spotters who have been trained to identify enemy aircraft based on a checklist of distinctive features. In fact, unbeknownst to the spotters, this checklist does not distinguish a certain type of aircraft X, which the pilots are able to identify, from another type of aircraft Y, which is much rarer and less dangerous. The modification of the checklist to cope with type Y aircraft (rare and not very dangerous) would complicate the identification procedures to the point of seriously hampering the timely identification of type X aircraft. Thus, a spotter, using his list, will identify a certain flying object as an aircraft of type X. But in fact, the distinguishing features on the basis of which he bases his identification do not enable him to distinguish X planes from Y planes. The spotter's assertion, "It is an X-plane" will certainly be accepted by the command since it is the result of a flawless application of the procedure. Nevertheless, *strictly speaking and independently of all practical considerations*, it cannot be said that the spotter *knows* that the aircraft he has spotted is of type X. Clarke's example is of course connected to the distinction that must be made between two questions that can be asked about any assertion. One can ask: "Is it true?" and one can ask: "Is it asserted in an appropriate, justified and reasonable way?" The example illustrates the fact that one cannot infer the truth of an assertion from its justified and reasonable character—any more than one can infer its falsity from its unjustified or unreasonable character. The spotter's assertion is perfectly justified given the voluntary omissions in his identification manual, but it does not follow that the assertion is true.

Clarke maintains that our situation in ordinary life is analogous to that of the spotters: if we cannot exclude that we are dreaming or that we are brains in vats or other more or less far-fetched eventualities, then *strictly speaking and independently of all practical consideration*, we do not know all the things we think we know. Naturally, we have excellent reasons to exclude or rather not to even consider these extravagant sceptical hypotheses, but no conclusion follows concerning the real status of our knowledge.

The lesson Clarke intends to draw from the spotters' example is that as long as we accept the idea of a logical leap between, on the one hand, the conditions of *appropriate and justified utterance* of an assertion and, on the other hand, the conditions of its *truth*, we will not be able to legitimately draw conclusions about the conditions of *knowledge* on the sole basis of considerations of normal usage or practice. The sceptic is well aware that the doubts she raises in the course of her reflection would not be considered appropriate or justified in everyday life. But, again, this is not enough to show that, in her investigation, she has engaged in a semantic sleight of hand similar to that involved in the example of the miraculous doctors.

When the Cartesian sceptic is summoned to appear before the court of appeal of ordinary usage, the hearing granted to him may therefore seem rushed and deaf to his genuine intellectual motivations. According to Austin, as we have seen, the sceptic's reasoning involves a rather crude fallacy, an illegitimate shift from the possibility of an *occasional* failure of knowledge to the possibility of a *permanent* failure in a normal context (when the object is in full view and we are in full possession of our means of perception and understanding); under such conditions, no doubt about the very existence of the object arises. But it is not clear that the sceptic is unaware of or has forgotten what the ordinary language philosopher would like to teach him or remind him of. He is well aware that specific reasons are needed to cast doubt on the existence of the perceived object; he is also aware that his conclusion contradicts common sense; he also concedes that from a practical point of view, his questioning of knowledge in general can be ignored. To the anti-sceptical arguments drawn from ordinary usage, the sceptic replies, on the one hand, that the deviation from ordinary language is quite innocuous insofar as every competent speaker can understand the discourse that narrates the emergence of doubt (after all, as Cavell notes, the beginning of Descartes' *Meditations* is not a particularly obscure text), and on the other hand, that one of the things one might discover, or think one discovers, in the course of a Cartesian meditation is that ordinary language may not be entirely trustworthy. In sum, the philosopher of ordinary language and the sceptic in the Cartesian tradition seem to be arguing past each other.

Santayana's Singularity

To the three "canonical" reactions to scepticism that I have reviewed, Strawson opposes, as I mentioned, a "naturalist" reaction, which he attributes to Hume and Wittgenstein. Santayana's response, as presented in *Scepticism and Animal Faith*, falls squarely within the scope of "naturalism" in Strawson's sense but displays unique features that I will highlight in the last two sections of this chapter.

Henry Levinson writes that "realists and naturalists in the United States generally characterized [*Scepticism and Animal Faith*] as a definitive statement of Santayana's critical realism [...]. They construed it as an attempt to sweep modern philosophy clean of metaphysics by establishing a naturalistic theory of knowledge linking mind to the world" (Levinson 1992, 205). In a sense, as Levinson notes, one only needs to read the famous first lines of the preface—certainly one of the most effective instances of *captatio benevolentiae* in the whole philosophical tradition—to realize that such a reading is misguided:

> Here is one more system of philosophy. If the reader is tempted to smile, I can assure him that I smile with him, and that my system–to which this volume is a critical introduction–differs widely in spirit and pretensions from what usually goes by that name. (Santayana 1923, v)

"One more system of philosophy!" And not, as Santayana expects the reader to assume, a better one. The smile Santayana alludes to is the smile that the term "philosophical system" is likely to elicit in a clear-headed, sane reader. How, indeed, is it possible to keep a straight face after so many philosophical wrecks? How not to react with amused condescension when one compares the ambitions traditionally displayed by philosophical systems to their actual achievements and to their inability to garner, even momentarily, an educated and *bona fide* consensus? Santayana hopes to transmute the reader's condescending (or perhaps pitying) smile, by assuring him "that [he] smile[s] with him," because his philosophical system's aims have little in common with those of traditional philosophical systems: "This system is not mine nor new," it is "no system of the universe," it is "not metaphysical," and it is "no phase of any current movement" (Santayana 1923, v–viii). Thus, the work renounces in advance all that its "target public" (as one would say today), however philosophically blasé, would have expected from it: it doesn't provide a new description of the link between words (or minds) and things and does not constitute a contribution to the burning epistemological controversies of the moment. Santayana is "merely attempting to express for the reader the principles to which he appeals when he smiles" (Santayana 1923, v).

These principles are no more (and no less) than what Santayana describes as "a certain shrewd orthodoxy which the sentiment and practice of laymen maintain everywhere" (Ibid.); that is, the fundamental convictions of common sense that have been justified "in all ages and countries, by the facts before every man's eyes" (Ibid., 10), or, to use Lachs' apt phrase, "the tenets of animal faith" (Lachs 1988, 42). The road he takes to try to make these principles explicit involves an exercise in radical scepticism, in the strict sense of the phrase. Instead of trying to line up arguments against the sceptic, his strategy is to go wholeheartedly along with him in order to see where the full development of the sceptical position may lead. Convinced that sceptical programs as a rule do not go beyond what is required to dismantle the dogmas of rival schools or reaffirm desirable conclusions, Santayana considers that the sceptic should not waver at the last moment, no matter how credible and attractive the beliefs he is about to strike down appear. Thus, in chapters III through XI of *Scepticism and Animal Faith*, he sets out to strain "[all] dogmas through the utmost rigours of scepticism" (Santayana 1923, 7). A detailed examination of the precise steps of the sceptical exercise Santayana undertakes would require more space and patience than I have available; thankfully, it is its terminus that we should focus on here. At the end of the examination, all the beliefs of which one could have the slightest reason to doubt have apparently been abandoned by Santayana: not only the clearly optional beliefs of religion and politics; not only, classically enough, the belief in an internal criterion of truth for sensory experience or for memory; not only, quite obviously, the Cartesian belief in a doubting and thinking "I," an entity that, as Hume pointed out, is never encountered as such among the objects of consciousness ("The persuasion that in saying 'I am' I have reached an indubitable fact, can only excite a smile in the genuine sceptic" [Santayana (1923), 290]); but even the belief in the veracity of the intuition of change and, more radically still, the belief in the existence of anything that can be given immediately to consciousness ("*Nothing given exists*" [Santayana 1923, Chapter VII]), all this goes overboard.

What is the outcome of such an uncompromising and devastating sceptical program? Nothing less, as is well known, than a "solipsism of the present moment." The efforts of such a solipsist "are concentrated on *not* asserting and *not* implying anything, but simply noticing what he finds" (Santayana 1923, 16). He doesn't *believe* anything, but his mind is not empty; he contemplates intuited contents that present themselves somehow stripped of epistemic import. ("colours, sounds, shapes, sizes, excellences, and defects" might constitute a minimal list of the simplest ones [Santayana 1923, 81].) These sensuous or conceptual elements which are devoid of transitive knowledge value constitute Santayana's realm of *essences* (or at least the fragment of that realm accessible to human consciousness). To put it in Aristotelian terms: the quiddity, the *what*, that remains as an immediate object of consciousness after all beliefs have been removed, is an essence. The sceptic that refuses to "set accidental limits to his scepticism" (Santayana 1923, 290) ends up in "the realm of immediate illusion," except that the data that constitute this realm "cease to be illusions cognitively, since no existence would be suggested by any of them" (Santayana 1923, 65). In Saatkamp's words: "Santayana's contention is that if we reduce our knowledge to the actually evident, we may discern an awareness that is infallible and indubitable; but this infallibility and indubitability characterize such a restricted state of consciousness that it cannot be described as knowledge in any form and therefore cannot provide the basis for the reconstruction of knowledge on self-evident beliefs or knowledge claims" (Saatkamp 1980, 138). But one could argue that Saatkamp's formulation does not go far enough, for if no description in terms of knowledge can be applied to the states of consciousness in question, it is also pointless to apply to them such eminently epistemic terms as "indubitable" or "infallible." Santayana writes that "whereas transitive knowledge [...] may always be challenged, intuition, on the contrary, which neither has nor professes to have any ulterior object or truth, runs no risk of error" (Santayana 1923, 70). Where there is no risk of error there can be no chance of knowledge.

Here we begin to glimpse how much the function of scepticism in Santayana's philosophy deviates from its traditional function in modern post-Cartesian philosophy, and also begin to discern the affinities with the thinkers that Williams groups under the label "New Sceptics" (Williams 1996, 10; cf. supra 1). Scepticism does not lead, in *Scepticism and Animal Faith*, to indubitable beliefs from which one could reconstruct, on more solid bases, the edifice of knowledge. As Tiller says, "the [...] sceptic who has descended into solipsism of the present moment has no inferential exit" (Tiller 2000, 51). What, then, other than the discovery of a realm of self-identical "essences" are the results of Santayana's uncompromising scepticism?[5]

A central point Santayana aims to demonstrate through his exercise in radical scepticism, is that someone who would refuse to accept any belief for which he does not have an explicit rational justification, would be reduced to adopting the stance of the solipsist of the present moment. As Sprigge explains:

> Anyone who is not a solipsist of the present moment—and that includes all who speak to persuade—believes some things for which he can offer no rational ground. [...]. Santayana's ultimate point is not to recommend solipsism of the present moment, but to insist that unless one is a solipsist of the present moment one cannot hold it against any theory of the world merely that it has foundations which cannot be demonstrated or verified. (Sprigge 1995, 35)

Seventeen years after the publication of *Scepticism and Animal Faith* Santayana himself wrote that the book "was not an invitation to the public to become solipsists or a pretence that [he] had become one, but a demonstration that demonstration in matters of belief is impossible [...]" (Santayana 1940, 517); a demonstration, in other words, that the foundationalist ideal of knowledge, with its demand for apodictic certainty in the foundations, ends up, when pushed to its ultimate limits, in solipsism, and consequently proves unrealistic and unreasonable; a demonstration that "an honest philosophy demands standards different from absolute certainty" (Hodges & Lachs 2000, 10). In short: Santayana offers a kind of *reductio* of the foundationalist premises of methodological scepticism, but not a *reduction ad absurdum* of scepticism, a demonstration of its incoherence. Not a *reduction to logical absurdity* of scepticism but rather a *reduction to animal absurdity*: scepticism is humanly impracticable.

Santayana's "Tenets of Animal Faith" and Wittgenstein's "Hinge Propositions"

At the beginning of Chapter XI, Santayana writes: "I have now reached the culminating point of my survey of evidence, and the entanglements I have left behind me and the habitable regions I am looking for lie spread out before me

---

[5] The cogency of Santayana's theory of essences is a matter of controversy on which I deliberately refrain from taking a position in this chapter.

like opposite valleys" (Santayana 1923, 99). Thus, from this point onward, Santayana begins to develop his alternative to the foundationalist ideal by referring to "animal faith": however dubious our ordinary beliefs may appear in principle (and, as a matter of fact, in principle only), we are constantly driven, whether we want it or not, to believe a great many things, to exceed the purely intuitive grasp of "essences," to maintain a spontaneously trusting epistemic relationship with the world. The reason Santayana calls "animal faith" the set of propensities and reactions that, *volens nolens*, eventuate in, or rather, amount to belief, lies in the fact that these dispositions to believe manifest themselves in the most incontrovertible way in our condition as animals evolving in an intractable environment that holds threats and allurements.

The animality of human beings and of the mind ("I believe profoundly in the animality of the mind" [Santayana 1940, 601]) is central to Santayana, and animal faith, insofar as it comes under the purview of science, falls within the explanatory scope of evolution: the beliefs constitutive of animal faith are first of all those that adapt an animal for survival and reproduction in a given environment. In this sense, the implicit beliefs that Santayana's philosophy of animal faith discerns are those that our *actions* reveal. (On this question of the epistemic primacy of action, Santayana is evidently very close to the pragmatists and to Wittgenstein. For the latter, justification necessarily comes to an end, "but the end is not an ungrounded presupposition: it is an ungrounded way of acting," "the end is not certain propositions' striking us immediately as true, i.e. it is not a kind of seeing on our part; it is our acting, which lies at the bottom of the language-game" [Wittgenstein 1969, §§110, 204]).

The essential point to which Santayana returns repeatedly is that it is as futile to argue against the background propensities and reactions constitutive of the human animal's condition, as it is to try to strengthen the commitments of animal faith by "founding" them. Like Hume, he deems scepticism both irrefutable and untenable: irrefutable in the context of the rational reconstruction of knowledge but untenable from the point of view of an animal engaging in action. In this respect, Santayana's animal faith is like Wittgenstein's "forms of life" (*Lebensformen*), which are "what has to be accepted" (Wittgenstein 1953, 192). One cannot provide any foundational reasons for or against the beliefs that pertain to animal faith, for the very activity of providing reasons already presupposes these implicit beliefs.[6]

This congruence between Santayana, Hume, and Wittgenstein is indeed striking. The status of Santayana's "tenets of animal faith" is very close to that of Hume's "natural beliefs," which in turn are reminiscent of Wittgenstein's "hinge propositions."[7] Strawson argues that, unlike Hume, Wittgenstein does

[6] For a systematic and enlightening exploration of the similarities between the thought of Wittgenstein and the philosophy of Santayana, see Hodges and Lachs (2000).

[7] Wittgenstein calls "hinge propositions" those propositions, such as "I know I have two hands" or "the world has existed for more than five minutes" that are "in deed not doubted" (Wittgenstein 1969, §342); the term "hinge" suggests an analogy with the function of door hinges: "If we want the door to turn, the hinges must stay put" (Ibid., §343).

not explicitly appeal to Nature in order to distinguish between those propositions that are genuinely doubtful in the light of reason and experience and those that are "exempt from doubt" (Strawson 1985, 14). It seems to me, however, that there is an unmistakable "naturalistic" streak in Wittgenstein. It shows up, for example, when he writes that "it is always by favour of Nature that one knows something" (Wittgenstein 1969, §505) or when he mentions a type of certainty that "[he] want[s] to conceive [...] as something that lies beyond being justified or unjustified; as it were, as something animal" (Ibid., §395), or again when he declares that "[he] want[s] to regard man here as an animal; as a primitive being to which one grants instinct but not ratiocination" (Ibid., §475). But whatever the textual concordances, it seems indisputable that Hume, Santayana, and Wittgenstein share similar views on how to deal with the problem of scepticism in relation to foundationalism. They agree that "at the foundation of well-founded belief lies belief that is not founded" (Ibid., §253); that, as Santayana says, the tenets of animal faith "are neither founded nor doubtful." All three thinkers

> have in common the view that our "beliefs" in the existence of body [...] are not grounded beliefs and at the same time are not open to serious doubt. They are, one might say, outside our critical and rational competence in the sense that they define, or help to define, the area in which that competence is exercised. To attempt to confront the professional sceptical doubt with arguments in support of these beliefs, with rational justifications, is simply to show a total misunderstanding of the role they actually play in our belief-systems. (Strawson 1985, 15)[8]

Hume, Wittgenstein, and Santayana all three resort to what might be called the "standard naturalistic argument" against foundationalism. According to this argument, any belief rests on substantial presuppositions that can only be verified or justified by procedures that already presuppose them. Some beliefs are at least as secure as any justification we could put forward in favor of them. Thus, Wittgenstein writes: "My having two hands is, in normal circumstances, as certain as anything that I could produce in evidence for it. That is why I am not in a position to take the sight of my hand as evidence for it" (Wittgenstein 1969, §250). Hume, for his part, holds that "we may well ask, *What causes us to believe in the existence of body?* But 'tis in vain to ask, *Whether there be body or not?* That is a point, which we must take for granted in all our reasonings" (Hume 1888, 187). Santayana also makes repeated use of this type of argument. With regard to the notion of substance, he considers that "belief in substance is [...] identical with the claim to knowledge, and so fundamental that no evidence can be adduced for it which does not presuppose it" (Santayana 1923, 185). Referring to the "first principles of discourse" (i.e., logical principles), he writes: "They can never be discovered, if discovered at all, until they

---

[8] Strawson is thinking here of the "profound community" between Hume and Wittgenstein; I am adding Santayana to the club.

have been long taken for granted, and employed in the very investigation which reveals them [...]; so that the mind must trust current presumptions no less in discovering that they are logical—that is, justified by more general unquestioned presumptions—than in discovering that they are arbitrary and merely instinctive" (Santayana 1923, 2).

In the second part of *Scepticism and Animal Faith* (from Chapter XI onward), Santayana gradually restores the common sense beliefs that scepticism has labored to dismantle. As Sprigge explains,

> the path back from scepticism [...] is not a path determined by deductive or inductive argument, it is neither a rationalist nor an empiricist re-erection of human knowledge on logically secure foundations, it is rather a path in which resistance after resistance is broken down by the fact that habits of mind which one cannot long suspend have beliefs in matters of fact implicit in them. (Sprigge 1974, 8)

Just as I did not dwell on the individual steps of the sceptical dissolution undertaken in the first part of *Scepticism and Animal Faith*, I will not dwell on the steps that lead to the restoration of animal faith. The general thrust of Santayana's argument is clear enough. I would be remiss, however, not to point out that one of the first steps on this path is the restoration of realism: animal action commits us to the existence of an external world. This commitment is not itself subject to inquiry, because it is presupposed when anything is believed. When Santayana sets forth his belief in substance (Santayana 1923, Chapter XIX), that is his belief that "there are things and events prior to the discovery of them and independent of this discovery" (Santayana 1942, 186), he cannot help exclaiming: "I shall be thought a silly philosopher to mention this, as if it were not obvious; but why do so many wise philosophers ignore it, and defend systems which contradict it?" (Santayana 1923, 209). Good question!

The Epistemic Status of Animal Faith and "Hinge Propositions"

Let us return briefly, to conclude, to the problem of the epistemic status of Santayana's "tenets of animal faith" and Wittgenstein's "hinge propositions." Wittgenstein suggests that the concept of knowledge is not applicable to hinge propositions: "If the true is what is grounded, then the ground is not true, nor yet false" (Wittgenstein 1969, §205); this idea is also taken up in §151 and §136:

> I should like to say: Moore does not know what he asserts he knows, but it stands fast for him, as also for me; regarding it as absolutely solid is part of our method of doubt and enquiry.

> When Moore says he knows such and such, he is really enumerating a lot of empirical propositions which we affirm without special testing; propositions, that is, which have a peculiar logical role in the system of our empirical propositions.

The logical role to which Wittgenstein alludes consists in delimiting the framework or backdrop within which empirical questions are raised and resolved; these are the "hinges" around which our inquiries, justifications, and judgments revolve; being always presupposed, they cannot in turn be justified.

As I pointed out above, Santayana does not carry out in *Scepticism and Animal Faith* a *reduction to logical absurdity* of scepticism but rather a *reduction to animal absurdity*. On this point, as Guy Bennett-Hunter has rightly observed, Santayana and Wittgenstein seem to diverge (cf. Bennett-Hunter 2012, 152–154). Wittgenstein starts from (and in a sense ends with) the logical observation that whenever we doubt anything, there must always be something that is not doubted, something that is taken for granted as the background against which the doubt can arise. Such is the structure of inquiry. "A doubt that doubted everything would not be a doubt" (Wittgenstein 1969, §4540). Universal doubt is incoherent. In this sense, his response to scepticism is more formal, less "substantive," than Santayana's: what determines that certain beliefs function as "hinge propositions" is simply that they are "off the route of inquiry" (Ibid., 147), that "they are in deed not doubted." Wittgenstein leaves open the question of their precise nature and content. Santayana, for his part, never condemns solipsism of the present moment on account of its alleged incoherence: "So far is solipsism of the present moment from being self-contradictory that it might, under other circumstances, be the normal and invincible attitude of the spirit; and I suspect it may be that of many animals. [...] A creature whose whole existence was passed under a hard shell, or was spent in a free flight, might find nothing paradoxical or acrobatic in solipsism" (Santayana 1923, 17). What determines for Santayana the inclusion of a belief among the tenets of animal faith is the fact that we *act on it*. Hodges and Lachs have argued that Santayana follows the principle that "whatever has existential primacy should enjoy epistemic prerogatives as well" (Hodges & Lachs 2000, 65). Given Wittgenstein's reluctance to construct positive philosophical doctrines, he would balk at asserting such a principle. Nonetheless, as Hodges and Lachs also maintain, "the centrality of what we do for what we should think stands as a common foundation" (Ibid., 67). If only for this reason, the Wittgensteinian category of what "is in deed not doubted" and the Santayanian one of "what you cannot help believing" must overlap.

As we saw in the introduction, the "moral" of scepticism, as Cavell would have it, is that "the human creature's basis in the world as a whole, its relation to the world as such, is not that of knowing, anyway not what we think of as knowing" (Cavell 1979, 241), or, as he observes elsewhere, that our relationship to the world's existence is "closer than the ideas of believing and knowing are made to convey" (Cavell 1980, 145). But how can hinge propositions, or articles of animal faith, be factual, given that our relations with them must remain, in an important sense, non-epistemic? Michael Williams is probably right to note that "the difficulty is to see why [naturalism] is a refutation of radical scepticism rather than another expression of it" (Williams 1996, 157). What the proponent of naturalism has yet to show is that the absence of foundations and justification "is not a lack" (Ibid.). Santayana and Wittgenstein, each in his own way, try to do this, but even if we consider that they succeed rather well in this endeavor, we may lack compelling arguments to refute those who think that the naturalistic "solution" to the problem of scepticism is merely a verbal maneuver aiming to exorcise the permanent threat of scepticism. This possibility is no doubt part of what "The New Sceptics" mean by "the truth of scepticism."

References

Austin, J.L. 1961. Other Minds. In *Philosophical Papers*. Oxford: Oxford University Press.
Baker, G.P., and P.M.S. Hacker. 1985. *Wittgenstein Rules, Grammar, and Necessity*. Oxford: Basil Blackwell.
Bennett-Hunter, G. 2012. A Pragmatist conception of Certainty: Wittgenstein and Santayana. *European Journal of Pragmatism and American Philosophy* IV: 2.
Bouveresse, J. 1976. *Le Mythe de l'intériorité*. Paris: Les Éditions de Minuit.
Carnap, R. 1950. Empiricism, Semantics and Ontology. *Revue Internationale de Philosophie* 4: 20–40.
Cavell, S. 1979. *The Claim of Reason: Wittgenstein, Scepticism, Morality and Tragedy*. Oxford: Oxford University Press.
Clarke, T. 1972. The Legacy of Skepticism. *The Journal of Philosophy* 69: 20.
Descartes, R. 1911. *Meditations on First Philosophy* [1641]. In *The Philosophical Works of Descartes*, Translated by Elizabeth S. Haldane. Cambridge: Cambridge University Press.
Hodges, M., and J. Lachs. 2000. *Thinking in the Ruins: Wittgenstein and Santayana on Contingency*. Nashville: Vanderbilt University Press.
Hume, D. 1888. In *A Treatise of Human Nature [1739]*, ed. L.A. Selby-Bigge. Oxford: Oxford University Press.
———. 1975. *Enquiries concerning Human Understanding and concerning the Principles of Morals* [1748,1751], ed. L.A. Selby-Bigge, revised by P.H. Nidditch. Oxford: Clarendon Press.
Kant, I. 1998. *Critique of Pure Reason* [1787], Translated and edited by Paul Guyer and Allen W. Wood. Cambridge: Cambridge University Press.
Lachs, J. 1988. *George Santayana*. Boston: Twayne Publishers.
Levinson, H.S. 1992. *Santayana, Pragmatism and the Spiritual Life*. Chapel Hill and London: The University of North Carolina Press.
Malcolm, N. 1949. Defending Common Sense. *The Philosophical Review* 58 (3): 201–220.
Moore, G.E. 1959. "A Proof of an External World" [1939] and "A Defence of Common Sense" [1925]. In *Philosophical Papers*. London: Allen & Unwin.
Nagel, T. 1986. *The View from Nowhere*. Oxford: Oxford University Press.
Putnam, H. 1981. *Reason, Truth and History*. New York: Cambridge University Press.
Saatkamp, H. 1980. Some Remarks on Santayana's Scepticism. In *Two Centuries of Philosophy in America*, ed. Peter Caw. Rowman and Littlefield: Totowa, NJ.

Santayana, G. 1923. *Scepticism and Animal Faith: Introduction to a System of Philosophy.* New York: Charles Scribner's Sons.

———. 1940. Apologia Pro Mente Sua. In *The Philosophy of George Santayana, The Library of Living Philosophers*, ed. P.A. Schilpp. Evanston and Chicago: Northwerstern University Press.

———. 1942. *Realms of Being.* One-Volume Edition. New York: Charles Scribner's Sons.

———. 1986. *Persons and Places: Fragments of Autobiography*, ed. W.G. Holzberger and H. J. Saatkamp, Jr. The MIT Press: Cambridge, Mass and London.

Sprigge, T.L.S. 1974. *Santayana: An Examination of his Philosophy.* London and New York: Routledge.

———. 1995. *Santayana: an Examination of His Philosophy.* London and New York: Routledge.

Strawson, P. 1959. *Individuals: An Essay in Descriptive Metaphysics.* Abingdon and New York: Routledge.

———. 1985. *Scepticism and Naturalism: Some Varieties.* Abington: Routledge.

Stroud, B. 1984. *The Significance of Philosophical Scepticism.* Oxford: Clarendon Press.

Tiller, G.A. 2000. *Peirce, Santayana, and the Presuppositions of Belief.* Unpublished doctoral dissertation, University of Toronto.

Wahman, J. 2007. Corpulent Or a Train of Ideas? Santayana's Critique of Hume. *Overheard in Seville, Bulletin of the Santayana Society,* 23.

Williams, M. 1996. *Unnatural Doubts: Epistemological Realism and the Basis of Scepticism.* Princeton, NJ: Princeton University Press.

Wittgenstein, L. 1953. *Philosophical Investigations.* Translated by G.E.M. Anscombe. Malden, MA and Oxford: Blackwell Publishing & Ltd.

———. 1969. *On Certainty*, Edited by G.E.M. Anscombe and G.H. von Wright. Translated by Denis Paul and G.E.M. Anscombe. Oxford: Basil Blackwell.

Knowledge as a Leap of Faith

Jessica Wahman

> "There is no avenue to the past or the future, there is no room or breath for progressive life, except through faith in the intellect and in the reality of things not seen."
> —SAF, 29

George Santayana's account of knowledge as grounded in animal faith is a noteworthy, original, and sadly underappreciated achievement. While arguments in favor of scepticism are as old as academic philosophy itself, and while American pragmatists have long exposed the quest for certainty as an unreasonable epistemological goal, Santayana stands out for his establishment of certainty as, in principle, incompatible with the pursuit of knowledge. According to Santayana, knowledge and faith are not opposed avenues to the formation of belief but are instead wholly bound up together. In any claim, Santayana argues, thought transcends the immediate object of its attention to make assertions about what is not, at that moment, given to it: the past, the future, or some material fact. Because, as he establishes, one cannot be certain about anything other than the present moment, and because all acts of cognition transcend that moment, knowledge and certainty—despite longstanding assumptions and desires to the contrary—in actuality have nothing to do with each other. It does not follow from this that knowledge is impossible; on the contrary, it is both possible and real. The feeling of certitude is simply unrelated to the achievement of understanding, the latter involving inevitable and

---

J. Wahman (✉)
Department of Philosophy, Emory University, Atlanta, GA, USA
e-mail: jessica.tabor.wahman@emory.edu

© The Author(s), under exclusive license to Springer Nature Switzerland AG 2024
M. A. Coleman, G. Tiller (eds.), *The Palgrave Companion to George Santayana's Scepticism and Animal Faith*, Palgrave Companions,
https://doi.org/10.1007/978-3-031-46367-9_6

uncertain beliefs. In calling attention to the unavoidable dogmas of our animal existence—belief in memory, demonstration, experience, a self, substance, and, ultimately, nature—Santayana effectively reconstructs the concept of knowledge as a leap of faith in things unseen.

A productive means of shedding light on Santayana's analysis of the dogmatic belief inherent to all understanding is to contrast it with aspects of similar investigations in two other major epistemological works: Rene Descartes's *Meditations on First Philosophy* and G. W. F. Hegel's *Phenomenology of Spirit*. All three philosophers take a moment of pure and certain presence and follow a step-by-step procedure that takes the reader beyond that starting point to establish that thinker's further claims. In so doing, each work serves as a sort of preliminary exercise, a rethinking of epistemology that clears the way for the philosopher to generate his broader philosophical claims. Moreover, and most importantly, Santayana's analysis deliberately—and, in the case of Descartes, explicitly—subverts both the methods and conclusions of the other two thinkers. He exposes the fact that contrary to Descartes's and Hegel's methods and aims, awareness of a datum cannot serve as an epistemological foundation or even a logical point of departure, for nothing follows necessarily from it. In addition, knowledge is not about an idea wholly capturing its object but involves a transitive leap beyond a given thought to something that thought can never wholly assimilate. In addressing what he terms "the solipsism of the present moment" (SPM) (*SAF*, 15) and our inability to move beyond that moment without a leap of faith, Santayana exposes Descartes's scepticism as half-hearted, demonstrates that no logical inference—whether deductive or dialectical—can be an infallible one, argues that the object of understanding is precisely what is *not* available to consciousness, and thus implies that Descartes's and Hegel's treatises are not logical analyses of ultimate knowledge but imaginative exercises in literary psychology.

The Value of Criticism

Scepticism and Animal Faith is a propaedeutic to Santayana's ontological treatise, *Realms of Being*.[1] Its point is to clear the way for discussion of speculative matters—realities other than the experiential—which modern philosophy and the work of his contemporaries had long declared anathema. Santayana dubs much of the modern thought to which he is opposed either *transcendentalism* or *psychologism*. While the two concepts are not identical, their treatment of experience as, quite literally, the substance of philosophy is the shared basis for his disagreement with them. Santayana thus takes on one of the sacred tenets bequeathed by late modernity, the notion that experiences are the true subject matter of philosophy. To do so, he must expose the error in Descartes's subjective turn, which made a personal consciousness the foundation of all inquiry.

---

[1] The book ends with an invitation to the reader to investigate the realms of being made available by establishing knowledge as animal faith (*SAF*, 309).

The focus on experience, Santayana believes, and the search for its necessary conditions is the result of a failed criticism of knowledge that began with Descartes's embrace of his own conscious attention as the one certain foundation on which to build a new ontological framework. *Scepticism and Animal Faith* aims to show, by contrast, that a proper criticism exposes knowledge as without certain foundation, whether its object is experience or material existence. Thus, scepticism is always tenable and important as an exercise for examining one's own beliefs more clearly, but it cannot establish a first principle on which to build an unshakable edifice.

Descartes's critical motive was a good one—his desire to question Scholastic dogma and to doubt the reliability of everyday sensory experience as a source of scientific information exposed longstanding superstitions and helped to move natural science in important new directions. At the same time, however, his expectation that knowledge of fact should entail the same certainty and precision that he found in mathematics caused him to sneak in, unawares, many of his own idols. Among these are two mistaken assumptions: (1) that scepticism can be overcome by finding and building on one certain truth, and (2) that knowledge involves indubitable logical progression from one certain building block to another. Santayana argues that a wholesale criticism will instead expose the fact that nothing it examines—no perception, concept, or inference—is certain. He notes that "[t]he only critical function of transcendentalism is to drive empiricism home, and challenge it to produce any knowledge of fact whatsoever. And empirical criticism will not be able to do so" (*SAF*, 4). A sufficiently close attention to experience, Santayana believes, will expose the fact that while foci of attention—what he terms the *data* of awareness—may be indubitable insofar as they simply are whatever appearance they are, any claim about their nature, meaning, or how they may be combined and compared takes us beyond the immediate and out of the locus of certainty. There may be facts to be learned about a given datum, but a present datum cannot, by itself, be an established fact. Therefore, the presumption "that knowledge should be intuition of fact ... must be revoked" (*SAF*, 171). We cannot deduce any necessary conditions for the possibility of experience or make claims about actual facts—whether or not those facts are experienced ones—merely by focusing on what is before us.

Criticism is thus important precisely because, done properly, it exposes the uncertainty of all knowledge claims. Santayana explains: "the scepticism I am defending is not meant to be merely provisional; its just conclusions will remain fixed, to remind me perpetually that all alleged knowledge of matters of fact is faith only, and that an existing world, whatever form it may choose to wear, is intrinsically a questionable and arbitrary thing" (*SAF*, 49). So, while Descartes's sceptical reduction to the cogito was merely a hyperbolic exercise in order to establish indubitable conclusions,[2] the scepticism Santayana defends is, he

---

[2] At the end of the *Meditations*, Descartes refers to his initial doubts as "exaggerated" and, indeed, "laughable" (Descartes 1984, 61).

claims, unassailable. In this sense, Santayana has something in common with the sceptics of ancient Greece and Rome. Unlike the ancient sceptics, however, Santayana does not conclude that knowledge is impossible. Instead, there is such a thing as knowledge, and it is inherently uncertain.

The Solipsism of the Present Moment

To understand why Santayana argues that all knowledge must be uncertain, it is important to attend closely to what he terms the solipsism of the present moment (hereafter SPM) and why he thinks any move beyond it entails a leap of faith. Essentially, the SPM is the mere presence of a datum to consciousness. To be clear, the SPM does not refer to the natural fact that people have experiences and that these experiences involve what contemporary philosophers of mind would term *qualia*, though Santayana's concept of a datum is comparable, in some ways, to such phenomena. It instead refers to an exercise in scepticism from a first-person perspective and its discovery that the datum alone is present and beyond doubt. Santayana's point is that if we are to take the sceptical exercise seriously and not admit anything about which we are not certain, then all that is certain is that which is immediately given at the very moment in which it is given.[3]

The witnessed datum, that "manifest being ... will seem an event in no world, an incident in no experience. The quality of it will have ceased to exist: it will be merely the quality which is inherently, logically, and inalienably is. It will be an ESSENCE" (*SAF*, 73–4). Santayana's concept of essence is—contrary to his pronouncements—unusual and somewhat complicated (indeed, Santayana gives it an entire realm in his ontology and devotes a book to it), but for present purposes we may think of it as the infinite variety of all possible characteristics, qualities, or—loosely speaking—forms. Santayana argues that essences are the only possible immediate objects of our attention. All else—matter, truth, and spirit (conscious awareness)—can only be an object of belief. When intuited, or given, an essence is equivalent in meaning to a datum or object of awareness. Scepticism reduces to a solipsism because, in short, nothing but a given essence, or datum, is present: in that moment of attention, there is no duration, no context, no self-awareness, and no claim to belief.

To fully grasp how radical a scepticism Santayana is positing, a comparison with the moments of certainty established by Descartes and Hegel—the cogito and sense-certainty, respectively—may be fruitful. For, while some may argue that Descartes's awareness of his own thinking, for example, is a simple and certain intuition of his existence, Santayana shows that this is not so. In the claim "I think, therefore I am," Descartes smuggles in many unsubstantiated beliefs; in his first deduction from that claim, he smuggles in even more. And, while Hegel's sense-certainty similarly takes nothing but the immediately given

---

[3] As I explain below, the presence of the datum is certain only in a vacuous sense, as the SPM does not involve any claim that the given is, in fact, given.

as its object, it nonetheless includes more in this moment—specifically, consciousness and its highly mediated experience—than Santayana will admit into the SPM.

In his progressive act of doubting, Descartes makes a distinction between appearance and reality that becomes increasingly focused on the certitude of the apparent while doubting the existence of anything else. He concludes that, even if all is a dream or an evil deception, it is nonetheless indubitable that he, Descartes, is having that dream or experiencing that deception. Thus, the fact of his own subjective experience is taken as certain while the veracity of that experience with regard to anything other than itself remains in question. Santayana's own exercise takes a similar course in noting that sceptical analysis, in doubting all knowledge of existence, will eventually land on an immediately given object of attention. The difference, however, is that Descartes's cogito includes a claim about a subject—*I* think—which Santayana stresses cannot be indubitably asserted: "a thorough criticism of knowledge ... would demand that the ideas of self, of activity, and of consciousness should be disintegrated and reduced to the immediate. In the immediate, however, there is no transcendental force nor transcendental machinery, not even a set of perceptions nor an experience, but only some random essence, staring and groundless" (*SAF*, 304). The SPM is not a cogitation *about* the present moment, which would require a temporal progression of thought and would thus transcend the presently given. It is nothing other than that present moment of attention. To be properly sceptical, then, there can be no assumptions about what or to whom the datum is given, much less how that datum comes about. Descartes's cogito, in other words, contains an unproven assumption about himself as a thinking entity, which becomes evident when he builds on his supposed foundation to infer that he is—indubitably—"a mind, or intelligence, or intellect, or reason. ... A thinking thing" (Descartes 1984, 18). In this inference, while claiming not to admit anything he has not already established as certain, Descartes assumes several unproven facts: that anything exists, that there is a process called reasoning which is legitimate in seeking truth, that there is truth, that there is time or duration through which an inference can be made, that there is a single subject to whom these different moments of thinking a premise and conclusion pertain, that there are entities or substances (at least one), and that properties and processes (in this case, cognitive ones) may be predicated of substance. Far from being certain knowledge or established fact, Descartes's foundation is, Santayana claims, a supposition chock full of "gratuitous dogmas" (*SAF*, 14).

Similar to Santayana, Hegel characterizes the epistemological starting point of his own exercise as the presence of a datum whose being simply is whatever it is. In sense-certainty, consciousness "has the object before it in its perfect entirety" and its certainty consists in nothing but the fact "that it *is*; and its truth contains nothing but the sheer *being* of the thing" (Hegel 1977, 58). Like Santayana, Hegel claims that such certainty is not knowledge at all (though he does so for different reasons). However, Hegel still finds more in the purely present than Santayana will allow. For example, Hegel asserts that "[c]onsciousness ... is in this certainty ... as a pure 'I'" (58). Like Descartes but unlike Santayana, Hegel claims to find an *I* along with the object in the present moment of awareness, and he asserts that both consciousness and object, however inadequate to complete knowledge, are nonetheless experienced as certain. Of course, on reflection, Santayana would attest that the SPM is a moment experienced by a conscious thinker. But this is a fallible knowledge claim distinct from the SPM as it is experienced. Santayana insists that there is no immediate awareness of one's own awareness. "I" am not, he claims, "a datum to myself. I am a somewhat remote and extremely obscure object of belief" (*SAF*, 290). In the solipsism of the present moment, in other words, there is only the immediately given object.

A second difference between the SPM and sense-certainty is that the being of the object in this initial stage of Hegel's dialectic turns out to be far more complex than the datum of the SPM. Hegel claims that a certain present awareness is an "instance" among other instances of certainty, which results in a "distinction between immediacy and mediation" that can be found "within sense-certainty itself" (Hegel 1977, 59). In other words, Hegel argues, the apparently pure and simple moment of awareness turns out to contain multitudes. Not only is there an *I*, but there is an implied *This*, *Here*, and *Now* that logically implies other such instances, rendering the apparent simplicity a "*mediated simplicity*, or a *universality*" (61). By contrast, Santayana argues, the SPM entails no internal complexity and—whatever it may suggest to one who witnesses it—implies nothing in and of itself, as the datum is simply the intuited essence that it is. Any analysis of that essence would be a new and—supposedly but uncertainly—related one, not a component found within the SPM. Moreover, any thought about an intuition of a datum is not part of the SPM but is instead a later moment that recalls what was previously given. Santayana stresses that "knowledge can never lie in an overt comparison of one datum given at the same time; even in pure dialectic, the comparison is with a datum believed to have been given formerly" (*SAF*, 167). Thus, any claims about an object of attention or even about that previously present moment of attention itself—the sort of claims Hegel attributes to consciousness within sense-certainty—have transcended the SPM and, Santayana argues, involve faith in both duration (the belief that there is a time that attention traverses) and memory (the belief that one's present thought is actually about a previously intuited datum).

Ultimately, Santayana's solipsism of the present moment has the "this, here, now" characteristic of sense-certainty but is simpler than Hegel describes. While Hegel's is an epistemological claim about what consciousness takes to be its proper object of knowledge, the SPM is not a claim at all but a bare noticing. Thus, its so-called certainty is not so in any epistemological sense. The datum is not known; it is only undeniably there. The second that one's attention moves beyond the SPM to posit the datum as an object of one's attention, much less to make any claim about it (e.g., "this datum is the object of which

I may be certain"), one has introduced uncertain beliefs. He notes: "To take the leap from one intuition to another, and assert that they view the same essence, or have the same intent, I must take my life in my hands and trust to animal faith. Otherwise all dialectic would be arrested" (*SAF*, 117). Thus, there is no way in which the SPM can serve as a necessary condition for other knowledge, whether as an epistemological foundation, as Descartes argued, or as a dialectical point of departure on the road to Absolute Knowing, as Hegel surmised.

Certain knowledge, it turns out, is an oxymoron. Scepticism cannot help to establish an indubitable domain in which a philosopher may more securely move about, however psychologically reassuring that might seem. It is "an exercise, not a life; it is a discipline fit to purify the mind of prejudice and render it all the more apt, when the time comes, to believe and to act wisely ..." (*SAF*, 69). For actual knowledge to take place, one must give up on the desire for certainty and embrace the inevitable dogmas on which knowledge is based.

KNOWLEDGE INVOLVES FAITH IN WHAT IS ABSENT

Given that Santayana finds scepticism to be unassailable and all knowledge to be uncertain, it can be tempting to align his thought with either ancient scepticism or the mitigated scepticism of modern philosopher David Hume. Indeed, there are important temperamental similarities here. All three philosophical positions caution against aspiring to complete and absolute knowledge, and all three present common sense as a saner approach to knowledge than arguments involving highly arcane terminology or technical and abstract logical proofs. However, to take Santayana for a sceptic is to misunderstand his original and important contribution to epistemology. The point of *Scepticism and Animal Faith* is not to declare knowledge impossible, as the ancient Sceptics would have it, nor to decry knowledge of matter and retreat within the bounds of the empirical, as Hume might propose (or, at least, as Santayana believed Hume was proposing).[4] Rather, it is to expand the realm of what can be known beyond the empirical by reconstructing the concept of knowledge so as to better recognize its true purpose and accomplishments. Characterizing knowledge as a leap of faith in what is not present to consciousness—in a sense, in what is absent—does not undermine the legitimacy of our inferences, he claims, but puts them in the proper context so as to better understand what those inferences actually achieve.

In following doubt to the point of solipsism, Santayana establishes that what is immediately present to consciousness may feel certain; indeed, this feeling of beholding the datum is all that certainty can be. However, such a feeling has

---

[4] In "Corpulent or a Train of Ideas? Santayana's Critique of Hume," I argue that Santayana did not fully appreciate the similarities between Hume and himself (Wahman 2007). It is possible that William James's more radical empiricism caused Santayana to misunderstand the modern thinker and to overstate Hume's focus on the experiential as philosophical subject matter.

nothing to do with being in possession of a fact, and giving in to the sentiment amounts to adoration of an illusion, not knowledge: "Being without irrational expectation (and all expectation is irrational) and without belief in memory (which is a sort of expectation reversed), [the mystic] will lack altogether that sagacity which makes the animal believe in latent events and latent substances, on which his eventual action might operate. ..." (*SAF*, 31). Upending the usual notion of the mystic as a sage in possession of higher truth, Santayana claims that those who focus intently on the being of pure presence are dupes of their own fascination with immediate objects. Real wisdom, he argues, comes from placing one's faith in common sense assumptions, namely, that an experienced phenomenon indicates that some event has happened or will happen and that such events are occurrences existing on their own terms and in their own way, more and other than their appearing.

After establishing that the epistemological search for an indubitable foundation dead ends in the solipsism of the present moment, Santayana engages in progressive analysis of increasingly broad and more generally encompassing beliefs, all of which are leaps of faith in the sense that they may be doubted in principle but must be believed in order to attain any knowledge of fact. Among these objects of belief are: (1) temporal trains of thought through which an essence may be repeated (belief in both identity and duration); (2) the possibility of logical inference (belief in demonstration); (3) conscious attention and intent (belief in intuitions); (4) experience (the belief that our intuitions exist and are somehow informative); (5) a self (the belief that there is someone to whom this experience is happening); (6) memories (the belief that present experiences are informative about one's own previous ones); (7) substance (the belief that something subtends all this experience); and (8) nature (the belief in an existing world that, through experience, can be studied and known). We can see in this list many items that Descartes and Hegel took to be present in the immediately given. Santayana insists, however, that all are absent from the present moment, only fallibly affirmed, but nonetheless required for any knowledge to take place. In considering belief in memory, for example, Santayana describes the basic claim to having remembered something as a belief that one is "taking cognisance," not of a present datum but of an experienced event that occurred in the past and on the plane of material existence. Such cognizance, he asserts, constitutes the "leap, which renders knowledge essentially faith" (*SAF*, 164). Even the most everyday perception "*is* faith; more perception may extend this faith or reform it, but it can never recant it except by sophistry" (*SAF*, 69). In so stressing, Santayana underscores that an intuition is not equivalent to a perception and that perception is instead, like the knowledge derived from it, a cognitive achievement that depends on a host of faith-based beliefs.

Ultimately, the difference between the intuition of a datum and an everyday perception that forms the basis for knowledge claims is how the essence given to our attention is treated. Because all that is immediately available to consciousness is the datum, and because intuition of a datum is not knowledge, cognition must treat what appears as a tool for its use rather than as itself the object of understanding. The immediately given, then, is assumed to be a sign that informs us in some way about an existing thing, event, or experience. Santayana asks: "Does not the existent profess to be more than apparent: to be not so much the self-evident as that which I am seeking evidence for, in the sense of testimony?" (*SAF*, 43). Perception involves an assumption, *based* on what appears, that something is *there*, and it further assumes that the given appearance is informative about that thing. This is why Santayana refers to knowledge as faith mediated by symbols (*SAF*, 164). He notes that "[i]n order to reach existences intent must transcend intuition, and take data for what they mean, not for what they are; it must credit them, as understanding credits words, accepting the passing vision as a warrant for something that once was, or that will be, or that lies in an entirely different medium, that of material being, or of discourse elsewhere" (*SAF*, 65). The datum, taken in this sense, serves as evidence regarding the nature of some thing or event, which testifies, in some manner, as to its properties and behaviors. A perception is a sort of communication, with essences serving as the medium through which the interaction between knower and known takes place. As such, knowledge is transitive; it is an activity that takes what appears and attributes it to some existing reality that is more, other, and beyond that appearance. The object of knowledge, then, is something to be reached or aimed for rather than merely present or given.

The fact that knowledge treats what appears as a sign of what exists can perhaps be more easily illustrated in cases of scientific experiments where some observable phenomenon is taken as evidence for a less perceptually accessible operation, such as when an fMRI scan displays images that represent measurements of relative levels of magnetism, which are used to infer relative levels of blood oxygenation and to further infer areas of greater and lesser brain activity. In such a case, the observed data are taken as a sign of something going on that is related to but also other than the data. But a scientific experiment is merely a more precisely organized and controlled version of our everyday perceptions. To take a commonplace example, let us say I have misplaced my keys. The chain contains a decorative metal disc, and as I cast my eyes about the room, something shiny and about the right size appears to wink at me from the far table. "Aha!" I think. Taking the small flash as a sign of the entity I seek, I believe myself to have found my keys. This belief will be either confirmed or rejected as I approach it, depending on the other signs given to me by the object. As things come into focus, I may confirm the object as my keys, or instead to be a coin or keys that belong to my husband rather than to me. Even these more clear and definite perceptions I experience on approach are, Santayana argues, leaps of faith insofar as the witnessed shapes and colors are taken to represent and derive from a material entity, either the one I am seeking or some other. Just as with scientific experimentation, then, perception is a sort of inquiry; moreover, the data utilized in acts of perception are like scientific information in that they serve as signs of what exists, where things are located, and what they are doing.

The act of knowing anything, then, is essentially a leap of faith from a given phenomenon to that which transcends it, and the basis for this leap is animal life: "Knowledge accordingly is belief: belief in a world of events, and especially of those parts of it which are near the self, tempting or threatening it" (*SAF*, 179). Living makes specific demands on a sentient organism: it must believe that objects of its awareness are situated in some existing here and now; that—whether it pursues what it desires or flees what it fears—it can move from that presently situated location to some other one; and that what it seeks or fears is an existing thing with which it can interact, something on the same plane of existence as itself, an entity that can truly help or hurt. This animal faith does not undermine our capacity for knowledge. Instead, it is what makes knowledge, and indeed living, possible.

Santayana's characterization of animal faith as a dogmatic belief that the present datum symbolizes some matter of fact that transcends it is not a criticism of the understanding's possibilities but an explanation of its nature, of what we are actually doing when we attain knowledge of something. He notes: "The experience of essence is direct; the expression of natural facts through that medium is indirect. But this indirection is no obstacle to expression, rather its condition. ..." (*SAF*, 102). Describing knowledge as indirect access to natural things and events depicts cognition as an ability to move beyond mere appearances and make claims about existing, formerly existing, or impending matters of fact. The ability to do so is a matter of life and death to animal beings; we make sense of our physical, social, and intellectual environments in order to live well within them. Thus, "[t]he function of perception and natural science is, not to flatter the sense of omniscience in an absolute mind, but to dignify animal life by harmonizing it, in action and in thought, with its conditions" (*SAF*, 104). Santayana's description of knowledge as essentially a leap of faith is a means of reminding the philosophically inclined that knowledge is a human undertaking with practical goals. Its purpose is not to illuminate all of reality but to enable us to live and thrive as best as possible.

What Santayana's Epistemology Achieves for Philosophy

Philosophy, in its original sense, is the love of wisdom. The purpose of *Scepticism and Animal Faith* is to return philosophy to these roots. Descartes's subjective turn and the empiricist and transcendental epistemologies that eventually followed led philosophers, according to Santayana, to despair of speaking about natural facts in common sense ways and, in so doing, made a folly of their attempts at wisdom. Accepting that neither sensory data nor logical categories could be infallibly attributed to material things in themselves, the philosophers of late modernity instead tried to formulate a logical science of experience, transforming given sensations and concepts—essences—into the ultimate object of knowledge. Santayana's propaedeutic aims to return common sense to epistemology and make room for his more poetically speculative ontology. However, as himself a child of modernity—in *Dialogues in Limbo*, Santayana has Democritus chide him for as much (*DL*, 88)—he cannot simply overlook the influence of Cartesian scepticism. As a result, Santayana is obligated to explain, via his sceptical reduction to the solipsism of the present moment, why there cannot be a science of the given and why all knowledge involves a leap of faith in something beyond it. Philosophical analysis of experience, in focusing on essences, cannot, by his lights, be knowledge but is instead a subfield of what he calls literary psychology—"the art of imagining how [animals] feel and think" (*SAF*, 252). One of the achievements of Santayana's epistemological reconstruction is to show that all philosophy, in reflecting on the meaning and worth of human experience in all its variety, takes the form of this sympathetic art. If the field of philosophy can give up its pretense to certain knowledge, philosophers become free to take their place as composers of worldviews and artists in the service of human wisdom.

To see how Santayana uses his epistemology to rethink the aims of philosophy, it may be useful again to contrast his position with the methods and aims of Descartes and Hegel. Their argumentative processes—similar in their attention to consciousness, logical precision, and believed necessity—each involve the ambitious goal of bringing the world's ultimate nature within the purview of human understanding. Descartes's interest in mathematics inspired him to derive a method whereby, in first establishing specific intuitive and precise truths and building on them with logical precision, one could, in principle, develop a complete knowledge of the whole. Corporeal substance—the natural world—was, for Descartes, an enormous machine that could be completely understood so long as one engaged in careful mathematical measurements and calculations of its essence (i.e., extension). Hegel's method similarly aims at absolute knowledge, though the procedure and object are quite different. The dialectical progression of the *Phenomenology* is based on the claim that knowledge seeks the complete adequation of concept and object—a concept that omits nothing, leaves nothing uncognized—and results in an absolute knowing where the object of consciousness is its own essence, namely "an authentic Science of Spirit" (Hegel 1977, 57). For both Descartes and Hegel, then, it is assumed that the goal of knowledge is to wholly grasp its object and to aim at what is total and complete, in other words, to possess concepts that capture and assimilate into one's understanding the ultimate nature of reality. Furthermore, for both, a certain starting point and precise logical attention to essences is said to make ultimate knowledge possible. Now, as literary psychology, the works of Descartes and Hegel display great ingenuity in describing the ways in which one thought might incline one's attention to another thought, and we may derive insight by considering how philosophical problems seem to them. Despite their ambitions, however, these philosophers are not building a science by reflecting on relations among essences. Santayana effectively undermines such claims by tracing scepticism to its extreme, thereby demonstrating that mere possession of an essence is not knowledge and that the aim of knowledge is to come into a functional agreement with an object, not to possess it in its totality.

"[W]hen consciousness itself grasps this its own essence, it will signify the nature of absolute knowledge itself" (Hegel 1977, 57). In so claiming, Hegel echoes the Aristotelian notion that ultimate theoretical knowledge entails thought thinking itself. As Santayana notes, "philosophers capable of intense contemplation—Aristotle, for instance, at those points where his thought becomes, as it were, internal to spirit—have generally asserted that in the end essence and the contemplation of essence are identical" (*SAF*, 126). Santayana recognizes, of course, that in the solipsism of the present moment all that presents itself is an essence—there is no *I* that is given, nor is there a judgment about the essence intuited—but this witnessing of a datum is hardly the pinnacle of contemplation. What has been taken to be the highest form of knowledge is actually an abdication of knowledge and rapt engrossment in the object of one's attention. Hegel's absolute knowing is at the opposite end of the dialectical progression from sense-certainty, of course, and contemplation of essences is not the same thing as the solipsism of the present moment. Santayana's point, nonetheless, is that while we may have a spiritual desire for oneness with an all-encompassing essence, this is not an apt description of knowledge: "If philosophers wish to abstain from faith, and reduce themselves to intuition of the obvious ... they will thereby renounce all knowledge and live on passive illusions" (*SAF*, 167). Knowledge is a practical engagement with essences not unity with them. The only way to be one with an essence is to stare at it and ask nothing more of it.

As it turns out, then, absolute knowledge is not possible, and philosophers who aspire to it have been playing in an aesthetic world of illusions. But, Santayana argues, this is not a problem for philosophy so long as it recognizes the capabilities that cognition actually does possess. Santayana explains that "[i]f I now ... consider the prospect open to animal faith, I see that all this insecurity and inadequacy of alleged knowledge are almost irrelevant to the natural effort of the mind to describe natural things. The discouragement we may feel in science," namely, that we cannot be certain to have captured nature absolutely and indisputably, "does not come from failure; it comes from a false conception of what would be success" (*SAF*, 101). Santayana demonstrates that both everyday knowledge and specialized science are experimental, transitive, and fallible leaps from the given to something beyond it. Sceptical conclusions about the possibility of knowledge stem from the confused assumption that our claims must be certain in order to be classified as known. But acts of knowing are, in actuality, adaptive achievements that enable us to live in the world with other existing things and—at times and to a limited extent—to bend them to our use. In his characterization of knowledge, Santayana illuminates the wisdom of placing faith in an existing world, one we cannot master but that possesses the capacity to sustain us for a lifetime.

Though scepticism is, taken on its own terms, invincible, it in no way undermines either our everyday folk theories or our more carefully constructed scientific ones. Too many philosophers, Santayana claims, "have identified science with certitude, and consequently entirely condemned what I call knowledge (which is a form of animal faith) or relegated it to an inferior position. ... But in doing so we should all be missing the truth," namely, that intuition of a datum is not knowledge and that all real knowledge of the world, oneself, and others is inherently fallible and involves a set of unprovable but practically imperative beliefs (*SAF*, 171). Scepticism is reasonable as a reminder that knowledge is inherently uncertain and that all knowledge claims are true only insofar as they continue to be confirmed by experience, that is, by the symbols through which existence expresses itself. However, to note that knowledge is neither certain nor absolute is not at all the same thing as declaring knowledge to be impossible. Ultimately, when knowledge is understood to be inherently experimental, philosophers can better recognize the purpose of knowledge and the important distinction between it and the art of philosophizing. Santayana's epistemology of animal faith provides access to what lies beyond the immediate, recognizes that the forms and models we use to understand the world are but symbols, and acknowledges how nature is able to teach us about itself via the signs we receive from it. At the same time, it recasts philosophy as works of art aimed at greater self-knowledge and wise engagement with our natural and social environments.

References

Descartes, Rene. 1984. Meditations on First Philosophy. In *The Philosophical Writings of Descartes, Vol. II*. Translated by John Cottingham, Robert Stoothoff, and Dugald Murdoch. New York: Cambridge University Press.

Hegel, G.W.F. 1977. *Phenomenology of Spirit*. Translated by A.V. Miller. New York: Oxford University Press.

Santayana, George. 1923. *Scepticism and Animal Faith*. New York: Dover Publications, Inc. [1955 reprint].

———. 1948. *Dialogues in Limbo, with Three New Dialogues*. New York: Charles Scribner's Sons.

Wahman, Jessica. 2007. Corpulent Or a Train of Ideas? Santayana's Critique of Hume. *Overheard in Seville: Bulletin of the Santayana Society* 25 (25): 1–9.

Animal Faith and Its Object

John J. Stuhr

> *I would lay siege to the truth only as animal exploration and fancy may do so .... I should not be honest otherwise.*
> —George Santayana (*SAF*, vi)

AGAINST CERTAINTY

Many classical American philosophers strongly rejected the possibility that human beings can *know with certainty* anything at all about the facts of their world. The central consequence of this shared rejection of "the quest for certainty," to use John Dewey's phrase, amounted to a *naturalization of epistemology and ontology*—naturalized accounts of human knowledge as always fallible, perspectival, partial, and never in principle free of future revision or replacement; and naturalized accounts of existence as temporal, evolving, relational, and never fixed such that there exists nothing eternal, static, absolute, and wholly sure for human animals to be wholly certain about.

This rejection of the possibility of epistemic certainty is a dominant theme or motif in, across, and throughout the writings of philosophers such as Charles Peirce, William James, Dewey, and George Santayana—as well as many earlier

---

J. J. Stuhr (✉)
Department of Philosophy, American Studies Program, Emory University, Atlanta, GA, USA
e-mail: jstuhr@emory.edu

© The Author(s), under exclusive license to Springer Nature Switzerland AG 2024
M. A. Coleman, G. Tiller (eds.), *The Palgrave Companion to George Santayana's Scepticism and Animal Faith*, Palgrave Companions, https://doi.org/10.1007/978-3-031-46367-9_7

American thinkers and many later ones.[1] For these thinkers, human beings do not have, and cannot acquire, epistemic certainty about matters of fact. Instead, humans have more or less adequate hypotheses that inform our action and, in turn, always may be modified by the results of that action. This is faith, often but not always confirmed, that the consequences of action will warrant having undertaken that action. This is a matter of faith, not certainty, because the consequences that warrant an action have not occurred and are never known before the action itself. And this situation continues on and on: Knowing an action's consequences is itself simply another action the consequences of which exist and are knowable always only after the action itself. This is a faith in our ability to fund future experience by means of the results of past experience, a faith not in our possession of certainty but in our ability bit by bit and imperfectly to act so as to accomplish our aims. This faith is experimental and contingent, the faith of human animals in their lives and practical powers in the natural world.

I here offer up this sketch of uncertain knowers engaged in uncertain knowing in uncertain environments without further elaboration or step-by-step argument, relying instead on the ability of my readers to complete this drawing on the basis of their familiarity with the pervasive anti-certainty theme in this tradition. Let one brief example from each of these authors suffice for present purposes.

In his 1908 "Neglected Argument for the Reality of God," Charles Peirce contrasted certainty in belief with everyday incomplete and inexact hypothesis-like knowledge crucial for animal life:

> [M]an, like any other animal, is gifted with the power of understanding sufficient for the conduct of life. This brings him, for testing the hypothesis, to taking his stand upon Pragmaticism, which implies faith in common-sense and in instinct, though only as they issue from the cupel-furnace of measured criticism. (Peirce 1998/1908, 445–46)

Sounding a similar theme in two early essays, "The Will to Believe" in 1896 and "The Sentiment of Rationality" in 1882, William James argued:

> [T]o *know* is one thing, and to know for certain *that* we know is another. One may hold to the first being possible without the second. ... When we as empiricists give up the doctrine of objective certitude, we do not thereby give up the quest or hope of truth itself. ... Faith means belief in something concerning which doubt is still theoretically possible; and as the test of belief is willingness to act, one may say that faith is the readiness to act in a cause the prosperous issue of which is not certified to us in advance.... The only escape from faith is mental nullity. ... We cannot live or think at all without some degree of faith. Faith is synonymous with working hypotheses. (James 1979a/1896, 20, 23, 76, 78, 79)

---

[1] My claim here is not intended as a rule, but its best-known exception is the philosophy of Josiah Royce.

Identifying the source of these hypotheses with the power of intelligence, Dewey concluded his 1917 "The Need for a Recovery of Philosophy" this way:

> Faith in the power of intelligence to imagine a future which is the projection of the desirable in the present, and to invent the instrumentalities of its realization, is our salvation. And it is a faith which must be nurtured and made articulate: surely a sufficiently large task for our philosophy. (Dewey 1980/1917, 48)

In a similar spirit, in his late-career *Persons and Places*, George Santayana claimed that it is animal faith rather than the possession of any certainties that is the source of human knowledge. He wrote:

> If, then, we are to see or to believe in anything, it must be at the bidding of natural accidents, by what I call animal faith; and the alternatives open to pure spirit are not open to rational belief. Rational belief must have other guides than sheer imagination exploring infinite possibilities. Those guides can be, logically, nothing but accidents; but they have a compulsory presence and evoke an inescapable adhesion, confidence, and trust; which trust is fortified by experiment and found trustworthy. ... Beliefs have an earthly origin and can be sanctioned only by earthly events. ... Only animal faith can lead us to reality. (Santayana 1986/1944, 1953, 171, 443)

These thinkers do not sound the same, identical note, but they do speak in harmony here: Human beings are not able to know *with certainty* anything about their world. The upshot of the quest for epistemic certainty in all its motivations and all its forms can be stated in a single word: failure.

Scepticism

If certain knowledge of our world is not possible, must we be sceptics? Should we be sceptics? Can we be sceptics? What does it mean to be a sceptic and what would be involved in actually living as a sceptic?

Scepticism has at least two meanings. In the first, *psychological* sense, scepticism denotes an attitude or disposition or feeling. In this sense, for example, someone might approach a get-rich-quick offer made online by strangers with an unconvinced *attitude* toward the promised amazing results, a *disposition* to ignore all such offers without even fully reading them, or an unconfident *feeling* that the offer is probably much riskier and more speculative than its backers claim. To be sceptical in this sense is to have an attitude of doubt and incredulity, a disposition to withhold assent and to find conclusive evidence lacking, and a feeling of uncertainty, distrust, misgiving, and absence of faith sufficient for action.

Four points are worth briefly noting here. First, understood psychologically, any particular instance of scepticism may be affirmed by a single individual, a family, a small group, a class of people, a nation, or a culture. For example, despite the confident feeling of die-hard fans that "this is the year," professional sportswriters might feel a lot of misgivings and uncertainty about how the team will fare as the new season begins. Some but not all jury members might be disposed to disregard the testimony of a witness because the witness had been granted immunity. Some might embrace at face value recommendations of online influencers, while others remain unconvinced and withhold assent. Here being sceptical is always the attitude, disposition, or feeling of a particular sceptical person or persons.

Second, psychological scepticism admits of degrees. It need not be all or nothing. A manager might be merely a little sceptical of an employee's annual self-assessment because of confirmation bias, or students might be highly sceptical of what they see in a photograph because they know some classmates are highly skilled at using artificial intelligence to create deceptive "deep-fake" images. Understood psychologically, being sceptical is always being more or less sceptical.

Third, as even these few examples illustrate, psychological scepticism can be directed at any assertion, belief, or proposition about existence. A child might be sceptical about a parent's stories of what life used to be. Competitors might be sceptical about another television network's proclaimed commitment to news rather than entertainment. Citizens might be sceptical about a politician's campaign claims or their government's stated justification for war. A relative might be sceptical about fad diets, climate change, or public health pronouncements. Business leaders might be sceptical of a company's IPO, the value of some new technology, or an investment firm's risk tolerance with pension funds. I might be sceptical about the wisdom of banning books or having state legislatures determine public school curricula. In theory, it is possible to be sceptical about anything. Why, you might even be sceptical about a particular interpretation of *Scepticism and Animal Faith*. Here being sceptical is always being sceptical about something or lots of things—anything—in particular.

Fourth, and perhaps most important, while it is possible to be psychologically sceptical of anything, it is not possible to be sceptical of everything all at once. To be psychologically sceptical of a person or undertaking or belief or assertion is to be doubtful, unsure, unconvinced, incredulous, and awaiting sufficiently compelling, conclusive proof. However, doubting any assertion is possible only by believing some other assertion—some other assertion that one does not doubt at that time. Citizens might be sceptical of a politician's campaign claims because they believe the politician has a history of documented lies—and are not sceptical of this belief. A couple of workers might be sceptical about the belief that human actions have impacted the earth's climate because they non-sceptically believe their co-workers are pretty smart and because they non-sceptically believe all these co-workers view climate change concerns as a hoax. I might be sceptical about the political value of banning books because I believe unquestionably that this only increases their online readership by larger numbers.

This is the point that Peirce made so forcefully in his 1868 "Some Consequences of Four Incapacities": Universal doubt, being sceptical of everything, is impossible. Unless we are sceptical about a belief on the basis of some other belief that we do not doubt at that time, our scepticism is simply self-deception rather than real scepticism, and our doubt is fake doubt rather than real doubt. In an often-quoted passage, Peirce explained that it is not possible for human beings to take a psychologically sceptical, doubting, untrusting, assent-withholding stance toward all belief at any given time:

> We cannot begin with complete doubt. We must begin with all the prejudices which we actually have.... These prejudices are not to be dispelled by a maxim, for they are things which it does not occur to us can be questioned. Hence this initial scepticism will be a mere self-deception, and not real doubt.... A person may, it is true, in the course of his studies, find reason to doubt what he began by believing; but in that case he doubts because he has a positive reason for it.... Let us not pretend to doubt in philosophy what we do not doubt in our hearts. (Peirce 1992b/1868, 28-29)

Santayana shared this view that even the most would-be sceptical human animal is always a creature of belief and faith rather than one of complete doubt, withheld assent, and distrust. In "Dogma and Doubt," the second chapter of *Scepticism and Animal Faith*, Santayana observed that human beings have a "vital compulsion to posit and to believe something, even in the act of doubting":

> Scepticism is a suspicion of error about facts, and to suspect error about facts is to share the enterprise of knowledge, in which facts are presupposed and error is possible. The sceptic thinks himself shrewd, and often is so; his intellect, like the intellect he criticizes, may have some inkling of the true hang and connection of things; he may have pierced to a truth of nature behind current illusions. Since his criticism may thus be true and his doubt well grounded, they are certainly assertions; and if he is sincerely a sceptic, they are assertions which he is ready to maintain stoutly. Scepticism is accordingly a form of belief. (*SAF*, 8-9)

When scepticism is thus understood as a belief—it is after all an "ism"!—it has a second, *epistemic* sense. Here scepticism is not understood psychologically in terms of the attitudes, dispositions, and feelings of a believer but, rather, epistemically in terms of its truth or falsity as a belief. Understood epistemically, the important questions concern justification and truth: Is scepticism true and is belief in scepticism justified?

A short course in experience is likely to suggest that scepticism is justified by a particular person or persons to a greater or lesser degree about one or more statements of fact. Statements about the future seem anything but certain. How can scientists be wholly certain that sea levels will rise by 0.33 meters by 2050 or ticket-buyers that they'll win the next Powerball lottery? (Hmmm ... if one could be certain about the future, the practice of gambling would be impossible.) Statements about the past also seem anything but certain. Is it absolutely certain whether Shakespeare wrote all the plays now attributed to him, or how many people were killed in the Russian Revolution? Statements about the present similarly might be uncertain. Are you now watching the magician move the upside-down cup with the ball in it or only an empty cup, and is that an eagle you see or is it a hawk? And am I really feeling jealous right now, or is it actually fear? All kinds of experiences seem to justify scepticism about specific factual claims that might issue from them: There are memory lapses, drug-induced delirium, poor eyesight and failing hearing, dreams, AI voice cloning and deep-fake images, gaslighting, confirmation bias, and incomplete, always incomplete data—and much, much more. These experiences appear to justify case-specific scepticism.

These kinds of cases and the scepticism specific to them have held little interest for almost all philosophers, particularly those who have taken epistemology to be a quest for certainty. It seems obvious that there are many cases in which particular people are justified in believing that particular claims *are not certain* epistemically (even if sometimes they may feel certain psychologically). The issue, therefore, is not whether human beings sometimes fail to have certainty about matters of fact; the issue, instead is whether human beings sometimes do have certainty about matters of fact. Put differently, the issue is not whether scepticism sometimes is justified; the issue is whether scepticism sometimes is not justified. As Santayana wrote, the issue is how far scepticism can be pushed (*SAF*, 10).

Philosophers of both so-called empirical and rationalist traditions have answered that scepticism cannot be pushed all the way—that some matter-of-fact beliefs are certain. What beliefs? There are intramural differences, of course, but most all philosophers who think they have successfully completed their quest for certainty have focused on supposed datum of immediate consciousness or experience—for example, beliefs that at present, I am thinking, or that doubting is going on; beliefs that I now feel pain or that I am seeing too orangely (in contrast to "I am seeing an orange"). This datum, according to these philosophers, halts scepticism—and Santayana thus called their scepticism "halting" (*SAF*, 45).

In the first eight chapters of *Scepticism and Animal Faith*, Santayana demonstrated that this view is false. No dogma withstands scepticism. In every battle of scepticism versus dogma, scepticism wins. He showed that the claims of both religion and inductive, empirical science are not matters of certainty (*SAF*, 11–15). He explained that present-moment solipsism is "wayward" and in the end not scepticism at all because the very identities of a person and a present moment imply duration and other moments (*SAF*, 15–20). This is, Santayana noted, not scepticism but only "infatuation": "They take their revenge on the world, which eluded them when they tried to prove its existence, by asserting the existence of the remnant which they have still by them, insisting that this, and this only, is the true and perfect world, and a much better one than the false world in which the heathen trust" (*SAF*, 20). He showed that present-moment appearances given in intuition are one thing but that beliefs, reports, accounts, descriptions, or knowledge of them at a later, changed moment are something else entirely—something about which there can be no certainty. "*Belief* in change," he wrote, "asserts that before this intuition of change arose the first term of that change had occurred separately. This no intuition of change can prove" (*SAF*, 27). Beliefs about self-consciousness and its appearances provide no defense against scepticism. The thoroughgoing sceptic must say with Santayana: "Having renounced my faith in nature, I must not weakly retain my faith in experience" (*SAF*, 26). Even the experience of change does not prove, against the sceptic, that change certainly is real:

> If you feel that earlier state [from which you suppose you have passed into your present state] now, there is no change involved. That datum, which you now designate as the past, and which exists only in this perspective, is merely a term in your present feeling. It was never anything else. It was never given otherwise than as it is given now, when it is given as past. Therefore, if things are such only as intuition makes them, every suggestion of a past is false. (*SAF*, 28–29)

Santayana thus affirmed an "ultimate scepticism," a scepticism about the existence of any datum: "Belief in the existence of anything, including myself, is something radically incapable of proof, and resting, like all belief, on some irrational persuasion or prompting of life" (*SAF*, 35).[2] A datum by its own nature says nothing; there may be no facts at all. Accordingly, anyone seeking certainty finds only scepticism.

ANIMAL FAITH AND KNOWLEDGE WITHOUT CERTAINTY

Does the victory of scepticism in the battle for certainty demonstrate that human beings have no knowledge?

No. Or, more precisely, the answer to this question depends on what one takes knowledge to be. If knowledge is or is derived from certainty, then the absence of certainty obviously entails the absence of knowledge. But if knowledge is not or is not derived from certainty, then belief in Santayana's ultimate scepticism does not show that human beings cannot or do not have knowledge. It only shows the complete irrelevance of concern with certainty to the nature and acquisition of knowledge. Moreover, it only shows the need for an account of *knowledge as something other than certainty*. I take this to be the practical upshot of the first ten "scepticism chapters" (including the chapters on the discovery of essence and the uses of this discovery) of *Scepticism and*

---

[2] Compare John Dewey's claims that the mere occurrence of mystical experience does not constitute immediate knowledge, but only a site for possible future inquiry: "The difference between mystic experience and the theory about it that is offered to us must be noted. The experience is a fact to be inquired into. The theory, like any theory, is an interpretation of the fact." Dewey added that the "fact" of occurrence of any experience is not simply a bare fact but already the product of imagination and symbolization. See Dewey (1986/1934); particularly chapter 2, "Faith and Its Object."

Animal Faith. It is in large part the task that constitutes the focus of the final seventeen "animal faith chapters," as Santayana noted:

> If I now turn my face in the other direction and consider the prospect open to animal faith, I see that all this insecurity and inadequacy of alleged knowledge are almost irrelevant to the natural effort of the mind to describe natural things.... Complete scepticism is accordingly not inconsistent with animal faith; the admission that nothing given exists is not incompatible with belief in things not given. (*SAF*, 101, 105)

So, what is the prospect open to animal faith? Looking prospectively, looking ahead, a turn from concern with certainty to concern with animal faith makes possible an alternative account of knowledge as "faith mediated by symbols." This account of knowledge has three parts: the claim that knowing is an *animal* activity; the claim that knowledge is animal *faith*; the claim that this faith is *mediated by symbols*; and the claim that belief in knowledge is identical to belief in *substance*. First, human knowledge is an activity of an animal, the human animal in its environment. It is simply one of the things that human beings by nature do—along with eating, sleeping, loving, playing, fighting, moving, resting, associating, aging, dying, and so on (*SAF*, 167). Knowing is a natural activity, a habit of adjustment to a world.

Second, knowing is a particular kind of natural activity: It is an act of faith, a species of faith. It is an act of faith because it is something never wholly certain, always possibly open to doubt and challenge, and a projection of future realities "out of view now" (*SAF*, 170).

And, third, just as Peirce earlier claimed that human beings cannot think without signs (and thus cannot know without signs) (Peirce 1992a/1868a, 23–24), Santayana held that knowledge is faith mediated by symbols because knowledge claims describe a present reality not as (or in its) immediacy but as sign of something else: that pain is a symptom of lung cancer, this painting's palette shows it is a Picasso, higher wages are a cause of inflation. Thus, Santayana argued:

> Discourse is a language, not a mirror. The images in sense are parts of discourse, not parts of nature.... The truth which discourse can achieve is truth in its own terms, appropriate description: it is no incorporation or reproduction of the object in the mind.... It takes the essences before it for messages, signs, or emanations sent forth to it from those objects of animal faith; and they become its evidences and its description for those objects. (*SAF*, 179–80)

The Objects of Animal Faith

Much more could be said here—whole dissertations can and have been written!—about the nature of symbols, the differences between true and untrue descriptions, and natural science as the "ideal of knowledge" (*SAF*, 181). Even so, in all this, it is the notion of animal faith that is fundamental. The central question here, as Santayana recognized is this: What is the *object* of animal faith? Put differently, what is animal faith, this faith founded not in reason but precipitated in all action (*SAF*, 106), faith *in*? Santayana addressed the issue this way: "I propose now to consider what objects animal faith requires me to posit, and in what order; without for a moment forgetting that my assurance of their existence is only instinctive, and my description of their nature only symbolic" (*SAF*, 106).

Consider this question: What objects does animal faith require positing? It is worth asking several questions about this question. First, does animal faith require positing any objects at all? How and why? Second, if animal faith does require objects be posited, what is the nature or status of this requirement? Is it the requirement of logical necessity, or practical usefulness, or temperamental preference, or some yet other kind of requirement? Third, why think that it is "objects" of any sort that animal faith finds itself required to posit? If this is an empirical claim, on what evidence does it rest? If instead it is simply a definitional stipulation—animal faith is not animal faith unless it requires the positing of objects—then how does Santayana avoid exactly the "dialectical physics" and metaphysical systematizing that he rejects in the writings of others? Fourth and finally, a posit—for example, a claim about objects posited on the basis of animal action—is a statement made on the assumption that it will be proven true. Are claims about objects asserted to be required by animal faith proven to be true—and if so by what proof? Or are the objects taken to be required posits of animal faith simply described, perhaps poetically described, even though the posit of them is never shown to be true?

Santayana characterized animal faith as instinctive and "natural" opinion at work in all action. It is instinctive belief without rational proof or certain foundation. I think it is helpful to think of this natural opinion or belief as a power, as an animal capacity—the power of belief in things not given in sheer immediacy, the power to take essences as signs of something else. Just as we might conclude that animals with the capacity to eat, fight, or age require us to posit food, opponents, or duration, so the power of animal faith requires us to posit an environment in which it is at work. These two factors—animal and environment—are antecedent to animal faith (which thus requires us to posit them). The environment is not part of animal faith, but both animal and its environment are required for animal life and its animal faith (*SAF*, 22, 23).

Santayana typically characterized this environment or field of action as "external" to, and "independent" of, the acting animal. It is matter independent of mind. He viewed it as a basic, fundamental, and action-structuring assumption at work in all animal instinct and action. For Santayana, conscious animal life is directed to, and points at, an external world; animal faith is faith in objects, not faith in that faith itself. An animal has faith—animal faith—in its existence. As a terminological matter, this may well seem odd: a field of particular action is only that particular field of action in relation to the action—not independent of it or external to it. Santayana took this natural belief in an external, independent world to be unquestioned—because unquestioned and, he thought, necessarily assumed by animal action. Accordingly, for Santayana, whether or not there is such an external world is only an issue for metaphysical fancy and pretend doubt, never an issue in action, practice, life. Santayana's project, rather, was the description of distinguishable aspects of this external. And this project proceeded by means of the concepts and categories he found most useful to employ—particularly his four "realms of being." In *Scepticism and Animal Faith*, he addressed these kinds of questions: Given animal faith and the external, independent world it presupposes: What is experience (chapter 15)? What is the self (chapter 16)? What is memory (chapter 17)? What is knowledge (chapter 18)? What is substance (chapters 19 and 20)? What is nature (chapters 22 and 23)? What is truth (chapter 25)? What is spirit (chapter 26)?

Scholarly attention to each of these questions as they arise in this context is a fine thing and it constitutes, to at least a significant degree, a thinking *with* Santayana, a sharing in his reasons "which are but prejudices and human" (*SAF*, 107). In the end, I find myself unable to do that—and so I must take up the offer implicit in Santayana's remark in the "Preface" to *Scepticism and Animal Faith*: "I do not ask any one to think in my terms if he prefers others," even as I decline to agree with his claim a couple pages later that "my philosophy is justified, and has been justified in all ages and countries, by the facts before every man's eyes" (*SAF*, vi, ix). I am not interested in or concerned to think *against* Santayana. Instead, I want to proceed *otherwise than* Santayana.

More specifically, I return to the claim that animal faith requires us to presuppose or posit an environment, a something that confronts me (*SAF*, 106; see also 133), *external* to, and *independent* of, human action. Does it? As noted above, Santayana answered in the affirmative. In contrast, radical empiricists (such as James and Dewey) have answered in the negative. Now, the answer to this question depends *in part* on what it means for an environment to be *external* to animal faith and what it means for an environment to be *independent* of animal life. The truth or falsity of a belief depends in part on the meaning of the ideas it employs. This is a pragmatic point, one stressed by Peirce in "How to Make Our Ideas Clear" and by James in "What Pragmatism Means." At the same time, it is crucial not to treat this question—is animal faith the faith in an external and independent environment?—as a *wholly* metaphysical question in the sense Santayana rejected: "my system, save in the mocking literary sense of the word, is not *metaphysical*. ... Metaphysics, in the proper sense of the word, is dialectical physics, or an attempt to determine matters of fact by means of logical or moral or rhetorical constructions" (*SAF*, vii).

Two important consequences follow from this commitment to avoid dialectical physics. First, we should understand the objects of any posits claimed to be required by animal faith to be physical objects, not metaphysical objects. We should understand any objects claimed to be external to and independent of human action as physical objects. Second, whether and how physical objects alleged to exist actually do exist is a scientific question, not a philosophical one. As Santayana observed, "*It is for science and further investigation of the object to pronounce on the truth of any belief*" (*SAF*, 296), although scientific investigation is never complete, and its findings are never epistemically certain. Philosophers, even those who write well-crafted essays about Santayana, perhaps pleading their preferred dogma, cannot by their rhetoric and logic alone establish anything at all about existence.

Imagining the different names that different people have called the moon, Santayana wrote:

> What that object is in its complete constitution and history will never be known by man; but that this object exists in a known space and time and has traceable physical relations with all other physical objects is a fact posited from the beginning; it was posited by the child when he pointed, and by me when I saw him point. (*SAF*, 177)

All this sits well with pragmatists, of course—the stress on experimental inquiry, the focus on consequences rather than origins and genealogy (*SAF*, 296), the commitment to fallibility as well as rejection of scepticism. So, if there is to be a scientific investigation concerning the existence of physical objects external to, and independent of, animal life, the practical or operational meanings of "external" and "independent" must be spelled out. Now, if an animal's positing objects "external" to itself simply means that in and through its action the animal believes its environment of field of action contains objects *other than* itself, we can ask biologists, psychologists, and other scientists if evidence supports this belief. However, if this belief is in fact experimentally warranted, it does not in any way justify or necessitate Santayana's materialism. It is, for example, wholly compatible with Dewey's instrumentalist naturalism and his claim that "experience is *of* and *in* nature"—the version of naturalism that Santayana famously called "half-hearted" and "short-winded" (Santayana 1925, 12).[3]

Similarly, if an animal's positing objects "independent" of itself simply means that these objects are classified by the animal as part of its environment rather than as part of itself, we can once again ask scientists if in fact this is so. However, here too any experimental warrant for this view—this "physics" rather than "dialectical physics"—provides no reason to believe that Santayana's version of naturalism alone is consistent with the facts. Such facts are or would be entirely compatible with James's pragmatism in which truth is understood not in terms of supposedly experience-external and experience-independent posited objects or substances or matter but simply in terms of the pointing, leading, guiding

---

[3] Santayana's critical review of *Experience and Nature* was titled "Dewey's Naturalistic Metaphysics" (Santayana 1925). Dewey's response to this review was published a little more than a year later as "Half-Hearted Naturalism" (Dewey 1927). I have discussed at some length this exchange and the underlying philosophical and temperamental differences in "Experience and the Adoration of Matter" (Stuhr 1997, 13–46).

function of cognition within experience—a bodily "working touch" with reality.[4]

This view that animals functionally distinguish themselves from their environment—and thus are other than that environment—is also entirely compatible with Dewey's pragmatic account of the organism/environment distinction as a functional rather than metaphysical one. Dewey spelled out this alternative throughout his later work. The following passages are representative:

> An organism does not live in an environment; it lives by means of an environment.... The processes of living are enacted by the environment as truly as by the organism; for they are an integration.... Natural operations like breathing and digesting, acquired ones like speech and honesty, are functions of the surroundings as truly as of a person. They are things done by the environment by means of organic structures or acquired dispositions. (Dewey, Bentley 1989/1949, 100)

> In actual experience, there is never any such isolated singular object or event; *an* object or event is always a special part, phase, or aspect, of an environing world—a situation. The singular object stands out conspicuously because of its especially focal and crucial position at a given time in determination of some problem of use or enjoyment which the total complex environment presents. (Dewey 1986/1938, 41)

> The idea that human nature is inherently and exclusively individual is itself a product of a cultural individualistic movement. (Dewey 1988/1939, 77)

These passages indicate that pragmatism might well be seen as having a commitment to animal faith and animal life in a more thoroughgoing way than does Santayana's materialism: Rather than claiming that animal faith is required to posit realms of being external to, and independent of, animal faith, it holds that the only objects that animal faith must posit are experienced objects as they come to be known fallibly and without certainty by the animals' own power, application, and development of intelligence.

Santayana claimed that "the original articles of the animal creed—that there is a world, that there is a future, that things can be found, and things seen can be eaten"—must endure as long as animal life lasts (*SAF*, 180). Fine. As such, animal faith at work in action constitutes no philosophical problem. It is simply a fact of animal life. Philosophical problems arise not in animal faith as it exists and operates but in the "posits" that Santayana takes to be required from it. These posits, despite Santayana's disavowal of metaphysics, are thoroughly metaphysical (rather than physical). They are not reports about the facts of animal life as established by science. Instead, they are transcendental claims about (unexperienced) conditions alleged to be necessary or required posits given the facts of animal life.

---

[4] For a fuller discussion of this point, see my "The Temperament of Pragmatism" (Stuhr 2023, 147–182).

Santayana thought that this objection amounted to the view "that if direct observation offered no illustration of the permanent, nothing permanent could exist in fact, or could be reasonably believed to exist" (*SAF*, 192–93). If "direct observation" means simply experience or animal life, then indeed this is the objection. Is Santayana correct that there is and must be "permanence behind change" (*SAF*, 195) or is what he calls "permanent" simply a relatively slower rate of change—like tectonic plates of earth's outer shell that are not fixed but simply move more slowly than human eye movements? Is he correct that in animal life "the flux touches the eternal at the top of every wave" (*SAF*, 195), or does flux touch only other flux in a world of ever-changing relations? Santayana asserted we are forced to believe in external and independent substance because we perceive continuing objects even though our perceptions are momentary, interrupted, and discrete (*SAF*, 196). We recognize, he wrote, that objects are permanent even though our glimpses of the object are intermittent (*SAF*, 197). Again, there is no question that this experience occurs. As such, it is simply an occurrence. It is, of course, an acquired experience: Infants must learn object permanence. More important, this experience does not establish that there are objects external to, and independent of, experience. It establishes only that we experience objects as existing when we are not observing them. This is not a fact about something independent of experience; it is a fact about how things are experienced as. Santayana confused the thesis of the radical empiricist—whose claim is not that things are only *when* they are experienced but, rather, that things are what they are *as* they are experienced.

Belief in objects external to, and independent of, animal life is not a requirement of animal life. It is not logically required, as Santayana recognized. It is not practically required, as Santayana failed to recognize. Instead, it is simply a transcendental posit about what allegedly must be so, given the realities of animal lives in their environments, the realities of experience in nature. It is better understood, I think, as a matter of real temperament rather than unjustified doctrine. From a perspective of temperament, Santayana's belief in the objects he believes are required by animal faith appears to be intended as both a comfort and a scold—and in these two ways persons with temperaments similar to Santayana may find it, as he noted in the "Preface" (*SAF*, vi), a category of things worth distinguishing.

The comfort: Animals are compelled to believe in change (*SAF*, 30), Santayana stressed, but the category of substance contains "the notion of permanence behind change" (*SAF*, 195). We see here not the "quest for certainty" that Santayana so devastatingly criticized but a quest for permanence. Unable to locate any permanence in animal life itself, Santayana claims animal life must posit permanence—external and independent permanence. This ontological impoverishment of animal faith, experience, and life is transcended by materialism's posit of substance. In the penultimate paragraph of *Scepticism and Animal Faith*, Santayana wrote that he lived "when human faith is again in a state of dissolution" and that in response he has "frankly taken nature by the hand" (*SAF*, 308). Here, in a time of disbelief, the felt necessity of the supposed posits of animal faith constitutes a particular will to believe. While James called this kind of endeavor to establish permanence external to, and independent of, experience "faked" from the start and "abstraction worship" (James 1975/1907, 119–20, 128), the comfort it may provide to temperaments very different from James is nonetheless real. That noted, it is worth recalling Santayana's caution that "the brute necessity of believing something so long as life lasts does not justify any belief in particular" (*SAF*, 9–10).

The scold: Belief in external and experience-independent substance allows human beings to avoid egoism, anthropocentrism, uncritical humanism, and the "conceited notion" that human beings or human reason or human morality is "the centre and pivot of the universe" (*WD*, 214). For Santayana, unlike James, the trail of the human serpent is definitely not over everything, and it is pragmatically dangerous to believe otherwise—as the state of the world makes clear today. Philosophical humility: That would be a change—a change that in a world of unsure flux does not require impermanent animals in impermanent environments to believe in reasoned certainty or posited permanence. In this light, animal faith in animal environment is an always unfinished activity of honest reconstruction rather than "restoration" (*SAF*, 304).

References

Dewey, John. 1927. Half-Hearted Naturalism. *Journal of Philosophy* 24 (2): 57–64.

———. 1980/1917. The Need for a Recovery of Philosophy. In *John Dewey: The Middle Works, 1899–1924*, ed. Jo Ann Boydston, vol. 10, 3–48. Carbondale, IL: Southern Illinois University Press.

———. 1986a. In *A Common Faith, John Dewey: The Later Works, 1925–1953*, ed. Jo Ann Boydston, vol. 9, 1–58. Carbondale, IL: Southern Illinois University Press.

———. 1986b. In *Logic: The Theory of Inquiry, John Dewey: The Later Works, 1925–1953*, ed. Jo Ann Boydston, vol. 12. Carbondale, IL: Southern Illinois University Press.

———. 1987/1935. In *Experience and Nature, John Dewey: The Later Works, 1925–1953*, ed. Jo Ann Boydston, vol. 1. Carbondale, IL: Southern Illinois University Press.

———. 1988/1939. In *Freedom and Culture, John Dewey: The Later Works, 1925–1953*, ed. Jo Ann Boydston, vol. 13. Carbondale, IL: Southern Illinois University.

Dewey, John, and Arthur F. Bentley. 1989/1949. In *Knowing and the Known, John Dewey: The Later Works, 1925–1953*, ed. Jo Ann Boydston, vol. 16. Carbondale, IL: Southern Illinois University Press.

James, William. 1975/1907. In *Pragmatism: A New Name for an Old Way of Thinking*, ed. Fredson Bowers and Ignas K. Skrupskelis. Cambridge, MA: Harvard University Press.

———. 1979a. The Will to Believe. In *The Writings of William James: The Will to Believe and Other Essays in Popular Philosophy*. Cambridge, MA: Harvard University Press.

———. 1979b. The Sentiment of Rationality. In *The Writings of William James: The Will to Believe and Other Essays in Popular Philosophy*. Cambridge, MA: Harvard University Press.

Peirce, Charles. 1992a. Questions Concerning Certain Faculties Claimed for Man. In *The Essential Peirce: Selected Philosophical Writings*, ed. Nathan Houser and Christian Kloesel, vol. 1, 11–27. Bloomington, IN: Indiana University Press.
———. 1992b. Some Consequences of Four Incapacities. In *The Essential Peirce: Selected Philosophical Writings*, ed. Nathan Houser and Christian Kloesel, vol. 1, 28–55. Bloomington, IN: Indiana University Press.
———. 1998/1908. A Neglected Argument for the Reality of God. In *The Essential Peirce: Selected Philosophical Writings*, ed. Nathan Houser and Christian Kloesel, vol. 2, 434–450. Bloomington, IN: Indiana University Press.
Santayana, George. 1923. *Scepticism and Animal Faith*. New York: Charles Scribner's Sons.
———. 1925. Dewey's Naturalistic Metaphysics. *Journal of Philosophy* 22 (12): 673–688.
———. 1986/1944, 1953 *Persons and Places: Fragments of Autobiography*. Cambridge, MA: The MIT Press.
———. 1971/1912. *Winds of Doctrine*. Gloucester, MA: Peter Smith.
Stuhr, John. 1997. *Genealogical Pragmatism: Philosophy, Experience, and Community*. Albany, NY: State University of New York Press.
———. 2023. The Temperament of Pragmatism. In *No Professor's Lectures Can Save Us: William James's Pragmatism, Radical Empiricism, and Pluralism*, 147–182. New York: Oxford University Press.

Natural Knowledge and Transcendental Criticism in *Scepticism and Animal Faith*

Paul Forster

The rise of the naturalistic attitude in philosophy is commonly viewed as signalling the death of transcendental methods. For Santayana, however, the situation is not so clear. Like proponents of naturalism, Santayana eschews first philosophy, starts from beliefs he sees no reason to question, recognizes his claims are fallible and sees the anticipation of causal feedback on our bodies as the sole test of knowledge about nature. At the same time, he views transcendental criticism as fundamental to the philosophy of knowledge and reality, relies on the method of doubt and sceptical arguments to scrutinize the nature and limits of human knowledge and insists there are principles of knowledge that cannot be justified by natural science since they are presupposed by it.

It is tempting to view Santayana's persistence in transcendental criticism as retrograde and no more than a way station on the road to the more mature, unhesitating naturalism of the mid- and late twentieth century. It might even seem that the argument in *Scepticism and Animal Faith* (1923/1955) [hereafter, *SAF*] encourages this view. Insofar as Santayana's transcendental critique vindicates, rather than answers, sceptical doubts about human knowledge it seems to bolster the conviction that there is no justification for natural

---

I am grateful for comments by Andrew Lugg and Glenn Tiller.

P. Forster (✉)
Department of Philosophy, University of Ottawa, Ottawa, ON, Canada
e-mail: pforster@uottawa.ca

knowledge firmer or deeper than natural knowledge itself and nothing for philosophers to uncover beyond what the methods of natural knowledge can reveal. Santayana would have us consider, however, that in the rush to rescue philosophy from transcendental metaphysics and untenable views concerning the foundations of knowledge, naturalistic philosophers uncritically assume that a complete account of human knowledge is accessible to naturalistic investigation. Rather than pit empirical and transcendental methods against each other, Santayana draws on both in crafting an account of knowledge that he considers to be more comprehensive and compelling than either naturalism or transcendentalism provides on their own.

Transcendental Logic Versus Empirical Psychology: Kant and After

Santayana's distinction between transcendental and empirical criticism is informed by challenges to Kant's contrast between transcendental logic and empirical psychology that emerged at the close of the nineteenth century and it is helpful to consider the significance of his work in this context.

Kant on Transcendental Logic and Empirical Psychology[1]

On Kant's view, transcendental logic provides an *a priori* foundation for ontology. Reflecting on the logical structure of empirical judgements, he finds general principles at work in human knowledge—principles assumed in ordering appearances in space and time, in representing things, properties and relations in states of affairs and in subsuming states of affairs under laws. Noting that the principles of human knowledge have objective application only if the world is isomorphic to them, Kant claims that their truth presupposes notions of objects, properties, relations and facts that are basic to reality, at least insofar as it is an object of human knowledge. The isomorphism between the logical structure of human judgements and the ontological structure of the world that knowledge requires is, for Kant, neither fortuitous nor divinely established. Rather it is guaranteed rationally as a precondition of there being judgements that answer (or fail to answer) to the way things are. That there are eight planets and the acceleration due to gravity is independent of mass are contingent matters—that the world might have been otherwise is conceivable. By contrast, a world in which appearances are not ordered in space and time, there are no objects with properties or relations, or no states of affairs covered by laws is inconceivable. Kant thinks our efforts to contemplate such a world falter because the notions basic to human understanding lack application leaving us bereft of tools by which to conceive of it. Purported descriptions of such a world prove on critical analysis to break the bounds of sense.

---

[1] See Kant (2003) and Forster (1994).

On Kant's view, transcendental logic and empirical science have distinct subject-matter. Principles of transcendental logic are necessarily true—they must hold in the world if there are to be judgements with truth values hinging on matters of fact. They do not, however, determine which of the logically possible ways the world might be is the case. The actual state of the world is an *a posteriori* matter determined through judgements warranted by experience. Since empirical judgements (true and false) presuppose the isomorphism of human judgements and the world secured *a priori* by transcendental logic, the truth of these logical principles is prior to and independent of empirical knowledge.

Kant thinks his distinction between transcendental logic and empirical science forces us to recognize two distinct branches in the science of human nature. As knowers human beings are endowed with cognitive capacities that are subject to inquiry in transcendental logic. Yet as creatures with mental lives that unfold in time and attach to bodies that move through space, they are also the subject of empirical investigation in psychology. The principles of transcendental logic, being *a priori* and independent of any knowledge of the natural world, provide no basis for anticipating empirical findings in psychology. Conversely, the findings of empirical psychology, being *a posteriori*, lack the necessity and *a priority* of the principles of transcendental logic they presuppose. As Kant sees it, we confuse transcendental logic and empirical psychology at our peril, their shared reference to human nature notwithstanding.

Naturalism and Logicism as Responses to Kant

Criticism of Kant's conception of transcendental logic and empirical psychology as branches of the science of human nature arose around the end of the nineteenth century from two distinct quarters.[2] The "naturalistic" attack on Kant—pressed in various ways by William James (1981), John Dewey (1917, 1930a) and others—was inspired by developments in the behavioural sciences—biology, physiology and human psychology. The "logistic" response to Kant—developed especially by Frege (1956) and Russell (1903, 1997)—was rooted in advances in mathematical logic.

Like Kant, the naturalists think logic aims at uncovering normative principles of human cognitive rationality, rather than the purely descriptive generalizations disclosed in empirical psychology and natural history. Unlike him, however, they take the study of logic to go hand in hand with empirical inquiry in psychology and other behavioural sciences. Drawing on the theory of evolution, they view human cognition as an organic capacity and its principles open to investigation by the same methods used to uncover the principles of respiration, circulation and other organic functions. They claim that biology,

---

[2] I ignore the critique of Kant advanced by T. H. Green, F. H. Bradley and other advocates of absolute idealism, notwithstanding its influence on the development of naturalism, logicism and Santayana's philosophy.

psychology and physiology provide insight into the limits of cognition and the conditions of its optimal performance, just as they provide insight into the limits and optimal conditions of vision. On this view, the normative principles of logic are justified by reference to empirical knowledge of human cognitive capacities and the environment in which they function. Conversely, knowledge of human cognitive capacities and their environment is justified through inquiry guided by the norms uncovered in logic. *A priori* investigation of the principles of human cognition in transcendental logic goes by the boards and good riddance.

The logicists, by contrast, retain Kant's view of logic as a foundation for metaphysics. Like him, they hold that judgements have a logical structure isomorphic to reality and the analysis of terms, propositions and inferences yields insight into the nature of objects, properties, facts and relations basic to ontology. They also follow Kant in distinguishing logic from the empirical sciences. For them, there is no deriving the truth of logical principles from more basic truths since the very notions of derivation and truth are explicated in terms of them. Taking logical principles to govern all that is actual and possible, the logicists hold there are no facts outside the scope of logic and no empirical discoveries at odds with its findings. To their way of thinking, Kant is right to claim that logic is *a priori*. While this leads them to endorse Kant's distinction between logic and psychology, they push it further than Kant himself by severing the connection between logic and the science of human nature. As they see it, the terms, propositions and inferences studied in logic are neither physical nor mental entities but rather abstract denizens of a third realm of being, and wholly unconditioned by humanity's grasp of them. The logicists recognize that human thought is part of the natural world and a product of evolution open to investigation in the behavioural sciences, as the naturalists maintain. However, they deny that this insight has any bearing on the nature of logic. For them, it is one thing to account for the emergence and operation of the capacity for logical thought in human beings, quite another to explain what this capacity is a capacity for. As they see it, the subject-matter of logic, being outside space and time, lies outside the scope of inquiry into the emergence of human cognition, the regularities that govern sequences of psychological states (e.g., laws of association) and the conditions for improving human cognitive function that the naturalists pursue.

A Clash Among "Special Schools of Philosophy"

While Santayana does not give a full discussion of the debate between the naturalists and the logicists in *Scepticism and Animal Faith*, his views of empirical and transcendental criticism provide a telling response to it. The debate has all the earmarks of what he calls a clash among "the special schools of philosophy" (*SAF*, v).[3] Each side starts from insights uncovered in some specialized branch

---

[3] See also Santayana (1915).

of inquiry—behavioural science for the naturalists, mathematical logic for the logicists. Looking to capitalize on progress in these fields, each side extends the methods of the relevant specialty to the study of philosophy and interprets questions in epistemology, metaphysics and value theory so that they fall within their scope. The opposing view is then rejected as ill-suited to the problems of philosophy so understood. The insights that motivate the competing position are not ignored. Rather, they are reinterpreted to render them consonant with the preferred understanding of philosophy and the resulting view is proffered as a complete and systematic account of knowledge and the world.

In the case of the naturalists, for example, advances in the science of human behaviour are traced to the use of experimental methods in biology, physiology and psychology. The naturalists' claim that human cognition is a biological capacity is part and parcel of their extension of these methods to philosophical questions about knowledge and its footing in the world. Having set their sights on an empirically informed account of the function and norms of human cognition, the naturalists view the logicists' method of uncovering logical principles through *a priori* analysis as a serious mistake. They fear the logicists' approach encourages speculation about knowledge and justification without due regard for what behavioural science tells us about human capacities and the environment in which they function. They worry, moreover, that in promoting the view that logical principles are necessarily true, the logicists foster the misconception that norms of human cognition are eternal and immune to revision, rather than capable of refinement and improvement as the theory of evolution suggests all organic functions are. The naturalists do not dispute the value of the methods of logical analysis that inspire the logicists but they construe them as tools of theory construction. While they recognize that logical analysis helps uncover and resolve conceptual difficulties in theories and render inferences precise and systematic, they deny that the logical reconstruction of a theory has any bearing on its claim to truth. For them, to formulate a theory in an exact language is one thing, to show a theory so understood represents the natural world another. Just as the justification of theoretical principles of bridge building rests ultimately on the performance of the bridges they are used to build, naturalists think the justification of logical principles depends in the end on the predictive reliability of the theories in which they figure. For them, all knowledge is natural knowledge and subject to experimental justification—the principles of logic included.

Reasoning from a contrary starting point, the logicists stick to their guns and turn back the naturalists' critique. In promoting the efficacy of *a priori* methods of logical analysis they point to advances in non-Euclidean geometry, transfinite arithmetic, the rigorization of the infinitesimal calculus and the doctrine of chances, the definition of number in logical terms, the resolution of antinomies in the notion of continuity and the development of the propositional calculus. Their view of reality as comprising a basic ontology grounded in logic is of a piece with their extension of these methods to philosophical inquiry. Given the strict criteria of definition and proof involved in logical analysis, they see no basis for the naturalists' charge that their methods encourage unbridled speculation and dogmatic pronouncements. Noting that the results of logical analysis are justified without appeal to claims about human beings, their capacities, or their natural environment, they insist they are *a priori* and write off the naturalists' reservations about *a priori* knowledge as the result of a crude empiricism. Taking the principles of logic to hold independently of contingent facts about nature, the logicists think it a mistake for the naturalists to pursue logic through inquiry in the behavioural sciences. For them, resting a theory of the structure of reality on principles by which one species of animal in one small corner of the vast universe forms beliefs about their environment is anthropocentric in the extreme. What is more, by tying metaphysics to the theory of human knowledge, the naturalists conflate investigation into reality as it is apart from human understanding with inquiry into the processes by which it comes to be known. The naturalists' rejection of logical analysis as a method for investigating nature is well-taken, the logicists acknowledge, but it is irrelevant, it being no part of their project to uncover insights into human beings, their capacities and their environment by *a priori* means. The logicists do not deny the findings about human behaviour and cognition uncovered in the behavioural sciences that inspire the naturalist view. To the contrary, they view them as grist to the analytical mill. Accepting them as part of our best grasp on reality (pending evidence to the contrary) they endeavour to analyse the concepts they contain and unpack the *a priori* principles on which their truth logically depends. Their goal is to unite knowledge gained through empirical inquiry with more comprehensive transcendental principles of metaphysics grounded in logic in a comprehensive and rigorous theory of the world.

Santayana's Rejection of First Principles of Criticism

Starting from either the naturalists' or the logicists' conception of the aims and methods of philosophy, the case against the other view seems hard to dispute. The logicists' reliance on *a priori* methods of logical analysis is as ill-suited to the naturalists' inquiry into the conditions for optimizing human cognitive capacities as the naturalists' reliance on experimental methods is to the logicists' reconstruction of knowledge as a logical system. To rely on the requirements of one project in discrediting the aims and methods of the other begs the question of the proper task of philosophy and ignores the fact that proponents of the contrary view are free to return the favour.

It might be suggested, in an experimental spirit, that each school should be left to its own devices and a final verdict on their disagreement withheld pending further evidence of their fruitfulness as programs of research. However, it is difficult to see how advances in the behavioural sciences or mathematical logic might settle this controversy. Neither the naturalists nor the logicists dispute the knowledge gained in these fields. Their debate is rather about the significance of these insights for philosophy. The naturalists have no problem welcoming new findings in logical analysis so long as they are viewed as contributing to the construction of precise, systematic predictive theories, and not as grounded in *a priori* knowledge of a non-natural reality. Similarly, the logicists can embrace whatever facts about human cognition the behavioural sciences might turn up while insisting that they fall within a space of possibilities circumscribed by necessary principles of definition and proof uncovered *a priori* through logical analysis. The difficulty is that in elucidating the deeper significance of various discoveries in the special sciences each side invokes a conception of the aims and methods of philosophy that the other side repudiates.

However tempting an idea, Santayana holds out little hope of deciding the issue by appeal to principles that stand apart from both views. As he sees it, neither the naturalists' nor the logicists' position is plausibly viewed as justifiable in this way. The naturalists' understanding of logic rests on claims about the origin and function of human cognition and these claims, Santayana insists, can only be evaluated by "begi[nning] in the middle" (*SAF*, 2) of things— accepting such evidence and beliefs about human beings and their evolution as seems credible given current methods of studying such things. While he thinks the logicists are free to devise systems of axioms and postulates "*ad libitum*" (*SAF*, 2), he insists that any "pure logic" "posited in the air" has "no necessary application to anything" and is "otiose" in philosophy "unless we find or assume that discourse or nature actually follows it" (*SAF*, 2–3). To show a system of logic "lends cogency to actual discourse," he argues, the logicists have no choice but to trust "current presumptions" (*SAF*, 2). They must adhere to the very principles they defend as basic to logic and test the adequacy of their reconstruction of human knowledge against beliefs and habits of reasoning already deemed credible. In pursuing either approach—the naturalists' or the logicists'—"we should ... be beginning with things as we find them in the gross, and not with first principles" (*SAF*, 3) and uncovering the principles basic to knowledge only at the conclusion of our philosophical investigation, if at all.

Deciding the debate between the naturalists and the logicists by appeal to a neutral conception of the aims and methods of philosophy is similarly a dead end, according to Santayana. Appeal to a third view of philosophy is no less question-begging against the naturalists' and the logicists' views than their views are against each other. A justification of beliefs that is higher and deeper than empirical science is precisely what the naturalists claim the science of human cognition precludes. Similarly, a critical perspective more basic than logic is ruled out by the logicists' given their view that the notions of "truth," "proposition," "argument," "object," "relation" and "fact" derive their content from logic.

Rather than despair the lack of an absolute perspective from which to adjudicate the dispute over philosophical fundamentals between the naturalists and the logicists, Santayana takes this realization in stride, embracing it as an important insight into the nature and limits of philosophical inquiry. For him, the pursuit of a unified system of the world continues but no longer encumbered by one of philosophy's most enduring myths—the dream of a universal or absolute perspective. "[A]nimated by distrust of all high guesses" (*SAF*, v), he sees no option in philosophy but to "follow the maxim of epic poets and ... plunge *in medias res*" (*SAF*, 1). Unable to stand above or aloof from controversies in science and common sense, he insists philosophers can "lay siege to the truth only as animal exploration and fancy may do so, first from one quarter and then from another" (*SAF*, vi). Rather than "pretend to place [himself] at the heart of the universe [or] at its origin, [or] to draw its periphery" (*SAF*, v–vi), Santayana "stand[s] in philosophy exactly where [he] stand[s] in daily life ... accept[ing] the same miscellaneous witnesses, bow[ing] to the same obvious facts, mak[ing] conjectures no less instinctively, and admit[ting] the same encircling ignorance," all in an effort "to think straight in such terms as are offered to [him], to clear [his] mind of cant and free it from the cramp of artificial traditions" (*SAF*, vi).

It is important to note, however, that Santayana does not take his abandonment of first philosophy to signal victory for the naturalists over the logicists. As he sees it, the logicists no more begin from an absolute perspective than the naturalists do. Both work *in medias rebus*. But if, as Santayana contends, neither first principles of criticism nor inquiry in the special sciences will resolve this debate, what will? How can we adjudicate the conflict between the naturalists and the logicists when the nature of the standards of philosophical criticism is precisely what is at issue? For Santayana, the answer lies in closer scrutiny of the motivations and assumptions on which the naturalists and the logicists rely.

SANTAYANA ON THE AIM AND METHOD OF EMPIRICAL CRITICISM

For Santayana, the force of the naturalists' position derives from the genetic explanation of knowledge it draws on. Agreeing that philosophy must start from current knowledge, Santayana embraces the naturalists' account of the origin and growth of knowledge in human organisms. He accepts that human beings are part of the natural world they seek to know. Situated in space and time, their behaviour is prompted by, and continuous with, broader physical processes. Far from shedding light on higher cognitive functions, he thinks appeals to disembodied mental processes only mystify them, there being, as he sees it, no credible explanation of natural processes in non-physical terms. Rather than attribute evident differences between sentient creatures and insensate matter to the presence of an unseen animus, Santayana follows the naturalist in tracing the distinction to differences in observable behaviour. Organisms—typified by what he calls "psyche"—are such that their patterns of response are shaped by physical interactions with their surroundings. Their behavioural dispositions are selective—i.e., responsive to certain sorts of stimuli and indifferent or inhibited by others—yield actions that culminate in characteristic outcomes and are modified by their physical effects. Habitual behaviour impeded by recalcitrant experiences evolves or is extinguished, while responses that proceed uninhibited are more likely to be repeated on similar occasions in future. The adaptation of habits to environmental pressures is the main mechanism of animal learning.

While acknowledging complexities in human knowledge introduced by reflective understanding, abstract thought, enculturation and the use of language, Santayana follows the naturalists in viewing common sense and scientific inquiry as an extension and refinement of more rudimentary processes of animal exploration. On his view, as on the naturalists, theories of nature are tested by comparing the predictions they imply with actual events. Discrepancies manifest ignorance or gaps in knowledge that prompt efforts to explain and remedy them in inquiry. Revising beliefs under the control of natural occurrences to "reduce conventional belief to the recognition of matters of fact" is the task of what he calls "empirical criticism of knowledge" (*SAF*, 3).

On Santayana's understanding of empirical criticism, even high-level theorizing retains something of the instrumental character of animal learning. Bringing symbolic representations of the world into line with the order of events is, for him, of a piece with the adaptation of responses to environmental pressures observed in the behaviour of even the simplest organisms. All too aware of the prevalence of expedient falsehoods and prosperous dogmas (*SAF*, 7, 8), however, Santayana balks at identifying the search for truth with the search for effective habits or useful beliefs. Nevertheless, he insists that the agreement (or discrepancy) of predictions with the order of events is the sole test of empirical knowledge and the only indication that nature is (or is not) as we think. So far as natural knowledge is concerned, seeking out and correcting failures to anticipate events is all we can do to "clear our intellectual conscience of voluntary or avoidable delusion" (*SAF*, 3). Even rightly conducted empirical criticism can lead us astray—no theory, however successful, can be secured against revision in the face of unanticipated experiences—but uncertainty about empirical beliefs is to be addressed by further empirical inquiry leading to the replacement of deficient beliefs by better established ones. Our susceptibility to error notwithstanding, Santayana agrees with the naturalists that natural knowledge demands no more of the world than that it unfold as predicted. To the extent that our beliefs meet this standard, they are beyond reproach. "If what we call a fact still deceives us, we feel we are not to blame; we should not call it a fact, did we see any way of eluding recognition of it" (*SAF*, 3). To require more by way of justification for natural knowledge than empirical criticism can deliver is, as the naturalists claim, bootless and a confusion.

Santayana on the Aim and Method of Transcendental Criticism

Seeing no constructive role for transcendental argument in the pursuit of natural knowledge and no standard of correspondence between beliefs and facts outside the scope of empirical criticism, Santayana thinks the naturalists are on safe ground in rejecting the logicists' attempt to "determine matters of fact by means of logical … constructions" (*SAF*, vii). For him, there is no route to knowledge of nature or the structure of reality through *a priori* metaphysics. However, he does not think this spells the end for transcendental methods in philosophy. As he sees it, liberating philosophy from the confusions of transcendental metaphysics is one thing—and all to the good—but following the naturalists in the single-minded pursuit of empirical criticism in philosophy is something else. Once purged of its metaphysical ambitions and its claim to supersede natural knowledge, he thinks transcendental criticism remains an important source of philosophical insight.

When we step back from the empirical pursuit of truth and reflect on "the tangle of human beliefs, as conventionally expressed in talk and literature," Santayana thinks it is easy to distinguish two factors at work in knowledge (*SAF*, 3). The first is "a compulsory factor called facts or things," the second "a more optional and argumentative factor called suggestion or interpretation" (*SAF*, 3). The former is manifest in our receptivity to the world—our capacity as believers to be affected by, and answerable to, a world independent of our understanding of it. The latter factor is rooted in spontaneous conceptual capacities—our ability in imagination and hypothesis to generate representations of the world that are not passively determined by environmental pressures (*SAF*, 8, 263). Were all knowledge reducible to mere copies of things or traces impressed on us by facts, there could no more be a discrepancy between beliefs and their objects than there can be between a thumbprint and the whirls and lines on the digit that leaves it or between a footprint and the shape and size of the foot that produces it. In cases of error, however, where there is "a contrast between what I find I know and what I thought I knew" (*SAF*, 4), what I take to be the case is not actually there to supply the content or grounds of my false belief. Santayana reckons that "if nothing in the facts justified my [mistaken] beliefs, something in me must have suggested them" (*SAF*, 4). To "disentangle and formulate" the "principles of interpretation" and "habits of inference" at work in our "tendencies to feign," objectivity is to make explicit our "unconscious transcendental logic" (*SAF*, 4). This, he claims, is the aim of "transcendental criticism of knowledge" (*SAF*, 4).

In uncovering the subjective contributions to human knowledge, Santayana invokes a method of sceptical doubt. He considers it uncritical to assume, as Kant and the logicists are wont to do, that "tendencies to feign must be the same in everybody, that the notions of nature, history, or mind which they [lead] people to adopt [are] the right or standard notions" and the isomorphism between the logic of human judgement and the structure of nature guaranteed *a priori* (*SAF*, 4). Given this, he thinks it fair to question whether knowledge emerging from the interplay of spontaneity and receptivity has a firm foothold in facts, as we are apt to think when, in less reflective moments, we are focused on fashioning beliefs to match the order of events. As he puts it:

Just as inattention leads ordinary people to assume as part of the given facts all that their unconscious transcendental logic has added to them, so inattention, at a deeper level, leads the empiricist to assume an existence in his radical facts which does not belong to them. (*SAF*, 4)

The "critical function of transcendentalism," then, is "to drive empiricism home, and challenge it to produce any knowledge of fact whatsoever" (*SAF*, 4).

Santayana begins his transcendental critique of knowledge by asking what at this "juncture in the life of reason ... he is most certain of, and what he believes only on hearsay or by some sort of suggestion or impulse of his own, which might be suspended or reversed" (*SAF*, 110). His pursuit of this question produces a ranking of beliefs in "the *order of evidence*" according to their vulnerability to sceptical doubts (*SAF*, 110).

First to succumb, he claims, is religious belief. However important faith may be as a source of ideals and values, he thinks the arbitrariness of religious accounts of the significance of events is evident from the persistence of contrary creeds, the variability of dogma over time and the indifference and plasticity of religious orthodoxy in the face of advances in science. Even "[w]ithout philosophical criticism," he contends, "mere experience and good sense suggest that all positive religions are false, or at least ... that they are all fantastic and insecure" (*SAF*, 12).

Santayana argues the claim of dramatic history to a basis in facts is similarly questionable. Far from taking past occurrences to be equally significant, narrative histories single out certain events as beginnings, turning points and endings. What is more, they classify outcomes as victories or defeats and historical figures as heroes or villains—all based on interests and ideals that go beyond any catalogue of events (*SAF*, 12).

As for chronicles of history free of dramatic flourishes and evaluations, Santayana puts them on a par with knowledge of physical facts. Rather than providing grounds for belief in a spatio-temporal world, he thinks knowledge of the past presupposes it. Our knowledge of history comes to us by way of physical objects—documents, artefacts, human remains, fossils and the like—and these function as evidence only on the understanding that they are of remote origin and reliably preserve something of an earlier time or place. Even personal reminiscences place experiences in their physical settings and identify them by public dates and scientifically discoverable characteristics (*SAF*, 13). History and memory both presume the general "postulates in which empirical knowledge and inductive science are based" (*SAF*, 14). That is, they take for granted "that there has been a past, that it was such as it is now thought to be, that there will be a future, and that it must, for some inconceivable reason, resemble the past and obey the same laws" (*SAF*, 14).

Santayana claims that the belief in a spatio-temporal order on which physical knowledge depends—knowledge of history included—can coherently be dismissed as "gratuitous dogmas" (*SAF*, 14) by acquiescing in solipsism of the present moment. Taking immediate appearances—what he calls "essences"—to be nothing more than what they are experienced to be and "lopping off everything else" (*SAF*, 18), he thinks reliance on what is present as a sign of something beyond itself must be rejected as fanciful (*SAF*, 16, 25). Once the interpretation of essences as evidence of natural occurrences is undercut, knowledge of human beings and their place in the natural world—the knowledge on which the naturalists rest their philosophy—is cast into doubt.

It is often thought that distrust in the existence of the physical world sown from the solipsistic point of view leaves various forms of *a priori* knowledge intact. However, Santayana sees room for doubt here as well. He argues, for example, that a sceptic who sticks to immediate experience must reject as presumptuous the posit of a thinking subject as its bearer (*SAF*, 21f.). Neither the fact of an essence's being apprehended nor the conditions of its being known is given in present experience (*SAF*, 23). What is more, the relations of similarity and difference necessary to classify an immediate experience as an event within a single consciousness are likewise extraneous to it (*SAF*, 22). Confined to the realm of essences, the consistent sceptic rejects claims to knowledge of their own minds as doubtful.

Even granting the sceptical doubts defended to this point, it might be thought that at least the shifting appearances and "passing unrest" (*SAF*, 22) felt in immediate experience provide an inkling of a process unfolding in time. However, Santayana considers this too a mistake. While granting that immediate content "may fade and lapse of its own accord" (*SAF*, 24) he insists that to take the bare feeling that something is happening as evidence of change is to "assert something not at all involved in the present being" (*SAF*, 24). As he sees it, real change implies that there is something prior to, and distinct from, its subsequent states (*SAF*, 25). Yet relations to something previous cannot be included in what is present. In their immediacy, feelings of change are but "pictures of motions and ideas of events" (*SAF*, 30). They "play idly before me" but offer no grounds for belief in a genuine passage from one state to another (*SAF*, 30).

To Santayana's way of thinking, the sceptic's doubts about consciousness and change extend to the *a priori* knowledge on which the logicists rely in crafting their view of philosophy. The logicists train methods of analysis on terms, propositions and inferences with eternal meanings, truth values and logical relations. However, the ability to grasp these entities on different occasions "presupposes ability in thought to traverse time without confusion, so that having lived through two intuitions I may correctly distinguish them as events, whilst correctly identifying their common object" (*SAF*, 112). The logicists suppose, for example, that Euclid's proof of the Pythagorean Theorem is an object of study to which knowers can return, its content unaffected by being apprehended. Santayana argues, however, that the identity of the meanings considered on different occasions of thought is "not properly predicated of essence in its own realm" (*SAF*, 112). So far as immediate appearances are concerned "my memory need not retain the first intuition so precisely that its disparity from the present one can be sensible to me now" (*SAF*, 112). From the standpoint of the apprehension of essences, the stability of meanings available to be contemplated that logical analysis requires is an "immense postulate" involving "ambitious and highly questionable dogmas" (*SAF*, 112).

The upshot of Santayana's transcendental critique is that, rigorously pressed and pushed to its limits, "[s]cepticism may ... be carried to the point of denying change and memory, and the reality of all facts" (*SAF*, 40). The "dogma that nothing exists"—that there are no entities, states of affairs or passing events to be right or wrong about, that what is immediately evident and luminous is a mere dream—proves "tenable intuitively" (*SAF*, 40). What is given provides "absolute assurance of nothing save the character of some given essence" and "the rest is arbitrary belief or interpretation added by my animal impulse" (*SAF*, 110). So long as our immersion in the immediate is consistently maintained, scepticism provides a "sanctuary from grosser illusions" and remains "irrefutable" (*SAF*, 40).[4]

The Naturalists' Critique of Transcendental Criticism

It might be thought Santayana's willingness to work alternately from the empirical and transcendental points of view betrays an unresolved tension in his thought. The suggestion is that his commitment to the naturalists' view of knowledge is half-hearted—since undermined by his endorsement of sceptical doubts about natural knowledge pressed from the transcendental point of view—and likewise that his scepticism is less than heart-felt—since qualified by his endorsement of the natural knowledge certified through empirical criticism.[5] It is important to see, however, that Santayana does not see his transcendental critique of knowledge as in any way opposed to his commitment to the naturalists' account of knowledge. What he professes from the standpoint of empirical criticism he does not take back from the transcendental point of view.

Consider, for example, the suggestion that if Santayana were to stick firmly to the naturalists' account of knowledge, he would reject the transcendental critic's sceptical doubts as disingenuous or merely verbal. The idea is that true naturalists recognize that philosophical thought experiments portraying knowers as victims of wholesale deception fail to instil real doubts about common

---

[4] As Santayana makes clear: "I do not ask anyone to believe in essences. I ask them to reject every belief, and what they will have on their hands, if they do so, will be some essence. And if, believing nothing, they could infinitely enlarge their imagination, the whole realm of essence would loom before them. This realm is no discovery of mine: it has been described, for instance, by Leibniz in two different ways; once as the collection of all possible worlds, and again as the abyss of non-existence ... 'all those things which do not exist at all are included in the non-existent, and those which no longer exist have returned to the non-existent.' It suffices, therefore, to deny a thing for us to recognize an essence, if we know at all what we are denying. And the essence before us, whether we assert or deny its existence, is certainly no abstraction; for there is no other datum, more individual or more obvious, from which the abstraction could be drawn. The difficulty in discerning essences is simply the very real difficulty which the practical intellect has in abstaining from belief, and from everywhere thinking it finds much more than is actually given" (1921, 211).

[5] See Dewey (1927 and 1930b) and the discussion in Forster (2007).

sense and scientific belief and this is not because we are irredeemably dogmatic but rather because we are on solid ground in claiming knowledge of our surroundings. Were Santayana resolute in taking the obstacles confronted in experience to attest to the existence of a surrounding world that is not of our making and success in predicting and controlling events as evidence that we know something of how the world we live in works, he would share the naturalists' view that the conditions for reasonable doubt about the existence of the world and the possibility of our knowing it are lacking.

Santayana accepts this line of thought as far as it goes but he does not think it counters the transcendental critic's reasoning. He grants the naturalists' observation that we have "a vital compulsion to posit and to believe something" (*SAF*, 9) and that this makes complete suspension of belief unsustainable. However, the mere fact that the conditions of life make wholesale scepticism unliveable does not show that the sceptic is wrong, from the standpoint of the realm of essences, to view knowledge claims as open to question. He argues that "[t]he brute necessity of believing something so long as life lasts does not justify any belief in particular" (*SAF*, 9–10). Nor does it assure us that to live and believe is epistemologically more responsible than to withhold belief. "To be dead and have no opinion would certainly not be to discover the truth; but if all opinions are necessarily false, it would at least be not to sin against intellectual honour" (*SAF*, 10). Having opted for life, Santayana agrees with the naturalists that we can do no better than fix our beliefs by the methods of empirical criticism. However, to dismiss the transcendental critic's line of argument merely because sceptical doubts are foreign and inimical to the pursuit of empirical criticism is to assume, rather than show, the authority of the naturalistic attitude. The point that needs stressing is that the beliefs the naturalists rightly consider to be firm from the engaged perspective of empirical criticism are nevertheless doubtful from the purely reflective perspective of the transcendental critic and there is no contradiction in recognizing this.

It might still be insisted that if Santayana were to adhere to the naturalists' account of empirical criticism consistently, he would set sceptical doubts about natural knowledge aside by challenging the notion of justification they involve. In calling natural knowledge into question the transcendental critic seems to assume that beliefs are not justified unless secured against any possibility of error—that empirical justification, being fallible, is not justification enough. They furthermore seem to suppose that beliefs are unwarranted unless they can be derived from present experience. Were he fully on board with the naturalists, Santayana would consider both of these assumptions unreasonable given what current science tells us about our cognitive capacities and the way they function in the natural environment. If Santayana finds the sceptical doubts of the transcendental critic compelling, it can only be that he has abandoned the naturalists' conception of empirical criticism.

For Santayana, however, the transcendental method does not presume a precise conception of justification. On his view, we saw, the transcendental critic is not driven by anxiety about the possibility of error to seek a foundation for natural knowledge firmer than that provided by empirical criticism. Rather the transcendental critic is led by reflection on the nature of error to the realization that even the firmest natural knowledge is a product of the compulsive force of fact and spontaneous conceptual interpretation. Finding principles at work in our system of belief that go beyond what facts impress on us, the transcendental critic asks what, if anything, might be said for them to someone who does not already accept them—someone immersed in solipsism of the present moment. While exploration of the coherence of wholesale doubts about beliefs leads the transcendental critic to rank beliefs on a scale ranging from the arbitrary to the indubitable, no precise standard of reasonable belief or model of justification is assumed at the outset of this process. What is and is not coherently doubtful and on what grounds only becomes clear in the course of the transcendental critic's line of questioning. For present purposes, the crucial step is the recognition that the inferences that justify beliefs in common sense and science lose their force if, with the sceptic, we deny the claim that essences occurring at one time and place provide evidence of what occurs at other times and places. It is only after having discovered a perspective from which this presupposition can be doubted that Santayana's transcendental critic is compelled to ask how it might be warranted and to consider whether justification in terms of immediate experience is possible. In short, the transcendental critic's doubts derive their force from the internal logic of the method of doubt and not from any antecedent theories about the nature of knowledge, justification or the natural world.[6]

Finally, it might be argued that if Santayana were firmly committed to the naturalists' view of knowledge, he would challenge the transcendental critic's assumption that methods of empirical criticism are doubtful absent some grounding in principles that do not presuppose them and that a naturalistic justification of empirical criticism is insufficient since viciously circular. In pursuing a foundation for common sense and science firmer and deeper than empirical criticism provides, the transcendental critic seems to run afoul of Santayana's own strictures on first philosophy.

For Santayana, the foregoing objection is also a misunderstanding. As he sees it, the transcendental critic does not cast doubt on knowledge from a standpoint independent of common sense and science. Nor do they tear down our current system of belief in a bid to start fresh. To the contrary, the transcendental critic works *in medias rebus*, recognizing that the only grounds for doubts about a belief is some other belief. As he explains:

> Scepticism is a suspicion of error about facts, and to suspect error about facts is to share the enterprise of knowledge, in which facts are presupposed and error is possible... . Since [the sceptic's] criticism may thus be true and his doubt well grounded, they [sic] are certainly assertions; and if he is sincerely a sceptic, they

---

[6] In this section I have drawn on competing discussions of scepticism by Marie McGinn (1989) and Michael Williams (1986).

are assertions which he is ready to maintain stoutly. Scepticism is accordingly a form of belief. (*SAF*, 8)

It is precisely because the sceptical challenges pressed by the transcendental critic are rooted in beliefs and standards "which it has not yet occurred to the sceptic to doubt" (*SAF*, 9) that they are compelling and not easily set aside. "[I]n the confused state of human speculation," Santayana thinks, the "embarrassment" of persisting in a system of belief that contains within it the seeds of sceptical doubts "obtrudes itself automatically" (*SAF*, 9). For this reason, "a philosopher to-day would be ridiculous and negligible who has not strained his dogmas through the utmost rigours of scepticism, and who did not approach every opinion, whatever his own ultimate faith, with the courtesy and smile of the sceptic" (*SAF*, 9).

Nor is Santayana's transcendental critic guilty of self-contradiction in drawing on the authority of contemporary knowledge while at the time calling it into question.[7] It is true that in defending solipsism of the present moment as a consistent position immune to sceptical doubt, the transcendental critic relies on contemporary claims to knowledge. However, the version of solipsism that emerges from this line of thought is not a system of belief at all. It is rather the attitude of immersing oneself in immediate experience while concentrating "on *not* asserting and *not* implying anything, but simply noticing what [one] finds" (*SAF*, 16). So long as beliefs are held in abeyance—belief in solipsism included—Santayana insists "the attitude of the sceptic is not inconsistent; it is merely difficult" (*SAF*, 16). Even when it proves impossible to sustain, he insists "the impossibility is only psychological" (*SAF*, 16).

Having shown that in pressing the sceptical arguments of the transcendental critic Santayana is not contradicting or even weakening his commitment to the naturalists' view of empirical criticism, we are better positioned to appreciate his allegiance to both methods. Taken as rival accounts of the human epistemic condition, there is no squaring transcendentalism and naturalism. The former view takes our knowledge to be grounded in immediate experience, if at all, and the latter takes it to be justified experimentally, by testing hypotheses against the order of natural events. If, however, we follow Santayana in viewing transcendentalism and naturalism as methods of criticism pursued from distinct points of view and guided by different questions and interests, then there is no need to choose between them.

Taking this line, Santayana views the empirical critic as immersed in common sense and scientific knowledge and pursuing a set of beliefs adapted to the order of nature for the purposes of prediction and control. In this context, he wholeheartedly embraces the naturalist's view of "the *order of genesis*" (*SAF*, 110) of our beliefs. In light of our best theory of the evolution and growth of human knowledge, he accepts unreservedly that there is no knowledge of nature to be gained from sources and methods higher and deeper than

---

[7] For a fuller discussion of this objection see Dewey (1915, 1930b) and Forster (2007, 2014).

empirical criticism provides. At the same time, however, he insists that the order of evidence uncovered by the transcendental critic shows that natural knowledge—including knowledge of the origins of knowledge—rests on the assumption of a world in which things and events function as reliable signs of what lies beyond them. This assumption is coherently doubted by a sceptic resolutely ensconced in the realm of essences—that there is the sort of world empirical criticism requires cannot be derived from immediate experience. Yet to justify the assumptions of empirical criticism—as the naturalists do—by appeal to the data of experience is to beg the question against the sceptic by assuming the conditions that legitimate this sort of inquiry. Rather than being grounded in facts about nature, the naturalists' reliance on empirical criticism is an "animal faith."[8]

Transcendental Criticism, Logicism and Naturalism

At this juncture the naturalists might still be inclined to think that their view of philosophy remains unscathed by Santayana's transcendental critique. To them it might seem that having undermined the logicists' appeal to *a priori* analysis in metaphysics, repudiated the idea of a source of natural knowledge that rivals or supersedes empirical criticism and reassured us that there is no improving on the methods of common sense and the empirical sciences, Santayana has only advanced their cause. They might suppose that Santayana's claim that natural knowledge is founded in animal faith amounts to nothing more than the realization that transcendental philosophy leads nowhere. Santayana seems to leave us with the choice of either immersing ourselves in essences and withholding all belief—thereby abandoning philosophy—or pursuing empirical criticism and working to improve methods of inquiry in light of natural knowledge of our capacities and environment.

This line of thinking underestimates the philosophical significance of Santayana's transcendental criticism, however. To see this, consider the resolution of the debate between the naturalists and the logicists that he thinks emerges from his account of the clashes between special schools in philosophy, the rejection of first principles of criticism and the transcendental critique of knowledge.

The naturalists and the logicists find themselves at odds because they each advance an account of knowledge informed by a view of philosophy that the other side rejects. Yet they arrive at their philosophical positions by a similar route. As noted, the naturalists point to successful cases of experimental inquiry in behavioural science in a bid to clarify their method and subject-matter. From their analysis of exemplary cases, they formulate a fully general account of knowledge and reality. They stress the importance of testing beliefs through action—by carrying out experimental procedures and gauging their effects—and take the correlations among beliefs, actions and the order of events revealed

[8] See Santayana (1925).

through experimental inquiry to be the objects of legitimate scientific inquiry. The notions of method, truth and fact implied by this view are then used to evaluate, and ultimately reject, the logicists' position. The logicists proceed in the same way. They draw on views of method and subject-matter in paradigmatic cases of logical analysis in developing a general account of the nature of knowledge and reality, one that stresses the importance of *a priori* apprehension of abstract objects and relations. The conceptions of method, truth and reality informed by their account provides the grounds for their rejection of the naturalists' view. Each side is convinced of the strength of their philosophical position because it has a legitimate footing in exemplary cases. Yet the general views of justification, truth and reality derived from these special cases lack critical force when considered by the standards of the opposing view. Lacking a neutral perspective from which to adjudicate this conflict, the debate persists and even seems intractable.

As Santayana sees it, the risk in proceeding from cases of inquiry in the special sciences to a general philosophical account is that "each [resulting view] squints and overlooks half the facts and half the difficulties in its eagerness to find in some detail the key to the whole" (v). By generalizing views appropriate to a particular domain to all cases of inquiry regardless of subject-matter, the naturalists and the logicists assume (even if only by way of hypothesis) that the authority of the views of method and subject-matter they extrapolate are not anchored in the specific contexts in which they have come to light. Put otherwise, the naturalists and the logicists take an understanding of a certain type of inquiry to be credible independently of the questions, constraints and conditions that are specific to the field in which they operate. It is their claims to universality that force us to view the naturalists and the logicists as offering competing accounts of a common subject-matter—viz. the nature of knowledge and reality in general. This compels us to opt for one view and draw on it in dismissing the rival account or conclude that there is no neutral resolution of this conflict to be had.

It is at this point that the transcendental critic can be called on to play the role of honest broker. As Santayana pursues it, transcendental criticism puts the lie to the claims of exclusivity pressed by the logicists and the naturalists alike. Judicious application of the method of doubt reveals that neither the naturalists' nor the logicists' view is couched in a language that provides knowledge of reality that is free of presuppositions and interests. Were the naturalists and the logicists to purge their beliefs of subjective principles of interpretation and tendencies to feign objectivity, they would be left contemplating essences and devoid of any grounds for belief, true or false. Transcendental criticism makes clear that the only way either view gets off the ground is by embracing an ungrounded faith that the conditions required by their preferred method of inquiry obtain. Once the assumptions underlying their views are made clear, Santayana thinks we can view the logicists and the naturalists as engaged in different, albeit complementary, enterprises and find room for both projects in a broader philosophical account of knowledge and reality.

As noted, Santayana thinks transcendental criticism shows that the logicists do not study essences with an innocent eye.[9] Taken immediately, as objects of pure contemplation, essences and their connections all are on a par. None is inherently more basic, axiomatic, important or interesting than any other. Rather than trace the order of essences from the standpoint, say, of one's personal stream of consciousness or consider—as a poet might—which essences are evoked by others, the logicists study essences from the standpoint of what Santayana calls "discourse" (*SAF*, 120). Guided by the demands of a logical system, they focus on enduring meanings, relations of equivalence assumed in defining one term by means of others, the combinations of terms in propositions and the logical relations among propositions in gapless proofs. The logicists' method posits these elements as subject-matter that subsists independently of our apprehension of it. Absent terms and propositions with stable meanings and relations, Santayana observes, discourse would be impossible—"we could not say or think anything on any subject" (*SAF*, 114). Yet, as the logicists themselves admit, the assumption of a domain of objects in discourse is "impossible to prove or even defend by argument, since all argument presupposes it. It must be accepted as a rule of the game, if you think the game worth playing" (*SAF*, 114). From the standpoint of transcendental criticism, the logicists' views of the logical world and the methods by which it is known are so interwoven with one another that neither can justify the other. Nor can they be viewed as a finding of logical analysis itself. As presuppositions that are not susceptible to deeper justification, they constitute the logicists' faith.

Santayana thinks transcendental criticism similarly undermines the naturalists' claim to know nature as it is free of presuppositions. Rather than intuit essences in their immediacy or contemplate their eternal meanings and logical relations in discourse as the logicists do, the naturalists broach essences from the standpoint of an organism implicated in, and dependent upon, the environment in which it lives. On Santayana's account, natural knowledge is "curiosity" moved by the "insecurity and instinctive anxiety of the animal whose spirit it is" (*SAF*, 125). Prompted by unfulfilled needs and behavioural uncertainty in a precarious world, the empirical critic views essences with an eye to predicting and controlling events. This assumes, the transcendental critic reveals, not only a domain of stable meanings and logical relations, as in discourse, but also that there are "self-existing fact[s]"—facts not of the organism's making, broader than its experience and "open to description from the point of view of other events" (*SAF*, 182). Absent the assumption of a world in which events at one place and time are reliable signs of occurrences elsewhere, the inferences that justify the naturalists' beliefs about human beings, their capacities and their function in nature lose their authority. Yet this assumption is not a hypothesis verifiable by the "external pressure" of facts, since the very practice of venturing beliefs and testing them against the order of events—the very project of adapting beliefs to external pressures—assumes it (*SAF*, 185). As he puts it:

---

[9] See also Santayana (1911).

> In recognizing any appearance as a witness to substance and in admitting (or even in rejecting) the validity of such testimony, I have already made a substance of the appearance; and if I admit other phenomena as well, I have placed that substance in a world of substances having a substantial unity. (*SAF*, 185)

On Santayana's view that "external things exist, that I exist myself, and live more or less prosperously in the midst of things" (*SAF*, 106) is "identical with the claim to knowledge, and so fundamental that no evidence can be adduced for it which does not presuppose it" (*SAF*, 185). The naturalists' empirical defence of empirical criticism assumes that the world is such that this sort of justification is possible. This is not itself an empirical finding but rather a presupposition or animal faith.

From the point of view of Santayana's transcendental criticism, the naturalists and the logicists cannot be viewed as proffering rival theories about a common domain of independent facts. They are better seen as pursuing inquiry into distinct subject-matters, guided by questions, methods and interests informed by articles of animal faith. Instead of searching for evidence independent of these two perspectives in a bid to swing our allegiance toward one project to the exclusion of the other, Santayana looks "to retain the positive insight of each" view while "keeping it in its place" (viii). On his view, the conceptions of method and subject-matter advanced by the naturalists and the logicists are each sovereign in their own domain of inquiry but neither one regulates the entire field.

When it comes to discourse, Santayana considers the logicists to be on safe ground in claiming that logical analysis operates independently of the search for natural knowledge. The objects and relations disclosed in analysis are eternal, not contingent on the vagaries of the spatio-temporal order. Confined to the examination of conceivable possibilities, analysis has nothing to say about the natural world. Indeed, from the standpoint of pure discourse, the "existence of changing things or events in nature [is something] I may still deny or doubt or ignore" (*SAF*, 124). While logical inquiry is still motivated by animal interests—as all human behaviour is—it proceeds without regard for the practical imperatives that drive empirical criticism. In discourse, the concern to predict and control the environment is subordinate to the apprehension of eternal forms. Logical inquiry thus has a life of its own and is not merely instrumental to the adaptation of beliefs and behaviour to the natural order, as the naturalists would have it.

In the context of empirical criticism, however, Santayana thinks the naturalists are right to insist that the logicists' priorities be reversed. "[I]f discourse were always a pellucid apprehension of essential relations, its existence would be little noted" (*SAF*, 123). In empirical criticism, the methods for improving clarity, coherence, rigour, elegance and simplicity in logic (which the naturalists accept as a legitimate stage in inquiry) are put to use in meeting the demands of a system of symbols that facilitate the prediction and control of events. From the engaged perspective of empirical criticism, discourse is ancillary to the adaptation of beliefs and behaviour to the environment that animal life requires. In common sense this means mathematical logic is largely irrelevant to the formation and evaluation of beliefs and rightly disregarded. In advanced physical science, however, it proves a powerful and indispensable tool.[10]

It is important to recognize that in reconciling the logicists' and the naturalists' views by viewing discourse and empirical criticism as distinct but related pursuits, Santayana does not claim to be adjudicating the debate from a disinterested or absolute point of view. Consistent with the findings of his transcendental criticism, he accepts that there is no way to proceed in philosophy impartially and that this is no less true when reflecting on the nature and methods of philosophy itself. As he sees it, different philosophers offer "vistas [that] give glimpses of the same wood" (*SAF*, ix) but their transcendental logic—their tendencies to feign—"like language, is partly a free construction and partly a means of symbolising and harnessing in expression the existing diversities of things" (*SAF*, vi). While "some languages, given a man's constitution and habits, may seem more beautiful and convenient to him than others," Santayana cautions that "it is a foolish heat in a patriot to insist that only his native language is intelligible or right" (*SAF*, vi). Accordingly, he does not claim his views are rationally binding on the logicists or the naturalists. As he says:

> I do not ask any one to think in my terms if he prefers others. Let him clean better, if he can, the windows of his soul, that the variety and beauty of the prospect may spread more brightly before him. (*SAF*, vi–vii)

At the same time, however, Santayana claims to be articulating a sort of universal wisdom. Rather than appeal to technical concepts and findings drawn from specialized domains of inquiry—as the naturalists and logicists do—he draws on an "orthodoxy which the sentiment and practice of laymen maintain everywhere" (*SAF*, v). Guided by broad but informal notions of experience, inquiry, truth and meaning that he considers "well grounded," if "ill expressed" (v), he seeks to make explicit "principles to which [every critic] appeals" even when expressing doubts about his views (*SAF*, v). While acknowledging the contingency of his starting point and that his opinions are "formed under the fire of contemporary discussions" (*SAF*, viii), he claims only to "spread a feast of what everybody knows" (*SAF*, ix). For him, "exact science and the books of the learned are not necessary to establish my essential doctrine, nor can any of them claim a higher warrant than it has in itself: for it rests on public experience" (*SAF*, x). His philosophy is "justified, and has been justified in all ages and countries, by the facts before every man's eyes; and no great wit is requisite to discover it, only (what is rarer than wit) candour and courage" (*SAF*, x). Were he to write in a different time and place, he concedes, "my language and my borrowed knowledge would have been different" (*SAF*, x). Yet "under

---

[10] See Kerr-Lawson (1988).

whatever sky I had been born, since it is the same sky, I should have had the same philosophy" (*SAF*, x).

Conclusion

I have explained how Santayana squares his commitment to naturalism and his rejection of first philosophy with his pursuit of transcendental criticism and his reliance on the method of sceptical doubt. Rather than view empirical and transcendental criticism as rooted in contrary accounts of the human epistemic condition, Santayana pursues both as methods of criticism, recognizing the scope and limits of each and confining them to their proper domain. I have further argued that on his view the lesson of transcendental criticism is not merely negative. The point is not to realize that philosophy falls into place as a branch of natural science as the naturalists would have it. Focussing on Santayana's discussions of scepticism, logicism and naturalism, I have suggested that, for him, transcendental criticism provides the basis for a constructive reconciliation of the seemingly contradictory views traditionally associated with these labels. Stripped of their claims to an absolute, complete or exclusive philosophy, the insights gained from each of these partial perspectives can be granted and incorporated in a view of knowledge and reality that Santayana considers to be richer and more compelling than any one of them provides on its own.

References

Dewey, John. 1915. The Existence of the World as a Logical Problem. In *The Collected Works of John Dewey, 1882–1953 (2nd Release) Electronic Edition, The Middle Works*, ed. Jo Ann Boydston, vol. 8, 83–97. Carbondale: Southern Illinois University Press.

———. 1917. The Need for A Recovery of Philosophy. In *The Collected Works of John Dewey, 1882–1953 (2nd Release) Electronic Edition, The Middle Works*, ed. Jo Ann Boydston, vol. 10, 3–48. Carbondale: Southern Illinois University Press.

———. 1927. Half-Hearted Naturalism. In *The Collected Works of John Dewey, 1882–1953 (2nd Release) Electronic Edition, The Later Works*, ed. Jo Ann Boydston, vol. 3, 73–81. Carbondale: Southern Illinois University Press.

———. 1930a. From Absolutism to Experimentalism. In *The Collected Works of John Dewey, 1882–1953 (2nd Release) Electronic Edition, The Later Works*, ed. Jo Ann Boydston, vol. 5, 147–160. Carbondale: Southern Illinois University Press.

———. 1930b. Conduct and Experience. In *The Collected Works of John Dewey, 1882–1953 (2nd Release) Electronic Edition, The Later Works*, ed. Jo Ann Boydston, vol. 5, 218–235. Carbondale: Southern Illinois University Press.

Forster, Paul. 1994. Realism and the Critical Philosophy: Kant's Abstentions in the "Refutation of Idealism". *Idealistic Studies* 24 (1): 21–41.

———. 2007. Animal Faith or Natural Knowledge?: Why Dewey and Santayana Can't Agree About Philosophy. In *Under Any Sky: Contemporary Readings of George Santayana*, ed. M. Flamm and K. Skowroński, 44–61. Newcastle Upon Tyne: Cambridge Scholars Publishing.

———. 2014. Doing Epistemology Scientifically: Dewey versus Russell. *Cognitio: Revista de Filosofia* 15 (1): 73–88.
Frege, Gottlob. 1956. The Thought: A Logical Inquiry. *Mind* 65 (259): 289–311.
James, William. 1981. Principles of Psychology, vol. 1 and 2. In *The Works of William James, Electronic Edition, vols. 8 and 9*, ed. F. Burkhardt et al. Cambridge: Harvard University Press.
Kant, Immanuel. 2003. *The Critique of Pure Reason*. Translated by N. Kemp-Smith (2nd rev. ed.). New York: Palgrave Macmillan.
Kerr-Lawson, Angus. 1988. Turning Towards Santayana. *Overheard in Seville: Bulletin of the Santayana Society* No. 6 (Fall): 30–38.
McGinn, Marie. 1989. *Sense and Certainty: A Dissolution of Scepticism*. Oxford: Blackwell.
Russell, Bertrand. 1903. *The Principles of Mathematics*. Cambridge: Cambridge University Press.
———. 1997. *The Problems of Philosophy*. Oxford: Oxford University Press.
Santayana, George. 1911. Russell's Philosophical Essays. *The Journal of Philosophy, Psychology and Scientific Methods* 8 (3): 57–63.
———. 1915. Philosophical Heresy. *The Journal of Philosophy, Psychology and Scientific Methods* 12 (21): 561–568.
———. 1921. On My Friendly Critics. *The Journal of Philosophy, Psychology and Scientific Methods* 18 (26): 701–713.
——— 1923. *Scepticism and Animal Faith: Introduction to a System of Philosophy*. New York: Dover Publications, Inc. [1955 reprint].
———. 1925. Dewey's Naturalistic Metaphysics. *Journal of Philosophy, Psychology and Scientific Methods* 22 (25): 673–688.
Williams, Michael. 1986. Descartes and the Metaphysics of Doubt. In *Essays on Descartes' Meditations*, ed. A. Rorty, 117–140. Berkeley: University of California Press.

Santayana's Naturalism at the Junction of Epistemology and Ontology

Ángel M. Faerna

The very title of *Scepticism and Animal Faith* bills itself as an "introduction to a system of philosophy." Perhaps this is the first surprise of the book, for by the time Santayana published it, the practice of constructing "systems of philosophy" had fallen into decline for a variety of reasons. On the one hand, by then empirical science was itself furnishing us with ever more complete and synoptic views of the world, making those devised in the systems of the old philosophers seem like products of a purely speculative imagination, or sandcastles in the air. On the other, professionalization had led to the fragmentation of philosophical questions and methods as philosophers sought to carve out their own territory. This led to the separation of its subjects into independent branches or subdisciplines, each with its own interests and analytical tools, and to the abandonment of more general theories. However, as is well known, Santayana resisted all these changes: the increasing professionalization of philosophy was one of the very reasons why he left university, and, while he did not rule out the possibility that the sciences would one day produce a true "scientific system," he still saw it as a long way off.[1]

---

[1] "There is now a great ferment in natural and mathematical philosophy and the times seem ripe for a new system of nature.... I wish such scientific systems joy, ... but what exists to-day is so tentative, obscure, and confused by bad philosophy, that there is no knowing what parts may be sound and what parts merely personal and scatter-brained" (*SAF*, ix).

Á. M. Faerna (✉)
Universidad de Castilla-La Mancha, Toledo, Spain
e-mail: Angel.Faerna@uclm.es

The book's second surprise does not take long to materialize, as Santayana brings it to the reader's attention in the Preface. There he says that his system of philosophy "differs widely in spirit and pretensions from what usually goes by that name," for three fundamental reasons: (1) it does not set out to rectify "the old prejudices and workaday opinions of mankind," but rather to better articulate them; (2) it "is no system of the universe," but merely the result of "my personal observation of the world," that nobody else need share; and (3) it "is not metaphysical," not being "an attempt to determine matters of fact by means of logical or moral or rhetorical constructions" (*SAF*, v–vii). Taken together, these remarks cast a shadow of ambiguity over the whole "system" that is not easily lifted, because in a way they act as a disclaimer against possible objections to any of its theses. Given Santayana's modest ambitions, how ironic is it for him to call the book's contents a "system of philosophy"? Just how much *scepticism*, therefore, does the book itself harbor toward the task it sets out to achieve?

Alternatively, however, one could ignore the author's caveats and take the ideas expressed in the book at face value. After all, Santayana's Preface is merely a commentary on his own system of philosophy, not a part of it. The latter can therefore be considered in isolation, no matter whether it agrees or not with the ultimate meaning that Santayana himself intended to convey. Here, I should like to focus on one feature that the system outlined in *Scepticism and Animal Faith* has in common with other philosophical conceptions, by which I mean all those that fall within the family of "naturalism." This concept can be construed in a number of ways, so some clarifications are in order. Firstly, we might distinguish between an ontological and an epistemological version of naturalism—or, indeed, between an ontological naturalism and an epistemological one, for it is possible to hold either one without necessarily subscribing to the other. Ontological naturalism is a thesis about the sorts of entities that exist in an ultimate or fundamental sense—which would be only those of a physical nature, whether bodies, movements, processes, interactions, and so on—and is sometimes known as "materialism."[2] Epistemological naturalism, meanwhile, is a thesis about the status of our knowledge and likewise has two versions.

The first contends that our knowledge of the world we are a part of—or, in common philosophical parlance, our empirical knowledge—is self-sufficient and does not rest on some other deeper or more certain knowledge of another kind. As such, this form of epistemological naturalism is a rejoinder to those who believe that empirical knowledge must have some non-empirical guarantee or foundation, as well as to those who believe that we lack true

---

[2] In fact, that is the term Santayana prefers to use to describe his "cosmology or natural philosophy," which is how he designates what I call here "ontology." However, the word "matter" seems too strongly colored by one specific conception, both scientific and metaphysical, of nature itself. Santayana was aware of this and did not commit himself to any one conception in particular (*SAF*, vii–viii), yet he was unwilling to relinquish the term.

knowledge of the world to which we belong because they doubt the existence of such a guarantee. The naturalist, in turn, maintains that empirical knowledge neither has nor needs one.[3] Yet, another version of epistemological naturalism holds instead that the world we are part of is just as our empirical knowledge describes it; here the epistemological thesis leads directly to another ontological one of the same naturalistic character—there is no existence beyond that of empirically known physical entities—since to claim otherwise would be tantamount to denying that empirical knowledge can ever be sufficient.[4]

Now, "empirical knowledge" can be taken to mean either the kind of familiarity with the surrounding reality gained from our first-hand dealings with it, or the more rigorous and systematic knowledge provided by the various empirical sciences. So there would be a common sense epistemological naturalism and another of a scientistic variety, depending on which of these two notions of "empirical knowledge" is taken as a reference. From the standpoint of the first version of epistemological naturalism I have outlined above, the distinction affects only the relations of epistemic priority between common sense and science: scientific knowledge can be thought of as something akin to "organized common sense," a mere aid to manipulation and prediction, without overriding our common sense beliefs; or it could be felt that common sense beliefs can and should be supplanted by corresponding scientific claims where truth, and not just the most immediate practical interest, is really at stake. By contrast, from the second version's standpoint, the ramifications of opting for either science or common sense as the referent of the term "empirical knowledge" extend much further, for they bind us to wholly different ontologies: one composed of the obvious qualitative entities and relations we interact with on a daily basis and another where only the objects and processes postulated in scientific theories are accepted as real.

In my opinion, one of the merits of *Scepticism and Animal Faith* is that it addresses head-on all the lingering questions in the distinctions and alternatives I have just raised. So to this day it remains a text of great relevance to the discussion of philosophical naturalism, despite the time that has elapsed since its publication. What is more, examining the work through the lens of these distinctions and alternatives is also a good way to try to grasp the meaning of Santayana's system of philosophy and to weigh up its coherence and real significance. The broad ideas I sketch out below are intended to guide such an exercise in interpretation, an exercise that only a deep dive into the reasoning of *Scepticism and Animal Faith* could fully accomplish.

---

[3] This is the concept of naturalism used by Peter Strawson in Strawson (1985), a work that, unfortunately, failed to count Santayana among the philosophers studied (mainly Hume and Wittgenstein) despite his obvious parallels with both. The similarities and differences of Santayana's naturalism with this and other anti-sceptical approaches are discussed at length in Faerna (2007).

[4] Here "sufficient" does not mean "complete" or "definitive." In this kind of epistemological naturalism, the content of empirical knowledge can be modified, expanded, or amended endlessly, as long as this is based on *more or better empirical knowledge*.

One initial idea is that, although Santayana is a self-avowed "materialist" (or ontological naturalist), *Scepticism and Animal Faith* is no treatise on ontology, nor does its system rest on ontological assumptions of any kind. Instead, such materialism emerges from the book's own analysis of knowledge. In other words, and in keeping with my first distinction, conditions of an epistemological nature induce Santayana to subscribe to a naturalist ontology in his system. The question should then be, which of the two versions of epistemological naturalism that I have distinguished is the one that Santayana can best represent?

One of the epistemological theses most vigorously upheld in *Scepticism and Animal Faith* is that empirical knowledge can in no way be said to portray the world as it truly is, but that there is an inexplicable "leap" between what appears to the mind (or "spirit") and the mode of being of material things, which our knowledge cannot help but substitute by immaterial symbols.[5] Ontologically, "I am a physical being in the midst of nature, and my knowledge is a name for the effects which surrounding things have upon me.... For the naturalist [materialist] there is accordingly no paradox in the leap of knowledge other than the general marvel of material interaction and animal life" (*SAF*, 164–5). *Epistemologically*, however, all there is underpinning such an ontological self-description is a "faith *mediated by symbols*" (emphasis mine) that the images of my spirit are of existing things and will properly guide my action among them.

We must therefore reject the idea that Santayana's epistemological naturalism dovetails with the second version, that is, that the world itself is as portrayed by empirical knowledge; quite the contrary, his thesis is that our knowledge is forever doomed to fall short of its own ambitions.[6] In "animal faith," the word determining the whole meaning is "faith," which must be interpreted as an express denial of the possibility of a *justifiable* transition from the epistemological to the ontological thesis of naturalism. The qualification of this faith as "animal" is not in itself justifiable, as goes without saying, since it implies explaining it in terms—those of our organic life and the bodily "psyche" that animates it—that are unknown to us on the basis of the prevailing epistemological thesis. Here again, although the materialist's ontological description would be that the "spirit, with knowledge and all its other prerogatives, is intrinsically and altogether a function of animal life," such a description cannot be established as a fact of knowledge, since "it is not one that spirit could ever find of itself" (*SAF*, 166).

In reality, this means that "animal faith" is a hybrid expression from a logical point of view, for it combines an assertion that in Santayana's system is deemed demonstrable (insofar of course as his definitions of the four "realms of being" are acceptable) with another that the system itself holds to be an unverifiable assumption. This need not be fatal to the system's internal coherence, but it

---

[5] See especially chapters XI and XVIII. Santayana had already put forward this thesis much earlier, in *EGP*.

[6] Santayana's famous observation that "life is a succession of second bests" (*LGS*, 5:125) also applies to the human pursuit of truth.

does pose a serious interpretative challenge, which could be summarized as follows: from which point of view does Santayana "perceive" what the spirit will never be able to "find of itself"? In other words: only with a foothold in the truth of materialism can we discover that knowledge is in fact faith mediated by symbols, but at the same time, the truth of materialism is not something that the spirit, discursive reasoning, can attain by itself. Now, a system of philosophy is undeniably *discourse*, so how does the discourse in *Scepticism and Animal Faith* arrive at its findings?[7]

The chances of Santayana having overlooked this problem are slim, for he himself observes it in all the philosophers of the Modern tradition, from Descartes onwards, in the concluding chapter of *Scepticism and Animal Faith*. For example, on Hume he shrewdly remarks:

> Having explained how, perhaps, early man, or a hypothetical infant, might have reached his first glimmerings of knowledge that material things exist, or souls, or causes, we are supposed to have proved that no causes, no souls, and no material things can exist at all. We are not allowed to ask how, in that case, we have any evidence for the existence of early man, or of the hypothetical infant, or of any general characteristics of the human mind, and its tendencies to feign. (*SAF*, 295)

Admittedly, Santayana, unlike Hume, makes no claim to have *proven* the idea that knowledge is a function of animal life, but the matter of the "point of view" governing his system remains unsettled. In a nutshell: if, in Santayana's estimation, Descartes' philosophical system suffered from naivety in applying criticism to knowledge,[8] and Hume's from insincerity, in his own system there is an ambiguity issue, since in his discourse the ontological and epistemological perspectives are entangled in a way that is difficult for the reader to assess. For example, one is free to discard my initial interpretation and regard *Scepticism and Animal Faith* as a treatise on ontology, or that its discourse is at least built on certain ontological assumptions, and the problem would then disappear. But that does not seem to be Santayana's way of structuring the reasoning in his book, in which he claims to have "adopt[ed] the method of Descartes" (*SAF*, 292).

What is abundantly clear, sticking with the interpretation I am testing out here, is that Santayana's epistemological naturalism sidesteps the ontological dilemma of what today would be called the debate around "scientific realism." As I mentioned earlier, this is an inescapable conundrum for those who subscribe to the second version of epistemological naturalism, faced as they are

---

[7] The difficulty I wish to draw attention to relates directly to Santayana's distinction between the four realms of being: matter, essence, spirit, and truth. I have explored what for me are its most problematic aspects in Faerna 2014 (see esp. 54 ff.). The specific problem of perspective or "point of view" in Santayana's philosophy has been discussed in Faerna (2011).

[8] "Thinking is another name for discourse.... But discourse, no less than the existence of a self, needs to be posited, and the readiness with which a philosopher may do so yields only a candid confession of personal credulity, not the proof of anything" (*SAF*, 291).

with the choice between one or other of the interpretations of empirical knowledge—as a common-sense belief system or as a scientific description of the world—in their thesis that the world is as described by empirical knowledge. This is a particularly satisfying feature of Santayana's brand of naturalism, because who wouldn't rather dodge a problem than have to deal with it? Alas, Santayana does not provide such a neat answer to the question of the epistemic priority between common sense and science, which those anchored in the first version of epistemological naturalism have to grapple with.

As we have seen, neither the objects of science nor those of common sense can be identified with material things as they really are, since both types of objects are mere metaphors, essences posited by the spirit to describe something that, on the material plane, somehow affects the living organism. In that sense, some are no truer than others, if by "truth" we mean literal knowledge, or the direct intuition of those things and material facts. Now, taken as products of symbolic knowledge—in Santayana's view, the only one that does not render the very notion of knowledge absurd—the objects of science would appear to have epistemic priority over those of common sense, since they are more appropriate descriptions of what happens to the organism on the material plane. They are, as it were, better metaphors, because in them "the sensuous and rhetorical vesture of these notions is stripped off, and the dynamic relations of events, as found and posited by material exploration, are nakedly recorded" (*SAF*, 179). In conclusion, "the effort of knowledge is to discover what sort of world this disturbing world happens to be. Progress in knowledge lies open in various directions, now in the scope of its survey, now in its accuracy, now in its depth of local penetration. The ideal of knowledge is to become natural science" (*SAF*, 181).

However, while affirming this, Santayana also holds that "a sensation or a theory, no matter how arbitrary its terms (and all language is perfectly arbitrary), will be true of the object, if it expresses some true relation in which that object stands to the self, so that these terms are not misleading as signs, however poetical they may be as sounds or as pictures" (*SAF*, 180). This second idea apparently now places scientific and common sense constructs on an equal footing, in what could be considered an instrumentalist perspective on the epistemic value of both: as long as it is not "misleading as signs"—that is, so long as it avoids frustrating the action of the organism toward the intended object—any description is true in its own terms. The scale of the object seems to play a pivotal role here: "It is only things on the scale of the human senses and in the field of those instinctive reactions which sensation calls forth, that can be the primary objects of human knowledge" (*SAF*, 175). For this reason, "when the constitution of the objects which the animal encounters is out of scale with his organs, or quite heterogeneous from his possible images" (*SAF*, 175), both common sense and science resort to poetic imagination to construct their respective objects, which must nevertheless remain controlled by outer facts. Perhaps, then, what Santayana is getting at is that, as far as the "primary objects of human knowledge"—i.e., macroscopic bodies and their directly observable qualities—are concerned, science is nothing more than organized common sense, whereas, when it moves above or below the human scale, scientific theories are not unlike mythologies, just far more elaborate in their scope, accuracy, and depth of local penetration.

If we cast our minds back to the remark in the Preface where Santayana expresses his sympathy "with the old prejudices and workaday opinions of mankind," we may well think that these various characterizations do no more than try to reproduce the vague and not entirely coherent way the average person blends scientific and non-scientific descriptions into her beliefs, depending on whatever the occasion calls for—all the more so if, as it happens, the remark is also a rebuke to "the special schools of philosophy, each of which squints and overlooks half the facts and half the difficulties in its eagerness to find in some detail the key to the whole" (*SAF*, v). Then again, what may be sagacious as an observation about human psychology may be somewhat less than satisfactory within a "system of philosophy" if it detracts from its clarity or precision. The notion that the ideal of knowledge is to become natural science seems to be suggested by Santayana's ontological naturalism, because natural science, in stripping off its notions of "the sensuous and rhetorical vesture," comes closer to "the relations posited by material exploration." Instead, the idea that any description may be true in its own terms appears to be more in keeping with the perspective of an epistemological naturalism that sees no need to bolster our common-sense beliefs more firmly or deeply. Santayana's stance can therefore be construed alternatively as a defense of scientistic naturalism or as a naturalism of the Humean or Wittgensteinian persuasion,[9] depending on whether we are inclined to read *Scepticism and Animal Faith* ontologically or epistemologically.

One of the reasons my interpretation leans toward the second option is that it allows us to tease out an anti-sceptical argument from *Scepticism and Animal Faith* that deviates in important respects from the line taken by other philosophers who have also argued that our "natural beliefs" are self-sufficient (and obviously the scientistic naturalist cannot wield that sort of belief in their own support). On the one hand, Santayana's reasoning chimes with other better known arguments—specifically those of Hume and Wittgenstein—in condemning radical scepticism in terms that do not entail *demonstrating* its material falsity. On the other, however, he does not join them in invoking a supposed psychological or logical-linguistic impossibility of questioning our natural beliefs—in the external world, in the reality of the past, and so on and so

---

[9] In the sense Strawson indicates (see note 3 above). Although mentions of Hume in Santayana's work are relatively scarce, and none too enthusiastic, he did admit to a certain affinity with him: "I have a great esteem for both Berkeley and Hume.... As a man of the world and a historian [Hume] felt as I do.... He was a sceptic in official philosophy but a naturalist in his real convictions" (*LGS*, 8:426). Then in his autobiography he harks back to his years as a student at Harvard, noting: "I also studied Locke, Berkeley, and Hume under William James.... Hume was the one I least appreciated; yet [George Herbert] Palmer once said that I had Hume in the bones" (*PP*, 238).

forth—which makes Santayana's line of reasoning an original contribution to epistemological naturalism.[10]

According to the most widespread interpretation of Hume's position on scepticism, his claim was twofold: firstly, that there is no rational argument to counter the sceptical thesis that questions the existence of things outside the mind; and, secondly, that nature has implanted in our minds an irrepressible impulse to believe in such things.[11] In other words, radical scepticism is logically unbeatable, but psychologically impracticable. In Santayana's language, this would mean that discourse has not the arms to defeat the sceptic, but nor can we dispense with animal faith, so there is no possibility of the sceptic ever being able to persuade us. Well now, here we are conflating two planes that Santayana would keep strictly separate: the first is that of discourse, where we affirm or deny at will with no limitations other than those imposed on us by the relations of some thoughts with others, which determine whether we are persuaded by them or not; and the second is the beliefs with which we operate when, instead of speculating on thoughts and their relations, we move among the things found by our experience. "The attitude of the sceptic is not inconsistent; it is merely difficult, because it is hard for the greedy intellect to keep its cake without eating it" (*SAF*, 16). In other words, to Santayana radical scepticism is nothing other than a speculative movement of the spirit, which could not even have begun without first suppressing the impulses of our nature, and which halts as soon as some external necessity compels us to heed them again; whereupon Hume's twofold reply, far from persuading the sceptic, concedes the point entirely.

Meanwhile, Wittgenstein, again in one of the most widespread interpretations of his second philosophy, sought to rebut scepticism by showing that the mere enunciation of its claim violates the rules of usage of verbs such as "believe," "know," and "doubt." According to his theory that words only take on meaning within the language-games in which they are played, and that, when we justify beliefs, we are in a language-game that ends, not in certain unprovable truths, but in ways of acting,[12] propositions that affirm or presuppose the existence of material things, of my own body, or of the past, can be neither meaningfully denied nor even doubted, because our whole way of behaving invariably takes them for granted. Santayana could not have been aware of the attempts, later to become commonplace in philosophy, to steer clear of the sceptical challenge by resorting to some specific theory of meaning, but he does expressly rule out meeting such a challenge by calling upon a

---

[10] Here I can only very briefly introduce Santayana's argument and explain what distinguishes it from the anti-sceptical arguments of Wittgenstein and Hume. For a full exposition of this point, see Faerna (2007).

[11] "A faculty which nature has antecedently implanted in the mind, and render'd unavoidable" (Hume 1978, 183).

[12] "Giving grounds, however, justifying the evidence, comes to an end;—but the end is not certain propositions' striking us immediately as true, i.e. it is not a kind of *seeing* on our part; it is our *acting*, which lies at the bottom of the language-game" (Wittgenstein 1979, §204).

putative self-contradiction in the terms used by the sceptic to enunciate it. In his opinion, "the sceptic is not committed to the implications of other men's language; nor can he be convicted out of his own mouth by the names he is obliged to bestow on the details of his momentary vision" (*SAF*, 15). Perhaps nowadays we would insist on somewhat more precision in what is meant here by "implications," for even the sceptic's discourse demands logical coherence—indeed, logical coherence is all that sustains it—but Santayana's remark clearly heads off in another direction, pointing once again to the intrinsically speculative character of sceptical claims. There is no denying that the sceptic's discourse *is* discourse, otherwise there would be nothing to reply to, and what would then be self-contradictory is to try to show by some sophisticated theory that the discourse to which one is replying cannot be produced. Michael Williams has made a very similar point in recent times:

> The very fact that a theory contradicts something much more intuitively appealing than itself will always, in the long run, prevent it from carrying conviction. This is particularly clear when theories of meaning are invoked to deny intelligibility to sceptical claims. Our sense that we *do* understand the sceptic—well enough, for example, to understand how we might argue *against* him—will eventually wear down the credibility of theories that imply that we don't. (Williams 1996, 18)

Arguably, Wittgenstein's reasoning proves too much, while Hume's proves not enough, at least if we concede to Santayana that scepticism is a thesis that moves exclusively on the plane of discourse and is speculative through and through. Such a concession might be excessive if we were to extend it to the history of philosophical scepticism as a whole. Applied, however, to the kind of radical scepticism that Descartes placed at the heart of concerns about an appropriate reconstruction of empirical knowledge, it seems to fit the bill. Both arguments appeal to the way we do believe, or speak, or act, which for Santayana is nothing more than our animal faith at work; the sceptic's discourse in no way denies the existence of such faith, but, as Wittgenstein himself did not fail to see, one cannot check a piece of news by buying a second copy of the same newspaper (Wittgenstein 1981, §265).

In contrast, Santayana's argument in *Scepticism and Animal Faith* does not deprive the sceptic of her right to *speculatively suspend* the activity of animal faith—however psychologically impossible such a suspension may be to achieve—nor to formulate questions in discourse that expressly contradict our justification practices—since it is those very practices that the sceptic's questions undermine. What it does withhold, however, is her right to *answer* these questions with the *assertion* that we can know nothing about the physical world around us: "The critical attitude, when it refuses to rest at some point upon vulgar faith, inhibits all belief, denies all claims to knowledge, and becomes dishonest; *because it itself claims to know*" (*SAF*, 187, emphasis mine). In other words, the true result of a scepticism that maintained its discourse to the bitter end would not be the delegitimization of empirical knowledge, but the suspension of discourse itself as a means of affirming or denying anything. There is nothing new in the idea that the sceptic contradicts herself by holding what she herself asserts to be true, but it seems to me that Santayana makes the case for it in a novel and particularly cogent fashion, by first establishing the intrinsically speculative—and therefore *purely* discursive—nature of sceptical doubt. This, which ostensibly makes it indestructible against any assault from psychology or our effective linguistic practices, is in fact what makes it crumble of its own accord: the radical sceptic, in annulling the very possibility of discourse through her own criticism, unwittingly cancels retroactively, as it were, all earlier discourse that has led her there:

> Criticism is only an exercise of reflective fancy, on the plane of literary psychology, an after-image of that faith in nature which it denies; and in dwelling on criticism as if it were more than a subjective perspective or a play of logical optics, I should be renouncing all serious philosophy. (SAF, 187)[13]

If this anti-sceptical argument were to be taken as the axis of interpretation for the rest of the work, there could be no doubt that *Scepticism and Animal Faith* contains an elaborate defense of my so-called first version of epistemological naturalism, i.e., the contention that empirical knowledge neither has nor needs foundations and is self-sufficient. We would then have established what Santayana's book declares right from the title of the opening chapter: that "there is no first principle of criticism," and that any critical analysis of our empirical knowledge is "an after-image" of an earlier image in which the knower and the known are continuous parts of one and the same world. But, taken to its final conclusion, such an interpretation would ultimately compel us to cast aside the expression "animal faith" to refer to what brings about that earlier image, for it would no longer be an *image* at all, but the very *framework* within which the knowing-relation between the knowers and known objects takes place. Now, since we cannot simply do away with the notion of "animal faith" without twisting Santayana's intentions, we are bound to admit that this interpretation does not do justice to his entire system of philosophy; or, alternatively, that his system fails to unify its component parts into a truly coherent whole.

Even assuming that these interpretative difficulties finally prove that there is some crucial flaw in Santayana's philosophical system, I believe that *Scepticism and Animal Faith* would still be an enormously useful book for anyone

---

[13] I find it significant that Santayana uses the expression "intellectual suicide" in reference to the price of trying to "push scepticism as far as I logically can" (*SAF*, 10). Intellectual suicide literally is what a suspension of discourse amounts to, because "discourse" is nothing more than a synonym for "thinking." But suicide is not something you can come back from to tell the tale, and anyone who purports to do such a thing cannot be taken seriously. If this is, as I believe, the point that Santayana is making regarding radical scepticism, then *Scepticism and Animal Faith* could (also) be read as a brilliant piece of subtle philosophical mockery.

interested in philosophical naturalism. Let me close by mentioning two points in support of this claim.

The first point concerns the lesson that the naturalist can draw from these difficulties. It seems that a fully coherent epistemological naturalism has no choice but to equate the first version of its thesis with the second, i.e., it must be committed to the idea that if one holds that empirical knowledge needs no foundations, this also *means* holding that it is absolutely sufficient and that it really does describe the world of which we are a part. In simple terms, it must blur the boundaries between epistemology and ontology. Until this step is taken, the naturalist can never be completely freed from the web of sceptical challenge. Santayana was well aware of this, which is why his conclusions could not and would not be entirely anti-sceptical: "The scepticism I am defending is not meant to be merely provisional" (*SAF*, 49). In his opinion, showing that the sceptic's discourse disintegrates under its own critique did not imply that this speculative movement of the spirit should not be a mandatory apprenticeship for every true philosopher, since it reveals the dogmatic nature of any form of belief.[14] The naturalism that Santayana finally settles upon is a "compensatory dogma" that he merely considers "more credible" than other similarly dogmatic philosophies (*SAF*, 49). Conceding that the plane of discourse enjoys full autonomy serves to effectively reduce the sceptic to silence, but it also comes at a price: being able to only fill that silence with another discourse as far removed from its own object as any other "reflective fancy."

Santayana's choice is to not take that step and to try to marry the epistemological perspective to the ontological one, but without actually fusing them together. As we have seen, the notion of "animal faith" combines both outlooks—and similar could be said of that of "symbolic knowledge"—which makes his system of philosophy oscillate (or maybe hesitate) between one and the other. In this sense, his distinction between the four realms of being—and in particular, his definition of a "realm of truth"—acts as a buffer against any temptation to completely merge the two perspectives. This may be understandable as a way of safeguarding certain philosophical intuitions that Santayana considers inalienable, but it is paradoxical that he describes as "half-hearted" Dewey's version of naturalism, which *does* break down the barrier between the "world of nature" and the "world of experience" in order to reach a *full-fledged* naturalistic view.[15] The gist of the disagreement between Dewey and

---

[14] The metaphor from Wittgenstein's *Tractatus* about the ladder to be thrown away after having climbed it could well be applied here: the ladder is made of nonsense, but we need it to get "the right view." For parallels between Santayana and Wittgenstein's philosophies, see Hodges and Lachs (2000). However, as is clear from this exposition, my view is that there is a marked difference between Santayana's and Wittgenstein's treatment of scepticism; see my criticism of Hodges and Lachs on this point in Faerna (2007b).

[15] See Santayana (1989). Dewey pitted his theory against Santayana's in Dewey (1927), where he retorts by calling Santayana's naturalism "dislocated" and "broken-backed," and calls his own position "empirical naturalism, or naturalistic empiricism." For a comparison between the two philosophers' underlying philosophical conceptions on this issue, see Forster (2007).

Santayana is summarized in Dewey's contention that "a universe of experience is the precondition of a universe of discourse."[16] The way I see it, every naturalist should take a stand for or against this contention in order to find out what form her naturalism is going to take.

The second reason why I believe *Scepticism and Animal Faith* remains a very valuable book has to do with the lessons the sceptic can draw from it. A radical sceptic is unlikely to ever accept the terms in which a whole-hearted naturalist conveys her discourse. In a sense, the cost of jettisoning the distinction between "ontological" subject-matters and "epistemological" ones is to forgo a common vocabulary capable of persuading the sceptic that her tenets are untenable. To this dialectical aim, Santayana's approach seems to me superior to any other attempt made so far from naturalistic quarters.[17] All in all, Santayana may not be the most candid type of naturalist philosopher, but he certainly remains a most faithful ally of naturalism's philosophical task.

REFERENCES

Dewey, John. 1927. Half-hearted Naturalism. *Journal of Philosophy* 24 (3): 57–64.

———. 1991. *Logic: The Theory of Inquiry*. The Later Works of John Dewey 12: 1938, ed. Jo Ann Boydston. Carbondale and Edwardsville: Southern Illinois University Press.

Faerna, Ángel M. 2007a. Naturalism and Animal Faith: Santayana's Meta-Criticism of Scepticism. In *Under Any Sky: Contemporary Readings of George Santayana*, ed. Matthew C. Flamm and Krzysztof P. Skowroński, 62–75. New Castle: Cambridge Scholars Publishing.

———. 2007b. Instrucciones para arrojar una escalera: Wittgenstein y Santayana sobre el escepticismo. *Limbo, Boletín Internacional de Estudios sobre Santayana* 27: 55–69.

———. 2011. Santayana, o la ilusión de la mirada. In *Santayana: un pensador universal*, ed. José Beltrán, Manuel Garrido, and Sergio Sevilla, 125–138. Valencia: Prensas de la Universidad de Valencia.

———. 2014. Santayana's Descriptive Metaphysics and the 'Implied Being of Truth'. *Limbo, Boletín Internacional de Estudios sobre Santayana* 34: 47–60.

Forster, Paul. 2007. Animal Faith or Natural Knowledge? Why Dewey and Santayana Can't Agree About Philosophy. In *Under Any Sky: Contemporary Readings of George Santayana*, ed. Matthew C. Flamm and Krzysztof P. Skowroński, 45–61. New Castle: Cambridge Scholars Publishing.

---

[16] Dewey (1991, 74). It is most interesting that Dewey then clarifies that there is no contradiction in saying this *in the discourse*: "It *would* be a contradiction if I attempted to demonstrate by means of discourse, the existence of universes of experience. It is not a contradiction by means of discourse to *invite* the reader to have for himself that kind of an immediately experienced situation in which the presence of a situation as a universe of experience is seen to be the encompassing and regulating condition of all discourse" (Dewey 1991, 75). It is as if Dewey were guarding himself here against the same question I posed earlier regarding Santayana: "How does the discourse arrive at its findings?"

[17] Dewey's approach, on the other hand, relapses into the unconvincing strategy of denying meaning to the sceptic's discourse: "Discourse that is not controlled by reference to a situation is not discourse, but a meaningless jumble, just as a mass of pied type is not a font much less a sentence" (Dewey 1991, 74).

Hodges, Michael, and John Lachs. 2000. *Thinking in the Ruins: Wittgenstein and Santayana on Contingency*. Nashville: Vanderbilt University Press.

Hume, David. 1978. In *A Treatise of Human Nature*, ed. L.A. Selby-Bigge. Oxford: Clarendon Press.

Santayana, George. 1989. Dewey's Naturalistic Metaphysics. In *The Philosophy of John Dewey*, ed. Paul A. Schilpp and Lewis E. Hahn, 243–261. La Salle, IL: Open Court.

Strawson, Peter F. 1985. *Scepticism and Naturalism: Some Varieties*. Bristol: Methuen.

Williams, Michael. 1996. *Unnatural Doubts. Epistemological Realism and the Basis of Scepticism*. Princeton: Princeton University Press.

Wittgenstein, Ludwig. 1979. *Über Gewissheit / On Certainty*. Translated by D. Paul and G. E. M. Anscombe. Oxford: Basil Blackwell.

———. 1981. *Philosophical Investigations*. Translated by G. E. M. Anscombe. Oxford: Basil Blackwell.

Reconstruction from Ultimate Scepticism

Angus Kerr-Lawson

In the second half of *Scepticism and Animal Faith* (*SAF*), Santayana carries out his reconstruction of knowledge, which starts from the ultimate scepticism of "solipsism of the present moment" and finishes with his version of a minimal set of assumptions required for successful performance in the "field of action." He describes this reconstruction as an orderly compilation of those posits required by animal faith. Here is his stated goal:

> To consider what objects animal faith requires me to posit, and in what order; without for a moment forgetting that my assurance of their existence is only instinctive, and my description of their nature only symbolic. (*SAF*, 106)

If there is to be found in his discussion of epistemology an analogy to contemporary treatments of knowledge, it must be found in this second reconstructive half of *SAF*, rather than in the reductive part; the aims in the second half are partly similar—how might valid knowledge arise in the presence of powerful sceptical arguments? The arguments in the first half may better be seen as directed against classical theories of knowledge, like that of Descartes, which claim to discover some foundation of absolute truths, following a determined effort to drop any claims that cannot be proved. Descartes sought to establish certain and infallible knowledge, but today theorists of knowledge tend to avoid absolute claims and focus on reliable rather than infallible knowledge and on partial justifications rather than final proofs. They might accept without argument the negative conclusions Santayana draws about a foolproof

---

A. Kerr-Lawson (✉)
Department of Pure Mathematics, University of Waterloo, Waterloo, ON, Canada
e-mail: glenn.tiller@tamucc.edu

access to truth. In part due to the work of Charles Peirce, Santayana, and other pioneers, many have turned their attention away from the search for foundations and toward belief in probable knowledge. To the extent that an analogy may be found, this will be to Santayana's line of reasoning following the watershed of criticism. However, even the analogy here is severely limited; with Santayana, justification must in the end be provided by animal faith, which many would see as no justification at all.

As does Descartes, the outline of whose method he continues to follow, Santayana reverses the direction of his sceptical reduction in a reconstruction of knowledge, with the results of that reduction as the point of departure. As a quest for certainty, he sees his reduction as a success: we are certain that the essence intuited at any moment is what it is and not some other essence. Certain, yes; but empty of content. In this final sceptical stance, solipsism of the present moment, there is nothing other than uninterpreted intuitions. There is nothing in this certainty that can lead to knowledge, no foundational truth whose validity has been uncovered by the reduction, which could serve as the starting point for logical deduction. He has discarded any items of belief that might be tied to the intuitions of this solipsism, leaving no solid point of departure for a logical reconstruction. Something different is needed. He turns to animal faith and considers what objects must be posited and in what order, allowing persons to carry on effectively in the field of action. The justification given for belief here is merely that some posit is required in everyday activities.

In this positive second half of *SAF*, Santayana follows the "order of evidence" and works through a sequence of posits. The chief points appealed to in subsequent texts are found in the two chapters "Knowledge is Faith Mediated by Symbols" and "Belief in Substance." Much of this material coming prior to the introduction of substance is scarcely seen or mentioned elsewhere. His return from a comprehensive sceptical stance to a positive set of knowledge claims—chastened but solid—proceeds in two stages. In this second half of *SAF*, he works his way through various posits required by animal faith, leading to a revised notion of natural knowledge and the belief in substance. The second stage is deferred until his study of the realm of matter, where he formally announces his materialist conclusions; in his system, substance will be matter.

The development offered by Santayana in this reconstruction works its way up through a sequence of beliefs that he is prepared to accept: belief in identity, in memory, in discourse, and so on. This reconstruction continues Santayana's argument in *SAF* and works back from scepticism to a reconstituted notion of knowledge and belief. However, the early steps in this argument play almost no part in his other writings. He makes little appeal to his arguments involving identity, duration, demonstration, and experience in other works. Instead, his preferred approach to natural philosophy, presented on several occasions, starts instead with a general assertion of materialism as a hypothesis. For example, in the early pages of his *Apologia* in *PGS* he states that this is the basic premise of his thought. He works from a short assertion of a materialist principle taken as a hypothesis. This affirms little more than that we humans are within and a part of a material cosmos. What he does take from this reconstruction and appeals to frequently in other writings are his notions of knowledge and substance, as given in the later parts of *SAF*; these are assumed throughout the later writings. The special kind of scepticism he espouses is retained; we cannot have literal knowledge of things, but we find in us faith in their existence, and our successful interactions with these indicate that we have genuine knowledge of them. Thus a part of Santayana's reconstructive argument that is applied elsewhere deals with knowledge, substance, and the relation between the two.

As well, there is one other important theme that is picked up later. In the chapter "Doubts about Self-Consciousness," he argues that we have legitimate doubts about our existence as selves. Although we may be convinced that the belief we have in our self is confirmed by intuition, this is not the case. Pure intuition gives nothing other than a simple essence and yields no certainty other than that it is the essence that it is and not some other essence. Our enduring belief in ourselves as existences depends neither on logical deduction nor on intuitive certainty. It depends on our character as natural organisms and is the product of animal faith. The various issues that arise here are dealt with later in *Realms of Being*: in his study of matter he defines the psyche; and in his study of spirit in the last book he begins the pairing of psyche and spirit that underlies his entire discussion of mind.

Santayana's reconstructive argument in *SAF* leads to his analysis of knowledge and the introduction of substance. His attention throughout is directed at factual knowledge and not at *a priori* propositions, with simple perception as his chief example. He breaks with the tradition of assuming that *a priori* propositions like those of mathematics offer a suitable template for all assertions of knowledge. According to his definitions, claims to factual knowledge have a radically different structure from mathematical propositions and cannot be accommodated by the template they provide. In the chapter "Knowledge is Faith Mediated by Symbols," he asserts that we possess factual knowledge: a knowledge claim is an assertion that some thing or event exists and has a certain property. This thing or event is a "remote" substantial existence, in the sense that it is not open to direct intuition; and for this reason this cannot be literal knowledge. Factual knowledge is necessarily symbolic and non-literal.

In the reconstruction, Santayana continues to appeal to a sharp distinction between the content of intuition and the object of belief, except that he can now appeal to the notion of essence. At play in a claim to knowledge of fact are two essences: one is the content of intuition; and the second is the true essence of the object under scrutiny. Of course, those in the empiricist tradition are apt to be reluctant to countenance essences at all, and especially apt to dislike the second essence; this must be expected from those unwilling to speak directly of physical objects. This extreme parsimony leaves them with no recourse except to explain knowledge through the experienced first essence alone. It is Santayana's ardently held opinion that from this meagre resource no useful account of knowledge can arise. There will be some tie of the intuited essence to the true nature of the thing or event, and Santayana seizes on this, but there is no remotely plausible argument that intuition will reproduce the second essence.

Knowledge is faith, says Santayana, or more exactly it is faith mediated by symbols. While belief is acknowledged on all sides to be an essential ingredient of knowledge, few others are prepared to give it such prominence. He rejects the idea that belief is something that can be turned on or off depending on the accuracy of some description; animal faith is deeper and more visceral than this. If we claim to know some natural object, it is his view that our description of that object is bound to be imperfect in any case, and a second improved description will be better in the sense that it offers a more functional account of something whose existence is already believed. The change of description leaves the belief in effect and clarifies it, rather than serving as a reason for discarding the belief and dropping any claim to knowledge. This is not the standard accepted view of knowledge, where all is lost when a claimed conclusion turns out to be wrong. In his account, every knowledge claim is imperfect, and can always be improved. On this point, at least, his account is superior; for with the standard account it is awkward to deal with the commonplace truth that a knowledge claim can be improved.

A PRIORI KNOWLEDGE

One basic reason for Santayana's refusal to admit mathematical and logical theorems and the *a priori* is that, for him, every claim to knowledge is in part a claim of the existence of some object. In its full statement, a knowledge claim asserts the existence of some parcel of an existing substance such as matter (as believed through animal faith) that has certain properties (as defined by an essence); it is an assertion of existence, which in his system clearly rules out the theorems of logic and mathematics. These are essences, non-existent essences. In his opinion, the difference between factual knowledge and *a priori* "knowledge" is too large and too important for the latter to be included within his system as knowledge.

For Santayana, then, the assertion that seven is a prime number does not state a truth; we do not know that seven is a prime. This view is clearly at odds with customary usage, where the term "existence" is commonly applied to mathematical objects and "truth" is applied to mathematical theorems without demur. The cost of his way of recognizing the differences between the two cases is that our ordinary usage of the terms "truth" and "knowledge" is violated. On this point, at least, his goal of giving a philosophy grounded in common sense is not achieved. However, given that his chief interest is in factual knowledge, the kind of knowledge studied in physical science, he makes a good case that the template for knowledge that he offers is superior to one patterned on mathematical theorems.

Here is a second reason, closely tied to the first given above, for Santayana's refusal to consider mathematical and other *a priori* propositions as truths that might be known. In his account of knowledge, as given in *SAF*, what is known is always absent from intuition, although it is partially described or named: it is a "remote existence." With the proof of a proposition of logic or mathematics, however, there is no external posit, nothing that is remote from experience and subject to doubt. In principle, the entire formal proof can be followed through intuition. This too is a major difference, in his eyes.

I shall consider his general treatment of the *a priori* in terms of a mathematical example. Santayana was well aware of, and accepted, the contemporary conception of mathematics, which denies that its propositions are truths. Here is one of his statements of this doctrine in which he speaks of "the development of symbolic logic and of the doctrine that regards mathematics as hypothetical and not true; that is to say, not necessarily applicable to natural facts" (*PGS*, 498).

A mathematical proof is a development or elaboration with some hypotheses as starting point, following clearly defined rules. The entire proof is manifest, neither assuming nor yielding absent existences. He wants to see the full proof as a single complex essence, which is intuited rather than known, and offers this as his account of the *a priori*. Doubtless from his extensive readings, he was aware of the technical processes that have been invented for carrying out a process of this type, although he was certainly not in a position to follow the mathematical arguments.

Consider the Pythagorean Theorem and its synthetic proof using lines and triangles. What is commonly said to be a known truth has its justification in a formal proof, a proof from hypotheses. For Santayana, the statement of the theorem is an essence, and he envisages a complex essence which presents the entire proof and which justifies the theorem's acceptance, although not as an item of knowledge. The proof as presented in the context of mathematical logic is a finite sequence of individual sentences. Santayana treats propositions as essences, and, assuming some technical expertise, one can consider as an essence the sequence of the sentences in the demonstration. The proof and its conclusion can be represented as a large but clearly defined complex essence.[1] He sees this as an elaboration of essence, where the proof, the result, the logic used everything is open to intuition without external posits that generate doubt. According to his definitions, this does not qualify as knowledge.

Since he accepts the view that every claim to mathematical truth is a deduction from assumptions, he will naturally consider the Pythagorean Theorem as a deduction from hypotheses. It can be proved in Euclidean Geometry, but not in Projective Geometry since the proof (and even the statement of the theorem) requires metric properties. One must assume a particular setting for this proof. In Santayana's view, similar arguments will show that all mathematical and logical truths are proved through deductions from assumptions, usually unproved axioms. Every claim to demonstration in mathematics must

---

[1] Kurt Gödel was the first to carry out a similar procedure when he assigned integers constructively to all possible proofs in his famous incompleteness theorem. Modifications of this technique account for the widespread applications of computers to non-numerical problems of all sorts.

acknowledge that it is dependent on assumption. What might be seen as a knowledge claim is directed towards this complex essence. This stands in strong contrast to the object of a factual knowledge claim. One of his most serious attacks on the standard view, at least of empiricists and their followers, is that for them all knowledge claims have an idea as the object of knowledge. This is a blunder that persisted throughout modern philosophy, Santayana alleges; the object of a factual knowledge claim is the existing object posited in the claim. At least within his ontological system, there will be an object in the realm of matter.

As Santayana points out, this division of knowledge claims into two different kinds is well known and goes back at least as far as Locke's separation of knowledge of facts from knowledge of ideas. With Santayana's account of factual knowledge, the differences are so significant that *a priori* truths cannot be admitted as objects of knowledge. A factual claim assumes the existence of something not given, is always subject to doubt, and depends on animal faith; with *a priori* propositions, however, everything is given, nothing is subject to doubt apart from the possibility of error, and animal faith does not enter the picture. In my view, it would be preferable for him to retain the terms "knowledge" and "truth," in some qualified form. Thus he might better treat these propositions as formal truths that may be formally known. This would be a happier convention, although of course this is just a matter of definitions. From Santayana's perspective, the only crucial point here is that the distinction be maintained between the two kinds of knowledge, and this might better have been accomplished by allowing a second kind of knowledge, say formal knowledge. The introduction of new concepts through new definitions is, after all, at the heart of his discussion, and I think that one more would be helpful here. However this is very much a secondary point; for Santayana the major point is that his notion of factual knowledge not be corrupted, as it is by those many philosophers who take as their universal model of knowledge mathematical and logical theorems.

Factual Knowledge

Having eliminated *a priori* propositions as candidates for knowledge claims, so that these latter are exclusively claims to natural facts, Santayana is free to impose his own perspective on his concept of factual knowledge. He ties it closely to action and prefers examples tied closely to animal life and the pressing concerns of survival and prosperity in the cosmos. Presumably, it is from such claims that our present notion of knowledge evolved, and therefore these ought to be given extra weight. My example of knowledge follows Santayana's predisposition on this point: I envisage a person being chased by a grizzly bear and knowing this. The example is atypical, but it brings out some of the differences between Santayana's treatment of knowledge and more standard ones. Some of the atypical features of his notion of knowledge are seen more clearly in the setting of this example, whose properties stand in strong contrast to those of *a priori* examples and of those patterned on the *a priori* case. Nobody in the unfortunate situation of this example will see their belief as directed at an idea or a proposition; it is belief in a hostile and a looming, sharp-toothed existence. This stands in sharp contrast to the *a priori* case, where the object of knowledge is an essence. In the example, animal faith dominates over the other properties of knowledge and in particular is of greater importance than the description of the object of knowledge. Belief in the pursuer's existence is inescapable, but the person being pursued is not interested in working out an exact description of that predator, and little cares about improving a perhaps meagre understanding of that animal's type, size, colour, and ferocity.[2] The validity of a claim to knowledge here hangs on the correctness of a belief that there is indeed a ferocious animal in pursuit and not on a correct account of what kind of attacker it is. There is no more interest in verification than there is in improving the description; only the belief matters.

In sum, knowledge as understood by Santayana differs radically from the knowledge that would arise if based on a template tied to that of mathematical theorems; in these, belief in the correctness of a proof is notably unreliable, whereas for him belief is dominant. A claim to mathematical knowledge would illustrate a quite different approach to knowledge, as would a perspective on knowledge based on this prototype or template. According to knowledge in this sense, if one has a correct proof of the proposition, then one is justified in claiming to know it—one can believe it as a valid theorem. Whether or not it counts as knowledge and can be believed depends entirely on that correctness. The key point of this claim is that the proof is valid, that the description is correct. For the template favoured by Santayana, however, the crux of the matter is the presence of some external existence, perhaps a threat or an opportunity. Belief is more significant than description in his case, whereas it is not at all a determining factor of the truth of a mathematical theorem or a basic principle of logic.

It appears contrary to the most fundamental assumptions about knowledge to stress so strongly its reliance on belief. Of course, all parties recognize that belief is an essential part of knowledge; but Santayana gives it an unusual prominence and makes the description of the object known a strictly secondary feature, thus reversing the priorities commonly given to the properties of knowledge. This will prompt complaints and objections about this irregular facet of his account of knowledge. Not only is the description of the known object downplayed, but it is conceded in advance that the exact description of the object is not available for natural objects. Knowledge is going to be nonliteral, and so it completely fails to satisfy the common sense assumption that to know something one must possess an absolutely true description of that

---

[2] Although this point is not brought into his discussion here, Santayana argues elsewhere that in tense situations such as this the fleeing person will identify the bear with the essence he has hastily constructed in order to describe it. Or, perhaps without identifying the two, the description will be considered as the literal truth about the threatening animal.

thing. Knowledge, it appears, does not have to be true. Santayana presents his answers to these questions in some detail; he argues that unusual properties are forced on philosophers by the circumstances, much as they would prefer accounts more satisfactory to the logician in them. An important aspect of the defence he gives of his position is his tendency to go on the attack. His critics are unduly swayed by ways of thinking that are grounded on invalid empiricist dogma, or on techniques that are proper to transcendental idealism and of no authority outside that philosophy.

JUSTIFIED TRUE BELIEF

Frequently, Santayana says that knowledge is faith, as if it were faith without conditions. Here is one example, with my italics added: "All knowledge, *being faith* in an object posited and partially described, *is belief* in substance, in the etymological sense of this word" (*SAF*, 182). Thus knowledge is faith; it is belief. However, he makes it clear elsewhere that knowledge is more than this; it is accompanied by other properties, and in fact he endorses the customary view of knowledge as justified true belief. While he wishes to emphasize the importance of the faith, he retains the descriptive aspect of knowledge, and the need for some ground for that knowledge. When he says that knowledge is faith without further elaboration, he is at least, with a certain exaggeration, laying emphasis on his doctrine that animal faith is the most basic part of knowledge, and countering the more usual view that correct description is the dominant part. However, he does conform to the traditional view that knowledge is justified true belief, where the three properties are each necessary for knowledge and are jointly sufficient; in more recent years, some have argued that a fourth necessary condition is required to ensure the sufficiency, but there is nothing of this in his text. The fullest statement of this occurs in a three-page segment of *SAF* (179–181). First and certainly foremost, knowledge is belief or faith that is true in a special sense and is warranted by the manner in which the belief is generated.

> Knowledge is accordingly belief: belief in a world of events, and especially of those parts of it which are near the self, tempting or threatening it. This belief is native to animals, and precedes all deliberate use of intuitions as signs or descriptions of things; as I turn my head to see who is there, before I see who it is. (*SAF*, 179)

As he often does, Santayana notes that animals are party to belief as he understands it. This does not mean that all animals have genuine knowledge, due to the part that spirit has to play there. Again, he cannot resist saying or almost saying that knowledge is only belief; and again, the reader must recognize these insinuations as contrary to his reasoned view and an exaggeration. Characteristic of his view, then, is the precedence he assigns to belief. In making a claim to knowledge, one is claiming that something exists, and, as this passage suggests, one is calling on the fundamental naturalist assumption asserting the existence of a world of facts, things, and events. As seen above, he does not think of knowledge in the way one might know a mathematical proposition, where truth is the dominant characteristic and belief is largely irrelevant. Rather he gives as an example his knowing that there is a person behind him. It is a question of believing the material existence of an individual person. In his account, the awareness that a person is there precedes his turning to identify that person and attach descriptive content to that belief. The description of the thing on which we have faith is secondary to the faith itself. There are difficulties with this doctrine, some of which will be considered later.

Truth is a second characteristic of knowledge, but there are important qualifications here, touching on the kind of knowledge of the world that he thinks is accessible to animal life. By truth in this instance he cannot mean the objective literal truth about the object of knowledge, since this would contradict his sceptical position. Here he struggles a little to explain the part truth has to play in this three part characterization of knowledge.

> Furthermore, knowledge is true belief. It is such an enlightening of the self by intuitions arising there, that what the self imagines and asserts of the collateral thing, with which it wrestles in action, is actually true of that thing. Truth in such presumptions or conceptions does not imply adequacy, nor a pictorial identity between the essence in intuition and the constitution of the object. Discourse is a language, not a mirror. The images in sense are parts of discourse, not parts of nature; they are the babble of our innocent organs under the stimulus of things; but these spontaneous images, like the sounds of the voice, may acquire the function of names; they may become signs, if discourse is intelligent and can recapitulate its phases, for the things sought or encountered in the world. The truth which discourse can achieve is truth in its own terms, appropriate description; it is no incorporation or reproduction of the object in the mind. (*SAF*, 179)

In short, useful knowledge is accessible and reflects a true interaction of subject with object; but we cannot expect it to be a literally true representation of that object. Literal truth would signal an "identity between the essence in intuition and the constitution of the object," a "pictorial" identity; rather, the essences intuited can only be signs or symbols or names of external objects. Knowledge of material things is not true at all in the literal sense, but still merits the name "knowledge," inasmuch as it facilitates action and permits understanding. In fact, he says, useful knowledge about some thing would not be possible to someone who was swamped with the mass of literal truths about that thing. Thus in order for knowledge to be manageable and helpful, it must be what he calls "non-literal" or symbolic; and it is just this kind of knowledge that is accessible to us. In this passage he contends that such knowledge is in a sense true, although not true in the strong sense suggested by his notion of eternal truth.

His use of the notion of truth here is somewhat strained, and he rarely appeals to a notion of truth so much diluted in this way. Truth for him is the eternal, mind-independent ideal account of what was, is, and will be. As he clearly indicates, however, he is not thinking of the rigid eternal notion of truth in this particular case, but of "truth on its own terms, appropriate description." When he maintains that we do have knowledge of things, he is explicitly dealing with symbolic description and with non-literal knowledge. It is true, as he likes to say, in the sense that it truly reflects the effect on the observer of the object perceived, something that can be highly useful, but which can only be called true if these qualifications are noted.

This notion of non-literal knowledge, so crucial to his doctrine, might be questioned by his readers. It must be conceded, however, that he is addressing a question that arises for other accounts of knowledge; those who think that we have knowledge in the strong sense of absolute and literal truth about natural objects are making a sweeping claim about our access to the truth that is hard to justify and to believe. Some are led to back away from a strong notion of truth here; others weaken the part truth has to play in knowledge. Santayana upholds a concept of truth absolute and eternal, and in his response to those who find this metaphysical, he says that, no, truth for him is physical; it is the ideal record of all the happenings in the realm of matter. In fact, many of today's philosophers say less about truth and turn their attention to the question of justification. With this focus, the epistemologist can cope with the problem of the inaccessibility of absolute truth indirectly, by concentrating on this question. Justification may be better or worse, and does not have to yield a definitive affirmation of truth; the difficult tie between fallible knowledge and absolute truth might thus be avoided by steering away from truth altogether.

In the next passage, Santayana does not use the word "justified," and he certainly does not shower on that concept the attention given it today. This is his statement that there is a third necessary property of knowledge.

> Finally, knowledge is true belief grounded in experience, I mean, controlled by outer facts. It is not true by accident; it is not shot into the air on the chance that there may be something it may hit. It arises by a movement of the self sympathetic or responsive to surrounding beings, so that these beings become its intended objects, and at the same time an appropriate correspondence tends to be established between these objects and the beliefs generated under their influence. (*SAF*, 180)

In this brief passage, he describes a correspondence that must arise for there to be knowledge. Notable here is the absence of some account that would justify an observer in making a claim to knowledge, some argument for demonstrating a correspondence between the objects and the beliefs. For him, it is knowledge if there exists such a correspondence. This is not unreasonable, but he is ignoring what for many is the issue of first importance—the validation for some observer to a claim of knowledge; we see how radically his account differs from what most epistemologists consider basic to knowledge—that the correspondence is brought to light and shown to be real and valid.

As the dominant feature of knowledge, Santayana thus singles out faith and not justification. He is forthright in his treatment of the difficulty with truth and renounces any access to the literal truth about things and events. He admits a kind of functional knowledge and on this issue follows the pragmatists. Unlike them, however, he maintains the importance of retaining as one of his realms an eternal realm of absolute truth, which for him is a part of common sense discourse. He usually fits into his remarks a contrast between his notion of attainable symbolic or non-literal knowledge and the inaccessible literal knowledge seen as an "incorporation or reproduction of the object in the mind." Unwilling to revise his notion of absolute truth, he argues that knowledge must yield something less; even though the term "knowledge" remains appropriate; the ambition to acquire truth about natural objects in the objective literal sense is misguided.

Santayana's treatment of knowledge is unusual; but I find it plausible and wonder that others have not offered something similar. It is widely felt, in discussions of scepticism, that some way of averting it is called for; a complete nihilism is a dead end that is unhelpful to the philosopher. One way to look at Santayana's position (not without some distortion) sees the existence of things as unproven and doubtful, but even when we accept these through an appeal to animal faith our knowledge of the nature of those things is doubtful in a manner that is less histrionic and implausible. The knowledge we have of the true nature of those things, once we assume their existence, brings on doubts that carry genuine plausibility. This kind of scepticism, as described by Santayana, differs from the far-fetched claims that we are not animals situated in a natural cosmos, and informs his concept of a viable theory of knowledge.

References

Santayana, George. [1923] 1955. *Scepticism and Animal Faith: Introduction to a System of Philosophy*. New York: Dover Publications. Cited as *SAF*.

———. [1940] 1991. *The Philosophy of George Santayana*, ed. Paul Arthur Schilpp. Illinois: Open Court. Cited as *PGS*.

PART II

Ontology and Spirit

The Centrality of the Imagination in *Scepticism and Animal Faith*

Richard Marc Rubin

I start with two quotations from Santayana's later works. From *My Host the World*:

> Cultivate imagination, love it, give it endless forms, but do not let it deceive you. (*PP*, 427)

From the preface to *Realms of Being*:

> The imagination which eventually runs to fine art or religion is the same faculty which, under a more direct control of external events, yields vulgar perception. (*RB*, ix)

The first quotation, though written as he was turning eighty and published posthumously, is Santayana's report of a motto he decided to live by after undergoing the losses of his father, his friend Warwick Potter, and (as he saw it) his youth at the age of thirty—losses that brought about the change of heart

---

This chapter is based on two previous publications, listed in the references as Rubin 2018 and Rubin 2021. It incorporates passages that occur in those articles, but they have been reworked, extended, and in the case of the 2018 article revised to focus primarily on the book that is the subject of this volume.

R. M. Rubin (✉)
George Santayana Society, Saint Louis, MO, USA
e-mail: rmrubin@georgesantayanasociety.org

© The Author(s), under exclusive license to Springer Nature Switzerland AG 2024
M. A. Coleman, G. Tiller (eds.), *The Palgrave Companion to George Santayana's Scepticism and Animal Faith*, Palgrave Companions,
https://doi.org/10.1007/978-3-031-46367-9_11

he called his *metanoia*. This motto conveys the importance of the imagination in Santayana's life. The second quotation tells us, in a nutshell, the importance of the imagination in his philosophy. It appeared in the opening pages of the four-volume work that *Scepticism and Animal Faith* was an introduction to. The thread of the imagination weaves its way through *Scepticism* itself and the centrality of imagination there is a manifestation of a lifelong devotion.

The Imagination in Santayana's Life

The abiding influence of the imagination can be seen in how much of Santayana's writing is directed towards work that is overtly imaginative. His first published work was a book of poetry. His first philosophic work was on aesthetics and his second was on poetry and religion. He wrote three plays towards the start of his career and in his seventies published a best-selling novel. He died working on a translation of poems by Lorenzo de' Medici and left the manuscript of a movie scenario. His criticism includes analyses of such literary masters as Lucretius, Dante, Shakespeare, Goethe, Whitman, and Browning and also visual artists like Picasso and Sargent.

Yet the imagination held sway over Santayana's life long before he published anything, long before the metanoia when he was thirty. His father brought him from Avila, Spain, to Boston at the age of eight. He was placed with kindergartners for a year so that he might learn English. His father could not adjust to life in America and soon returned to Spain. Jorge, who was then newly called George, was not without friends, but he summed up his memory of life in America as a boy with the following:

> I know that my feelings in those years were intense, that I was solitary and unhappy, out of humour with everything that surrounded me, and attached only to a persistent dream life, fed on books of fiction, on architecture and on religion. (*PP*, 145)

So from his early years Santayana was drawn to the life of the imagination. The discomfort revealed in this passage lay at the core of Santayana's personality. In many ways, it guided his life. He continued:

> A certain backwardness, or unwilling acceptance of reality, characterises my whole life and philosophy, not indeed as a maxim but as a sentiment. (*PP*, 145)

In his teens, Santayana took it upon himself to go to a German Catholic Church, early on Sunday mornings before breakfast, where he found deeply moving the singing of hymns in unison by parishioners, mostly men. He preferred the "communal spirit of those people, devout and unspoiled" (*PP*, 160) to what he regarded as the bland, conventional, and bourgeois atmosphere of Unitarian services his family took him to later in the morning. Yet, even at this moment in his development, Santayana regarded the doctrines, traditions, and stories of the church as so many fables—as products of the imagination. Even then, he would not let the imagination deceive him: "I was at bottom a young realist; I knew I was dreaming, and so was awake" (*PP*, 167). Nevertheless, the dreams of the imagination were preferable to the world he lived in:

> According to my youthful heart, existence was profoundly ugly and wrong. The beautiful remained imaginary. My daily life had nothing to do with it. Reality meant a dull routine of getting up in the morning, walking to school, sitting there for five hours, walking home, eating not very palatable food, and going to bed again. (*PP*, 166)

To this he added:

> That the real was rotten and only the imaginary at all interesting seemed to me axiomatic. That was too sweeping; yet allowing for the rash generalisations of youth, it is still what I think. (*PP*, 167)

As he matured, George came to rely on humour, irony, and conviviality to take on the world that initially presented itself as alien. At Harvard, he was quite active socially. He performed in the Hasty Pudding revue and helped found the Harvard Lampoon. Even after his confrontation with the weight death places on life as he began his teaching career, the emerging philosopher "went on teaching and writing, drinking and travelling and making friends" (*PP*, 427). His continued determination to cultivate imagination came from a realization that there is "enthusiasm no less than resignation in an enlightened metanoia" (ibid.).

The mature Santayana was determined to find what in the world might make it as congenial as possible a place to contemplate both the fancies and the realities the imagination conjured up.

THE IMAGINATION IN SANTAYANA'S PHILOSOPHY

The double role of the imagination is explicitly specified in the second quotation at the start of this chapter—the one where Santayana said that "the same faculty" yields *both* "fine art or religion" and "vulgar perception." Albert William Levi raised the issue of these two aspects of the imagination in an essay that begins by saying, "The problem of the two imaginations haunts the development of Western epistemology" (Levi 1964, 188). By the two imaginations, Levi meant, on the one hand, the faculty that plays an essential role in all cognition and, on the other, the products of the "seething brains" of madmen, lovers, and poets.[1] To characterize the first he quoted Aristotle, who said of imagination, "It is not found without sensation or judgment without it" (*De Amina* 427^b; Levi 1964, 188). I'll call this essential faculty the *humdrum*

---

[1] The image is from *A Midsummer Night's Dream*. See further along in the paragraph.

imagination. To characterize the second Levi quoted Theseus's speech at the start of Act Five of *A Midsummer Night's Dream*, in which "the Lunatic, the Lover, and the Poet" are said to be "of imagination all compact." The madman sees devils everywhere, the lover sees Helen of Troy in an ordinary-looking woman, and the poet

> Doth glance from heaven to earth, from earth to heaven.
> And, as imagination bodies forth
> The forms of things unknown, the Poet's pen
> Turns them to shapes, and gives to airy nothing,
> A local habitation, and a name.
> (Levi 1964, 188; Shakespeare 5.1.1843–1847)

Levi used Kant to elucidate the difference between the two imaginations, seeing the first as predominant in *The Critique of Pure Reason* and the second in *The Critique of Judgment*. Santayana, it would be fair to say, endeavoured to bring the two together throughout his works—to emphasize the continuity between the humdrum imagination and that found in fine art. In an earlier essay (on which this chapter is partly based) I wrote that Santayana saw "the wide-ranging poetic imagination as an outgrowth of the imagination that infuses every moment of experience" (Rubin 2018). I now see that I had it backwards. Santayana regarded the poetic imagination as primary. In the preface to *Realms of Being*, after characterizing ordinary perception and the visions of fine art or religion as two products of the same faculty, Santayana, in the same paragraph, asserted this judgment boldly. He wrote:

> Poetic, creative, original fancy is not a secondary form of sensibility, but its first and only form. (*RB*, x)

He meant this remark to apply not just to moments of experience, but also to the growth of an individual and to the history of our species. We play with toys before we play with implements of work and war. Religious passion drives social organization. Dedication to a country or a cause is driven by the imagination. Clothing is not just protection, but decoration—an instrument of self-expression. Later in the paragraph, Santayana added:

> Fine art is thus older than servile labour, and the poetic quality of experience is more fundamental than its scientific value. (*RB*, x)

Furthermore, Santayana said that "existence"—and by that he meant lived existence paying attention to the world—"often reverts to play" (*RB*, x). Note that the word "reverts" suggests returning to an original state. This reversion is not avoidance of things that are of more worth. It is a recognition of where true worth lies. Santayana's preface continues until we reach a short sentence in which he embedded not just the high value of the imagination, but the importance of the realm of spirit in his philosophy:

> Facts for a living creature are only instruments; his play-life is his true life. (*RB*, xi)

The Imagination in *Scepticism and Animal Faith*

Bearing in mind the emphasis Santayana placed on the imagination, you can turn to almost any page in *Scepticism and Animal Faith* and find he has invoked the imagination, either explicitly or implicitly. The entire sceptical exercise of the first part of the book stretches the imagination to its limit. You are encouraged to pretend that all the things you cannot help believing in are fictitious. Later in the book when he gets to animal faith, Santayana acknowledges how compulsory those beliefs are. But in the sceptical phase, when at the ultimate moment of scepticism, when you imagine only you at the present moment exist—without a past, without other people or things, without events or surprises—Santayana then asks you to realize that you cannot even prove your own solitary existence. Surely, it is pushing the imagination to the extreme to go beyond Descartes and to doubt the doubter exists.

In going through this exercise, Santayana shows[2] how much imagination is involved in everyday perception and belief. The progress of the chapters that start *Scepticism and Animal Faith* is a gradual paring away of appearances from what they represent. Santayana used the term *datum* to refer to whatever holds the attention of consciousness at any particular moment. Datum, in this context, takes on its etymological meaning of something given. Data, to use the plural form, are what the mind receives. From what do data come? Most of animal life involves taking data to be coming from things and events in the world. But in the chapter "Ultimate Scepticism," Santayana finds something odd about this:

> The animal mind treats its data as facts, or as signs of facts, but the animal mind is full of the rashest presumptions, positing time, change, a particular station in the midst of events yielding a particular perspective of those events, and the flux of all nature precipitating that experience at that place. (*SAF*, 34)

The commonplace assumptions of everyday life are imaginative conjectures. Here Santayana characterizes the humdrum imagination as something rash, as though it has something deeply akin to the wildest fantasies. His point was to distinguish the datum from the existence it purports to represent. His argument is leading to the conclusion that the datum itself does not exist. As he put it:

> The datum is a pure image; it is essentially illusory and unsubstantial, however thunderous its sound or keen its edge, or however normal and significant its presence may be. (*SAF*, 34)

---

[2] My usual practice, when reporting about a historical figure, is to use the past tense. Here I adopt the present tense to convey both the chapter-to-chapter progression of *Scepticism and Animal Faith* and the sense that Santayana is still talking to us.

Calling it "unsubstantial" is a denial that it exists. The next chapter, "Nothing Given Exists," makes this certain. In this chapter, Santayana says he is using the word existence "to designate such being as is in flux, determined by external relations, and jostled by irrelevant events" (*SAF*, 42). The key attribute of existence is change. What sort of being—a term that for Santayana is wider in meaning than existence—does not change? You might think of numbers or colours as examples of things that don't change, but the complex image present to the mind at any moment—whether it represents something actual or something the mind invents—is also an unchanging datum, even though at the next moment it is replaced by another.

Santayana uses the word "intuition" to refer to the momentary reception of a datum. He is at pains to distinguish intuitions, which do exist, from data, which do not. He thinks it incumbent on him to explain how he is using the terms existence and intuition. In spelling out what he means by existence, Santayana specified intuitions as one of two kinds of existence. This distinction is fundamental in Santayana's philosophy. It is the distinction between the realm of spirit and the realm of matter. He wrote:

> I therefore propose to use the word existence (in a way consonant, on the whole, with ordinary usage) to designate not data of intuition but facts or events believed to occur in nature. These facts or events will include, *first*, intuitions themselves, or instances of consciousness, like pains and pleasures and all remembered experiences and mental discourse; and *second*, physical things and events, having a transcendent relation to the data of intuition which, in belief, may be used as signs for them. (*SAF*, 47)

The non-existence of data is critical to making the distinction between truth and falsehood. Suppose the opposite were true: that to appear to some conscious mind is enough (or even required) to make something exist. Santayana argues that the assumption that existence consists in being present to intuition leads to a *reductio ad absurdum*. This assumption would undermine both intuition and even existence itself. If that weren't enough, it would make imagination and fantasy impossible:

> Since presence to intuition would be sufficient for existence, everything mentionable would exist without question, the non-existent could never be thought of, to deny anything (if I knew what I was denying) would be impossible, and there would be no such thing as fancy, hallucination, illusion, or error. (*SAF*, 46–47)

I have skipped over the part of Santayana's *reductio* where he argues that his initial assumption leads to a denial of both intuition and existence,[3] because

---

[3] Santayana's initial assumption—the one he wants to prove false—is that "presence is existence." That phrasing is ambiguous and the passage quoted above shows the unacceptability of saying presence is *sufficient* for existence, meaning there could be unthought-of existences that are never present. But earlier in the same paragraph he wrote: "If presence to intuition were necessary to

here I wish to emphasize that imagination is impossible if anything that comes into the mind automatically exists. The complete argument, however, is fundamental to Santayana's overall direction. It makes the case for the title of his chapter. In showing that appearances are neither necessary nor sufficient for existence, he makes the case for what follows from that, namely that something can be an appearance only if it does not exist.

The Freedom of Imagination

Existence means being in flux. One quality replaces another. One thing comes into existence while another goes out. It takes energy and movement. The recognition that the data of intuition don't exist and are therefore independent of any worldly event is a discovery that gives the imagination its freedom.

> If nothing that appears exists, anything may appear without the labour and expense of existing; and fancy is invited to range innocently—fancies not murdering other fancies as an existence must murder other existences. While life lasts, the field is thus cleared for innocent poetry and infinite hypothesis, without suffering the judgement to be deceived nor the heart enslaved. (*SAF*, 55)

Santayana's sceptical excursion moves towards its conclusion in the chapter "The Discovery of Essence." There he repeated this observation with even greater force. Essence is, of course, one of the four realms of being that *Scepticism and Animal Faith* introduces. But Santayana has barely mentioned the term in the course of his sceptical journey. He is using scepticism as a way of approaching essence. An essence is any idea, image, meme, sensory input, or feeling. As each essence is what it is by definition,[4] the realm of essence could be thought of as the realm of meaning. An essence is a unit of meaning. The thrust of "The Discovery of Essence" chapter is to show that the data of intu-

---

existence, intuition itself would not exist; that is, no other intuition would be right in positing it." Another way of thinking about this is: if another intuition were needed to make an intuition exist, the first intuition would no longer be an intuition but a datum for some other intuition. And what then would make the other intuition exist? But if intuition is necessary for existence and there are no intuitions, then existence is impossible. So, the assumption "presence is existence" meant presence is equivalent to existence—both necessary and sufficient for it. Santayana has shown that appearance is neither necessary nor sufficient for existence. Sufficiency, to take one side of the argument, means that simply appearing implies that a thing exists. The only way that implication can be false is when something is an appearance but does not exist. It follows, then, that the refutation of sufficiency means that being an appearance means not existing. This conclusion is what the title of the chapter asserts. This conclusion has wide radiations in Santayana's philosophy. For example, it leads to a refutation of idealism, when idealism means that ideas are fundamental components of existence. Because ideas are present to the mind in thought, they cannot exist.

[4] Two quotations affirm that a definition determines an essence: "Each essence is certainly not two contradictory essences at once; but the definitions which render each precisely what it is lie in the realm of essence, an infinite continuum of discrete forms" (*SAF*, 97); "The being of each essence is entirely exhausted by its definition; I do not mean its definition in words, but the character which distinguishes it from any other essence" (*RB*, 18).

ition are essences. Each datum is eternal, unchanging, and non-existent, which is precisely what an essence is. Essences do double duty in Santayana's philosophy. In addition to being what comes to us as an appearance, essences are also exemplified by the physical world (Santayana's realm of matter). This exemplification is what makes it possible for us to know anything. Essences thus are the discrete units of both physical being and of awareness, of matter and of spirit. For the moment, the concern is discovering that the datum before the sceptic's mind is an eternal essence.

Remember the "solitary and unhappy" boy who was "attached only to a persistent dream life." Is it any wonder that Santayana began his exposition of his ontology with the solitary musings of a sceptic seeking to find some solid foundation for his beliefs by doubting everything until he finds something he cannot deny? This process approaches its end when the sceptic reaches the point of thinking only he exists and that the spectacle presented to his mind of history, of other people, and of places is a fabrication of his imagination. This spectacle with all its weight of nostalgia and regret, of hope and fear, may well be an illusion. Santayana says there are three ways to overcome this concern. The first is to die, so that the possible illusion disappears completely and is followed by no other. The second is to replace one spectacle or panorama with another, so that you have the illusion of movement—of progress or regression—or correction of an error. This replacement is how life normally proceeds because we take what appears to us to stand for actual things and events that affect us both overtly and inconspicuously. The third possibility is the great discovery that you can entertain the panorama before you without any regard to whether it represents anything factual. Bear in mind the adolescent Santayana who found existence "profoundly ugly and wrong" as we read the following:

> Deceit itself becomes entertainment, and every illusion but so much added acquaintance with the realm of form. For the unintelligible accident of existence will cease to appear to lurk in this manifest being, weighting and crowding it, and threatening it with being swallowed up by nondescript neighbours. It will appear dwelling in its own world, and shining by its own light, however brief may be my glimpse of it: for no date will be written on it, no frame of full or of empty time will shut it in; nothing in it will be addressed to me, nor suggestive of any spectator. It will seem an event in no world, an incident in no experience. The quality of it will have ceased to exist: it will be merely the quality which it inherently, logically, and inalienably is. It will be an ESSENCE. (*SAF*, 73–74)

At the moment when you can indulge in the imagination without any care that what it presents is found in any world, Santayana utters the magic word.

The Magnitude of the Imagination

The moment at which doubt becomes extreme is thus the moment when the imagination becomes the freest. Think again of the unhappy boy who was "attached only to a persistent dream life." To see the magnitude of the influence the imagination had on Santayana, we need only look at his description of it in *Interpretations of Poetry and Religion*:

> We have memory and we have certain powers of synthesis, abstraction, reproduction, invention,—in a word, we have understanding. But this faculty of understanding has hardly begun its work of deciphering the hieroglyphics of sense and framing an idea of reality, when it is crossed by another faculty—the imagination. Perceptions do not remain in the mind, as would be suggested by the trite simile of the seal and the wax, passive and changeless, until time wear off their sharp edges and make them fade. No, perceptions fall into the brain rather as seeds into a furrowed field or even as sparks into a keg of powder. Each image breeds a hundred more, sometimes slowly and subterraneously, sometimes (when a passionate train is started) with a sudden burst of fancy. (*IPR*, 7–8).

The Imagination and Knowledge

This celebratory description appears to regard the imagination as a faculty that takes us to places remote from ordinary understanding of the world and other people. It is the same wonder at the unending range of timeless possibilities that Santayana celebrates when his sceptic is led to the discovery of essence. But ordinary understanding is impossible without the imagination. Santayana has led us to the moment when imagination realizes that its scope is unlimited. Just at this moment his discourse pauses to consider where it has been and where it will go to. This pause is in the chapter "The Watershed of Criticism." It is where scepticism is held at bay and animal faith comes in. After the purgative exercise of extreme doubt, the possibility of knowledge emerges. Santayana sees a continuum between the unfettered imagination and the humdrum imagination needed to deal with the everyday.

Essences do not exist, so the imagination is free to explore them, entertain them, or indulge in them without being concerned about whether they are actual. Reality,[5] however, intrudes upon this reverie and forces the individual to believe that certain things do exist and, therefore, exemplify the essences that make up the content of perception. To these unavoidable beliefs in things like food, shelter, dangers, and enticements, Santayana gives the name *animal faith*. The physical things that are objects of these beliefs make up what Santayana called the realm of matter. To the consciousness that has those beliefs

---

[5] At this moment I am using "reality" as a synonym for existence, in Santayana's restricted sense of being in flux, which is to say, in the world and excluding essence. Although Santayana used the term ambiguously, he wrote, "What is reality? As I should like to use the term, reality is being of any sort" (*SAF*, 34). In this sense, essences also have reality.

and an imagination that is free to stray from them, Santayana gives the name of spirit. Spirit and matter are two dimensions of existence. They are not separate dimensions. A conscious intuition, which is a moment of spirit, and the corresponding bodily events in the sense organs, muscles, nerves, and brain (which Santayana gathers together under the term *the psyche*) can be regarded as different aspects of the same event. The essences that correspond to what happens in either existing realm constitute the realm of truth.

Animal faith does not abandon the imagination. It merely tames it. Santayana's epistemology breaks down into two parts: external observation and the imaginative reconstruction of what goes on in another mind. The latter he calls literary psychology. But the imagination comes into play not just when we understand other people or when we imagine what babies or animals are thinking. Even the most scientific investigation demands that the inquirer develop an imaginative sympathy with how things work in order to arrive at genuine understanding. Organizing data, developing hypotheses, designing experiments, and interpreting results all require imaginative construction.

IMAGINATION AND OTHER MINDS

Although the imagination plays a role in all knowing, this role is first apparent in the case of literary psychology. Santayana distinguishes scientific from literary psychology as follows:

> Scientific psychology is a part of physics, or the study of nature; it is the record of how animals act. Literary psychology is the art of imagining how they feel and think. Yet this art and that science are practised together, because one characteristic habit of man, namely speech, yields the chief terms in which he can express his thoughts and feelings. Still it is not the words, any more than the action and attitude which accompany them, that are his *understanding* of the words, or his *sense* of his attitude and action. These can evidently be apprehended only dramatically, by imitative sympathy; so that literary psychology, however far scientific psychology may push it back, always remains in possession of the moral field. (*SAF*, 252)

The introduction here of the moral sphere indicates that it is through the imagination that we are able to discern the life of spirit:

> When a man believes in another man's thoughts and feelings, his faith is moral, not animal. Such a spiritual dimension in the substances on which he is reacting can be revealed to him only by dramatic imagination. (*SAF*, 221)

This identification of the moral field with the spiritual dimension may seem anomalous to those who read a work like *Platonism and the Spiritual Life* as separating morality from spirituality. But what is important here is that discernment of spirit is fundamentally an imaginative process that forms a key part of Santayana's epistemology. Knowledge that comes primarily from observation may be accurate as far as it goes. It is always based on mental symbols—the contents of our perceptions and calculations—that are not the same as and, for all we know, do not resemble the things they represent, however accurately, and so observational knowledge is only approximate. But in imagining another mind, when we get it right, the ideas that we use to represent the ideas of the other or the feelings we have when we are accurately empathetic are identical to those experienced by the other person:

> Knowledge of discourse in other people, or of myself at other times, is what I call literary psychology. It is, or may be, in its texture, the most literal and adequate sort of knowledge of which a mind is capable. (*SAF*, 173–174)

IMAGINATION IN KNOWLEDGE OF THINGS

The distinction between scientific and literary psychology is the epistemological parallel of Santayana's ontological distinction between matter and spirit. Notice that both methods are needed and are directed towards the same object: conscious experience. The strength of imagination as a tool of knowledge extends beyond the discernment of mental life. In the passage where he distinguishes the two kinds of psychology, Santayana regarded the imaginative approach to knowledge as different from the scientific approach. The scientific approach is rooted in our common-sense perceptions from a standpoint outside the object. Perception depends upon memory. In the chapter called "The Cognitive Claims of Memory," Santayana asserts that without memory "intuition regards essence only" (*SAF*, 150). In order to have knowledge of the world, intuition must be both "directed by memory on the past" and "by animal faith on the future or external things" (ibid.). Implicit in this observation is that at any moment when intuition is directed upon existence intuition must fuse both immediate memory and expectation of intuitions that just occurred and are about to occur with the long-term memory of the past and anticipation of the future which gives context to the life of the creature undergoing the experience. Santayana makes this point later in the chapter when he writes, "The immediate past is continuous with the present" (*SAF*, 160), but his initial discussion of memory focuses on long-term memory as its model. Santayana is careful to distinguish between memory in which past experience is recalled with the sense that it is definitely over and the vivid sort of memory in which it seems as if the experience is relived. The one helps place current experience in context whereas the other is a form of fantasy:

> If the reversion to the past seems complete, it is not because the facts are remembered accurately, but because some subtle influence fills me with a sentiment wholly foreign to my present circumstances, and redolent of a remote past; and that dramatic shift seems to lift all the details of the picture out of the perspective of memory into the foreground of the present. It is the fancy that comes forward, producing a waking dream, not the memory that sinks back into an old experience. (*SAF*, 153)

Memory proper is the faculty in which the past is weighed and judged from a perspective that is impossible in the moment it originally occurred:

> Memory has fundamentally the same function as history and science—to review things more intelligently than they were ever viewed. (*SAF*, 157)

The distinction of memory from fancy is similar to the distinction between literary and scientific psychology. It is as if perception of the world is one thing and the imagination is another. But the difference is one of belief and direction, not of process. Santayana observes that it seems somewhat paradoxical that memory is always a reconstruction of past experience, yet that is not what memory is usually about. He tells us:

> It seems natural to say that a man may remember his own *experience*, and can remember nothing else; and yet it is not his *experience* that he commonly remembers at all, but the usual object of his memory is the object of his former experience, the events or the situation in which his earlier experience occurred. The object of a man's memory is most often not the experience itself. (*SAF*, 158; italics Santayana's)

The result is that:

> When I remember I do not *look* at my past experience, any more than when I think of a friend's misfortunes I look at his thoughts. I imagine them; or rather I imagine something of my own manufacture, as if I were writing a novel, and I attribute this intuited experience to myself in the past, or to the other person. (*SAF*, 158)

So, memory is like writing a novel! Santayana reemphasizes this point on the next page:

> There is a great difference conventionally between memory and fancy, between history and fiction, and the two things diverge widely in their physical significance, one regarding events in nature and the other imaginary scenes; nevertheless psychologically they are clearly akin. It is only by an ulterior control that we can distinguish which sort of fancy is memory and which sort of fiction is historical. (*SAF*, 159)

Memory is a subspecies of fancy and history a subspecies of fiction. In "The Watershed of Criticism," just as Santayana starts to leave the contemplation of essence for the discovery of nature and spirit, Santayana stipulates the importance of the imagination in learning about the world. He describes how our knowledge grows through repeated observations. But comprehending the world comes not just from the gathering of facts, but by creatively assimilating observations into a picture that conveys a feeling for the way nature works. He presents us an image borrowed from Schopenhauer:[6]

> Signs identify their objects for discourse, and show us where to look for their undiscovered qualities. Further signs, catching other aspects of the same object, may help me to lay siege to it from all sides; but signs will never lead me into the citadel, and if its inner chambers are ever opened to me, it must be through sympathetic imagination. (*SAF*, 106)

There are several things worth noting in this passage. The first is that you build knowledge of objects by repeated observations (laying siege from all sides). This is the beginning of both everyday common-sense knowing and also—when observation is controlled and measured—of scientific investigation. The second thing is that observation alone is not enough. You assemble your observations in your imagination and then make a sympathetic leap to imagine what the object in itself might be—what it is apart from your observations. The result is that you start to have a feel for the way things are. The third thing is that the imagination we bring to nature is the same sort of imagination we use in understanding other people. To emphasize the point, Santayana adds that when the object is "a sympathetic mind" our knowledge will be "as complete and adequate as knowledge can possibly be" because "the given essence will be the essence of the object meant" (*SAF*, 107). Yet it is not just understanding others, but grasping the intricacies of anything, that requires imaginative penetration. Moreover, it is *sympathetic* imagination. You must feel the way nature moves from the inside. It is what Einstein must have meant when he said his aim was to learn the secrets of the "Old One." A baseball outfielder leaping for a fly ball doesn't calculate the angle and curve of the ball's flight as a precision instrument might, but acquires an intuitive feeling for the ball's movement. Yet it is not only magical achievements in sports, grand scientific insights, painstakingly wrought philosophic systems, or the comprehensive visions of great art and literature that reveal the imagination at work. Every moment of experience—every perception, memory, and expectation—is an imaginative, which is to say creative, act. Santayana, rather than fret about the gap between the humdrum moments of imagination and the great ones, takes ordinary moments as cousins of the unencumbered moments that lead to the great ones.

Philosophy and the Imagination

That poetic fancy is the "first and only form of sensibility" (see "The Imagination in Santayana's Philosophy," above) is borne out in the pages of *Scepticism and Faith*. This idea carries forward into the four volumes that are its sequel. In

---

[6] From *The World as Will and Representation*: "A way *from within* stands open to us to that real nature of things to which we cannot penetrate *from without*. It is, so to speak, a subterranean passage, a secret alliance, which, as if by treachery, places us all at once in the fortress that could not be taken by attack from without" (Schopenhauer [1819], 2:195).

Realms of Being the imagination continues to play a role in divining both nature and mind. In *The Realm of Matter*, for example, we read, "The study of nature is the most picturesque of studies, and full of joy for the innocent mind" (*RB*, 233). In *The Realm of Truth*, dramatic and moral truths are truths of spirit. In dramatic truth, especially, the life spirit lives in the bodies necessary for its existence are often conveyed by ignoring facts or inventing imaginary circumstances. Yet all these observations about ideas found in Santayana's writing do not address the issue of how philosophy itself is imaginative and what the upshot is of its being so.

In the first place, philosophy, like all other human endeavours, has an imaginative component. Santayana acknowledges this at the start of *Scepticism and Animal Faith* when he says,

> The Realms of Being of which I speak are not parts of a cosmos, nor one great cosmos together: they are only kinds or categories of things which I find conspicuously different and worth distinguishing, at least in my own thoughts. (*SAF*, vi)

That is to say, his realms are imaginative constructions—the ones that best enable him to clean "the windows of his soul." This observation is intertwined with his philosophy. Animal faith teaches him that he lives in a world that is largely not him and often does not serve his interests. Furthermore, however much he learns about it is but a glimpse of a vast and complex world from a narrow perspective. All philosophic systems emerge from efforts to develop a comprehensive framework for understanding and coping with that vastness and that complexity. But ideas are not facts and different philosophies can build different frameworks and express them in different vocabularies while still being true to the facts. Although the tools are intellectual, the purpose of philosophy is aesthetic and moral.

Moreover, philosophy has this moral and aesthetic disposition because it is an expression of personal and social values that are driven by each philosopher's nature and circumstances. Santayana acknowledged this when he wrote in "Apologia Pro Mente Sua" that his philosophy is built on "the fundamental presuppositions that I cannot live without making" (*PGS*, 505).

So for Santayana, philosophy yields an imaginative bounty when it teaches us how to live—that is, when philosophy guides us to creatively adjust to the world. Such adjustment requires the understanding that observation and imagination make possible. Understanding the truth about both mental life (spirit) and physical reality (matter) is of fundamental importance to what might be regarded as Santayana's overriding moral project. An often-repeated quotation is his observation that "there is no cure for birth and death save to enjoy the interval" (*SE*, 97). To follow that maxim, you have to be clear about what you enjoy and what possibilities there are for fulfilment. In other words, you must come to terms with your situation in the world and plumb the depths of your own desires so that, in learning what the world can afford you, you can strive to live as well as you might. This coming to terms also involves facing up to the limits of what can be had and what can be done. Facing up to the troublesome constraints under which life is often lived requires a deepening of spiritual insight. It means probing your immediate desires and overt interests to discover your overriding passion—an imaginative exercise of high order. What benefits the individual also benefits society, where an imaginative grasp of the variety of interests in a community leads to an exploration of what organization and what rethinking of interests will result in the greatest harmony among them.

Yet moral benefit is only one facet. The imagination has no single home or purpose. It pervades every moment of experience. It is the bridge that takes spirit to matter, linking the two existing realms. Yet it is also how spirit gets to explore the infinity of essence and to meditate on the also infinite subset of essence Santayana calls truth. In *Scepticism and Animal Faith* Santayana makes clear that the imagination is necessary if knowledge is to be more than superficial. In *Realms of Being* he asserts that the humdrum (the "vulgar") imagination is an offshoot of the poetic. This insight opens the possibility that each intuition, however mundane, may blaze with an aura of suggestion.

References with Abbreviations

Santayana, George

IPR. [1900] 1990. *Interpretations of Poetry and Religion*. Edited by William G. Holzberger and Herman J. Saatkamp, Jr. Vol. 3 of *The Works of George Santayana*. Cambridge: MIT Press.

PGS. [1940] 1951. *The Philosophy of George Santayana*. Vol. 2. of *The Library of Living Philosophers*. Edited by Paul Arthur Schilpp. La Salle, Illinois: Open Court Press, 2nd edition.

PP. [1944, 1945, 1953] 1986. *Persons and Places*. Edited by William G. Holzberger and Herman J. Saatkamp, Jr. Vol. 1 of *The Works of George Santayana*. Cambridge: MIT Press.

RB. 1942. *Realms of Being*. One-Volume Edition, with a New Introduction by the Author. New York: Scribner's.

SAF. 1923. *Scepticism and Animal Faith: Introduction to a System of Philosophy*. New York: Charles Scribner's Sons.

Other References

Aristotle. 1964. *De Anima*. Translated by J. A. Smith. Quoted in Levi.

Levi, Albert William. 1964. The Two Imaginations. In *Philosophy and Phenomenological Research*. Vol. 25, No. 2 (Dec. 1964), 188–200.

Rubin, Richard M. 2018. Character and Philosophic Creativity–the Example of Santayana. *Overheard in Seville: Bulletin of the George Santayana Society* 36: 89–98.

———. 2021. 'The Imagination in *Scepticism and Animal Faith*.' A Subsection of Richard M Rubin and Phillip L Beard, The Other Side of the Mountain: Wallace Stevens's Poem and 'The Watershed of Criticism.' *Overheard in Seville: Bulletin of the George Santayana Society* 39: 152–153.

Schopenhauer, Arthur. [1819, 1844, 1859], 1958, 1966. *Die Welt als Wille und Vorstellung*. Translated as *The World as Will and Representation* by E.F.J. Payne. Indian Hills, Colorado: The Falcon's Wing Press, 1958. Reprint edition. New York: Dover Publications, 1966. 2 vols.

Shakespeare, William. 1964. *A Midsummer Night's Dream*. Quoted in Levi.

Spiritual Exercises and Animal Faith

Martin A. Coleman

Introduction

In *Scepticism and Animal Faith* (*SAF*), Santayana took up Descartes's method of universal doubt and "sought to carry it further" (*SAF*, 292). Santayana, similar to Descartes, intended his scepticism to "purify the mind of prejudice" (*SAF*, 69); and both thinkers sought that which cannot be doubted (McDermid 2009, 1, 6). But for each thinker the end of doubting (both its cessation and its goal) was different.[1] Descartes claimed to find reasons to doubt all that he believed about the world and himself, yet he thought this very act of doubting entailed the existence of the self as a thinking thing. This supposedly indubitably existing self became an Archimedean point of certainty on which to rest a lever of methodical inquiry that could raise knowledge to new heights (Descartes 2006, 13).

Santayana thought Descartes's result dubious because his scepticism was incomplete, never doubting the principle of sufficient reason or the existence of discourse. A complete sceptic, who suspended all beliefs, would be an unbelieving spectator of only what immediately appears to consciousness,

---

Thanks to Glenn Tiller for helpful suggestions for this essay.

[1] The second sentence of Santayana's Preface to *SAF* announces that the system of philosophy introduced in the book "differs widely in spirit and pretensions from what usually goes by that name" (*SAF*, v).

M. A. Coleman (✉)
Indiana University Indianapolis, Indianapolis, IN, USA
e-mail: martcole@iupui.edu

© The Author(s), under exclusive license to Springer Nature Switzerland AG 2024
M. A. Coleman, G. Tiller (eds.), *The Palgrave Companion to George Santayana's Scepticism and Animal Faith*, Palgrave Companions, https://doi.org/10.1007/978-3-031-46367-9_12

resulting in "solipsism of the present moment" (*SAF*, 15). Going beyond Descartes's assumed existences, the sceptic discovers nothing but the immediate datum of consciousness, or what Santayana called essence. Intuiting essence, in itself, conveys nothing about existence, asserts nothing, and never is in error[2] since it always is exactly what it appears as; so, it cannot be doubted (*SAF*, 74–75). An essence may be taken up in a context different from that of its immediate appearance (namely, in a context of beliefs) and put to work as a symbol for some absent thing or some existence not open to intuition (*SAF*, 45).[3] When an essence is used to symbolize some existing object posited in action based on animal faith, then it may be used to make believable (or doubtable) assertions. But an essence in itself is no instance of knowledge, has no value, and is without meaning, and so brings doubting to an end.

Descartes believed his scepticism arrived at true knowledge—something indubitable because known with certainty. Santayana claimed his scepticism arrived at essence—something indubitable because not capable of being known in itself but only intuited. The difference in the conclusions of doubting for Santayana and Descartes reflects a divergence in their philosophical projects. In aiming to establish an item of certain knowledge as an immovable foundation for all further knowledge, Descartes's work inaugurated a preoccupation with epistemology in European philosophy that continues today. Santayana's divergence from this project is well attested, but this essay considers where the divergence leads.

An Epistemology Book

It is understandable that *SAF* would be regarded as a work of epistemology, and it has happened frequently enough. Contemporary reviewers read it as "an inquiry into the nature, the roots and the justification of knowledge" (Adams 1925, 193); and as "Santayana's ... contribution to the solution of the knowledge problem," which addresses "the most fundamental question ... : How is it possible to posit an object which is not a datum, and how, without knowing positively what this object is, can I make it the criterion of truth in my ideas?" (Ten Hoor 1923, 658). Bertrand Russell had concerns, relevant to this

---

[2] Santayana wrote of essences in themselves that they are "free from error ... devoid of truth" (*SAF*, 65).
[3] Intuition is the function of consciousness; to be conscious is to intuit an essence. Santayana distinguished this from perception, which involves the bodily organs and has existing things—not essences—for its object.

fundamental question, and suspected a disregard for science that rendered Santayana's notions of essence and substance problematic (Russell 1923, 281).[4]

Herman Saatkamp clearly articulated *SAF's* turn away from typical epistemological problems. Though *SAF* seems to suggest that Santayana attempted "an epistemology from an 'intuition-out' perspective and [was] asking how does one explain going beyond the mere intuition of essence" to the known object, Saatkamp pointed out that "Santayana did not view this as the task of his philosophy." Rather, Santayana thought that discerning essences that symbolize what we actually believe is more beneficial (*PGS*, 580, cited in Saatkamp 2021, 14). In considering how Santayana's philosophy related to contemporary epistemology, Saatkamp concluded that "if [Santayana's scepticism is] correct, it is a thorough defeat of any foundationalism based on infallible and indubitable knowledge and at the same time it serves to introduce Santayana's own description of knowledge" derived from animal faith (Saatkamp 2021, 23).

John Lachs also explained how Santayana's scepticism and the resulting solipsism of the present moment challenged certain epistemological positions by demonstrating what is wrong with scepticism. Santayana's thoroughgoing scepticism demonstrated how the search for a foundation of knowledge to end doubting undercuts all inquiry because it leads to "something not open to doubt, but ... unable to ground anything" (Lachs 2006, 14). The problem with scepticism lies in assuming universality and necessity as criteria for knowledge. Santayana demonstrated the implausibility of these criteria. He discredited the epistemological aims of scepticism in order to advocate for "our ordinary practices with their sound and ordinary standards of knowledge" (Lachs 2006, 16); practices developed in actual living and subject not to standards of certainty but to the faith of the animal in what its life activities compel it to believe.

Like Saatkamp and Lachs, T. L. S. Sprigge thought Santayana departed from the concerns of contemporary epistemology. Sprigge contended that Santayana did not regard epistemology as necessary for the ontological system articulated in the four-volume work to which *SAF* is an introduction, *Realms of Being*. But, according to Sprigge, Santayana "thought that the philosophical climate of his time was such that the ontologist must begin by disposing of all

---

[4] In contrast to Russell's concerns, one scientist found the theory of essence particularly agreeable. This scientist's favorable review was remarked by Santayana's biographer, John McCormick: "In a review of the book for the British scientific journal *Nature*, H. W. Carr seized upon the theory of essence as having peculiar importance to contemporary scientific theory, in which, following Einstein, constancy and nineteenth-century positivism gave way to the principle of relativity, and the route was prepared for the even later principle of inconstancy. Carr cited Santayana's belief that existence is not a datum, since what is given to the mind is not the existence of objects but their essence. 'Santayana's doctrine, therefore, which does not reject existence but denies that it is a datum and excludes it from knowledge, is singularly in accordance with the theory that in physical science we are not contemplating absolute existence but co-ordinating phenomena by means of invariants.... All data and descriptions, all terms of human discourse, are essences, inexistent.... The distinction cuts science free from all the perplexities and antinomies which arise when reality is identified with existence'" (McCormick 1987, 259; Carr 1923, 572–73).

sorts of epistemological objections to his enterprise" (Sprigge 1995, 30). Sprigge characterized *SAF* as presenting an epistemology and defining knowledge as belief that, first, has as its object a world of events of import to the self, second, is true, and, third, is grounded in experience or controlled by fact (*SAF*, 179–80; quoted in Sprigge 1995, 52). Sprigge, consistent with the interpretations of Saatkamp and Lachs, understood that true belief was based not on a justification but on animal faith and an unjustifiable compulsion.

Each of the three interpretations by Saatkamp, Lachs, and Sprigge, following Santayana's lead and appropriate to their own philosophical climates, situates *SAF* in an epistemological context, that is, a context of philosophical problems of knowledge, its nature and reliability, and methods for securing it. These three interpretations are far more insightful and understanding of Santayana's philosophy than some of Santayana's contemporaries who, according to Henry Samuel Levinson, read *SAF* hoping to find a system of the universe revelatory of hidden connections between discourse and nature and articulating conditions for knowing the external world (Levinson 1992, 206).[5] The epistemological expectations of Santayana's contemporary readers risked distorting Santayana's philosophy in a way that the epistemological context taken up by later commentators' does not.

Yet, we can jettison the expectations *and* the context, dropping epistemology altogether and reading *SAF* as, to use Levinson's term, anti-epistemology. More positively, we can read the book as "a stylized presentation of" variations on age-old, self-transforming spiritual disciplines and "a book of exercises ... to restore a sense of life-at-first-hand" (Levinson 1992, 206–7).

For Levinson, this means reading *Scepticism and Animal Faith* as presenting a four-part ritual process[6]: First, announcing the nature of *SAF* in the "Preface" communicates the "playful or imaginative status" of Santayana's philosophy, denying that it is novel, personal, universal, metaphysical, or part of any school; rather, it is a philosophy expressed in terms of "what everybody knows," the discovery of which requires not great wit but honesty (*SAF*, ix). Second, scepticism detaches you from roles and expectations that constrain or distort consciousness. Third, acknowledging animal faith reveals a kinship with others and is "an avowal of humankindness" or community wider than political society (Levinson 1992, 209). Fourth, taking up previously suspended common sense enables you to engage practical matters with consciousness clarified of delusion.

Levinson's interpretation subordinated epistemology in Santayana's philosophy to the hygienic virtues of scepticism (Levinson 1992, 213, 216), the liberating effects of the discovery of essence (Levinson 1992, 214), and the

---

[5] Levinson wrote elsewhere that this group of readers was "universally disappointed" (Levinson 1987, 293). He seemed to class Lachs in this group (Levinson 1992, 208), a judgment that might be modified on a broader consideration of Lachs's comments on *SAF* than appear in Levinson's text.

[6] Levinson explained that "The depiction of philosophical discipline that Santayana gives in *Soliloquies* [in *England and Other Soliloquies* (1922)] conforms structurally to the 'ritual process' identified by Victor Turner" in *The Ritual Process: Structure and Anti-Structure*, Ithaca, NY: Cornell University Press, 1969 (Levinson 1984, 61n20).

humanizing import of animal faith (Levinson 1992, 216–17). In other words, Levinson emphasized philosophy's contribution to happiness: to living free from anxiety and distraction, humanely, and sanely. Levinson's interpretation gives point to Santayana's claim that his ontological system—his categories of essence, matter, truth, and spirit—is not exhaustive, universal, or articulating parts of a cosmos but rather categories he found "worth distinguishing", their particular worth being the support they provide for a life in which thinking is devoted to truth and sanity (*SAF*, vi). In other words, his ontology supports the exercises of *SAF*.

Levinson articulated the purpose and the outcome—the meaning—of the exercises is *SAF*; and, in particular, suggested the importance of sceptical exercise for liberation through discovery of essence and the necessity of animal faith for restoring common sense. But a reader of *SAF* still may wonder: *What exactly are the distinctive exercises of SAF and how might I practice them to transform consciousness and restore a sense of life at first hand?*

A Book of Exercises

The exercises of *SAF* eliminate confusion and doubt, liberate spirit, and, ultimately, cultivate sane living. "Spirit" is the word Santayana favored when writing about consciousness. To liberate spirit is to free consciousness from delusion and distractions such as fear, anxiety, and regret that result in madness of varying degrees. Freed from distractions we can pursue wisdom and live sanely.

Levinson remarked that Santayana challenged himself to become abnormally sane (Levinson 1992, 166), and Daniel Moreno wrote a valuable and insightful study of Santayana that takes the pursuit of sanity as an organizing theme of Santayana's intellectual life (Moreno 2015). According to Santayana, normal or conventional sanity consists in "those habits and ideas ... which are sanctioned by tradition and which, when followed, do not lead directly to the destruction of oneself or of one's country" (*DL*, 46). This normal sanity is equivalent to what Santayana called normal madness in that it embraces beneficial illusions (or takes intuited essences to be existences). These are exemplified in "images in sense, love in youth, and religion among nations" (*DL*, 46) and are functionally distinct from the abnormal madness of destructive "belief in the imaginary and desire for the impossible" (*DL*, 46). Abnormal sanity goes beyond conventions and the minimal avoidance of destruction; it aims to realize the potential of human consciousness undistracted by animal concerns and liberated from the confusion of mad beliefs and desires.

Scepticism, intuition, and animal faith work together to eliminate confusion, liberate spirit, and promote sane living. Scepticism, a special exercise not occurring naturally, is a way of avoiding error. Intuition is a natural function that, when refined or clarified through disciplined exercise, can liberate spirit. Animal faith is similar to intuition in being natural, but unlike intuition it cannot be developed or refined; in fact, it is no exercise at all, setting it apart also from scepticism. Animal faith compels an attitude of a creature toward its environment; but awareness of animal faith and the exercises of scepticism and intuition together make possible a distinctive exercise. Animal faith is a means to animal life; scepticism and pure intuition liberate spiritual life; together they enable an exercise of self-knowing, serving the end of living a sane human life.

Scepticism

Scepticism may describe a temperament or natural tendency; but as systematic or conscious analysis of belief it is not natural.[7] Scepticism is more exclusive than the other exercises, meaning that not everyone is a sceptic. According to Santayana, we naturally and haphazardly collect all kinds of opinions about things as we move through the world encountering various conditions. We carry on dogmatically until some opinion conflicts with another indicating error among our beliefs. We become doubtful of what some opinion asserts about facts, and investigation might lead to revising our collection of opinions. But dogmatic belief persists: active life compels us to go on believing many things as we maintain our bodies, interact with others, and perceive the world. We eat food, greet people, and put a foot out for our next step, often with barely any awareness of, let alone reflection on, what we believe about what is edible, worthy of respect, or stable.

This persistent, compulsive dogmatism justifies no particular beliefs, making confusion, conflict, and error unavoidable; and any belief always is, to some extent, suspect. One way to escape error would be to simply cease living, but this would not achieve any understanding or determine the truth of any belief (and it is the esteem for understanding and truth that gives point to a concern with error). Another option would be continual correction of erroneous opinions, bringing a greater degree of reliability to living; but convention still would determine many opinions so that chance would remain a factor in avoiding conflicting opinions. The situation would make any "philosopher ... ridiculous and negligible who had not strained his dogmas through the utmost rigours of scepticism" (*SAF*, 9), since, for Santayana, being a philosopher means committed regard for truth (*SAF*, 105, 227; *PP*, 421).

Rigorous scepticism, Santayana remarked, is not disbelief; disbelief is belief in the falseness of an assertion. "The true sceptic," he wrote, "merely analyses belief, discovering the risk and the logical uncertainty inherent in it" (*PGS*, 516). The sceptic withholds belief and disbelief from opinions dubious in even the slightest degree. Of course, this would undermine religious belief, history, science, perception, and memory, and result in "solipsism of the present moment" (*SAF*, 15), in which the sceptic merely observes an immediate appearance. Santayana found no contradiction is this solipsism, but he thought it impossible to sustain in a human life (*SAF*, 17). He observed that past philosophers had employed scepticism to jettison whatever was not bound up with

---

[7] "People are not naturally sceptics, wondering if a single one of their intellectual habits can be reasonably preserved; they are dogmatists angrily confident of maintaining them all" (*SAF*, 11–12).

their deepest feelings or thoughts while preserving whatever idea expressed these unscrutinized depths. So, for example, the mystic retained "the feeling of existence" and the romantic solipsist their "personal history and destiny" (*SAF*, 33).

Beyond this limited and "wayward scepticism" lay "ultimate scepticism." In solipsism of the present moment, the sceptic finds no existence or personal narrative, no principles of reason, no discourse, and no thinking thing; but rather only the immediate appearance. This intuited datum is, wrote Santayana, "embraced in a single stroke of apperception" (*SAF*, 34); everything that is not the datum, is nothing for the sceptic. The immediate datum presents only itself; all beliefs, including a belief in existence, are bracketed; and the datum is only what it appears as. And it really *is* what it appears as, but its reality is distinct from existence. Existence entails change and external relations, and ultimate scepticism has found the datum to have a fixed character and only internal relations.[8] Hence, ultimate scepticism leaves untouched the reality of the immediate datum but finds in it no existence. Any sense of existence, such as the mystic clings to, is due to something other than intuition of the datum.

Ultimate scepticism enables intuition of familiar appearances untethered from belief in existence. Santayana acknowledged that denial of existence, while false and epistemologically inadequate, is "tenable intuitively and, while it prevails, is irrefutable"; and Santayana found it helpful as an exercise for protection against illusion (*SAF*, 40). By introducing the practitioner to essence in itself, the sceptical exercise ends doubting, eliminates error, and opens to consciousness the infinite realm of essences, which can be the only thing of interest to spirit not distracted by animal needs or deluded by desires or aversions. Scepticism, in introducing intuition of essence as essence, makes possible an exercise in imagination, not in the service of fantasy and wish fulfillment, but in the service of broader acquaintance with reality, namely, with the infinite realm of essence.

Scepticism for Santayana was not especially oppressive or threatening to life through a disregard for values. To be a living creature is, prior to advocating or rejecting particular values, to be attracted to some things and averse to others according to how they influence the creature's life. And scepticism is not a life. Santayana was explicit: scepticism is an exercise. (And if some deeper pathology denies life in an attempt to live scepticism, that is no defect of scepticism.) Scepticism is not an end in itself but a means to a richer and freer human life: "a discipline fit to purify the mind of prejudice" (*SAF*, 69), which makes possible a further exercise, an intentional exercise of purified intuition.

---

[8] "The datum is an idea, a description; I may contemplate it without belief; but when I assert that such a thing exists I am hypostatising this datum, placing it in presumptive relations which are not internal to it" (*SAF*, 35).

Intuition

Intuition, unlike scepticism, is common to every conscious being, since being conscious entails intuiting essences.[9] But typically, we take an intuited essence naively as the thing it symbolizes; that is, it often is identified with the existing thing that has stimulated organs of sense that in turn have prompted consciousness to intuit some particular—who knows why?[10]—essence. Encountering my friend at a coffee shop—seeing him, hearing him call my name, feeling his embrace, smelling the chai he habitually drinks, tasting my own latte—prompts an essence that includes all sorts of traits, histories, and future actions. Taking this intuited essence as the substance of my friend leads me to assign to the existing human being what I only imagine about him: he is comforting, pleasant, and wise; he is one with whom I have shared adventures, he is the one I'll enjoy talking to or the one I am anxious not to hurt inadvertently. Confusing the essence with my actual friend can make me insensitive to the existing human being in front of me and to my immediate physical response: Anxiety can diminish the perception of "the congenial rate of vibration" that Santayana identified as fundamental to the experience of friendship (*LR2*, 95); expectation of a humorous story or an ego-pleasing compliment can block awareness of my friend's distress that could be addressed with attention undistracted by ideas about my friend.

Santayana thought that wisdom lay in the ability to distinguish between existing things (the human being who is my friend) and the appearance of things (the essence that I intuit when I perceive my friend) (*DL*, 37, 45); while to confuse them and take intuited essences as material existences is madness (which could be destructive of relationships with people I misunderstand or neglect) (*DL*, 41). So, the discovery of essence introduces the possibility of sanity and wisdom. The ultimate sceptic is able to entertain the appearance without being taken in by what can be only illusory[11] for one dogmatically believing in its existence; the sceptic simply observes what they intuit without holding beliefs about its power to please or disappoint and so without risk of deception. Negatively, intuiting essence as essence frees us from anxiety that comes with believing we directly intuit existence, which leads us to believe stories we make up about threats and benefits for which there is no material basis. Positively, intuiting essence as essence broadens acquaintance with the endless possibilities of reality, and we may come to appreciate reality as more varied and extensive than the limited round of the material animal. Pure

---

[9] Santayana regarded intuition as "the common property of all mental life or as the light of consciousness itself" (*PGS*, 578).

[10] Santayana wrote that the question of why some particular essence is intuited is "a question which could only be answered by plunging into a realm of existence and natural history every part and principle of which would be just as contingent, just as uncalled-for, and just as inexplicable as this accident of my being" (*SAF*, 73).

[11] According to Santayana, all intuited essences are illusory (*SAF*, 34, 54).

intuition is an antidote to deception and distraction, a taste of freedom from anxiety, and a glimpse of the infinite range of imagination.

Just as intuition is common to all of us, so are, thought Santayana, moments of pure intuition free from deception and anxiety. Such moments of freedom occur in everyday life without presupposing or promising salvation (*RB*, 746). Celebration, laughter, or understanding may be occasions in which consciousness is absorbed in the intuited essence and freed from distraction. Such spiritual freedom "overflows in the play of children" (*RB*, xxxii) and may be found in absorption in inquiry. But the momentary freedom is fleeting because of a habitual tendency (an "original sin") of conscious beings to take intuitions as direct revelations of what truly exists (*PP*, 418–19).

This habitual tendency to confusion and error can be countered by scepticism and pure intuition of essence: the former reveals essence, and the latter ends delusion. Disciplined sceptical exercise relaxes natural dogmatism and reminds us that essence presents no revelation of existence and no voucher for truth. Disciplined exercise of pure intuition adds constancy to the experience of liberation, enabling spirit to realize its nature as observer of essences apart from their significance for the material creature.[12] Experience still includes illusory essences, but with the benefit of pure intuition you are no longer deceived by them and can appreciate them in themselves. Liberated spirit does not exempt you from the vicissitudes of material existence, but it is a vital contribution to wisdom and sane living.

Animal Faith

Animal faith, like intuition, is common to all; but it is prior to intuition, and so extends to creatures lacking intuition altogether. Animal faith, unlike intuition, is not in itself an exercise; rather, it is "a sort of expectation" (*SAF*, 107)[13] that channels basic sensations such as hunger, pursuit, shock, or fear toward existing things (*SAF*, 214). That is, animal faith instinctively determines an attitude that presumptively orients the living creature with regard to existing things and their arrangement in relation to the creature. Non-living existences react to other existences without variation and depend for preservation of structure on the weakness of any disrupting influence relative to the integrity of the material organization, but the animal has a living faith that orients it in response to

---

[12] Santayana maintained that the experience of liberation is not different in kind whether it occurs spontaneously in the laughing partygoer and playing child or in "the saint or the sage" who cultivate it through exercises; the latter stand apart from the rest of us in the constancy of the experience of liberation, which pervades their thoughts and actions turning the "material circumstances [of the experience] into almost indifferent occasions" (*RB*, 746).

[13] As expectation, animal faith is irrational (*SAF*, 31), and, in spite of expectations, "sometimes a surprise comes, and sometimes nothing" (*SAF*, 36).

other existing things in a way that preserves its vital structure. So, when bodily sensations call forth instinctive reactions that pick out particular objects to pursue or avoid, animal faith lies behind these particular actions as the orienting attitude of the active creature; and these actions compel beliefs that then may be articulated (*SAF*, 16, 175; *PGS*, 581).[14,15] Saatkamp characterized animal faith as providing "the basis for action, belief, and knowledge" (Saatkamp 2021, 281); and Santayana called it "the presupposition of all curiosity and discovery" (*PGS*, 582): while intuition surveys non-existent essences, animal faith is the precondition for exploring existence. Further consideration of animal faith in relation to the exercises of scepticism and intuition will clarify its contribution to living sanely.

Awareness of animal faith comes with the discovery of essence in the exercise of ultimate scepticism. Ultimate scepticism, in revealing the non-existent nature of all that is intuited, also reveals, indirectly and on reflection, animal faith as the "irrational persuasion or prompting of life" on which all belief rests, rendering our beliefs "radically incapable of proof" (*SAF*, 35). The connection between the discovery of essence as non-existent and the awareness of animal faith can be observed in the claim that experience is illusory or life is a dream. To fully give up belief in life and experience would eliminate any prompting to make claims about the illusory nature of experience; essences are no illusions to the sceptic (*SAF*, 65, 99). But to take an intuited essence to be illusory is to put it in relation with something outside of it (that thing which is misrepresented—as existing or changed or not existing—by the essence), and *this action* of positing something external to the essence compels belief resting ultimately on animal faith. Animal faith—influencing the living and acting that give point to distinguishing illusions—provides the basis for the contrast between life and dream when you pursue sane living.

Animal faith limits the pure intuition or liberated spirit arising from scepticism. Spirit is impartially interested in all essences and "ready to be omniscient and just" to everything it beholds (*SAF*, 214). Animal faith, in contrast, orients the animal relative to other existing things; it is an orientation that expresses particular biases determined by the needs, desires, and aversions of the animal. So, liberating spirit from the distraction of animal interests carries risk: Santayana acknowledged that if the pure function of spirit as observer of essences were taken by someone to be their singular ambition—a tendency he observed in saints and some philosophers—animal interests would be

---

[14] "We believe," wrote Santayana, "because we act, we do not act because we believe" (*PGS*, 581).

[15] Sprigge found Santayana's usage of the term "animal faith" ambiguous and thought it could be interpreted as a compulsion to believe or as that which is compelled (Sprigge 1995, 53). Without directly refuting Sprigge's charge of ambiguity, I find textual support for inclining toward the first rather than the second interpretation. It seems more accurate to claim that action (with its particular form resulting in part from how the active animal is oriented toward the world by its faith) compels belief; animal faith compels an attitude or orientation of the creature toward the world. On this view, animal faith is never articulated; only the belief resulting from action is articulated.

condemned in themselves as "vain or sinful" for serving no direct interest of spirit (*SAF*, 215). Other practical consequences of separating animal concerns from consciousness can include pathological dissociation, as might occur in those who have endured trauma. Dissociation can be helpful as a spontaneous or even intentional (as among prisoners and other victims of ongoing torture) strategy for surviving extreme trauma; but if unacknowledged or practiced with limited understanding, it can become problematic in navigating the world and relating to others.

Animal faith is a counter[16] to fanatical self-denial or persistent and uncontrolled dissociation, providing—as a prompting of life—a connection to existence that spirit lacks and can never justify in itself. Santayana wrote, "the suasion of sanity is physical: if you cut your animal traces, you run mad" (*SAF*, 283). Animal faith lies behind basic maintenance behaviors (consuming edible things, avoiding speeding vehicles), and it may contribute to a conscious alteration of instinctive reactions (*SAF*, 175). But conscious correction of errors and abnormal sanity are not easy or automatic, and they require an *awareness* of animal faith. When animal faith remains unacknowledged in the language-using creature, confusion of essence and existence still is likely as demonstrated by the history of European philosophy.[17] The resulting belief in false substances and burden of anxieties and distractions can result in madness ranging from normal and functional to fanatical or lethal.

The importance of acknowledging animal faith suggests how the exercises of *SAF* work together to promote sanity. The exercises of scepticism and pure intuition make us aware of the distinction between essence and existence, and this brings awareness of animal faith; but animal faith is not in itself an exercise. So, *what is the third distinctive exercise of SAF that involves animal faith?* Sprigge read *SAF* as proposing that the compelling nature of animal faith leads us to respond to doubt not by rejecting doubtable beliefs (being a sceptic) but by determining through reflection what beliefs we actually hold; consciousness of animal faith makes it reasonable to inquire rather than suspend belief (Sprigge, 53). But is there a distinctive method of inquiry that follows acknowledgment of animal faith?

Lachs seemed to think so when he wrote that Santayana's "method of animal faith" is comparable in significance with philosophical methods proposed by Plato, Descartes, Hume, Kant, Hegel, and Nietzsche. According to Lachs,

---

[16] Animal faith is a counter *in action* to pure intuition or dissociation; it is what keeps the fanatic or completely detached person acting in ways conducive to living insofar as they do. But animal faith is not on its own a cure to pathologies, though it is a basic condition for sanity. Abnormal sanity requires awareness of animal faith.

[17] In Chapter XXI of *SAF*, "Sublimations of Animal Faith," Santayana listed examples of "the chief false substances which human faith may rest on when the characteristic human veil of words and pictures hides the modes of matter which actually confront the human race in action, and which therefore, throughout, are the intended object of its faith" (*SAF*, 218). This confusion of essence and matter or of words and existence results in bad philosophy and is remedied, thought Santayana, by checking intuition through attention to action and subsequent articulation of beliefs.

the method is to examine actions to figure out the beliefs assumed in performing them. This yields a philosophy that consists of all the carefully stated general beliefs the actions imply (e.g., "space is continuous," and "there are things existing independently of us"). Lachs thought Santayana's method the best ever proposed for justifying the claims of philosophy because it ensures that philosophical reflection attends to daily life and arrives at conclusions that "keep faith with our actions" (Lachs 2011, n.p.). But Lachs criticized Santayana for failing to notice that the method of animal faith does not require the discovery of essence, and Lachs thought that marrying the idea of essences to animal faith distorts the method. The method begins, thought Lachs, not with essence, but with human agency in a world of space and change (Lachs 2009, 485–6).

An anti-epistemological reading of *SAF* regards scepticism, intuition of essences, and animal faith as related in their contributions to living sanely. Animal faith's contribution to a sane life *does* require the discovery of essence as distinct from existence. An anti-epistemological interpretation is not primarily concerned with implications and justifications of philosophical claims because it is not concerned with animal faith as the basis for an epistemology. According to Santayana, the persuasiveness of animal faith renders philosophical doubts about the reliability of *knowledge in general* mostly irrelevant to our actual efforts to make sense of nature (*SAF*, 101). Animal faith is, *in general*, secure and adequate enough on its own. This makes epistemology mostly superfluous[18]—many journalists, scientists, medical diagnosticians, tour guides, treasure hunters, foragers, documentary filmmakers, and others carry on reasonably well without attending carefully to theories of knowledge—and suggests that the compiling of carefully stated, generalized beliefs is unlikely to be the most significant philosophical outcome of acknowledging animal faith. And if animal faith is not the basis for a new method of securing belief, then it seems unlikely that scepticism and intuition are merely prefatory to epistemological debates about method. Instead, the exercises work together *continually* to liberate spirit and promote sane living.[19]

---

[18] There remains a place in philosophy for epistemological questions, as for theological questions, if only in virtue of the history of the subject and its influence on intellectual culture. Perhaps anti-epistemology should be called anti-philepistemy ("philepistemy" comes from Alexander 2013, 4) to indicate what should be obvious: philosophy is not the love of knowledge but the love of wisdom, and philosophical questions of knowledge ought to serve a love of wisdom.

[19] Diana Heney claimed in her contribution to the present book that "the structure of *SAF* cannot be a symmetrical journey—an ascent to the great heights of sceptical clarity and a triumphant descent to a secure system of knowledge—some form of scepticism remains a companion on the return journey. Instead of a step-wise recovery from one indubitable truth to a system of knowledge, the structure of *SAF* reflects the way in which an enduring scepticism is the expression of a responsible sense of one's own limits—limits that nonetheless do not render us unable to go on" ("Laying Siege to the Truth: Santayana's Discourse on Method," 61). Scepticism remains because it is a beneficial exercise not for establishing an epistemological theory (after which scepticism may be safely disregarded) but for living sanely.

Regarding the exercises of *SAF* as separable—as practicable and beneficial in isolation—diminishes the potential of the exercises and hinders a full appreciation of animal faith. Lachs's characterization of the method of animal faith as independent of Santayana's notion of essence and his ontology more generally would be a method that could be practiced by the naïve, if reflective, person of action who takes what is given in intuition as an existing thing. What Lachs called the method of animal faith, then, would seem, at least initially, to be of little help in going beyond normal madness. Its significance for Santayana's pursuit of abnormal sanity would remain obscure.[20]

But Lachs's interpretation is quite sensible in an epistemological context. Both Lachs and Saatkamp's interpretations show how Santayana's ideas displace foundationalist epistemology and, in Lachs's words, replace it with "our ordinary practices with their sound and ordinary standards of knowledge" (Lachs 2006, 16). It is true Santayana's philosophy does this,[21] and it seems reasonable and beneficial to replace the search for epistemological foundations with attention to actions and the assumptions they express (such a methodological revolution could make many academic philosophy courses more humane, relevant to actual living, and conducive to a genuine love of truth). Furthermore, Santayana's philosophy does not condemn normal madness,[22] and Lachs has written persuasively of the virtue of leaving people alone to pursue their interests and enjoy their pleasures (Lachs 2012, 115–72). If Lachs's interpretation of animal faith supports this virtue by inviting people to acknowledge the priority of their actions over philosophical doctrine as a method of understanding themselves and the world, all the better. The alternative interpretation of animal faith proposed in this essay recognizes and seeks to understand an interest in abnormal sanity (which, for Santayana, would include acknowledgment of a plurality of legitimate interpretations[23]).

---

[20] What would an isolated method of animal faith contribute to a life that entertains "the illusion without succumbing to it" (*SAF*, 72)?

[21] See Daniel Pinkas's essay, "Scepticism, Anti-scepticism, and Santayana's Singularity," (57–94), in this book.

[22] Santayana wrote that his "philosophy is not urgent or 'militant': you can manage perfectly without it, but you will find a quiet solidity in it at the end" (*LGS*, 8:127).

[23] Lachs commented on the social significance of recognizing and honoring this plurality (rather than imposing or acquiescing to a single dogma): "In a dynamic society critique is a compliment and the greatest engine of progress. To criticize people is to take them seriously, that is, to respect them as intelligent friends traveling with us on the road to a less error-prone and more humane universe" (Lachs 2012, 140).

Animal Faith, Auscultation of Psyche, and Criticism

Animal faith, then, need not be regarded as a special method of inquiry[24] or an exercise. It is not strengthened or refined; it remains what it is—irrational faith—to the end. But the *awareness* of animal faith is extremely important for sanity. In an abnormally sane life, animal faith grounds, not certain conclusions with true premises, but liberated spirit in the material body.[25] The distinctive exercise involving animal faith that grounds liberated spirit is an exercise of self-knowing that Santayana called "auscultation of psyche" (*RB*, 335). Psyche, for Santayana, is the organization of matter that maintains the living creature, the hereditary pattern of vital operations of the organism, including the operation that presents essences to consciousness.[26] It is the necessary, material ground for anything you identify as the self. While you may have a direct sense of psyche as "personal momentum [or] a pervasive warmth and power," its structure and mechanism remain hidden (*RB*, 337). As the generator of essences—of thoughts and images arising in psyche's interaction with other things—psyche presents no thoughts and images of itself (*RB*, 337). But you can observe it through the sensible effects of its interactions with the world, analogous to how you can investigate internal organs by listening for sounds that indicate their functioning, for example, when the heart pumps blood through the body or the lungs exchange gases with the external environment.

Katazyrna Kremplewska called auscultation of psyche "everyday phenomenology," carried out "by way of a detour, via the world" (Kremplewska 2019, 55).[27] Animal faith, the material creature's direct route to acting on the world, is the mind's route of detour for interpreting the world. The terms of interpretation are essences, which, according to Santayana, "help out [animal faith] and lend it something to posit" (*SAF*, 107). Animal sensation—an operation of psyche—presents signs to the conscious animal: "These signs are miscellaneous essences—sights, sounds, smells, contacts, tears, provocations" (*SAF*, 175).[28]

---

[24] On Santayana's account all inquiry, including scientific, *presupposes* animal faith (*PGS*, 582).

[25] Truth is not thrown over in pursuit of sanity, which would be madness. Santayana wrote, "there is no sacrifice of truth to utility [which could include health and freedom from distraction on some interpretations]: there is rather a wise direction of curiosity upon things on the human scale, and within the range of art. Speculation beyond those limits cannot be controlled, and is irresponsible; and the symbolic terms in which it must be carried on, even at close quarters, are the best possible indications for the facts in question" (*SAF*, 105). Sanity requires honesty and sincere inquiry, and "the truth is the realm of being to which the earnest intellect is addressed" (*SAF*, 227).

[26] Regarding the mind, consciousness, and intuition, Santayana wrote that "there is no mental machinery; the underground work is all done by the organism, in the psyche, or in what people call the unconscious mind" (*PGS*, 580).

[27] Kremplewska's *Life as Insinuation: George Santayana's Hermeneutics of Finite Life and Human Self* (2019) has inspired much of my thinking about auscultation of psyche.

[28] According to Santayana's manuscript of *SAF*, "tears" in this sentence should be "fears." His essay, "Three Proofs of Realism" (in *Essays in Critical Realism: A Cooperative Study of the Problem of Knowledge*, London: Macmillan, 1920, 171), parts of which he used in *SAF*, includes "fears" in this sentence. In the first edition of *SAF*, used for citations in the present volume of essays, the sentence reads "tears." There is no evidence that Santayana authorized changing "fears" to "tears," and the critical edition of *SAF* produced by the Santayana Edition reinstates "fears" based on the authority of the manuscript and "Three Proofs of Realism."

Mind, in attempting to understand[29] the object of sensations, takes up these essences, in the context of beliefs; mind then can describe the object by taking essences as symbols for the objects that animal faith, through action, compels belief in. This enables exploration of the world, and, in turn, indirect inquiry into psyche.

Indirect investigation of psyche proceeds by exploiting what is accidental and partial in psyche due to its history, interests, and perspectives,[30] which become apparent in cumulative results of inquiry. Santayana wrote, "all the errors ever made about other things, if we understand their cause, enlighten us about ourselves" (*RB*, 336). This is because psyche is "the ground of refraction, selection, and distortion in our ideas" and introduces much that is arbitrary and accidental into our investigations (*RB*, 337). But if we systematize and clarify our knowledge in any field through sustained inquiry, criticism, and correction of error, then whatever is thrown out—"whatever may be arbitrary in it, based on human accidents" such as the mythical, sentimental, and partial—is revelatory, indirectly, of psyche (*RB*, 336). Accordingly, indirect inquiry into psyche may involve not only awareness of generalized beliefs about the world but also of the results of historical, scientific, or aesthetic inquiries, among others.

Indeed, Santayana thought that "all that is called knowledge of the world, of human nature, of character" contributes to self-knowledge (*RB*, 335). Because knowledge and inquiry are social, my indirect realization of my partialities and biases involves animal faith orienting me toward the world of other inquirers; and, I become aware of limitations common to all humans. This recalls Levinson's characterization of animal faith as Santayana's confession of "his sense of *generic humanity*" (rather than "a credo or manifesto of belief") that "binds him to his kind, establishing a sense of community," giving social life "its ultimate concern or point" because the social has no significance for the ultimate sceptic lost in pure intuition of essences (Levinson, 217).[31] Animal faith grounds liberated spirit in the material body *and* the community, "lend[ing] ballast to ... social life" (Levinson 1992, 218).

The connection between self-knowing and other inquiries rests in the nature of experience, because when you gain knowledge of the world through experience, you develop your ability to cultivate the self. So, your refined inquiry into the natural world enables the self-conscious development of yourself, for

---

[29] To understand is, at a very basic level, to respond consciously to an object as existing and as distinct from intuited essences. This understanding leads to (and becomes) descriptions that are regarded as symbolic of material existence; understanding continues in the refinement of those descriptions through intensified observation, criticism, and correction of errors in actual dealings with material existence.

[30] These would include cognitive biases or heuristics, determined indirectly through various experimental situations, like those presented in Kahneman (2011).

[31] Santayana alludes to this social character in the beginning of *SAF* in acknowledging the influence on our beliefs of custom, the social articulation of shared expressions of animal faith (*SAF*, 6). Thanks to Richard Rubin for drawing my attention to this text.

example, as a scientist through the practice of this sort of inquiry. This sort of self-cultivation can itself be refined to enable greater self-knowledge, not as another science but a way of living an abnormally sane life. Understanding how this works requires understanding Santayana's notion of experience.

According to Santayana, experience is more than a rambling run of ideas or mere recall. He identified experience with "a fund of wisdom gathered by living" (*SAF*, 138), which depends on intuition of essences. Intuition of essences enables psyche to extend its "action with more circumspection, into what we call the arts" understood broadly as any intelligent modifications of patterns or organizations of existence "concentric with those of health in the psyche" (*RB*, 352). The pause of spirit for wonder and contemplation of essences is an opportunity for psyche to "pause for breath" and survey conditions through organs of sense, modify impulses, and become more sensitive and effective in its activity, consolidating power over its environment (*RB*, 352).[32] Intuition of essences modifies psyche not directly by altering material patterns of the living creature, but indirectly by illuminating beneficial possibilities and taking the creature beyond the mechanical round of purely material activity (*LR1*, 4). Santayana wrote that the instinctive reactions of psyche, called forth by sensations and expressive of animal faith, "may be modified by experience, and the description the mind gives of the object reacted upon can be revised" (*SAF*, 175). Psyche modified by experience influences the creature's orientation prompted by animal faith; it is an orientation resulting in keener discrimination of essences, sharper attention to the most relevant essences, and greater sensitivity and judiciousness of a psyche able to recover from and correct mistaken reactions to conditions, three things Santayana identified as requisite for experience (*SAF*, 138).

These requirements for experience or wisdom are deliberately cultivated by the scientist, artist, or disciple. Specialized activities of scientific investigation, artistic creation, or religious discipline are experiences that modify psyche in ways that condition further experience. That is, the activities cultivate discrimination, attention, and sensitive judgment with respect to those things that support the particular aim or ideal: a botany student experiences more diverse plant structures; the beatmaker, more distinct rhythms and new complexities in their interactions; the religious devotee, divinity running through all of it. These kinds of experience—scientific, artistic, or religious—can serve auscultation of psyche, but an explicit pursuit of abnormal sanity modifies psyche in a distinctive way. Accordingly, the exercises of *SAF* differ from those of science, art, and religion in, first, bracketing all assumptions in a thoroughgoing sceptical exercise rather than assuming a set of special propositions; second,

---

[32] Of course, wonder and contemplation of essences may tempt one to neglect material activity altogether and escape into fantasy, undercutting further experience and development of psyche altogether. More typically, animal faith is not willfully opposed and operates to ensure a normal madness enabling perceptions to become significant (registered as essences symbolic of existence, whether acknowledged or not); then a creature may become aware of purposes and act intentionally, having more illuminating experiences.

discriminating essence itself rather than discriminating among essences of a particular type, say, plants or beats or manifestations of the divine; and, third, inquiring into psyche or that which conditions inquiry in any of the other fields. Psyche modified by the exercises of *SAF* becomes an actively exploring and plastic psyche, responsive to expressions of its own character.

The exercises of *SAF* culminate in auscultation of psyche, which depends on the continued operation of scepticism and intuition of essences as essences. Scepticism loosens fixation on a favored identity that impedes self-knowing. Distinguishing essence from existence renders intuition clearer and psyche more sensitive. Pure intuition keeps spirit less entangled in the business of psyche. Auscultation of psyche also supports the other exercises: first, in acknowledging animal faith it emphasizes the nature of scepticism as an exercise rather than a life; second, in its indirect exploration of psyche the exercise of intuition comes to discriminate essences more finely and to continue to discriminate essence from existence.

As auscultation of psyche is carried out, there is greater sensitivity to the body, its changing orientation to the world, and its expressions of animal faith in particular actions; which then, with intuited essences taken symbolically, may be articulated as beliefs, which contributes to self-knowing.

The continued exercises render the human being less distracted and deluded, moving through the world more confidently and competently. Spirit attends to essences without delusions of power and undistracted by material tasks it cannot attend to; and psyche better accomplishes the material tasks that sustain the creature. Consciousness has no control over what it intuits and can observe only what psyche presents: "it is the body that speaks, and the spirit that listens" (*RB*, 338). The liberated spirit is the best listener to what the body has to say (the best auscultator of psyche), and in listening carefully the spirit enables the psyche to exercise its executive functions, becoming more sensitive and judicious as it does. The ideal result is a life of equipoise that liberates consciousness and honors animal faith as necessary for cultivating such a life.

The ongoing auscultation of psyche also is called by the more familiar term "criticism." Santayana was explicit that he did not mean the criticism of knowledge that pervaded European thought in the three centuries prior to his work. He substituted for epistemological criticism "criticism of myself," which, though it may make use of systematic knowledge and theories, is not necessarily scholarly or scientific. Criticism consists in considering "what I believe in my active moments, as a living animal, when I am really believing something"; and Santayana characterized it as "the discipline of my daily thoughts and the account I actually give to myself from moment to moment of my own being and of the world around me" (*SAF*, 305). It is a continual exercise of self-knowing involving scepticism, intuition of essences, and awareness of animal faith. It is a continual exercise of cultivating sanity or "assurance and peace in being what one is, and in becoming what one must become" (*DL*, 40). In other words, auscultation of psyche or criticism serves sanity as a continual inquiry into the changing limits of my life—as an active acceptance of the facts of change and limit, of life and death.

To be able, through criticism of myself, to discern what I believe in active moments is an antidote to habitual prejudgments, to what might be called self-deception, to the mostly functional delusions and neuroses that attenuate experience and diminish consciousness. Such criticism, as a "discipline of my daily thoughts," is helpful, for example, when I meet my friend for coffee, and find myself suddenly anxious that I have unwittingly hurt his feelings. Perhaps I have and have interpreted a look or a gesture to support this judgement; or perhaps I have misinterpreted some stirring of the psyche unrelated to my friend. In any case, an anxious response could be problematic for addressing the situation. But the slackening of natural dogmatism through sceptical exercise helps me recognize my description of the situation—say, a situation marked by my thoughtlessness and my friend's apparent withdrawal—as merely an essence and not identical to a blight on my moral character or a permanent wound to the relationship (which could not be concluded at this point). The exercise of pure intuition enables me in the particular case not merely to distinguish and contemplate essence as essence, but, with the benefit of awareness of animal faith, to distinguish the essence of my catastrophic elaboration from the essences of immediate perceptions—the essences that stand for the actions large or small that express "what I believe ... as a living animal." These latter could initially include the simple sensations of standing on solid ground or breathing, which could be articulated as active beliefs in immediate stability and vital power and contribute to clarified consciousness; and with those immediate resources, I could further attend to my friend.

This is an auscultation of psyche and indirect inquiry (by way of the world that animal faith orients me toward) into what is really going on. And this stops the undisciplined amplification of barely articulable feelings that suggest vague emotions of fear or shame. The spirit is better able to listen to the body. The exercises attend to the present activity of the psyche, to immediate animal living. And with this attending to experience I am better able to carry on attending to the living friend in front of me: either to the distress he may be experiencing, acknowledging it as *his* (and not as a prop for rehearsing my stories about a fixed self with which I identify) and inquiring in a caring (and minimally self-centered) way what would help him; or, on realizing there is no immediate problem, enjoying our mutual pleasure in each other's company.

This exercise of criticism has immediate benefits as described here, but it is part of an ongoing discipline that reveals the actions articulated in beliefs, and so indirectly reveals psyche. What you find might be described as a succession of orientations to the world prompted by animal faith and symbolized by essences that, insofar as they are articulated, become masks for the changing self. To identify them is never to identify candidates for a true self; rather, broad and sustained attention reveals masks of the self but more importantly it reveals how and where these are frozen and inhibit the exercise of criticism. Continuing the auscultation can help find these inhibited identities not to get to a final truth but to make the inquiry wiser and more skillful; self-knowing becomes not a final story but an ongoing exercise that clarifies consciousness, refines the sensitivity of psyche, and enables an enactment of animal faith freer of delusion and superstition and more conscious. The intuited essences never capture the entire self, though finer, more discerning criticism can begin to follow a developing narrative, a continuing story of change and growth, that has an end not yet known. But there is no hurry to complete the story; the exercises in refining attention and consciousness provide you "assurance and peace in being what one is," namely, a conscious animal that is subject to change and limitations; and understanding of your actual living that extends the assurance and peace to "becoming what one must become" (*DL*, 40).

Spiritual Practices

SAF presents three exercises—scepticism, pure intuition, and auscultation of psyche or criticism—that, together, contribute to a life of abnormal sanity. But how you might *practice* these exercises is not explicitly addressed in *SAF* or in Santayana's other works. Commenting on his own exercise of pure intuition and contemplation of essence as essence, Santayana wrote: "I happen to be able to do this trick and to enjoy doing it" (*PGS*, 542), seeming to suggest his own ability is a matter of chance. But, acknowledging moments of liberated spirit are common to humans and may come to almost anyone, he contrasted saints and sages who "add ... constancy" to those moments with "the least disciplined or integrated of us" (*RB*, 746) whose moments of liberation are fleeting. This idea of being more or less disciplined suggests that practice can develop facility with these exercises. Santayana also distinguished "spiritual directors ... [and] their catechumens," the former having "an art of clarifying intuition" and the latter having not-so-clarified intuition; and he suggested that "we might establish an art of eliciting intuition," by which teachers could guide students in developing pure intuition (*PGS*, 580).

So, which practices cultivate or develop scepticism, pure intuition, and auscultation of psyche or criticism?[33] The question does not seek a definitive statement of how to achieve liberation: dictation of the means to freedom is at least distracting to spirit and at most destructive of the freedom they aim to achieve. The question seeks examples of relevant practices, always assuming their

---

[33] I take it to be idiomatic and relatively uncontroversial to distinguish exercise, as the more general activity I engage in for some purpose, from practice, as a particular activity I do to develop my ability to perform the exercise (to perform it correctly, to improve performance of it, or to expand the range of conditions in which I can perform it). For example, I might exercise in order to be healthy and strong by lifting weights or swimming or riding my bicycle. To develop an ability to perform an exercise, I might practice my form—the placement of my feet, the position of my spine, my grip on the bar—to perform a deadlift; to improve my ability to perform an exercise, I might practice flip turns for a more sustained effort in a swim workout; or to expand the range of conditions in which I can perform an exercise, I might practice shifting gears to better ride a bicycle on especially diverse terrain.

efficacy depends on experience, temperament, and culture. Accordingly, the essay surveys recent work about practices related to Santayana's philosophy (not specifically addressed to the exercises of *SAF*), makes some observations, and speculates on how to think about practicing the exercises of *SAF*.

In his book *Stoic Pragmatism*, Lachs combined the apparently incompatible philosophies of acquiescent stoicism and ameliorative pragmatism, characterizing the stoic pragmatist as one who makes efforts for a better life while being prepared to accept conditions when further attempted change becomes futile. Lachs thought Santayana's naturalistic account of the human condition—the condition of being both a spirit whose nature is to observe whatever arises with stoic calm and equanimity and a psyche that attempts to pragmatically turn the changing conditions of an indifferent world to its material advantage—could provide philosophical support for stoic pragmatism. Lachs wrote that stoic pragmatism "captures [Santayana's] attitudes, practices, and portions of his theoretical position" (Lachs 2012, 143).[34]

Steven Miller and Yasuko Taoka remarked that even though Lachs presented stoic pragmatism as a way of living, the book reveals "little about what particular practices this might involve" (Miller and Taoka 2015, 152). Miller and Taoka proposed to amend this lack with ancient stoic practices enriched with insights of American pragmatism, which, I think, could serve the exercises of *SAF*. The practice of *leaving others alone to live their lives as they wish but paying attention to them to increase understanding* could promote awareness of dogmatism when you suspend judgment of others and are open to learning from them. The practice of *distinguishing what is up to us and what is not in order to achieve the good enough* could support distinguishing the nature of psyche and spirit. The practice of *self-reflective meditation to review the events of today and prepare for tomorrow* could contribute to clarifying intuition. The complimentary practices of *oikeiosis*,[35] to understand our connections with other human beings, and *analysis of impressions* could prepare us to become aware of animal faith in both its affirmation of humanity and its influence expressed in the actions each of us undertakes and the subsequent beliefs. Miller and Taoka's thoughtful and intelligent essay offers more detail and more suggestions than included here about practices relevant to the exercises of *SAF*; but an important general point that their essay demonstrates is how a shared tradition and

---

[34] The practices Lachs mentioned here seem to be "the rich, embodied activities of animals trying to survive in a treacherous environment" (Lachs 2012, 65).

[35] Miller and Taoka explained that "Oikeiosis ... asks us to imagine ourselves at the center of a series of concentric rings comprised of all humanity, and it is the task of this practice to bring these circles closer to the center: those from the third ring should be treated as if they are in the second ring, the fourth in the third, and so on" (Miller and Taoka 2015, 161). They continued, incorporating pragmatists' insights articulated by Marilyn Fischer, "the individual practitioner cannot understand him- or herself independently of the members of other circles and their effects. The different circles also cannot be understood without reference to one another," but, Fischer pointed out that, even though mortality is common to all human beings, actual occurrence of death—its timing and manner—is not shared.

community in which techniques are preserved and passed on can be a generous source of practices: recall Santayana's comment that an art of clarifying intuition would likely be exemplified in a pedagogical setting of spiritual director and catechumens (*PGS*, 580).

Drawing on a tradition shared across centuries and around the world, Hector Galván's important unpublished 2019 essay, "Mindfulness and the Spiritual Life," argues for using mindfulness as described in the early Buddhist text the *Satipatthana Sutta*[36] to gain practical understanding of Santayana's notion of spiritual liberation. Drawing on interpretations of contemporary teachers, Galván characterized mindfulness as clear awareness of whatever arises in consciousness free from attachment or bias; and cultivating this awareness contributes to liberation from suffering, that is, to *nibbana* (or nirvana).

Though Galván referred to mindfulness as a practice, I would suggest it can be considered an exercise in service of liberation from suffering. His essay described how mindfulness can be developed through the practice of concentration meditation, in which you restrict attention to a single object, such as the breath (but the object could be any idea or deliverance of the senses; in Santayana's terms, any intuited essence). When attention is drawn to something else, as often happens, you can practice mental noting and identify the distraction as "sensation," "thinking," "planning," "remembering," or some other generic mental event. This can prevent you from being swept away by the distracting object and, instead, take it up as a new focus of attention. These practices together help you develop the open and choiceless awareness of mindfulness. And when you develop mindfulness and exercise it, then, according to the *Satipatthana Sutta*, you abide "independent, not clinging to anything in the world" (Goldstein, 40, 415; quoted in Galván 2019, n.p.).

Galván thought that mindfulness has much in common with Santayana's notion of pure intuition, suggesting that practices to develop mindfulness may similarly promote pure intuition. He also thought that the detachment and disinterest of mindfulness correspond to aspects of pure intuition, which has no bias or existential stake in what arises. And finally, he thought that mindfulness as an ongoing exercise develops a habit of mind in which you continually let go of attachment to whatever arises in consciousness similar to how the discovery of essence and pure intuition enable you to appreciate illusions without succumbing to them (*SAF*, 72). So, to use an example of Galván's, instead of *being* angry and *identifying* with the anger, you are aware of the emotional disturbance in the body and of the images that arise in consciousness. You then can observe sensations without immediately interpreting them and believing in the values they would impose, about, say, who is an enemy. Galván identified this habit of mind with what Santayana, in *Realms of Being*, called disintoxication. While he did not think mindfulness corresponds exactly to Santayana's philosophy, the general similarities in addition to the great variety of interpretations of

---

[36] For a translation of this text see Goldstein (2016, 405–415).

the tradition he appealed to suggest the potential for finding modifications and refinements of practices that could support the exercises of *SAF.*

In Michael Brodrick's *The Ethics of Detachment in Santayana's Philosophy*, the approach to spiritual practice departs from traditions of deliberate practice such as mindfulness in favor of the natural capacity, common to conscious beings, for spontaneous moments of liberated spirit. He called such moments spirituality, defined as "a form of contemplative activity that occurs when consciousness is fully absorbed in immediacies without any concern for their significance" (Brodrick 2015, 8). Brodrick distinguished spirituality from religion and its beliefs and practices; and while he acknowledged that beliefs and practices—religious and non-religious—may be means to achieving spirituality (e.g., seated meditation or a long walk) (Brodrick 2015, 44); he insisted, rightly, on the possibility of spirituality without practice.

One reason Brodrick valued spontaneous spirituality is his belief that it may bring relief to dying people tormented by regrets and anxieties, and in particular, advanced cancer patients with only days or weeks to live. In such cases, he thought spirituality superior to mindfulness as described by Galván because spirituality is spontaneous. Developing mindfulness would require time not available to a person about to die, but he thought a "modicum of spirituality" could be "induced by those caring for the dying person.... [perhaps by] facilitating non-demanding activities that foster present-focused absorption" (Brodrick 2015, 155). The activities he had in mind included, for example, spending time with beloved pets.

While Brodrick read Santayana as supporting the idea that "practice yields greater control in spirituality" (Brodrick 2015, 153),[37] the minimal practice—mainly that of a caregiver who induces spirituality, perhaps by fetching a pet or arranging some other significant experience—would seem to yield little control or reliable liberation from anxieties and regrets. Santayana acknowledged spontaneous spirituality that may come unbidden "to ne'er-do-wells, poets, actors, or rakes" and other undisciplined sorts including most of us, but he continued, "the spark dies in the burnt paper" (*RB*, 746). Without spiritual understanding or practices intended to relax dogma, purify intuition, and develop criticism in service of sane living, control of and benefits from spontaneous spirituality seem extremely limited. Of course, the experience of spirituality is qualitatively distinct from mere distraction, but the effects in many cases would be barely distinguishable. This sort of minimally cultivated spirituality would seem to do little for promoting less confusion and fear beyond the moment, with the further risk of exhausting its sources: I could imagine my own undisciplined mind

---

[37] Surprisingly, the offered textual support is the claim that spirituality is "a trick I do well" (Brodrick, 153), which recalls the above-quoted text, "I happen to be able to do this trick and to enjoy doing it" (*PGS*, 542), that suggests Santayana sometimes thought of his own exercise of pure intuition and contemplation of essence to be a matter of chance. The text quoted in *The Ethics of Detachment* appears without citation, so it is uncertain which Santayana text Brodrick had in mind.

becoming increasingly agitated and upset as death approached, rendering neutral or even irritating the previously comforting company of my beloved pet.

And, yet, solely focusing on spontaneous spirituality *is* a practice with historical precedent. It recalls the experience of sudden awakening found in the Indian Buddhist tradition but more often associated with the East Asian tradition of Chan Buddhism and known in Chinese as *dunwu*. Gaining awareness of spirituality, perhaps from reading Santayana or Brodrick, could turn your attention to those moments of liberated spirit that you previously did not notice or appreciate; and with increased attention you certainly will notice them more frequently than previously, which will contribute to relatively purer and more discriminating intuition. This may seem less helpful to a person near death, but no one can count on having more time than a person expected to die within days; and—here is the point—if awareness of spontaneous spirituality as a practice works at all it is because you are not closed off to the immediate accessibility of spirituality—it is a beneficial practice *right now*.

The problem of time that Brodrick responded to by emphasizing the spontaneity of spirituality emphasizes the significance of the idea that philosophy is preparation for dying and worth dedicating your life to, however long or short it may be.[38] And, indeed, Levinson thought that "for Santayana, philosophy was basically a discipline that permitted an individual to learn to live triumphantly with death.... a religious discipline" (Levinson 1984, 60).[39] To live triumphantly with death is another way of achieving "assurance and peace in being what one is [mortal and limited in strength and understanding], and in becoming what one must become [realizing the particular potentials that material existence has presented you and the facts of transformation and dissolution]" (*DL*, 40)—that is, of living abnormally sanely.

Levinson's further characterization of Santayana's philosophical work suggests it could be an art of eliciting intuitions that Santayana thought spiritual guides might practice with catechumens: Levinson thought that Santayana, in *Soliloquies in England and Other Soliloquies*, came to "identify philosophical meditation with" the performances of Carnival in that both opened "an imaginative world in which delight, joy, harmony, proportion, and beauty displaced the shadow of death"—there was no triumph over the *fact* of death but there was liberation from death's distracting domination of the spirit (Levinson 1984, 61). Levinson wrote that "just as the masks of Carnival depicted and evoked, through their disciplined presentations, a sort of fundamental human community able to make even tragedy festive" so too did Santayana's writing— as a sort of "philosophical 'mask'"—depict and evoke a human community, sharing a common animal faith, that could transform limitation into

---

[38] See Plato, *Phaedo*, 63e–64a (Plato 1961, 46).

[39] In *Winds of Doctrine*, Santayana asserted "that the spectacle of death was the first provocation to philosophy" (*WD*, 66), citing Schopenhauer. Compare Arthur Schopenhauer, *World as Will and Representation*, Vol. 3, trans. R. B. Haldane and J. Kemp (London: Kegan Paul, Trench, Trübner and Co., 1909), 249.

celebration of liberated spirit (Levinson 1984, 61). Santayana's written work, according to Levinson, "was presented in ways that did not simply depict triumphant self-transformation, but evoked it by luring the reader into the same sort of discipline" (Levinson 1984, 61). Hence, the spiritual practice is reading Santayana's work.

Conclusion

Santayana characterized his philosophy expressed in *SAF* and *Realms of Being* as "like that of the ancients a discipline of the mind and heart, a lay religion" (*RB*, 827). As religion it addresses the large facts of human existence that everyone encounters including facts of human limitations, death, imagination, and human community; and so is not personal. But as religion it is idiosyncratic and particular,[40] and his lay religion was articulated in his style and reflected his interests and abilities.

This tension between the large facts and the particular articulations of them is reflected in the opposing character of the practices surveyed here, each of which may cultivate spiritual liberation, but each going about it in a different way: both Stoic and Buddhist practices are grounded in tradition and community; but Brodrick's recommendation of spontaneous spiritual freedom rejects traditional disciplined practice, emphasizing the radicality—the basicness to individual human experience—of spirituality. The practice identified by Levinson seems to contain its own version of the tension: his anti-epistemological interpretation distinguished Santayana's thought more than it already was from a large segment of contemporary academic philosophy, while his recommended practice is that favored activity of the professional scholar of philosophy, namely, reading. (This approach is subversive; this approach is easily co-opted; or epistemologists are doing more than they or their critics realize, and definitely less than they know.)

Stoic and Buddhist approaches provide the guidance of teachers, the support of a community of practitioners, and scholarly traditions, all of which can expand and deepen understanding of Santayana's ideas in addition to supporting intense spiritual practice. Brodrick's emphasis on spontaneous spirituality lessens the risks of rote rehearsal of practices, exploitation by leaders, and factionalism and fanaticism that may infect communities committed to diverging interpretations of texts and traditions; and it offers an immediate freedom that characterizes sane living. Levinson's approach may take us closest to Santayana himself as a practitioner. It invites further inquiry into Santayana's writing as his spiritual practice,[41] that is, a specific practice of auscultation of psyche or criticism and a distinctive example in the tradition of spiritual writing.

---

[40] Santayana wrote that "the attempt to speak without speaking any particular language is not more hopeless than the attempt to have a religion that shall be no religion in particular" (*LR3*, 3).
[41] Levinson thought Santayana considered "philosophy as a kind of writing" (1984, 48).

So, there are practices, and they are various, for living sanely—undogmatically, consciously and free of delusion, and actively curious and aware of particular limits and potentials. This sanity requires awareness of the limits imposed by the material world on any living human, but it also requires that you live your particular and distinctive life. Sanity requires animal faith, and animal faith will orient your particular psyche in a way that sustains your individual organism. Liberating and sane practices must be chosen freely, but must not isolate the practitioner from their body, species, or world; and attention to the variety of practices, experimentation in practice, and criticism serve this end.

References

Works by Others

Adams, George P. 1925. Review of *Scepticism and Animal Faith*, by George Santayana. *The Philosophical Review* 34 (2): 193–197.

Alexander, Thomas. 2013. *The Human Eros*. New York: Fordham University Press.

Brodrick, Michael. 2015. *The Ethics of Detachment in Santayana's Philosophy*. London: Palgrave Macmillan.

Carr, H.W. 1923. Review of *Scepticism and Animal Faith: Introduction to a System of Philosophy, The Life of Reason: Or the Phases of Human Progress. Nature* 112: 572–573. (Cited in McCormick 1987, 259).

Descartes, René. 2006. *Meditations on First Philosophy*, in *Meditations, Objections, and Replies*, eds. and trans. Roger Ariew and Donald Cress, 46–103. Indianapolis and Cambridge, Massachusetts: Hackett.

Galván, Hector. 2019. Mindfulness and the Spiritual Life. Paper presented at the Annual Meeting of the George Santayana Society, New York, January.

Goldstein, Joseph. 2016. *Mindfulness: A Practical Guide to Awakening*. Boulder, Colorado: Sounds True.

Heney, Diana. 2023. Laying Siege to the Truth: Santayana's Discourse on Method. *The Palgrave Companion to George Santayana's* Scepticism and Animal Faith. London: Palgrave Macmillan.

Kahneman, Daniel. 2011. *Thinking Fast and Slow*. New York: Farrar, Straus and Giroux.

Kremplewska, Katarzyna. 2019. *Life as Insinuation: George Santayana's Hermeneutics of Finite Life and Human Self*. Albany: SUNY Press.

Lachs, John. 2006. *On Santayana*. Belmont, California: Thomson Wadsworth.

———. 2009. Animal Faith and Ontology. *Transactions of the Charles S. Peirce Society* 45:4, 484–90, Symposium on the Work of Angus Kerr-Lawson, ed. Glenn Tiller.

———. 2011. The Method of Animal Faith. In *George Santayana, Santayana: un pensador universal*, eds. José Beltrán, Manuel Garrido. CD-ROM appendix. Valencia: Publicacions de la Universitat de València.

———. 2012. *Stoic Pragmatism*. Bloomington and Indianapolis: Indiana University Press.

Levinson, Henry Samuel. 1984. Santayana's Contribution to American Religious Philosophy. *Journal of the American Academy of Religion* 52 (1): 47–69.

———. 1987. Meditation at the Margins: Santayana's *Scepticism and Animal Faith*. *The Journal of Religion* 67 (3): 289–303.

———. 1992. *Santayana, Pragmatism, and the Spiritual Life*. Chapel Hill and London: The University of North Carolina Press.
McCormick, John. 1987. *George Santayana: A Biography*. New York: Alfred A. Knopf.
McDermid, Douglas. 2009. Santayana or Descartes? Meditations on *Scepticism and Animal Faith*. *Overheard in Seville: Bulletin of the Santayana Society* 27: 1–8.
Miller, Steven A., and Yasuko Taoka. 2015. Toward a Practice of Stoic Pragmatism. *The Pluralist* 10 (2): 150–171.
Moreno, Daniel. 2015. *Santayana the Philosopher: Philosophy as a Form of Life*. Translated by Charles Padrón. Lewisburg, Pennsylvania: Bucknell University Press.
Pinkas, Daniel. 2023. Scepticism, Anti-scepticism, and Santayana's Singularity. In *The Palgrave Companion to George Santayana's Scepticism and Animal Faith*. London: Palgrave Macmillan.
Plato. 1961. *The Collected Dialogues of Plato, Including the Letters*. Edited by Edith Hamilton, Huntington Cairns. New York: Bollingen Foundation.
Russell, Bertrand. 1923. A New System of Philosophy, review of *Scepticism and Animal Faith*, by George Santayana. *The Dial* 75: 278–281.
Saatkamp, Herman. 2021. *A Life of Scholarship with Santayana: Essays and Reflections*. Edited by Charles Padrón and Krzysztof Piotr Skowroński. Leiden and Boston: Brill Rodopi.
Sprigge, T.L.S. 1995. *Santayana: An Examination of His Philosophy*. rev. ed. London and New York: Routledge.
Ten Hoor, Marten. 1923. Review of *Scepticism and Animal Faith*, by George Santayana. *The Journal of Philosophy* 20 (24): 653–665.

Works of George Santayana

George Santayana. 1905a. *The Life of Reason: Reason in Common Sense*. Book 1, Vol. VII, *The Works of George Santayana*, critical edition, eds. Marianne Wokeck, Martin Coleman. Cambridge, Massachusetts, and London: The MIT Press.
———. 1905b. *The Life of Reason: Reason in Society*. Book 2, Vol. VII, *The Works of George Santayana*, critical edition, eds. Marianne Wokeck, Martin Coleman Cambridge, Massachusetts, and London: The MIT Press.
———. 1905c. *The Life of Reason: Reason in Religion*. Book 3, Vol. VII, *The Works of George Santayana*, critical edition, eds. Marianne Wokeck, Martin Coleman. Cambridge, Massachusetts, and London: The MIT Press.
Santayana, George. 1913. *Winds of Doctrine*. New York: Charles Scribner's Sons.
———. 1923. *Scepticism and Animal Faith*. New York: Charles Scribner's Sons.
———. 1940. Apologia Pro Mente Sua. In *The Philosophy of George Santayana*, ed. Paul Arthur, 495–605. Schilpp. Evanston and Chicago: Northwestern University.
———. 1942. *Realms of Being*. New York: Charles Scribner's Sons.
George Santayana. 1948. Normal Madness. Chapter 3 in *Dialogues in Limbo: With Three New Dialogues*, 36–57. New York: Charles Scribner's Sons.
———. 1986. *Persons and Places*. Vol. I, *The Works of George Santayana*, critical edition, eds. William G. Holzberger, Herman J. Saatkamp. Cambridge, Massachusetts, and London: The MIT Press.
———. 2008. *The Letters of George Santayana: Book 8, 1948–1952*. Vol. VIII, *The Works of George Santayana*, critical edition, ed. William G. Holzberger. Cambridge, Massachusetts, and London: The MIT Press.

The Cries of Spirit: Santayana in Dialogue with Andrey Platonov

Matthew Caleb Flamm

Crying with Chagataev's Camel: Or Why Epiphenomenalism is a Pseudo-issue

What is the connection between suffering and spirituality? A pat dismissal of religion argues that people only find God at the height of suffering—that is, out of moral convenience, vain cowardice, or some other "failure of nerve." Such a criticism is obviously too easy and, as discussed here in relation to the philosopher's question of "epiphenomenalism," a result of the same pseudo-reasoning that leads people to wonder whether consciousness matters at all.

Anyone can mock and with good reason dismiss the disingenuous conversion of a scoundrel, one who with little more than a verbal declaration of repentance on his deathbed hopes to be delivered from cosmic judgment after a life of lasciviousness and criminality. But the "little more" here is key. If we *do* see genuine anguish in the repentant sufferer's heart, has he not begun to fulfill the divine injunction to "rend his heart and not his garments"?[1] Whether or not we are obliged to authorize him worthy of cosmic forgiveness, his genuine anguish surely lends a human sympathy to the idea that, even at the apex of suffering, he is on the verge of faith.

---

[1] Joel 2:13.

M. C. Flamm (✉)
College of Arts and Humanities, Rockford University, Rockford, IL, USA
e-mail: MFlamm@rockford.edu

© The Author(s), under exclusive license to Springer Nature Switzerland AG 2024
M. A. Coleman, G. Tiller (eds.), *The Palgrave Companion to George Santayana's Scepticism and Animal Faith*, Palgrave Companions,
https://doi.org/10.1007/978-3-031-46367-9_13

Though rare, and whether or not we forgive, we sometimes *do* see anguish in the repentant heart and when we do, we recognize what Santayana calls spirit and spirituality. "We must admit," he writes in *SAF*, "that spirit is not in time, that the perception of flux (or of anything else) is not a flux, but a synthetic glance and a single intuition of relation, of form, of quality" (*SAF*, 161). Spirit is out of time, witness to the material flux, capable of intuitively arresting aspects of that flux that are invisible to others (these *aspects* are what Santayana calls "essences," intuitions of "relation, form, quality"). Spirit is not a material existence, but since it is the crying witness of an existing material body, its aspect can be discerned in other spirits, just as sound is heard emanating from an instrument: "spirit is physically the voice of the soul crying in the wilderness."[2] The anguish we see in the repentant heart is a glimpse of just such a phenomenon: in his suffering we see what he sees, *that* he has "intuited" a relation creating in him recognition of an overwhelming moral responsibility.

The connection between spirituality and suffering is thus implied in (perhaps especially) experiences of human empathy which have the power to syncretize a wide array of otherwise disparate, even nonhuman forms of life. A stunning illustration is provided in Andrey Platonov's profound short novel *Soul* or *"Dzhan."* The Dzhan is an ancient tribe of Central Asia living in the most reduced circumstances imaginable. The protagonist Chagataev—appropriately, an economist commissioned by the Soviet state to bring socialism to his people—is journeying from Moscow back to his birthplace.[3] Entering the territory of the Amu-Darya river delta he comes upon a strange sight, a "camel sitting like a human being, propped up on his front legs in a drift of sand" (Platonov 2007, 26). Chagataev interprets that the camel, hairless and emaciated from "illness and need," has been abandoned by its caravan, or perhaps its master has died and "until he had expended his own reserve of life, the animal was going to wait for him" (27). No longer having the capacity to raise himself by his front legs, and because he will not be able to get back up if he "sinks back and lies down" (27), the camel remains positioned oddly as described, eyeing dead stems of grass and tumbleweeds with a wistful hope that he can snatch them in his teeth as they drift past.

Platonov describes the eyes of the camel (seen through those of Chagataev) as resembling a "sad, intelligent human being." At one point, while the camel spies an approaching tumbleweed, a cross wind blows the weed in another direction, prompting him to close his eyes "because he did not know how he was meant to cry" (28). At times the camel looks to Chagataev as though "ready either to weep or to smile, and tormented because he did not know how" (28). These emotions are presented by Platonov in a way that resists

---

[2] *RB*, 568, underlining mine.
[3] A journey that takes him southeast from Moscow through modern Kazakhstan, wending at its southern border near Tashkent, turning south-westerly towards the northern border of Afghanistan.

interpretive closure: are these anthropomorphic "projections" of Chagataev? Of the author Platonov? Are they meant to literally express the "inner emotional state" of the camel? Platonov leaves such questions to the reader to decide, so whether or not the reader will "feel with" Chagataev the reality of the situation becomes a matter itself of spiritual capacity.

Chagataev winds up gathering tumbleweed for the camel and, as night is coming on, hugging close to the animal for warmth. Platonov describes Chagataev's mood as he settles in to sleep with the camel:

> Everything in the existing world seemed strange to him; it was as if the world had been created for some brief mocking game. But this game of make believe had dragged on for a long time, for eternity, and nobody felt like laughing any more. The desert's deserted emptiness, the camel, even the pitiful wandering grass—all this ought to be serious, grand and triumphant. Inside every poor creature was a sense of some other happy destiny, a destiny that was necessary and inevitable—why, then, did they find their lives such a burden and why were they always waiting for something? (Platonov 2007, 27–28)

What are they waiting for? The encounter with the camel enables Chagataev to achieve a point of view that precisely illustrates Santayana's description of spirituality as "enlarg[ing one's] acquaintance with true being" (*SAF*, 75). The "desert's deserted emptiness" ought to be "serious, grand and triumphant": this could be taken to mean that its vast, barren bleakness ought to evoke a heroic sense of surviving struggle. Instead, it evokes in Chagataev a realization of the vanity and pointlessness of the cruel suffering struggles of all "poor creatures" such as those of the dying camel. The camel *does not know how he was meant to cry or laugh*—expressions he is on the verge of achieving and appears to desire. Apparently he cannot achieve such expressions because he is a non-human animal, coping with the direst struggles, as such creatures are apt to do, with what appears from the human standpoint to be an eerie, indifferent equanimity.

This aspect of the camel responding to its extreme suffering (with eerie equanimity) describes other human characters Chagataev will encounter on his journey to come. One important such character is Sufyan, a "forgotten old man" who had "passed his days in a shelter dug out from a hillside":

> And he lived on small animals and the roots of plants that grew in the crevices on the plateau. Ancient age and the hardship of life had nearly deprived him of human form. He had lived far beyond the human life span, all his feelings had been satisfied, and his mind had studied and memorized the world around him with the precision of long-exhausted truth. Through habit he knew even the stars by heart, many thousands of them, and they bored him. (Platonov 2007, 30)

Mostly out of indifference and want of a better thing to do (Chagataev is the first human Sufyan has apparently seen in quite some time), Sufyan will join Chagataev on his journey to find his long-lost mother and birthplace. Later in his journey when Chagataev is reunited with his mother Gyulchatay, she will exhibit the same indifferent sort of feral openness to existence, an attitude shared by most of the other diminished (*or are they enlarged?*) inhabitants of this materially wasted and dying homeland. For example, similar to Sufyan, there is among them an outsider, a Russian "Ivan the Old" for whom "Almost every day, for sixty years, his life should have come to an end, but he had not yet died even once and, having lost faith in the power of death and every kind of disaster, he now lived with indifferent equanimity" (71, underlining mine).

A conventionally religious reader is disturbed by these images because of the revaluation of the motif of sacredness of the desert wanderer. Among other traditions, Platonov's *Soul* can be read as reevaluating the Biblical tale of Moses leading the Israelites out of Egypt.[4] In one respect, desert solitude and spiritual isolation seem to do little for what might be called the *humanity* of these characters: the Dzhan wanderers immediately and without reflection consume wet clay to sate their thirst, as well as dead human and animal bodies, drinking the blood before it gets cold. But it is just this question of "humanity," a question conventional minds tend to associate with things like civic virtue and the preservation of established values, that tends to put to trial the deepest considerations of what is also named "soul" and "spirit."

The camel encounter is the beginning of Chagataev's spiritual journey. Chagataev is moved to stay with the camel, to share his anguish, and to mourn on his behalf the sufferings of all "poor creatures." Chagataev cries *for-and-with* the camel, and we readers are enjoined to cry with them both. Chagataev's is no mere act of sentimental sympathy. In fact, it would be a mistake to think of it as an "act" at all. An "act" involves some relation of a singular object or locus, yet Chagataev's encounter with the camel opens to him the possibility of a spiritual relation to all things. The experience of Chagataev with the camel is a *happening* that determines all that is to come for him. An "astonishment at strange reality" overtakes him as he falls asleep with the camel (Platonov 2007, 28). This sets in motion a spiritual journey to his childhood home (what began as an errand for the socialist State has turned into something altogether different).

Chagataev's spiritual destiny in the greater narrative is perhaps foreshadowed in Platonov's description of the protagonist's outlook as the story develops: "[Chagataev] cared for everything that existed, as if it were sacred, and his heart was too thrifty not to notice whatever might serve as consolation" (29). Chagataev is an economist (thus, a good materialist), and Platonov's narrative deploys the adjectives of "economy" and "thrift" to describe various characters' survival strategies; their existences having been pared down to primal levels, it is a *material* necessity to mercilessly select what they value most. Chagataev discovers in this state of material deprivation that he values

---

[4] Interpreters of Platonov's *Soul* have seen Sufist elements—the mystical aspect of Islam that importantly influences aspects of the history and culture of Iran and Central Asia. For more interpretive angles on the interfacing of traditions in Platonov's works, see Livingstone 2001.

everything that exists, which can only be valued with the thriftiest of hearts—a heart that does not waste its love on the unlovable but finds in the latter whatever tiny morsel there is deserving of human consideration.

This astonishing text of Platonov's contains exquisite descriptions of precisely what Santayana means by spirituality and sets up an understanding of its relation to suffering: most particularly how *crying* is an opening to spirit. But the shift from a humanistic-literary reference point to a formal philosophical one is jarring and begs accounting. The spiritual relation here is what in starchy philosopher's terms would be called a "mind-world relationship," and as such, introduces considerations of relevance to a rather abstract (if related) preoccupation in Santayana scholarship. An unsettled question among interpreters of Santayana's thought is that of the relation of, and distinction between, psyche and spirit. And just here is an interesting, perhaps ironic paradox in our Platonov-Santayana cross comparison because Santayana introduces the distinction to avoid the "poetical word ... soul, laden with so many equivocations," and labels psyche and spirit "two levels of life" (*RB*, 331). We shall see that Santayana himself identifies "soul" with *psyche* and so does not perhaps altogether evade the "equivocations" he hoped to avoid. (The comparison with Platonov will serve to show that this is a good thing.) Suffice here to say that the "two levels" of what Santayana calls psyche and spirit are material and spiritual.[5]

Anyone familiar with abiding controversies in philosophy will immediately and correctly think here of the specter of dualism: the so-called mind-body problem, the bugbear legacy of Cartesianism which divides individual persons into two irreconcilable realms, one "material" and the other "mental" or "conscious." Among Santayana interpreters this question has been addressed for the most part in relation to the question of his purported "epiphenomenalism," the view that consciousness has no causal relation to the material world (a view he endorses throughout his writings).

Robin Weiss has made a plausible case for ceasing to characterize Santayana as an "epiphenomenalist" and to call him a "compatibilist" (a concept from the parlance of contemporary philosophy of mind).[6] Certainly *compatibilism* is the correct label if one is motivated to "update" Santayana's thought for contemporary understanding, to fit him within the fashionable lingo of a specialized sub-discipline of philosophy. Compatibilism, as I understand the label, is basically the idea that freewill and determinism are both true. That is, compatibilists hold that humans are, in a special sense, *free* to direct the course of their

---

[5] As will be discussed in the next section, psyche is the material "level of life" here and is a "habit in matter"; meantime spirit is the "light of consciousness," or "the ultimate invisible emotional fruition of life in feeling and thought" (*SE*, 25).

[6] Robin Weiss. "Santayana's Epiphenomenalism Reconsidered." *European Journal of Pragmatism and American Philosophy*. XII-2, 2020: https://journals.openedition.org/ejpap/2138. Weiss is critically responding to the views of Jessica Wahman ("Why Psyche Matters." *Transactions of the Charles S. Peirce Society*. 2006 Winter); and Michael Brodrick ("Santayana's Amphibious Concepts." *Transactions of the Charles S. Peirce Society*. Spring 2013).

own lives, and yet in another special sense, their minds and choices are *determined* by some, usually material, cause. So to call Santayana a "compatibilist" is only to say that he falls in line with this double-allegiance to both freewill *and* determinism.

I have two issues with this approach to Santayana's view of consciousness. First, it is unnecessary. His position on consciousness is not in need of help from recently invented labels from contemporary philosophers of mind that are supposed to resolve the freewill-determinism debate: it is the other way around. That is, contemporary philosophers of mind could stand to adopt Santayana's understanding to treat with more subtlety the freewill-determinism puzzles they entertain.[7] "Compatibilism" is a new *sounding* label for a very old position held by, for example, Aristotle, who would undoubtedly have thought such a label, or any such like it, odd and unnecessary. It never occurred to Aristotle that what we call "freewill" is somehow *incompatible* with or in need of reconciliation to what we call "determinism."[8]

Second, and more important for purposes to come, approaching Santayana's view of consciousness in the manner of Weiss manufactures and makes *appear* to be a "problem" what has already been well-addressed and resolved in Santayana's greater doctrine of spirit. For what is the epiphenomenalism debate centrally about? (It is perhaps too embarrassing to admit, so one never hears anyone in philosophy say it.) *It is about whether consciousness matters.* Even the most zealous "epiphenomenalist" (let us suppose he has finally and decisively proven that consciousness has no causal influence on the world), every moment of his everyday life, maintains faith that *his* consciousness matters: that it influences the world. His faith that his thoughts have influential relation to the

---

[7] I believe Jessica Wahman comes closest to showing this in her work—that is, how and why contemporary philosophers of mind/psychologists, etc., *need* Santayana and not vice versa (see, for example, "Why Psyche Matters" by Jessica Wahman (*Transactions of the Charles S. Peirce Society*. 2006 Winter; 42(1): (133)).

[8] Just here one should keep in mind that Santayana's view of consciousness/spirit is basically that of Aristotle's notion of "entelechy" (Greek *entelecheia*, that which realizes or makes actual what is potential): "spirit," Santayana writes, "is an entelechy, or perfection of function realized; so that (if I may parody Aristotle), if a candle were a living being, wax would be its substance and light its spirit" (*SAF*, 217). Earlier in *SAF* Santayana writes, "The contemplation of so much of essence as is relevant to a particular life is what Aristotle called the entelechy or perfect fruition of life" (*SAF*, 130). As Santayana says, he may be "parodying" Aristotle somewhat—Aristotle's use of "entelechy" seems to pertain to what is imperfectly translated as "soul" or "psyche," which as we shall discuss are given separate distinction by Santayana—but we have more indication yet of Aristotle's influence in Santayana's earlier work *Life of Reason: Reason in Common Sense* (which he wrote when arguably *most* under the influence of Aristotle): "Mind is the body's <u>entelechy</u>, a value which accrues to the body when it has reached a certain perfection, of which it would be a pity, so to speak, that it should remain unconscious; so that while the body feeds the mind the mind perfects the body, lifting it and all its natural relations and impulses into the moral world, into the sphere of interests and ideas" [underlining mine] (*The Life of Reason: Introduction and Reason in Common Sense*. Critical Edition, MIT Press, co-edited by Marianne S. Wokeck and Martin A. Coleman, 2011: 125).

world will betray at every point his vain proof that consciousness "has no causal power."[9] Of what use to life then is the philosopher's proof?

The same hypocrisy is operative in the person highlighted at the opening who dismisses religion because of the disingenuous repentant heart. Like the passionate "epiphenomenalist," he conveniently pronounces the irrelevance of an entire sphere of value and meaning based on a single poor sample of its fulfillment. These critics are only exposing their cynicism about the meaningfulness of consciousness, something they actually never doubt—they clearly think consciousness matters—but it is apparently easier for the sake of intellectual comfort to pretend otherwise.

Although Santayana was perhaps not the only "living materialist" (as he joked),[10] he might have been the last philosopher to have believed in the spiritual capacity of mind from a materialist point of view. Because just here it should be acknowledged that the question of epiphenomenalism appears less ridiculous when posed in relation to the broader consideration of the status of spirit and spirituality in Santayana's thinking.[11] This is because for Santayana consciousness *is* spirit, and what he calls the life of spirit is given premium status in his thinking.

Santayana's so-called life of spirit is sometimes accused of being a spectatorial, contemplative retreat from the world, rendering mind impotent in relation to material life. Although there are critics in this direction,[12] I defend here (with the aid of Platonov's *Soul*) a contrary position. It is helpful here to cite a lengthy passage from the preface of *The Realm of Spirit*:

> What I call spirit is only that inner light of actuality or attention which floods all life as men actually live it on earth. It is roughly the same thing as feeling or thought; it might be called consciousness; it might be identified with the *pensée* or *cogitatio* of Descartes and Spinoza. Yet there is an important circumstance that leads me to prefer the term spirit. In modern philosophy the notion of mind has become confused and treacherous, so that in whatever direction we press it into consistency, mind ceases to be mind. Pushed inwards, it may be reduced to a vanishing ego, the grammatical counterpart, impersonal and empty, of all feelings and objects alike. Driven outwards, mind may be lost in its objects, and identified with the existence and movement of a phenomenal world or the history of events. Again, mind may be conceived dynamically, called will or life, and turned into a magic law or impulsion supposed to compel things to become what they are. And it may be conceived analytically and dissolved into a multitude—nowhere

---

[9] William James makes this point forcefully in "The Dilemma of Determinism" (James 1977).

[10] "In natural philosophy I am a decided materialist—apparently the only one living ..." (*SAF*, vii).

[11] As Michael Brodrick attempts in "Santayana's Amphibious Concepts" (*Transactions of the Charles S. Peirce Society*. 2013 Spring 2013; 49 [2]). Another important recent essay in this direction (one that does not focus on epiphenomenalism but offers resources for those addressing the question) is Drew Chastain. "Liberating Spirit from Santayana's Spectatorial Spirituality" (*OiS* 2018).

[12] See Chastain (*OiS* 2018).

assembled—separate data, or a series of feelings each feeling itself, and none feeling any other. Or instead of data, which after all are thinkable and given, mind may be dissolved into a diffused unconscious substance still paradoxically called feeling, out of which organic bodies and centres of apprehension might be composed. Yet all these results are abdications, and living mind is none of those things. It is a moral stress of varying scope and intensity, full of will and selectiveness, arising in animal bodies, and raising their private vicissitudes into a moral experience. This inner light is indeed requisite for focusing impressions and rendering them mentally present, but it is biologically prior to them, vital and central, a product of combustion, a leaping flame, a fountain and seat of judgment. I therefore call it spirit; not that I think it either a substance or a physical power, or capable of existing by itself, but that it is a personal and moral focus of life, where the perspectives of nature are reversed as in a mirror and attached to the fortunes of a single soul. (*RB*, 549–50, underlining mine)

So much in this comprehensive passage addresses foregoing considerations. Two to mention: the compatibility of mind/spirit with both free *and* determined features of existence (mind is both a combustive "product" of matter, and "biologically prior" to those causal processes); and the various ways in which modern conceptions can be seen as *abdicating* living mind (suggesting the need to draw from a richer tradition such as Santayana draws from Aristotle).

The crucial theme of this passage for present purposes, however, is that spirit (Santayana's preferred word for "mind/consciousness") is a "moral stress/focus of varying scope and intensity," and that spirit emerges from the "perspectives of nature" with those perspectives "reversed" and "attached to the fortunes of a single soul." This means that for Santayana spirit is not an impotent spectator. Spirit is borne of suffering and its share of existence comes in the form of the *personal, moral stakes* existence has for living beings. "The great characteristic of human spirit," he writes in the introduction to *Realms of Being*, "is its helplessness and misery, most miserable and helpless when it fancies itself dominant and independent; and the great problem for it is salvation, purification, rebirth into a humble recognition of the powers on which it depends, and into a sane enjoyment of its appropriate virtues" (*RB*, xxxii).

To put a final important point on the triviality of the question of epiphenomenalism in relation to this, there is the much-referenced but still underappreciated 1913 Santayana letter to Horace Kallen which contains Santayana's succinct consideration of the label "epiphenomenalism" applied to his thought. He explains his objection to the label as follows:

[I]t is based ... on idealistic prejudices and presuppositions. An epiphenomenon must have some other phenomenon under it: but what underlies the mind, according to my view, is not a phenomenon but a substance—the body, or nature at large. To call this is [sic] a phenomenon is to presuppose another thing in itself, which is chimerical. Therefore I am no epiphenomenalist, but a naturalist pure and simple, recognizing a material world, not a phenomenon but a substance, and a mental life struck off from it in its operation, like a spark from the flint and steel, having no other substance than that material world, but having a distinct existence of its own (as it is emitted continually out of bodily life as music is emitted from an instrument) and having a very different kind of being, since it is immaterial and moral and cognitive. This mental life may be called a phenomenon if you like, either in the platonic sense of being an instance of an essence (in which sense every fact, even substance, is a phenomenon) or in the modern sense of being an observable effect of latent forces; but it cannot be called an epiphenomenon, unless you use the word phenomenon in the one sense for substance and in the other sense for consciousness.[13] (*LGS*, 2:127, to Horace Meyer Kallen, Madrid, April 17, 1913)

One sees from this letter that Santayana's objection centers on the word "phenomenon," which has a special significance in philosophy: he is concerned with its distinction from what he understands as "substance." Santayana's own understanding of the concept "phenomenon" is rooted in its historical inception, in modern philosophy from Hume through Kant and Hegel. He explains this in *Scepticism and Animal Faith* (*SAF*), where he charges that Modern philosophers "deny substance in favour of phenomena, which are hypostatised essences, because phenomena are individually wholly open to intuition" (*SAF*, 183). For Santayana the only thing "open to intuition" is what he calls *essence* or appearance (the "given" of reality). The underlying substance or matter (the ground of appearance) is a feature of *intent* or belief and is not open to intuition (to spirit).

This then is a critique of the entire gamut of Modern philosophers from Hume through the Kantian and Hegelian traditions, which posit "phenomena" in replacement of what was traditionally understood as substance. The concept "phenomenon"—among others such as "sensations" and "experience" Santayana reviews in the chapter "Belief in Substance"—is a "hypostatized" essence. To "hypostatize" in a simple sense is to treat something that is abstract as concrete,[14] to make substantial that which lacks substance. Santayana's view is that Kant was guilty of this in his own "phenomenonalism."[15]

---

[13] Note here the repeated invocation of music as emitted from an instrument being akin to spirit/consciousness. As Robert Chandler observes in the book's introduction, Platonov's *Soul* also "devotes considerable attention ... to music." I just highlight the musical connection here and delay for a moment further important comment in order to extrapolate Santayana's letter.

[14] This suggests that essences are "abstract," but it is misleading to leave it there: in exactly what sense essences are "abstract" is a matter of further consideration that runs afield of this discussion, but Santayana has a beautiful explanation of this feature of his doctrine of essence (see the chapter "Some Uses of this Discovery" in *SAF*).

[15] One should recall here that Kant was inspired by the phenomenalism of Hume. Hume's empirical critique of knowledge entailed the demolition of all "abstract" ideas not traceable to original sense impressions. The only reliable knowledge for Hume derives from directly known sense particulars (so Hume was a nominalist), and these "sense data," as they are called, are the ground of Hume's phenomenalism. From Santayana's point of view, Kant adhered to this phenomenalism because, although he purported to be establishing for mind a "single grammar" of "categories, and schemata, and forms of intuition," these were all in actuality "pompous titles for what Hume had satirically called tendencies to feign" (*SAF*, 300); he elaborates that "the only pure doctrine of Kant" (like that of Hume) "was that knowledge is impossible" (*SAF*, 301).

By the historical time phenomenalism had traveled through Kant into the Hegelian tradition, the project had become one of developing a *phenomenology* of spirit (knowledge of the absolute through the dialectical systematization of direct experience—to say nothing of the so-called dialectical materialism of Marx). In other words, from Santayana's point of view all Modern philosophers through the German idealist tradition remained committed to a critical project reducing what in common sense is called "matter" and "substance" to some hypostatized ideal essence.[16]

All this serves to show that attempting to justify or condemn Santayana's perceived epiphenomenalism tends in my view (to borrow a sentiment of Santayana's) to "squint too much at the facts."[17] What is needed is not an apology for Santayana's epiphenomenalism but a robust understanding of Santayana's understanding of spirit. This I now turn to directly—focusing on the experience of crying in order to think through Santayana's understanding of the interrelation of psyche and spirit.

Manikin Nature

Here is an unforgettable image from *Scepticism and Animal Faith* (*SAF*), the image of a child crying at the discovery of a manikin formerly assumed to be a living man:

> Imagine a child accustomed to see clothes only on living persons and hardly distinguishing them from the magical strong bodies that agitate them, and suddenly carry this child into a costumer's shop, where he will see all sorts of garments hung in rows upon manikins, with hollow breasts all of visible wire, and little wooden nobs instead of heads; he might be seriously shocked or even frightened. How should it be possible for clothes standing up like this not to be people? ... Just as the spectacle of all these gaunt clothes without bodies might make the child cry, so later might the whole spectacle of nature, if ever he became a sceptic. (*SAF*, 70–71)

---

[16] From the above letter one might be led to wonder whether it is acceptable to call Santayana an "epi-materialist," making his objection to epiphenomenalism something of a verbal quibble (replace the word "phenomenon" with "substance" or "matter"). This would in my understanding of Santayana be a mistake. By my reading there is no "epi" anything—no category in Santayana's ontological system supervenes on another or "stands out" for inspection in the background of which another realm resides. This follows from Santayana's clear indication of his intent in calling his identified realms (essence, matter, truth, spirit) "ontological": "The Realms of Being of which I speak are not parts of a cosmos, nor one great cosmos together: they are only kinds or categories of things which I find conspicuously different and worth distinguishing, at least in my own thoughts" (*SAF*, vi); he says as well that the realms have "inherent differences in them which nothing can ever obliterate" (*RB*, 184). In other words, ontology is not taxonomy of realities but of forms, qualities of being, discriminated by spirit (an irreducible moral center).

[17] "[each of the 'special schools of philosophy'] squints and overlooks half the facts and half the difficulties in its eagerness to find in some detail the key to the whole" (*SAF*, v).

If ever he became a sceptic. The imaginative credulity that sets the child up for metaphysical shock interacting with living beings foreshadows a parallel shock for the sceptical adult about the whole of nature. Why scepticism? Why the "whole *spectacle*, of nature?"

The context of the above quote is the "Discovery of Essence," chapter nine of *SAF*. Santayana describes the discovery of essence in terms of pure spirit, as an opening "into fields of endless variety and peace," out of the "gorges of death" and "into a paradise where all things are crystallised into the image of themselves. ..." (*SAF*, 76). Sounds somewhat like Chatagaev's discovery in the desert, yet the description of the manikin-traumatized child hardly exhibits any discovery of this grandiose sort. The fact that the experience is potentially traumatizing for the child has not (as yet) to do with any kind of intellectual, sceptical commitment on his part. It would be strange and presupposing to conclude that he has himself "discovered essence"; rather, the child's trauma is due to stark natural facts crashing into his naïve imaginative life. If the hypothetical child cries, it cannot be from any discovery of the sort Santayana describes of the spiritual release accompanying acquaintance with essence (the child clearly feels no sense of peace or paradise). Clearly, rather, his cry indicates a significant loss.

But *now* what will the child do? The general process of personal and intellectual maturation apparently entails, ontologically speaking, an increased generalized scepticism. Or, if "scepticism" is too strong, *formal* a word, one can agree that the crying child, if he is to avoid the perverse absurdity of perpetually being shocked by the basic facts of life and nature, will come to need to abstain from believing certain falsehoods. At the very least, *some* sceptical maturation is required if the child is to develop flourishingly. In order to avoid perpetual shock and trauma, a person must start placing diverse realities in correct relations; one must start to, as it were, ontologically separate clothes from bodies and living persons from their inanimate counterparts. One must come to separate realities from appearances. And as shall be seen, this is precisely where a counterbalancing influence from spirit is needed. If the maturing child is to avoid the bad consequences of the other extreme, excessive scepticism, spiritual understanding is essential.

Imagine the shocked child prolonging in immaturity. He would inevitably meet with increased levels of trauma; persisting in imaginative credulity, he would eventually have to devise greater and greater delusional strategies to cope. Perhaps he populates his world with races of manikin spirits vexing and taunting their human counterparts. If the child wishes to avoid a world of illusion, perhaps inevitably a world of increasing *delusion*, scepticism, whatever its informal manifestation, becomes a basic coping skill.

While the persistently credulous child creates a world of illusion, the increasingly sceptical adult must come to terms not with *delusion* but with *disillusion*. However much trauma the credulous child comes to endure, his world is at least still alive with color, passion, blood, and drama. The survival of these living elements comes at the cost of a delusional world, a world populated by imagined entities. By contrast the world of a growing sceptic, should he become over-zealous, risks losing what gives *it* meaning and worth (risks losing the world's color, passion, blood, and drama).

Historically, intellectually, there has been no shortage of such over-zealous sceptics. They are very often reductive materialists, perhaps also cynics who, like the critic referenced in the opening, dismiss religion for its disingenuous professors of faith. Such philosophers will perhaps always find newer, creative ways to rid the world of its unexpected shocks and wonders to make room for the fantasy of the permanent peace of certitude. One is reminded here of William James's favorite foil W. K. Clifford, who proclaimed that the highest treason is to believe on insufficient evidence; or chortlers like Baron d'Holbach who claim without irony that "invariable truth … can never harm" a person. Their worlds, constructed as they are in platitudes of arrogant self-righteousness, utterly drained of imaginative speculation and poetic insight, lack precisely what makes life worthy, even, of sorrow or love. The irony here is that it is obvious to anyone that the truths of the world these two so dogmatically covet—and insist cannot harm—must have very much harmed them (and must now be more capable than ever of harming them); what else could have produced in them such willing intellectual servitude?[18]

Such worlds are precisely those Santayana has in mind in his allusion to the "whole spectacle of nature" which, no less than the vulnerable child's manikin, would be apt to horrify an over-zealous Cliffordian, Holbachean sceptic. What is obvious here is that the persistent sceptic, no less than the credulous child, is primed for a fall, for a shock of terror. Whether such a shock should arise for the sceptic depends on considerations no less operative in the imaginative child. How receptive is he to the world and its complexities? How much does his intellectual bias hold up in the face of that receptivity? And finally, what relation to the world awaits that is apt to send the whole house of cards crashing?

Psyche as the Echo-Locator of Matter

The manikin-traumatized child and nature-jilted sceptic need to return to their psyche-spirit centers: like Chagataev with his camel, they need a good cry. Freud might say the manikin-traumatized child and nature-jilted sceptic have experienced the *uncanny*: "Uncanny is in reality nothing new or alien, but something which is familiar and old-established in the mind and which has become alienated from it …"[19] Freud's analysis of the uncanny is an apt reference point because he diagnoses the phenomenon as a result of the interface of

---

[18] Paul-Henri Thiry, Baron d' Holbach (1723–1789): "An organized being may be compared to a clock, which, once broken, is no longer suitable to the use for which it was designed" (*The System of Nature*). W. K. Clifford (1845–1879): "It is wrong always, everywhere, and for anyone, to believe anything upon insufficient evidence" (*The Ethics of Belief*).

[19] Sigmund Freud. "The Uncanny." *The Standard Edition of the Complete Psychological Works of Sigmund Freud*. Trans. James Strachey. Vol. XVII. London: Hogarth, 1953: 241.

"over-accentuated" psychic "reality," with a usefully similar sense of "psyche" to that put forth in Santayana's thinking:

> [A]n uncanny effect is often and easily produced when the distinction between imagination and reality is effaced, as when something that we have hitherto regarded as imaginary appears before us in reality, or when a symbol takes over the full functions of the thing it symbolizes ... The infantile element in this ... is the over-accentuation of psychical reality in comparison with material reality—a feature closely allied to the belief in the omnipotence of thoughts. (Freud 1917–1919, 224)

The Freudian psychoanalysis of "uncanny" has at its base a materialist conception of mind that overlaps with but in a crucial sense diverges from what Santayana calls "psyche." Santayana calls psyche "the specific form of physical life," "a system of tropes, inherited or acquired, displayed by living bodies in their growth and behaviour." The inherited material "seeds" constituting the animal psyche grow into a unified complex, a "habit in matter," and this habit constitutes "the dynamic life of [what is conventionally called] both body and mind" (*RB*, 331).

Psyche is Santayana's concept for the "nucleus of hereditary organization" in living, sentient animals (*ES*, 14). An important reason he distinguishes this concept from the narrower concept "body" is because he aspires toward non-reductive materialism, a materialism certainly less reductive than that of contemporary philosophers—"physicalists," "eliminative materialists," and so forth—whose reductionism entangles them in questions about "qualia" and intractable puzzles about the nature of "mental" phenomena.

For Santayana, mind is not a "problem" but is rather a fact begging correct ontological positioning in the existential matrix of life. The subjectivity that emerges in self-awareness is the beginning of what Santayana calls spirit, the inner light of awareness, a "moral illumination" that exists "invisibly, in a manner of its own, by virtue of an intrinsic moral intensity" (*RB*, 572–73). Santayana characterizes spirit as both glorious and profound, "glorious" (*RB*, 603) in its "transformation" (out of matter) into "an actuality [that] has extraordinary ontological privileges"; and profound in the fact that its "power" is "natural": "spiritual power is profoundly natural" (*SE*, 24).

More should be said here on the "ontological privileges" of spirit and the "profoundly natural powers" it enjoys. Clearly "natural powers" in this context is not causal. We must be willing here with Santayana to gleefully accept the concession to epiphenomenalism highlighted in the opening section. The power and privilege of spirit comes from its wise, expansive interpretive standpoint. Think here of the peaceful aspect and ironic posture of the decorated senior member of a long-successful team toward his combative teammate underlings. The newcomers join the group with momentous powers of talent, ability, and force but, as so often happens, also a naïve and ignorant grasp of the politics and history of the team and its particular group dynamics. If junior members can be said to represent the *psychic* potential of the team, the accomplished senior member possesses what we might call the team's *spiritual* capacity: he is able to appreciate the entire team in its various relations and to potentially guide it to success more wisely than his junior peers.

Many of the former quoted characterizations of spirit come from Santayana's formal ontology, *The Realms of Being*, but the last comes from an overlooked but important short piece called "Cross Lights" in *Soliloquies in England*, a book Santayana composed in Port Meadow, Oxford, during WWI under the "whirr of airplanes ... daily casualty list," and "the constant sight of the wounded" (*SE*, 1). "Cross Lights" and many of the other pieces in the book show that Santayana is at his best describing spirit when he is in the poetic mode. Leaving aside as it does the necessity of technical precision (as is the objective of *Scepticism* and *Realms*, in which the chapters contain technical terminological clarifications and glossaries of terms), *Soliloquies* perhaps illustrates a sense of living spirit that is easier to appreciate than in the altitudes of Santayana's formal ontology. *Soliloquies* certainly provides a vital means of understanding the psyche-spirit relation and the materialist conception of spiritual life that is, in my understanding, Santayana's most important philosophic insight.

In the book's prologue Santayana offers the following insight into the spiritual power that pervaded him while composing the poetic, free-form pieces that make up *Soliloquies*:

> The human mind at best is a sort of <u>song</u>: the <u>music</u> of it runs away with the words, and even the words, which pass for the names of things, are but poor wild symbols for their unfathomed objects.. So are these Soliloquies compared with their occasions; and I should be the first to hate their verbiage, if a certain spiritual happiness did not seem to breathe through it, and redeem its irrelevance. Their very abstraction from the time in which they were written may commend them to a free mind. Spirit refuses to be caught in a vice; it triumphs over the existence which begets it. (*SE*, 2, underlining mine)

Here is the true power and privilege of spirit. This passage and its context, with its emphasis on music, calls to mind the likely apocryphal story of Nero and his infamous "fiddling" (apocryphal beyond the fact that fiddles would not exist for centuries after 64 CE).[20] Stuck in the "vice" of wartime England, Santayana (unfairly accused by some of his peers to be something of a twentieth-century "Nero") let his spirit soar in a manner apropos of the "free mind" whose function is to "redeem the irrelevance" of its singing amidst the horrors of human conflict. Spirit is indeed the *only* source of liberation in such a position of entrapment.

---

[20] Roman historian Suetonius reports how Nero was so moved by the burning of his city that he climbed atop the city walls and wept while reciting lines describing the destruction of Troy by the Greeks.

The very text of *Soliloquies* testifies to the existence, power, and potency of spirit, as Santayana understands the concept. "Cross Lights" in particular provides as close to a full sense as one could hope of Santayana's attempt to show how it is that, while spirit is rooted in and fated to expire in matter[21]—and is therefore correctly understood as a natural phenomenon—its visions, insights, and moral sufferings are not reducible to any specific idea of nature or matter, whether nebulous or rigorously scientific: "Apart from its roots in animal predicaments, spirit would be wholly inexplicable in its moods and arbitrary in its deliverance" (*SE*, 25); inexplicable, because the louder its cries and jubilations, the closer spirit comes to intoning the very voice of matter: "The more ecstatic or the more tragic experience is, the more unmistakably it is the voice of matter" (Ibid). This fits perfectly with Santayana's own sense of matter, regarding which both critics and defenders have raised important issues. Santayana provides different interesting conceptions of matter, contending in one context that "[the order of matter] is that of actual generation and existential flux, something that happens and is not conceived" (*RB*, 189), and in another that "existence itself is a surd" (*RB*, 109).

Taking Santayana as much as possible at his word, if the order of matter is something that happens and is not conceived, and the flux of existence of which matter is but a place-holding concept, an unintelligible surd, it would have to be the echoes of matter, or the tremors and pulsations of the matter-rooted psyche that offers spirit—the immaterial illuminating eye—its inspirations.

Recall how Santayana alleges that the emergence of spirit occurs when the various "perspectives of nature are reversed as in a mirror and attached to the fortunes of a single soul" (*RB*, 550). This "single soul" is psyche (recognizing in this context that this goes somewhat against his aforementioned wish to avoid the "poetical word" "soul") for, as Santayana is at least clear on this point, "The same thing that looked at from the outside or biologically is called the psyche, looked at morally from within is called the soul" (*RB*, 570). Santayana contends that psyche is "not another name for consciousness or mind" (Ibid). The "other" name he proposes for those concepts is "spirit." And here Santayana departs from or rather ontologically amplifies the Freudian concept of psyche previously discussed.[22] From a Santayanan point of view, Freud's account of the "uncanny" as being due to an "over-accentuation of psychical reality in comparison with material reality," although diagnostically

---

[21] That spirit expires in matter follows from a couple of points, first, from Santayana's assertion that "spirit ... needs the being and movement of matter, by its large sweeping harmonies, to generate it, and give it wings" (*SAF*, "Discernment of Spirit" 288); second, by his assertion that "The possible liberation of the spirit is not a liberation from suffering or death, but through suffering and death" (*RB*, 761). Finally too it bears mentioning here that Santayana asserts that psyche expires in matter: "[psyche] is no supernatural principle, but only a moving harmony or equilibrium maintaining itself more or less perfectly in each organism until death breaks it down altogether" (*RB*, 679).

[22] Freud wrote "The Uncanny" in 1919, and we know from Santayana's letters that he was reading Freud in 1915 and *Interpretations of Dreams* was in his official library.

sound, is too reductive; it fails to give ontological due to the cries of spirit that afford persons an interpretive reckoning with confounding and tragic realities.[23]

To put it more succinctly, for Santayana there is no such thing as what in Freudian terms can be termed "mental machinery," but rather the *psychic* "machinery of growth, instinct, and action" that is the basis, or ground (not a directly determining feature), of whatever may or may not be the "essential" nature of mind. As a matter of fact, mind is left somewhat mysterious by Santayana, necessarily so given what he suggests can be known of its alleged "nature": "Artists have their place," he writes in SAF, "and the animal mind is one of them" (SAF, 87). The "mind" in Santayana parlance is only "known" by its creative endeavors. This is why Santayana approaches mind from the standpoint of ontology: mind cannot be "known" from within but only poetically from without. Mind is sight, and body, psychic attachment, is an echolocating devise for the seeing mind.

Unlike Freud, Santayana understands mind as deserving ontological distinction—especially from matter—because, as the more contemporary non-reductive materialist John Searle (an *in*compatibilist!) has argued, what happens at the level of mind/spirit is not directly causally determined by what is happening at the level of psyche.[24] In effect, what is of relevance or pertains to spirit is not directly, and indeed may be wholly out of scale with, what is of relevance or pertains to psyche. This amounts to a paradoxically bifurcated-yet-related relationship between what is conventionally called "body and mind."

---

[23] It will be of help here to consider Freud's understanding of psyche as compared to Santayana's. Freud was influenced by energy conservation theory of nineteenth-century physics, conceiving mind as emerging out of a "psychic energy system"; he submits that mind is the product of "neuronal inertia," an idea attempting to make psychology a form of natural science. This view of mind fits within a trajectory of similar views traceable back to what is labeled (somewhat simplistically) "reflex-arc," the stimulus-response model of human action and behavior. Freud's view of psyche is thus in league with what was then a growing tradition attempting to conceive mind in terms of "mental machinery," accounting for all psychological phenomena as features of constant physiological processes. As such, although masterful in his literary psychology regarding psychological concepts such as the uncanny (to say nothing of the more well-known and infamous concepts including oedipal complex, penis envy, castration theory, and so forth), Freud is more reductive about the psyche than Santayana. "Psychical reality" for Freud is mind, is mental reality. For Santayana "psychical reality" is material reality; it is, to put it in Spinozistic terms, mind under the aspect of matter. The ontological category of spirit—mind under the aspect of spirit—signifies Santayana's attempt to conceive mind in non-reductive terms.

[24] Causal explanations of human action and behavior occur for Searle along "two levels of description" (mental and physical): see chapter one, "The Mind-Body Problem" in *Minds, Brains and Science* (Searle 1984).

From Distraction to Liberation: Hearing the Cries of Spirit

Having argued in the first section how squinting and beside-the-point is the question of epiphenomenalism (risking dismissal of the significance of mind), and in the second and third sections how precarious is the relation between material and spiritual realities (risking dismissal of the significance of nature), my concluding concern here is to explore the liberating possibilities open to the suffering spirit. And just here we should consider the point in conjunction with another unforgettable image from Santayana, expressed in the final sentence from "Normal Madness" in *Dialogues in Limbo*: "The young man who has not wept is a savage, and the old man who will not laugh is a fool."[25] This pithy maxim expresses a powerful truth in a single poetic insight, capturing the nature and meaning of spiritual maturation through the cries of spirit. For Santayana's child crying at the manikin, and Platonov's Chagataev crying with the camel, there is hope. How might crying in the early stages of spiritual development indicate philosophically healthy dispositions? How might laughter in maturity do the same? If there is hope for the child crying at his unfair suffering, there is an equally promising consolation for the adult laughing at the same. Achieving philosophic reconciliation will require a correct calibration of what Santayana terms "scepticism and animal faith."

As Santayana enthusiasts know, *Scepticism and Animal Faith* was published in 1923, a dramatic preface to his system of philosophy that sheds ontological insight on these questions. The work's very conjunction, scepticism *and* animal faith, suggests a solution to the quandary at hand. Identifying four realms of being, "kinds or categories of things" he finds "conspicuously different and worth distinguishing" (*SAF*, vi), Santayana claims that these ontological categories are "distinguish[ed] in [his] personal observation of the world" [ibid] and that they constitute "no system of the universe," nor "parts of a cosmos, nor one great cosmos together." Moreover, as he assures his "reader who is tempted to smile" at his attempt to put forth "one more system of the universe," that he smiles with them.

Such sentiments of humility should be considered in light of the rhetorically technical, even *scholastic* categories Santayana goes on to elucidate—ontological *realms of being* with formal philosophic names: essence, matter, spirit, and truth. The reader who smiles with Santayana at the outset of *SAF* will continue to smile, even as Santayana elaborates his ontological "system," so long as, beneath each of their respective "overt parrot beliefs," the "friendship" they maintain is "built" on "convictions in the depths of their souls" (*SAF*, v).

This appeal has its strongest prospects—that is, Santayana's thinking most readily connects to the philosophically curious reader—in relation to the interplay of what Santayana calls psyche and spirit. In particular, it is real, *psychic*, moral suffering, exemplified in the various cries of spirit, that affords the

---

[25] *DL*, 57.

opportunity to achieve philosophic liberation. Chagataev's journey in Platonov's *Soul* provides a vivid illustration of this precise phenomenon. Toward the end of the narrative Platonov includes the following analysis of the ironic origin of the word *Dzhan* or "soul" for the desert tribes among whom is classified Chatagaev's own people:

> "What tribe are you from?" Chatagaev asked an old Turkmen who looked older than everyone.
> "We're Dzhan," replied the old man, and it emerged from his words that every little tribe, every family and chance group of the gradually dying people living in the empty places of the desert, the Amu-Darya and the Ust-Yurt, called themselves by the same name: Dzhan. It was their shared name, given to them long ago by the rich beys [Governors of Turkish provinces], because *dzhan* means soul and these poor, dying men had nothing they could call their own but their souls, that is, the ability to feel and suffer. The word *dzhan*, therefore, was a gibe, a joke made by the rich at the expense of the poor. The beys thought that soul meant only despair, but in the end it was their *dzhan* that was the death of them; they had too little *dzhan* of their own, too little capacity to feel, suffer, think and struggle. They had too little of the wealth of the poor. (Platonov 2007, 141)

As seems to occur throughout the greater narrative of *Soul*, Platonov is subjecting a concept that has a canonical burden—in this case "Blessed are the poor"—to reevaluation. His narrative framing of that motif in the above passage reveals that the typical mis-estimation of the poor by the rich is due not to any idle home-prejudice or inherent principle of selfishness but to their mis-aligned relationship to *being*—that underlies all perceptions of the "other who suffers."

The "wealth" that is "too little possessed" by the condescending beys is no mere spiritual "ideal" or aspiration: theirs is the incapacity to feel, to suffer; a devastating incapacity for the beys, spiritually speaking. The projection by the beys of pejorative pity on the impoverished *dzhan* comes from a tragic, *willful* inability to even try to identify with their suffering; indeed, doing so (trying to identify with the suffering of those "lesser" others) would upset their very relation to being. The reduction of the suffering of others to a pitiable "physical" status—seeing them as only capable of being preoccupied with material things—results from an ironic projection: it says more about what the bey value than the *dzhan*. Platonov in other words reveals what is truly tragic about the outlook of the bey, and it is not at all to do with the suffering tribes they demean with the name "dzhan" (although to be sure in their condescension they tie themselves fatally to the dzhan, as any oppressor does to those they oppress). What is tragic is their withholding *from themselves* an opportunity at spiritual liberation. Santayana writes: "The possible liberation of the spirit is not a liberation from suffering or death, but through suffering and death" (*RB*, 761). Opening oneself meaningfully to the possibility of this spiritual transfiguration results in the possibility of a transformed relation to the very attachments which gave rise to suffering in the first place: "Our sufferings will chasten and transfigure our attachment to the circumstances and passions that caused those sufferings" (Ibid).

Santayana's boy cries at the human-like manikin because he has discovered this very possibility. The thing he naively took previously to appear to be "him," to be *like* others like him, is capable of being *not* the life-filled entity he always assumed it to be. "It" is now recognized for the first time "*as* an it"; formerly we might say it was a "that," a phenomenon of imaginative reaction yet to be considered for its own sake, distinct from the surrounding world. The newly defined "it" could now be lifeless or as devoid of consciousness as other surrounding objective entities. This is why the child cries. He has come to see (rudely and without notice) that there may be no "there, there" when it comes to his presumed relation to being, and the proof of this is the value his spirit has placed on otherwise unproven realities.

Now of course Santayana's proverbial child is unlikely ever to come to such a clear realization of his shock. We are waxing philosophical here, and unless the child is a remarkable philosophic type such as Santayana or Platonov was, he just cries, he knows not precisely why. He cries for the same reason all of us cry when suddenly confronted with contradictions in our basic ontological understanding: there is no explanation of the phenomenon and what is more, the unexpected phenomenon undermines the character of the expected reality. The reason for this conflict is the friction between psyche and spirit, an inevitable and, if at the same time potentially debilitating, also potentially liberating friction.

And this is why the interface between psyche and spirit is so crucial for understanding the moral suffering of the sort illustrated so vividly in the crying of Santayana's manikin-traumatized child and of Platonov's protagonist. Santayana argues provocatively that the greatest struggles in life are not with "cosmic fatalities" such as "war and death," rather: "The worst entanglements from the spirit's point of view, arise within the psyche, in what in religious parlance is called sin" (*RB*, 568). "Psyche," he continues, "is primarily directed upon all sorts of ambitions irrelevant to spirit, producing stagnation, inflation, self-contradiction, and hatred of truth." Sounds like our child, but equally, if from another direction, Platonov's Chagataev who, after having successfully helped his Dzhan nation to live "without an everyday sense of its death, working at finding food for itself … just as most of humanity normally lives in the world," finds nonetheless that he is "not satisfied with the ordinary, meager life his nation had begun to live" (Platonov, 2007, 108–9). Yet Chagataev eventually comes to see that "people can see for themselves how best to live," that it was "enough that he had helped [his people] to stay alive" and lets them go to find their own happiness. After deciding this, "He set off slowly back, and on the way he began to cry" (Platonov 2007, 118). The moral release offered by the crying response comes from spirit's protest to the contradictory position in which it is placed.

And this crying release is precisely where spirit comes closest to intoning the *voice of matter*.[26] The "vicarious admonishment of the soul" that becomes spirit's eventual role is everywhere reflected in nature in nonhuman animals and other sentient forms of nonhuman life. Here again, Platonov's *Soul* is a veritable guidebook to Santayana's materialist conception of spiritual life. Platonov permits even animals and plants their own inner dignity, equal in spiritual value and without the need of human justification. One is forced to acknowledge the spiritual capacity of nature, "Otherwise one would have to assume that true enthusiasm lies only in the human heart—and such an assumption is worthless and empty, since the blackthorn is imbued with a scent, and the eyes of a tortoise with a thoughtfulness, that signify the great inner worth of their existence, a dignity complete in itself and needing no supplement from the soul of a human being" (Platonov 2007, 120). If we are to appreciate the materialist conception of spirituality we must be prepared to entertain the possibility that nonhuman organic life too has not only psyche but also spirit.

The crucial thing to note here is that psyche is, yes, a distraction *from* but crucially also *for* spirit. Psyche is, as Martin Coleman puts it, "concerned with threats to animal life"; it "distracts spirit from its proper activity" (*ES*, 263). Yet as Santayana asks rhetorically in the chapter following "Distraction" in *RB* from which this important point is drawn, "From what does distraction distract the spirit?" (*RB/RS*, 736). "What," he asks, is the "better and deeper thing" from which spirit is estranged in its psychic entanglements? Traditional religions have of course long provided the obvious answer: spiritual resurrection and salvation. Not dissimilar from Platonov's reevaluation of religious traditions, Santayana will proceed in the "Liberation" chapter to perform his own reevaluation of the historical concepts of resurrection and salvation, and translate the religious meaning of those concepts, preserving what he deems noble and best in them, into his naturalistic framework.

Adapting those translated concepts—of resurrection and salvation—to our example, the child undergoes psychic distraction, and the "proper activity" of spirit this distraction thwarts is the liberating attitude of what Santayana terms in one context to be "entranced love" (*RB*, 551). This creates for spirit a "congenital" "longing": "at first for happiness and at last for salvation" (Ibid): setting up this harmonic closing passage from Platonov, "Chagataev patiently went on living, bringing ever nearer the day when he could begin to realize the true happiness of shared life, without which nothing is worth doing and the heart feels ashamed" (Platonov 2007, 112).

---

[26] "[W]hilst spirit is physically the voice of the soul crying in the wilderness, it becomes vicariously and morally the voice of the wilderness admonishing the soul" (Santayana RB, 568).

References

Brodrick, Michael. 2013. Santayana's Amphibious Concepts. *Transactions of the Charles S. Peirce Society* 49 (2, Spring): 238–249.

Chastain, Drew. 2018. Liberating Spirit from Santayana's Spectatorial Spirituality. *Overheard in Seville: Bulletin of the Santayana Society* 36 (36): 99–114.

Freud, Sigmund. 1953. The Uncanny. In *The Standard Edition of the Complete Psychological Works of Sigmund Freud*. Trans. James Strachey. Vol. XVII (1917–1919). London: Hogarth.

James, William. 1977. The Dilemma of Determinism. *The Writings of William James: A Comprehensive Edition*. Edited with an introduction by John M. McDermott. Chicago: University of Chicago Press: 605–606.

Livingstone, Angela, ed. 2001. 'A Hundred Years of Andrei Platonov'. Platonov special issue (vol. I). *Essays in Poetics: The Journal of the British Neo-Formalist Circle* 26 (Autumn): 1–167.

Platonov, Andrey. 2007. *Soul and Other Stories*. New York Review Books.

Santayana, George. 1905–1906. *The Life of Reason: or, the Phases of Human Progress*. Five volumes. New York: Charles Scribner's Sons; London: Constable and Co. Ltd.

———. 1922. *Soliloquies in England and Later Soliloquies*. New York: Charles Scribner's Sons; London: Constable and Co. Ltd.

———. 1927–1940. *Realms of Being*. Four volumes. New York: Charles Scribner's Sons; London: Constable and Co. Ltd.

———. (1923) 1955. *Scepticism and Animal Faith*. New York: Dover Publications, Cited as *SAF*.

———. 1957. *Dialogues in Limbo*. University of Michigan Press.

———. 2009. *The Essential Santayana: Selected Writings*. Compiled and with an introduction by Martin A. Coleman. Indiana University Press.

Searle, John. 1984. *Minds. Brains and Science*: Harvard University Press.

Wahman, Jessica. 2006. Why Psyche Matters. *Transactions of the Charles S. Peirce Society* 42 (1, Winter): 132–146.

Weiss, Robin. 2020. Santayana's Epiphenomenalism Reconsidered. *European Journal of Pragmatism and American Philosophy* XII (2) https://journals.openedition.org/ejpap/2138.

Fumbling Toward the Animal in "Animal Faith"

Charles Padrón

The publication in 1923 of Santayana's *Scepticism and Animal Faith* (*SAF*) was a milestone of sorts, both for Santayana personally and the legacy of his philosophical *œuvre*. First of all and arguably the most significant takeaway is the *formal*, published and public, appearance of what for lack of a more apt phrase is his *mature* philosophy. In a letter to his lifelong US publisher Charles Scribner's Sons a couple of years before its publication, Santayana wrote that he was "at work—slowly—on a much more considerable book, in which I endeavour to clear up, as far as I can, all the fundamental questions concerned in these theories" (*LGS*, 3:6). The "fundamental questions" found in "these theories" Santayana had subsumed under "the whole nature of fiction, expression, and representation" (*LGS*, 3:6) found in *SB*, *LR*, and *SE*. From the above quote we can infer a continuity between his early and later ideas, and I tend to be of the opinion that there were no major, radical departures in Santayana's evolution as a thinker. However, that complex question is not my emphasis in this piece. The interesting question of one or two Santayanas, like the similar conundrums of two Wittgensteins, two Sartres, or two Heideggers, is an intriguing line of investigation and argument, but not the focus here. Rather, that primary focus lies in one half of the compound noun found in the title of the work under discussion: *animal*, of animal faith.

The author would like to thank Daniel Moreno for his assistance in the completion of this piece.

C. Padrón (✉)
Gran Canaria, Spain

© The Author(s), under exclusive license to Springer Nature Switzerland AG 2024
M. A. Coleman, G. Tiller (eds.), *The Palgrave Companion to George Santayana's Scepticism and Animal Faith*, Palgrave Companions, https://doi.org/10.1007/978-3-031-46367-9_14

As an entry point into the discussion of the centrality of *animality* in *SAF*, I would like to quote a passage from a letter that Santayana wrote to his half-sister Susana in the year of its publication (1923): "I see you are puzzled by the title of my last book. It has nothing to do with religion: by 'animal faith' I mean the confidence one has, for instance, that there will be a future, that you will find things where you have hidden them, etc. It is a technical book and not intelligible unless you have a very analytic mind, but I will send you a copy if you wish" (*LGS*, 3:150). Apart from the fact that the recipient of this letter was his older half-sister, who once had spent six months in a convent and was not overly receptive to (or capable of sincere interest in) his philosophical overtures, Santayana, I claim, had inadvertently revealed two aspects of his own strain of the refutation of scepticism: his own animality ("a rational instinct or instinctive reason, the waxing faith of an animal living in a world which he can observe and sometimes remodel. This natural faith opens to me various Realms of Being ..." [*SAF*, 309]) and his understanding of the surrounding world and us humans amidst it originating and framed by matter though not determined by that matter. Here the bond between a material, natural grounding (*animal faith*), and the ontology of *RB* is evident, where, for example, *essences* and *truth* and *spirit* are discussed in depth. This aggregation of matter and non-matter can even be thought of as the source of Santayana's naturalism. P. F. Strawson makes a distinction in his *Skepticism*(Strawson, 1985) *and Naturalism: Some Varieties* that helps clarify what I understand as characteristic of Santayana's naturalism. He distinguishes between *reductive* (or *hard*) naturalism, and *catholic* or *liberal* (*soft*) naturalism. As I see it, the former does not include Santayana, for in no way does Santayana ever reduce anything to merely something else. Strawson's "*soft* naturalism" is more fitting. It bestows a non-dogmatic tint to Santayana's naturalism. Santayana's "rational instinct or instinctive reason," though emerging from matter, is not *defined* by that matter (Strawson, 1985, 1–2).

Bringing into the interpretative frame Santayana's own explanation in "Apologia Pro Mente Sua" (1940), where he identifies "essences" as solely originating from matter indirectly, as they are *not* material entities, we can establish a firm bond to *LR*:

> [B]ut essences are non-existent, they cannot manifest themselves of their own initiative, and it is only in matter, or in a mind fed on matter, that they can shine in all their concreteness and splendor. For my essences are not washed out; they are the *whole* of what is actually visible, audible, imaginable or thinkable; and these manifestations in their pungency can come to a warm soul from a world of matter. This was my interest in composing the *Life of Reason*, with an eye open to all concrete perfections. ... (*PGS*, 501–2)

Another passage supporting the claim that Santayana's early and later works (*LR* and *SAF* and *RB*) are to be understood as consistent and continuous despite variations, is a pithy sentence at the beginning of the chapter "Charity" in *LR3*: "Spiritual men, in a word, may fall into the aristocrat's fallacy; they may forget the infinite animal and vulgar life which remains quite disjointed, impulsive, and short-winded, but which nevertheless palpitates with joys and sorrows, and makes after all the bulk of moral values in this democratic world" (*LR3*, 129). Amazingly enough, Santayana's stated source of values (and thus the provenance of his aesthetics, ethics, and politics) nearly twenty years later became the source of his epistemology, metaphysics, and ontology. However, my use of these concepts is straightforward, even pedestrian. By *epistemology*, I understand matters related to knowledge, beliefs, and justification; by *metaphysics*, I borrow a definition put forth in a manner more precise than I can muster: "[O]ne way of construing metaphysics is to say that it is concerned to set out in the most general terms what must hold good of conscious beings and the world in which they live if that world is to constitute reality for them" (Hamlyn 1984, 8); as for *ontology*, I think along the lines of what *is*, of being-as-being, *in se*.

The Sceptical Threat and Santayana: How Serious?

The historical evolution of scepticism, from its origins in the Hellenistic Greek period with Pyrrho of Elis (*c*. 360–*c*. 270 BCE) and Arcesilaus (315–240 BCE), through Descartes and Hume and Kant up to Stanley Cavell (1926–2018), is a powerful, compelling phenomenon. Some philosophical scholars understand it as one of the most, if not *the* most, proliferant and problematic elements in the history of Western philosophy, troubling, oftentimes crippling, yet always provoking and inspiring many philosophical giants as well as countless other thinkers and scholars. Two of these philosophical scholars, Julia Annas and Jonathan Barnes, have provided us with a historical schema of the extent of this impact, this menacing, inexplicable "anxiety of influence": "In 1562 the French scholar and publisher Henri Etienne brought out the first modern edition of Sextus Empiricus' *Outlines of Pyrrhonism*. ... It was the rediscovery of Sextus and Greek scepticism which shaped the course of philosophy for the next three hundred years" (Annas and Barnes 1985, 5). After quoting passages from Descartes, Hume, and Kant, Annas, and Barnes conclude their assessment of the historical import of scepticism in ominous language, identifying the expansive chasm between *ancient* and *modern* scepticism:

> Those quotations from Descartes, Hume and Kant could be matched by a thousand others from philosophers of humbler talents. Scepticism was the philosophical disease of the age, and the disease had been transmitted by Sextus Empiricus' *Outlines of Pyrrhonism*. Even if scepticism is no longer the first problem for a philosopher, it is still an issue which no philosopher will avoid. ... Modern scepticism frequently represents itself as issuing a challenge to *knowledge*. ... The ancient skeptics did not attack knowledge; they attacked belief. They argued that, under skeptical pressure, our belief turns out to be groundless and that we have no more reason to believe than to disbelieve. (Annas and Barnes 1985, 7–8)

The pressing question arises as to the extent to which Santayana understood scepticism as an intellectual (I hesitate to include *physical*) threat, even as an illness, to be overcome. The answer is a convincing *yes*—it was a threat, a centuries-old specter that compelled him to come to grips with it, and if he were incapable of surmounting and subduing it, then "even at the price of intellectual suicide" (*SAF*, 10), to forever live with the awareness that one's beliefs, claims, and opinions were subject to doubt and uncertainty. Is life worth living with this understanding? Why would Santayana, having already completed a five-volume work of sustained thought (*LR*) without any confrontation with scepticism, now, after nearly two decades, turn his intellectual attention to the "disease"? Why had he to settle accounts with it? And after the reckoning and confrontation, what was the aftermath? A claim of a successful refutation or an acknowledgment of *living one's scepticism*? Having resolved that there are no "first principles of criticism," that is, no agreed upon fundamental, basic "axioms and postulates," no authoritative "living discourse" that we carry within us in our everyday lives and use when we want or need to, Santayana proceeds to jettison convention, and all strains and forms of dogma: "To me the opinions of mankind, taken without any contrary prejudice (since I have no rival opinions to propose) but simply contrasted with the course of nature, seem surprising fictions; and the marvel is how they can be maintained" (*SAF*, 7). Diverse dogmas, in search of a more extended reach in influence and relevance, run up against other dogmas, and *educated* exchange and competition breed the discourse of *criticism*. "Criticism" is Santayana's term for our claims and language that we create and apply in our attempts to understand the world and in our interactions with it, which Santayana, in the second chapter of *SAF*, separated into *empirical criticism* and *transcendental criticism*. The former are everyday beliefs corresponding to the facts, while the latter is the effort to "disentangle and formulate ... subjective principles of interpretation" (*SAF*, 8).

Santayana distinguishes between two types of scepticism in *SAF*: *wayward* and *ultimate*. He defines by example what he calls "wayward" sceptics. There are three types. The first is the individual who reduces all immediate concentration and mental zeal into a singular momentary now, a *this very moment* that discards "everything that is not present in their prevalent mood, or in their deepest thought" (*SAF*, 18), and *absolutizes* it. The second is the mystically inclined person who also absolutizes immediacy in an oceanic oneness with the moment, thereby negating "all natural facts and events, which he calls illusions," with the extreme claim that "pure Being is, and everything else is not" (*SAF*, 19). The third example is the prototypical bookish mind who denies the meaningfulness of the tactile world of phenomena, yet who absolutizes it via *knowledge*—reducing his "so limited" world to an "after-image of his learning" (*SAF*, 19). Each is "wayward," in the Santayanan understanding, for denying the world and beliefs about it *not* by living one's scepticism honestly and modestly but by fleeing from it—and taking refuge in a separate sort of escapist glorification of the *self* even though it might appear that the self has been obliterated.

"Ultimate" scepticism is far more serious and pathological. It is the living legacy of the sceptical tradition that Santayana was a part of in his own life, stemming back to the Hellenistic Greeks, especially Pyrrhonian scepticism. It involves not only the denial of (or doubting) the content of thought but our own personal *beliefs* regarding those thoughts. In moving toward identifying what Santayana considers to be "ultimate scepticism," he claims we can reject all *data*, those givens which are "the whole of what solicits my attention at any moment" (*SAF*, 35). This is that movement to "push scepticism as far as I logically can" (*SAF*, 10). Here he makes a crucial distinction, as I understand it, between what is in my thinking mind when I think, and what I might *believe* about what I entertain in that mind (or have entertained, accessed by memory). For "belief in existence, in the nature of the case, can be a belief only. The datum is an idea; a description; I may contemplate it without belief" (*SAF*, 35). Even in my denial of being an existent being, or doubting that I am one, I am still existing. The risk here is that without a belief in or of something other than my own self, *solipsism* is a tempting lure. Timothy Sprigge, in his study of Santayana's thought, identified something quite germane to this in the following passage: "Since there is nothing within my experience to guarantee the existence of a real material world (some part of which it apprehends), or of any other centre of experience, it seems that if I refuse to take anything on mere trust, I shall end up in solipsism, that is, in the belief that the discoursing and feeling mind which I am exists, but that possibly nothing else exists" (*SAEP*, 32). Santayana writes:

> What is reality? As I should like to use the term, reality is being of any sort. If it means character or essence, illusions have it as much as substance, and more richly. If it means substance, then sceptical concentration upon inner experience, or ecstatic abstraction, seems to me the last place in which we should look for it. (*SAF*, 24)

This is a metaphysical claim and one of singular importance. In short, Santayana is affirming that the material, natural world surrounding humans in its everyday, phenomenal sense does *not* have a monopoly on the *real*. But do I, as a human being, then seek out security and what degree of certainty I can possibly secure in my existence, immersed in "sceptical concentration upon inner experience, or ecstatic abstraction"? A rich and variegated group of thinkers had done so throughout history, and for Santayana, at least, were continuing to do so in his own day. However, that option path did not win over Santayana. Understanding it through the metaphor of an *illness*, one can assert that he put up sincere efforts to resist it and to overcome it, confronting *ultimate scepticism*, which is Santayana's reformulated version of the Cartesian demand (to doubt everything I have learned in my life and the sources of that knowledge). What emerges, in my reading of the "Ultimate Scepticism" chapter in *SAF*, is not only the first usage of the concept of *animal faith* in the book but the increasing presence of Santayana's response to the threat and disease of unbridled scepticism (*SAF*, 24).

Before embarking on a discussion of Santayana's *philosophical* counter (*animal faith*) to this presence, there are three issues in Santayana's counter to scepticism that need to be mentioned. One is the factor of *insularity*. The second is Santayana's unintentional dismissal of the *epistemic regress argument*, or the *infinite regress argument*, and all chains of epistemic dependence that justify any degree of *foundationalism*, in chapter one of *SAF*. And the third is the irrefutability of scepticism in the final say and of the necessity of *living one's scepticism*.

Philosophical insularity is not absolute. It is a relative idea. To what degree is my philosophical outlook or orientation or informed *beliefs* regarding my life and its surrounding totality one and the same with that physical existence which is my embodied self? In other words, do I *live* my philosophy in step with my twenty-four-hour, seven-day-a-week everydayness, or is it separate, isolated, distinct, a pastime I engage in, or a specified body of time I spend thinking about it *outside* the rest of my life, and then somehow fit it in, attach it to my life and to the world as a whole? We can never completely think *inside* our bodily, present moment existence ("solipsism of the present moment"), for that would not allow us those moments that are reflective and not engaged in what lies at hand, which bestow on us the endowed gift of perspective, nor can we be completely outside, for that would belie that fact that our embodiment allows for reflective thought in the first place. Timothy Sprigge has offered the following with respect to his reading of Santayana's own assertion (in the chapter "Wayward Scepticism"): "If, for instance, the solipsist says that nothing but the *present moment* exists, he says something incoherent, for a moment can be called present in contrast to other moments, which are past or future. The solipsist simply rejects the idea of there existing anything but *this* and *these*" (*SAEP*, 35). Herman Saatkamp claims something similar in his "Some Remarks on Santayana's Skepticism": "In more contemporary terms (but uglier and far less dramatic) Santayana's contention is that if we reduce our knowledge to the actually evident, we may discern an awareness that is infallible and indubitable; but this infallibility and indubitability characterize such a restricted state of consciousness that it cannot provide the basis for the reconstruction of knowledge on self-evident beliefs or knowledge claims" (Saatkamp 2021, 19).

What Santayana achieves is a frank, up-front confession of where he considers himself to be on this continuum, and he does so at the very outset of his book, before diving into his *theoretical* reflections: "I would lay siege to the truth only as animal exploration and fancy may do so, first from one quarter and then from another, expecting the reality to be not simpler than my experience of it, but far more extensive and complex. I stand in philosophy where I stand in daily life: I should not be honest otherwise" (*SAF*, vi). Echoing the Humean assault on intransigent ("excessive") sceptics who argue that active, relentless scepticism is a viable, livable philosophy found in Part II, Section XII of Hume's *An Enquiry Concerning Human Understanding* (1748), Santayana clarifies immediately that he is making a forthright attempt to be consistent and *not* insular. A consummate, though sad, example of an individual at the opposite extreme from where Santayana claims he is, is found in this example provided by Myles Burnyeat in his "The Sceptic in His Place and Time":

> Nowadays, if a philosopher finds he cannot answer the philosophical question 'What is Time?' of 'Is Time Real?', he applies for a research grant to work on the problem during next year's sabbatical. He does not suppose that the arrival of next year is actually in doubt. Alternately, he may agree that any puzzlement about the nature of time, or any argument for doubting the reality of time, is in fact a puzzlement about, or an argument for doubting, the truth of the proposition that next year's sabbatical will come, but contend that this is of course a strictly theoretical or philosophical worry, not a worry that needs to be reckoned with in the ordinary business of life. Either way he *insulates* his ordinary first order judgements from the effects of his philosophizing. (Burnyeat 1984, 225)

In entreating us to make a philosophical plunge into an honest orientation to knowledge and life, Santayana lets us know at the beginning of *SAF* that there is no *foundational ground* for any certainty in knowledge or in his terminology, "there is no first principle in criticism" (see *SAF*, 1). His reasoning can be convincing, if we think along with him. He claims that no matter where we attempt to establish an inferential link to grounding what we think we know (there is always another *before* any before, and more *after* following any projection into the future), these "principles of discourse" can be described only after long, lived experience, and we need to work with the what we have at hand—the *facts*. "To reduce conventional beliefs to the facts they rest on—however questionable those facts themselves may be in other ways—is to clear our intellectual conscience of voluntary or avoidable delusion" (*SAF*, 3). Rather than intellectually seek out and pine for a secure epistemological anchor on which to build an honest outlook on the world, acknowledging that there is none is the first step. It is not a dead end, fractured and tormented by sceptical forebodings, but a momentary respite on a trajectory of sanity and engagement with the everyday.

Living one's scepticism is not a defeat of any sort. It is a recognition of and a coming to grips with a philosophical position that entertains certain irrefragable truths, but those truths are not delimiting or oppressive unless stretched to the extreme of *ultimate scepticism*. According to Santayana, "Scepticism, if it could be sincere, would be the best of philosophies. But I suspect that other sceptics, as well as I, always believe in substance, and that their denial of it is sheer sophistry and the weaving of verbal arguments in which their most familiar and massive convictions are ignored" (*SAF*, 186). Crispin Sartwell thinks it even more dishonest than that: "So a philosopher who continues to produce such utterances while claiming on paper to doubt that there are objects external to the mind does not believe what he is saying, or else he does not believe what he is writing. And as a matter of fact, he does not believe what he is writing. This does not show what is written is false, but it does show that the writer is a hypocrite" (Sartwell 1991, 189). Finally, Burnyeat, in an even more comprehensive assessment, asserts: "When one has seen how radically the skeptic must detach himself from himself, one will agree that the supposed life without belief is not, after all, a possible life for man" (Burnyeat 1983, 141). A prehensive individual can avoid the contradictory trappings of scepticism by establishing, or reestablishing should it be the case, trust in the facticity of this world and our existent bodies as the *foundational wellspring* of quotidian life, and that includes mental life. One cannot, nor should one, deny the *substantial* basis of our material lives, including our mental lives. Viewed objectively, the solipsistic self embeds itself in an impotent, immature situation, an enfeebled starting point vis-à-vis the environing world and shared human congruity, circumscribed by action and the overall commonweal. Solipsism is an embodiment of immature stubbornness and an avoidance of a world larger than oneself. And scepticism *can* breed solipsism, but not necessarily. For the entrenched sceptic (the "excessive" one, employing Humean language), human possibility and language expand, ebbing and flowing, in a sphere of what they are *not*, not what they *are*. At some unspecified impasse, at some critical juncture in the career of an individual self, one is eventually forced to affirm rather than deny (unless one should perish in a sustained sequence of enlightened solipsism or become frozen in a singular trance of Nirvana, i.e., nothingness). It could very well be the case that affirmations are made every single day, even every hour, but without recognition as such.

Solipsism, as an epistemological position, is completely barren in what it can induce and meaningfully help enact. It is an ego-centered (although it recognizes no ego), carnivalesque play of thought, engaging for the individual living it, yet grossly inadequate for a fulfilling human life. On the other hand, scepticism is, at the end of the day, an existential and intellectual dead end, for it generates no motives or inspiration for meaningful, coherent action. If taken to the extreme, it eventually stifles human potentiality. Santayana tells us that "scepticism is an exercise, not a life; it is a discipline fit to purify the mind of prejudice and render it all the more apt, when the time comes, to believe and act wisely" (*SAF*, 69). Though highly valuable, even desirable, in the development of a human life, as a mature and honest way of approaching the vast extent of the world one is a part of, it fails miserably. It needs to be tempered and folded into the parameters of animal life and action.

Animal Faith as an Antidote to Scepticism

The opening up of the universe of *essences* through the recognition that the immediate material environment need not be divorced from the immaterial phenomena that transpire in our brains was a key insight that Santayana propounded in "The Discovery of Essence" (Chapter IX) and "Some Uses of This Discovery" (Chapter X). Essences are the vehicles of human knowledge and human discourse, and knowledge, for Santayana, in *SAF* is at bottom treated as *belief*, as he writes in a later chapter ("Knowledge is Faith" Chapter XVIII): "Knowledge accordingly is belief: belief in a world of events, and especially those parts of it which are near the self, tempting or threatening it. ... Furthermore, knowledge is true belief" (*SAF*, 179). *Essences* also serve as a place for refuge and solace in the face of *shocks* (a favorite Santayanan term), setbacks, disappointments, and failures amidst the phenomenal world. Nevertheless, at bottom, there is no categorical chasm between the intellectual understanding (knowledge and *essences*) and the "fevered activity of animal life" (*JLGS*, 117), as both are wedded and are part and parcel of the human predicament. There is no priority among them—they are distinctions. Consciousness, *essences*, knowledge, and the bodily material are inextricably intertwined, but the last is the provenance of the previous three for Santayana. Subsuming the first three into the conceptual term of *mind* and leaving the latter with the concept of *body*, we neutralize mind/body separation via an epiphenomenal "compromise position designed to salvage what is viable in mind-body dualism and to avoid the absurdities of the reductive materialist" (*JLGS*, 117). *Animal faith* partakes of both.

In the course of an outstanding work on the philosophy of mind, and one influenced by, and arguing in support of, Santayana's thought, Jessica Wahman in her *Narrative Naturalism: An Alternative Framework for Philosophy of Mind* puts forth an insight that could serve as a *grounding* for an understanding of *animal faith*. She writes that "Santayana's epistemology of animal faith is geared toward asserting that no knowledge claim is identical to the existence it describes, and so our more narrative and poetical descriptions of life have their contribution to make to our understanding as well" (Wahman 2015, 103). Consonant with Santayana's own understanding of his philosophical writings as a whole, and his general non-dogmatic tenor of mind, I claim that Santayana's *animal faith* is *suggestive*, a conceptual reinforcement that not only aids in understanding scepticism, knowledge, belief, and certainty but helps to contextualize each individual human being and the respective limits and limitations that circumscribe one throughout a lifetime. One is always at liberty to dismiss it outright or ignore it altogether, as Santayana was pleased to share his natural tendency not to feel slighted or piqued by disagreement: "but I do not ask any one to think in my terms if he prefers others. Let him clean better, if he can, the windows of his soul ..." (*SAF*, vi).

What distinguishes *animal faith* for Santayana, and what are the argumentative affirmations? Some of the most insightful commentary on this concept in Santayana's thought comes from the writings of Santayana scholar John Lachs. One of these insights goes right to the heart of the matter and establishes *action* as the wellspring of *animal* faith and human existence in a material world: "The central emphasis here and throughout Santayana's discussion of the starting point for his own philosophy is on the preconscious reality of action. Like Lucretius and other naturalists, he thinks we must begin with the birth and death, the dark natural struggle of the threatened animals" (Lachs

1987, 149). In a philosophical work that begins with an inauguration of the implacable threat of scepticism in the cast of an intellectual challenge, the discussion devolves into Santayana's version of a response to or even a "refutation" of scepticism's pitch by confronting life itself on life's terms as one giant perennial threat, as something that intimates endings and mortality, that spreads an enveloping factor of risk to all that we do and engage in. In actuality, scepticism's threat, in *SAF*, has not been refuted or eliminated, but rather has been disarmed under the habituation of a far more serious menace—life itself. Those who could maintain that, given a choice of whether *doubt* or not being alive are in any sense equivalent, are frankly being disingenuous. With this in mind, doubt and *living one's scepticism* appear as rather innocuous considerations. As stated by another philosophical critic of Santayana: "Moreover, in animal faith's postulation of the existence of a mind (self) and an external world, there is a sense in which the world has priority. For to distinguish between appearances in our mind and an external reality they purport to represent, we must distinguish between external reality and our ideas of it. " (Shirley 1996, 139). Santayana, who maintained a firm unity in life and thought ("I stand in philosophy where I stand in daily life"), exhibits in the second part of *SAF* a tenacity in his orientation away from what until his day had been representative of scepticism in the Western tradition, in favor of an unambiguous shift toward life, armed with a practical compass that, truth be told, steers all mortals in their contingency. Only action allows us to subsist and persevere, and affords us the greater part of the modicums of certainty we could ever possess.

There is a passage in *SAF* that both gives us an unequivocal take on *animal faith* and bolsters Jessica Wahman's claim capturing the general Santayanan suggestion that *knowledge* is not the equivalent of what its claims envelop: "So the whole realm of being which I point to when I say existence might be described more fully; the description of it would be physics or perhaps psychology; but the exploration of that realm, which is open only to animal faith, would not concern the sceptic" (*SAF*, 42). Why would the sceptic show no interest in this enterprise? Primarily because, like any exploratory enterprise, being open and setting forth in a move to understand the world and one's place in it involves action and belief, at the very minimum. And though we fumble and stumble in our everyday lives like animals, which we are, learning here, forgetting there, and trying as best we can to eat nutritiously and tend to our needs, we wake up each day and initiate movement with the *belief* that, everything else being more or less equal, we will do it again, pretty much like yesterday. Why would anyone want to doubt this? First of all, Santayana asserts that "the most perfect knowledge of fact is perfect only pictorially, not evidentially, and remains subject to the end to the insecurity inseparable from animal faith, and life itself" (*SAF*, 107). Yes, we live, even thrive, with contingency everywhere. And what would press us to doubt that contingent change is *real*? A friend whom I had known for seven years, whose funeral service I attended a week ago, is no longer living. How do I know? Apart from my memory that

I can tap to recall the image of his face at the wake, I can walk over to his nearby house and see the vans and cars moving another family's possessions into the home where he formerly invited me in. I do not require further confirmations or explanations. I can let go of doubt at a certain point. I can have *faith* in the *belief* that what my human (animal) eyes, mortal and becoming less acute with the passing of the years, have absorbed, is good enough for me to be as certain as I can be, to hold a justified true belief, that José cannot be reached by phone tonight. Santayana tells us:

> In regard to the original articles of the animal creed—that there is a world, that there is a future, that things sought can be found, and things seen can be eaten—no guarantee can possibly be offered. I am sure these dogmas are often false; and perhaps the event will some day falsify them all, and they will lapse altogether. But while life lasts, in one form or another this faith must endure. It is initial expression of animal vitality in the sphere of the mind, the first announcement that anything is going on. It is involved in any pang of hunger, of fear, or of love. It launches the adventure of knowledge. The object of this tentative knowledge is things in general, whatsoever may be at work (as I am) to disturb me or awaken my attention. The effort of knowledge is to discover what sort of world this disturbing world happens to be. … The ideal of knowledge is to become natural science: if it trespasses beyond that, it relapses into intuition, and ceases to be knowledge. (*SAF*, 180–81)

This is consistent with Santayana being quite content to let the *hard science* scientists tell him what the world consists of. For the rest of us, or for those of us who are *not* trained in the hard sciences, we are left with essences, intuitions, beliefs, language, and *animal faith*.

WHERE IS THE ANIMAL IN *ANIMAL FAITH*?

The word "animal" appears in every chapter of *SAF* except one—the first one, "There is No First Principle of Criticism." The word and the notion of *animality* are part and parcel of the entirety of *SAF*, including the very title. Most philosophical critics and commentators have concentrated on *animal faith* when discussing *SAF* and justifiably so (see Lachs 2009, 484–90, and Saatkamp 2021, 280–90). I too think it is the key to Santayana's disarming of the threat of scepticism, as set forth in *SAF*. But *animal faith* is inextricably tied up with animals, or as I am using in this piece, *animality*. *Animal faith* is a belief in objects that somehow goes beyond the immediate impression of the senses in the moment, in the *here*, the *now*. *Animality* is what makes it all possible, its *sine qua non*. I have in mind one of the definitions that the *OED* gives for this term as "animal nature, animal life, as opposed to that of vegetables, or of inorganic matter" (*OED* 1991, 53). Humans fall within these definitional parameters. Even Bertrand Russell agrees with this, as he wrote in a review of *SAF*: "By 'animal faith' is meant something that we share with other animals: the belief of the cat in the mouse, and of the mouse in the cat; the habit of taking our fleeting perceptions as signs of 'things,' and generally those fundamental beliefs without which daily life is impossible. Animal faith can be purified and systematized by philosophy, but cannot be abolished except on pain of death" (Russell 1923, 280). That which differentiates Mr. President from Flipper, or Lassie, can never be completely removed from our considerations in our relationship with another species of animals. But what is shared in common is convincing and recognizable also. And it was for Santayana.

I am in agreement with Justus Buchler's claim in his "One Santayana or Two?" that Santayana's outbursts of commentary and thoughts in general outside the pages of his published works, belie and reveal much, intentional or not. He was surprised at "how much went on in his [Santayana's] reflection that failed to appear either in his theoretical work or his autobiography" (*AFSL* 69). Buchler also points out that Santayana "always fancied that his own variety of methodological skepticism was uniquely and safely worked out, that it was purgative and normal and desirable. He thought of it as an auxiliary device, and remained unaware of the fact that it threatened to devour his naturalism" (*AFSL* 71). It might have "threatened" to overwhelm his "naturalism," but it did not menace his animality. The subtending animality in *SAF* remained secure from the sceptical *scandal* (see Cavell 2005, 132–54).

Early in *SAF* Santayana attempts to define "existence." In the chapter "Nothing Given Exists" he states that he employs *existence* "to designate not data of intuition but facts or events believed to occur in nature" (*SAF*, 47). Existence is a trait we share with animals and " is accordingly not only doubtful to the sceptic, but odious to the logician. ... If this whole evolving world were merely given in idea, and were not an external object posited in belief and in action, it could not exist or evolve. ... I shall attribute existence to a flux of natural events which can never be data of intuition, but only objects of a belief which men and animals, caught in that flux themselves, hazard instinctively" (*SAF*, 48–49). Though he distinguishes between humans and animals in this last phrase, in another one he does not. Santayana likens the whole tradition of Western thought and its acolytes to the work of intelligent beasts, when in comparison to that august, serene image of the Indian sage, he asserts: "How like unhappy animals western philosophers seem in comparison" (*SAF*, 53). What is in fact very clear is that humans and animals, the human animal and other animals, exist. We share this *fact*, and Santayana quite unhesitatingly attributes it to animals as well as humans. Toward the conclusion of *SAF*, in the final chapter "Other Criticisms of Knowledge," this becomes abundantly clear. Writing of transcendentalism as an epistemological criticism he affirms: "Yet this attitude, seeing that man is not a solitary god but an animal in a material and social world, must be continually abandoned" (*SAF*, 303), and in distinguishing his *naturalized* epistemological criticism from the German conception of it in *Wissenschaft*, he confesses that his "criticism is criticism of myself. I am talking of what I believe in my active moments, as a living animal ... it is the discipline of my daily thoughts and the account I actually give to myself from moment to moment of my own being and of the world around me" (*SAF*, 305).

The projected distances that humans conceive of as various lengths of separation between them and other species of animals are far-ranging and creative. This collective product of discontinuous reasoning attempts to wall off, to separate as something inexorably unique, the human animal. This capacity for establishing discontinuity seems ingrained in most of us. It is understandable, as the idea that *we* cannot be beings that emerged from the primal slime and piles of muck and dirt and savagery is more pleasant to ponder over and presume. But suppose that those missing links and gaps in the evolutionary chain of being were clearly known to us, in scientific fashion with ocular proof, and we could know precisely where the human animal did indeed become *human*, and where *homo sapiens sapiens* left behind *homo sapiens*? Would we not be more understanding of creatures not like us and more appreciative that we have so much in common? Would we not, like Santayana, grow accustomed to calling ourselves *animals*, like he showed himself quite at ease with in *SAF* calling himself an *animal*? Perhaps there is one fundamental, bedrock certainty that can help us bridge this divide, even though, of course, we can never be totally convinced, categorically inoculated, as it were, from doubt concerning it. That is a side effect of *living one's scepticism*. As one contemporary philosopher, Gary Steiner, has asserted as a conceivable conviction: "To accept our mortality is to recognize our shared kinship with animals. It is to open ourselves to what Karl Löwith calls a 'cosmo-political' perspective that freely acknowledges the priority of our belonging to nature over our belonging to a human social whole" (Steiner 2008, 138). In this vein, Santayana in *SAF* has fulfilled his part—his partial part.

In the final analysis, Santayana equates *animality* with an aspect of what it means to be human. It is a semblance of what lies deepest and is what is more elevated and sublime, in all of us, in contradistinction to our cerebral trajectories and achievements. Curiously enough, it is in a passage in Chapter XIV ("Heathenism") in *Egotism in German Philosophy*, published some seven years prior to *SAF* in 1916 (though first published in a magazine a year before in 1915), where we first formally come into contact with *animal faith*, and comprehend how long Santayana must have been wrestling with its centrality in how he understood the world. These words betray the entrenched conviction of the animal-in-human, or *animality*, as I have been using it. He writes:

> Man used to be called a rational animal, but his rationality is something eventual and ideal, whereas his animality is actual and profound. ... I have sometimes watched a wild bull in the ring, and I can imagine no more striking, simple, and heroic example of animal faith...when he follows the lure again and again with eternal singleness of thought, eternal courage, and no suspicion of a hidden agency that is mocking him. ... Later, when sorely wounded and near his end, he grows blind to all these excitements. He smells the moist earth, and turns to the dungeon where an hour ago he was at peace. (*EGP*, 148–49)

Humans have also cultivated other humans, as they have and still do cultivate the *toro bravo*, to fight in arenas for the entertainment of certain other humans: *gladiators*. Could the above passage from Santayana apply to them also? Whether one thinks so or not, what it does open up is a meaningful conversation as to similarities and distinctions we persist in enacting in our reflections on humans, animals, the human animal, and what we see in animals as the *human*.

Works Cited I (Works by Santayana)

Santayana, George. 1916. *Egotism and German Philosophy*. London and Toronto: J. M. Dent & Sons Limited. Cited as *EGP*.
———. 1923. *Scepticism and Animal Faith: Introduction to a System of Philosophy*. New York: Charles Scribner's Sons. Cited as *SAF*.

Works Cited II (Works by Others)

Annas, Julia, and Jonathan Barnes. 1985. *The Modes of Scepticism: Ancient Texts and Modern Interpretations*. Cambridge: Cambridge University Press.
Burnyeat, M.F. 1983. Can the Skeptic Live His Skepticism? In *The Skeptical Tradition*, ed. Myles Burnyeat, 117–148. Berkeley and Los Angeles: University of California Press.
———. 1984. The Sceptic in His Place and Time. In *Philosophy in History*, ed. Richard Rorty, J.B. Schneewind, and Quentin Skinner, 225–254. Cambridge: Cambridge University Press.
Cavell, Stanley. 2005. *Philosophy the Day After Tomorrow*. Cambridge, MA: Harvard University Press.
Hamlyn, D.W. 1984. *Metaphysics*. Cambridge: Cambridge University Press.
Lachs, John, ed. 1967. *Animal Faith and Spiritual Life: Previously Unpublished and Uncollected Writings by George Santayana with Critical Essays on His Thought*. New York: Appleton-Century-Crofts.
———. 1987. Belief, Confidence, Faith. In *Mind and Philosophers*, ed. John Lachs, 141–156. Nashville: Vanderbilt University Press.
———. 2009. Animal Faith and Ontology. *Transactions of the Charles S. Peirce Society* 45 (4): 484–490.
Russell, Bertrand. 1923. A New System of Philosophy: A Book Review of George Santayana's *Scepticism and Animal Faith: Introduction to a System of Philosophy*. *The Dial, September 1923*: 278–281.
Saatkamp, Herman J., Jr. 2021. In *A Life of Scholarship with Santayana: Essays and Reflection*, ed. Charles Padrón and Kris Skowroński. Leiden and Boston: Brill.
Sartwell, Crispin. 1991. Doubt and Faith: Santayana and Kierkegaard on Fundamental Belief. *Transactions of the Charles S. Peirce Society* XXVII (2): 179–195.
Shirley, Edward S. 1996. Animal Faith: Santayana and Strawson. In *Frontiers in American Philosophy*, ed. Robert W. Burch and Herman J. Saatkamp Jr., 133–142. College Station, TX: Texas A & M Press.
Sprigge, Timothy L. S. 1995. *Santayana*. London and Boston: Routledge. Cited as *SAEP*.

Steiner, Gary. 2008. *Animals and the Moral Community: Mental Life, Moral Status, and Kinship*. New York: Columbia University Press.
Strawson, P. F. 1985. Skepticism and Naturalism: Some Varieties. New York: Columbia University Press.
The Compact Oxford English Dictionary. 1991. Oxford Clarendon Press. Cited as *OED*.
Wahman, Jessica. 2015. *Narrative Naturalism: An Alternative Framework for Philosophy of Mind*. Lanham, MD: Lexington Books.

A Tension at the Center of Santayana's Philosophy

Michael Hodges

It is well known to all who study Santayana's work that he distinguishes four "realms of being"—Matter, Essence, Truth, and Spirit. Each realm is supposed to be a distinctive aspect of our world. Perhaps the most problematic of these realms is matter. Matter, as we shall see, is contrasted with essence and so nothing can be said about it—it has no essence—but what place can a something about which nothing can be said have in a systematic philosophical view? In what follows I will try to explain how we should understand Santayana here. I believe this expresses one of his deepest insights. Perhaps it is best understood as a moral notion since it encapsulates his understanding of our place in the cosmos. Human existence and, in fact, all existence is radically contingent and without meaning or purpose. Santayana's notion of matter is very much in keeping with his overall philosophy and encapsulates his sense of the limited degree to which thought can penetrate the ultimate mystery of existence. Earlier philosophers, Lucretius for example, have attempted to literalize this inexplicability in his notion of the swerve. While Santayana applauded the insight he rejects the literalization, seeing it instead as a piece of poetry. The "idea" of matter is his alternative, but it does not escape from being ironic and

---

I wish to thank my colleague John Lachs for his invaluable assistance on this chapter. There were many interesting, productive, and happy conversations.

M. Hodges (✉)
Department of Philosophy, Vanderbilt University, Nashville, TN, USA
e-mail: michael.p.hodges@vanderbilt.edu

its own bit of poetry. It has the form of an explanation—matter is what explains existence—but functions as an empty placeholder. In so doing it conforms to the limited vision that he expresses in the Preface to *Scepticism and Animal Faith*, when he says:

> I stand in philosophy exactly where I stand in daily life; I should not be honest otherwise. I accept the same miscellaneous witnesses, bow to the same obvious facts, make conjectures no less instinctively, and admit the same encircling ignorance. (Santayana, *Skepticism and Animal Faith*, (1923) *Preface*, vi 1923 hereafter SAF)

His notion of matter is part of that "encircling ignorance."

It is necessary to distinguish between matter and the realm of matter, for obviously he has a great deal to say about the realm of matter[1] and nothing can be said about matter. Matter is the "principle of existence" and the realm of matter is the domain in which it is at work.

Along with the realms, Santayana's philosophy is stated in terms of the commitments of animal faith—those commitments that animal existence forces upon us. At the heart of animal faith is the world of substance that exists independently of us in the same plane as our bodies and awaits discovery and interaction. It will be my concern to try to clarify the relation between these two systems, if they are two, for that is a contentious claim itself. Some interpreters contend that they are but two ways of characterizing a single system (Kerr-Lawson 2009, 596). I do not believe that such a view can be maintained. To bring this out I will focus on the role that matter plays in relation to substance—the most important and probably the first posit of animal faith.

Santayana does not claim that the realms that he identifies are exhaustive. He does not know how many other realms there might be,[2] but these are ones that "are conspicuously different and worth distinguishing" (*SAF*, vi.). Unfortunately, he does not tell us why they are worth distinguishing. Perhaps we are to discover this for ourselves by seeing what light they bring to the discussion. We shall see! However, when we come to the categories of animal faith, we are told exactly how they arise. They are the beliefs that animal action commits us to—what we take for granted in action. Santayana is at pains to give us the context in which the various distinctions operate. It is the very project of *Scepticism and Animal Faith* to reject a "view from nowhere" since, as the sceptical side of the book shows, such a vision is empty, leading, as it does, to a "philosophy of silence." No judgments survive the sceptical reduction (Hodges and Lachs, 2000). But such a "philosophy" cannot be honest. We cannot live by it. "Willingly or regretfully, if I wish to live, I must rouse myself from this open-eyed trance into which utter scepticism has thrown me ... I must consent to be an animal" (*SAF*, 111). The satisfaction of animal needs requires action

---

[1] There is a whole book written about it.
[2] Is this a reference to Spinoza?

and beliefs are essential for action. Shall I go down this path or that? Which will lead me to lunch? We must, practically, form beliefs and therefore we need a standard of acceptable belief—knowledge—that will serve us in that. We cannot *live* without belief.[3] But Santayana is clear that, for all we know, the best course may be death. He does not abandon scepticism even when he takes up the positive task of laying out the commitments of animal faith.

And we must not forget that there is a "practical side" to scepticism and that is the discovery of essence and with it the possibility of the spiritual life. Scepticism allows us to see that all claims are open to doubt, and the only certainty is to be found in beliefless direct and immediate apprehension of the content of consciousness—the contemplation of essence for its own sake. This is a strange form of certainty, since it does not involve belief at all. While nothing is of value in the realm of essence or from the perspective of pure contemplation, such contemplation has a practical place in a well-lived life. It gives us an escape from the "treadmill" of daily life. It is a mode of awareness that is free of desire and satisfaction—a temporary respite from our animal existence. But the rumblings of our animal natures will call us back to the practical all too soon (Hodges 2018).

The sceptical reduction allows us to see where we stand in the world and what assumptions are practically necessary. But what about the realms? What is the perspective from which they are "worth distinguishing"? Here we are left in the dark. This seems to be a view from nowhere! But if the task of *Scepticism and Animal Faith* is to undercut the idea of a view from nowhere in favor of an epistemological standard that is grounded in action, why is ontology not "reined in" in the same way? Surely the "kinds of things" we find depend on what our purposes are. Differently interested persons will see different sorts of things in the same domain. Even a pile of junk will be sorted differently by individuals who bring different purposes to the job. The commonplace "one man's trash is another man's treasure" attests to this fact.

At least Santayana does not claim that his ontological categories are the only right ones or, as we have seen, the only ones. He says, "I do not ask anyone to think in my terms if he prefers others. Let him clean better, if he can, the windows of his soul, that the variety and beauty of the prospect may spread more brightly before him" (*SAF*, vi–vii). But what are we to make of this claim? Is Santayana proposing an aesthetic standard for an acceptable philosophy?[4] This seems far-fetched! That a prospect is beautiful does not imply that it is right! Is he suggesting that individual human differences may make different prospects appropriate to different individuals? This is an interesting possibility in light of Santayana's views on ethics, in which individual differences are taken with the utmost seriousness. But it would imply that ontology is a personal enterprise and that seems antithetical to the historical aim of an ontological investigation

---

[3] Hume also noted that scepticism evaporates as soon as we leave the study.
[4] He does claim that the identification of the realms is not a matter of truth, but more about this later.

itself. Perhaps the vocabulary in terms of which it is expressed might be individual, but the underlying view should not be exclusively so. Or is he simply challenging anyone to do better than he has? But this brings us back to the question, "What is he doing?"

Santayana thinks that his revised epistemology gains great plausibility through its presentation as an incremental development from the most minimal hypothesis of the identity of intuitions over time to a full-blooded commitment to nature as a system of substances which exist on the same level as one's body and with which we interact. This positive presentation takes its structure from the deconstructive side of the argument. Just as Santayana slowly rejects systems of belief as failing to meet the standard of certainty endorsed by the tradition until he reaches the position that nothing given exists, he slowly builds up the structure of beliefs by adding new elements in accord with the "new" standard of acceptability, which is animal faith—beliefs implicit in the press of animal action. Thus, his constructive development is controlled by his deconstructive strategy. He presents the reconstruction as an incremental build-up from "Nothing given exists" to "Belief in Nature."[5] This is a distorted view, since it is certainly not how animal faith would express itself. Animal faith "operates" wholistically, engaging a world of objects with which we interact and the structure of which is to be revealed in action and by investigation and ultimately by systematic science. Nowhere do we see this version of animal faith expressed in its own terms.

If this is correct, then Santayana does not "break free" of the tradition and instead implicitly allows himself to be controlled by what he is attempting to displace. However, this does not imply that the reductive analysis is misplaced or unnecessary. First, it shows the bankruptcy of the traditional epistemological project, which leads not to a robust theory of knowledge but to silence. Of course, silence is not a living philosophy. And as we have seen, we must decide, willingly or not, to admit to being animals and honestly accept the unavoidable consequences of that admission. At the same time, reductive analysis may be seen as the key to understanding "where" the ontological analysis of the realms comes from. In these "postmodern days" we have become philosophically suspicious of views from nowhere and Santayana's own critique of the Cartesian standard of knowledge confirms that suspicion. But this leaves us with the question, what perspective do they presuppose? And the reductive analysis itself offers us one answer.

The realms are exposed as distinct aspects of our world by the deconstructive analysis itself. This is clearest for the cases of spirit and essence, both of which are highlighted via the sceptical reduction. Spirit and essence come to light in the possibility of the "spiritual life" or the immediate contemplation of essence, which involves no belief—essence as the content of contemplation and spirit as the awareness implicit in such contemplation. And *the realm* of matter

---

[5] Certainly, animal faith does not see "knowledge" in such terms. It would speak in terms of success. See especially "The Implied Being of Truth," Chapter 25, *SAF*.

as the realm of existing things becomes clearly isolated via the reduction as well since the difference between mere possibility—essence—and actuality or existence is a basis for systematic doubt for, as Santayana puts it, "Nothing Given Exists" (*SAF*, Chapter VII). Even truth might be implied in this difference, although this is not how Santayana actually thematizes it (*SAF*, Chapter XXV). The realm of truth is simply the intersection between matter and essence taken in its totality and from an eternal perspective. It is a set of essences and, in that sense, is not a hybrid notion. It is the set of essences which have been touched by matter but it, in itself, is a set of essences. If we follow this line, then the legitimacy of the realms would stand or fall with the legitimacy of the reduction itself. What the reductive analysis allows us to see clearly is different moments of emphasis, which would likely go unnoticed without the teasing apart that the destructive analysis provides.[6]

A second path to the realms can be envisioned in a more traditional way via the analysis of God as conceived by Leibniz, for example. One way that the problem of existence has been approached from the earliest[7] is *via* God and forms as models for creation. Leibniz states this clearly in terms of his doctrine of possible worlds. On this view, God contemplates an infinite number of possible worlds in infinite detail and chooses, for existence, the possible world that is the best of all. Here we have three elements of Santayana's ontological analysis. We have the "realm of essence" as the possible worlds:[8] these are possibilities that do not "exist." For that we need the creative power of a necessarily existing being which, from the perspective of Christian theology, is also necessarily good and so would choose the best of the possibilities set before it. The emphasis of existence which is imparted by God[9] is "matter" on this view and the realm of truth is the created order seen from the perspective of eternity. This leaves out spirit, but spirit is an "outlier" in Santayana's view as well. There might have been a universe without consciousness. Spirit is a function of there being complex biological[10] creatures and there might not have been such creatures. That there are such creatures is a contingent fact about the material order. After all, we "can see" that in vast stretches of the existing universe there are no conscious creatures and so it might have been the case that none came to exist. There are two considerations about this view. First, of course, if there were no spirit or consciousness there would be no awareness that there was

---

[6] There are other approaches to the realms as well.

[7] See Plato's *Timaeus*.

[8] It should be clear that Santayana does not organize the realm of essence in terms of possible worlds, but that does not subvert the comparison. In fact, the determinateness of "possible worlds" might be thought to bring to the fore Santayana's notion of "specific" universals. Brick red shade 23 is just as much a universal—a repeatable—as is red itself.

[9] How this is done is not explained, but since God exists, it is assumed that such a being can "impart" existence to others. Perhaps this accounts for the unfortunate "constructionist" language here, which Santayana clearly rejects. We know how all this is done when a human being constructs a pot from clay!

[10] Whether such creatures must be biological is an interesting question raised for us by ever increasingly complex computers (AI).

such a universe. While we can conceive of such a possibility as things stand now, the very act of conceiving of it proves it to be false.

Second, it will be argued that such a world would not be the "best of all possible worlds," because a world without consciousness would lack a "perfection," since God is perfect, and God is conscious. I will not contest this argument here since it is not directly to my purpose. I am only interested in drawing out the comparison between Santayana's realm and a more traditional ontological picture. His realms are a simpler, more parsimonious variant of this traditional picture. First, the traditional picture takes existence for granted. It begins with an existing being and one whose existence is self-explanatory—one which exists necessarily. It does not account for existence but presupposes it. It pretends to do so via God's creative agency but that already presupposes existence. And Santayana's notion of matter, as we shall see, does not offer an "explanation" of existence at all. So it is perhaps informative to see Santayana's realms as inspired by this traditional picture purified for his purposes, expressing his own spartan commitments. In that regard it is in line with the "more honest" stand that he takes.

For now, we need to pick up the strands of the discussion. We are not to imagine that the realms are "parts of the cosmos or one great cosmos together" (*SAF*, vi). We should not construe the realms as constituting "a system of the universe." In other words, we are not to think of the realms as building materials that, when assembled, will make up a universe.[11] Santayana wants to reject the idea that each of the realms exists independently so that when they "come together" we get a universe. Instead, they are aspects of the world as we find it.

The realm of spirit names an aspect of the world as we find it. "Spirit" names consciousness. And we are all witnesses to the fact that consciousness exists. Essence too fits this description. The "realm of essence" names the infinite set of properties, numbers, and other abstract entities in their separation from things existent. There is a difference even between a particular whiteness (say pale white shade 12) and a particular white thing. Pale white shade 12 has a status independently of the existence or nonexistence of anything that is pale white shade 12. That whiteness taken by itself is a mere possibility for existence which is itself indifferent to existence and might never come to characterize any existing thing. As D. C. Williams puts it,

> Essences are natures, but the whole point of the distinction between essence and existence [matter] is lost if any nature is assigned to existence. Matter or existence is the plain fact or status of occurring; and occurrence is the irreducible circumstance that essences enter into external relations. (Williams 1954, 39)

Here we find both an agreement with Plato and a fundamental difference. Santayana is certainly a Platonist in holding that there are essences and that

---

[11] How this differs from Dewey's project in *Experience and Nature* is a fascinating question that I will not pursue here. Santayana certainly thinks it does differ.

they are independent of the existence or nonexistence of things.[12] But there are also two great differences as well. For Plato, there are only generic universals—human being—but for Santayana, there are both generic and specific universals.[13] There is an essence of Michael Hodges, consisting of all the features that characterize him, as well as one of human being. This is exactly why Santayana's essences cannot function as standards, as Plato's do. In any case, that there are entities of this sort seems obvious so long as we do not worry over the meaning of "there is" too much. And of course, second, Plato thinks that a preexisting creative agency is also necessary. Forms do not embody themselves. There must be an agent that brings this embodiment about, whereas for Santayana existence is an "irreducible fact."

The final two of the realms do not fit so easily into the picture we are considering. Consider Truth! In *Scepticism and Animal Faith*, truth is not thematized until late in the story. Truth is discussed in Chapter XXV and there its existence is "implied."[14] What appears first is success, not truth. Santayana says,

> It might seem, perhaps, that truth must be envisioned even by the animals in action, when things are posited ... Certainly, truth is there, if the thing pursued is such as the animal presumes it to be ... [but] he would want to be successful, not to be right. (*SAF*, 263-264)

There are two things to note here. First, the distinction between success and truth is not one that arises from animal faith itself. The animal is concerned with success and not truth. But if animal thought ends with success or failure where does the notion of truth come from? In strict consistency, success should be identified with truth and failure with falsehood. But this would give us a pragmatic conception of truth, which Santayana so clearly rejects. Therefore, the very distinction between success and truth is not one made from the perspective of animal faith. It seems to be a second-order interpretation of animal success. This means that the realm of truth is not a posit of animal faith and its presence in a list of "The realms of being" is problematic if that list is to reflect animal faith.[15]

Truth only comes into focus obliquely when some falsehood is uttered about one's self, for example. The difference between success and truth becomes clear in that context, since no matter of success hangs in the balance. It is just a matter of "getting at the truth"! Again, Santayana assumes that there

---

[12] This will become very important as we approach the discussion of matter.

[13] Perhaps this is brought out most clearly in the comparison with Leibniz, above. The possible worlds talk makes it clear that there must be specific universals.

[14] As we have seen, the structure of the second part of the book does not itself follow the path of animal faith. Instead, it mirrors the sceptical reduction of the first part. If one were to present matters from the point of view of animal faith, the identity of essence over time would not be the first "discovery" of animal faith.

[15] See my more complete discussion of The Realm of Truth in *Santayana at 150*, "The Realm of Truth in Santayana," Chapter 12 (Lexington Books, 2013).

is a difference between what is successful and what is true, and while the two may track together, he does not identify them. He is not a pragmatist! But there is no argument for that here. He just assumes it. In fact, one might argue that this, by itself, implies that the realms are not identical with the categories of animal faith, since for the engaged animal no difference would be discovered. Or to put it another way, the natural "theory of truth" for the engaged animal is a pragmatic one, not a realist theory. Even this is wrong. The active animal has no theory of truth. Its thinking stops with success. But Santayana argues that a realist theory is implicit because without it there would be no distinction between illusion and truth itself.

Neither spirit nor essence are posits of animal faith *per se*. Rather they come to light via the sceptical reduction. And the same can be said for truth. As Santayana argues in *The Realm of Truth*, truth is implicit in the very idea of appearance since, without the realm of truth, immediate appearances would be the final arbiter. Or to put it another way, there would be no arbitration! Without the realm of truth—the set of essences that have been "chosen" by matter—there could be no distinction between appearance and truth and it is the sceptical analysis that lets us see this (*RT*, Chapter I).

The realm of truth is derivative in the sense that it is a hybrid realm, involving as it does reference to both essence and matter. But it is a set of essences that has been touched by matter—in other words, those essences which have existed, are existing, and will be existing. This is an eternal and infinite set of essences but still a subset of all essences. I want to stress the fact that it is a set of essences, not a set of in-mattered essences. The latter set is a constantly changing one in each successive moment. But the realm of truth is eternal and therefore unchanging. It is what allows for the difference between seeming and being. If there were not an objective order, every "mere opinion" would be acceptable or true.

And this leads us to the question of what "accounts" for the fact of existence? Here we encounter Santayana's notion of "matter," which is the principle of existence. Matter marks the difference between a mere possibility and an actuality. But we must proceed carefully, because matter is the other of essence and that means that it can have no nature at all. But then what is it? As essence's foil, it cannot have a "nature," since it is precisely the other of any nature. It cannot be described because any description would invoke some essence. This makes it a very strange notion to be included in a philosophical account. It is a "something" about which nothing can be said,[16] and yet it is an "essential" element in the total account of things since without it there would be no difference between possibility and existence. It is nothing that is supposed to explain something. But it cannot be nothing since without it there would only be the eternal realm of essence. One might contend that matter is

---

[16] Even though Santayana seems to have written a whole book about it, which is primarily a description of the "realm" of matter or the order of existence, not matter itself. See the Preface to *The Realm of Essence*.

power itself.[17] But of course, power is also an essence and essences do not change. They are eternally the same. So it is certainly not the essence of power that accounts for change. But if it is existing power, we again have the problem of presupposing what we are trying to explain.

Classical accounts of essence—Plato's, as we have seen—appeal to some being that is supposed to explain the fact of existence. However, it is not matter itself but some creative agency. In Plato's *Timaeus*, for example, the ontology is not complete without a creative agency that operates with a vision of the good.[18] Creation involves the application of forms (essences) to matter by an agent with a view of the good in mind. Here we have the realms, such as they are, as independent parts of a creative process. But on this view, matter does not have power, since an agent is required and that agent already exists. In fact, this sort of understanding takes existence as a given. The agent exists and somehow manages to bring other things into existence, although there is no discussion of what this amounts to. It is easy to see that this sort of picture is borrowed from the context of human creation—a potter at the wheel—and while matter is an essential part of the story so conceived, Santayana does not want to accept any such analogy. He rejects such an account in the preface to *Scepticism and Animal Faith*. First, it treats the realms as "parts of a cosmos." And it appeals to an already existing agent to "explain" existence at all. And nothing is said about the very difference between the formal and the material. This is Plato's famous doctrine of participation, but we find no development of this metaphor that escapes from the "construction" metaphor.

In Aristotle's view, by contrast, matter is not so much an explanation of existence as a part of the analysis of an existing thing and its changes. After all, what counts as matter for Aristotle is always dependent on the identification of the relevant form and vice versa. There is a glass bottle, so we have matter—glass—and form—bottle—but the glass itself has a form and a matter, etc. Pure form and matter are merely logical termini of the conceptual process. The problem here is that Aristotle's view again takes existence as a given, and the categories of matter and form analyze it without explaining the mere fact of existence.

Angus Kerr-Lawson, one of the more systematic and astute critics of Santayana's work, misses a fundamental point here. The identification of matter with substance which he proposes, would violate what Williams called "the whole point." If essences are natures then matter cannot have a nature, but of course substances do. We have the classical distinction between the "what" of existence—essence—and the "that" of existence—matter. Perhaps it could be said that the *realm* of matter is the field of action. It is the reality in which matter is "at work." But that is not matter. It is not existence itself—which does not have and cannot have any nature. Kerr-Lawson says: "I do not find plausible any claim that matter, because it is a realm of being, must be disjoint from

---

[17] Michael Brodrick in conversation.
[18] Leibniz all over again.

essence, so that matter cannot both serve as a source of agency and have a form" (Kerr-Lawson 2009, 604).

He contends that he does not find it plausible to say that because matter is a realm it must be disjoint from form or essence. But if it were not "disjoint" it would not be a distinct aspect of the world as we find it. It would not explain the fact of existence but would already take it for granted as a given. Of course, a philosophy can do that. Aristotle's does, for example, but in so doing it becomes incomplete, leaving unexplained the very thing it is posited to explain. If it serves as a source of agency and has a form it cannot be in virtue of that form that it is the source of agency because no form, considered in its own right, can have power or agency because each essence is eternally the same. What Kerr-Lawson has done is smuggle into the story a principle that he claims to overtly reject. The *Realm* of Matter is the realm of existence or, in other words, substance. We have already seen that substance is a category of animal faith. If we accept this account of matter, then it does seem to be Aristotle's notion of a substance—a composite of matter and form—but then the doctrine of essence should model Aristotle's notion of form; but we know that that is not the case. For Aristotle, forms exist in things, whereas for Santayana essences are Platonic, in the sense that their being is independent of existence. This forces on Santayana the issue of existence itself. Aristotle begins with existing things and analyzes them and their changes. He offers no account of their coming to be as such. Of course, Aristotle does explain the coming to be of things. But his account shares in common with the modern scientific account that it always begins with something already existing and explains how something else comes from that. In short, both science and Aristotle take existence as a given. However, it is precisely in this context that Santayana's notion of matter does very important work. More about this shortly.

Kerr-Lawson suggests that the realm of matter should be understood simply as the order of existing things and there is no independent notion of matter as such (Kerr-Lawson 2009). There are certainly many places where Santayana seems to identify the two—matter and substance. There is even a sense in which it is true as a matter of convenient terminology. The realm of matter is the realm in which matter is at play. In that sense, while matter is the "principle of existence," the realm of matter is the order of existing things. And notice that in the previous quotation Kerr-Lawson claims both things—that matter is the "principle of existence" and that matter simply refers to the order of existing things. I do not believe that he can have it both ways. The study of the realm of matter is the study of the material order of the world as we discover it. Matter as the principle of existence is without characteristics and there is nothing to say about it. So, of course, we would expect that any talk would be about the realm of matter, not about the principle of existence. Thus, Santayana says,

> I wait for the men of science to tell me what matter is, in so far as they can discover it, and am not at all surprised or troubled at the abstractness and vagueness

of their ultimate conceptions: how should our notions of things so remote from the scale and scope of our senses be anything but schematic. (*SAF*, viii)[19]

Here "men of science" are not studying matter as such, but matter as it manifests itself in the "gross objects that fill the world"—in the realm of things as they exist. We may therefore agree to the terminological stipulation mentioned above. Matter is the "principle" or brute fact of existence and the realm of matter is the sphere of existence. The former is unintelligible but matter informed—the order of substances—is open to investigation. For Kerr-Lawson, by taking the realm of substance as the end point of explanation, he accepts the more traditional Aristotelian interpretation, which offers no account of existence itself. On the other hand, Santayana is a Platonist on this very point.

Even if we identify the *realm* of matter with substance in Santayana's system, this does not solve the problem. As we have said, substance is the primary posit of animal faith and it is the order of existence that is continuous with animal bodies. It is the world in which animals exist and seek their fortune. It awaits discovery but exists independently of such discovery. However, substance is not merely essence. It is embodied essence and that means that it involves matter. This means that for the realms to provide an adequate account, matter is an "essential" element. At the same time, matter, as the foil for essence, cannot explain anything, and so one might wonder what there is to insist upon here. I will come to that, but for the present I want to insist that Kerr-Lawson's view makes Santayana out to be an Aristotelian, and that is not compatible with his treatment of essence, which is Platonic.

The realm of essence is infinite, including all natures. It is totally indifferent to existence and each essence remains eternally the same in all respects. Of course, they (essences) do not exist and that is the point. Only a subset of the entire realm comes into existence and it is not via any rational agency. But there is an undeniable difference between an existing red patch and the mere possibility of such a patch, which is an essence. It is this difference that Santayana is marking with the term "matter."

Consider for a moment the category of spirit. There might not have been any consciousness in the entire cosmos. I am not making a point about the fact that consciousness makes no causal difference in the material order—Santayana's epiphenomenalism. Rather I am pointing out that consciousness arises from particular contingently *existing* biological structures, what Santayana calls "psyche," which might never have come into existence. In fact, as was noted earlier, it appears that such structures have not come into existence in vast parts of the universe. After all, it is a function of which essences have been selected for existence or what is in the realm of truth. Nothing might have existed, at least in the sense that there can be no ultimate reason why one essence is selected and another not, since matter is without any nature at all.

---

[19] For an explication of this idea, see *The Immense World*, by Ed Yong (Random House, 2022).

This does not deny that scientific explanations can provide us with information to understand and control the world. Of course, science may proceed, and Santayana applauds that but it takes as a given what exists. All scientific explanation proceeds from one given state of things to another and so offers no explanation of existence itself. It explains the existence of one state of affairs given another. Even the "Big Bang" is such an explanation. While it may explain the structure of the cosmos as we know it now, it does not proceed from nothing. It does not offer an explanation akin to the sort that theology seeks. There is no creation *ex nihilo*.

Substance is or substances are the things that exist in the natural world waiting to be encountered by living animals. So substances are, in Santayana's view, a composite of matter and essence. Here is his radical "materialism."[20] Given the "nature" or better the non-nature of matter, existence is radically contingent and inexplicable. "Matter" is Santayana's way of marking the unintelligibility of existence. In that sense, it is a moral category as well as an ontological one. It is a rejection of any theistic or transcendent meaning, including the principle of sufficient reason. There is no ultimate reason why something exists and another does not. There is no reason why anything exists at all. That is a brute fact outside the possibility of intelligibility.[21]

What this implies is that Santayana's materialism is not what might be called a scientific materialism, at least not in the first instance. It is not a view based on the findings of modern science. That is not to say that Santayana is not a materialist in that sense as well. He certainly sees the "drift of science" as evidence for the fact that in so far as explanation is possible, it will be in scientific terms. But his materialism is deeper than that. It is the rejection of all explanations when it comes to existence itself. What he calls "matter" is the bruteness of existence. Nothing explains existence itself. Rather, it is the starting point of all explanations.

Matter is the foil of essence and so is empty in any positive way. But this means that it cannot explain anything and thus we must take it on its negative side as a denial or perhaps more fittingly the enactment of that denial of the possibility of explanation. Santayana's notion of "matter" does not explain anything. Rather, it marks the place where all explanations end. To draw the line between essence and existence is no more than to notice the difference between what a thing is and that it is, between its character or kind and its occurrence as a case of the kind, between the rosiness of the rose and the fact that this is a rosy rose.

One might think that this shows the failure of Santayana's system, since it depends on a nonsense notion at its very center. Given his account, essences have no power to instantiate themselves. But how can a nothing about which nothing can be said be a part of a rational system of philosophy? How can it "account" for anything? It is an ingenious device that stands at the limit of

---

[20] Santayana says that he is the only materialist alive at the time.

[21] It would be very interesting to compare Santayana and the early Wittgenstein on this point.

thinking. "Matter" fills a space where an explanation should go while at the same time reminding us of the impossibility of explanation. The human intellect cannot penetrate the mystery of existence. However, this is not a weakness of the intellect. It is not a mystery to be solved. It is the "encircling ignorance" (*SAF*, vi). All that can be done is to "name" that mystery but in such a way that the mystery does not disappear or become transparent. Other systems of thought are not "honest" at this point. Instead of recognizing the unintelligibility of existence, they invent a being that is "self-explanatory." God is said to explain everything, even itself. But what can this mean? We do not know. And that is admitted even by the proponents, when they admitted that we do not and cannot comprehend "the divine essence."[22] And of course, as an essence, it cannot include its existence. The attempt to forge that connection—the ontological argument—fails (Aikin and Hodges 2014). But if that is true, then nothing has been explained by an appeal to such a divine being and we are still in the dark. But this admission is deadly, for it means that such a being cannot function as a part of the explanation of existence. At best, it marks a boundary of intelligibility.

An explanation of existence via the idea of God—an existing being—is, of course, empty, since precisely the thing that is to be explained is the fact of existence. Think in terms of the classical question, "Why is there something rather than nothing?" It cannot be answered by appeal to something that exists, since that would beg the question. And to appeal to a "necessarily existing being" is to appeal to what is nonsense. All necessity for Santayana is a function of internal relations and limited to the realm of essence. As D. C. Williams puts it in the earlier quotation, "Matter or existence is the plain fact or status of occurring; and occurrence is the irreducible circumstance that essences enter into *external relations*" (Williams 1954, 39, emphasis my own). Essence cannot account for existence without introducing total unintelligibility. Essences do not exist and cannot therefore account for existence. Something else is required—the irrational surd of existence or matter.

Santayana does not employ any of the trickery of self-existent beings or confusion about the relation of matter to the realm of matter. He simply honestly recognizes that the lofty aims of classical philosophy are founded on the attempt to "paper over" the unintelligible. Now we can see that the doctrine of matter is part of the whole enterprise of *Scepticism and Animal Faith*, which is to clip the wings of an over-optimistic philosophical standard for knowledge. The standard of absolute certainty is empty. Not even the simplest judgment, for example, "red, here, now," can survive such a test. We operate in our lives based on animal faith, not Cartesian Certainty, which might be an acceptable standard for a disembodied mind but will not serve an engaged animal. We should apply the same deflated vision in coming to terms with the Realms and specifically with existence or matter.

[22] It certainly become apparent when Descartes contends that God could have modified the laws of logic.

In the preface to *Scepticism and Animal Faith*, Santayana rejects such non-explanations as a self-existent being when he says, "I stand in philosophy exactly where I stand in daily life. I would not be honest otherwise. I accept the same miscellaneous witness, bow to the same obvious facts, make conjectures no less instinctively and *admit the same encircling ignorance*" (*SAF*, vi, emphasis my own). The term "matter" embodies that encircling ignorance.

Marking this sort of limit is always dangerous in philosophy, because it seems that recognizing the limit must involve transgressing the limit. How can you mark a limit without knowing that it is a limit and that would mean knowing that there is nothing on the other side? But that is to deny that it is a limit at all.[23] Santayana's solution is a term which embodies the unintelligibility which it marks. This is very much in keeping with the poetic nature of his philosophical thinking and the irony that he builds into his system.

Santayana says that his philosophical categories are not part of the realm of truth. They do not describe any facts which are themselves part of the realm of truth. The "realm of truth" is not a further part of the realm of truth. It is not true or false that there is a realm of matter.[24] Rather, such terms as "Spirit," "Essence," "Matter," and "Truth" are like buckets that bring a certain order to the water they contain. They do not add to the water at hand, but they make the water more useful by organizing it. Buckets are convenient ways to convey it from one place to another. In the same way, the "realms" are ways to organize our beliefs. They provide useful ways to express our ultimate situation. But if that is true, in what sense are they justified at all? What standard ought we to apply in assessing them? As we noted earlier, Santayana himself seems to propose an aesthetic standard. He says, "I do not ask anyone to think in my terms if he prefers others. Let him clean better, if he can, the windows of his soul, that the variety and beauty of the prospect may spread more brightly before him" (*SAF*, vi). In the end, I don't think that is what he means. Rather, he is offering a pragmatic criterion in the broadest sense. For Santayana, philosophy is about making an honest assessment of the human situation. This is where he "takes his stand." Human existence, like all existence, is ultimately unintelligible. To live resolutely in the face of that is our "destiny"!

But this leaves me with a question that I believe might challenge the way that Santayana characterizes his philosophical vision. If we say, as I have suggested, that Santayana's "account" of matter is best understood as a moral story about the limits of explanation and the honesty of a philosophy that respects those limits, how are we to understand his claim that his "ontology" of the realms is not true but a useful way of organizing what is true. "No language or logic is right in the sense of being identical with the facts it is used to express" and "it is a foolish heat of a patriot to insist that only his native language is intelligible or right" (*SAF*, vi). How, then, might we adjudicate between Santayana's vision and

---

[23] This is the fundamental problem that faces Wittgenstein's *Tractatus*. See my *Transcendence and Wittgenstein's* Tractatus (Temple University Press, 1990).

[24] See my essay in *Santayana at 150*.

that of William James at the end of "The Will to Believe" (James 2011)? There James argues for our "right to believe" in what he calls the "religious hypothesis," which says that the universe is organized around the good and so, at the end of the day, the good will obtain. And, second, that it is better even now to believe the first, since it is better to live with hope than not. He ends his discussion by saying that "there is no better way to face death than to act for the best, hope for the best and take what comes." Santayana's "view" seems to be obviously different. There is no hope. But why then should we prefer his view to James's? After all, according to Santayana himself, it is not a question of truth but of the pragmatic value one has over the other. Why is one "bucket" to be preferred to the other? Both carry the water and serve us in the moment of death. One provides stoic resolve and the other combines that with a bit of hope. Neither can be tested directly. Are they but two ways of expressing the same limit? James certainly does not think so and in various places offers considerations in favor of a religious outlook ontologically understood.[25] But perhaps I am making too much of the difference. Perhaps it is a foolish heat to try to decide between them except in a completely personal way. Or, finally, the difference may not be open to judgment on this narrow front. Perhaps, we must look at the complete picture to see how the whole vision makes sense of things, and in that way come to a final judgment. I confess I find Santayana's comprehensive vision highly plausible and tempting.

References

Aikin, Scott, and Michael Hodges. 2014. St. Anselm's Argument as Expressive. *Philosophical Investigations* 37 (2): 130–151.

Hodges, Michael. 2018. Lachs on Transcendence: Art's Relation to the Life of Reason. In *John Lachs's Practical Philosophy, Value Inquiry Book Series Online*, ed. Krzysztof Piotr Skowroński, vol. 315, 1–15. https://doi.org/10.1163/9789004367647_002.

Hodges, Michael, and John Lachs. 2000. Displacing Skepticism. In *Thinking in the Ruins*. Nashville: Vanderbilt University Press.

James, William. 2011. The Will to Believe. In *The Pragmatist Reader*, ed. Robert Talisse and Scott F. Aikin. Princeton, NJ: Princeton University Press.

Kerr-Lawson, Angus. 2009. Responses to Friendly Critics. *Transactions of the Charles S. Peirce Society* 45 (4): 596–648.

Santayana, George. 1923. *Scepticism and Animal Faith: Introduction to a System of Philosophy*. New York; London: Charles Scribner's Sons; Constable and Co. Ltd.

Williams, D.C. 1954. Of Essence and Existence and Santayana. *The Journal of Philosophy* 51 (2): 31–42.

---

[25] For example, see *Varieties of Religious Experience*, Chapters 16–18.

Truth and Ontology

Glenn Tiller

I

Santayana's materialist system of philosophy comprises four ontological categories set out in his four-volume *Realms of Being* (*RB*). In *Scepticism and Animal Faith* (*SAF*), three of these categories or realms, namely essence, truth, and spirit, are introduced in dedicated chapters. Although Santayana references "material substance" in *SAF*, and materialism is the leading principle of his system, the realm of matter is not presented and developed until the sequel.[1]

Santayana is not a reductive materialist, so matter is not the only kind of reality for him. Following Democritus, he admits immaterial, powerless

---

I thank Martin Coleman and Paul Forster for their comments.

[1] In *SAF*, Santayana defends the belief in substance. In his system, "substance" is a more generic term than "matter" since it stands for whatever is the object of instinctive belief or animal faith. Idealist philosophers who reject the existence of matter still believe in substance, but the substance is mental. In Santayana's view, the proper object of animal faith is implicated in action. Such a substance has certain "indispensable properties." It is external to thought, in flux, unequally distributed, has parts, and composes a unified field of action (*RB*, 202–203). He maintains that a substance possessing these properties "has a familiar name: it is called matter" (*RB*, 234), the only source of power and potentiality in the universe and the subject of physics (*SAF*, viii, *PGS*, 522). For a different interpretation of Santayana's realm of matter, see Lachs (1988) and (2003) and Hodges (2014) and in this volume. Cf. Kerr-Lawson (2003) and Sprigge (1974).

G. Tiller (✉)
Department of Philosophy, Texas A&M University-Corpus Christi,
Corpus Christi, TX, USA
e-mail: glenn.tiller@tamucc.edu

© The Author(s), under exclusive license to Springer Nature
Switzerland AG 2024
M. A. Coleman, G. Tiller (eds.), *The Palgrave Companion to George Santayana's Scepticism and Animal Faith*, Palgrave Companions,
https://doi.org/10.1007/978-3-031-46367-9_16

realities into his ontology (*PGS*, 509). Essence, "the infinite multitude of ideal terms," is an immaterial realm of being (*RB*, viii). So is spirit, the morally charged "awareness natural to animals, revealing the world and themselves in it" (*RB*, 572).[2] When spirit grows cognitive and forms beliefs about nature and discourses with other minds, Santayana claims it recognizes another immaterial reality: the realm of truth, "to which the earnest intellect is addressed" (*SAF*, 227).

In what follows, we first look at how *SAF*'s epistemology introduces *RB*'s ontology and Santayana's notion of a "realm of being." Next, we situate the realm of truth within his categorial ontology. We note some of the core traits of the realm of truth and differentiate it from his account of true belief or judgment.[3] We conclude by looking at the place of individual truths in Santayana's system.

II

Santayana's sceptical analysis of knowledge in chapters I–VII of *SAF* demonstrates that belief in the existence of anything is "radically incapable of proof" (*SAF*, 35). No beliefs are certain; none possess intrinsic warrant. The sceptic who engages in radical, thorough doubt is led to the conclusion that scepticism is "invincible" (*SAF*, 101).

The terminus of radical scepticism is not the retention of some attenuated, residual belief. It is the cognitive exit from all belief. The "romantic solipsist" (*SAF*, 13), maintaining the belief in memory, present experience, and expectation, is driven to solipsism of the present moment, a wholly aesthetic state in which the sceptic is absorbed in whatever essence is given to consciousness but without recognizing the fact that essence is given to consciousness.

For Santayana, radical scepticism clears the ground of any epistemological objections to a sincere statement of the beliefs presupposed in daily activities and the realities recognized in ordinary reflection. Belief cannot be long suspended in animal life. And the critic of knowledge must have beliefs and admit some realities to exit the terminus of radical scepticism. However, radical scepticism shows admitting the beliefs implicated in action and the realities encountered in experience are only possible by an instinctive, involuntary act of "animal faith," which Santayana says might otherwise be called "cognitive instinct, empirical confidence, or even practical reason" (*PGS*, 586).

Another way *SAF* introduces *RB* is characterized by Santayana's analysis of "transcendentalism," or what he calls the subjective critique of the principles of knowledge.[4] In his analysis, transcendentalism has two phases. The first, scepti-

---

[2] Other names for spirit include "consciousness, attention, feeling, thought, or any word that marks the total inner difference between being aware or asleep, alive or dead" (*RB*, 527).

[3] Santayana often uses "belief," "opinion," and "judgment" interchangeably. We will mainly refer to "true belief."

[4] "Transcendentalism" is "looking for reality in one's own breast" and searching for the reality of all things "in one's memory and experience" (*EGP*, 21–22).

cal phase leads to the suspension of belief. In the second, assertive phase, scepticism is abandoned for the beliefs and categorial realities of common sense. Recognizing these is done in awareness that one is operating without proof or denying the validity of radical doubt. The critic of knowledge gives up the quest for finding a rationalist foundation of knowledge and "substitute[s] the pursuit of sincerity for the pursuit of omniscience" (*OS*, 100). It is in the assertive phase of transcendentalism that Santayana announces and delineates his realms of being.

The phrase "realms of being" has the ring of metaphysics. Santayana, however, does not consider his system metaphysical. While recognizing that others (e.g., idealists) will disagree with his terminology, he takes "metaphysics" to signal "an attempt to determine matters of fact by means of logical or moral or rhetorical constructions" (*SAF*, vii). An example of this sort of metaphysics is Plato's idea that the Good is a form possessing creative power.[5] Instead of being an example of "metaphysics" in that sense of the word, Santayana's realms of being are intended to express the ontological commitments of *common sense*, which he separates from *common opinion* (*RB*, 832). Common opinion might refer to any fantastic, widespread belief—true or false—such as the power of an immaterial soul to command the body. In contrast, common sense refers to the unavoidable convictions implicated in action. Santayana's categories are grounded in common sense since they are spontaneously employed and revealed in reflection "by an animal mind in the presence of nature" (*RB*, xxvi). They express the convictions that lie beneath all "overt parrot beliefs" (*SAF*, v) and all the "special systems" of philosophy (*RB*, 826). These convictions cannot be doubted without undermining our everyday actions and common-sense thinking. From this perspective, he asserts (hinting at his aristocratic tendencies) that if materialism or the "belief in the existence of hidden parts and movements be metaphysics, then the kitchen-maid is a metaphysician whenever she peels a potato" (*SAF*, viii).[6]

In the preface to *SAF*, Santayana writes, "The Realms of Being of which I speak are not parts of a cosmos, nor one great cosmos together: they are only kinds of categories of things which I find conspicuously different and worth distinguishing, at least in my own thoughts" (*SAF*, vi). Despite the word "things," which suggests a material object, this statement is liable to give the impression that his categories are conceptual only, or a kind of folk-ontology akin to "folk-psychology" in the philosophy of mind, referring to "things"

---

[5] A contemporary example of "metaphysics" in Santayana's sense of that word is found in Leslie's neo-Platonic hypothesis that "the actual world of people and objects is a good one and *it exists simply because it ought to*. Its ethical requiredness—the fact that there is an ethical need for it—*is itself creatively effective*" (Leslie 2007, 2, italics preserved).

[6] Santayana does not think materialism is metaphysical, but he does regard it as a form of naturalism since the physical cosmos is a unified field of action. Any supernatural world, if it exists, would be "only ultra-mundane, an extension of this world on its own plane, and a recognition of forces ruling over it not reckoned with in vulgar commerce" (*RB*, 196). See also "The Appeal to the Supernatural" (*GTB*, 18–29).

eliminable by a superior theory. Moreover, by writing "my own thoughts," he suggests his categories are personal or idiosyncratic. So understood, his categorial ontology would be a form of mental autobiography, probably without purchase in other minds.

The notion that Santayana's ontology is but a useful set of conceptual categories is not without support. His aims are relatively modest compared to other categorial philosophers, such as Kant. Santayana does not claim to discover the *a priori* universal categories of reason. He allows there might be other categorial realities "to which I have no approach or which I have not happened to distinguish in my personal observation of the world," and he concedes an element of personal expression in his terminology (*SAF*, vi). There is more to reality than he or any person can conceive, and the categories he singles out for emphasis express our instinctive interests. Given the comparative modesty of ambition and scope for his ontology, commentators such as Buchler have a point when they judge that "Santayana conceives a system philosophy to be a personal work of art which serves, for the philosopher, to unify the various phases of his experience" (Buchler 1939, 410).

We should not, however, place too much emphasis on the word "personal." Santayana states, "I think it reasonable to suppose that the beliefs that prove inevitable for me, after absolutely disinterested criticism, would prove inevitable also to most human beings" (*RB*, xxv). To the critic who smiles at such a pretentious claim, he replies that he aims to articulate "the principles to which [the critic] appeals when he smiles" (*SAF*, v). So, while his ontology is meant to unify the various phases of his experience or "clean the windows of his soul" (Ibid.), this is not an exercise in autobiography only; it is also an attempt to articulate a shared ontology of human experience. Support for this interpretation is found in his claim that unlike his novel, *The Last Puritan*, which he thought no one else could have written since it gives the emotions of his experiences living in America, his realms of being "might perfectly well be described by some future writer better than I should do it" (*LGS*, 5:37). A future writer might better describe the realms he identifies since they are present in human experience in general and not only his personal experience.

Still, we might ask, are the categories simply ways we organize our thoughts? Or are they "things" in the sense of being indicative of what is real? In other words, do we just think with the categories, or do they reveal realities? A plausible reply to these questions is that his ontology has both functions. On the one hand, his realms make explicit the ontological realities encountered in experience. On the other hand, they are conceptual distinctions continually contrasted in discourse to expose their differences and throw them into sharp relief.[7]

One might object that the only reality indicated by Santayana's categorial scheme is material substance. He states that "the only belief that I myself

---

[7] Here I agree with Goodman's interpretation of Santayana's ontology (Goodman 1943). See Kerr-Lawson (2004) for a discussion of Santayana's contrastive method.

entertain, because I find it irresistible, is the belief in a realm of matter, the expectation of persistence and order in a natural world ... But the realms of truth and of essence are in quite another case. To them I assign no existence; in them I demand no belief" (*RB*, 453). This statement fits with his position that "technically ... to believe in anything means to believe that it exists" (*PGS*, 527). However, setting aside the fact that elsewhere he asserts that the realm of truth is "an object of belief" (*SAF*, 100), it would not be accurate to say that his other three categories are merely conceptual in the sense of being instrumentally useful but not revelatory of reality. Despite the above passage, his categories pick out realities, even if these are not implicated in action in the same way as matter.

Take, first, the realm of essence. In contemporary terminology, essences would be classified as "abstract objects." They are non-causal entities that do not depend on matter or mind. For Santayana, essences possess being but do not exist in space or time.[8] He explicitly argues against critics who object that essences only come into being when instantiated by matter (*PGS*, 535). Indeed, he claims the being of essence is ontologically necessary insofar as essences are immutable forms impossible to banish given their ideal status. "To deny the being of essence," he writes, "because it may happen to be unrealised, is self-contradictory: for if it is not realised, it must have a quality, distinguishing it from realised forms" (*RB*, 22). Denying the being of essence or that something exists implicitly acknowledges the being of essence. So, although we do not believe in the existence of essence, we admit the reality of essence the moment we contemplate any quality or relation.

As for spirit, Santayana does not think it is merely a convenient and eliminable folkway for talking about the mental. Spirit does not exist in the same way as matter since it does not have parts or power. Instead, it is an entelechy, a manifestation of the body's activity. A moment of spirit or an "intuition" "is generated at some particular point of space and time and expresses a material predicament of some animal" (*OS*, 207). It manifests existence insofar as it has "actuality." Such "intuitions are not ... existences in the same sense as natural things," he writes, "nor events after the fashion of natural events; and yet we must say of them pre-eminently that they exist and arise, unless we are willing to banish spirit from nature altogether and to forget, when we do so, that spirit in us is then engaged in discovering nature and banishing spirit" (*OS*, 208). Thus, spirit is both a category of thought—the category of thought itself—and denotes the reality of conscious experience.

The claim that Santayana's ontology picks out kinds of reality might seem to clash with his position that philosophy is fundamentally a literary pursuit, a branch of the humanities rather than the sciences. This is Singer's view, who,

---

[8] The distinction between existence and essence is Santayana's most fundamental ontological distinction. He holds that "we learn in the Timaeus that the first of all distinctions is that between what is always identical with itself and immutable and what, on the contrary, is in flux and indefinable. This is the precise distinction I should make between essence and existence" (*PGS*, 544).

like Buchler, holds that "Santayana's philosophy was intended to be an expression of the author's *personal experience* and imaginative interpretation of *his life* as he lived it" (Singer 2000, 2, italics added). Any clash here, however, seems superficial. To be sure, Santayana did not regard philosophy as a science. And he did not claim to be an expert in "natural or mathematical philosophy"—he could "only spread a feast of what everybody knows" (*SAF*, ix). However, it does not take a scientist to recognize the existence of the realm of matter or a mathematician to recognize the realm of essence. Anyone might recognize the realms of spirit and truth. His realms do not belong to the specialist.

For Santayana, essence, matter, and spirit are irreducibly different kinds of reality. One category is not definable in terms of another. Although his terminology might be somewhat non-standard, these three categories have some claim to being not only the orthodox categories of common sense but also the basic categorial realities recognized, albeit with significant differences in formulation, by philosophers from the ancient to the modern era. As basic categories, his realms are not exotic. Philosophers regularly recognize non-material realities, such as universals and numbers. Santayana finds "kindred doctrines" to his realm of essence in the philosophies of Plato, Spinoza, Leibniz, Whitehead, Husserl, and others (*RB*, 155–180). Philosophers commonly admit the reality of spirit or consciousness—the subject of the "hard problem." And many Western philosophers are materialists or "physicalists" of some sort, sometimes excluding all other types of reality. Had Santayana kept to his original plan in 1911 of writing a "system of philosophy to be called 'Three Realms of Being,' … namely Essence, Matter, and Consciousness" (*LGS*, 2:37), his ontology would be generally in line with much of past and present philosophical speculation. It is the realm of truth that makes his ontology unique.

III

Santayana's realm of truth is unusual in contemporary philosophy in that it does not define truth primarily in terms of belief or judgment. Most contemporary philosophers tend to agree in one way or another with Ramsey's deflationary thesis that it is "obvious that if we have analyzed judgment, we have solved the problem of truth" (Ramsey 1999, 106). Although many eschew Rorty's eliminativist view that "truth is not the sort of thing one should expect to have a philosophically interesting opinion about" (Rorty 1982, xiii), contemporary philosophers have, by and large, sought to extirpate any notion of truth divorced from belief or judgment and the norms of linguistic practice. Santayana's ontological account of truth inverts this perspective. For him, the primary, common-sense meaning of "truth" is that there is a way things are independent of our thoughts, and the way things are can be distinguished from things themselves as well as our beliefs about those things. His ontological account of truth is thus closer to classical accounts in which truth is an aspect or part of reality than contemporary accounts of truth rooted in the philosophy of language.⁹

The realm of truth is also unique within Santayana's system since it is the only category defined in terms of two other categories. Essence, matter, and spirit are *sui generis* aspects of reality (although matter and spirit involve essence). Significantly, all three of these categories figure among the seven meanings of the word "is" that Santayana distinguishes in his essay, "Some Meanings of the Word 'Is'" (*OS*, 189–212), published a year after *SAF* and which he regarded as the best summation of his system. Essence is defined by the "is" of "identity," matter by the "is" of "existence," and spirit by the "is" of "actuality." The realm of truth, in contrast, does not correspond to one of the meanings of the word "is." Instead, it is constructed from the realms of essence and matter. Hodges nicely puts this point by saying the realm of truth is an ontological "hybrid."¹⁰

To arrive at Santayana's realm of truth, we need first note his claim that "whatever exists, must have some essence" since a "being without any essence is a contradiction in terms. The existence of something without quality would not differ in its absence nor from the existence of anything else" (*OS*, 116–117). Accepting that whatever exists must have some essence, we then note that unlike his philosophical "master," Spinoza, Santayana did not hold that all essences are "realized somewhere at some time in the life of nature" (*RB*, 22). Only some essences are instantiated by matter. The totality of instantiated essences is the realm of truth or "that segment of the realm of essence which happens to be illustrated in existence" (*RB*, xv). Two metaphors help indicate what he means by the hybrid nature of the realm of truth. He describes truth as "the splash any fact makes, or the penumbra it spreads, by dropping through the realm of essence" (*SAF*, 267). And he writes that "existence, as if charged with electricity, turns a whole region of essence into a magnetic field" (*RB*, 451). We return to these ideas below.

The core traits that characterize Santayana's realm of truth are adumbrated in chapter XXV of *SAF*, "The Implied Being of Truth," and then more fully in *RB*. One of these traits is that truth is mind-independent (*SAF*, 267). He refers to the "reality of an actual truth, comprehensive and largely undiscovered" (*RB*, 402). Truth's comprehensive and largely undiscovered nature implies that it is not bound up with belief. It is that to which belief must answer, but it outstrips belief and most truth we shall never know.

---

⁹ Szaif (2018). Santayana's realm of truth sounds much like a secularized version of Augustine's account of truth. "You will not deny that there is unchangeable truth, containing everything that is unchangeably true. You cannot call it yours or mine or anyone else's. Instead, it is present and offers itself in common to all who discern unchangeable truths, like a light that is miraculously both public and hidden. Who would claim that everything present in common to all who reason and understand pertains to the nature of any one of them in particular?" (Augustine 2010, 56). See also Cameron (2018).

¹⁰ Hodges (2014).

Although the realm of truth is mind-independent, Santayana regularly and confusingly characterizes it in terms of propositions and assertions. He writes that truth is "what omniscience would assert" and "the sum of all true propositions" (*RB*, 420) and states that the "standard comprehensive description of any fact which neither I nor any man can ever wholly repeat, is the truth about it" (*SAF*, 266). These sorts of statements, and there are many others like them, are ways of elucidating ontological truth, but they cannot be taken literally, there being no omniscient judge or asserter of the sum of all true propositions.[11] A possible complication here is that Santayana asserts that truth is "something that only a mind can detach" and that it is "something ... addressed essentially to mind" (*RB*, 471), which appears to contradict the idea that truth is mind-independent. However, in the same passage, he makes clear that in the "order of genesis it is the being of truth, the fact that facts exemplify essences and have relations ... makes it possible that animals should ... discover some part of the truth" (Ibid.) "Truth," he writes, "is ontologically no more mental than physical" (Ibid.). And the fact that it is a "standard" or that "to which correct judgments conform" is incidental to the realm of truth (*SAF*, 267). Conformity to the realm of truth is what makes our beliefs true, but it does not make the realm of truth. Ontological truth is nothing mental or physical but the "form, an essence, that intelligence may find in an object, or in a system of objects" (*RB*, 471).

Given that the realm of truth is mind-independent, there is some irony in the fact that Santayana tells us "from the beginning of discourse there is a subtle reality posited which is not a thing: I mean the truth" (*SAF*, 262) and proposes that the "experience which perhaps makes even the empiricist awake to the being of truth, and brings it home to any energetic man, is the experience of other people lying" (*SAF*, 266). If I am falsely accused and "represented as thinking what I do not think, I rebel against that contradiction to my evident self-knowledge" and "learn that a report may fly in the face of the facts" (Ibid.). I then clearly see that there is "a comprehensive standard description for every fact, which those who report it as it happened repeat in part, whereas on the contrary liars contradict it in some particular" (Ibid.). This recognition happens even if a third party decides against me—the realm of truth is independent of the community of believers. If falsely accused, we become viscerally aware of the differences between assertion, belief, and truth. We conceive the way the world is independent of the lying description.

The example of lying also helps explain why truth is typically taken as inseparable from judgment. Since the "being of truth ... seems to be first clearly posited in disputation" over the right answer, which is one way in which the truth is "implied," Santayana holds that "a consequence of this accident (for it is an accident from the point of view of the truth itself under what circumstances men most easily acknowledge its authority) is that truth is often felt to

---

[11] Kerr-Lawson (1997) discusses why "Moore-Russell propositions" are too psychological a notion for Santayana's realm of truth. Cf. Atkins (2018).

be somehow inseparable from rival opinions; so that people say that if there was no mind and consequently no error there could be no truth" (*SAF*, 266). This last thought contradicts the mind-independence of truth. The being of truth might be first broached in discourse, but this does not mean that it is an artifact of language, as many have concluded.

Another trait of the truth is that it is all-inclusive or comprehensive. Some philosophers countenance the idea that there might be facts without truth and truth without facts (Hookway 2000, 56–81). Santayana rejects this possibility; for him, every fact is reflected in the truth. Truth is not "accidental" "since by existing the world fatally determines the truth about itself" (*RB*, 445). This is another way truth is "implied": it is automatically implicated by material existence. Material facts fix truth, but ontological truth is not the facts themselves but the form of those facts. This means there are no "gaps" in the realm of truth. In Santayana's estimation, pragmatists are led to absurdities, such as denying the truth about the past, because they conflate ontological truth with an "empirical analysis of true judgment," where a "true judgment" is one that is verifiable (*COUS*, 90–91).

The all-inclusive nature of truth gives Santayana another reason for distinguishing ontological truth from true belief. A final, true belief that aspired to be all-inclusive would be a new event. It would therefore add something to the world not included in the final judgment. Rejecting the identification of truth with an absolute, all-inclusive belief, Santayana argues that "in order that even a superhuman survey of history should be complete, the last of future events would have had to occur and show its colours. Therefore an actual survey (which would be a fresh event) could not supervene; or if it supervened it could not be all-inclusive, since by arising, this survey itself would have added an important event to history" (*RB*, 485).

The notion that a final belief cannot supervene over the totality of the realm of matter is related to a key trait of ontological truth: eternality. Santayana defines "eternal" as "that which without existing is contemporary with all times," which he states "contains everything that is not temporal at all; in other words, the whole realm of essence, as well as the realm of truth" (*SAF*, 271). This definition does not clearly distinguish the *eternality of truth* from the *eternality of essence*. Here we can note that for Santayana, the "eternality of truth is inherent in it: all truth—not a few grand ones—are equally eternal" (*SAF*, 268). He grants that it "might seem ... that the truth changes as fast as the facts which it describes" (*RB*, 489). However, the realm of truth does not change with events but is an eternal record of them. The eternality of truth distinguishes it from the material flux. "The truth about existence differs altogether in ontological quality from existence itself. Life and motion are gone ... all ages equally present" (*RB*, 486). Truth is a "frozen history" or "synthetic image of time" (*SAF*, 271), and so the truth about the past, present, and future is definite and unchanging. "If Julius Caesar was alive at a certain date," he holds, "it was then true, it had been true before, and it will be true always that at that date he was or would be or had been alive" (*RB*, 489). As McHenry observes, Santayana's position on the eternality of truth is complemented by his "eternalist" theory of time. Under this view, "past, present, and future must all have an equal ontological status, regardless of which particular date we choose as our point of departure" since "the past is only past in relation to what we call our present" (McHenry 2000, 220–222).

It is hard to overstate the importance of the eternality of truth in Santayana's philosophy. He defends the idea with vehemence.[12] It is one of the reasons for his decision to add the realm of truth to his initial three categories. He protested that the "category of truth in particular has been lately subjected to rough usage" (*RB*, 401). For him, some of this "rough usage" came from the rising tide of pragmatism. In opposition to James, who held there is "no 'eternal' edition of [the truth] to draw comfort from" (James 1911, 226), Santayana thought we could draw some comfort from eternal truth. Along with Emerson, he thought it possible for the cruel facts of life to become benign objects of contemplation when taken as essences in the eternal realm of truth. For this reason, eternal truth is central to Santayana's account of secular spirituality and his notion of ideal immortality. In *Reason and Religion*, he argued that "the more we reflect, the more we live in memory and idea, the more convinced and penetrated we shall be by the experience of death; yet, without our knowing it, perhaps, this very conviction and experience will have raised us, in a way, above mortality" (*LR3*, 154). We are raised in a way above mortality since we recognize our lives enshrined in the eternal truth. "Apprehension, which makes man so like a god, makes him in one respect immortal; it quickens his numbered moments with a vision of what never dies, the truth of those moments" (*LR3*, 156). Without the eternal realm of truth, his vision of the spiritual life would be undercut and transformed beyond recognition.

The last key trait of truth is contingency. Santayana argues that anyone who recognizes the infinite realm of essence will also acknowledge the contingency of material existence and the truth about it.[13] For if essences are "infinite in number and variety," then "it follows that every particular fact is contingent ... since infinite alternatives were open to existence, if existence had chosen a different form" (*RB*, 407). Since matter is the only source of power in the universe, nothing compels matter to "choose" a different form. A related point is Santayana's rejection of the principle of sufficient reason. This is "a principle," he maintains, "for which there is no reason at all" (*SAF*, 289). Hence, "[t]here is no reason why a particular fact should exist rather than any other, or none at

---

[12] After asserting the eternality of truth, Santayana makes *ad hominem* attacks against those who deny it, claiming they fail to see the "sublime" nature of truth. "I am sorry," he writes, "that the word eternal should necessarily have an unction which prejudices dry minds against it, and leads fools to use it without understanding" (*SAF*, 268). Cf. James: "The truth *happens* to an idea. It *becomes* true, is *made* true by events" (James 1911, x, italics preserved).

[13] Contingency also applies to mathematical and logical "truths," which Santayana regards as consistent only or "idiomatically true" (*RB*, 426). For a discussion of Santayana's treatment of math and logic, see Kerr-Lawson, "Truth and Idiomatic Truth in Santayana" (Kerr-Lawson 1997) and "Turning to Santayana" (Kerr-Lawson 1988).

all," and "there is also no reason why it should not exist" (*SAF*, 134). For Santayana, that *anything* exists is a brute fact. The brute fact of existence infects the entire realm of matter, and there is no logical necessity why any fact must exist or continue to exist.[14] Santayana would agree that in daily life, we assume that facts and events have causes. So, the principle of sufficient reason is a regulative assumption of animal faith: we could not get far in life without it. Still, the principle is open to doubt and its truth is indemonstrable.

Having reviewed some of the key traits of truth, one might conclude that ontological truth is not a necessary consequence of animal faith, so an animal might live contentedly in the world without recognizing the being of truth. In fact, this is Santayana's view. Animal faith is not a sufficient condition for recognizing the being of truth. For a human animal concerned only with the exigencies of successful action, ontological truth might "not come within his purview, nor distinguished among his interests" (*SAF*, 264). A person might be wholly absorbed in intentional experience. In such a case, the "active object posited alone interests the man of action," not the rightness of the action, so the "recognition of a truth to be discerned may thus be avoided" (Ibid.). Discerning the realm of truth happens only after much experience and reflection—well after the impulse to action is translated into a belief about material substance.

IV

Despite Santayana's claim that common sense is "technically sounder than the special schools of philosophy" (*SAF*, v), it may seem that he broke with common sense by not defining truth in terms of belief or judgment. Pragmatists

---

[14] The contingency of matter seems to make the eternality of truth different from the eternality of essence. Sprigge touches on this issue when he states, "Sometimes one feels that Santayana thinks that he has established the eternity of truth on the ground that essences are eternal" (Sprigge 1997, 128). In *SAF*, Santayana says that "facts are transitory ... and when they have lapsed, it is only their essence that subsists" (*SAF*, 267). The word "subsists" suggests there is an intermediate mode of reality between the being of essence and the existence of matter, but that violates his ultimate ontological distinction between existence and essence upon which his philosophy is founded as well as his position, stated four chapters earlier, that the realm of truth, "if not a substance, is a luminous shadow or penumbra which substance, by its existence and movements, casts on the field of essence: so that unless a substance existed which was more physical than truth, truth itself would have no nucleus, and would fade into identity with the infinite essence of the nonexistent" (*SAF*, 227, italics added). This claim about truth fading into identity with the infinite essence of the non-existent seems to impinge on the eternality of truth, since it says that if matter were annihilated, truth would go with it, but the eternality of the realm of essence would remain. Contrary to his position expressed throughout *SAF* and *RB*, in *LR*, he held that there would be truth even without the existence of matter. "The notion that it might have been true that nothing existed," he wrote, "is a perfectly clear notion." He added that if we suppose a "universe did not exist ... it would then be true that all existences were wanting, yet this truth itself would endure" (*LR*, 5:18). For the Santayana of *LR*, truth is not an existence; nevertheless, it is a kind of reality that would "endure" in the absence of a material world. His view of truth in *LR* might be more in step with the aims of his later ontology. See Kerr-Lawson (2009) and Tiller (2011).

inspired by Peirce will object that Santayana's realm of truth is unnecessary, if not incoherent. They will agree that when it comes to truth, "all you have any dealings with are your doubts and beliefs. ... Your problems would be greatly simplified if, instead of saying that you want to know the 'Truth,' you were simply to say that you want to attain a state of belief unassailable by doubt" (*CP*, 5.426).

However, along with his ontological account of truth, Santayana also presents a rudimentary account of true belief which has much in common with pragmatic views. He accepts correspondence with reality as a basic formulation of true belief (*SAF*, 239). But along with Peirce and other pragmatists, he rejects the thesis that a true belief must copy reality. Before Rorty dismissed the notion of the mind as a "mirror of nature" (Rorty 1979), Santayana wrote that a true belief "does not imply ... pictorial identity between the essence in intuition and the constitution of the object. Discourse is a language, not a mirror" (*SAF*, 179). "Our worst difficulties," he held, "arise from the assumption that knowledge of existences ought to be literal, whereas knowledge of existences has no need, no propensity, and no fitness to be literal" (*SAF*, 101). Instead of being literally true, the true belief part of knowledge is symbolic. Our beliefs are "symbolic initially, when a sound, a smell, an indescribable feeling are signals to the animal of his dangers or chances" (*SAF*, 102). Importantly, symbolic knowledge is not compensation for lacking literal knowledge. On the contrary, Santayana holds that symbolic knowledge "fulfills its function perfectly—I mean its moral function of enlightening us about our natural good—if it remains symbolic to the end" (Ibid.).[15]

Santayana also shares in outline the model of belief-doubt-inquiry-belief that Peirce presents in "The Fixation of Belief." Both philosophers agree that we begin inquiry *in media res* (*SAF*, 1). They also agree that we naturally incline toward belief. Santayana writes that "intelligence is naturally forthright; it forges ahead" (*SAF*, 7), while scepticism is an "accident of human history" (*SAF*, 9). They also agree that our beliefs guide our actions since "ideas become beliefs only when by precipitating tendencies to action they persuade me that they are signs of things" (*SAF*, 16). If our beliefs are good guides to action, "the machine runs on prosperously until some hitch comes along, or some catastrophe" (*SAF*, 265), or, as Peirce has it, we have an experience counter to our expectations (Peirce 1992, 114). With the experience of doubt, we are left "defenseless and undecided in the presence of oncoming events" (*SAF*, 17). However, staying in a state of doubt is not an option due to the "brute necessity of believing something so long as life lasts," and our "naturally forthright" intelligence leads us to form a new belief (*SAF*, 9–10). And just as Peirce holds the right way to fix our beliefs is "by nothing human, but by some external

---

[15] Santayana holds that "we inevitably assume a sufficient indicative truth [for our beliefs], without minding their conventional symbolism and extreme inadequacy" (*PGS*, 539). Beliefs "have to be symbolic and inadequate because they are phases of animal life and not reproductions of their objects" (Ibid.).

permanency—by something upon which our thinking has no effect" but that "affect[s] our senses according to regular laws" (Peirce 1992, 120), Santayana holds that a "true belief is grounded in experience, I mean controlled by outer facts. ... It arises by a movement of the self sympathetic or responsive to surrounding beings ... and at the same time an appropriate correspondence tends to be established between these objects and the beliefs generated under their influence" (*SAF*, 180). Finally, Santayana accepts a pragmatic criterion of warrant for our beliefs. "How should [our beliefs] be false if they describe the efficacious order of nature," he asks, "by which our existence and health and power of speech and thought are notoriously controlled? *What better criterion have we of truth than pertinence to action and implication in the dynamic order of nature*" (*RB*, 442–443, italics added). This last point about true belief shows that despite his rejecting the label "pragmatist," there is a strain of pragmatism running through Santayana's philosophy.[16]

For Santayana, an account of true belief does not obviate the need for ontological truth since the possibility of true belief is predicated upon the being of the realm of truth. The truth is something true beliefs must answer to and get right, although "getting right" does not mean mirroring or copying. As a result, any denial of ontological truth also denies the notion of a true belief. "If there were no absolute truth, all-inclusive and eternal," he argues, "the desultory views taken from time to time by individuals would themselves be absolute. They would be irrelevant to one another and incomparable in point of truth because they are not answerable to a common subject matter, each being without any object but the essence which appeared in it. If views can be more or less correct, and perhaps complementary to one another, it is because they refer to the same system of nature, the complete description of which, covering the whole past and the whole future, would be the absolute truth" (*RB*, xv). In other words, without ontological truth, our beliefs would not be about anything; they would have no "standard." Santayana argues that if we try to do away with the realm of truth, then another word, perhaps "fact" or "reality," would then be the standard "to which our correct judgments conform" (*SAF*, 267).[17] However, in Santayana's analysis, neither "facts" nor "reality" designate a "description," that is, the totality of essences embodied by material

---

[16] In a letter to his former student, Horace Kallen, Santayana wrote "I am afraid, in spite of your better opinion of me, I am no pragmatist" (*LGS*, 2:263).

[17] If we ask how one compares beliefs with the truth, Santayana replies that when "opinions are reported to a third person he may easily compare them, *in their ideal deliverance*, with their intended objects, provided these objects have been independently reported to him also by perception or science or history. In this way every man continually compares people's opinions, including his own, with the facts; and this without instituting any ultimate criterion either for the truth of memory and history, which report opinions, or for the truth of perception and science, which report the facts. We inevitably assume a sufficient indicative truth in both reports, without minding their conventional symbolism and extreme inadequacy" (*PGS*, 539, italics preserved).

reality.[18] Both "fact" and "reality" designate existence, and existence is transitory and contravenes the eternality of truth. Truth cannot "be identified with the facts to which it relates, since they are in flux, and it is eternal" (*SAF*, 268).

V

Critics of Santayana's realm of truth argue that it either fails to make sense of certain individual truths (e.g., mathematical truths, counterfactual truths) or individual truths in general.[19] Here we briefly look at the latter criticism. It is advanced most forcefully by Sprigge. He objects that Santayana "does not do justice to the fact that the most, or one of the most basic, sorts of truths are truths to the effect that a certain specified object has a certain specified character (or stands in specified relations to other specified objects)" (Sprigge 1997, 121). Sprigge's objection involves two claims. The first is that Santayana's realm of truth is monistic. Santayana suggests there is a single realm of truth, the complete truth about the universe, not a plural realm of truths.[20] Sprigge concludes that Santayana "really has no place for truths, just for truth. It turns out that the realm of truth has just one member" (Sprigge 1997, 123). The second claim is that individual truths are not locatable in the realm of truth since an essence that is a constituent of a complex essence is not identical in isolation from that complex. For example, if we assert "The sapphire is blue," Sprigge contends that Santayana can at best say the essence "blue" is "virtually" the same as the "blue" in the complex essence "sapphire." "At most there is a strong affinity," he writes, between two such essences (Sprigge 1997, 124). They are never identical.

Without taking up the issue of identity and complex and simple essences,[21] it seems that even if individual truths do not belong in Santayana's monistic realm of truth, they have a place in his account of true belief. For Santayana, beliefs "are true or false by repeating or contradicting some part of the truth about the facts which they envisage" (*SAF*, 267). However, we have seen that the "repeating or contradicting" involved in belief is non-literal. Sprigge's criticisms seem better directed at claims of literal knowledge. In the context of symbolic knowledge, we hope for a "strong affinity" between the signs of human cognition and the essences embodied by the intended object of knowledge.

---

[18] On this point Kerr-Lawson comments, "the truth about a fact or event in the material world does not require any explicit internal reference to that which is true, no identification within the truth of the portion of the world being alluded to. Apparently this is already taken care of, presumably because the setting in the realm of matter sufficiently fixes the bond between the essence (which is the truth) and the thing embodying that existence (which the truth is about)" (Kerr-Lawson 1997, 101).

[19] Lachs (1988), Sprigge (1995 and 1997), and Hodges (2014).

[20] *SAF*, 267 and *RB*, 420.

[21] See Sprigge (1995, 1997) and Sopuck (2021).

Santayana's treatment of "conventional" truth helps illustrate his position on individual truths. His example of conventional truth is: "Sun rises 7:35 a.m, sets 3:58 p.m." (*RB*, 455). He writes that such a truth may "be conveyed in conventional terms which in themselves are loose and inaccurate. Implications as to what has happened physically, and hypotheses as to what might have happened psychologically, may be placed before the human mind in a figure of speech that will not bear pressing, yet is unequivocal enough for human purposes" (*RB*, 456).

Just as conventional truth is symbolic, other sorts of individual truths can be seen as figures of speech fit for human purposes. Presumed individual truths, taken as beliefs that are instances of symbolic knowledge, would be evaluated by their pertinence to action. Although they would not "bear pressing" as literal truths, they might function as pragmatically good guides to action. If they were good guides to action, they would conform in some manner to ontological truth.

If Santayana is to account more fully for individual truths, his account of true belief must be developed. More generally, since his account of true belief must be constructed in light of his theory of symbolic knowledge, his philosophy would benefit from a general theory of signs. Santayana holds that knowledge is symbolic, but unlike Peirce, he never developed a theory of signs to support his theory of symbolic knowledge.[22] A general theory of signs is also called for since there is no indication Santayana limits symbolic knowledge to states of belief. Sensations also convey truth insofar as they are "signs ... [or] ... indications of further realities and not dead objects in themselves" (*LSK*, 105). Furthermore, Santayana holds that any moment of spirit, be it a propositional belief, a sensuous experience, or some other state, is an "index to an internal psychic life" (*RB*, 152). Our beliefs and sensations symbolize the truth about things, but all mental states are indices of the truth about the body.

VI

In 1887, when Santayana was a student at Harvard, he wrote that "it is impossible to abandon the postulate of one eternal and objective truth" (*LGS*, 1:63). Decades later, he turned this postulate into a realm of being in his categorial system of philosophy. Along with being a postulate impossible to abandon, objective, eternal truth plays a crucial role in his system. His theory of secular spirituality and his notion of ideal immortality depend on it. Consequently, any problems or tensions with his construal of a "realm of truth" would not, for him, vitiate the postulate. After all, as Santayana states, another writer might well exhibit the postulate better than he did.

Santayana grants not everyone will admit the being of truth. Truth is not a power; it cannot cause events or coerce thought. The tragic nature of the truth is often starkly present in the mind of mortals and it is not an ultimate good.

[22] Houser (2009) discusses Santayana's intriguing relationship to Peirce. See also Atkins (2024).

Individual interests and preferences determine the recognition and moral value of the truth. Certainly, not all intellects are earnestly addressed to the truth. And some philosophers earnestly deny some portion of it (e.g., the past), and some deny it altogether.[23] In Santayana's view, such fundamental philosophical disagreements are irresolvable. In response to critics of his categorial system, he replied, "as to the contrary principles or preferences that dictate our different views, it would be chimerical and ill-natured to argue. You cannot refute a principle or rebut a preference, you can only indicate its consequences or present alluringly the charms of a rival doctrine" (*PGS*, 604). If a critic rejects the postulate of objective, eternal truth, the incommensurability of philosophical theories must be accepted. In such a case, "the only question will be how [the critic] will get on; what sort of intellectual dominion and intellectual life he will achieve; also whether he will really be using other categories in his spontaneous and successful contacts with the world, or only a different jargon in his professional philosophy" (*RB*, 453). For the philosopher who reckons with the radical scepticism of *SAF*, answering these questions depends on animal faith and the pursuit of sincerity.

REFERENCES

WORKS BY SANTAYANA

[1] 2011. *The Life of Reason: Reason in Common Sense*, eds. Martin Coleman and Marianne Wokeck. Cambridge, MA: MIT Press. Cited as *LR1*.

[1905] 2014. *The Life of Reason: Reason in Religion*, eds. Martin Coleman and Marianne Wokeck. Cambridge, MA: MIT Press. Cited as *LR3*.

[1915] 1936. *Obiter Scripta*, eds. Justus Buchler and Benjamin Schwartz. New York: Charles Scribner's Sons.

[1920] 1955. *Character and Opinion in the United States*. New York: George Braziller. Cited as *COUS*.

[1923] 1955. *Scepticism and Animal Faith: Introduction to a System of Philosophy*. New York: Dover Publications. Cited as *SAF*.

[1932] 1977. *The Genteel Tradition at Bay*. New York: Haskell House Publishers. Cited as *GTB*.

[1940] 1991. *The Philosophy of George Santayana*, ed. Paul Arthur Schilpp. Illinois: Open Court. Cited as *PGS*.

1942. *Realms of Being*. One-volume edition, with a new introduction by the author, contains the four books: *The Realm of Essence: Book First* (1927); *The Realm of Matter: Book Second* (1930); *The Realm of Truth: Book Third* (1938); and *The Realm of Spirit: Book Fourth* (1940). New York: Charles Scribner's Sons. Cited as *RB*.

2001–2008. *The Letters of George Santayana*. Volumes 1–VIII, ed. William G. Holzberger. Cambridge, MA: The MIT Press.. Cited as "*LGS*, n:m" – to volume n, page m.

---

[23] See Santayana's discussion of "Denials of Truth" (*RB*, 525–536).

WORKS BY OTHERS

Atkins, Richard Kenneth. 2018. Santayana on Propositions. *Overheard in Seville: Bulletin of the George Santayana Society* 36: 26–39.

———. 2024. C. S. Peirce and Josiah Royce. In *The Oxford Handbook of George Santayana*. Oxford: Oxford University Press.

Augustine. 2010. In *On the Free Choice of the Will, On Grace and Free Choice, and Other Writings*, ed. Peter King. Cambridge: Cambridge University Press.

Buchler, Justus. 1939. Charles Peirce, Giant in American Philosophy. *The American Scholar* 8 (4): 400–711.

Cameron, Margret. 2018. Truth in the Middle Ages. In *The Oxford Handbook of Truth*, ed. Michael Glanzberg. Oxford: Oxford University Press.

Goodman, Arthur. 1943. Santayana's Ontology of Realms. *Philosophy and Phenomenological Research* 3 (3): 279–302.

Hodges, Michael. 2014. The Realm of Truth in Santayana. In *George Santayana at 150*, ed. Matthew Caleb Flamm, Guiseppe Patella, and Jennifer A. Rea. Maryland.: Lexington Books.

Hookway, Christopher. 2000. *Truth, Rationality, and Pragmatism: Themes from Peirce*. Oxford: Oxford University Press.

Houser, Nathan. 2009. Santayana's Peirce. *Transactions of the Charles S. Peirce Society* 45 (4): 516–531.

James, William. 1911. *The Meaning of Truth*. New York: Longman Green and Co.

Kerr-Lawson, Angus. 1988. Turning to Santayana. *Overheard in Seville: Bulletin of the Santayana Society* 6: 30–37.

———. 1997. Truth and Idiomatic Truth in Santayana. *Transactions of the Charles S. Peirce Society* XXXIII (1): 91–111.

———. 2003. Santayana on the Matter of Aristotle. *Transactions of the Charles S. Peirce Society* 39 (3): 349–371.

———. 2004. The Absence of Argument in Santayana. *Overheard in Seville: Bulletin of the Santayana Society* 24: 29–40.

———. 2009. Responses to Friendly Critics. *Transactions of the Charles S. Peirce Society* 45 (4): 596–648.

Lachs, John. 1988. *Santayana*. Boston: Twayne Publishers.

———. 2003. Substance and Matter: A Response to Kerr-Lawson. *Transactions of the Charles S. Peirce Society* 39 (3): 373–381.

Leslie, John. 2007. *Immortality Defended*. Oxford: Blackwell Publishing.

McHenry, Leemon B. 2000. The Ontology of the Past: Whitehead and Santayana. *The Journal of Speculative Philosophy*. 14 (3): 219–231.

Peirce, Charles Sanders. 1931–1958. *Collected Papers of Charles Sanders Peirce*. Volumes 1–6, eds. C. Hartshorne and P. Weiss; Volumes 7–8 ed. A. Burks. Cambridge: Harvard University Press. References are of the form "CP, n.m" – to volume n, paragraph m.

———. 1992. In *The Essential Peirce*, ed. Nathan Houser and Christian Kloesel, vol. 1. Bloomington and Indianapolis: Indiana University Press.

Ramsey, F.P. [1927] 1999. On Facts and Propositions. *Truth*, eds. Simon Blackburn and Keith Simmons. Oxford: Oxford University Press.

Rorty, Richard. 1979. *Philosophy and the Mirror of Nature*. Princeton, NJ: Princeton University Press.

———. 1982. *Consequences of Pragmatism*. Minneapolis: The University of Minnesota Press.
Singer, Irving. 2000. *George Santayana, Literary Philosopher*. New Haven and London: Yale University Press.
Sopuck, Adam. 2021. Santayana on Colour: Collisions with Contemporary Thought. *Overheard in Seville: Bulletin of the Santayana Society*, No. 29: 40–67.
Sprigge, T.L.S. [1974] 1995. *Santayana*. London: Routledge.
———. 1997. Kerr-Lawson on Truth and Santayana. *Transactions of the Charles S. Peirce Society* XXXIII (1): 113–130.
Szaif, Jan. 2018. Plato and Aristotle on Truth and Falsehood. In *The Oxford Handbook of Truth*, ed. Michael Glanzberg. Oxford: Oxford University Press.
Tiller, Glenn. 2011. The Assumption of Truth. *Limbo* 31: 31–46.

PART III

Philosophical Relations

On Gnats and Barnacles, or Some Similarities Between Santayana's Idea of Change and Ancient Greek Thought

Andrés Tutor de Ureta

> *The gnat may begin with a sense of flux, like Heraclitus ... and the barnacle may begin, like Parmenides, with a sense of the unshakable foundations of being.*
> —(*SAF*, 29)

Santayana and *Scepticism and Animal Faith* in Ancient Greece

Santayana's *Scepticism and Animal Faith* is one of the most important books in the philosophical career of the Spanish thinker. For many reasons. First, as he himself tells us in the title, because it is an "Introduction to a System of Philosophy"; thus, *SAF* is the most accessible path available to anyone who wants to enter his complex and original epistemological world, as later detailed in the four volumes of *Realms of Being*. Secondly, because the most basic epistemological ideas in Santayana's thought, the categories of matter, essence,

---

A. T. de Ureta (✉)
University of Tsukuba, Tsukuba, Japan
e-mail: tutor.andre.fu@u.tsukuba.ac.jp

truth, and spirit[1] are discussed and briefly explained in *SAF*, and, as it commonly happens, summaries often offer the clearest definitions and explanations about a particular topic. Finally, because, as Santayana often stresses (*SAF*, v–x), any philosophical method or perspective—scepticism, idealism, naturalism—is nothing if it is not honest, we can assert that the thoughts reflected in *SAF* accurately convey not only his system of philosophy but also his view of how the world truly works.

SAF was published in 1923 and that is why we are now celebrating the anniversary of Santayana's epistemological masterpiece. However, in many ways it could have been written around two thousand years earlier, let us say, in 323 B.C., only a few days after Alexander the Great died.[2] By that time Aristotle's death had closed Ancient Greece's great metaphysical era and a change of mind and interests ensued. The immense philosophical systems of Plato and his disciple were to be followed by numerous movements and schools that abandoned the all-embracing metaphysical views, substituting for them instead more practical approaches to human life (Guthrie 1962, 16). Precisely right there, among the philosophies of Pyrrho, Epicurus, or Democritus, we could locate Santayana's reflections in *SAF*, especially as far as the question of change is concerned.

Indeed, there are many reasons, both vital and intellectual, some of which will appear in this chapter, that link Santayana's thought and temper to the tenets of ancient Greek philosophy. Some of the most conspicuous are[3]:

Santayana assumes substance as unproblematic, in the sense of something that is there when the quest for knowledge starts. In opposition to Christian thought, there is no need to justify the existence of the world.

Nature, matter, substance... The idea that Santayana holds of the world is also akin to that of the first philosophers, who thought of it as a mother, or creative principle.

Even though in the end the world may be adequately described as chaotic or irrational, our reality is understandable, meaning that, up to a certain point, matter can be bent in our favor, turning chaos into cosmos in the Greek sense of this word, that is, transforming an irrational sprout into an ordered and law-abiding world.

Thus, it is no wonder that, together with Indian philosophy and Spinoza, Santayana often confessed his admiration for the Greek naturalists, considering they had been the only ones "right on the chief issue, the relation of man and of his spirit to the universe" (*SAF*, viii). Precisely regarding the topic of knowledge and reality, one of those ideas, the idea of change, will be analyzed here.

---

[1] We will use the capitals "E," "M," "T," and "S," in Essence, Matter, Truth, and Spirit for the situations in which we are talking about the names of the Realms; all other cases will be written in lower-case letters.

[2] Of course, not in every way, since Santayana's reflections include lessons from and discuss many other authors who lived thousands of years after the time of Alexander the Great, such as Descartes, Hume, or Kant.

[3] This part is mostly based on the description of the basic assumptions of ancient Greek philosophy given in Marías 1980 (11–61).

The main aim of this chapter is to expose the roots of the clear connections that the concept of change, absolutely key in *SAF*, has with ancient Greek philosophy. Acknowledging that the world around us is constantly changing, or, better said, distinguishing when objects change and what exactly it means to change (*SAF*'s Chapter XII: "Identity and duration attributed to essences") is the most evident realization around which the whole epistemological building introduced in *SAF* is developed. In exposing those roots, it will be shown that Santayana's view of time and change, which deeply influences his description of both the Realm of Essence and the Realm of Matter, shares with ancient Greek thought many philosophical and mathematical tenets. Moreover, that idea of change confirms the existence of an inevitable chasm between what exists and what we know, between reality and the epistemological world in Santayana's philosophy. To achieve our goals, we will mainly contextualize Santayana's whole epistemological enterprise placing it in the ancient Greek debate about movement, permanence, and knowledge, initiated once the consequences of the doctrines of Heraclitus and Parmenides started to spread.[4] Here, it will be suggested that Santayana's process of knowledge together with his division between a Realm of Matter and a Realm of Essence can be better understood relating it to that classical paradox where swift-footed Achilles loses his race to the tortoise. By tracing Santayana's ideas of time, matter, flux, and essence back to their pre-Socratic origins, we will clearly realize how his description of the epistemological process that turns intuitions into beliefs, as well as the Realm of Essence and its components, intuited within the Realm of Matter, are indeed logical constructs. These logical constructs are built under the mathematical premise of divisible leaps, combining the existence of a continuum with the analysis of that continuum via discrete units. We will thus confirm how Santayana's philosophy was influenced by ancient Greek thought, while at the same time we will provide an example and a detailed explanation of Santayana's process of intuition and belief, as well as of his theory of essence and its interaction with the Realm of Matter.

The text is divided into three parts: first, we will start by reconstructing Santayana's theory of knowledge, framing it around the problem of change in ancient Greek philosophy. Having introduced Santayana's epistemological outlook, in a second section we will qualify both the notions of matter and of essence indicating their undeniable pre-Socratic scent, as they are clearly based on the philosophies of Heraclitus and Parmenides. In a third and final part, Zeno's paradox of Achilles and the tortoise will be brought forward in order to confirm our hypothesis and demonstrate how three crucial elements in Santayana's theory, the process of knowledge, the Realm of Matter, and the Realm of Essence, share the paradox's perspective according to which it is (logically) possible to divide a continuum into eternally divisible, discrete units.

---

[4] There is another obvious possibility for framing the arguments in Santayana's *SAF*, which is Descartes' methodic doubt. Save for some basic allusions, due to lack of space only the first one will be developed here, although both options are not exclusive but rather complementary.

The conclusions will together enable us to evaluate Santayana's effort in *SAF*, highlighting its many merits and qualifying it as an extremely attractive work of a serious thinker.

Santayana's Theory of Knowledge and the Problem of Change in Ancient Greek Philosophy

The titles of some of *SAF*'s first chapters—Chapter II: "Dogma and doubt"; Chapter V: "Doubts about change"—lay bare Santayana's aim in this book: "To clear our intellectual conscience of voluntary or avoidable delusion" (*SAF*, 3).[5] Thus, from the very beginning his intent tackles the basic epistemological discussion about the reality of the world. We can frame that discussion in many different ways, all of them problematic: *What exists? What do I know? How do I know?* How does Santayana answer these questions?

For Santayana, knowledge is never direct but symbolical. Whenever we claim to know something—the door is closed, my feet are cold, Sydney is far from Madrid—what we know is not what it is, but what it is through a translation into terms that we, as humans, can understand. Probably the clearest metaphor employed by Santayana to convey what he means by knowledge is the one that compares our ability to know with our ability to speak different languages, all of them acceptable:

> Discourse is a language, not a mirror. The images in sense are parts of discourse, not parts of nature: they are the babble of our innocent organs under the stimulus of things;. ... A sensation or a theory, no matter how arbitrary its terms (and all language is perfectly arbitrary), will be true of the object, if it expresses some true relation in which that object stands to the self, so that these terms are not misleading as signs, however poetical they may be as sounds or as pictures. (*SAF*, 179–180)

Knowledge being symbolical, that means that we need at least two elements: first, the object we want to talk about; secondly, the sign we will use to convey that object; the first ones, the objects, are known to us through the second ones, the essences, which work as terms of our epistemological discourse.

---

[5] This sentence reflects not the first but the second of Santayana's ideas in *SAF*. Before reaching this point, Santayana has already made the claim that "there is no first principle of criticism" (*SAF*, 1), nor are there first principles of discourse either, meaning that our knowledge must start, as Homer's *Illiad* does, *in media res*. As we have said, this mind-set clearly identifies Santayana's outlook with ancient Greek thinkers, for whom the notion of creation *ex-nihilo* was totally absent (cfr. Parmenides' view infra, and also Sorabji 1983, 193–194).

On the other hand, to be perfectly honest, the quotation offered does not reproduce any explicit statement made by Santayana about the objective of *SAF*. However, having located a point in time from where to begin our epistemological adventure—no other but the one that nature has assigned us—our next step needs to be to distinguish facts from interpretation, "factual elements" from "uncritical assumptions" (*SAF*, 4). In this sense, the quotation provided in the text does summarize Santayana's global aim and explains why he considers that we must doubt.

Essences are then "ideal terms at the command of fancy and of the senses ... as words are at the command of a ready tongue" (*SAF*, 81), names we use to refer to the material elements that we happen to encounter around us (*RE*, 35) or, simply put, "terms used in perception" (*SAF*, 94). Maintaining a strong materialism, Santayana will accordingly state that "things will not be unknown since notice will have been taken of them and their appearance, in some respect, will have been recorded; we shall understand that there is one strain, at least, in their constitution and movement fitted to provoke our perception and to render our description applicable and correct" (Santayana 1923, 16). Substance then exists and the proof that there is an object in front of me is that somehow it triggers my perception, that trigger ("any reaction focused upon that thing— any turning, or visible contemplation, or defensive movement, or pursuit—" [Santayana 1923, 23]), once made conscious, roughly being what we call knowledge. The language metaphor can be substituted for a musical one, which is also quite clear: "Calling substance unknowable, then, is like calling a drum inaudible, for the shrewd reason that what you hear is the sound and not the drum" (Santayana 1923, 16). I know that there is a drum because I can hear its sound, even if its sound and the drum can be considered two different entities. In other words, Santayana is saying that we know matter because the effect it casts upon us; matter's intrinsic character may remain unknown, but that is something that should not worry us, since the key in knowledge, as in language, is not to be identical to the object but relevant to the subject (*SAF*, 88). In short: "The experience of essence is direct; the expression of natural facts through that medium is indirect. But this indirection is no obstacle to expression, rather its condition" (*SAF*, 102).

Many interpretations and connections can be made out of this seminal epistemological view, but here we will only focus on how with this perspective Santayana is actually providing an answer to the old problem of movement and change as it appeared in the first Western philosophers. To do that, we must go back a couple of thousand years to introduce the topic following the language of Parmenides and Heraclitus.[6]

According to the doctrine of Parmenides, logic tells us that one thing cannot be and not be at the same time. As it is known, the philosopher from Elea exposed this far from tautological idea, as it was told to him by a goddess, in an exceedingly cryptic poetic composition:

> Come now, I will tell (and do thou lay up my word when thou hast heard it) the only ways of inquiry that are to be thought of. The one, that it is, and that it is impossible for it not to be, is the path of Persuasion (for she attends on Truth). The other, that it is not, and that it must necessarily not be, that I declare is a

---

[6] Besides the customary warning point about our fragmentary knowledge of what pre-Socratic thinkers actually said and thought (Guthrie 1962, 24–25), it is necessary to add that the presentation of their ideas in such a limited space as a book chapter should be expected to provide a rather summarized view of their thought.

wholly indiscernible track; for thou couldst not know what is not—that is impossible—nor declare it; for it is the same thing that can be thought and that can be.

What can be spoken and thought of must be, for it is possible for it to be, but impossible for nothing to be. This I bid thee consider, for this way of inquiry is the first from which I <hold thee back>.

But also from this one, on which mortals, knowing nothing, wander two-headed; for helplessness in their own breasts guides their erring mind. They are borne along, both deaf and blind, mazed, hordes with no judgment, who believe that to be and not to be are the same and not the same, and the path of everything is one that turns back upon itself.

For this shall never prevail, that things that are not are, but thou keep thy thought from this way of inquiry; ...

One way alone is yet left to tell of, namely that "It is." On this way are marks in plenty that since it exists it is unborn and imperishable, whole, unique, immovable and without end. It *was* not in the past, nor yet *shall* it be, since it now *is*, all together, one and continuous. (Guthrie 1962, 13–26)

Since It is, and it is impossible that It originated from its opposite, we have here an argument to justify the existence of matter, making no sense to question where It comes from: matter just is. At the same time, since It cannot turn into what is not; what is, just is, and cannot help but being; thus, movement (change) is impossible. Popper (1999, 103) can help us to summarize Parmenides' reasoning from "being is" to the impossibility of movement in six steps:

(1) Only being is (only what is, is)
(2) The nothing, the non-being, cannot be.
(3) The non-being can also be understood as the absence of being, that is, the void.
(4) According to (2), there can be no void.
(5) Since there is no void, the world is full, it is a block.
(6) As a conclusion, movement is impossible.

That being the case, there is no possibility of explaining the world around us, where, contrary to our senses, everything is moving.

Precisely that last idea of constant change is what another pre-Socratic, Heraclitus, asserted when he warned us that "you cannot step twice into the same rivers; for fresh waters are ever flowing in upon you" (Burnet 1920, 100). Herein lies the doctrine according to which the reality of the world is a constant opposition of contrary elements—day and night, war and peace, wet and dry, life and death—both of them equally necessary, that resolve themselves in a synthetical process (Burnet 1920, 100). We cannot develop further this point about the correlation of opposites; however, for our purposes, Heraclitus' doctrine as it is expressed by the sentence about the river perfectly represents the view we are interested in, according to which movement is all there is.

These are, summarized, the perspectives of immutability and change as they were seen thousands of years ago. Now, before going back to Santayana, we should explain why the problem of movement and change is actually a major problem and how both "nothing changes" and "everything changes" are equally lethal to human knowledge. We can start with the most obvious one, which is probably Heraclitus' position. The explanation of the problem here is easy and Aristotle is already one of the first to state it clearly: there can be no science, no sure knowledge of elements that are always changing into a different thing (Aristotle, *Metaphysics*, Γ, 5 1010a 1). If we want to be able to know, the object of our knowledge must be stable. The bridge I am talking to you about today must be the same bridge I saw yesterday, and the same you are expected to cross tomorrow. If they were all different, my information about the first bridge—the one I saw—might not be relevant for the second and third bridges—the one I am talking to you about and the one you are planning on crossing tomorrow. Even more, the Idea of Bridge must be roughly the same for you and me, and again, constant, if we both consider the task, for example, of building one. The dilemma that the existence of change and movement cast upon knowledge, however, was far from simple, since neither of the two available options seemed to be satisfactory. To confirm that, let us now turn to Parmenides. If we reject Heraclitus' position and think that Parmenides was right, we must accept that movement itself does not exist, which basically implies that our senses are permanently providing us with wrong information, thus making both nature and the study of nature (physics), broadly understood as the knowledge of the surrounding world, equally a chimerical and inherently flawed enterprise. In short: if Heraclitus is right, we can have no knowledge; if Parmenides is right, our knowledge is untrustworthy.

The depth and importance of the problem is confirmed by the fact that it did not stop with these two thinkers or their followers, but it was afterward reflected and tackled both in Plato's and Aristotle's philosophies: Plato saw the sensible world as an image of Heraclitus' ever-changing river, but, in order to make knowledge possible, he built an intelligible world of Ideas following Parmenides' notion of permanence. On the other hand, Aristotle started from the undeniable reality of change and developed an original view of the Being that differentiated actuality from potentiality, thus incorporating the idea of movement back into our world (Guthrie 1962, 12). Be that as it may, it is plain to see that the problem of knowledge in ancient Greece was a problem of movement, and change was the key element that differentiated a world where knowledge was not possible from a world where we could know. If everything moves and changes, we cannot know anything, but if we must accept that there is a contradiction between the information provided by our senses, where everything is changing, and the conclusion of our logical deduction, where what is cannot turn into what is not, knowledge of the world is just apparent and deceiving. How is it then possible for us to accurately know reality? Precisely at this point Santayana enters: following Plato—and probably like him, following both Heraclitus and Parmenides—Santayana built a realm of immutable, perfect, and universal essences, separated from this world of material existence, which in its turn was considered a world of change, motion, and different perspectives.[7] To introduce Santayana's answer to the former epistemological question, let us put him alongside these ancient thinkers: first, Heraclitus' river will help us to understand Santayana's Realm of Matter; afterward Parmenides' permanent Is will clarify some of the most important characters of essences.

THE RIVER OF MATTER AND THE PARMENIDEAN ESSENCES

So far we have only covered the first epistemological steps described in *SAF*: whatever substance is, we know about its existence thanks to essences, which give away substance's presence around us in a way that we can understand. Now, in order to go deeper into Santayana's gnoseological theory, we need to make a distinction between essences when intuited and essences when used in discourse, that is, essences building up knowledge. This is exactly where the Realm of Matter and the Realm of Essence start to show their practical implications, and it is also the point where the notion of change turns into a key element in Santayana's epistemology.

Once the level and extent of scepticism that Santayana considers possible and, even more, advisable has been established, we arrive in Chapter IV of *SAF* at the first realization from which every other one can be accepted, "namely, that I know and can survey the *movement* of my existence, and that I can actually have lapsed from one state into another" (*SAF*, 24). What we are about to explain is bound to happen to any essence we talk about, since essences, when used by us to talk about substance, are always disguised as facts or events; however, Santayana's example refers specifically to the notion of movement as an essence—thus confirming the importance of that term. Santayana explains that in order to be able to speak about change, we must differentiate the essence of change from change as it is perceived by us. In other words, the essence of change can be intuited in a specific moment t_1, but to realize that intuition and use "change" as a term in discourse, we must have moved to moment t_2; having done that, we are now in t_2 using change in t_1 "as a report" of something that already happened:

> One thing is the *feeling* that something is happening. ... Another thing is the *belief* that what is found is a report or description of events that have happened already. ... In a word, specious change is not actual change. The unity of apper-

---

[7] In that sense, it is perfectly understandable to find Santayana describing himself as "a Platonist in logic and morals" (*SAF*, viii–ix), although without the ethical bias that led Plato to locate the Good or the Beautiful as the highest of Ideas (*RE*, 93).

ception which yields the sense of change renders change specious, by relating the terms and directions of change together in a single perspective, as respectively receding, passing, or arriving. In so uniting and viewing these terms, intuition of change excludes actual change in the given object. If change has been actual, it must have been prior to, and independent of, the intuition of that change. (*SAF*, 25)[8]

That this is a Heraclitean outlook through and through can be confirmed by comparing Santayana's approach to the philosophy of another ancient Greek thinker, Cratylus, for whom nothing should be said, since the time when one speaks refers to an object or idea located in a different time, an object that, in the lapse of time used to utter our words, has already changed (Aristotle, Metaphysics, Γ, 5 1010a 10). This outlook precisely defines Santayana's view of the Realm of Matter, seen as a perennial flux where anything that can be thought or said must, inevitably, depend on time and memory. Thus, to be able to state something as simple as "this has changed," a huge number of assumptions are involved and needed: there must be a unity of apperception—a psyche, in Santayana's terms—there must be a permanent object that endures time, remaining the same in some respects, but changing in others from t_1 to t_2, it has to be accepted that my memory in t_2 of what I intuited in t_1 is correct. ... In Santayana's own words, having asserted "this, and again this with a variation" (*SAF*, 113), we must be ready to accept as irrefutable that "it is known to me that what now is was not always, that there are things not given, that there is genesis in nature, and that time is real" (*SAF*, 26).

We have reached the bedrock of knowledge as this enterprise is presented in *SAF*, which according to Santayana is no other thing but movement, that is, change. All knowledge is thus constructed upon "a sense of at least possible change. ... The flux and perspectives of being seem to be open within me to my own intuition" (*SAF*, 24).[9] Santayana's idea of flux refers to the movement of matter, that movement being exactly what the ancient Greeks called κίνησις, understanding with this word any kind of change, from a change of place to a change of quantity, quality, and *pace* Aristotle (Aristotle, *Physics*, V, 224a 19 and fol.), even a substantial change, or, in Parmenides' words, a change from it is to it is not and vice versa. Obviously, this view of the world as a perennial flux is Heraclitean. To say, as Heraclitus did, that "cold things become warm, and what is warm cools; what is wet dries, and the parched is moistened" (Burnet 1920, 100) is, basically, to state that everything changes and nothing stands still. Santayana's view of matter clearly reproduces, then, Heraclitus' view of the world. This, however, is only half of the picture. If we want to fully

---

[8] As the former quotation shows, herein faith has rushed in in a way that Santayana considers inevitable. Indeed, "[a]ctual change, if it is to be known at all, must be known by belief and not by intuition [...] The belief is irresistible in animal perception" (*SAF*, 26–27).

[9] For all the possibility and existence of the Realm of Spirit, this last sentence should not lead us to think that Santayana considered the self as a component of a different Realm than the Realm of Matter; cfr. *SAF*, 278: "I myself am a substance in flux."

understand change, we need something that does not change, a permanent basis that allows us to say that the object in front of us is the same object as before, but slightly different[10]; we need essences; we need Parmenides' wisdom now.

That stable element that is needed is provided by Parmenides' theory of immutable being and, as we shall see in the next part, best exemplified in Zeno's paradoxes. As for Parmenides, offering a reasonable translation of one of his own sentences, his philosophical theory is frequently presented as "what is is, what is not is nothing." As it happened between Heraclitus' river and Santayana's matter, Santayana's idea of essence closely replicates Parmenides' idea of "what is" and the attributes attached to it: essences are thus unchangeable, eternal,[11] and each of them is different from the neighbor up to the smallest detail (*SAF*, 113–114).[12] Accordingly, when we intuit an essence, no matter how simple or complex, every little aspect makes it what it is, so every tiny variation in the essence means we are facing a different essence: "Every landscape seen, as actually seen ... is an eternal and indivisible unit; the least derogation from its complete essence substitutes a different essence for it. *That* spread of light, *that* precise emphasis of line ... form the very individuality of the composition momentarily intuited" (*RE*, 71). Moreover, when Santayana defines the Realm of Essence he says that it is "an infinite plenum or continuum, in which every essence is surrounded by others differing infinitesimally from it in character" (*RE*, 78), consequently forming "an infinite continuum of discrete forms" (*SAF*, 97).[13] The Realm of Essence is populated by an infinite number of essences, each of them an element different from the next one if even by just a minuscule variation.

Movement—change—as we can see, is thus a crucial element in both Realms: in the Realm of Matter, because, as Heraclitus exposed, everything changes; in the Realm of Essence, because, following Parmenides, essences never have and never ever will change—if, in this Realm, we happened to say, "This essence has changed," what we would actually be saying is, "These are two different essences." Nevertheless, even more than Parmenides' sentences perhaps, Zeno's paradoxes show how powerful the former's theory truly is and

---

[10] That, in order to speak about change we need something that does not change was already stated by Aristotle (*Metaphysics*, 1069b), is also accepted by Santayana (*SAF*, 30–31; 232) and is evidently confirmed by anyone who approaches the problem of change itself (cfr. Popper 1958, 12).

[11] We will not analyze here the minute distinction between "timeless" and "eternal." For that, see *SAF* 270–271.

[12] Obviously, for Parmenides this last sentence would not apply, since any change in the structure of being, even the slightest conceivable, is impossible. Having said that, what makes his theory applicable to Santayana's idea of essence is that each essence is, in itself, an example of the Parmenidean being.

[13] Faerna's comparison (Faerna 2011) between Santayana's Realm of Essence and J. L. Borges' Babel library in the famous tale of the Argentinian writer is sharp and original, as is Borges' story itself. However, since that library, though immense, is not infinite and neither is it expanding, as we are told the universe is, Zeno's logical construct, which does hold the infinite within it, seems to be a more apt metaphor.

allow us to combine both Heraclitus and Parmenides, exposing how the interaction between the Realm of Matter and the Realm of Essence actually happens. We have reached our third part, where we will fully explain how change, understood as an interplay between a continuum and various discrete elements applied to it, works in Santayana's system of philosophy.

Divisible Leaps, or the Possibility of Combining the Discrete with the Continuum

From all the aporias that we are told Zeno exposed (Sorabji 1983, 321–335), probably the most famous is the one called "Achilles and the tortoise." In it we are told that swift-footed Achilles, having given the slow tortoise a certain advantage before starting the race, will never catch the happy chelonian, since the time invested by Achilles to reach where the tortoise was when he started moving will be used by the tortoise to move further in the direction to the goal. Since Achilles will always need a certain amount of time to reach where the tortoise was and that same time will be used by the tortoise to abandon that place and move forward, our Greek hero will always be closer to the tortoise, but he will never be able to catch it. On the one hand, it is true that, as Sorabji (1983, 330) mentions, mathematics does solve the particular problem of the race: if Achilles gives the tortoise, say, a hundred-yard start and runs ten times as fast, at 111 1/9 yards he will catch the tortoise. On the other hand, as the same author also states (1983, 325), even if this paradox is solved because "infinite divisibility does not imply infinite length, ... more can be made of Zeno's paradox than that." Indeed, a simple mathematical operation shows the conundrum within this paradox: take a limited amount, say, one (1). Divide it into two (1/2 = 0.5); divide it again (0.5/2 = 0.25); and again (0.25/2 = 0.125); and again (0.125/2 = 0.0625). ... No matter how many times you do it, each time you will get closer to, but will never reach 0, that is, you will never stop being able to divide the result. In other words, you can do unlimited divisions within a limited amount, showing that a finite amount contains an infinite series: that is the paradox's core. This mathematical logic behind the paradox is the part that is important to our study: we can imagine both space or time as forming a limited continuum—what we identified as one (1); applying the series of divisions that we have just mentioned, it is mathematically possible to divide that unit into an infinite series of elements, none of which, no matter how small, will ever be zero.[14]

What we have here is a view according to which we are combining a continuum—the space separating Achilles from the tortoise—with discrete elements—for example, the exact point where Achilles reaches where the tortoise

---

[14] A different version of the paradox, called "the dichotomy, or the half distances" (Sorabji 1983, 321–322), also represents this problem: movement is impossible since, in order to go from point A to point B you would first have to go halfway, but, before that, you would also need to go half the remaining distance, and before that, go again half of that half ... and so *ad infinitum*, meaning you actually never move.

was; these elements, the different places from or at where Achilles leaves or reaches, are seen at the same time as specific points in the continuum, but also as infinitely divisible themselves, since space, taken as a quantity and no matter how small, can always be logically divided. This is the point where the theory of divisible leaps (Sorabji 1983, 53 and foll.) appears, implying the possibility of counting a continuum in discrete units. Not only space but also time can be viewed under this light. In Sorabji's words, we can, for example, think that

> time is a countable aspect of change because we count periods, when we count instantaneous stages in change. What is discrete here is the stages which we choose to count. But time is not itself a discontinuous thing merely because we can divide it by picking out instantaneous stages. On the contrary, it is infinitely divisible, in the sense that we can divide it at stages as close together as we please, and its infinite divisibility is precisely a mark of its continuity. (Sorabji 1983, 89)

Now we can illustrate through an example both the flux and movement that happen within the Realm of Matter, together with the process of apprehending that change through essences stemming from the Realm of Essence. Let us say we are outside as the sun sets. To begin with, we can look at the horizon and identify an essence, say, the color blue in the sky. However, the Realm of Matter is in a flux and the night is approaching. We close our eyes for a while and later, when we watch again, we see how the same object,[15] the sky, has changed; it has adopted a new essence, this time a lighter shade of blue, progressively turning yellow and later on, orange. According to Santayana, what is happening here is the usual process: "Existence at every step casts off one essence and picks up another" (*RE*, 23), or, in more poetic terms: the sky is dressing itself in different clothes (see *SAF*, 70–72). The change of the color in the sky is undeniable and although it may be extremely difficult, if not impossible, for us to exactly identify at what particular moment the color blue turned to yellow, or this last one changed to orange, for every moment there is an essence. The fact that we cannot agree on the question of at what exact moment the color we are seeing is no longer "blue" but "yellow," or no longer "yellow" but "orange," or the fact that we cannot see or distinguish certain shades of color does not affect the core of the theory, since in those cases we are referring to human conventions—the names we assign to different colors we see—and to human limits—the range of colors our eyes are able to identify; Santayana is crystal clear on the relativity that affects the presence of certain essences: "Another man, a different animal, a spirit native to another world may even now be greeting essences which it has not entered into my heart to conceive" (*RE*, 20). What is crucial, however, is the expression "every moment." What does that mean? In an identical way to what we have just applied to Zeno's paradoxes, since "every moment" corresponds to an essence and both time and the shades of color can be, logically speaking, infinitely divided, we could, in

---

[15] Or "substance." The fact that this word could also be used confirms Aristotle's influence over Santayana. Besides, there is no doubt about the possibility of adapting this whole explanation and build two Aristotelian Realms: one of Matter and another Realm of Form (cfr. Guthrie 1962, 467).

principle, identify infinite shades of color, ranging from blue to orange, corresponding to an infinite number of essences.[16]

How exactly are Santayana's Realm of Matter and Realm of Essence based on a notion of change that shares the same mathematical idea that supports Zeno's paradox? According to Santayana's theory, there is an undeniable reality, the flux of matter; then—here comes the epistemological approach—we intuit an essence that is representing the existence of a substance and we turn that intuition into knowledge by—there is no other option left—believing in that intuition, a process that repeats itself with successively appearing essences. Essences are then unique, and in our intuition we pass from one to the next, managing discontinuity—since each essence is one element—within the continuity of matter. In fact, through our analysis we realize that Santayana's theory is applying the view of a continuum as something presented in discrete units not once but three times: first, we can find it in the idea of time that he uses to describe the process of intuiting and turning that intuition into knowledge, because we refer to the intuition of an essence (t_1) and to the belief in that intuition (t_2) as different moments in the flux of matter, both of them considered as discrete, individual stages; besides, it is also possible to identify this perspective again in the explanation of the elements through which we apprehend the flux, the essences, but here even at two levels: on the one hand, since essences are themselves like indivisible atoms inside their own continuous Realm, we can see it applied within the Realm of Essence itself; on the other hand, since essences are the discrete elements that allow us to describe the Realm of Matter, that same idea of a continuum described through discrete units is repeated. In this last case, to correctly apply Sorabji's explanation to Santayana's theory we should identify the references to time and number respectively with matter—the continuous whole—and essences—the instantaneous stages we use to perceive matter in flux. If we go back to our particular example, we can easily confirm how it would work: matter—the sky—is limited and continuous, while essences—the different colors and shades of color we see—are various, unique, and, logically speaking, always divisible elements.[17]

In summary, both the way our intuition and belief work, and the way essences function in the Realm of Matter as well as in their own Realm are based on the notion of an existing continuum—limited but in permanent flux the former, endless but never changing the latter—described through discrete elements—essences in both cases. This is, briefly explained, Santayana's theory of knowledge.

---

[16] Logically, but not actually, since, paraphrasing Sorabji's former solution to Achilles' paradox, "infinite divisibility does not imply infinite duration."

[17] Essences in their own Realm stay in an infinite mathematical continuum but, depending on the perspective, we should call them divisible or indivisible. In our example the colors form an infinite series, since the different shades of yellow could be, as we mentioned, potentially divided *ad infinitum*, therefore, essences can be infinitely divided. However, in practice, from our point of view each essence represents a singular element and, even though from a different perspective several essences might be distinguished inside what we call one essence, for us that essence works in the Realm of Matter as an atomic element, that is, it is indivisible.

Conclusions: Santayana's Roots in Ancient Greek Thought

In our chapter we have seen that one of the most fundamental problems in the philosophical world of ancient Greece was related to the question of movement. According to the doctrine of some of the first philosophers in the Western intellectual tradition, such as Parmenides, or Zeno of Elea, movement, understood as the indubitable fact that things around us are constantly changing, is logically unsound. On the other hand, philosophers such as Heraclitus defended the claim that change is all there is, a doctrine that also brought catastrophic consequences to the collective enterprise of human knowledge. This discussion about change, our perception of it, and the possibility of knowledge is taken up by Santayana and incorporated in the structure of *SAF*.

Certainly, for Santayana change is the first element from which scepticism can be overcome, but exactly what idea of change is Santayana using? As we have seen, change in Santayana is supported by a view of time, of the Realm of Essence, and of the apprehension of the flux of the Realm of Matter identical to the one present in Zeno's aporia of Achilles and the tortoise: to move, to change, is to stop being in one point to start being in another, which is based on the idea of a mathematical continuum being apprehended through divisible leaps. When Santayana talks about belief and intuition, when he describes the Realm of Essence, and when he explains how we use essences to convey knowledge about the Realm of Matter, he is always thinking about continua that can be divided into successive points. If we had to look for a metaphor in particular for the process that relates essences and matter, we could say that it is the same that takes place in films: a movie is made of several, individual pictures; each frame would constitute an essence, and all put together would convey the film, the flux of matter.[18] In conclusion, we can say that what Santayana is doing in *SAF* is trying to put together discontinuity—infinite, separate essences—with continuity—the Realm of Matter.

Santayana's naturalism is undoubtedly the main principle in which all his philosophy is rooted. Matter is always the primary element, the ἀρχή on which to build our life, so even when aiming at the spirit, humans should never forget from which that Realm originates: "Art is secondary, life and perception are primary; since it is only the fascination exercised over us by real things that can suggest to us the possibility of their ideal perfection" (*AFSL*, 402). As for

---

[18] It is somehow strange to find barely any opinion of Santayana about an invention that provides such an apt metaphor for his epistemology as film does. In a letter to Mrs. C. F. Lama, in October 1944, Santayana says that "[t]he instantaneous photographs now in vogue are violent and good only when strung together in a film, so that the eye may compose its own synthetic image out of a lot of them, as it always does by nature" (*LGS*, 7:94). This idea, later repeated in a letter to George Sturgis the day after, is one of the few references that seems to exist about this topic. (For Santayana's comments on photography, which could be applied to filmmaking, see "The Photograph and the Mental Image" in *AFSL*, 391–403, and also Singer 1977.)

Matter and Essence, this sentence summarizes both Parmenides' and Heraclitus' philosophies and identifies the exact epistemological problem that change and the lack thereof cause:

> If discrete altogether, without a continuous substance or medium, events will not follow one another, but each will simply exist absolutely; and if a substance or medium be posited ... in so far as the substance or medium permeates the events nothing will happen or change. (*SAF*, 31)[19]

If matter were actually a series of consecutive essences, it would be a constant sequence of births and deaths—exactly what Heraclitus thought; on the other hand, were matter just the substance that undergoes the change, everything would be changeless—and Parmenides and Zeno would be right. On the one hand, it seems as if it were a question of perspective, which allows us to agree with Heraclitus on rightly defending that matter is in a constant flux, while at the same time also sharing Parmenides' view about the essence of the world as being one unchangeable unit. As the second part of the quotation that opens this book chapter goes, "after all, the mind of Heraclitus, seeing nothing but flux, would be as constant a mind as that of Parmenides, seeing nothing but rest" (*SAF*, 29–30), which means that all in all both gnats and barnacles have the same experience of the universe. On the other hand, we are neither gnats nor barnacles, so maybe we could elaborate an integrated view about the world, building a logical explanation of how we perceive reality. That is exactly what Santayana tries to do in *SAF*.

As it happens with other issues—respect for Christianity and atheism, belief in spirit and materialism, an American life without renouncing his Spanish origins—Santayana is here in between two apparently irreconcilable sides: as a materialist, he must defend the flux, since matter is, in fact, always changing; however, to make science and the life of reason possible, he needs to build an object of knowledge that is stable; thus, he is also a believer in an eternal and never changing form via individual essences.[20] This last opposition between two more contradictory beliefs, gnats and barnacles, Heraclitus and Parmenides, adds one more example to that list, in the same way that it adds one more reason to defend Santayana's intellectual legacy, both in itself and as a marvelous representative of what a contemporary discussion of correctly assimilated classical philosophy should be. As we mentioned in the introduction to our chapter, one feature in the line of that classical heritage is Santayana's belief in the existence of chaos at the origin of the universe, a chaos that could nonetheless

---

[19] Cfr. *RE*, 14–15: "Were there nothing but essence [...] there would be no possible movement, no events, no life, and no preference [...] without it [matter] there could be no manifestation of essence, whether in nature or in discourse."

[20] We have barely touched the subject of spirit but incorporating it might certainly offer an even more complicated view about change: "We must admit that spirit is not in time, that the perception of flux (or of anything else) is not a flux, but a synthetic glance and a single intuition of relation, of form, of quality" (*SAF*, 161).

be seen—should be *believed to be*, we had better say—as an orderly cosmos. As this chapter has shown, the system of philosophy presented in *SAF* is one excellent attempt at building that cosmos. As a system, it is certainly not just "one more" (*SAF*, v), and for all its slips and quirks it still represents one of the most valuable philosophical contributions to the history of philosophy. That is exactly one of the main reasons to be celebrating *Scepticism and Animal Faith* today. George Santayana is one of those few thinkers who make true those beautiful words of his contemporary, the Spanish philosopher, Xavier Zubiri, words that will close this chapter in Spanish to honor an intellectual tradition that started in Greece and in Greek thousands of years ago and, thanks to intellectuals like Santayana, continues alive in our world today in many different languages: "los griegos somos nosotros" (Zubiri 1963, 312).

References

Aristotle. 2014a. *The Complete Works of Aristotle, Volume 1: The Revised Oxford Translation*. Princeton: Princeton University Press.

———. 2014b. *The Complete Works of Aristotle, Volume 2: The Revised Oxford Translation*. Princeton: Princeton University Press.

Burnet, J. 1920. *Early Greek Philosophy*. London: A&C Black.

Faerna, Á. 2011. Santayana o la ilusión de la mirada. In *Santayana: un pensador universal*, ed. J. Beltrán, M. Garrido, and S. Sevilla, 125–138. Valencia: Universidad de Valencia.

Guthrie, W. K. C. 1962. *A History of Greek Philosophy. The Earlier Presocratics and the Pythagoreans*. 6 vols. Vol. 1. Cambridge: Cambridge University Press.

Marías, J. 1980. *Biografía de la Filosofía*. Madrid: Alianza.

Popper, K. 1958. Back to the Pre-Socratics: The Presidential Address. *Proceedings of the Aristotelian Society* 59: 1–24.

———. 1999. *El mundo de Parménides. Ensayos sobre la ilustración presocrática*. Barcelona: Paidós.

Santayana, G. 1923. *The Unknowable. The Herbert Spencer Lecture*. Oxford: Clarendon Press.

———. 1927. *The Realm of Essence*. New York: Charles Scribner's Sons. (*RE*).

———. [1923] 1955. *Scepticism and Animal Faith. Introduction to a System of Philosophy*. New York: Dover. (*SAF*).

———. 1967. *Animal Faith and Spiritual Life. Previously Unpublished and Uncollected Writings by George Santayana with Critical Essays on His Thought*. New York: Appleton-Century-Crofts. (*AFSL*).

———. 2006. *The Letters of George Santayana, Book Seven, 1941–1947*. Cambridge, MA: MIT Press. (*LGS*)

Singer, I. 1977. Santayana and the Ontology of the Photographic Image. *The Journal of Aesthetics and Art Criticism* 36 (1): 39–43.

Sorabji, R. 1983. *Time, Creation and the Continuum: Theories in Antiquity and the Early Middle Ages*. London: Duckworth.

Zubiri, X. 1963. *Naturaleza, Historia, Dios*. Madrid: Editora Nacional.

The Ideal of a Philosophic Redemption: Baruch Spinoza's Place in Western Philosophy and in Santayana's Thought

Lydia Amir

> *I will not attempt to describe here the many lessons that I learned in the study of Spinoza, lessons that in several respects laid the foundation of my philosophy.*
> —Santayana, *PP*, 233–234

Introduction

Scepticism and Animal Faith contains the most striking eulogy of the seventeenth-century Jewish-Dutch philosopher, Baruch Spinoza, at the same time that it rejects Spinoza's main ideas, the identification of essence with substance and of nature with God. Elsewhere, Santayana discards additional central Spinozean views, such as the determinism he endorses and the mind-body parallelism he advances; moreover, Santayana's mature philosophy, as presented in *SAF* and additional works, differs from Spinoza's.

We may thus wonder at the soundness of the invitation to the tercentennial meeting at The Hague which Santayana received in 1932 to deliver a lecture in honor of Spinoza, whose content is disclosed in "Ultimate Religion" (1936). True, Santayana maintains that he adheres to Spinoza's psychology and that he admires his naturalism, yet he thoroughly criticizes and significantly alters these views. Spinoza is no moral relativist, no humanist, and no materialist; even on

---

L. Amir (✉)
Department of Philosophy, Tufts University, Medford, MA, USA

© The Author(s), under exclusive license to Springer Nature Switzerland AG 2024
M. A. Coleman, G. Tiller (eds.), *The Palgrave Companion to George Santayana's Scepticism and Animal Faith*, Palgrave Companions,
https://doi.org/10.1007/978-3-031-46367-9_18

the notion of truth these two differ, which strikes me as an important divide for philosophers.

I argue that a reevaluation of the relevance of Spinoza to Santayana's thought, notwithstanding the compliments he pays him in *SAF* and on additional occasions, is in order, and as it is especially relevant to Santayana's mature philosophy, I undertake it in this essay.

I begin by explaining the six references to Spinoza in *SAF*, followed by an evaluation of the accuracy of Santayana's judgement, when needed. I continue by attempting to understand, through the use of additional resources, the puzzling relationship that Santayana entertains with his "hero" and "master," whose philosophy he discards and whose personality he often censures, yet with whom he entertains an ongoing dialogue from his student days in Berlin till the very end of his life. The clarification of Spinoza's role in modern philosophy leads me to conclude that the key to Santayana's own philosophic project lies in the relationship that he entertains with Spinoza. This in turn helps to elucidate Santayana's place in modern philosophy.

Santayana refers six times to Spinoza in *SAF*. While he eulogizes him at the beginning and the end (vii, 305), he criticizes him in the work: the Index points to two criticisms (16, 129), I have found two more (203–209, 237). This is not the sole instance of Santayana beginning and finishing a work with Spinoza in mind.[1] It is an indication of the significance of the Jewish-Dutch philosopher for Santayana, which this essay attempts to shed light on, beginning with the six telling references to *SAF* but also necessarily going beyond those in this work.[2] Santayana's sustained and systematic criticism of Spinoza problematizes the continual eulogy, a problem that I will pose and solve, following an attentive clarification of each reference and an evaluation of the accuracy of its content.

Reference Six

Both the first and last references set the tone toward Spinoza. I begin with the latter because it accurately singles out Spinoza in modern thought and reveals Santayana's project in its entirety. It reads: "Merely learned views are not philosophy; and therefore *no modern writer is altogether a philosopher in my eyes, except Spinoza*" (*SAF*, 305; emphasis added).

Santayana explains that knowledge, *Wissenschaft* in German, is no more than learning. Rather than a choice between artificial theories—a "learned pursuit"—his criticism is, to the contrary, self-criticism:

> It is the discipline of my daily thoughts and the account I actually give of myself from moment to moment of my own being and the world around me. I should be ashamed to countenance opinions which, when not arguing, I did not believe.

---

[1] See, for example, *The Idea of Christ in the Gospels* (Santayana, ICG, 5–6; 207–209).
[2] I use Santayana's works, letters, and biography.

It would seem to be dishonest and cowardly to militate under other colours than those under which I live. (*SAF*, 305)

The critics of knowledge are particularly targeted here, for being "as feeble morally as they are technically" (*SAF*, 305); *SAF*'s very enterprise attempts to show that their conclusions cannot pass the test of validity, because being unlivable they are also unbelievable. As merely learned views are not philosophy for Santayana, only Spinoza is a philosopher "in the better sense," as the index qualifies him in referencing this passage (*SAF*, 313).

True, the Santayanan view of the philosopher's nature was not fashionable in modern times; even those who advanced views of philosophy as a way of life, such as Arthur Schopenhauer or Friedrich Nietzsche, denied the necessity or the capacity of the philosopher to follow his own recipe. Schopenhauer famously rejected it as similar to the demand that a sculptor should be as beautiful as his sculpture[3]; Nietzsche did insist on the necessity of writing with one's blood and philosophizing with a hammer, but ended up differentiating in his intellectual autobiography between his writings and himself.[4] Even more telling is David Hume's attitude toward philosophy: having attempted to live his scepticism, he renounced "the philosophic malady" which was bringing him to the verge of depression; getting better or living well meant forgetting philosophy altogether.[5]

This passage reveals not only Santayana's view of philosophy but also his isolation among philosophers, which explains Spinoza's importance for him. Spinoza lived his philosophy, as did Santayana. This may be the main reason for the special bond Santayana felt with Spinoza, whom he famously called "his hero" and "master,"[6] and to whom he often alluded in his various works, his autobiography, and his letters.

Santayana's portrayal of Spinoza is accurate, as far as we know. Living as the first modern man, outside of any religious community, the Jewish-Dutch philosopher followed the philosophy he devised, being convinced of its soundness. He lived quietly enjoying the peace of mind he reached by the means he recommended. Beginning with the search for a stable joy that he would enjoy forever, as described in the *Treatise on the Emendation of the Intellect*, he ended up with the method to secure it with his theory of immanent redemption or liberation as expounded in the *Ethics*. I emphasize the accuracy of Santayana's first evaluation, because we may dispute the correctness of the following one.

The remaining five references to Spinoza disclose the content of Santayana's philosophy. The first *eulogizes* Spinoza again for his role in modern philosophy, but for a different reason; it contextualizes his thought by associating it with

---

[3] Schopenhauer, *The Word as Will and Idea*, 1966, vol. I, sec. 68, 495.
[4] Nietzsche, *Ecce Homo* (1967) 1989, "Why I Write Such Good Books," sec. 1, 259: "I am one thing, my writings are another matter."
[5] Hume, *Traité de la nature humaine*, (1739) 1995, bk. 1, 303, 362.
[6] Santayana, *PP*, 521–522; 235; for these affirmations, see Spiro 2009.

the ancient Greeks and with the Indians and enables Santayana to avail himself of this legacy for his view of the human being and of his spirit in relation to the universe. Additional references *criticize* Spinoza on four points; although dissimilar, they indicate Santayana's distinctive and restrictive view of existence and of substance.

REFERENCE ONE

The first reference in *SAF* to Spinoza reads:

> The first philosophers, the original observers of life and nature, were the best; and I think only the Indians and the Greek naturalists, together with Spinoza, have been right on the chief issue, the relation of man and of his spirit to the universe. (*SAF*, viii)

Santayana intends in this passage to emphasize his own naturalism and to point to that which he sees as primordial in any naturalistic view: the situation of the human being in the universe as a natural being and of his spirit as a natural occurrence. The passage is somewhat misleading insofar as the Greek naturalists did not refer to spirit, nor did Spinoza; the Indians did but denied the existence of matter, while Santayana defined himself as a materialist.

In various places in *SAF*, Santayana elaborates on his materialism; he explains the similarity between the Greek naturalists, whom he considers to be religious and spiritual thinkers, and the Indians. He especially probes the latter's views, in order to explain what he endorses and why, and how he can relate to them at all given that they see spirit as primary and matter as nonexistent. Yet he does not explain in this work what is Spinoza's view of man and his spirit, and how his own materialism and his view of spirit as immaterial set him apart from the naturalism of Spinoza.

Spinoza is no materialist; he is a monist, a proponent of one substance which we apprehend as matter and as thought, but which can be conceived of in an infinite number of ways; and he has no concept of spirit, but of mind, which parallels the body as its idea, one's self being conceived, as is everything else, either as matter or as thought, in two different languages out of the infinite ones that describe us as part of the one substance. Spirit and body for Santayana do not entertain the same relations as mind and body for Spinoza; nor is the Santayanan spirit similar to the Spinozean mind; Santayana's naturalism is not similar to Spinoza's (or to the Greek atomists'), nor to the Indians' who are not materialists.

Yet, Santayana includes himself in a lineage, which despite the confusion it may create aims at emphasizing that the spirit (a reality that needs to be posited) is immaterial, strictly speaking non-existent, yet natural. Since Santayana, rather than directly enlighten us on his thought, harmonizes each of the schools of thought mentioned above until they are recognizable no more, the purpose of their grouping together should be clarified. I believe it is to set them and himself apart from any view that assumes a supernatural *origin* of spirit. This makes Spinoza "right on the chief issue," as the Index lists this reference (*SAF*, 313).

That Santayana believed that the Greeks and the Indians had the same thought (of which Christianity was the heir)[7] need not occupy us here; but insofar as for him this lineage culminates in Spinoza, this reference tells us that Santayana saw Spinoza as a mystic.[8] Santayana supposedly despised mysticism, when unrealistic or supernatural, but accepted the appellation "Castilian mystic."[9] Spinoza's thought has been compared to Indian thought by other commentators, most profitably to Buddhism, when the goal of philosophy as deliverance from suffering was emphasized; but it has also been compared to Hinduism when his thought was read as mystical. The latter reading is not accurate, but the former is correct.[10]

Santayana understands Greek philosophy as the heir of Indian thought, Christianity as the heir of both, and Spinoza as the successor of them all in providing salvation or liberation. He himself follows in those steps: as he explains in *The Realm of Spirit*, spirit "longs at first for happiness and at last for salvation" (*RS*, ix); and indeed, "salvation is demanded, and in one sense is possible, because by virtue of his intelligence man already has one foot in eternity" (*RS*, 213). In his "General Confession" in *The Philosophy of George Santayana* he sums up his whole message in these terms:

> That is all my message: that morality and religion are expressions of human nature; that human nature is a biological growth, and finally that spirit, fascinated and tortured, is involved in the process, and asks to be saved.... What is salvation? ... Some organic harmony in forms and movements is requisite for life; but physical life is blind and groping and runs up continually against hostile forces, disease and death. It is therefore in the interests of life to become more intelligent and to establish a harmony also with the environment and the future. But life enlightened is spirit, the voice of life, and therefore aspiring to all the perfections to which life aspires, and loving all the beauties that life loves; yet at the same time spirit is the voice of truth and of destiny, bidding life renounce beauty and perfection and life itself, whenever and wherever these are impossible. (*GC*, 23)

Santayana refers to it as "this philosophic salvation" in his autobiography (*PP*, 428); in *Platonism and the Spiritual Life*,[11] as an ascent of spirit, which is reprised in the last chapters of *Realms of Being*. The movement is as follows:

---

[7] This is not stated in *SAF*; but elsewhere, Christianity is introduced as the heir of both Indian thought (i.e., *RB*, 766) and Paganism (*LR3*, Chapter 7).

[8] This view is repeated in *Reason in Religion*, 87, 101, and in "The Ethical Doctrine of Spinoza" (1957, 81), among other places.

[9] Santayana, "Apologia pro Mente Sua," 1940, 603–604.

[10] On this point see Amir forthcoming b. For a discussion of Spinoza and Buddhism, see, for example, Wetlesen 1979; for a discussion of Spinoza and Hinduism, see, for example, Hessing 1977.

[11] *PSL*, XIX, 71.

ascending from the realm of existence to the eternal image of the realm of truth, and then to the realm of essence.

Thus, this first reference in *SAF* completes the previous one, which concludes the book: philosophy needs to provide salvation, which should be actualized by the philosopher; philosophy as lay religion is a way of life.[12]

Reference Two

The four remaining references are critical of Spinoza. The points they make are linked insofar as they point, first, to Santayana's view of existence and, second, but relatedly, to his view of substance. The critical reference I begin with defends Santayana's scepticism against Spinoza's dogmatism and is therefore relevant to the entire project of *SAF*.

Spinoza "thinks ideas beliefs" (*SAF*, 16), the index tells us (*SAF*, 313). Santayana takes Spinoza to mean that scepticism is impossible. To the contrary, Santayana considers that the solipsism of the present moment (which makes the agent "an incredulous spectator of his own romance," who "thinks his own adventures fictions") is "an honest position"; moreover, certain attempts to refute it he sees as self-contradictory (*SAF*, 15). The further explanation he gives of this kind of scepticism, which he qualifies as ascetic, is opposed to the "voracious dogmatist," Spinoza, whose "greedy intellect" refuses scepticism:

> Scepticism is not concerned to abolish ideas; it can relish the variety and order of a pictured world, or of any of them in succession, without any of the qualms and exclusions proper to dogmatism. Its case is simply not to credit these ideas, not to posit any of these fancied worlds, nor this ghostly mind imagined in viewing them. The attitude of the sceptic is not inconsistent; it is merely difficult because it is hard for the greedy intellect. Very voracious dogmatists like Spinoza even assert that it is impossible, but the impossibility is only psychological, and due to their voracity; they no doubt speak truly for themselves when they say that the idea of a horse, if not contradicted by some other idea, *is* a belief that the horse exists. (*SAF*, 16)

I am not sure that the last sentence describes accurately Spinoza's view of ideas, at least not all instances of ideas. "Idea" is used in many different ways by Spinoza; further investigation may be needed, which exceeds the scope of this article. Spinoza refers also to "ideas of non-existent individual things",[13] Paul Kashap argues, "what we normally describe as fictions of the mind or imaginations, which would include dreams" (Kashap 1977, 60). And, the notion of "non-existent individual things" would also "include things that may be said to be possible and/or in the future as well as those that existed in the past" (Kashap 1977, 60), such as "various thoughts, beliefs (i.e., ideas) about, say,

---

[12] "My philosophy is like that of the ancients: a discipline of the mind and heart, a lay religion" (Santayana, *RB*, 827). For Santayanan philosophy as a way of life, see Moreno 2015.

[13] Spinoza 1985; *Ethics*, Book II, Proposition 8.

immortality or life after death without stating (uttering or writing) them. I might also utter the sentence and thereby state that 'the chair I am sitting on is on fire,' without believing that the chair is in fact on fire. Or, I might simply make a verbal mistake in the course of making a statement of my belief" (Kashap 1977, 70n2).

For a long time, however, the prevalent opinion among commentators was that the very nature of Spinoza's philosophy excludes the possibility of scepticism. This would explain Santayana's characterization of Spinoza's philosophy as necessarily anti-sceptical. That this is no longer the case can be seen in recent publications (Serrano 2018; Viljanen 2020).

Santayana criticizes the accuracy of the view that "the idea of a horse, if not contradicted by some other idea, *is* a belief that the horse exists," which he ascribes to Spinoza. This would be so, he argues, if the will or impulse or tendency to action were involved; this is indeed the case, Santayana argues, but it needs to be counteracted by the poised philosopher:

> but this would not be the case if they felt no impulse to ride the imagined horse, or to get out of its way. Ideas become beliefs only when by precipitating tendencies to action they persuade me that they are signs of things; these things are not those ideas simply hypostatized, but are believed to be compacted of many parts, and full of ambushed parts, entirely absent from the ideas. (*SAF*, 16)

Reflection should discount the latent mechanical reaction of the body producing the idea. It may not be avoided, but "this confused and terrible aspiration of life" needs to be probed "to the bottom" by a philosopher, as a poised and experienced person. It is this aspiration of life, which Santayana considers "terrible," which links the next reference to this one.

Reference Three

The last indexed reference I comment on is critical of Spinoza, who rightly defines "the realm of essence" (*SAF*, 313) as "an infinite number of kinds of being, each having an infinite number of variations," yet is mistaken in calling "this infinity of being *substance*" (*SAF*, 129). The rest of the quotation tells of Santayana's philosophy: "as if at once to weight it all with existence (a horrible possibility) and to obliterate its internal distinction." The latter is the very meaning of essence as "distinction, infinitely minute and indelible distinction of everything from everything else, is what essence means"; and the prejudice against the non-existent is sheer positivism: "People suppose that whatever is non-existent is nothing—a stupid positivism, like that of saying that the past is nothing, or the future nothing, or everything nothing of which I happen to be ignorant" (*SAF*, 129).

That existence is qualified as a horrible possibility calls for an elaboration of what existence means for Santayana. He is aware that his view of existence has particular relevance to his project since "in scepticism … everything turns on the meaning of the word existence" (*SAF*, 42). As he had explained earlier in *SAF*, existence designates such being as is in flux, determined by external relations, and jostled by irrelevant events (*SAF*, 42). The exploration of that realm, with the purpose of describing it more fully, would be the domain of physics or perhaps psychology, but does not concern the sceptic (*SAF*, 43). "A conjunction of natures in adventitious and variable relations" (*SAF*, 48), existence is also described as the locus of "the struggle of assertion and counter-assertion" (*SAF*, 43). More specifically, that which exists are

> facts of events believed to occur in nature, including, *first*, intuitions themselves, or instances of consciousness...and all remembered experiences and mental discourse; and *second*, physical things and events, having a transcendent relation to the date of intuition, which in belief, may be used as signs for them. (*SAF*, 47)

From the point of view of knowledge, existences are facts or events affirmed, not images seen or topics merely entertained, which yields the following conclusion:

> Existence is accordingly not only doubtful to the sceptic, but odious to the logician. To him it seems a truly monstrous excrescence and superfluity in being, since anything existent is more than the description of it, having suffered an unintelligible emphasis or materialization to fall upon it, which is logically inane and morally comic. At the same time, existence suffers from defect of being and obscuration; any ideal nature, such as might be exhaustively given in intuition, when it is materialized loses the intangibility and eternity proper to it in its own sphere; so that existence doubly injures the forms of being it embodies, by ravishing them first and betraying them afterwards. (*SAF*, 48)

It is now clear why Santayana objects to Spinoza's burdening with existence the "infinity of being" that essence is by making it a "*substance*" (*SAF*, 129). Contrasting Leibniz's view of essence with narrow views of it and with Spinoza's view of essence as substance, Santayana sides with the former: the non-existent is infinite, is everything, is "the realm of essence." However, it is not the power or worth in actual things, but rather "as the form of everything and anything" (*SAF*, 129).

The sceptic is confined to "a sort of play with the non-existent, or a game of thought … to this mirage of the non-existent, or intuition of essence" (*SAF*, 75), which yields the contents of Santayana's liberation, a paradise, a peaceful solitary freedom where anxiety and torment have no reach:

> Thus, a mind enlightened by scepticism and cured of noisy dogma, a mind discounting all reports, and free from all tormenting anxiety about its own fortunes or existence, finds in the wilderness of essence a very sweet and marvelous solitude. The ultimate reaches of doubt and renunciation open out for it, by an easy transition, into fields of endless variety and peace. As if through the gorges of

death it had passed into a paradise where all things are crystallized into the image of themselves, and have lost their urgency and their venom. (*SAF*, 76)

Santayana had expressed his sympathy with the Indians' hope of escaping from the "universal hurly-burly into some haven of peace" (*SAF*, 54). He notes that the philosopher has a haven in himself because "he has pleasure in truth, and an equal readiness to enjoy the scene or to quit it" (*SAF*, 54). Although "liberation is never complete while life lasts, and is nothing afterwards; … it flows in a measure from this very conviction that all experience is illusion, when this conviction is morally effective, as it was with the Indians" (*SAF*, 54).

The ideal of cognitive life is sacrificial: "it aspires to see each thing clearly and to see all things together, that is to say, under the form of eternity" (*SAF*, 128). And, "to cease to live temporally is intellectually to be saved; it is … to fade or to brighten into the truth and to become eternal" (*SAF*, 128).

This kind of understanding yields a form of love, which Santayana ascribes in *SAF* to the Indians and describes in the following terms: "How infinite, how helpless, how deserving of forgiveness creative error becomes in the eyes of understanding, that loves only in pity, and has no concupiscence for what it loves!" (*SAF*, 53)[14] Elsewhere, Santayana will appropriate this love as his ideal, christening it "charity" and defining it as a disillusioned sympathy, a perception and a love of "the possible perception in all other things," letting people simultaneously take themselves and their own with a grain of salt while appreciating the alien other (Santayana, *RB*, 759). It brings a sense of well-being by "detaching us from each thing with humor and humility, and attaching us to all things with justice, charity, and pure joy" (Santayana, *RB*, 745). So far as they engage in spiritual discipline, people need to suspend the practice of judgment and replace it with understanding, with seeing and appreciating things for their own sake. The spirit's choice is intelligence, sympathy, universality. Morally, the whole natural world, with us as people in it, will be removed to a distance. It will have become foreign. It will touch us, and exist morally for us, only as the scene of our exile, and as being the confusion from which it hopes to be delivered (*RS*, 188).

REFERENCES FOUR AND FIVE

There are two additional references to Spinoza, which are not indexed. One takes issue with Spinoza's view of *substance* (*SAF*, 203–209) and the other with his identification of that substance, nature, with God, or *Deus sive Natura* (*SAF*, 237).

The first objection is to the metaphysical approach to substance, which Spinoza shares with Aristotle and Plato, Santayana notes (*SAF*, 203), but which

---

[14] The passage continues: "How like unhappy animals western philosophers seem in comparison, with their fact-worship, their thrift, their moral intolerance, their imaginative poverty, their political zeal, and their subservience to intellectual fashion!" (*SAF*, 53).

I will address here only in relation to Spinoza. Substance, as "an independent object" (202), as self-existent (203), and borrowing Spinoza's definition, as that which is understood through itself (208), does exist according to Santayana. Yet he sees it as physical (*SAF*, 201, 209), rather than metaphysical, that is, dialectical or moral. As such, substance is only fact, a surd (*SAF*, 208) devoid of meaning, contingent, and irrational. Knowledge of fact or substance leaves it unattained, posited but unpossessed (206). Substance is "something challenging respect and demanding study" (206), yet childish to spirit (205). While it remains a mystery as is the existence of the self (*SAF*, 207, 208), unfathomable, and almost incredible (211), Santayana insists on the difference between himself and the world, "which is not mine nor like me" (212), and identifies himself with "light," rather than with "this dark Substance," as a "poetical and superior spirit prefers dialectic over knowledge of fact (which is knowledge of substance)" (205):

> Only essences please this jealous lover of light, and seem to it sufficient; it hates faith, existence, doubt, anything ulterior. Substance and truth offend it by their unnecessary claims.... What ghostly thing, it says to itself, is ... this dark Substance behind the fair appearance? Substance interrupts and besets the spirit in its innocence, and in its mad play; one substance, which it calls the flesh, torments it from below, and a kindred substance, which it calls matter, prods, crushes, and threatens it from without. God also, another substance, looms before it, commanding and forbidding; and he is terrible in his wrath and obscurity, until it learns his ways. (*SAF*, 206)

The second objection to Spinoza (*SAF*, 237) follows directly from Santayana's view of substance: it cannot be what we mean by God. But his objection to Spinoza's view of *Deus sive Natura* runs deeper: while it may be a poetic exclamation pointing at the mystery of nature, a philosopher should know better than to use the word God in vain.[15]

Beyond *SAF*: The Relationship with Spinoza

At this point, the reader may wonder at the meaning and the value of the eulogy of Spinoza at the beginning and the end of *SAF*, since Spinoza's more particular views, which we commonly call his philosophy, are being clearly rejected. Indeed, all of Spinoza's views are rejected if not here, then elsewhere,[16] yet Santayana writes: "I will not attempt to describe here the many lessons that I learned in the study of Spinoza, lessons that in several respects laid the foundation of my philosophy."[17]

---

[15] Pantheism is rejected by Santayana in other places as well, and in other forms. See, for example, *The Idea of Christ in the Gospels*, where both Stoicism and Spinozism are rejected.
[16] For the additional Spinozean views that Santayana rejects, see Amir 2023.
[17] *PP*, 233–234.

The systematic discarding of all of Spinoza's views and the sustained criticism of the Dutch philosopher, "his master" and "hero," is a puzzle, which needs resolving. The quotations from *SAF* point to the direction of the solution: Spinoza is called upon at every juncture of the liberation that Santayana offers as the content of his philosophy, because as different as this liberation may be from Spinoza's, the very idea that (modern) philosophy should offer liberation is Spinozean, as is the idea that this philosophy and the liberation it affords are to be lived. Moreover, the blueprint of the liberation that Santayana offers follows Spinoza's: it involves love and an alternative to eternal life.

Many a commentator has noticed Santayana's engagement with Spinoza, and some have noted it in the contexts that I emphasize. For example, Angus Kerr-Lawson remarks that on the topic of liberation the similarities between Santayana and Spinoza are most striking (2000). Santayana's view of love, as best described by Irving Singer in his monumental *The Nature of Love* (1987, vol. 3), is associated with the release he offered. Finally, quoting Santayana on eternity in his contribution to Arthur Schilpp's *The Philosophy of George Santayana*, Bertrand Russell noted the similarities between Spinoza and Santayana.[18]

However, Singer maintains that Santayana's thought is a synthesis of various philosophies (Singer 2000), and Kerr-Lawson asserts more specifically that Santayana takes from Spinoza whatever he likes (Kerr-Lawson 2000). Such a practice does not sit well with Santayana's denial in *SAF* of an eclecticism that would explain his thought (*SAF*, ix). Russell immediately associates Santayana with Spinoza as philosophers who should be read on account of their respective views of "what constitutes the good life," and of the "standard of values in art and morals"; yet he clarifies that "neither his opinions nor his values resemble Spinoza's," who failed in Santayana's eyes to constitute the life of reason; rather, "the likeness to Spinoza consists in concern for the life of reason, not in the theory as to what it consists of." "Fundamentally ethical" philosophies of this kind should be also evaluated for consistency and the importance of the point of view, Santayana's ranks high on both counts, and Spinoza on the latter (Russell 1940, 453–454).

Timothy Sprigge has given a thorough analysis of Santayana's attitude to Spinoza in various publications (1993), including the introduction he wrote to the latter's *Ethics* (1910), where his own views rather than Spinoza's are stated. However, none of the above commentaries fully explain what Santayana owes to Spinoza and why. The following quotation may give us a clue about Spinoza's significance for Santayana: "Spinoza was not only a complete naturalist, but, by a rare combination, also a spiritual man, seeing and accepting the place of the human heart in the universe."[19] Yet Santayana takes issues with his capacity to guide us in the spiritual life, deeming Spinoza "narrow and inadequate" for not

---

[18] See Russell, "The Philosophy of Santayana," 1940, 469; also of relevance here is Spiro 2009.
[19] Santayana, *PP*, 235.

embodying a wide tradition.[20] Spinoza's view of Christ as a moralist misses on the symbol of the embodied spirit, which Christ represents. Santayana rejects the Spinozean pantheism, which, following Schopenhauer, he deems Jewish and optimistic. He prefers the Greeks and Catholicism to Spinoza, yet refrains from endorsing the reconstruction of Christianity which Schopenhauer offers, especially his liberation from the denial of the will; he offers, instead, a variation on the latter's aesthetic contemplation of the world by the spiritual life that he defines. He reduces Schopenhauer to Spinoza and thus explains away his infatuation with the former, which he qualifies as short-lived (*PP*, 239).

Finally, Santayana sets out to capture the esoteric core of Christianity (*RB*, 845), which alone interests him and translates the truth of the religion in philosophic terms.[21] The same project has been undertaken by Spinoza. After criticizing its shortcomings, Santayana follows Spinoza's blueprint of an immanent liberation or salvation, whose ties with love and with an alternative to eternal life he emulates.[22]

The significance of Spinoza's philosophy for Santayana's thought, notwithstanding the compliments he pays him in *SAF* and on additional occasions, can now be reevaluated. For the purpose of reevaluating the relationship of Santayana and Spinoza, the role played in modern philosophy by the latter should be further elucidated. Its impact on Santayana, as mediated by German idealism (Vaysse 2007) and especially by Schopenhauer, whose relevance to Santayana's thought has been established (Flamm 2002; Brodrick 2015, Chapter 5), would be clarified.

Spinoza not only provides a successful example of a philosophic project which other philosophers emulate, but also a rationale for undertaking such a project which determines the course of Western philosophy (see Yovel 1989). In line with ancient and Hellenistic philosophers, whose view of philosophy as an alternative to established religion he endorses, and as heir to Judaic and Christian influences on Western civilization Spinoza redefines philosophy's role after the Medieval reign of Christianity and its ideal (salvation in another world by God's grace, through love of God which grants eternal life): Philosophy should provide the individual with a philosophic redemption, a personal redemption which captures the truth of monotheistic religions and offers an alternative to religious salvation. To be effective, the liberation and blessedness

---

[20] Santayana, *PP*, 235–236.

[21] "In Christianity the idea of prosperity is abandoned for that of salvation in the world to come; and incidentally there is much aspiration towards spiritual perfection and many a master of it; yet this spiritual discipline is in some sense esoteric" (*PP*, 409). "The incidental esoteric discipline, which is all that I respect in Catholicism, terminates in the same inward liberation and peace that ancient sages attained under all religions or under none. The question is whether the paraphernalia of salvation are not in all cases accidental" (*PP*, 409). The various references in Santayana's Letters to his attitude toward Catholicism as a religion do not refute the point I make. See, for example, Letter to Susan Sturgis de Sastre, 29 April 1906 (*LGS*, 1:343); to William Roscoe Thayer, 29 May 1900 (*LGS*, 1:218); to William Lyon Phelps, 1936 (Santayana, *LGS*, 5:297).

[22] See Amir (2023).

which constitute this philosophic redemption are worked through alternatives to Christian views of love and eternity. The idea of taking religious concepts, such as salvation, love of God, and eternal life, and infusing them with meanings that offer a path for the individual to reach the highest ideals, which only religion offered till now, is the legacy that Spinoza left to Western philosophy.[23]

The backbone of this project, which Spinoza fleshed out through his own version of redemption, love, and eternity, has been endorsed by Schopenhauer and later by Nietzsche,[24] each in debt to Spinoza for various additional views. Santayana contends with Nietzsche for the place of the true affirmative thinker that answers best Schopenhauer's pessimism.[25] As an alternative to the established Christian religion, with new content poured into the notions of redemption, love, and eternity, Santayana's philosophy follows closely Schopenhauer's yet also has affinities with Nietzsche's. The emphasis on suffering that the three philosophers share contrasts with the Glory that Spinoza's view of *Deus sive Natura* emphasizes.

Were it not for Spinoza, however, none of these philosophies could be formulated in those terms, because the very project of replacing established religion's salvation by modern philosophical means was explicitly formulated by him. The emphasis on love as the path to redemption and on a variety of eternity as part of one's blessedness—the specifics of the Spinozean contribution to the new concept of philosophic redemption—were read as requirements for the new, modern, philosophic alternatives which were to rival the contents of the ideal advanced by established religions. Spinoza's philosophy served as a blueprint to be followed, at the price of erasing its contents. This explains how Spinoza is revered at the same time that he is rejected by all his followers, including Santayana.

By disclosing in these terms Santayana's debt to Spinoza and to Schopenhauer's previous use of Spinoza for the formulation of the "most Christian philosophy" (as Schopenhauer refers to his own worldview),[26] we help to clarify the idea that unifies Santayana's contributions. These include his view of the role of philosophy and of his own thought as philosophic; his view of religion and the reason why various notions associated with it, such as the flesh, the world, the devil (RB 673–735), prayer (RB 797–801), Christ (RB 757–766), and the Trinity (RB 845–854) are redefined within his thought; and his rethinking of the notions of love (RB 783, 788, 791–766) and eternity

---

[23] See Amir (forthcoming-b).

[24] For Spinoza and Nietzsche, see Amir forthcoming-b; for the role of Schopenhauer in Nietzsche's thought, see Swift (2005).

[25] For Santayana and Nietzsche, see Amir (2020–2022) and Amir (forthcoming-a).

[26] For Schopenhauer and Spinoza, see Bouriou 2007; Rousset 2007.

(*SAF*, 267–271; *RB*, 112–114)[27] to fit the unwritten requirements of a successful philosophic personal redemption, as undertaken and exemplified, if not formally defined, by Spinoza.

By emphasizing philosophic personal redemption as the modern equivalent of individual liberation, the analysis proposed here clarifies Santayana's position in modern philosophy: a follower of Spinoza, and of Schopenhauer, whom he assimilates to Spinoza, Santayana is a contender for Nietzsche's place as heir of both.

References

Santayana Works

George Santayana. 1910. Introduction. *Everyman edition of Spinoza's Ethics and De Intellectus Emendatione*. Translated by Andrew Boyle. London, J. M. Dent & Sons, Ltd.; New York, E. P. Dutton & Co.

Santayana, George. 1923. *Scepticism and Animal Faith: Introduction to a System of Philosophy*. New York: Charles Scribner's Sons.

George Santayana. 1936. Ultimate Religion. In *Obiter Scripta: Lectures, Essays and Review*, eds. Justus Buchler and Benjamin Schwartz. New York: Scribner's; London: Constable.

Santayana, George. 1940a. Apologia pro Mente Sua. In *The Philosophy of George Santayana*, ed. Paul A. Schlipp. New York: Tudor.

———. 1940b. General Confession. In *The Philosophy of George Santayana*, ed. Paul A. Schlipp. New York: Tudor.

———. 1942. *Realms of Being, One-Volume Edition, with a New Introduction by the Author*. New York: Scribner's.

———. 1946. *The Idea of Christ in the Gospels; or, God in Man, A Critical Essay*. In *New York: Scribner's*. Toronto: Saunders.

———. 1957a. *Platonism and the Spiritual Life*. New York: Harper Torchbooks.

George Santayana. 1957b. *The Idler and His Works, and Other Essays*, edited with a preface by Daniel Cory. New York: Braziller.

Santayana, George. 1962. *Reason in Science*. London: Collier.

———. 1982. *Reason in Religion*. New York: Dover Publications.

———. 1987. *Persons and Places: Fragments of Autobiography*. Cambridge, MA: MIT Press.

George Santayana. 2001–2008. *The Letters of George Santayana*. Edited by William G. Holzberger. Cambridge, MA: The MIT Press.

---

[27] For Santayana's view of love, see Singer 1987, vol. 3, Chapter 7; for his view of eternity, see Woodward 1988. See also Lovely 2012, whose view of Santayana's philosophy of religion contains valuable comments which are relevant to my argument; especially pertinent is the comparison he draws between Santayana's view of love and Spinoza's love of God, and in general his view of salvation with Spinoza's philosophy as expressed in "Ultimate Religion" (155–163).

ADDITIONAL REFERENCES

Amir, Lydia. 2020–2022. The Democritean Tradition in Santayana, Nietzsche, and Montaigne. Part I–III. *Overheard in Seville: Bulletin of the Santayana Society*, 38: 74–92; 39: 116–140, 2021; 40: 88–99, 2022.

———. 2023. Individual Liberation in Modern Philosophy: Reflections on Santayana's Affiliation to the Tradition Inaugurated by Spinoza and Followed by Schopenhauer and Nietzsche. *Ruch Filozoficzny* LXXIX (1): 43–77.

———. forthcoming-a. *Laughter and the Good Life: Montaigne, Nietzsche, Santayana, Bergson*. Albany, NY: State University of New York Press.

———. forthcoming-b. *Redemptive Philosophies: Spinoza versus Nietzsche*. Monographien und Texte zur Nietzsche-Forschung. Berlin: de Gruyter.

Bouriou, Christophe. 2007. Conatus spinoziste et volonté schopenhaurienne. In *Spinoza au XIXe siècle*, ed. André Tosel, Pierre-Francois Moreau, and Jean Salem, 163–180. Paris: Publications de la Sorbonne.

Brodrick, Michael. 2015. *The Ethics of Detachment in Santayana's Philosophy*. London: Palgrave Macmillan.

Flamm, Matthew Caleb. 2002. Santayana and Schopenhauer. *Transactions of the Charles S. Peirce Society* 38 (3): 413–431.

Hessing, Siegfried. 1977. Prologue with Spinozana. In *Speculum Spinozanum 1677–1977*, ed. Siegfried Hessing, 1–64. London: Henley.

Hume, David. (1739) 1995. *Traité de la nature humaine*. Translated by Baranger Philippe and Saltel Philippe. Paris: GF: Flammarion.

Kashap, S. Paul. 1977. Spinoza's Use of 'Idea'. *The Southwestern Journal of Philosophy* 8 (3): 57–70.

Kerr-Lawson, Angus. 2000. Freedom and Free Will in Spinoza and Santayana. *The Journal of Speculative Philosophy* 14 (4): 243–267.

Lovely, Edward W. 2012. *George Santayana's Philosophy of Religion: His Roman Catholic Influences and Phenomenology*. Lanham, MD: Lexington.

Moreno, Daniel. 2015. *Santayana the Philosopher: Philosophy as a Form of Life*. Translated by Charles Padrón. Lewisburg, PA: Bucknell University Press.

Nietzsche, Friedrich. (1967) 1989. *On the Genealogy of Morals*. Translated by Walter Kaufmann and R. J. Hollingdale, and *Ecce Homo*, translated by Walter Kaufmann, edited with Commentary by Walter Kaufmann. New York: Vintage Books.

Rousset, Bernard. 2007. L'image schopenhaurienne du spinozisme: *causa sive ratio cur*. In *Spinoza au XIXe siècle*, ed. André Tosel, Pierre-Francois Moreau, and Jean Salem, 181–191. Paris: Publications de la Sorbonne.

Russell, Bertrand. 1940. The Philosophy of Santayana. In *The Philosophy of George Santayana*, ed. Paul A. Schilpp, 453–474. New York: Tudor.

Schopenhauer, Arthur. 1966. *The World as Will and Idea*. 2 vols. Translated by E. F. J. Payne. New York, NY: Dover.

Serrano, José María Sánchez de León. 2018. The Place of Skepticism in Spinoza's Thought. *History of Philosophy Quarterly* 35 (1): 1–20.

Singer, Irving. 1984–87. *The Nature of Love*. 3 vols. Chicago, IL: University of Chicago Press.

———. 2000. *George Santayana, Literary Philosopher*. New Haven, CT: Yale University Press.

Spinoza, Benedict. 1985. Treatise on the Emendation of the Intellect. In *The Collected Works of Spinoza,* trans. and ed. by Edwin Curley, vol. 1. Princeton, NJ: Princeton University Press.

———. *Ethics.* In *The Collected Works of Spinoza,* trans. and ed. by Edwin Curley, vol. 1. Princeton, NJ: Princeton University Press.

Spiro, Daniel. 2009. Santayana and His "Hero." Lecture Delivered on September 14, 2009 to the Washington Spinoza Society.

Sprigge, Timothy. 1993. *Spinoza and Santayana: Religion without the Supernatural.* Delft, the Netherlands: Eburon.

Swift, Paul A. 2005. *Becoming Nietzsche: Early Reflections on Democritus, Schopenhauer, and Kant.* Lanham, MD: Lexington.

Vaysse, Jean-Marie. 2007. Spinoza dans la problématique de l'idéalisme allemand. In *Spinoza au XIXe siècle,* ed. André Tosel, Pierre-Francois Moreau, and Jean Salem, 65–74. Paris: Publications de la Sorbonne.

Viljanen, Valtteri. 2020. The Young Spinoza on Scepticism, Truth, and Method. *Canadian Journal of Philosophy* 50 (1): 130–142.

Wetlesen, Jon. 1979. *The Sage and The Way: Spinoza's Ethics of Freedom.* Assen: Van Gorcum.

Woodward, Anthony. 1988. *Living in the Eternal: A Study of George Santayana.* Nashville, TN: Vanderbilt University Press.

Yovel, Yirmiyahu. 1989. *Spinoza and Other Heretics.* Princeton, NJ: Princeton University Press.

G. Santayana (*Scepticism and Animal Faith*, 1923) and E. Husserl (*Cartesianische Meditationen*, 1929), Readers of R. Descartes

Daniel Moreno
Translated by Clare Murray

Abbreviations

CM   (*Cartesian Meditations*)
Ideen   (*Ideen zu einer reinen Phänomenologie und phänomenologischen Philosophie*)
SAF   (*Scepticism and Animal Faith*)

Introduction: Santayana and Phenomenology

Much has been written about Jorge/George Santayana's relationship with the Pragmatists and American philosophy in general, as well as his tenuous relationship with Spanish philosophy. Both these relationships bring to light something that is in itself remarkable. Few philosophers share the distinction of featuring prominently in *two* Histories of Philosophy, the American and the

---

D. Moreno (✉)
Department of Philosophy, IES Miguel Servet, Zaragoza, Spain
e-mail: dmoreno@unizar.es

© The Author(s), under exclusive license to Springer Nature Switzerland AG 2024
M. A. Coleman, G. Tiller (eds.), *The Palgrave Companion to George Santayana's Scepticism and Animal Faith*, Palgrave Companions,
https://doi.org/10.1007/978-3-031-46367-9_19

Spanish.[1] This essay, however, belongs to an as yet underexplored interpretative current: Santayana's relationship with European philosophy and phenomenology in particular. Having received his philosophical training not only at the Harvard of William James and Josiah Royce, but also in neo-Kantian Germany, it is noteworthy that Santayana would go on to devote important works to his European contemporaries, Bertrand Russell and Henri Bergson, as well as some important commentaries on Edmund Husserl's *Ideen zu einer reinen Phänomenologie und phänomenologischen Philosophie* 1913.[2] These contributions, however, have not been given the attention they deserve.

As a matter of fact, the secondary literature highlights the overlap between Santayana and Husserl or, more precisely, between Santayana and phenomenology more broadly, as much in terms of method as of essences. José Beltrán Llavador paved the way by setting out, in the first all-encompassing monograph in Spanish, *Celebrar el Mundo: Introducción al Pensar Nómada de George Santayana*, the key texts on Santayana and Husserl's relationship, and by establishing that Santayana had performed "an exercise in translation, whereby the terms used to devise a given construct are translated into another type of conceptual architecture in order to test their structural soundness" (Beltrán Llavador 2002, 48).[3]

In the section "Evidence of a Phenomenological Approach" in the third chapter of his book *George Santayana's Philosophy of Religion: His Roman Catholic Influences and Phenomenology*, Edward W. Lovely gathers references to Santayana's relationship with phenomenology in both the Santayanian secondary literature and in histories of phenomenology, in particular H. Spiegelberg's *The Phenomenological Movement: A Historical Introduction* (1960) (Lovely 2012, 92–97). In fact, Lovely himself acknowledges that his book opens a new interpretative avenue in need of further development (Lovely 2012, xvi). He discerns a certain kinship between Santayana and phenomenology as far as the intuition of essences, the initial radical scepticism, and the somewhat descriptive approach are concerned, although he views Husserlian transcendental idealism as being removed from Santayana's realism, naturalism, or materialism (Lovely 2012, 102–104, 111–112). After comparing Santayana's "Literary Psychology" and Husserl's thoughts on intersubjectivity and experience of the other, he concludes that "Santayana's entire mature philosophical

---

[1] Max H. Fisch included Santayana in *Classic American Philosophers: Peirce, James, Royce, Santayana, Dewey, Whitehead* (1951), and Alfonso López Quintás included him in *Filosofía española contemporánea* (1970). These pioneers were joined by John J. Stuhr, who included Santayana alongside Charles S. Peirce, William James, Josiah Royce, John Dewey, and Herbert Mead in *Classical American Philosophy: Essential Readings and Interpretative Essays* (1987), and José Luis Abellán, who included Santayana in the monumental *Historia crítica del pensamiento español* (1989). More recently, Professor Manuel Garrido gave him a place of honor in *El legado filosófico y científico del siglo XX* (2007) and, together with Miguel de Unamuno and José Ortega y Gasset, in *El legado filosófico español e hispanoamericano del siglo XX* (2009).

[2] Cf. *The Philosophy of M. Henri Bergson* and *The Philosophy of Mr. Bertrand Russell* (*WD*, 58–109, 110–154); *Postscript* (Santayana 1927, 171–174).

[3] See also Beltrán Llavador (2002), 178–180.

project may be considered an unstructured phenomenology, and more specifically, a phenomenology of the spirit. If we consider *Realms of Being* to be, at its core, not a descriptive psychology, but a description of the conflict in the human spirit between fact and illusion, intuition and absolute apprehension and the work of the imagination vs. the truth of nature then such a broad categorical term may be appropriate" (Lovely 2012, 123–124).

Katarzyna Kremplewska's recent book *Life as Insinuation. George Santayana's Hermeneutics of Finite Life and Human Self* has shed new light on this issue. Professor Kremplewska draws a comparison between the role of the *self* as an agent, as a centre of power, decisions, and will in both Santayana and Husserl, and finds Husserl's transcendental *ego*, while logical-ontological, to be closer to a strong conception of the self than Santayana's interpretation, which is materialistic, psychologistic, and, as such, more fragile. Kremplewska does, however, acknowledge that, unlike other materialists, Santayana never completely renounces the important role of the self, as either psyche or spirit (Kremplewska 2019, 13–16, 37–38). Indeed, reductive materialism, upon discovering that the mind is nothing more than the brain, holds that the mind no longer has theoretical value. Nothing could be further from Santayana's approach.

Parallels between Santayana and Husserl

Thanks to the critical edition of Santayana's letters we can pinpoint exactly when Santayana began to read the Husserlian *Ideen*, in its second 1922 edition. In a letter of March 17, 1927, to his friend and philosopher Charles A. Strong, he says that, having rewritten *The Realm of Essence*, he means to add an appendix on those thinkers who have themselves recently written about essence: R. Guénon, A. N. Whitehead, and E. Husserl. He declares that Husserl "is wonderfully coincident with my notions, although approached from the psychological side" (*LGS*, 3:323). And in a letter dated April 12 of the same year, he mentions what their main connection was: "When an entity is put in parenthis, it is no longer viewed in external relations, but as a framed picture: i.e. as an essence" (*LGS*, 3:327).

Indeed, Husserl, in *Ideen zu einer reinen Phänomenologie und phänomenologischen Philosophie*, that is, his presentation of the phenomenological method—a method that marked an epoch—and of phenomenology as a system—a system heralded in this book but that never saw the light of day—literally defines *phenomenology* as the science of essences: *phainomenon*, what is manifested; *logos*, knowledge. *Phenomenology*, therefore, literally means science or knowledge about what is manifested, that is to say, about essences. For, like Santayana, Husserl does not understand essence in the sense of Aristotelian second substance—*x* is the essence of *y*—but in the Platonic sense of *eidos*, the aspect, that which is seen. In fact, before including Husserl's quotations on essence in his 1927 "Postscript," Santayana provides his own definition of *essence*: "an essence, far from being an abstraction from a thing, is the whole of that thing as it ever can be directly given, or spiritually possessed" (*RE*, 173).

As such, both Husserl and Santayana are in agreement in emphasizing the immaterial and incorruptible nature of essences, as opposed to the material and changeable nature of the objects that make up the world around us. In reading *Ideen*, Santayana also notices the parallel between the Husserlian *epoché* and the suspension of animal faith he had discussed in *Scepticism and Animal Faith* (1923):

> All the emphasis falls on the word *pure*; objects, in order to enter the realm of this phenomenology, must be thoroughly *purified*. This purification consists in reducing the object to its intrinsic and evident character, disregarding all question of its existence or non-existence, or of its locus in nature; or, in my language, it consists in suspending animal faith, and living instead contemplatively, in the full intuition of some essence. (Santayana 1927, 172–173)

At this point we bid a brief farewell to agreement between the two authors, as Santayana raises two objections to Husserl in his "Postcript"—somewhat unfairly, as we shall see later: (1) for being overly interested in emphasizing the cognoscitive role of the essences, thus forgetting the merely *possible* essences; and (2) for assuming that intuition extends to all essences. Moreover, by understanding Husserlian transcendental idealism as a variation of Berkeley's idealism—an interpretation favoured by many but dismissed out of hand by Husserl[4]—Santayana supposes that the mind would remain, in Husserl's eyes, isolated within itself, since Husserl would have denied that external reality is an ontological entity. According to Santayana, therefore, Husserl would be unable to ask the question typical of all naturalists: "to look for the genesis and meaning of immediate experience in the material and animal world, where a malicious transcendentalism, one that isolates mind in mind, cannot consistently look for them" (*RE*, 174). Santayana, being a naturalist, does pose this question and answers it from the perspective of his own particular materialism. But Husserl's was a different question: he does not seek the genesis of the immediate in the material world, but the aprioric presuppositions of all immediate experience. Husserl is no naturalist but a transcendentalist.

The fact that Santayana's and Husserl's philosophical paths did not actually cross until the spring of 1927 further underscores the uncanny parallels in aspects of their respective earlier intellectual journeys. Born Edmund Husserl in 1859 in the Moravian town of Prostejov, and schooled in F. Brentano's Aristotelianism, his training as a mathematician and logician drew him to Plato

---

[4] "If anyone reading our statements objects that they mean changing all the world into a subjective illusion and committing onself to a 'Berkeleyan idealism,' we can only answer that he has not seized upon the *sense* of those statements. They take nothing away from the fully valid being of the world as the all of realities, just as nothing is taken away from the fully valid geometrical being of the square by denying that the square is round (a denial admittedly based, in this case, on what is immediately obvious)" (Husserl 1983, 129).

and placed him on the fringes of modern philosophy. Jorge Santayana was born in 1863 in Madrid and trained in the pragmatism of W. James. Against the grain of contemporary philosophical thought, he turned to the Greeks, and Aristotle in particular, who were omnipresent in his early philosophical system, *The Life of Reason* (1905–1906). As a poet, he had always felt a natural affinity with Plato. As contemporaries of the cultural realm of positivism, both Husserl and Santayana proved to be internal critics, more authentic positivists in a sense, since they tackled fields that scientific positivism brushed all too blithely aside.

However, Husserl and Santayana hailed from different philosophical traditions, Kantism and pragmatist naturalism, respectively. Therefore, as we shall see later, after finding some common ground around essence and how to attain it, their paths once again diverged: one towards Husserlism as a *sui generis* unfinished phenomenology and the other towards Santayanism as Platonic materialism. And curiously enough, neither thinker has a strict philosophical following. In Husserl's case, this is because his many followers shone in their own right upon distancing themselves from the master, and in Santayana's, because his followers are not just first-rate philosophers, but his "ambassadors," to borrow the term coined by Matthew Flamm for Herman Saatkamp Jr., a leading modern-day Santayanian scholar.[5]

To illustrate the pertinent parallels between Husserl and Santayana, I should like to draw attention to something on which the two thinkers agree, and which is by no means trivial. Santayana and Husserl were well aware of philosophy's great problem of the time, especially after it emerged as an academic discipline set apart from other branches of knowledge as a defence against the rise of positivism. With positivism having made sciences of many questions that, since Greece, had fallen under the broad umbrella of philosophy, seen as total wisdom—or, to use Descartes' terminology, philosophy as *mathesis universalis*—ontological, gnoseological, ethical, logical, and aesthetic matters became, in turn, a *sui generis* academic discipline, philosophy in the narrower sense of the term. This was a new meaning for the public at large to get to grips with and accounts for the growth of a new publishing niche over the last hundred years: books entitled "What is philosophy?" which, as it happens, all seem to describe quite different disciplines. This exacerbated a longstanding problem: the mutual incomprehensibility of different philosophies.

It is not without irony that Husserl, alluding to the fashion for philosophy congresses, wonders in *Cartesianische Meditationen*: "But how could actual study and actual collaboration be possible, where there are so many philosophers and almost equally many philosophies? To be sure, we still have philosophical congresses. The philosophers meet but, unfortunately, not the philosophies" (*CM*, 5). Meanwhile, in May 1908, Santayana was thinking of attending the Third International Congress to be held from August 31 to

---

[5] Cf. Flamm (2021).

September 5 in Heidelberg.[6] In the end he did not go because, as he wrote in a letter from Avila on August 8 to his friend Albert von Westenholz: "In my talks with the philosophers, and especially with [Charles A.] Strong, I have seen that my project of going to the Congress at Heidelberg was strange and foolish. I can hardly understand how I came to entertain it seriously. It would be to add one to a gathering of very ugly men talking at cross-purposes about subjects on which they are, for the most part, as ignorant as the rest of the world" (Santayana 2021, 230). A glance at the dates shows that Santayana and Husserl could easily have met at the Heidelberg congress, but they did not.

Faced with this mutual incomprehensibility of philosophies, we know that, taking his cue from Descartes, Husserl proposed a strict science of absolute knowledge, namely phenomenology, to be accepted by all. Santayana, on the other hand, accepting that all philosophical systems are individual elaborations that treat merely partial knowledge as if it were complete, dismisses this option, so dear to Husserl, out of hand: "of comprehensive synthesis; a speculation so evenly inspired and broadly based that it should report the system or the medley of known things without twisting any of them" (Santayana 1915, 563), and prefers something more modest: choosing sincerity over the search for omniscience and confessing "that a system of philosophy is a personal work of art which gives a specious unity to some chance vista in the cosmic labyrinth" (Santayana 1915, 564). As we can see, Husserl and Santayana are on the same page in their diagnosis of what ails philosophy, but differ in their choice of remedy. And as is well known, Husserl's approach was to no avail. Indeed, not only did phenomenology not become his hoped-for *strict science*, but it also spawned a whole host of phenomenological approaches, quite the "movement," as the title of Spiegelberg's aforementioned volume suggests. Santayana, however, did achieve his goal, no doubt because it was far more modest: to complete *his own* philosophical system and present it as one option among countless others. It was arguably the most all-encompassing philosophical system of the twentieth century, comprising *Realms of Being* (1927–1942), *The Idea of Christ in the Gospels* (1946), and *Dominations and Powers* (1951). It was a philosophy that dealt with essence, matter, truth, and spiritual life as well as including a philosophy of religion, Catholicism in particular, without shying away from the thorny questions of freedom, society, and government.

HUSSERL AND SANTAYANA AS READERS OF DESCARTES

However, the most significant parallel between Santayana and Husserl lies in their common endeavour of revisiting Descartes in a bid to rescue Cartesianism from the impasse into which it had fallen after morphing into the various

---

[6]The congress was attended by three hundred philosophers, among them: W. Windelband, J. Royce, Xavier Léon, B. Croce, É. Boutroux, and H. Münsterberg. Germany was the most represented country and the main topics were logic, epistemology, history of philosophy, ethics, and politics; less coverage was given to aesthetics and the philosophy of religion (cf. Fullerton 1908). Compare this with today's world congresses.

currents of idealism. While as a scientist Descartes was far from being trapped in his methodological scepticism,[7] he certainly prioritized the theory of knowledge over ontology, leading philosophers to regard knowledge as the knowledge of ideas and to believe that reality itself was unknowable. Well, following in Descartes' own footsteps, both Santayana and Husserl showed that this was far from self-evident. It was to this subject that Santayana dedicated his 1923 book *Scepticism and Animal Faith* (*SAF*), and it was the *leitmotiv* of the lectures that Husserl gave, in German, at the Sorbonne in February 1929, entitled *Cartesianische Meditationen* (*CM*): four "Cartesian" meditations[8] in which Husserl embarked on the ambitious task of summarizing—and reformulating,[9] as was his wont—the phenomenological method and science unveiled in *Ideen*. Both works, incidentally, are presented as "Introductions": "to a System of Philosophy," in Santayana's case, and "to Phenomenology," in Husserl's. Once again, we see here some similarity in their diagnoses of the philosophical problems, but very different presuppositions and inferences drawn by the two philosophers, as were their later philosophical paths.

Although, as Santayana says, "A philosopher is compelled to follow the maxim of epic poets and to plunge *in media res*" (*SAF*, 1), he is willing to trace the path of scepticism towards the evidence set in motion by Descartes and proposes the intellectual exercise of pushing "scepticism as far as I logically can, and endeavour to clear my mind of illusion, even at the price of intellectual suicide" (*SAF*, 10). Husserl, likewise, who had posited "Back to the things themselves" as a way around post-Cartesian paradoxes, proposes: "Must not the demand for a philosophy aiming at the ultimate conceivable freedom from prejudice, shaping itself with actual autonomy according to ultimate evidences it has itself produced, and therefore absolutely self-responsible—must not this demand, instead of being excessive, be part of the fundamental sense of genuine philosophy?" (*CM*, 6).

Husserl accepts the Cartesian criticisms of sensitive experience and the being of the world insofar as they are not absolutely self-evident. He also accepts the *ego* of the pure *cogitationes*, recognizing it as "a kind of solipsistic philosophizing" (*CM*, 3) that goes "from naïve Objectivism to transcendental subjectivism" (*CM*, 4), although what most interests him is the Cartesian quest for a

---

[7] Cf. Moreno (2017).
[8] These four meditations were not published until 1931, in the French translation, *Méditations cartésiennes*. For this edition, the famous, and lengthy, "Fifth Meditation" was added, where Husserl defends himself against solipsistic criticism by explaining—rightly, in my opinion—that only a cursory reader could have taken his transcendental idealism to be Berkeleyan idealism.
[9] A comparison of Husserl's *Ideen* and later *Cartesianische Meditationen* reveals two reformulations: (1) In *CM* phenomenology is no longer defined as the science of essences, since Husserl uses *essence* in its Aristotelian sense; hence the terms *eidos* (pure eidetic phenomenology, eidetic analysis), *cogitationes*, and *cogitatum qua cogitatum* come to the fore; (2) *CM* constantly alludes to the *correlate* between the transcendental-eidetic sphere and the empirical-factual sphere both in the mind and in the world, including therein the human being as a psycho-physical, social, and cultural entity, which is never called into question. In this way, *CM* insists on distancing itself from Berkeleyan idealism by never overlooking the empirical-factual sphere.

foundation for science: "Let the idea guiding our meditations be at first the Cartesian idea of a science that shall be established as radically genuine, ultimately an all-embracing science" (*CM*, 7). Santayana, meanwhile, begins by adopting the pre-philosophical standpoint. From there, and also in a very Cartesian manner, he questions different beliefs, because they are not absolutely evident: religious beliefs, history, inductive science, time, and romantic solipsism—"in which the self making up the universe is a moral person endowed with memory and vanity" (*SAF*, 13). In this way, he arrives at the *solipsism of the present moment*, where "all his [the sceptic's] heroic efforts are concentrated on *not* asserting and *not* implying anything, but simply noticing what he finds" (*SAF*, p 16). If, therefore, our quest is total evidence, in this solipsism of the present moment there is neither time, nor doubt, nor anguish, nor self; such a state of concentration is, in reality, impossible to achieve completely, beyond the *sensation* of reaching it for a few seconds, however long that may seem.

Santayana picked the Cartesian "ego cogito, ego sum" apart with a fine-tooth comb, taking matters several steps beyond where Descartes' own scepticism ended. Santayana's ultimate scepticism *discards* the affirmation that any self can be a member of the human family existing in the world; it also *discards* the subject-object relationship, since in the face of doubt the only indubitable thing in the thought is the thought itself, single, absolutely unconditioned, and groundless; beneath the supposed analytic-logical *necessity* of the *cogito-cogitationes* relationship, Santayana uncovers the echo of a biological necessity: the organized body capable of detecting stimuli and the stimuli necessary for all experience. Transcendentalism is thus accused of the temptation "to assign a metaphysical status and logical necessity to a merely material fact" (*SAF*, 23). Husserl, meanwhile, accepts the principle of transcendentalism of confining oneself only to what comes from experience: "It is plain that I, as someone beginning philosophically, since I am striving toward the presumptive end, genuine science, must neither make nor go on accepting any judgment as scientific *that I have not derived from evidence*, from 'experiences' in which the affairs and affair-complexes in question are present to me as '*they themselves*'" (*CM*, 13). This principle compels him to confine himself to the *ego cogito* and not to affirm the existence of the world or of other selves or of the past, which is not to say that they are nothing: "Here too the philosophically reflective Ego's abstention from position-takings, his depriving them of acceptance, does not signify their disappearance from his field of experience" (*CM*, 20). Husserl, therefore, would not be compelled, as Santayana presupposes, to linger in the solipsism of the present moment. The phenomenological reduction treats everything as mere phenomena, not as pure nothingness, but as the *cogitatum* of a *cogito*.

So, for Husserl the *cogito-cogitationes* relationship is basic and unquestionable; it cannot be put in brackets. The fact is Santayana also holds that it is impossible to remain in the solipsism of the present moment because the thinking self immediately appears, rendering the suspension of the subject-object relationship untenable. Thus, the two philosophers' positions are not as divergent as one might think. However, Santayana's criticism would not concern Husserl because, for the latter, reducing himself to the given-reality does not imply denying the existent-reality, as Santayana presupposes, but rather looking at it from the phenomenological side, when he writes, "I thereby acquire myself as the pure ego, with the pure stream of my *cogitationes*" (*CM*, 21). This is why I believe that Santayana would support this Husserlian formulation: "In such experience the ego is accessible to himself originaliter. But at any particular time this experience offers only a core that is experienced 'with strict adequacy,' namely the ego's living present (which the grammatical sense of the sentence, *ego cogito*, expresses); while, beyond that, only an indeterminately general presumptive horizon extends, comprising what is strictly non-experienced but necessarily also meant" (*CM*, 22-23). To that *horizon* belong the past, the faculties of the self and all that is proper to the self, and external perception; but that horizon is *adequate*, not *apodictic* (*CM*, 22). The distinction between adequacy and apodicticity is precisely what Santayana finds lacking in Kantian transcendentalism. Husserl is thus spared Santayana's criticism. It seems to me that on this point they would readily agree.

They would also be of one mind regarding the relationship of the *ego cogito* to the world and the natural self: according to Husserl, these do not rely on the *ego cogito* for their *existence*—as a naïve idealist would argue—but for their *meaning* and *validity*—"its whole sense and its existential status" (*CM*, 26-27). Also Santayana, following Democritus, believed that the values that human beings project on reality, which is neutral in itself, come from the human being, not from reality; in his oft-quoted phrase: "We are condemned to live dramatically in a world that is not dramatic" (*RB*, 463).

As for time, Santayana once again considers that a consistent sceptic would have no choice but to deny it since it can, in theory, be doubted—"if things are such only as intuition makes them, every suggestion of a past is false" (*SAF*, 28-29)—although, time immediately makes its presence felt as soon as the sceptic changes the subject, since the temporal horizon is inescapable. Here Husserl would once again evade Santayana's criticism for, although what is given to consciousness can be considered in itself, and is as such static, it will always belong to the stream of consciousness that is constitutive of the transcendental ego, of the life of consciousness: "The *fundamental form* of this universal synthesis, the form that makes all other syntheses of consciousness possible, is the all-embracing *consciousness of internal time*" (*CM*, 43).

This, according to Santayana, is how ultimate scepticism is achieved. The sceptic sees experience—that which is given to intuition or manifested to consciousness—as the only thing that undoubtedly exists. Santayana, nevertheless, believes that the sceptic is the victim of an illusion, since what is given is precisely what does not exist: "existence comports external relations, variable, contingent, and not discoverable in a given being when taken alone: for there is nothing that may not lose its existence, or the existence of which might not be conceivably denied" (*SAF*, 37). In reality what is given *is* but does not *exist*.[10] It is the thinking human animal that ascribes existence to what is given, that transforms what is given into the *appearance* of substance, but in itself what is given is the whole of the surface with no reference to anything *beyond* it. *All* existence, on the other hand, can be doubted. One can even—and Santayana takes it further than Descartes (or is a little more refined in saying so)—doubt the existence of the intuition of doubt: "the existence of his [the sceptic's] own doubt is not given to him then: all that is given is some ambiguity or contradiction in images; and if afterwards he is sure that he has doubted, the sole cogent evidence which that fact can claim lies in the psychological impossibility that, so long as he believes he has doubted, he should not believe it. But he may be wrong in harbouring this belief, and he may rescind it" (*SAF*, 40).

What is given, therefore, belongs to a realm of being that is distinct from facts; in the realm of what is given everything is obvious, in the realm of facts there is room for truth and error. This is something that Husserl also brought to light in *Ideen*: "*Positing of* and, to begin with, intuitive seizing upon, *essences implies not the slightest positing of any individual factual existence; pure eidetic truths contain not the slightest assertion about matters of facts.* And thus not even the most insignificant matter-of-fact truth can be deduced from pure eidetic truths *alone*" (Husserl 1983, 11). And Santayana also asserts this in *Scepticism and Animal Faith*:

> Any motion seen will be but a fixed image of motion. Actual flux and actual existence will have their appropriate and sufficient seat in my thought; I shall conceive and believe, when I reflect on my rapt contemplations, that I have been ruminating, and passing from one to another; but these objects will be only the several essences, the several images or tunes or stories, each always itself, which my mind picks up or invents or reconsiders. (*SAF*, 124)

In *Cartesian Meditations*, Husserl stresses that evidence is attained when the natural attitude, an attitude that regards what is given as existent, is suspended. *Epoché* involves changing one's attitude and adopting a transcendent point of view:

> In *transcendental-phenomenological reflection* we deliver ourselves from this footing, by universal epoché with respect to the being or nonbeing of the world. The experience as thus modified, the *transcendental experience*, consists then, we can say, in our *looking at* and describing the particular transcendentally reduced *cogito*, but without participating, as reflective subjects, in the natural existence-positing that the originally straightforward perception (or other *cogito*) contains or that the Ego, as immersing himself straightforwardly in the world, actually executed. (*CM*, 34)

---

[10] For the different meanings of the important word "is," see Santayana (1924).

Santayana calls this change of attitude, or epoché, *suspending animal faith*, which is the faith that believes in the existence of the surrounding world and the events occurring therein. But such faith can be subject to scepticism. So:

> When by a difficult suspension of judgement I have deprived a given image of all adventitious significance, when it is taken neither for the manifestation of a substance nor for an idea in a mind nor for an event in a world, but simply if a colour for that colour and if music for that music, and if a face for that face, then an immense cognitive certitude comes to compensate me for so much cognitive abstention. My scepticism at last has touched bottom, and my doubt has found honourable rest in the absolutely indubitable. Whatever essence I find and note, that essence and no other is established before me. I cannot be mistaken about it, since I now have no object of intent other than the object of intuition. (*SAF*, 74)

And in Husserl's words:

> Naturally everything depends on strictly preserving the absolute "unprejudicedness" of the description and thereby satisfying the principle of pure evidence, which we laid down in advance. That signifies restriction to the pure data of transcendental reflection, which therefore must be taken precisely as they are given in simple evidence, purely "intuitively," and always kept free from all interpretations that read into them more than is genuinely seen. (*CM*, 36)

Both Santayana and Husserl thus discover the *essence*. And it is around the theory of essence where we find the greatest—but not absolute, of course—philosophical meeting of minds between the two thinkers. Essence, of course, opens up a whole area, a *realm* in Santayanian terms. So the impression Santayana got from reading *Ideen* is not entirely accurate: "the fact that experience must play with terms or essences does not imply that all essences must figure in experience. No doubt the field of *possible* intuition, the range of pure spirit, is infinite, and none other than the realm of essence itself" (*RE*, 174). Indeed, Husserl, in *Cartesian Meditations*, states: "The universal Apriori pertaining to a transcendental ego as such is an eidetic form, which contains an *infinity* of forms, an *infinity* of apriori types of actualities and potentialities of life, along with the objects constitutable in a life as objects actually existing" [italics added] (*CM*, 74).

Santayana and Husserl Part Company

After that fleeting but fundamental meeting of minds, the two thinkers' paths diverged. Santayana tries to restore all that has been cast into doubt: the self, memory, substance, naturalization, and the others. However, the cognitive level of all these important philosophical categories is diminished, since they are now mere objects of belief, not of apodictic evidence. Husserl, however, aspires to complete the mapping of the entire realm of discovered evidence, seeks a science that encompasses the totality of the sciences, and strives to elaborate a complete noetic-noematic description of thought in the Cartesian sense.

All in all, Husserl can be said to describe the process of knowledge as he thinks, whereas Santayana seeks to eliminate thought as he thinks. Husserl arrives at the discovery of the structures that give thought consistency, whereas Santayana reaches nothingness. Following this *via crucis*—quite the exercise in intellectual asceticism—Santayana returns to everyday life more humble and spiritually renewed, while Husserl gains self-confidence as a transcendental *ego* as he works on his a priori map. In this sphere he finds—or thinks he finds—something that can never falter in the knowledge process, the basis of all knowledge, be that scientific or everyday.

Santayana approaches the psychological process of knowledge with an introspective and Cartesian-style method of self-analysis, in order to subject himself to the mental experiment of assuming that everything in doubt is denied. His approach is therefore existential, poetic, and bordering on the mystical. When he discovers essence, he assumes that everything else does not exist, not even essence itself, which only *is*. As we have seen, however, for Husserl the transcendental *ego* can never be placed in doubt, not even as a mental experiment. Santayana writes *Scepticism and Animal Faith* partly as a critical dialogue with Hume's sceptical idealism, which he accuses of *malice* for confusing the *experienced* world with the world just as it is, so that when Hume denies the former—the *experienced* world—he is surreptitiously taken to have also denied the latter—the world just as it is. Hence, when Santayana reads *Ideen*, he concludes that Husserl has also fallen victim to this kind of idealism. Nothing could be further from the truth. In actual fact, for Husserl, bracketing reality, whether of the world or of the psychological self, in no way implies affirming its non-existence.

This is a fundamental nuance. Husserl never imagines that what is subject to reduction does not exist; he always bears in mind the parallel, the *correlate*, between the two sides of the coin: the empirical reality and the transcendental reality. Both are *real*, the first in the sense of the Cartesian *res extensa*, and the second, which would be the Cartesian *res cogitans*, which in turn has two, not easily distinguishable levels: the psychological—both the experiential-personal and the pure psychological—and the transcendental or aprioric. In fact, the areas of most concern to Husserl were the different activities of the mind, the noetic, and the field of objects to which these activities apply, the noematic, both in their intentional effectiveness and in their multiple and inferred horizons. It is these very horizons that tended to remain hidden in analyses prior to Husserlian phenomenology. What Husserl was trying to steer clear of was positivism's purely psychological approach to logic, ethics, and aesthetics. This was a Herculean but unfinished effort—and about which there is no consensus among his followers. In fact, Husserl always considered himself a novice philosopher, albeit a *true* novice, but in order to become a philosopher, that is, a *wise man*, he would need—in his own words—to live to the age of Methuselah (Husserl 1931, 28).

Santayana would then be numbered among the group of readers Husserl criticised for not having understood his transcendental idealism, i.e., the implications of the change of perspective inherent in the ascent from worldly subjectivity to transcendental subjectivity—"anyone who misconstrues the sense and performance of transcendental-phenomenological reduction is still entangled in psychologism; he confounds intentional psychology and transcendental phenomenology, a parallel that arises by virtue of the essential possibility of a change in attitude; he falls a victim to the inconsistency of a transcendental philosophy that stays within the natural realm" (*CM*, 86–87).[11] In conclusion, Husserl would have classified Santayana as a *purely* naturalistic thinker.

Santayana further hit the nail on the head when he used one of his own memorable metaphors for Husserl. Santayana argues that what Husserl does in *Ideen* is akin to the work of seventeenth-century cartographers: after drawing the relevant territory, cartographers would add to the map the instruments they had used: the compass, the sextant, the telescope, even the vessel they had travelled on, and some of the antipodean inhabitants (*RE*, 172). And the curious thing is that Husserl considers himself to be the geographer of "a new continent" (Husserl 1931, 23). In Santayana's view, in other words, Husserl would be more concerned with describing the framework of the mind than with using it for knowledge. In this sense, the criticisms Santayana heaped on Kant would also apply to Husserl because, *grosso modo*, Husserl subscribes to German transcendentalism when he claims to describe apriori knowledge as being necessarily and universally valid, including as a legislator—"we surmise that there is also an apriori science, which confines itself to the realm of pure possibility (pure imaginableness) and, instead of judging about actualities of transcendental being, judges about <its> apriori possibilities and thus at the same time *prescribes rules a priori* for actualities" [italics added] (*CM*, 28). As a reader of Charles Darwin, however, Santayana recognizes that what transcendentalism regards as logically prior is of animal, changing, and contingent origin. Far from being resounding and grandiloquent discoveries, the great expressions of transcendentalism—in this case of phenomenology—would turn out to be, in Santayana's eyes, mere tautologies. In other words, once the specific definitions of the terms used are accepted, the phrase as a whole is obvious—too obvious, one might say:

---

[11] Furthermore, in the "Author's Preface to the English Edition" of *Ideas: General Introduction to Pure Phenomenology*, Husserl referred to those who had fallen into the same trap by alluding, without naming names, to his favourite but already wayward pupil, Martin Heidegger, and describing him as an *anthropologist* (Husserl 1931, 16). Indeed, in his similarly incomplete *Being and Time* (1927), Heidegger had applied the phenomenological method to describe the existential structures of his life as an example of a human being in the world, of his own space and time; whereas Husserl sought to describe the *general* structures of the human mind, those that make humanity *as a whole* distinctive in the universe. Husserl had aspirations for a general science, while Heidegger devoted his efforts to knowledge that was merely regional—and with an expiry date.

Transcendental principles are accordingly only principles of local perspective, the grammar of fancy in this or that natural being quickened to imagination, and striving to understand what it endures and to utter what it deeply wills. The study of transcendental logic ought, therefore, to be one of the most humane, tender, tentative of studies: nothing but sympathetic poetry and insight into the hang and rhythm of various thoughts. It should be the finer part of literary psychology. But such is not the transcendentalism of the absolute transcendentalists. For them the grammar of thought is single and *compulsory*. [italics added] (*SAF*, 301–302)

This demonstrates the unbridgeable gap in the basic assumptions of each philosophy. Therefore, even if Edmund Husserl and Jorge/George Santayana had met at the Third International Congress of Philosophy in Heidelberg, Husserl's prediction would have come true: "The philosophers meet but, unfortunately, not the philosophies" (*CM*, 5).

References

Beltrán Llavador, J. 2002. *Celebrar el mundo. Introducción al pensar nómada de George Santayana*. Valencia, Spain: PUV, Biblioteca Javier Coy d'estudis nord-americans. Segunda edición en 2008.

Flamm, M. 2021. Santayana's Ambassador. *Limbo. Boletín internacional de estudios sobre Santayana* 41: 131–139.

Fullerton, G. 1908. The Meeting of the Third International Congress of Philosophy, at Heidelberg, August 31 to September 5, 1908. *The Journal of Philosophy, Psychology and Scientific Methods* 5 (21,Oct. 8): 573–577.

Husserl, E. 1931. Author Preface to the English Edition. In Edmund Husserl, *Ideas: General Introduction to Pure Phenomenology* (1913), translated by W. R. Boyce Gibson, London: George Allen & Unwin/New York: The Macmillan Company.

———. 1960. *Cartesian Meditations. An Introduction to Phenomenology*. Translated by Dorion Cairns. The Hague/Boston/London: Martinus Nijhoff Publishers.

———. 1983. *Ideas Pertaining to a Pure Phenomenology and to a Phenomenological Philosophy* (1913), translated by F. Kersten. The Hague/Boston/London: Martinus Nijhoff Publishers. This edition does not include the "Author's Preface to the English Edition" (1931).

Kremplewska, K. 2019. *Life as Insinuation. George Santayana's Hermeneutics of Finite Life and Human Self*. Albany, New York: SUNY Press.

Lovely, E.W. 2012. *George Santayana's Philosophy of Religion: His Roman Catholic Influences and Phenomenolopy*. Lanham, MD: Lexington Books.

Moreno, D. 2017. Gnoseología Cartesiana. *Laguna. Revista de filosofía* 40: 51–68.

Santayana, G. 1913. *Winds of Doctrine. Studies in Contemporary Opinion*. New York: Charles Scribner's Sons.

———. 1915. Philosophical Heresy. *The Journal of Philosophy, Psychology and Scientific Methods* 12 (21, Oct. 14): 561–568.

———. 1923. *Scepticism and Animal Faith. Introduction to a System of Philosophy*. New York: Charles Scribner's Sons.

———. 1924. Some Meanings of the Word 'is'. *The Journal of Philosophy, Psychology and Scientific Methods* 21 (14, Jul. 3): 365–377.

---. 1927. *The Realm of Essence. Book First of Realms of Being.* New York: Charles Scribner's Sons.

---. 1942. *Realms of Being. One-Volume Edition, with a New Introduction by the Author.* New York: Charles Scribner's Sons.

---. 2002. *The Letters of George Santayana. Book Three (1921–1927).* Edited by William G. Holzberger. Cambridge, MA: The MIT Press.

---. 2021. *Recently Discovered Letters of George Santayana/ Cartas recién descubiertas de George Santayana*, bilingual edition by Daniel Pinkas, with a Presentation by José Beltrán, and translated by Daniel Moreno. Valencia, Spain: PUV, Biblioteca Javier Coy d'estudis nord-americans.

Spiegelberg, H. 1960. Excursus: Santayana's Ultimate Scepticism Compared With Husserl's Phenomenological Reduction. In *The Phenomenological Movement: A Historical Introduction*, 2 vols., Springer-Science, vol. I, 138–139.

Hermes as an Interpreter and the Guide to Hades: Re-reading "The Lord Chandos Letter" with Reference to Santayana's *Scepticism and Animal Faith*

Katarzyna Kremplewska

> "It is alarming and yet salutary to notice how near to radical scepticism are the gates of Hades."
> —(*SAF* Triton, 132)

> "I am a sensitive creature surrounded by a universe utterly out of scale with myself: I must, therefore, address it questioningly but trustfully, and it must reply to me in my own terms, in symbols and parables, that only gradually enlarge my childish perceptions."
> —(*SAF* Triton, 171)

Scepticism and Animal Faith in the Context of Its Era

The early twentieth century witnessed the development of a variety of new—often competing with one another—trends in philosophy, which may be considered in the context of radical changes in society and culture, and the corresponding crisis of the nineteenth-century worldview. While some more traditional projects, like Neo-Kantianism, were still thriving, some others, like empiriocriticism, were oriented toward a renewal of philosophy, starting with the rejection of the residues of speculative metaphysics. What was common for the philosophy of *fin de siècle* and the following two or three decades was an

K. Kremplewska (✉)
Institute of Philosophy and Sociology, Polish Academy of Sciences, Warsaw, Poland

© The Author(s), under exclusive license to Springer Nature Switzerland AG 2024
M. A. Coleman, G. Tiller (eds.), *The Palgrave Companion to George Santayana's Scepticism and Animal Faith*, Palgrave Companions, https://doi.org/10.1007/978-3-031-46367-9_20

interest in experience, consciousness, meaning, and language, and an attempt to uncover their deeper "structure." There emerged some analytical projects, strongly inspired by scientific methods, such as logical positivism on the one hand and phenomenology on the other. The above examples are representative but by no means exhaust the variety of the then existing or emerging trends. Psychoanalysis, Bergson's philosophy of life, and American pragmatism formed alternatives to those more formalistic and analytically oriented schools. The influence of the bustling philosophical life of the era extended beyond philosophical circles, over intellectual and artistic life in general. Among the young writers and poets who sought inspiration there one may list Marcel Proust, Robert Musil, or Hugo von Hofmannsthal.

In 1927, five years after Wittgenstein's *Tractatus Logico-Philosophicus* was published, Heidegger's project of fundamental ontology in *Being and Time* saw daylight. In the background of the continuing intellectual ferment, George Santayana published *Scepticism in Animal Faith* (1923). The book, perhaps more than any other of Santayana's works, inscribed itself into the debates of its time.

One of the main claims of the book is that a thorough epistemological scepticism (which involves applying Descartes' method unwaveringly to the point of its ultimate consequences) is an untenable and unlivable position. The experiment starts with an assumption that anything worthy of the name of knowledge must pass the test of indubitability and proceeds by discounting all the beliefs that fail to withstand this test. Employing such rigorous criteria in practice leads to the suspension of one's spontaneously held convictions. The only thing saved from doubt is the presence of a datum, a "something-now" given to consciousness. Nothing further can be inferred about it and no existence ascribed to it. We are left mute, helpless as it were, immersed in the present landscape of consciousness, which signifies nothing—a position called *solipsism of the present moment* (SOPM). In practice, ultimate scepticism equals not only the rejection of common sense and suspension of judgment (all discourse indeed is recognized as untrustworthy) but also the suspension of symbolization and, hence, meaning.

> It will lead me to deny existence to any datum, whatever it may be; and as the datum, by hypothesis, is the whole of what solicits my attention at any moment, I shall deny the existence of everything, and abolish that category of thought altogether.... Belief in the existence of anything, including myself, is something radically incapable of proof, and resting, like all belief, on some irrational persuasion or prompting of life. (*SAF* Triton, 35)[1]

Showing the consequences of scepticism, Santayana opposes two uses of the term "knowledge": as belonging to ordinary life practices and as a sceptical

---

[1] Disclosing the consequences of scepticism undermines the bedrock of what is called foundationalist rationalism.

philosopher's tool. This opposition is not unrelated to his distinction of existence and essence. Humans have a privileged, intuitive, and immediate access to the latter and only a second-hand or mediated awareness of the former. Knowledge of existence runs the risk of error and involves a sort of transcendence—sometimes referred to as "leap" by Santayana—of the given.[2] As for essences, they form a medium more basic, universal, and versatile than language, which is rather a tool, a practical way of making use of the vehicular nature of essences by the discursive animal. Intuition of essences allows for discernment and abstraction. It

> first enables the mind to say something about anything, to think of what is not given, and to be a mind at all. A great use of the discovery of essence, then, is to justify the notions of intelligence and knowledge ... and to show how such transcendence of the actual is possible for the animal mind. (*SAF* Triton, 76)

Scepticism, by demanding of knowledge to be clear and indubitable, is ignorant of the above distinctions, yet an experiment in scepticism reveals them sharply. As Wittgenstein might have written, Santayana writes: "Dialectical difficulties ... are irrelevant to valid knowledge, the terms of which are irrational" (*SAF* Triton, 30). There are some striking resemblances between Santayana and the later Wittgenstein on this point. Both ascribe to traditional philosophy "advocating inapt, unreasonable, illusory, or absurd criteria of justification.... Seeking absolute assurance or transcendent grounding isolates philosophy from the concerns of life" (Lachs and Hodges 2000, 9).[3] But also in its own sphere, scepticism, Santayana notes, implicitly undoes itself. It conveys "a suspicion of error about facts, and to suspect error about facts is to share the enterprise of knowledge, in which facts are presupposed and error is possible" (*SAF* Triton, 13). Furthermore, to "argue, explain, prove [anything], is to believe in mental discourse" (*SAF* Triton, 108), the origins of which, according to Santayana, are irrational.[4]

As stated at the beginning, Santayana's main argument may be interpreted as aiming at displacing scepticism. Yet, this is only part of the picture. His ruminations, far from being limited to a dry philosophical argument, combine

---

[2] From the perspective of consciousness or spirit, one may speak of "the fatality which links the spirit to a material organ so that, in order to reach other things, it is obliged to leap; or rather can never reach other things, because it is tethered to its starting point, except by its intent in leaping, and cannot even discover the stepping stone on which it stands because its whole life is the act of leaping away from it" (*SAF* 148). The said "leap" originates in psychic intent, is the principle of animal faith, and is further manifest in attention, perception, presumption, and knowledge.

[3] As the authors later note, "Sceptics can offer us only alternative uses of words. ... They cannot expose the substructure of meaning, that is, analyze the ordinary sense of ordinary speech" (Lachs and Hodges 2000, 25). In other words, the sceptics try to stage an alternative form of life. One may say that these particular views of Wittgenstein are congruent with Santayana's position.

[4] Discourse or a train of thought originates in psyche's transactions with the environment. It is "a contingent survey of essence, partial, recurrent, and personal, with an arbitrary standing point and an arbitrary direction of progress" (*SAF* 120).

elements of different perspectives—epistemic, existential, phenomenological, psychological, and spiritual. We are presented with a sensitive and careful rendering of the subsequent stages on the path of a genuine sceptic—from criticism of knowledge, through the questioning of the existence of the external world and the reality of time and change, to doubting experience, discourse, and the self-same "I."[5] Consistent scepticism is ultimately rejected as an impracticable attitude but its value—both philosophical and existential—as a *process* and an *experiment* is not thereby denied. On the contrary, an experiment in scepticism is enlightening in that it leads to the distinction of essences, facilitates understanding the nature of consciousness, prompts one to redefine knowledge with regard to life. Furthermore, it reveals its own psychological (and irrational) motivation, which involves the love of security and the fear of error and change. Other than that, it brings to light the affinities between apparently unrelated areas of human activity such as poetry, mysticism, and the experiences and revelations that occur to someone on a sceptical journey. Finally, as a cathartic experience, it may prepare ground for a re-orientation of one's self in the world. This is what happens to Santayana's sceptic, who, armed with the lesson of scepticism, re-establishes his relation with reality on the basis of the promptings of life itself. The renewal involves restoring faith in intuition, experience, memory, discourse, and the self or person endowed with a certain nature or constitution. All these beliefs are preceded by a more primitive and instinctive kind of belief, namely—belief in substance.[6] Scepticism, one is led to conclude, may be harmonized with animal faith, common sense, and habit insofar as its limitations and a possible function in life are understood.

> I may yield to the suasion of instinct, and praise the arts with a humble confidence, without in the least disavowing the most rigorous criticism of knowledge or hypostatizing any data of sense.... It is precisely by *not* yielding to opinion and illusion ... that I aspire to keep my cognitive conscience pure and my practical judgment sane.... [Animal] faith ... takes advantage of that [sceptical] analysis to interpret this volatile experience as all animals do and must, as a set of symbols for existences that cannot enter experience, and which, since they are not elements in knowledge, no analysis of knowledge can touch—they are in another realm of being. (*SAF* Triton, 96–7)

As framed by Matthew Flamm, "Anyone engaging modernity must ... engage scepticism ... as a mode of purgation setting one back to the path of animal faith" (Flamm 2013, 39–44). In its broad, cross-disciplinary approach

---

[5] For a genuine sceptic to maintain that "a self or ego is presupposed in experience by its absolute fiat, is curiously to fail in critical thinking" (*SAF* 25).

[6] Animal watchfulness and alertness express this primary conviction, which is "an implication of action, and a conviction native to hunger, fear, feeding, and fighting" (*SAF* 177). As knowledge accrues, the instinctive belief in substance evolves and "becomes a map in which my body is one of the islets charted: the relations of myself to everything else may be expressed there in their true proportions, and I shall cease to be an egotist" (*SAF* Triton, 185).

to scepticism, where room is made for relating scepticism to sanity, art, and mysticism, *SAF* may be regarded as responsive to the intellectual and moral concerns of the era, and a promising source of reference for a philosophical re-reading of Hugo von Hofmannsthal's canonical piece of modernist prose—"The Lord Chandos Letter." Before I attempt such a reading, let me introduce the reader briefly to the cultural and historical circumstances of Hofmannsthal, which are immensely helpful for understanding his text.

Hofmannsthal and His Circumstances

While many masterpieces of literature have been subject to a philosophical interpretation, Hofmannsthal's *Ein Brief* (1902, in scholarship in English known as the Chandos letter)—"one of the key documents of Modernist movement"[7]—seems to be an obvious candidate for such a reading. A mirror of existential and philosophical concerns of the era, it may also be viewed as a literary rendering of the ancient problem of the tension between mind and reality, the soul and the world. It is said of Hugo von Hofmannsthal (1874–1929) that he was a marvelous child of European literary modernism, a star among the Viennese artists and intellectuals of the *fin de siècle*. His work, comprising poetry, short prose works, essays, dramas, and librettos (the latter two forms of literary expression became dominant in his mature years), reflects both the development of his individual genius and a number of influences that shaped his sensitivity and ideas—from romantic and symbolist poetry to the ideas of Plato, Novalis, Goethe, Schopenhauer, Nietzsche, Darwin, Freud, and Ernst Mach, to name just a few. Perhaps one should mention Calderon de la Barca as well, with whom Hofmannsthal shared the idea of dreaming as a profound form of world experience, which was reflected in a haunting, dream-like quality of disquietude permeating their writings (Kamińska 1984, 17).

This said, Hofmannsthal's style remains unique and, as discussed by Broch and Thomas A. Kovach, related to his personality and life circumstances (Broch 1984; Kovach 2002a). Among the characteristic features of his *oeuvre* one may list charm; a profound ambiguity; a sense of loneliness; a vision of life as a voyage toward some mysterious, mythical depths or a heart of nothingness. An antinomy between life and death, the self and the world, as well as an unceasing longing to recover a lost unity and return to a primordial innocence are the recurring themes in the Viennese writer's works.

Starting at a young age, Hofmannsthal was initiated into the artistic *bohéme* of Vienna at a time when the artist no longer played an orderly public function of serving the society's central values but rather stood outside the society, rebelled against its bourgeois values, and was committed to the creation of what is often called *l'art pour l'art* and considered by scholars a manifestation of a deeper crisis of the Western, modern worldview and moral consciousness.

---

[7] John Banville, Introduction in Hugo von Hofmannsthal, *The Lord Chandos Letter and Other Writings*, trans. Joel Rotenberg (New York: New York Review Books, 2005), x.

In the Austro-Hungarian Empire it converged with a political crisis and a powerful sense of the decline of the monarchy, which constituted the main axis around which Austrian self-understanding or identity was centered. The crown played a unifying function in relation to the whole multinational mosaic of more or less autonomous political units that the Habsburg empire consisted of. However, the conservatism, inertia, and isolation of the crown turned the Austrian state into a "specterlike skeleton of a theory in which no one any longer believed ... the state of vacuum" (Broch 1984, 72). Still, the emperor remained a "living point of orientation" for the aestheticizing middle class of Vienna with its cosmopolitan sympathies (Broch 1984, 80). According to Broch's theory of the relation between the ethical, the political, and the aesthetic dimensions of common life, there is an affinity between the first and the second and they are both marked by hostility toward the third. Accordingly, the Viennese cultural life happened to exhibit a tendency to depoliticization paralleled by aestheticization and hedonism. Being a decadent community, it was more likely to "follow mystical inclinations than revolutionary ones" (Broch 1984, 80).

Similarly, Claudio Magris sees Hofmannsthal's work as reflecting some features of the decaying Austrian culture at the time of the dissolution of the Habsburg Empire. Among them one may list: escapism, introspectiveness, a sense of exhaustion and fatality leading to a crisis of agency, fear of the disintegration of the self, sensuality and a refined aestheticism, a motive of life as a theater. To an extent aestheticism, which at some points takes the shape of a fascination with the ugly and the ordinary, may be viewed as a means of overcoming the crisis. Hofmannsthal, however, resorts to yet another way of evading the catastrophe, namely the idea of the return to an idealized past, which earned him an opinion of a "*grand-conservateur*" of the Austro-Hungarian civilization (Magris 2019, 331). This longing for retrieving the past may be associated with the myth of the golden age in history, which was followed by other ages in a descending order of perfection, but also with Plato's theory of the pre-existence of the soul and anamnesis. One may also associate it with the idea of a primary mythos and a primeval, universal (divine) language, which resurfaces in Chandos' obsession with meaning. Aleida Assmann recognizes Hofmannsthal as a forerunner of a hieroglyphic "mystique" of modernity—a kind of remedy to the modern disenchantment of the world. Upon this interpretation, Chandos discovers a new, non-alienating "speech"—a way of letting things speak on their own behalf (Assmann 2003, 272–274). This may also be viewed in the context of Hofmannsthal's hope that a revitalized humanism might be a response to the crisis of modern culture and the danger of dehumanization inherent in capitalism and the industrial civilization.

According to Hofmannsthal's biographers, the writer underwent a *metanoia* at the end of the nineteenth and the dawn of the twentieth century, leaving his aesthete's identity behind for a more socially engaged and ethically oriented attitude, manifest in his writings conceived after the Chandos letter. To an extent the text may be viewed as a crypto-testimony of a personal, intellectual, and creative crisis suffered by the twenty-eight-year-old writer in the midst of what was for him—not unlike for Santayana—a cultural and intellectual chaos, which "robbed the soul of the treasure of language, and reduced it to the 'wordless ego'" (Broch 1984, 95). The meaning of this experience of estrangement in Hofmannsthal's case is multilayered, ranging from the social isolation of the poet, "damned to the role of the eternal guest, someone constantly seeking admittance and without a home" (Broch 1984, 105), to the never-ending and multifaceted task of assimilation inherited from his Jewish great-grandfather.[8]

The metaphorical "homelessness" of the young artist brings to the fore the idea that the poet's home is language. It is his familiarity with language that retrieves the world for him, allows him to break through the isolation of his self, and, as Broch might add here, justify his social existence. Hence, the loss of language, or, perhaps, doubt in discourse and estrangement from speech, acquires an almost *apocalyptic* dimension for the poet, in particular when one views the poet's task as Hofmannsthal did.

In my reading I approach the Chandos letter as a fictional, epistolary confession—though clearly containing an element of a personal testimony[9]—of a profound, life-changing experience of a cognitive and existential crisis, which is at once (a) personal, (b) culture- and history-specific, and (c) in some measure existentially and philosophically universal. I analyze the stages of Chandos' crisis through the lens of the experiment in radical scepticism described by Santayana. This brings me to a conclusion that—to put it in most general terms—Chandos is undergoing a crisis of faith, including what Santayana calls "animal faith," leading to a temporary cognitive impairment, which is part of an overall existential crisis. The *metanoia* ultimately leads to a reorientation of the self and a renewal of the contract with life in response to the summons of life itself, in which Chandos is similar to Santayana's sceptic, who finds scepticism unlivable yet precious as an experience and a lesson. Along the path I shed light on a number of points relevant for both authors, such as the relation between scepticism, mysticism and poetry, faith and meaning, silence and suffering. I hope to offer new interpretive possibilities in regard to the Chandos letter as well as demonstrate—through *praxis*—a considerable hermeneutic potential of Santayana's elaboration on scepticism.

Nosce te Ipsum

It is kind of you, dear friend, to ignore my silence of two years and write to me as you have done. To express your concern about me, your disquiet at what you see as the mental paralysis into which I have fallen ... and express your belief that I

---

[8] The issue was never problematized by the writer himself, yet, according to Broch, should not be ignored by an inquisitive reader. "Even after an assimilation achieved through the course of several generations, a 'nobly isolated' externality is held onto" (Broch 1984, 90).

[9] Scholars today agree as to the presence of an autobiographic layer in the Chandos letter, even if it is by no means the only or the most important one.

need medicine not merely to cure my illness but to heighten my awareness of my inner state. (Hofmannsthal 2005, 117)

With these words, Lord Chandos, a young writer and a *porte-parole* of Hofmannsthal himself, begins his epistolary confession, dated 22 August 1603, to a friend, the philosopher, Francis Bacon. He has recently experienced a period of despair and personal disintegration, which has led him to an uncertainty about his own identity—"I hardly know if I am still the person your precious letter is addressing." But who is that person or that part of his former self Chandos feels detached from? As it turns out, it is an eloquent writer, a master of language and the author of "*The New Paris, The Dream of Daphne ...* those pastorals, tottering under the weight of their grand words." Those works, one learns, had impressed many a member of high society and brought fame to the talented young poet. Now, there remains only an ironic distance from the pompous style, the grandeur of those texts and the author's former self, which was constructed in the likeness of an abstract "edifice of Latin prose" (Hofmannsthal 2005, 117).

Formerly infatuated with rhetoric—so "overvalued" by his contemporaries—he now finds it vacuous and incapable of "getting at the heart of things" (Hofmannsthal 2005, 118). Likewise, his former narrative project of himself, which had laid a wager on eloquence and erudition, now seems artificial and egotistic, based on a naïvely idealistic and anthropocentric view of reality. It was thus bound to collapse under the wave of what I interpret to be an overwhelming and profound scepticism. This kind of experience, in contrast to the deliberate, philosophical exercise in scepticism offered by Santayana, seems to be a spontaneous, subterranean process. Both, however, consist of a few phases, share a number of features, and are thoroughly transformative in relation to the selves and worldviews of their subjects.

When writing the letter, Chandos feels separated both from his past works and the future ones, those that he once intended to write. The message from his friend has evoked some memories of the time spent together, when he was still playing with a vision of his future literary career. He recalls the experience of an all-encompassing unity, a perfect blending of the material and spiritual dimensions of reality and a sense of a spontaneous flow of creativity. He felt he possessed the knowledge (familiarity with the greatest texts of the intellectual tradition of the West, the Latin tradition in particular) and the ability to convey—through literature—a deeper, eternal order of things. Now this experience is but an oddly extravagant and lifeless memory, and—if it wasn't for his friend—he might as well doubt its reality.

In Santayana's vocabulary memory is a sort of "inverted expectation," where expectation—as manifest in intent—is a mode of being proper to the human psyche. Both memory and expectation (an intentional orientation toward the future) may be described as *modi* of an unceasing imaginative transcending of any here-and-now. This activity involves temporal synthesis, which manifests itself materially in the formation of habits and imaginatively as a narrative and a projection. Thus, an individual, conscious life, acting intelligently in a unified field of action, generates a more or less coherent self-narrative and a vision of a future. An important "structural" component of this vital dynamics is what Santayana calls *animal faith*—a number of tacit, instinctively made assumptions, such as belief in existence, substance, experience, time, and a continuous self. It is this sort of faith—a tool of survival indeed—that serves as a bedrock for thinking, discourse, knowledge, the very idea of "meaning," and anchors them in physical life. According to my reading of Santayana's theory of knowledge, symbols themselves, the vehicles of meaning, are called to life by animal faith and are sustained in their function by psychic intent, even though spiritual (conscious) mediation is indispensable in this process. Even in abstract thinking, say in mathematics, there is faith involved, that is faith in the possibility of symbolization and designation.[10]

The deconstruction of some of these assumptions, being part of scepticism, leads to the suspension of some others, and, ultimately, to the loosening or unmaking of this vital structure. *Underneath Chandos' doubts in memory, the possibility of planning, the continuity of his self and the relevance of language to reality there rests, I suggest, the loosening of the described by Santayana "fideistic" underpinning of conscious life, or, in other words, the crisis of faith.* Its dramatism is due to the fact that Chandos, unlike the deliberate, philosophical sceptic described by Santayana, is subject to an uncontrolled wave of scepticism. Still, he does not venture the final step of radical scepticism as described in *SAF*, namely denying existence to anything at all, which would reduce the mind to the *solipsism of the present moment* (SOPM).

According to Santayana, scepticism (a) feeds on high epistemological demands, (b) is itself a form of belief because it assumes the possibility of error, and (c) has a depth that tends to be proportional to the degree of dogmatism at the point of departure. The case of Chandos seems to confirm—loosely, as we are talking about a literary text and not a philosophical treatise—these remarks. Chandos' reflection on his former literary career, worldview, and state of mind illuminates the contrast between the previous apex and the later nadir. There is a certain disbelief in his voice about how hubristic he used to be. He was an idealistic projection of himself. Now he is exposing himself in front of his friend as a "freak," perhaps someone suffering from "a mental illness" (Hofmannsthal 2005, 118). "What is man," he asks, disillusioned, "that he conceives projects?" Those past projects, he confesses, now "dance before me like miserable mosquitoes on a dim wall no longer illuminated by the bright sun" (Hofmannsthal 2005, 119). These words may easily be read as an allusion to Plato's cave. Chandos woke up from a state of delusion and now is summarizing the bygone Platonic phase in his artistic and personal trajectory, the backbone of which was an idea of an eternal, symbolic unity of all reality and of

---

[10] "Whereas intuition, which reveals an essence directly, is not knowledge, because it has no ulterior object, the designation of some essence by some sign does convey knowledge ... of what that essence was" (*SAF* 151).

one's own privileged, cognitive position in it. The tacit, philosophical vision of reality he used to enjoy may be described as essentialist, cosmic, and anthropocentric at once. It was also eclectic, saturated with Platonic and Neoplatonic elements characteristic of the Renaissance worldview (which is understandable given the date of the fictional letter) as well as epistemological orientation and some traces of the encyclopedic enterprise of the Enlightenment (here Francis Bacon, the addressee of the letter, is a possible inspiration). One also finds in it a romantic, Faustian articulation of will and yearning for omnipotence—"I wanted. I wanted all sorts of other things" (Hofmannsthal 2005, 119). Chandos thought of himself primarily as a mind, a genius perhaps, and intended to write an all-encompassing book of timeless wisdom, the project of which became *spiritus movens* in his life. All this brings me back to a remark by Santayana that "the more perfect [and insulated] the dogmatism, the more insecure" (*SAF* Triton, 13). The idealistic edifice raised by Chandos was threatened by scepticism in a highest degree.

Insofar as Chandos may be viewed as representative of Hofmannsthal, it is interesting to see what were some of the latter's views on reality, cognition, language, and the role of the writer, the poet in particular. According to both Broch and Magris, he viewed reality as a manifestation of a deeper, symbolic realm—"the symbolic come to life"[11]—and was engaged in a life-long pursuit of the primary *mythos*, a divine matrix of reality or *Ursprache* of sorts. The poet's mission was to convey the essence of reality, which could be achieved through a "poeticizing dream"—a state, when the poet's imagination and the symbolic range of his language are confronted with the external world, and, more precisely, with the primary, virginal symbolism that shines through this world. During this interaction another symbolic level is being generated and "the task of poetry ... [which is] constant recreation of the world" is fulfilled (Broch 1984, 108). Creative writing thus understood engages the writer's soul in its entirety and involves a solemn cognitive commitment on his part while making him an accomplice of the truth itself. In a distant correspondence to Heidegger's view of poetry as disclosing Being, here poetry reveals by way of innovative creation and becomes "an ethical ritual," "the unveiling of the essential symbol" (Broch 1984, 108). Broch, if I understand him correctly, applies to art a specific understanding of ethicality in terms of *asserting the essential* or *genuinely revealing*, which, by the way, seems to me to be an interesting way of establishing a tripartite relation between the ontological, the aesthetic, and the ethical.[12]

---

[11] Poetry as such is defined here as "an interplay between external and linguistic reality" (Broch 1984, 108).

[12] One finds in Broch an important conclusion: "Artistic *art pour l'art* is at the same time always ethical *art pour l'art*, so that the development of art (not its nonexistent progress) at the same time serves ethical progress and participates in the mystical hope that it may exist and ultimately overcome global disaster. Without this secret faith, the 'internal' ethics of art, its demand for an absolute union with reality and its antipathy to every 'purpose,' of whatever nature or however socially-ethically appealing, cannot be explained" (Broch 1984, 183).

The mission of the poet, as described above, is particularly challenging in the view of reality as an infinite, abysmal "interpretability." Indeed, reality poses a threat of an infinite chain of significations, masks dropping only to reveal other masks, a risk of hermeneutic nothingness or incomprehensibility. The infinity of reality corresponds to the potential inexhaustibility of the human spirit (as reflected, for example, in the evolution of culture); the individual human life, however, is embodied and finite, and so is (at least in one sense) a concrete work of art. If the poet, whose medium of expression and home is language, becomes particularly sensitive to the restrictive impact that cognitive schemata and language—as part of internalized, cultural symbolism—exert on his imagination and hermeneutic capacity, he may desire "to wrestle … [himself] away from language" (Broch 1984, 113).

The poet thus committed to the revelatory function of art faces two major obstacles—the seclusion of the self, with its egotistic and narcissistic tendencies, as well as the conventionality, conservatism, and hence, restrictiveness of thought and language. A third obstacle, an external one, mentioned by Broch, is the "value vacuum" of a decadent culture. However, one may regard the said vacuum, as I am inclined to do, as triggering rather than inhibiting the creation of a new language that the poet is expected to be capable of. This may be particularly true about Hofmannsthal's poetic "metaphysics," where the reality of conventional symbols is founded on a mysterious, deeper well of a primal vocabulary. It is true that the presence of such an irrational, primordial dimension may pose a danger in an era of "value vacuum," but at the same time it may offer an opportunity for a genuine revelation in the work of an artist—perhaps a forerunner of a moral reorganization on a larger scale.

Before passing to the next section let me suggest that there is a tension between the great project of reconstructing a universal human wisdom pursued by Chandos before the crisis and another aim that he has set for his art, namely to let things speak for themselves. The latter aim requires—except for minimizing the influence of the ego and subjectivism[13]—being in the present and restricting the burden of the past, which stands in contradiction to the former, spiritual vision anchored in eternity. In the case of the former what is at stake is gathering and synthesis, in the latter—lived experience. In the mental landscape of Chandos before the crisis (and some of Hofmannsthal's works in general) time seems to be relativized to a mythical past, which is raised to the status of timelessness; the present is fallible and, metaphorically speaking, corrupt (even though it may be ennobled through poetic innovation); and the future is reduced either to an idealized projection or an apocalyptic premonition. This temporal specificity has a cultural context too—it is reinforced by the already mentioned premonition of a decline in the Austrian culture in Hofmannsthal's era.

The crisis begins when Chandos realizes the artificiality, vanity, and relativity of his previous project. It was a combination of linguistic confidence, cultural competence, and a commitment to a set of ideas, which—as Santayana would

---

[13] It is assumed that "confession is nothing, knowledge is all" (Broch 1984, 118).

likely say—formed a worldview, which, while it was very specific, aspired to universality. It depended to a large degree on the assumptions that there exists a meaningful unity of human culture, that culture may be a vehicle for an in-depth understanding of nature (or reality), and matter has no secrets to the spirit. In a striking semblance to the ideas contained in Novalis' canonical work *Novices of Sais*, Chandos wrote: "everywhere I was in the midst of it…. At other times I had the intuition that everything was symbolism and every creature a key to all others, and I felt I … could take hold of each" (Hofmannsthal 2005, 120). The desire for an in-depth understanding of reality blended in him with his collector's passion, both supported by a conviction that an ultimate knowledge about reality was possible.[14] Reality was assumed to be at bottom a human and ideal reality. Different and contrasting phenomena were perceived as mere differences in the symbolic articulation of a harmonious whole. They were, one might say, swallowed up by generality. Thus, the young artist was committed to a blend of influences that were more likely to inhibit the epiphany that he desired than further it. One of the most striking and illuminating details in the first part of the letter is a remark that the envisaged *opus magnum*, "the work as a whole was to be entitled *Nosce te ipsum*" (Hofmannsthal 2005, 120)![15]

The Crisis

The first symptom of Chandos' crisis is the dissolution of the ideas that used to play a unifying function in relation to the poet's worldview. Religious convictions "have boiled down to a grand allegory … [and] worldly ideas are retreating from me in the same way" (Hofmannsthal 2005, 121). As mentioned previously, I read Chandos' crisis in terms of loss of faith in Santayana's understanding of this term. One may speak here of two kinds of faith—a universal and tacit one, which is a condition of possibility of knowledge, discourse, and intelligent action, and a more or less explicit and ideal one, which co-determines a view of the world and oneself. This latter kind of faith may assume a form of a religious belief or a philosophy of life. Chandos' functioning in the world was strongly anchored in the second type of faith, to the point that he became a projection of himself mediated by the ideas and speech of others, which was reflected in his collecting famous "utterances" and "maxims." The dissolution of faith in his case started with the ideas he consciously enjoyed and then

---

[14] A longer quotation merits evoking here: "I planned to put together a collection of maxims. … My plan here was to assemble the most remarkable utterances which I had collected during my travels in my dealings with the learned men and clever women of our time … and also to combine beautiful classical and Italian aphorisms and reflections … and also to include … festivals and pageants, strange crimes and causes of dementia" (Hofmannsthal 2005, 119).

[15] The formula *Nosce te ipsum* takes us back to the philosophical heritage of, on the one hand, antiquity, and on the other, German romanticism and Novalis' credo that man's highest vocation is knowing, training, transforming, and expanding his self. As such, it illuminates a somewhat chaotic eclecticism in Chandos' worldview, its inner tensions and contradictions.

extended to the deeper, life-sustaining assumptions, like the one about the veridic function of language.

Summarizing his condition, Chandos writes: "I have completely lost the ability to think or speak coherently about anything at all" (Hofmannsthal 2005, 121). This confession makes sense in the light of Santayana's thesis that thought, discourse, and action depend on a number of tacit and ungrounded beliefs. It indicates consequences of a deeper process of the loosening of what I have called the fideistic structure. Except for its hermeneutic function, it also serves as a protective shield, a kind of immunity of the human psyche against the experience of chaos and the fear of death. What is more, from this perspective *scepticism is far more than an exclusive domain of philosophers and does not have to follow a purposive, critical, or deconstructive reasoning. Scepticism* sensu largo *is an existential condition and an existential possibility.*

What scholars call Chandos' "linguistic despair" starts with the loss of confidence when using general and abstract terms, such as "spirit," "soul," and "body," followed by the discovery of the relativity of morals and inability to produce moral judgments—"the abstract words which the tongue must enlist as a matter of course in order to bring out an opinion disintegrated in my mouth like rotten mushrooms." Chandos is amazed by what strikes him as the vacuity of all conventional opinions, "ordinarily offered casually and with the sureness of a sleepwalker" (Hofmannsthal 2005, 121). They seem "as unprovable, as false, as full of holes as could be" (Hofmannsthal 2005, 122). The reality seems to be this: an occasion triggers a reaction (a moral judgment), which is co-determined by habit, convention, and accident. Added to Chandos' growing awareness of the arbitrariness of language (loss of belief in meaning), he is haunted by an impression that people in social situations act like sleepwalkers. Moreover, the suspicion that certain general concepts lack real designates and his growing distrust in relation to language may be an indication that Chandos, probably unawares and rather abruptly, turns from a form of idealism toward some kind of nominalism—a change he was unprepared for. A broader context in which one might want to look at this stage of Chandos' crisis is the rejection of metaphysics common among the philosophers in the era of Hofmannsthal.

Another symptom of Chandos' crisis is a distortion of what Santayana considers as a function of animal faith, namely perception.[16] It consists of a certain deviation of attention from its ordinary functioning, a disintegration of the casual perspective and scale of looking at things. When talking to other people, bored and overwhelmed by a sense of absurdity or vacuity of conversation, he can't help focusing on accidental, material details—once he saw "through a

---

[16] "It is these instinctive reactions that select the objects of attention, designate their locus, and impose faith in their existence" (*SAF* Triton, 157). "Perception is faith; more perception may extend this faith or reform it, but can never recant it except by sophistry" (*SAF* Triton, 64). "Not the data of intuition, but the objects of animal faith, are the particulars perceived: they alone are the existing things or events" (*SAF* Triton, 86).

magnifying glass that an area of skin on my little finger looked like an open field with furrows and hollows." In relation to human affairs he could "no longer grasp them with the simplifying gaze of habit. Everything came to pieces ... and nothing could be encompassed by one idea" (Hofmannsthal 2005, 122).

What Chandos describes here, the loosening of the ordinary perceptual habits, may be viewed as a threshold to an (involuntary) discovery of essence—an important stage in radical scepticism as described by Santayana—the hygienic effect of which consists in the purification of the mind of unwanted prejudice and schemata. The "discernment of essence ... destroys the illusions of Platonism."[17] Whatever is given in intuition at any moment is a meaningless datum unless incorporated—with the support of animal faith—into a coherent, casual framework of existence. Santayana, guided by his imagined sceptic, discovers already at an early stage of their path that "[a]nything given in intuition is, by definition, an appearance and nothing but an appearance" (*SAF* Triton, 27). Besides, the awareness of this ethereal quality of what is present to consciousness may be accompanied by a sense of timelessness or dwelling in a dream-time, which happens to be part of Chandos' experience.

At one stroke the relativity of both human opinion and ordinary perception is exposed to Chandos. This contributes to his growing scepticism about any deeper relevance of human discourse to reality, or, at least, the reality that he is interested in. It dawns on him that the wholeness or unity implicit in notions such as "the world" or "humanity" may be a great delusion. Meaning now seems to be a meticulous construction, relative and to some extent arbitrary (it is not arbitrary only as a means of survival). Like Santayana's sceptic, Chandos, absorbed by his "pathological" perceptions, feels "not committed to the implications of other men's language" anymore (*SAF* Triton, 19).

Initially, the protagonist seeks therapy in the wisdom of the ancients, especially that of the Stoics, which he once valued as universal. But while he can still appreciate the internal coherence of those philosophies, they seem lifeless to him, so that, in the end, they only deepen the "feeling of terrible loneliness" that overwhelms him. One thing should not be overlooked when reading the Chandos letter, namely—that one of the themes of this text is *suffering and its relation to meaning*. I will return to this issue shortly.

To anticipate one of the conclusions of this interpretation, it merits noting that the focus on oneself and inner experience may suggest an affinity between Chandos and Santayana's *romantic solipsist*—a variety of sceptical attitude—for whom nothing exists save the reality of his own mind, or, in other words, the whole world is but his mind's projection (think of the idea of *Nosce te ipsum* as the title for the book of wisdom). This might be an adequate psychological description of Chandos before the crisis and might even be recognized as one of the factors that furthered the crisis. At the moment of writing the letter, while he is still absorbed by his inner state, his romantic solipsism, which is said

---

[17] Then Santayana concludes: "This is one hygienic effect of the discovery of essence: it is a shower-bath for the dreamy moralist, and clears Platonism of superstition" (*SAF* 74–75).

to rely on a coherent personal narrative, seems to have collapsed. Chandos is detached from his past, which he accepts only due to the residue of common sense that he retains and mainly for practical reasons.[18] Unlike a romantic solipsist, but also unlike a steadfast sceptic, he has not denied the existence of external reality nor explicitly reduced it to the content of his imagination, even though the boundary between the two is blurred. Chandos is also free from what tends to contaminate scepticism and is called by Santayana the *transcendental fallacy*—the assumption of the ego's absolute *fiat*—even though, before the crisis Chandos did enjoy a sense of an omniscient and pan-creative ego. At the moment of writing the letter, though, Chandos may be described quite accurately with reference to yet another sceptical figure described by Santayana, namely—*a romantic mystic*. The romantic mystic has rejected many commonsensical assumptions (but not all of them) and—unlike the romantic solipsist—his own personal narrative. Yet, his sense of vitality deters him from risking the final stage of scepticism. From the viewpoint of radical scepticism, "the same survival of vulgar presumptions which leads the romantic solipsist to retain his belief in his personal history and destiny," speculates Santayana, "leads the romantic mystic to retain, and fondly to embrace, the feeling of existence" (*SAF* Triton, 33–34).

To return to Chandos' crisis, the waning of animal faith and the consequent dissolution of the hermeneutic unity of the world manifest themselves as "an attack" of the external reality—the reality of those foreign "things" whose practical reference has been suspended—on consciousness. Ordinary life situations appear meaningless, as gestures and objects—without a function and out of context. Santayana refers to this aspect of the experiment in scepticism as follows: "it is to these actual and familiar, but now disembowelled objects, that scepticism introduces us, as if to a strange world" (*SAF* Triton, 66). All in all, deprived of the world-ordering schemata, the sceptic is threatened by a bare experience of something "unconditioned and groundless, impossible to explain and … to exorcise"[19] (*SAF* Triton, 26). This condition invites the sense of the possibility of nothingness and death. Chandos is haunted by (crypto-)apocalyptic fantasies. He finds the whole realm of human affairs distant and utterly insignificant. Images retrieved from memory enjoy a nearly identical temporal status as what presents itself as something external and currently encountered. The past and the present, which seem to have become merely *specious past* and *specious present*, merge in an uncontrolled flux of daydreaming. Like Santayana's "sceptic in his honest retreat," he "knows nothing of a future" (*SAF* Triton, 17–18).

---

[18] Similarly, Santayana's sceptic says: "The difficulties I find in maintaining it [solipsism of the present moment] consistently come from the social and laborious character of human life" (*SAF* Triton, 21).

[19] Elsewhere Santayana writes of experience: "a lingering thrill, the resonance of that much-struck bell which I call my body, the continual assault of some masked enemy" (*SAF* Triton, 169).

It is not unusual for scepticism to lead to a conclusion that everything is illusion and "life is a dream" (*SAF* Triton, 91). When reality acquires a phantom-like quality, one may assume an attitude of a poet and say: "It does not seem to me ignominious to be a poet, if nature has made one a poet unexpectedly" (*SAF* Triton, 92). But this answer of Santayana suggests being content with illusion and accepting that one is playing with (mere) surfaces, which may be acceptable from the perspective of, for example, imagist poetry, but is at odds with Chandos' romanticizing pursuit of depth. An alternative option, one more plausible for Chandos, is to be a mystic. Questioning the reality of time, the validity of ordinary perception, and the constancy of the self may be conducive to mysticism.

Meaning, Silence, and Suffering

Santayana once remarked that *what is ambiguous is meaning, not the given* (*SAF* Triton, 63–64). Suspicion and the sense of insecurity that Chandos is haunted by at the outset of the crisis are related to his assuming that everything that appears points to something else, as if the world as found was a gate to another, essential reality. In other words, as a poet and a visionary, he wants his *intuitions to be revelations*, which brings to the fore the idea of transcendence.[20] If we consider this in the light of Santayana's conception of knowledge as a leap we may reach a puzzling but telling result: "In order to reach existences intent must transcend intuition, and take data for what they mean, not for what they are" (*SAF* Triton, 62).[21] Only when this is accomplished—with the necessary support of animal faith—does a realistic context of our psychic being emerge. For Santayana, then, the (ordinary) world of things—as we perceive it—is, metaphorically speaking, *a revelation conditioned by (animal) faith*. For someone like Chandos, who assumes there to be a deeper reality, this is but the first and almost insignificant stage of transcending. Another stage means another leap—the transcending of the level of ordinary perception—via poetic language creation (or mystical experience) in search for a deeper, essential layer of reality. At this point ordinary perception retreats and the poet, like a mystic, "surrenders to totality" (Broch 1984, 94). It is so because poetic knowledge, for Hofmannsthal, means "complete identification with the object ... through the extinguishing of the ego, the entirety of being is known or, rather, newly

---

[20] To look at it from a different angle, Chandos desires to master a language of symbols that would be as rich, deep, and anchoring as religious symbolism, but, at the same time, as novel, immediate, and intuitive as only a poetic symbol can be. These two conditions can hardly be met simultaneously. A religious symbol, being nothing other than *hierophany*, as established by Eliade, is relatively constant (even if subject to an unceasing interpretation), rooted in a tradition, and provides for a sense of an overarching integrity (Eliade 2000, 468–477).

[21] For Santayana conscious experience is a revelation of things indeed (*SAF* 169), but things are "masked," clad in costumes made according to the scale and capacity of the conscious, cognizing body. It is so because substance is "on an entirely different plane of being from the immediate terms of experience" (*SAF* 183).

recognized in a wondrous, long-known familiarity, as if in total recall of a previous experience, in a total recollection" (Broch 1984, 118–119).[22] However, the surrender of the poet's ego cannot be tantamount to its annihilation because "[l]anguage creation ... can occur only from the ego" (Broch 1984, 124).

What Santayana frames as objects of belief (things perceived), then, are believed by Chandos to point to something deeper. The belief, then, and the hermeneutic transcendence are two-tier. Where Chandos first stumbles and falls is the initial, "ordinary" stage. It is precisely the translation of the given into the meaningful that Chandos becomes suspicious of because he fears that—because of the mind's schematism—it is not conducive to any further revelation. The field of action, where social actors play their roles while participating in useful language games, is of no interest for him. It gives him only boredom and fatigue. But it turns out soon that merely bypassing or bracketing this (commonsensical) stage does not readily transfer one to the essential realm. Instead, there opens a sphere of darkness and suffering. One should not ignore the fact that Chandos gives expression to pain in his confession. In my reading, the sceptical crisis discloses to Chandos the adaptive (and social) function of thought and language, which serve successful functioning rather than knowledge and truth as they are conceived of in Platonic tradition. Even though he mentions he has rejected Platonism and, as one guesses, his approach to language resembles nominalism now, at heart he has remained an essentialist in relation to reality and a maximalist as far as his tireless hermeneutic orientation is concerned. The effect of this awkward combination is his attempt to bypass language and rely on *experience* as a vehicle for revelation—something very Nietzschean and very modern indeed, like the whole ideal of immediacy. Abandoning writing and forgetting his Latin education is not too high a price for the realization of his ideal of an *unmediated understanding* of reality.

If everyday life is sustained by habits, including thinking and language habits, which serve survival and adaptation, habits must be bracketed to free experience and imaginative activity and make them vehicles of revelation. By doing so, by the way, one minimizes the influence of *the four idols* on one's thinking as famously enumerated and described in the first book of *Novum Organum* by Francis Bacon, the addressee of the letter, whose purpose was clearing the mind of error and bias.[23] After *metanoia*, Chandos ascribes the fact that he is still living normally in the eyes of his relatives and neighbors to his upbringing and routines, which continue to guide his behavior and action and give his life "a semblance of acceptable stability ... appropriate to [his] ... position." One can see that common sense has not abandoned him altogether and he is able to

---

[22] Note the aspect of retrieving something involved in re-cognition and re-collection.

[23] For an analysis of the numerous explicit and implicit references to Francis Bacon in the Chandos letter, see: H. Stefan Schultz's "Hofmannsthal and Bacon: The Sources of the Chandos Letter" (Schultz 1961). Note that the author—rather surprisingly regarding the main theme of the Chandos letter—does not mention Bacon's theory of *idols* at all.

perform his social role albeit absent-mindedly. "A life of scarcely credible emptiness" is what he calls it (Hofmannsthal 2005, 125). At its surface it does not appear very different from the lives of other people. Yet, he acts like a sleepwalker and his heart and consciousness become absorbed by a secret and intense imaginative life. Underneath the daily tedium there awakens an anxious curiosity—his gaze "is passing with silent longing over the rotten boards ... searching among all the shabby and crude objects of a rough life for that one whose unprepossessing form, whose unnoticed presence ... whose mute existence can become the source of that mysterious, worldless, infinite rapture." This may be understood in association with the pursuit of revelation and sublimity in the ordinary and the ugly—a tendency that appeared in the symbolist movement with Baudelaire and later in the decadent movement. "[M]y nameless joyful feeling will come not from contemplating the starry sky but more likely from a lonely shepherd's fire in the distance" (Hofmannsthal 2005, 126).[24] But there is more to it than that. There prevails an element of a powerful empathy toward the non-human, compared by the poet to Crassus' weeping over the death of his beloved fish. Letting oneself be overwhelmed by empathy may be viewed as a form of *katabasis* of thinking from the realm of abstraction and artifice into the realm of existence, the bodily sphere, which is one of (com)passion and death. He is quite explicit about the radicality of the change—"the whole thing is a kind of feverish thinking, but thinking in a medium more direct, fluid, and passionate than words." It touches the depth of Chandos' soul, "the lap of the most profound peace" (Hofmannsthal 2005, 127).[25]

At the outset of his moments of epiphany his attention is absorbed by an image, often a detail of the scenery of daily life. Anything—a stray dog or an abandoned farmhouse—may become the vessel of revelation. A perception or a memory triggers in him an intense, prolonged reaction of bodily, emotional, and imaginative nature at once, which culminates in an experience of merging with a mysterious, "bestial-divine" essence of nature. These revelations seem to come from beyond human culture in any customary understanding of this term. To illustrate it, Chandos recalls a recent event—spreading rat poison in his cellar and the experience that followed it. His imagination was filled, with an extreme vividness, with the dramatic scenes of the moments preceding the rats' death. Finding himself in the position of those dying creatures he experienced "much more and much less than pity—a vast empathy, a streaming across into those creatures, or a feeling that a flux of life and death, of dreaming and waking, had streamed into them for an instant." It is crucial to note that Chandos mentions the accompanying sense of being "*in the present, the fullest,*

---

[24] Thomas A. Kovach suggests that "his immersion in the most ordinary ... might ultimately be viewed as a kind of cosmic retribution for the aesthetic narcissism" of Chandos' former self (Kovach 2002b, 93).

[25] One may associate the new, more "bodily" or "physical" kind of thinking, as Chandos describes it, with the turn from the Cartesian view of the mind to the whole spectrum of theories highlighting embeddedness, interconnectedness, and embodiment.

most sublime present" (Hofmannsthal 2005, 124, emphasis added).[26] The revelation consists in an acute sense of "merging" with the time of existence as well as a deeply felt empathy toward the creatures being at the threshold of death and, hence, their metaphorical becoming one with fate. In the framework of Santayana's philosophy, which distinguishes between essence and existence, a detached contemplation and reflectiveness reveals and intensifies the distance between the spiritual aspect of the self and existence. Here this distance is overcome by the intervention and prevalence of feelings and dramatic imagination capable of recreating the experience of other living beings.[27]

As mentioned, Chandos is not a committed sceptic. His loss of trust stops in front of the mystery of existence precisely because—one may speculate—it is irrational and exerts a physical impact. The scepticism of Chandos, being, as I read it, an existential condition engaging his entire self and remaining (to some degree at least, just like in a case of a genuine religious conversion) beyond his control is not committed—to paraphrase Santayana—to the implications of a speculative philosopher's scepticism. After the crisis Chandos resorts to what has been saved in the process of *metanoia*—a particular psychic and imaginative potentiality and sensitivity as well as an emerging, tacit worldview, which I tried to characterize briefly with reference to nominalism, a peculiar essentialism and mysticism. His status of a newly born still depends on a hidden faith, partly transformed and articulated differently now, as evidenced by his quiet but profound revelations and the very fact—puzzling for scholars—that he is writing the letter, and, hence, composing a new self-narrative.

In Chandos' account of his epiphanic moments one may trace an attempt to approach and apprehend the condition of a speechless animal. Now it is there, in those mute, animal-like experiences that he pursues a deeper reality rather than in the world of literature and philosophy. It is as if the truth were shining through the pre-verbal and pre-human, a raw life with its convulsiveness, urgency, and determinacy. The rejuvenating sense of participation in a secret life of nature saves him from any further decomposition. But the "speechless animal" motif has its darker connotations too.

One of the themes of the letter is suffering. One may see a prophetic dimension in the despair of the young poet: "[t]he dread of the coming dehumanization, the dread of the coming silence of humanity ... the dread of human suffering ... this precompassion lay deep within Hofmannsthal" (Broch 1984, 164). To develop this remark by Broch, let me add that the crisis of the human medium (language) leading to silence, which makes man closer to an animal, intensifies his sense of participation in universal suffering. This may explain the spontaneous feeling of a "vast empathy" toward the non-human world.

---

[26] In the German original: "es war Gegenwart, die vollste, erhabenste Gegenwart" (Hofmannsthal 1991, 51).

[27] Such a dramatic recollection and an intense sense of re-living a past event or experience is described by Santayana as a feeling of a miraculous identity similar to what is said to occur during *transubstantiation* (*SAF* Triton, 138). This, however, is not living in the present *sensu stricto*, but rather a substitution of a waking dream for the present.

Whether one associates these experiences with a premonition of the dehumanization and the suffering that were to come in the twentieth century or not, one may find there a general suggestion of a connection between dehumanization, manifest in silence, and suffering. While on the one hand rationalization and verbal expression make suffering easier to cope with, on the other they easily condemn the suffering that cannot be voiced to oblivion or non-existence. Santayana describes pain without a meaning superbly in the following words: "a pain, when it is not sorrow at some event or the sign of some injury or crisis in bodily life, *becomes sheer horror, and a sort of wanton little hell, existing absolutely*, ... the organism has raised intuition [of pain] to an extreme intensity without giving it direction upon anything to be found or done in the world, or contemplated in the fancy" (*SAF* Triton, 61–62, emphasis added). Elsewhere the thinker notes that even though one can hardly imagine a human experience utterly divorced from discourse and even the most sudden, intense, and painful experiences are sublimated into some intuition (e.g., that of despair), they have a "suasion in them out of all proportion to their articulation, or, we might almost say, inversely proportional to it; as if the more an experience meant the less it cried out, and the more it cried out the less it meant" (*SAF* Triton, 127). This disquieting contention may be related to another memorable, concise passage, where Santayana connects suffering to the crisis of meaning and the loss of faith in the context of scepticism: "It is alarming and yet salutary to notice how near to radical scepticism are the gates of Hades" (*SAF* Triton, 132). Accordingly, the sceptical "episode" of Chandos was nearly a *self-destructive* or *self-erasing experience*, leading to the gates of nothingness. The above ruminations bring to mind an alternative: meaning or death. Santayana's words about the gates of Hades may be read as playing with the double role of Hermes, who was known as the god of interpretation but also performed the function of the guide to the underworld. This said, yet another key association should be brought to light at this point—one between animal faith and sanity. Santayana has no doubts that "reason is only a form of animal faith ... [so] if you cut your animal traces, you run mad" (*SAF* Triton, 252). Chandos' case illustrates this, too.

Spirit or consciousness, as described in *SAF*, is fueled by organic life and tends to be "thickened" by existence. In this bottom to top approach, spirit "is a fruition ... qualified by the types of life it actualizes, and is individuated by the occasions on which it actualizes them" (*SAF* Triton, 244–245). As a result of his sceptical phase, Chandos turns from the most abstract cultural registers and ethereal sphere of the spiritual realm of spirit to the irrational basis of conscious experience. Emotions and empathy now "thicken" his imagination. This felt intensification of experience contributes to the fact that Chandos is able to regain a sort of vital integrity, including discursive integrity, which might explain how he is able to talk about his experience at all. It would be naïve, of course, to think that all this is somehow pristine in the sense of being unmediated by culture—the search for immediacy and naked experience as well as the idea of letting things speak on their own behalf were among the fanciful themes of the intellectual and artistic life in Hofmannsthal's milieu. Perhaps the most concise expression of it is found in Chandos' phrase: "more divine, more bestial" (Hofmannsthal 2005, 124). In any case, the very idea of poetic knowledge for Chandos acquires a new sense—that of understanding as a revelation flowing from participation in a non-discursive, living "meaning," accompanied by a pervasive sense of an all-encompassing inter-connectedness:

> I feel a blissful and utterly eternal interplay in me and around me, and amid the to-and-fro there is nothing into which I cannot merge. Then it is as if my body consisted entirely of coded messages revealing everything to me. Or as if we could enter into a new, momentous relationship with all existence if we began to think with our hearts. But ... I am not able to say anything about it; I can no more express in rational language what made up this harmony permeating me and the entire world. (Hofmannsthal 2005, 125)

As the readers of Hofmannsthal are aware, Chandos declares in the letter that he is quitting writing. "I knew—not without a pang—that I would write no books either in English or in Latin in the coming year, the years after that, or in all the years of this life of mine" (Hofmannsthal 2005, 127). I suggest this be interpreted in terms of *the price*—very high indeed as it involved sacrificing a vital part of his self—to be paid for his transition into a mystical-ecstatic mode of being.

Another question I find interesting is: Why has the transformation made Chandos think of himself as incapable of writing? An obvious reason is that he found any conventional language too superficial, relative, and pragmatic to express what he came to see as the only thing worth expressing. The mysterious depth, or the new source of intoxication, as Santayana might say, is a source of inexpressible awe, something that might be conveyed by movements, gestures, cries, music, even tears rather than by words. The problem then rests in the inadequacy between the medium and the object (which suffers no mediation), especially in the light of the poet's aim—to express the inexpressible. Chandos in my view has remained a maximalist in that, first, he ascribes to poetry a task that is at once more and less than human; second, he sees it as an all or nothing game. My preliminary conclusion is that *learning the lesson of scepticism not without solemnity, which Chandos did in his own way, but without assuming the humility and the ironic distance advocated by Santayana, has led him to silence or, in other words, to the gates of Hades*. I will return to this issue in the last section.

Technically speaking, from the perspective of Santayana's philosophy, behind Chandos' silence there may be the discovery of the gap between the "now" of existence and the specious temporality of consciousness, let alone the "now" sublimated into a literary expression. Even something so intimate as one's inner discourse (the murmur of the self, as Santayana calls it) is more of a recollection or a projection than the living "now." The absolute present, then, which Chandos now claims to be experiencing ecstatically, is normally an object of faith rather than of conscious experience.[28] This single difference—time difference—turns out to be decisive and literally sabotages the effort to pinpoint and adequately convey existence. The apex of this effort is the desire to share in the experience of a speechless animal. If these speculations to some extent at least illuminate Chandos' reasons for quitting writing, they also explain his words about a "medium more direct, fluid, and passionate than words" and his remarks about the new way of thinking that feels more physical than mental. In any case, his old self—that of the philosophizing poet—has been deconstructed by scepticism and a new self is born, one immersed in what I propose to call *the vital abyss of the present moment* (VAPM) instead of *the solipsism of the present moment* (SOPM), where Santayana's sceptic has arrived. In both cases, Santayana might say, the momentary ecstasy is, in a sense, an illusion and brings about silence. Despite the articulation of the bodily and emotional intensity present in VAPM and the spiritual and luminous one in SOPM, they have something in common. In both cases the burden of linear temporality gives way to an intoxicating sense of being in the present, either "the absolute present" of existence or "the eternal now" of pure spirit, where "the living are as ghostly as the dead, and the dead as present as the living" (*SAF* Triton, 37). This, by the way, is a possible way in which the Nietzschean postulate of the eternal return of the same is realized. Chandos survived but he did so by the price of an intellectual, or literary suicide, even if he has found a new treasure along the way.[29]

Kovach suggests that behind Chandos' silence there is an indication of "the elusiveness of any text, the precariousness of the entire enterprise of writing which seeks to encompass a reality outside itself" (Kovach 2002b, 91). As for Chandos himself, he accounts for his withdrawal from literary activity in words that seem plain but, at the same time, multiply questions. The reason, he writes, is "a strange and embarrassing one":

> It is that the language in which I might have been granted the opportunity not only to write but also to think is not Latin or English, or Italian, or Spanish, but a language of which I know not one word, a language in which mute things speak to me and in which I will perhaps have something to say for myself someday when I am dead and standing before an unknown judge. (Hofmannsthal 2005, 127–128)

To unpack the above words, the substance of life leaks or slips through the categories, ideas, and concepts that thought uses and language refers to by means of words. For Chandos, cognitive schemata and language work like a wrong sieve—in the process of sifting the most precious substance seems to be

---

[28] For more on the function of the said time difference (the "failed now") for the dynamics of human self in Santayana's philosophy, see: Katarzyna Kremplewska, *Life as Insinuation. George Santayana's Hermeneutics of Finite Life and Human Self* (Kremplewska 2019, 71–75).

[29] Still, he has not given up faith in existence, experience, and nature. Added to an element of common sense—sustained by animal faith—it was enough for him to go on living and even to prosper in some way.

lost irretrievably. Overcoming them may open a poet to an apparently fuller experience of reality but, at the same time, mute him. His aim is no longer to possess and convey eternal wisdom (the very idea now seems grotesque) but rather to experience and merge with the absolute present—unique, unrepeatable, and, hence, unknowable and ineffable. Santayana's sceptic discovers the abstractness of essence and the isolation (or loneliness) of spirit. Chandos discovers existence in its temporal "otherness" in relation to language and mind.[30] Their paths converge in proximity to mysticism.

Santayana's Defense of Mediation and Ironic Knowledge

By existence Santayana understands the plane of material change, of which life is part and which is transcended within consciousness. The experiment in scepticism discloses the pure and meaningless content of consciousness at any given moment—an essence. "The discrimination of essence," he asserts, "has a happy tendency to liberalise philosophy, freeing it at once from literalness and from scepticism" (*SAF* Triton, 90). It also suggests that meaning has existential underpinning and is an outcome of a natural process, where animal faith, social interaction, and cultural context are involved. Here we touch upon a major difference between Santayana's naturalism and Chandos' (Hofmannsthal's) tacitly assumed poetic "metaphysics," in which—debatably—resurfaces some version of a priority of essence in relation to existence, even if modified by Nietzschean and Modernist influences. Existence, one may note, if understood strictly in the sense given to it by Santayana, is not exactly the object of knowledge pursued by Chandos. But if one asks what is it that is pursued, the answer, far from being precise, will oscillate somewhere in-between a secret meaning of being, the raw experience of existence as interconnectedness of all things, and the very heart of existence, which Chandos has tacitly equated with the essence of being. But despite the different ways they define the object of knowledge, in both cases scepticism grows out of anxiety about the possibility of error and self-delusion. Doubts arise with regard to meaning (of words or appearances) and truth, and this applies with equal force to Chandos and the sceptic from *SAF*. Accordingly, both Chandos during his crisis and the sceptic described by Santayana experience the uncanniness and the falling apart of the once familiar world.

The following words by Santayana convey aptly the ambiguity involved in witnessing the appearances and their status:

---

[30] Another way of explaining Chandos' involuntary discovery is by relating it to the fact that he strives to approach experience in itself, a living intuition springing from psychic existence. But, according to Santayana, intuitions are "spiritual facts," which themselves cannot be repeated or re-lived. A given essence may be encountered again but the intuition of it can only be memorized and re-imagined, which act constitutes a separate intuition. The difference between intuition and essence is "profound" (see *SAF* Triton, 120, and *SAF* Triton, 21–22).

The datum is apparent in the sense of being self-evident and luminous; and it is apparent also in the sense of merely appearing and being unsubstantial. In this latter sense, the apparent threatens to become the non-existent. *Does not the existent profess to be more than apparent*: to be not so much the self-evident as that which I am seeking evidence for, in the sense of testimony? (*SAF* Triton, 41–42, emphasis added)

The notion of "testimony" may be understood as suggesting a quest for certainty but also an expectation that "things" (the existent) will reveal themselves or speak on their own behalf.[31] Note that Chandos' epiphanies are triggered by a perception or an image.[32] But such expectations exceed the function and limitations of the mind. Existence "is something imputed and never found," concludes Santayana's sceptic (*SAF* Triton, 59–60). Whatever is given in intuition is beyond doubt but "[t]he immediate visionary datum is never the intended object, but always a pathological symptom, a term in discourse, a description proffered at that moment by that feeling for that object" (*SAF* Triton, 61). Santayana's distinction of essences articulates and at the same time explains this *caesura* between the mind and existence and influences the idea of knowledge. In short—while what is directly given in consciousness is always only an essence (ideal and timeless), the object of knowledge is existence (a material thing, an existential relation, an event). The proverb that human life is a dream is owed to the otherworldly (metaphorically speaking) nature of consciousness.

---

[31] The psychic origins of discourse, inner discourse, or a train of thought in particular, may suggest a sort of "immediacy" in two senses: (1) discourse as expressive of the spontaneity of psyche; (2) discourse as an inherent part of all (human) experience. Thus, inner discourse may be described as *intimate* and *authentic*. It also is, as I mention elsewhere, in some measure rooted in the bodily sphere. Vincent Colapietro in his engaging essay suggests the possibility of extending the scope of immediacy to a specific type of discourse, i.e., poetry, while understanding "immediacy" in a stronger, ontological sense. Poetry might even be viewed as an expression of things themselves, the author maintains, supporting this idea with an assertion that discourse is located within existence and it springs thence. This interpretation seems to me plausible only if "immediacy" is understood metaphorically. For Santayana, the "universe [is] utterly out of scale with myself" (*SAF* Triton, 171). Discourse is mediated by intuitions of essences and symbolization. If self-reflective, it is doubly mediated. Poetry may indeed be said to be immediate as having essences as its main object, i.e., immediate in the spiritual sphere, which is its domain (or, perhaps, as Colapietro notes, being a sort of discourse "in which discourse asserts itself"). Some sort of immediacy might be granted to it in the sense of being authentically *expressive* of some emotions or, in a generalized sense, of a psychic life (which is itself conscious and thus spiritually mediated). But it is not immediate in the sense of having an unmediated "access" to existence or even of directly conveying experience. If that were the case, the difference between essence and existence introduced and insisted on by Santayana would be merely decorative. When Santayana compares discourse to poetry, he means to emphasize its relative freedom and arbitrariness in relation to existence (symbolization is a matter of convention; see Colapietro 2013, 17–19).

[32] I leave aside the issue of the relation between what appears and language as it exceeds the scope of this essay. It may be the case that for Chandos no human language is capable of bearing the gravity of what appears, hence an image is allowed to act directly upon feelings and the body. This, by the way, is an indication of his symbolist inspirations.

This supernatural status and supertemporal scope of spirit are not prerogatives; they are deprivations; they are sacrificial conditions, from the point of view of natural existence, to which any faculty must submit, if it is to understand. Of course understanding is itself an achievement ..., but it must be bought at a price: at the price of escaping into a fourth dimension, of not being that which we understand. (*SAF* Triton, 146, my emphasis)

In other words, human cognition is irrevocably mediated—something that Chandos resists to accept, hence his disillusionment with language and ideas. Still, in my reading Chandos finally arrives at a similar conclusion albeit in a different, non-speculative way. Searching for a medium more fluid and less schematic than language, he finally locates it in the heart.

On Santayana's view scepticism need not lead to a complete disillusionment with human cognitive faculties. Knowledge of existence "has no need, no propensity, and no fitness to be literal. It is symbolic initially ... and it fulfils its function perfectly—I mean its moral function of enlightening us about our natural good—if it remains symbolic to the end" (*SAF* Triton, 93). What is more, the indirection of symbolic representation

is no obstacle to expression, rather its condition; and this vehicular manifestation of things may be knowledge of them, which intuition of essence is not. The theatre, for all its artifices, depicts life in a sense more truly than history ... and much in the same way the human medium of knowledge can perform its pertinent synthesis and make its pertinent report all the better when it frankly abandons the plane of its object and expresses in symbols what we need to know of it. (*SAF* Triton, 94)

Both science and arts, remarks Santayana, even though their methods and goals differ radically, rely on intuitions of essences and symbolic mediation, and both reveal, more or less adequately, some truths about nature. He is happy to admit that knowledge is symbolic and anchored in animal faith. The tacitly made assumptions spring from life and are its functions, like spirit is. But mere intuitions are not enough to know anything. *It is the living psyche who knows.*[33] Every user of language is a believer in this sense. It is not accidental then that what Broch calls "linguistic despair" is so prominent an aspect of the scepticism of Chandos. The problem is not so much that he is ascribing to art a revelatory function but that he desires a divine directness of a sort. This desire, combined with a Platonizing sense of reality, drives the young artist to despair. He loses faith in the capacity of thought and language to reach, let alone express, anything worth attention. One may indeed interpret this in a loose reference to

---

[33] The bodily dimension of knowledge is articulated in the following passage: knowledge is "not intramental nor internal to experience ... it has compulsory objects that pre-exist. It is incidental to the predicaments and labour of life. ... It expresses in discourse the modified habits of an active being, plastic to experience, and capable of readjusting its organic attitude to other things on the same material plane of being ... this attitude, physical and practical, determines the object of intent, which discourse is about" (*SAF* Triton, 154).

Santayana's well-known contention that nothing given exists, namely—as a premonition that *the existent somehow escapes the light of the mind and the scope of language*.

While Santayana is happy to accept—at least for a while and experimentally—the above conclusion insofar as it springs from his discovery of essences, Chandos, with his god-like idea of a poet, rebels against the suggestion that consciousness may be a sort of "deprivation" and blames language for the failure in capturing reality. Meanwhile, let me repeat, both before and after the crisis he is haunted by the idea that "everything seems to mean something, everything that exists" (Hofmannsthal 2005, 125), and he clearly understands by "meaning" something more than a human (adaptive and social) construct. Other than that, he lacks the ironic distance of Santayana, who is quite happy to note that "[i]f all data are symbols and all experience comes in poetic terms, it follows that the human mind, both in its existence and in its quality, is a free development out of nature, a language or music the terms of which are arbitrary" (*SAF* Triton, 90–91). Neither does he seem willing to embrace the possibility that *knowledge is inescapably ironic*, that it is—at best—*à propos* in relation to existence, and "the ideas we have of things are not fair portraits; they are political caricatures made in the human interest; but in their partial way they may be masterpieces of characterization and insight" (*SAF* Triton, 95). The fulfillment of the impossible literalness pursued by Chandos would require getting rid of symbols. He represents, one may also say, a cultural and intellectual temperament different from the ironic, disillusioned, and "relaxed" (or, perhaps, Mediterranean) stance of Santayana, his "smiling sadness," as some critics have characterized the thinker.[34]

At the moment of embarking on the path of his "mystical empiricism" (or a secularized variety of apophatic mysticism), Chandos may be viewed as approaching the condition of a nihilist, like those sceptics about whom Santayana writes that they "wish to abstain from faith, and ... thereby renounce all knowledge, and live on passive illusions ... so that we should be driven back to a nihilism which only silence and death could express consistently" (*SAF*

---

[34] An important quotation in which Santayana summarizes the effect that his theory of essences may have on one's epistemic stance merits evoking here: "If all data are symbols and all experience comes in poetic terms, it follows that the human mind, both in its existence and in its quality, is a free development out of nature, a language or music the terms of which are arbitrary, like the rules and counters of a game. It follows also that the mind has no capacity and no obligation to copy the world of matter nor to survey it impartially. At the same time, it follows that the mind affords a true expression of the world, rendered in vital perspectives and in human terms, since this mind arises and changes symptomatically at certain foci of animal life; so that, for instance, alternative systems of religion or science, if not taken literally, may equally well express the actual operation of things measured by different organs or from different centres" (*SAF* Triton, 90–91).

Triton, 150).³⁵ Yet, as mentioned previously, after reaching the nadir of his despair, Chandos renews his contract with life but does so on new terms. To an extent, his new practical-mystical attitude, which allows for leading a double life, confirms Santayana's conclusion that scepticism is not necessarily inconsistent with animal faith. Even "the admission that nothing given exists is not incompatible with belief in things not given":

> That such external things exist, that I exist myself ... is a faith not founded on reason.... This faith ... does no violence to a sceptical analysis of my experience; on the contrary, it takes advantage of that analysis to interpret this volatile experience as all animals do and must, as a set of symbols for existences that cannot enter experience, and which, since they are not elements in knowledge, no analysis of knowledge can touch—they are in another realm of being. (*SAF* Triton, 96)

A possible solution—one chosen by Chandos—in the light of this awareness is living as if nothing has changed and cultivating a hidden dreamworld at the same time.

Sympathetic Imagination and Literary Psychology as a Rescue

The silence of Chandos as a poet is a result of his realization that getting at the heart of things—which we may assume for the purpose of our discussion as roughly corresponding to Santayana's "existence"—requires a non-discursive medium. It is, to use Santayana's phrase, "another realm of being." The quasi-mystical states of emotional and imaginative rupture, described in the letter as neither mental nor purely physical, engage the vital center of Chandos' very being. Like a religious convert, he seems to have undergone a profound change and a renewal in the course of the crisis. Some light may be shed, as I'd suggest, on this new way of appropriating reality with the support of a few hermeneutic techniques described in *SAF*, such as *the animation of nature*, which stands for

---

[35] If considered in literary terms, the premonition of nihilism in the Chandos letter may also be viewed as a reflection of decadence absorbed by the symbolist movement, by which Hofmannsthal was influenced. The whole crisis of Chandos indeed may be read in terms of overcoming Parnassianism in favor of symbolism with a pronounced romantic component. Thus, silence would be the result of bearing the consequences of the symbolist poets' credo of expressing the inexpressible. The Parnassians, in turn, were seen by the younger generation as "coldly archeological in their treatment of ancient myths and fables," precluding all feeling and the "intense subjectivity" characteristic of both romanticism and symbolism (Dorra 1994, 13). For the influence of symbolism on Hofmannsthal, see for example Thomas A. Kovach's *Hofmannsthal and Symbolism: Art and Life in the Work of a Modern Poet* (Kovach 1985).

endowing nature with a capacity to first-person experience, and *imitative sympathy*, both closely related to literary psychology.[36]

Understanding the way other creatures think or feel can only happen by way of sympathetic imitation, which involves an imaginary taking place of or merging with them by assuming a certain (bodily) attitude, which is accompanied by a flow of images, emotions, and inner discourse. Behind animation, by the way, there is a tacit belief in oneself, in nature, with which one remains dynamically connected, and in experience, which is ascribed to other creatures too. Animation may involve a dramatic understanding of other (living) beings, which occurs through contagion and imitation. While it is a way of overcoming the seclusion of first-person experience, ironically, it may reveal predominantly the observer's inner discourse projected onto nature. But Santayana is far from dismissing animation as a form of spontaneous, non-scientific understanding of nature. On the contrary, attributing thoughts and feelings to non-human beings is "courteous or even humble," "inevitable," and is a way of recognizing non-human beings' "parity with myself" (*SAF* Triton, 220). To dismiss animation as naïve would be tantamount to exhibiting "insensibility to the actual life of nature." Poetry and myth "may do the life of nature less injustice than would do the only alternative open to me, which is silence" (*SAF* Triton, 220–221).

First-person experience in itself is, according to the philosopher, beyond the scope of scientific investigation. Likewise, "thought can be found only by being enacted" (*SAF* Triton, 226). Santayana claims that some philosophers who are interested in the scientific validity of knowledge and, for that end, dig into the very basis of conscious experience within this experience itself (he probably means both empiricists and phenomenologists), in fact practice literary psychology, not science, which would seek explanation on the material plane.[37] Yet, there is nothing derogatory about literary psychology. On the contrary—it

---

[36] Knowledge of existence is based on instinct and the interpretation of signs. But there also is a subtler component at play—"sympathetic imagination," a notion broader than "imitative sympathy." Signs reveal some aspects of existence, but "will never lead me into the citadel, and if its chambers are ever open to me, it must be through my sympathetic imagination." This sort of imagination involves a kind of a natural "syntony," "a unison between my imagination and its [nature's] generative principles" (*SAF* Triton, 98). Imitative sympathy seems to be a dramatic variety of sympathetic imagination and involves enacting and ascribing the capacity to experience to other beings. When understanding obtained through sympathetic imagination concerns other minds it is called by Santayana literary psychology. Here things are simpler due to the affinity of the object of inquiry (other people's minds) with its organ—"The only sphere in which clairvoyance is normal is the sphere of mental discourse" (*SAF* Triton, 185).

[37] By literary psychology, Santayana understands imaginative inquiry into the mental life of the psyche—"Knowledge of discourse in other people, or of myself at other times" (*SAF* Triton, 156). It is carried out "from within" and based on animal faith (more precisely, it is a moral sublimation of animal faith) and the inner flow of mental discourse, as opposed to the methods of scientific psychology, such as behavioral sciences (*SAF* Triton, 133; *SAF* Triton, 198–200). Psychological imagination, on which literary psychology thrives, requires a "fineness in instinct and in perception" (*SAF* Triton, 228). Santayana, by the way, considered psychoanalysis to be a variety of literary psychology in a naturalistic guise.

may be "in its texture, the most literal and adequate sort of knowledge of which a mind is capable" (*SAF* Triton, 156). Interestingly, "the poets and novelists are often better psychologists than the philosophers" (*SAF* Triton, 227), because they are unconstrained by the requirement of being "scientific" and practice psychology more freely, relying on emotions, empathy, and premonitions, which sometimes provide amazingly adequate insights. Moreover, to develop Santayana's argument, writers may convey by means of literary psychology much more than a glimpse into an individual experience—they may illuminate the mental landscape of a generation or a society in a given era—*vide* the Chandos letter. Finally, literary psychology "always remains in possession of the moral field" (*SAF* Triton, 224), which makes it an irreplaceable device for understanding the human world. Interestingly, Santayana relates the value of literary psychology—here he seems to be assuming the perspective of culture—to the artistic merits of its form.[38]

In every single perception, regardless of whether its context is poetic or scientific, spiritual mediation is at play—"there is an essence present which only poetry can describe or sympathy conceive" (*SAF* Triton, 229). Science treats essences merely instrumentally in its pursuit of facts and principles. Contemplation of essences, in its turn, may become "a sort of *gran rifiuto* in the life of mind, a collapse into lotus-eating and dreaming" (*SAF* Triton, 230). Literary psychology as an interpretive device makes concession both to facts and intuitions of essences. The author "feels the rush of emotion on the other side of the deployed events; he wraps them in an atmosphere of immediacy.... Literary psychology pierces to the light, to the shimmer of passion and fancy, behind the body of nature" (*SAF* Triton, 230). It thus restores experience in its vital integrity by *understanding* through sympathetic dramatization. Chandos attains it when he is envisaging and "enacting" the mother rat in the final moments of her life. Due to his poetic sensibility and the recent crisis he is overwhelmed by the power of the experience and finds it inexpressible in words. This sort of intimate understanding, even though it may be said to originate beyond discourse—in animal faith and intent—does involve *inner discourse, to which some sort of immediacy may be ascribed*, and may be given a literary expression, regardless of the fact that the relation between this further expression and its object is bound to be marked by a degree of arbitrariness, and this in a deeper sense than the arbitrariness related to the mere fact that language is conventional.[39] Santayana sometimes remarked that all discourse is

---

[38] "It is only when this philosophy is good literature that it is good for anything" (*SAF* Triton, 226). Thus, one may speculate that—in a certain sense—Marcel Proust was more successful in his literary rendering of conscious experience of time than Edmund Husserl, who aspired to be scientific. Still, the role of literary philosophy as a certain fundamental human *art* in Santayana's rendering of it is by no means limited to the realm of art. For a more comprehensive analysis of this issue, see Jessica Wahman's text, "Literary Psychology and Philosophical Method" (Wahman 2013, 29–38).

[39] "The inner patter of words which I sometimes hear in myself, and which mystics have called inspiration ... is not thinking; it is an object of perception ... the fountain of my thoughts, that is the self who thinks them, is my psyche, and the movements there guide my thoughts ... [and] dictate my feelings" (*SAF* Triton, 218).

at bottom, and in a most general sense, poetry—it springs from the fountain of life and is a sort of variation on experience (*SAF* Triton, 261). If this happens to be part of the discovery of Chandos, as well as one of the reasons for his *metanoia*, then one may say that his revelation was genuine and his transformation emancipatory. The price, however, that Chandos paid for it in the form of silence was not a necessary price; it did not flow from this emancipatory discovery itself. Rather, it was a choice which may be explained in the context of his specific circumstances and his other beliefs that I have described as maximalist. Lacking Santayana's seasoned, ironic distance toward the mind and the self, he found the writer's role degraded in the light of his discovery and chose to be a (half-hearted) mystic instead. This is not to say that this attitude precluded him from maintaining, in his own way, some sort of a "discipline of disillusionment" advocated by Santayana.[40] This is one of the conclusions one can arrive at when staging Chandos' and Santayana's temporary companionship.

Let me conclude with a remark concerning the issue that has hitherto bothered Hofmannsthal's scholars, namely: what to do with the fact that Chandos, who claims to have quitted writing for good, is writing the letter to Francis Bacon and happens to be composing one of the most memorable fictional letters in modern literature. My interpretation of this fact is as follows. Chandos distanced himself from the capital "W" Writing, writing as revelatory creation in the medium of language. Disillusionment with capital "L" Language and capital "T" Thinking anteceded his quitting Writing. His silently murmuring self, his inner discourse, which one cannot shrug off as long as one is alive and conscious, was not bothered by Language for it "knew" language is no less arbitrary than necessary for life. What is more, this arbitrariness, which makes it essentially poetic, as we know from Santayana, does not prevent it from performing its function and being adequately expressive, or, in other words, does not corrupt either the authenticity of discourse or successful communication. Regardless of the fact that Chandos abandoned his literary ambitions, not only was he still in touch with his inner self and, hence, inner discourse, but was enjoying a sense of intimate unity he had never experienced before. Obviously, he did not cease to be able to give it a verbal expression in a small "l" language, perhaps with a practical purpose in view, just like he was still living an ordinary life among his family and neighbors. Explaining himself in front of his friend was in fact a conventional and social act. Affording himself frankness in disclosing the story of his crisis was a practical, relieving, and therapeutic act. That one is creating a masterpiece as if unawares and by accident may come as a surprise but is perfectly thinkable.

---

[40] I borrow this phrase from Vincent Colapietro, who notes that one may learn from Santayana's philosophy that "happiness in disillusion" may be "the only sustainable happiness for a rational animal" (Colapietro 2013, 7).

References

Assmann, Aleida. 2003. Hofmannsthals Chandos-Brief und die Hieroglyphen der Moderne. *Hofmannsthal-Jahrbuch* 11: 267–279.
Broch, Hermann. 1984. *Hugo von Hoffmansthal and His Time. The European Imagination 1860–1920*. Translated, edited and introduction by M. P. Steinberg. Chicago, London: The University of Chicago Press.
Colapietro, Vincent. 2013. Literary Forms, Heuristic Functions, and Philosophical Fixations: Santayana's Emancipatory Example. *Overheard in Seville. Bulletin of the George Santayana Society* 31: 5–19.
Dorra, Henri. 1994. *Symbolist Art Theories. A Critical Anthology*. Berkley, Los Angeles, London: University of California Press.
Eliade, Mircea. 2000. Traktat o historii religii [A Treatise on the History of Religion]. Translated by Jan Wierusz Kowalski. Warszawa: KR.
Flamm, Matthew Caleb. 2013. Review of George Santayana's Philosophy of Religion. *Overheard in Seville. Bulletin of the George Santayana Society* 31: 39–44.
von Hofmannsthal, Hugo. 1991. Ein Brief. In *Hugo von Hofmannsthal. In Sämtliche Werke XXXI. Erfundene Gespräche und Briefe*, ed. Ellen Ritter, 45–55. Frankfurt am Main: Fischer.
———. 2005. *The Lord Chandos Letter and Other Writings*. Translated by J. Rotenberg. With introduction by J. Banville. New York: New York Review Books.
Kamińska, Krystyna. 1984. Introduction in Hugo von Hofmannsthal. In *Liryka, wiersze i dramaty* [Lyrical Poetry, Poems and Dramas], ed. and trans. Leopold Lewin. Warszawa: Państwowy Instytut Wydawniczy.
Kovach, Thomas A. 1985. *Hofmannsthal and Symbolism. Art and Life in the Work of a Modern Poet*. New York, Bern, Frankfurt am Main: Peter Lang.
———., ed. 2002a. *A Companion to the Works of Hugo von Hofmannsthal*. Rochester, NY: Camden House.
———. 2002b. Hofmannsthal's *Ein Brief*: Chandos and His Crisis. In *A Companion to the Works of Hugo von Hofmannsthal*, ed. Thomas A. Kovach, 85–95. Rochester, NY: Camden House.
Kremplewska, Katarzyna. 2019. *Life as Insinuation. George Santayana's Hermeneutics of Finite Life and Human Self*. Albany, NY: SUNY Press.
Lachs, John, and Michael Hodges. 2000. *Thinking in the Ruins*. Nashville: Vanderbilt University Press.
Magris, Claudio. 2019. *Mit habsburski w literaturze austriackiej moderny*. [The Habsburg Myth in Modern Austrian Literature]. Translated by E. Ugałła and J. Ugniewska. Kraków, Budapeszt, Syrakuzy: Austeria.
Santayana, George. 1937. Scepticism and Animal Faith. In *The Works of George Santayana*. Triton Edition. Volume XIII. New York: Charles Scribner's Sons. Cited as *SAF* Triton.
Schultz, H. Stefan. 1961. Hofmannsthal and Bacon: The Sources of the Chandos Letter. *Comparative Literature* 13 (1): 1–15.
Wahman, Jessica. 2013. Literary Psychology and Philosophical Method. *Overheard in Seville. Bulletin of the George Santayana Society* 31: 29–38.

The Conservative Disposition in Santayana's Philosophy

Michael Brodrick

American philosophers, like Americans in general, tend to be favorably disposed to progress. For evidence of this progressive disposition in American philosophy, one need look no further than Emerson's romantic idealism, William James's "strenuous mood" (James 1956, 211), or John Dewey's instrumentalism. "Men walk as prophecies of the next age" (Emerson 1888a, 285), said Emerson. "The only sin is limitation" (Emerson 1888a, 287). Emerson, James, and Dewey shared an instinct for progress, and they looked to the future with an optimism that comes naturally to visionaries, explorers, inventors, and entrepreneurs. Pragmatism, the philosophical movement they founded, epitomizes their pioneering spirit of progressive change.

The Spanish-born American philosopher George Santayana was cut from a different cloth. He praised Emerson, studied with James, and read Dewey, but he did not share their progressive tendency. Santayana harkened to the ancient Greeks. He sought understanding, as those great thinkers had done, not so much to change the world as to flourish within its permanent constraints. Although not a conventional believer, Santayana was at home in the traditions of the Catholic Church. He held fast to common sense opinions, even as his contemporaries invented bold, counterintuitive theories. In short, Santayana evinced a disposition to be conservative.

Scepticism and Animal Faith reveals how profoundly Santayana's conservative disposition shaped his philosophy. For in that work, Santayana pushed back against the romantic progressivism of the day by recovering belief in limits that

---

M. Brodrick (✉)
Institute for Humane Studies, George Mason University, Arlington, VA, USA

© The Author(s), under exclusive license to Springer Nature Switzerland AG 2024
M. A. Coleman, G. Tiller (eds.), *The Palgrave Companion to George Santayana's Scepticism and Animal Faith*, Palgrave Companions,
https://doi.org/10.1007/978-3-031-46367-9_21

permanently constrain human knowledge and prospects. The result is an epistemological framework for a sophisticated conservative worldview.

Let me begin by explaining what I mean by the conservative disposition. From there, I'll examine Santayana's autobiography for evidence of that disposition in Santayana himself. Next, I'll show how *Scepticism* articulates a philosophy of imperfection and limits that supports a conservative vision of human flourishing. I'll conclude by assessing the value of Santayana's conservatism today.

The Disposition to be Conservative

Political theorist Russell Kirk set forth six "canons" of the conservative creed (Kirk 1995, 8–9). But if conservatism is a creed, it is also, and more deeply, a disposition: a tendency to behave, to think, and to feel in certain ways. Wary of venturing into the unknown in search of more and better, the conservative would sooner cherish the everyday, the routine, the humdrum. This proclivity for quotidian fulfillments implies, if not a fully-fledged creed, then at least a generic belief. The conservative holds that both human nature and the world are inescapably—one might even say tragically—limited.

To be conservative, said the philosopher Michael Oakeshott, is to delight in what is, not in what was or what may be (Oakeshott 1962, 408). The conservative is very much aware of having something to lose that he has learned to care for (Oakeshott 1962, 408). Thus, he is warm with respect to enjoyment and cool with respect to change and innovation (Oakeshott 1962, 412). He does not lightly surrender a known good for an unknown better. "He is not in love with what is dangerous and difficult; he is unadventurous; he has no impulse to sail uncharted seas; for him there is no magic in being lost, bewildered, or shipwrecked" (Oakeshott 1962, 412). In short, the conservative is predisposed "to enjoy what is available rather than to wish ... or to look for something else" (Oakeshott 1962, 408).

Conservatism presupposes goods already possessed. The conservative disposition does not arise in a present devoid of goods, for such a present offers nothing worth conserving. A deeply troubled present, which calls forth the impulse to alter what is, cannot sustain the disposition to be conservative. But the goods already possessed need not be perfect. The conservative esteems them because they are familiar, not because they are unsurpassed. The maxim of conservatism is not Goethe's *Verweile doch, du bist so schön*, but instead, "*Stay with me because I am attached to you*" (Oakeshott 1962, 408).

Conservatism and Limits

The disposition to cherish imperfect goods already possessed, rather than hold out for progress or novelty, implies belief in permanent limits of the kind conventionally referred to as fallenness or finitude. The conservative perceives the ideal in light of those limits, ever conscious of the price of improvement. Life, in her eyes, is not the "sweet solipsism" it may appear to be to the young (Oakeshott 1962, 436)—or even to the philosopher spellbound by lofty rhetoric. Hidden constraints shape our destiny, even as we cast about to comprehend and control them. We may gain the upper hand for a while, but at last we are subject to the tradeoffs thrust upon us. Even if human ingenuity ushered in a future superior in some respects to the present, that future might turn out to be no better—or, indeed, worse—on balance. At best, new and improved goods impose the not inconsiderable cost of learning how to enjoy them. Weighing the promise of change against its inherent risks, the conservative chooses to resist the siren call of Emerson's "flying perfect" (Emerson 1888a, 281).

Thus, the disposition to be conservative implies a basic premise—indelible limits—of a philosophy sceptical of bold claims about the human capacity to know or the human ability to transform the world. Conservative philosophies of that ilk first arose in response to the radical ideas of the French revolutionaries. The revolutionaries believed the world was "an order which is intelligible to human reason ... and is responsive to human will, once reason has comprehended its structure" (O'Sullivan 1976, 10). Conservatives, meanwhile, were sceptical that "man's reason and will were powerful enough to regenerate human nature by creating a completely new social order" (O'Sullivan 1976, 9). To oppose that idea, they tried to show "that the world imposes limitations upon what either the individual or the state can hope to achieve" (O'Sullivan 1976, 11). Thus, conservatism has been defined as "a philosophy of imperfection, committed to the idea of limits" (O'Sullivan 1976, 12).

Santayana's autobiography affords ample evidence of his conservative disposition. In *Scepticism and Animal Faith*, responding to theories of knowledge not unlike the radical ideas of the French revolutionaries, Santayana would set forth his own philosophy of imperfection and limits.

Santayana's Conservative Disposition

The disposition to be conservative predominated in Santayana. For him, the philosophical heritage of the past, customs, traditions, everyday enjoyments, and what he called "spirituality" were goods already possessed—that is, they were already available and familiar to him—and he instinctively sought to conserve them. The lessons of the past, Santayana thought, were seldom straightforward, and critical intelligence was needed to apply them to the present, but to start afresh, to "live ever in a new day" as Emerson had urged (Emerson 1888b, 58), that Santayana could not do. "I was," he confessed, "a child of Christendom: my heritage was that of Greece, of Rome ancient and modern, and of the literature and philosophy of Europe. Christian history and art contained all my spiritual traditions, my intellectual and moral language" (*PP3*, 36). If not for those rich deposits from the past, neither the present nor the future would be intelligible and both would be poorer.

Transplanted from Spain to the United States as a boy, Santayana would eventually travel the world, living for extended periods in Germany, France, England, and Italy. He viewed those around him charitably—sympathetically, that is, but with detachment, a spectator more than a participant. These personal circumstances and traits might have made Santayana a pure cosmopolitan—not only adept at seeing the world through the eyes of others but equally at home everywhere and, chameleon-like, changing colors to match his environment.

But charity in Santayana was paired with a firm commitment to his own traditions. "The full-grown human soul," he wrote, "should respect all traditions and understand all passions; at the same time, it should possess and embody a particular culture, without unmanly relaxation or mystical neutrality" (*PP3*, 53). In America, he found he could not, as other Catholics and some Jews had done, simply assume a Protestant identity "and bury as deep as possible the fact that they were born Catholics or Jews" (*PP2*, 123). "I am not a man of that stamp," he wrote (*PP2*, 123). "And I refuse to be annexed, to be abolished, or to be grafted onto any plant of a different species" (*PP2*, 123).

For the romantic Emerson, customs and traditions were made to be broken, for they stood in the way of the individual soul in its journey of self-creation. "Nothing is at last sacred," Emerson wrote, "but the integrity of your own mind" (Emerson 1888b, 52). But in customs and traditions the conservative Santayana found not timeworn impediments to progress but vital centers of gravity that stabilize life in the present. The habits of imagination, belief, and feeling they transmit keep individuals on a steady course. Santayana observed as much with regard to his friend Julian Codman. Codman had "imbibed secret religious feelings," although they were "not so secret … that I wasn't perfectly aware of them" (*PP2*, 102). "I liked those feelings," Santayana added. "They were ballast, good for a young man of family who might otherwise dance too lightly on the summer waves" (*PP2*, 102).

Life in Santayana's native Avila was structured almost entirely by custom. Were a stranger to wonder at some ceremony or courtesy of theirs, the local people would state simply, "It is the custom." What a "great relief," Santayana recalled, "to hear that things were the custom, and not that they were right or necessary, or that I ought to do them" (*PP1*, 110). For what reason could there be for living, after all, "if it were not the custom to live, to suffer, and to die" (*PP1*, 110)? To Santayana, the people of Avila were "deeply civilized, not by modern conveniences but by moral tradition" (*PP1*, 110).

None of these goods—neither the intellectual heritage of the past, nor customs, nor traditions—were unalloyed. But Santayana consistently preferred a bird in the hand. We see this conservative propensity again in his preference for modest, everyday enjoyments. What Santayana loved best about Germany was *Gemütlichkeit*—"joy in hearty, fleshly, kindly, homely, droll little things" (*PP2*, 5). These things were nothing if not routine. To find more exotic ones would have been easy. Yet they were already available, and that was as good a reason as any to be satisfied with them. Here, as elsewhere, Santayana's ruling impulse was conservative: to enjoy the present, not to light out in search of improvement. *Gemütlichkeit* was a virtue, he said. It tended to "redeem the human soul from disorder, from servitude, and from spleen" (*PP2*, 5).

In Santayana's love of spirituality, we find the same inveterate preference for enjoying what is already at hand. Spirituality calls attention home to the immediate, without reference to the past, the future, or the hidden depths of nature. Forgetting those remote realities evaporates concern, letting consciousness rest in the present. This is at once a release and a positive fulfillment, for the qualities of the immediate shine forth to the quiet mind in their intrinsic uniqueness. Nor does one need to voyage into the unknown to discover these fulfillments. They are there in the pale daylight that peeks through the front window, in the familiar view to the garden, in the shadows that gather near the door. Spirituality unlocks the radiance of immediacy in the midst of the everyday.

For Santayana, to cherish the familiar was often the better part of wisdom. He had learned to care for learning—so much so that he left his professorship at Harvard to pursue, for life, the lifestyle of a wandering student. Yet he would wander only so far, wary of the point at which further adventures would diminish the life of the mind. Once, during a voyage, Santayana overheard an archaeologist describing a discovery in the mountains of Crete, which they had just seen from the ship. The idea of exploring those ruins tempted Santayana. "I felt the attraction strongly," he wrote (*PP3*, 44). Yet he "nursed no illusions about it and suffered only a theoretical pang at having to renounce it all" (*PP3*, 44). The reality of such an expedition would have been "a terrible bore and far beyond my physical endurance and agility" (*PP3*, 44). To discover the significance of ruins was to cherish a familiar activity—learning—that Santayana habitually enjoyed; to actually explore them was to risk trading that enjoyment for boredom and exhaustion. He would not be so rash.

Santayana's conservative disposition appeared to set him against the entire trajectory of Western civilization. For the world around him had turned away from the familiar goods of the present. Its gaze was fixed on the future, and it took for granted that progress should be measured by quantitative standards alone. Science was supposed to "make all mankind both rich and free from material cares" (*PP3*, 141). Soon, the proponents of science exulted, "practical wisdom would be secured together with fabulous material well-being" (*PP3*, 141). For Santayana, this "dream of the moderns" (*PP3*, 141) was a fool's errand. It demanded the familiar goods of today in exchange for the promise of a better tomorrow, but it couldn't say in what respects tomorrow would be better. For the dream "lacked altogether the essential trait of rational living, to have a clear, sanctioned, ultimate aim" (*PP3*, 141). Neither science nor industry could provide a guiding ideal by which to measure human progress. "The cry was for vacant freedom and indeterminate progress," Santayana wrote. "Onward! Full speed ahead! without asking whether directly before you was not a bottomless pit" (*PP3*, 141).

Elements of this crisis of Western civilization, Santayana knew, had been "working in the body-politic for ages" (*PP3*, 143). His diagnosis was clear: the cause of this "long fever" was "subjectivism, egotism, conceit of mind" (*PP3*, 143). To discover life's guiding ideals, one had to consider not the ego's raw demands but its underlying nature, what Santayana called the psyche, whose predominant impulses determine an individual's actual good. Nor do human natures hang in a void: to consider one's own nature is to consider the conditions of its existence, as well. Such considerations broach realities that, being independent of subjectivity, constrain opinion, balance egotism, and temper conceit of mind. But the world was not ready for sober reflections. The great hopes of the day—that humanity should have material abundance without material concerns—were "contradictory" (*PP3*, 141). For, in truth, neither human nature nor the conditions of existence would allow those outcomes to coincide.

In the romantic progressivism of those around him, Santayana met the antithesis of his own conservative disposition. Sheer enthusiasm for progress had pushed out all consideration of limits. The entire background of subjectivity—the psyche, the natural world, the truth—had been tossed aside. Unconstrained egotism threatened the very idea of human fulfillment with unintelligibility, for there were, apparently, no substantial selves whose specific natures could be fulfilled, no costs imposed by an environing world on selves in search of fulfillment, and no objective truth about the self, the world, or the conditions of flourishing. "The old ark of salvation might be broken up without fear of the deluge, and the whole menagerie of more or less tamed human passions and the keeper, human reason, might be cheerfully committed to the waves; for you were assured that the flood itself was simply your spirit thinking, and unraveling its destiny according to your own secretly omnipotent will" (*IW*, 30).

For Santayana, the times were "moving, rapidly and exultingly, towards ... chaos and universal triviality" (*PP3*, 135). The approach of those discords, he wrote, "sounded like distant thunder" (*PP3*, 135). In *Scepticism*, Santayana would restore consideration of limits to the forefront of philosophy, while setting forth an epistemological framework for a conservative vision of human happiness.

A Philosophy of Imperfection and Limits

Modern philosophers, like the French revolutionaries, tended to underestimate limits. In particular, modern epistemologies misleadingly equated knowledge with direct awareness of ideas or sensory data. Empiricists reduced the events of history to mere sensory images and then "attribute[d] existence to each scintilla taken separately" (*SAF*, 57). Idealists abolished existence by declaring *Esse est percipi*, calling upon "themes of intuition" to "absorb all reality" (*SAF*, 59). For them, a belief was no more than "a fresh datum in thought" (*SAF*, 59). Transcendentalists found existence "repugnant" (*SAF*, 61), "a ghost cut off from knowledge and from the breath of life in me here and now" (*SAF*, 61). Beneath these theories lay the conceit that all existence must be transparent to human intelligence in much the same way that all creation must be transparent to God. Subjectivity had taken center stage in an ill-advised attempt to make humanity the measure of all things.

Some of those responsible for this subjective turn were undoubtedly "men of genius" (*SAF*, 103) and "infant prodigies of reflection" (*SAF*, 103). But Santayana saw in their doctrines "a curious cruelty" (*PP1*, 87). "The sharp mind," he said, "finds things queer, perverse; it puns about them; and it doesn't see why they shouldn't be expected and commanded to be quite other than they are; but all this without much hope of mending them, and a sardonic grin" (*PP1*, 87–88). Their radical innovations in philosophy cut against human fulfillment by ignoring its natural conditions. They inflated the ego but channeled it in no particular direction. They invited endless striving but gave no sign of the hidden constraints poised to defeat it. They fueled ambition but supplied no larger perspective that might show it where to stop.

Santayana's friends not infrequently fell victim to the rampant egotism of the times. Santayana observed in Lionel Johnson a man driven by "emotional absolutism" and "hatred of everything not plastic to fancy" (*PP2*, 61). That unbridled impulse drove him "from Victorian England into Celtic poetry and Catholic supernaturalism" and even then it "kept him from accepting definition and limitation" (*PP2*, 61). Johnson simply "could not deny himself other dreams" (*PP2*, 61).

Lowes Dickinson was another untethered dreamer. "He prayed, watched, and laboured to redeem human life," but he "began by refusing to understand what human life is" (*PP3*, 24). "Too weak to face the truth," Dickinson "set himself a task too great for Titans: to shatter this world to bits and put it together again on a moralistic plan" (*PP3*, 24). The plan, hopelessly utopian, was "that no one should suffer, and that all should love one another: in other words, that no one should be alive or should distinguish what he loved from what he hated" (*PP3*, 24).

No less consumed by egotism was Frank Russell, brother of the famous Bertrand and perhaps Santayana's closest friend. Russell professed to want a happy marriage but couldn't live within those limits, destroying one marriage after another by pursuing affairs. "What folly," Santayana wrote, "after having found ... domestic peace with [a] good woman, and tested the union for so many years, that he should now drive her away, and not only launch upon a new and dangerous voyage, but destroy his home port" (*PP3*, 73). In an 1894 letter to Santayana, Russell confessed: "I am all for the emotional strife and struggle, however vague and however formless, as being at least a reaching toward some end unknown, and seen only by faith as existing at all" (*PP3*, 63).

Egotism, aided and abetted by philosophy, was a frontal assault on the foundations of happiness as understood by Santayana. Happiness, like subjectivity itself, depended on natural conditions utterly unlike subjectivity or consciousness. The dangerous fiction of an unbridled ego could be sustained only by ignoring the natural ground of subjectivity and the limits it imposed. Apart from a reckoning with those limits, happiness would remain forever out of reach. Philosophy could still awaken the modern world from "the Satanic dream that we were creators and not creatures" (*IW*, 34), but it would have to admit realities beyond the veil of sensory data. Philosophy would have to develop "naturalist convictions" (*PP2*, 6). For such convictions, Santayana wrote, "revealed the real background, the true and safe foundation, for human courage, human reason, and human imagination" (*PP2*, 6).

Naturalist convictions belong to the universal orthodoxy of common sense that Santayana sought to conserve in *Scepticism*. "I am animated," he declared in the Preface, "by distrust of all high guesses, and by sympathy with the old prejudices and workaday opinions of mankind: they are ill expressed, but they are well grounded" (*SAF*, v). Santayana would restore those old prejudices and workaday opinions to their rightful place in philosophy by making two pivotal moves: identifying knowledge with transitive intelligence, not direct awareness, and taking seriously the promptings of instinctive faith in things unseen.

For Santayana, modern epistemologies made a crucial error when they equated knowledge with direct awareness of immediate objects. Were knowledge actually reducible to thought or perception, there would be nothing else under the sun besides minds, ideas, and images. Subjectivity would have swallowed the entire real world. To expose the error, Santayana distinguished awareness—what he called "intuition"—from its objects.

Objects of intuition—what Santayana called "essences"—are distinct forms, such as the roughness of sandpaper, the gray of a winter sky, the Pythagorean theorem, or Hamlet's soliloquy. They are infinite in number. Related only by their differences, as blue and red are related only by not being the same color, each is equally central in its own right. There is no center or direction of survey intrinsic to essences, and no spatial or temporal relations inhere in them. Their very distinctness excludes all change. To allege that an essence exists, then, is to discover something not present in the datum itself. It is to discover intuition: "the finding, the occurrence, the assault, the impact of that being here and now" (*SAF*, 37). Intuition of essence repeated with the same intent—what Santayana called "discourse"—betrays something unlike any essence. A moving survey, discourse has its own focus and direction. Those additives—that is, a movement, a focus, and a direction of survey—do not belong to essences themselves and point to a type of being altogether different.

Nor can pure subjectivity be the type of being pointed to, for the selectiveness of discourse would be foreign to disembodied awareness. For Santayana, discourse betrays the vital interests of an organism—a living psyche beneath intuition and discourse, scouring essences for signs of ulterior events. This "animal soul" is "a center of organization and moral direction for the body of that creature and for all his arts" (*IW*, 42). But if discourse points to a type of being other than essence or subjectivity, then knowledge must be a transitive, not a direct, relation—a species of belief, not of vision. Belief in the existence of a real psyche beneath discourse inevitably constrains epistemological excess.

Objects not directly available to intuition can be known but imperfectly. One must take care not to be mistaken about oneself or others, and one's knowledge of them will be fraught with uncertainty. The transitivity of knowledge deals a powerful blow to the rampaging egotism Santayana hoped to subdue.

But if discourse suggests a real psyche, it also suggests a real world in which the psyche has arisen. Belief in the psyche is belief in substance "in the etymological sense of the term" (*SAF*, 182)—that is, "belief in a thing or event subsisting in its own plane" (*SAF*, 182). A mode of substance, the psyche is but the tip of an iceberg. If belief in the psyche constrains epistemological excess, belief in substance has the same effect in spades. Knowledge of substance is not just a matter of plumbing the depths of human organisms, it is also a matter of probing a vast non-human world. Humility and self-restraint, not egotism and self-assertion, are the appropriate posture in such a risky enterprise.

To belief in the psyche and substance Santayana added a third constraint on human knowledge. For just as a belief can be mistaken about the actual disposition of substance at any given time, a belief can also be mistaken about its past or future disposition. Knowledge of substance posits a "subtle reality" (*SAF*, 262) not itself a substance: the truth about the career of substance in time.

Most often recognized in the context of disputes, truth appears to be a property of opinion. The correct opinion—the truth—is "felt to be somehow inseparable from rival opinions" (*SAF*, 266). But this conception of truth is misleading in a way that feeds the very egotism Santayana sought to temper, for if truth is inseparable from rival opinions, then "people say that if there was no mind and consequently no error, there could be no truth" (*SAF*, 266). Here, again, philosophy faces the Promethean temptation to make all reality dependent on subjectivity. The romantics succumbed to that temptation, denying not only the independent existence of substance but also the independent being of truth (*SAF*, 265). "No substance exists, according to their view," Santayana wrote, "but only things as they seem from moment to moment; so that it is idle to contrast opinion with truth, seeing that there is nothing, not even things, except in opinion" (*SAF*, 265).

For Santayana, belief in the independent existence of substance meant truth could not be a property of opinion. An opinion might be correct or incorrect but only in relation to "the standard comprehensive description" of all facts (*SAF*, 266)—that is, only in relation to the truth. All opinion, whether of the past, the present, or the future, is thereby made answerable to a reality independent of subjectivity—an infinite reality, no less. For the comprehensive description of any fact includes all of its "radiations" (*SAF*, 267)—"all that perspective of the world of facts and of the realm of essence which is obtained by taking this fact as a centre and viewing everything else only in relation with it" (*SAF*, 267). Such a staggering prospect cannot but tame the ego. "Evidently," Santayana wrote, "no opinion can embrace it all, or identify itself with it" (*SAF*, 267).

Santayana's account of knowledge as belief in substance and truth—realities independent of subjectivity that forever constrain the knowledge enterprise—constitutes one pillar of his philosophy of imperfection. The other is his openness to the non-rational. A sophisticated sceptic might be persuaded to believe in substance and truth by following the thread of Santayana's ontology as outlined above. But humans are imperfectly rational, and we cannot live by reason alone. Ultimately, belief in substance rests on what Santayana called "animal faith": the "assurance of the not-given" that is "involved in action, in expectation, in fear, hope, or want" (*PGS*, 19). Belief in substance, Santayana wrote, "is the most irrational, animal, and primitive of beliefs: it is the voice of hunger" (*SAF*, 191). Those who reject belief in substance ignore "their most familiar and massive convictions" (*SAF*, 186). "I should be doing myself … violence," Santayana said, "if I denied the validity of perception, and asserted that a thunder-clap … was only a musical chord, with no formidable event of any sort going on beyond the sound" (*SAF*, 187–188).

Philosophers who demand a reason for everything make an unreasonable demand: "there cannot be a reason for everything" (*SAF*, 186). Yet if demanding reasons is "automatic" in the philosopher, not demanding them is no less automatic in the common person (*SAF*, 186). Santayana once again sides with universal human orthodoxy. Were human intelligence omniscient, there might be no need for common sense opinions founded on faith, but that is not the nature of the actual case. Knowledge is but one imperfect means by which finite beings make their way in a finite world. Faith is another. By conserving them, Santayana brought to heel the unconstrained egotism of modern epistemology, slaying what he playfully called "the romantic dragon" (*SAF*, 123).

Belief in the independent being of psyche, substance, and truth provides a framework for a constrained vision of human happiness. The specific nature of psyche holds impulse and opinion to account, for the indulgence of some impulses will prove detrimental to a nature so constituted, and opinions about the psyche, no matter how passionately held, will sometimes be incorrect. The objective nature of substance routinely brings down ambition to humiliating defeat. We may flatter ourselves that we are indispensable, but the truth hangs over us in silent judgment, and the mutability at the heart of substance, in time, will make that truth felt. Framed by such beliefs, happiness calls for self-knowledge, not self-aggrandizement, for accrued wisdom, not scientific or technological prowess. The goal is not to be carried away by our impulses but to observe how they trade off against each other, choose to cultivate only the best of them, and establish a pleasant harmony among them all.

This vision of human flourishing as moderation and compromise supports the ordinary, everyday fulfillments to which the conservative is predisposed. With human knowledge hemmed in by the obscure motions of psyche and substance, scepticism and prudence are in order. The great promise of tomorrow may disappoint. Better, therefore, to cherish to the fullest the familiar goods already available to us. For Santayana, spirituality was the quintessence of this attitude. "You give up everything in the form of claims," he explained; "you receive everything back in the form of a divine presence" (*PP3*, 12). In his youth, Santayana's sister had observed that he was by nature "detached"

(*PP1*, 88)—that is, disinclined to make claims for himself. Instead, it was the complete loss of self, the union of consciousness with immediacy, that for him was "the acme of life" (*SAF*, 126). To be so absorbed, he wrote, was to "cease to live temporally" and "intellectually to be saved" (*SAF*, 128). It was "life at its best" (*SAF*, 130). Santayana's love of spirituality still resonates today and points to the contemporary relevance of his conservatism.

Santayana's Conservatism Today

Conservatism has long been imbued with a kind of pessimism (Will 2019, 402), and Santayana's conservatism is no exception. Philosophers, he thought, are free to invent a world transparent to intelligence, ruled by our highest ideals cast as independent powers, or otherwise not subject to ordinary beliefs, but such armchair visions cannot stand up to action. No sooner do we act then we must believe again in that ancient and fallen world whose inherent constraints we know painfully well. This is the negative pole of Santayana's conservatism. But the same ontological distinctions that give rise to the doctrine of animal faith—and so to belief in a fallen world—also provide a foundation for the momentary transcendence of belief, opening a door to a kind of salvation. Taken together, these two poles offer a conservatism that is neither optimistic nor pessimistic but thoroughly joyous.

Starting from the distinction between intuition and its datum, Santayana provides ontological support for common sense opinions, reining in epistemological hubris. With belief in psyche and substance pointing unavoidably to human limits, those limits become harder to evade. But in becoming harder to evade they also become easier to accept and to forget. Preoccupation with altering the conditions of human life fades as attention turns, instead, to fulfillment. When the impulse to act predominates, data automatically signify the movements of substance, but the same essences, once distinguished, can be enjoyed for their own sake.

For Santayana, two ways of relating to essence enrich the present and make it worth conserving. Imagination is one. The stories we tell about what goes on in the world have a certain poetic meaning, but they are not exact transcripts of nature. Treating them as if they were invites a "means and ends" approach to intelligence. The purpose of intelligence, then, is simply to aid us in our efforts to control things. We sideline the intrinsic value of imagination in a rush to innovate around whatever conditions happen to stand in our way.

The problem is not instrumental intelligence as such. In fact, Santayana supported the use of science and commerce for the improvement of life (*LR5*, 239). But surging demand for scientific knowledge and innovation risks throwing out the baby with the bathwater, and the conservative Santayana hedged against that risk. Imagination, like science, has meaning with respect to psyche and substance. Yet the value of Orion's Belt or the myth of Sisyphus is expressive, not scientific. If intelligence were always instrumental, there would be a surfeit of contested meanings but no free play of imagination, no poetry, literature, or mythology. The loss would be devastating to human fulfillment. Santayana sought to conserve imagination as against encroaching scientific reductionism.

Inasmuch as it follows in the footsteps of science, philosophy, too, risks becoming reductionist. The discovery of objective truth cannot be the sole purpose of philosophy, for that is a recipe for technical controversies that fill the pages of professional journals but fail to enrich the present. To pursue objective truth presupposes that it can be known. To treat intellectual activity as a means of control presupposes an environment that can be controlled. The conservative Santayana rejected the first presupposition and pulled back from the second.

For Santayana, objective truth is forever closed to direct inspection. We can take control of life, but only at the margins and before the unaccountable flux of substance reverses human progress in a deluge. Still, the expressive value of imagination can be enjoyed even in the absence of control. Without imagination, life would be reduced to a meaningless mechanism. The conservative can live without direct access to objective truth but not without meaning. The works of human imagination, Santayana wrote, "alone are good; and the rest—the whole real world—is ashes in the mouth" (*PGS*, 7).

Spirituality enriches the present, too, albeit in a way more religious than literary. Spirituality, like imagination, can be distinguished only by prying apart what animal faith has glued together: I mean essences and the substantial events they symbolize. When invested with animal faith, data are not noticed at all. We see only what they indicate about events. But Santayana's doctrine of animal faith calls attention to the ontological complexity of knowing, distinguishing immediacy from ulterior objects. Once aware of that complexity, the data we miss when prompted by animal faith can be seen as they are in themselves. Thus, Santayana's doctrine, which conserves the common sense beliefs that ground the knowledge enterprise, also contains the means of transcending them.

Santayana understood by spirituality simply the clear seeing of immediacy, without reference to anything ulterior, such as the self or the world. Many religions take a similar view. One strand of Christianity, for example, invites us to transcend the cares of the world in the knowledge that God will provide. The birds of the air and the lilies of the field do this naturally. For the rest of us, such transcendence may require deliberate efforts to ignore the import of what we see and experience. What remains, in any case, is a bare essence, a mere image with no existence and no significance. Yet those who behold the immediate untouched by urgency, doubt, and confusion have their reward in the radiance of the present.

The quest for fulfillment leads us through the terrain of animal faith in hopes of modifying existence to accommodate our demands. Those efforts can be successful and have been increasingly, even astonishingly, so in recent times. But they are neither costless nor final. History tells of the fearsome cost of progress in blood and treasure, and the constant change that swirls within and around us means further progress must be made, with no end in sight. There is no such thing as complete fulfillment in the realm of action.

Spirituality offers such fulfillment to those willing to ignore the promptings of animal faith. This is apt to happen spontaneously as attention to ulterior things wanes. "As I was jogging to market in my village cart," Santayana wrote, "beauty has burst upon me and the reins have dropped from my hands. I am transported, in a certain measure, into a state of trance. I see with extraordinary clearness, yet what I see seems strange and wonderful, because I no longer look in order to understand, but only in order to see" (*RE*, 6–7). Such fulfillments do not last, but they lack any reference to the self with its voracious appetite for progress, making them complete in themselves.

But to transcend animal faith is one thing, to evade it another. Santayana instinctively resisted philosophical innovations that evaded animal faith. What he called "the subjective attitude in philosophy" was, he said, "always legitimate; because a mind capable of self-consciousness is always free to reduce all things to its own view of them" (*RM*, 1). But such evasions surrender the ground of common sense beneath our feet, and the price of surrender is confusion, anxiety, and want of fulfillment.

Standing firmly on the ground takes courage, for it means affirming the beliefs we take for granted in action: that we are but small creatures pitted against a vast world, borne by a power outrunning us on all sides, whose face we will never see, whose course we can hardly alter, and whose incessant transformations are destined to swallow us. But those articles of faith, once accepted, can set us free, for only then can we see and experience without trying to know or to control. Spiritual fulfillment, Santayana feared, would be lost were philosophy to break free of its anchorage in common sense opinion, sinking transcendence in the conceit of an unconstrained subjectivity.

Today, as in Santayana's lifetime, the world appears to be overwhelmingly on the side of progress. Emerson's "law of eternal procession" (Emerson 1888a, 293) thrills us. We live for a future better than the present. Material and moral improvement mean more to us than imagination or spirituality. We see the limits of time, space, and ignorance as temporary challenges, not permanent constraints inviting us to acquiesce in the good enough. To count imagination and spirituality among the highest goods suggests callous lack of concern for human suffering and injustice. Given the overwhelming appeal of this progressive attitude, what value, if any, can we find in Santayana's conservatism?

One lesson it offers concerns the cost of improvement. Progress is always relative to a particular value, so that progress in any direction necessarily incurs costs in others—that is, in terms of other values not realized. Santayana calls our attention to those mounting collateral costs. Frenetic pursuit of improvement leaves little time for individuality to develop, for the imagination to expand, or for the spirit to rise above the urgency of animal faith. "If," Santayana wrote, "I am compelled to be in an office (and up to business, too) from early morning to late afternoon, with long journeys in thundering and sweltering trains before and after and a flying shot at a quick lunch in between, I am caught and held both in soul and body; and except for the freedom to work and to rise by that work. ... I am not suffered to exist morally at all" (*COUS*, 210).

Nor can we leave Santayana's conservatism without being reminded of human finitude. Philosophers may amuse themselves by reducing all things to their own view of them, but animal faith gives the lie to that sort of classroom exercise. The real world, space, and time exist, and we must answer to those non-rational realities, not they to us. Better to reconcile ourselves to that fact than to avoid confronting it. It's only natural to try to work toward a better future, but that future, we must remember, may never come to be.

Reflection on the human predicament as adumbrated by animal faith won't make us optimists, but it shouldn't make us dour pessimists, either. Santayana's conservatism is not about the future or the past. Instead, such reflections should return us to the present with renewed appreciation of its intrinsic value. To be conservative, Oakeshott reminds us, is "to be equal to one's own fortune, to live at the level of one's own means, to be content with the want of greater perfection which belongs alike to oneself and one's circumstances" (Oakeshott 1962, 409). "I was never afraid of disillusion," Santayana wrote, "and I have chosen it" (*PGS*, 8). But the conservative disposition, properly understood, cannot be reduced to mere acceptance or resignation. On the contrary, acceptance for the conservative is but a necessary prelude to the joy of living fully in the present, finding fulfillment in the familiar rounds of life. "And the pismire is equally perfect," said Walt Whitman, "and a grain of sand, and the egg of the wren" (Whitman 1888, 53). If tomorrow should happen to bring something better, that would be a pleasant surprise.

References

Emerson, Ralph Waldo. 1888a. Circles. In *The Works of Ralph Waldo Emerson*, vol. II, 281–300. Boston: Houghton, Mifflin and Company.

———. 1888b. Self-Reliance. In *The Works of Ralph Waldo Emerson*, vol. II, 47–87. Boston: Houghton, Mifflin and Company.

James, William. 1956. The Moral Philosopher and the Moral Life. In *The Will to Believe and Other Essays in Popular Philosophy*. New York: Dover Publications.

Kirk, Russell. 1995. *The Conservative Mind from Burke to Eliot*. 7th rev. ed. Washington, DC: Regnery Publishing, Inc.

O'Sullivan, Noël. 1976. *Conservatism*. London: J. M. Dent & Sons LTD.

Oakeshott, Michael. 1962. On Being Conservative. In *Rationalism in Politics and Other Essays*. Indianapolis, IN: Liberty Fund.

Santayana, George. 1924. *Scepticism and Animal Faith: Introduction to a System of Philosophy*. New York: Charles Scribner's Sons. [Second Impression of 1923 Edition]. Cited as *SAF*.

———. 1927. *The Realm of Essence*. New York: Charles Scribner's Sons. Cited as *RE*.

———. 1928. *The Life of Reason: Or, the Phases of Human Progress, Vol. v, Reason in Science*. New York: Charles Scribner's Sons. Cited as *LR5*.

———. 1930. *The Realm of Matter*. New York: Charles Scribner's Sons. Cited as *RM*.

———. 1944. *Persons and Places: The Background of My Life*. New York: Charles Scribner's Sons. Cited as *PP1*.

———. 1945. *Persons and Places: The Middle Span*. New York: Charles Scribner's Sons. Cited as *PP2*.

———. 1951. A General Confession. In *The Philosophy of George Santayana*, ed. Paul Arthur Schilpp. New York: Tudor Publishing Company. Cited as *PGS*.

———. 1953. *Persons and Places: My Host the World*. New York: Charles Scribner's Sons. Cited as *PP3*.

———. 1957. Americanism. In *The Idler and His Works and Other Essays*, ed. Daniel Cory, 21–53. New York: George Braziller. Cited as *IW*.

Whitman, Walt. 1888. *Leaves of Grass*. Philadelphia: David McKay.

Will, George F. 2019. *The Conservative Sensibility*. New York: Hachette Books.

Index[1]

A

Agency, 27, 40, 41, 51, 204, 253, 262, 263, 265–267, 346

Animal, 1, 2, 5, 17, 18, 21–27, 30, 40, 62, 64, 65, 68, 88–92, 96, 102, 104, 105, 109, 110, 113, 116–122, 130, 132, 133, 137, 143–145, 152–154, 168–171, 169n2, 173, 181, 186, 195, 197–203, 202n15, 206, 209–211, 212n34, 220–222, 226, 231, 233, 234, 238, 241–254, 258–260, 263, 264, 267–269, 274, 275, 277, 280, 283, 284, 284n15, 301n8, 304, 317n14, 328, 334, 337, 343, 344, 344n6, 359, 360, 362, 366n34, 367, 370n40, 380, 382

Animal faith, 2, 5, 14, 18, 20–26, 29, 30, 40, 40n4, 42–44, 46, 47n17, 48, 49, 49n21, 51, 51n25, 54, 57, 61, 61n8, 63, 68, 89, 91–93, 95, 96n1, 101, 104, 106, 107, 109–122, 141, 144, 152, 156–159, 163–166, 168–170, 173, 181, 185–187, 190, 193–217, 235, 241–254, 258–260, 260n5, 263, 263n14, 264, 266, 267, 269, 273n1, 274, 283, 288, 328, 335, 343n2, 344, 347, 349, 353–356, 353n16, 360, 362n29, 363, 365, 367, 368n37, 369, 382–386

tenets of, 2, 49n21, 86, 88–92

See also Faith

Animality, 5, 6, 89, 242, 251–253

"Apologia Pro Mente Sua" (Santayana, 1940), 26, 63, 190, 242

Appearances, 15, 34–36, 39–42, 44–49, 47n18, 97, 99, 103, 104, 114, 115, 126, 135, 136, 144, 181, 183, 183n3, 184, 194, 198–200, 227, 229, 241, 250, 264, 297, 318, 334, 354, 363

Arcesilaus (315/4–241/40 BCE), 243

Aristotle (384–322 BCE), 18, 49, 106, 179, 224, 224n8, 226, 265, 266, 294, 299, 301, 302n10, 304n15, 317, 329

Art, 27, 105, 107, 177, 179, 180, 186, 189, 206n25, 208, 211, 213, 215, 276, 306, 319, 330, 344, 345, 350, 350n12, 351, 365, 369n38, 375, 380

Augustine (354-430), 279n9

Austin, J. L. (1911–1960), 73, 82, 83, 85

---

[1] Note: Page numbers followed by 'n' refer to notes.

© The Author(s), under exclusive license to Springer Nature Switzerland AG 2024
M. A. Coleman, G. Tiller (eds.), *The Palgrave Companion to George Santayana's Scepticism and Animal Faith*, Palgrave Companions,
https://doi.org/10.1007/978-3-031-46367-9

390 INDEX

B

Being, 2, 6, 12, 13, 15, 17–22, 26, 27, 34–36, 40, 41, 44, 46, 48, 49, 51, 52, 58, 60, 68, 74, 77, 79, 89, 90, 92, 98–100, 102–104, 109–116, 122, 126–128, 130–132, 136, 138, 141, 143, 150, 152, 156, 159, 168–170, 172, 182–185, 183n3, 183n4, 185n5, 190, 194, 197, 198, 200, 200n10, 201, 203, 209, 211–215, 212n35, 220, 221, 224n8, 225–227, 227n13, 228n16, 229, 230n18, 233, 233n21, 236–238, 243–245, 249–253, 257, 260–266, 261n9, 269, 270, 274n2, 275–281, 283–285, 283n14, 286n18, 287, 296–299, 301, 302n12, 303, 306, 307, 310–312, 315–318, 326, 328, 328n4, 331, 331n9, 333, 334, 337, 337n11, 338, 343, 346, 348–351, 356, 356n20, 356n21, 358–365, 364n31, 365n33, 367–370, 368n36, 374, 378–382, 386

Belief(s), 2, 17, 34, 59, 73, 95, 110, 125, 151, 164, 181, 193, 227, 243, 258, 273n1, 295, 314, 332, 342, 373

  natural, 20, 89

Bergson, Henri (1859–1941), 326, 342

Berkeley, George (1685–1753), 75, 155n9, 328

Body, 1, 20, 36, 37, 45, 45n13, 76, 79, 90, 127, 150, 154, 156, 180, 190, 198, 206, 207, 209, 210, 213, 217, 220, 222, 224n8, 226, 228, 229, 231, 234, 246, 248, 249, 258, 260, 267, 275, 277, 287, 312, 315, 332, 344n6, 353, 355n19, 356n21, 361, 364n32, 369, 380, 386

The Book of the Homeless (Wharton, 1916), 14

Bradley, F. H. (1846–1924), 38, 39n2, 48, 127n2

Buchler, Justus (1914–1991), 252, 276, 278

Buddhism, 215, 313, 313n10

C

Candide (Voltaire, 1759), 58

Carnap, Rudolf (1891–1970), 73, 80–82

Categories, 18, 25, 29, 40, 41, 53, 57, 59, 62, 92, 104, 118, 121, 190, 197, 227n15, 228n16, 234n23, 235, 258, 259, 264–268, 270, 273, 275–279, 282, 288, 293, 335, 342, 362

Catholicism, 14, 320, 320n21, 330, 373

Causation, 35, 42n7, 43

Cause, 15, 19, 27, 28, 37, 57, 66, 90, 110, 116, 141, 153, 180, 207, 224, 283, 287, 307, 352n14, 378

Cavell, Stanley (1926–2018), 74, 75, 83, 85, 92, 243, 252

Certainty, 17–19, 36–39, 40n4, 42, 44, 45, 47, 49–54, 74, 75, 79, 81, 83, 84, 88, 90, 95, 97–101, 106, 109–111, 114–116, 120–122, 164, 165, 193–195, 230, 245, 247, 249, 250, 253, 259, 260, 269, 335, 364

Change, 6, 14, 15, 25, 42, 43, 60, 87, 112, 115, 121, 122, 136, 137, 149, 166, 177, 181, 182, 199, 204, 210–212, 250, 265, 266, 281, 293–308, 333, 335, 337, 341, 344, 353, 358, 363, 366n34, 367, 373–375, 380, 384

Charity, 242, 317, 376

  See also Love

Christ, 320, 321

Christianity, 307, 313, 313n7, 320, 320n21, 384

Clifford, W. K. (1845–1879), 230, 230n18

Clinica della Piccola Compagna di Maria (Clinic of the Little Company of Mary)/ "Blue Nuns," 15

Codman, Julian (1870–1932), 376

Cogito, 36, 38, 39, 58n2, 59, 61, 66, 97–99, 332, 334

Common sense, 1, 2, 17, 22, 27, 40n4, 45, 50, 51, 65, 65n17, 85, 86, 91, 101, 102, 104, 110, 132, 133, 137, 139–141, 145, 151, 154, 155, 166, 169, 173, 187, 189, 196, 197, 228, 275, 278, 283, 342, 344, 355, 357, 362n29, 373, 380, 382–385

Compatibilism, 223, 224
Consciousness, 1, 2, 11, 19–21, 26–29, 46n16, 47, 87, 96, 98–102, 105, 106, 114, 136, 143, 181, 182, 185, 193, 194, 194n3, 196, 197, 199–201, 200n9, 203, 206, 206n26, 209–211, 213, 214, 219, 223–225, 224n8, 227, 227n13, 233, 237, 246, 249, 259, 261, 262, 267, 274, 274n2, 278, 316, 333, 342, 343n2, 344, 345, 354, 355, 358, 360, 361, 363, 364, 366, 377, 379, 383
Conservatism, 346, 351, 373–386
Continuum, 6, 183n4, 185, 246, 295, 302–306, 305n17
Cory, Daniel (1904–1972), 12, 15, 16
Cratylus (c. 450 BCE), 301
Criticism, 4, 5, 51, 52, 58, 82, 96–99, 104, 110, 113, 125–146, 153, 158, 159n14, 164, 178, 206–211, 207n29, 214, 216, 217, 219, 244, 247, 252, 276, 286, 296n5, 310, 319, 331, 331n8, 333, 337, 344
Critique of Pure Reason (Kant, 1781/1787), 78, 180
Crying, 5, 219–229, 235, 237, 238, 238n26

D

Datum, 38–44, 47, 96–104, 98n3, 106, 107, 114, 115, 137n4, 181, 182, 183n3, 184, 194, 195n4, 199, 199n8, 245, 342, 354, 364, 378, 380, 383
"A Defence of Common Sense" (Moore, 1925), 78
Delusions, 35, 133, 196, 197, 201, 209–211, 217, 229, 247, 296, 349, 354
Democritus (c. 460–c. 370), 105, 273, 294, 333
Demon, Descartes's, 35
Descartes, Rene (1596–1650), 2, 4, 5, 17, 57–62, 58n2, 59n4, 61n9, 64–67, 65n18, 75–78, 82, 83, 85, 96–102, 97n2, 104, 105, 153, 157, 163, 164, 181, 193, 194, 203, 225, 243, 269n22, 294n2, 295n4, 325–338, 342
Determinism, 223, 224, 309
Deus sive Natura, 317, 318, 321
Dewey, John (1859–1952), 12, 46, 46n16, 48, 63n12, 63n13, 109, 111, 115n2, 118–120, 119n3, 127, 159, 159n15, 160, 160n16, 160n17, 262n11, 373
D'Holbach, Paul-Henri Thiry (Baron) (1723-1789), 230, 230n18
Dickinson, G. Lowes (1862–1932), 379
Discourse on Method (Descartes, 1637), 57–69
Dogma, 2, 19, 20, 37, 39, 52, 60, 61, 86, 96, 97, 101, 114, 119, 133, 135, 137, 140, 170, 198, 205n23, 214, 244, 251, 316
Dogmatism, 38, 52, 198, 201, 210, 212, 314, 349, 350
Dominations and Powers (Santayana, 1951), 12, 330
Doubt(s), 2, 15, 19, 24, 34–39, 41, 44, 45, 45n13, 49–53, 50n23, 50n24, 58n2, 60, 61, 75, 76, 78–80, 82–85, 87, 90–93, 97–99, 97n2, 101, 110–114, 116, 118, 125, 134–140, 142, 144–146, 151, 156, 158, 165, 167, 168, 173, 181, 184, 185, 193–195, 197, 199, 203, 204, 225, 244, 245, 247, 250, 251, 253, 259, 261, 274, 275, 283, 284, 295n4, 296n5, 304n15, 314, 316, 318, 330, 332, 334–336, 342, 344, 347–349, 360, 363, 364, 384
Dreams, 35, 42, 77, 78, 99, 114, 132, 137, 178, 179, 184, 185, 187, 202, 314, 354n17, 359n27, 364, 377, 379, 380
Dualism, 45, 223, 249
Ducasse, Curt John (1881–1969), 21

E

Egotism, 378, 379, 381, 382
Egotism in German Philosophy (Santayana, 1915), 14, 69, 253
Eliot, Charles William (1834–1926) [president of Harvard, 1869–1909], 13

Emerson, Ralph Waldo (1803–1882), 282, 373, 375, 376, 385
Empiricism, 36, 37, 47n18, 48, 97, 101n4, 130, 135, 159n15
"Empiricism, Semantics and Ontology" (Carnap, 1950), 80
Empiricist, 34, 47n18, 91, 104, 110, 118, 121, 135, 165, 168, 170, 280, 368, 378
Entelechy, 224n8, 277
Epicurus (341–270 BCE), 46n15, 294
Epiphenomenalism, 19, 20, 219–228, 231, 235, 267
Epistemology, 2, 5, 53, 96, 97, 99, 104–107, 114, 129, 149–160, 179, 186, 194–197, 204, 205, 209, 243, 249, 260, 274, 300, 306n18, 311, 330n6, 344, 378, 380, 382
  anti-, 196, 204n18
Esse est percipi, 378
Essence(s), 2, 11, 39, 60, 87, 98, 115, 135, 153n7, 164, 183, 194, 220, 242, 257, 273, 293, 309, 326, 343, 380
  realm of, 6, 87, 136, 137n4, 138, 141, 183, 183n4, 199, 259, 261, 261n8, 262, 264, 267, 269, 277–279, 281, 282, 283n14, 295, 300, 302–306, 302n13, 314–316, 335, 381
Eternal, 44, 109, 121, 129, 136, 143, 144, 171–173, 184, 253, 261, 264, 281, 282, 282n12, 283n14, 285–288, 302, 302n11, 307, 314, 317, 319–321, 347–349, 361–363, 385
Eternity, 21, 221, 261, 283n14, 313, 316, 317, 319, 321, 351
Ethics (Spinoza, 1677), 311, 319
Euclidean Geometry, 167
Existence, 17, 34, 38–39, 60, 75, 96, 109, 135, 151, 163, 179, 193, 245, 257, 273n1, 294, 312, 328, 342, 378
Expectation, 24, 40, 42, 53, 62, 63, 97, 102, 187, 189, 196, 200, 201, 201n13, 274, 277, 284, 348, 364, 382

Experience, 1, 4, 21, 25, 27, 34–41, 44n12, 45–47, 46n16, 52, 53, 69, 77, 78, 80, 87, 90, 96–99, 102–105, 107, 110, 113–115, 115n2, 118–122, 127, 132, 133, 135, 136, 138–141, 143, 145, 156, 159, 160, 160n16, 164, 167, 172, 180–182, 184, 187–189, 191, 196, 200–202, 201n12, 207, 208, 208n32, 210, 212, 214–216, 220, 222, 226–229, 233, 245–247, 250, 274, 274n4, 276–278, 280, 282–285, 287, 297, 307, 316, 317, 326, 328, 331–335, 342, 344, 344n5, 345, 347–349, 351, 353–360, 355n19, 356n21, 359n27, 362, 362n29, 363, 363n30, 364n31, 365n33, 366–370, 366n34, 368n36, 369n38, 384, 385
External world, 4, 22, 75, 77, 79, 81, 91, 117, 118, 155, 196, 250, 344, 350

F
Facts, 2, 18, 38, 59, 77, 95, 109, 126, 150, 165, 180, 196, 222, 242, 257, 274, 296n5, 315, 326, 343, 376
Faith, 20–23, 25, 26, 40n5, 41, 42, 50, 51, 63, 64, 68, 78, 95, 97, 100–104, 106, 110, 111, 113, 115–118, 135, 140, 142, 143, 152, 153, 157, 158, 165, 166, 170, 171, 173, 186, 195, 201, 202n15, 203n17, 204, 206, 219, 222, 224, 230, 242, 251, 335, 344, 347, 349, 350n12, 352, 353n16, 359, 360, 362, 362n29, 365–367, 379, 380, 382, 385
Fallibilism, 34, 100, 107, 109, 119, 125, 138, 172, 351
Fichte, Johann Gottlieb (1762–1814), 40
Flux, 6, 44, 121, 122, 181–183, 185n5, 220, 233, 252, 273n1, 277n8, 281, 286, 295, 301, 301n9, 304–307, 307n20, 316, 334, 355, 358, 384
Form of life, 89, 220, 343n3

INDEX   393

Foundationalism, 62, 76, 76n2, 90, 195, 246
Foundation(s), 2, 17–20, 23, 37, 50n22, 50n23, 59, 62, 64, 65, 74, 76, 88, 90–93, 96, 97, 99, 101, 102, 117, 126, 128, 138, 139, 150, 158, 159, 163, 164, 184, 194, 195, 205, 250, 275, 318, 332, 379, 380, 383
Freewill, 223, 224
Freud, Sigmund (1856-1939), 230, 231, 233, 233n22, 234, 234n23, 345

G

"A General Confession" (Santayana, 1940), 313
Given, 19, 24, 39, 42, 43, 48, 53, 98n3, 103, 105, 106, 135, 137, 189, 195n4, 205, 227, 333, 334, 343, 356, 357
God, 18, 36, 37, 61n9, 69, 110, 219, 252, 261, 261n9, 262, 269, 269n22, 282, 309, 317, 318, 320, 321, 322n27, 360, 379, 384
Gödel, Kurt (1906–1978), 167n1
Goethe, Johann Wolfgang von (1749–1832), 178, 345, 374
Grammar, 81, 82, 227n15, 338

H

Harvard University, 11–15, 17, 155n9, 179, 287, 326, 377
Hegel, Georg Wilhelm Friedrich (1770–1831), 13, 50, 53, 54, 96, 98–102, 105, 106, 203, 227
Heraclitus (c. 500 BC), 6, 295, 297–303, 306, 307
Hinge proposition(s), 88–93, 89n7
Hofmannsthal, Hugo von (1874-1929), 6, 342, 345–354, 352n14, 356, 357n23, 358, 359, 359n26, 361–363, 366, 367n35, 370
"How to Make Our Ideas Clear" (Peirce, 1878), 118
Hume, David (1711–1776), 5, 20, 39, 39n3, 74, 75, 85, 87, 89, 90, 90n8, 101, 101n4, 151n3, 153, 155–157, 155n9, 156n10, 156n11, 203, 227,

227n15, 243, 247, 259n3, 294n2, 311, 336
Husserl, Edmund (1859-1938), 6, 278, 325–338, 369n38

I

Ideal(s), 6, 18, 44, 65, 69n24, 88, 89, 135, 154, 155, 172, 208, 209, 228, 236, 251, 253, 274, 277, 287, 297, 306, 309–322, 352, 357, 364, 374, 377, 378, 383
The Idea of Christ in the Gospels (Santayana, 1946), 12, 330
Idea(s), 4, 6, 19, 24, 34–36, 38–41, 40n4, 45–49, 47n17, 51, 53, 62, 63, 63n12, 66, 75, 81, 83, 85, 91, 92, 96, 99, 118, 120, 131, 136, 137, 141, 150–155, 158, 159, 166, 168, 169, 183, 183n3, 185, 187, 189, 190, 194, 197, 199, 199n8, 200, 204, 205, 207, 208, 211, 213–216, 219, 223, 224n8, 227n15, 233, 234n23, 241, 245, 246, 250, 252, 253, 257, 259, 262, 264, 269, 275, 279–282, 284, 293–309, 312, 314, 315, 319, 320n21, 321, 331, 332, 335, 345–347, 349, 351, 352, 354, 356, 360–366, 364n31, 375, 377, 378, 380
Identity, 22, 43, 60, 102, 114, 136, 164, 171, 209, 210, 260, 263n14, 279, 283n14, 284, 286, 346, 348, 359n27, 376
Illusion(s), 23, 35, 42, 45n13, 87, 102, 106, 113, 182, 184, 197, 199, 202, 205n20, 213, 229, 244, 245, 264, 317, 327, 328n4, 331, 333, 344, 354, 356, 362, 366, 377
Imagination, 1, 5, 68, 111, 115n2, 134, 137n4, 149, 154, 177–191, 199, 201, 216, 231, 314, 327, 338, 350, 351, 355, 358–360, 367–370, 376, 380, 383–385
Imperfection, 6, 36, 374, 375, 378–383
Impressions, 34, 35, 39–41, 212, 226, 227n15, 251, 275, 335, 353

Indubitable, 18, 20, 34, 37, 38, 43–46, 50n22, 53, 54, 61, 67, 76, 76n2, 87, 88, 97, 99, 101, 102, 139, 194, 195, 204n19, 246, 306, 332, 335, 343
In medias rebus, 132, 139
In medias res, 132
Intuition(s), 5, 6, 11, 20–26, 39, 44, 45, 48, 87, 97, 98, 100–103, 106, 107, 114, 115, 136, 154, 159, 164–167, 170, 171, 182–184, 182–183n3, 186, 187, 191, 194, 194n3, 195, 197–205, 203n16, 203n17, 206n26, 207–215, 214n37, 220, 227, 227n15, 251, 252, 260, 277, 284, 295, 300, 301, 301n8, 305, 306, 307n20, 316, 326–328, 333–335, 343, 344, 349n10, 352, 353n16, 354, 356, 360, 363n30, 364, 364n31, 365, 369, 380, 381, 383

J

James, William (1842–1910), 11, 40, 48, 51n25, 51n26, 63n13, 101n4, 109, 110, 118, 119, 122, 127, 155n9, 225n9, 230, 271, 282, 326, 329, 373
Johnson, Lionel (1867–1902), 379
Judaism, 13, 309–311, 320, 347, 376

K

Kallen, Horace (1882–1974), 18, 19, 226, 285n16
Kant, Immanuel (1724–1804), 51, 74, 78, 126–128, 134, 180, 203, 227, 227n15, 228, 243, 276, 294n2, 337
Kerr-Lawson, Angus (1932–2011), 5, 42n7, 59–61, 64, 64n15, 258, 265–267, 280n11, 286n18, 319
Kirk, Russell (1918–1994), 374
Knowledge, 2, 17, 34, 58, 73, 95–107, 109, 115–116, 125–146, 150, 163, 166–170, 185–189, 193, 228, 243, 259, 274, 294, 296–298, 310, 327, 342, 363–367, 374
  non-literal, 165, 169, 171–173

  symbolic, 49, 64n15, 68, 154, 159, 165, 171–173, 284, 286, 287, 296, 365
  traditional definition of, 5
  transitive, 87, 103, 106, 380

L

Lachs, John (1934–), 41n6, 44n11, 49n21, 60n7, 86, 88, 92, 159n14, 195, 196, 196n5, 203–205, 205n23, 212, 212n34, 249, 251, 258, 343, 343n3
Language, 12, 22, 23, 26, 29, 66, 81, 82, 116, 129, 133, 142, 145, 154, 156, 157, 171, 216n40, 243, 244, 248, 251, 261n9, 270, 279, 281, 284, 296, 297, 308, 312, 328, 342, 343, 346–351, 353, 354, 356, 356n20, 357, 359, 361–363, 364n32, 365, 366, 366n34, 369, 370, 375
  game, 89, 156, 156n12, 357
  ordinary, 82–85
The Last Puritan (Santayana, 1936), 12, 29, 276
Leap of faith, 5, 95–107
Leibniz, Gottfried Wilhelm (1646–1716), 58, 137n4, 261, 263n13, 265n18, 278, 316
Levinson, Henry Samuel (1948–2010), 5, 67, 68, 85, 86, 196, 196n5, 196n6, 197, 207, 215, 216, 216n41
Lewis, Clarence Irving (1883-1964), 40, 54n27, 63n13
Liberation, 197, 201, 201n12, 211, 213–216, 232, 233n21, 235–238, 311, 313, 316, 317, 319, 320, 320n21, 322
The Life of Reason (Santayana, 1905–1906), 329
Limbo: boletin de estudios sobre Santayana, 29
Limit(s), 6, 50, 61, 64, 67, 68, 82, 87, 88, 125, 128, 131, 137, 146, 181, 191, 202, 204n19, 206n25, 210, 217, 249, 268, 270, 271, 287, 304, 373–375, 378–383, 385
Locke, John (1632–1704), 48, 75, 155n9, 168

Logic, 18, 40, 51n26, 119, 127–131, 134, 135, 139, 144, 145, 166, 167, 169, 269n22, 270, 297, 300n7, 303, 330n6, 336, 338
Logical principles, 90, 127–129
Logicists, 128–132, 134, 136, 141–145
"The Logic of Fanaticism" (Santayana, 1914), 14
Lotze, Herman (1817–1881), 13
Love, 104, 177, 197, 204n18, 205, 223, 230, 238, 251, 313, 317, 319–321, 322n27, 344, 374, 377, 379, 383
See also Charity
Lowell, A. Lawrence (1856–1943) (president of Harvard, 1909–1933), 14

M

Malebranche, Nicolas (1638-1715), 51
Matter, 6, 60, 110, 126, 150, 184, 196, 242, 257, 273n1, 293, 311n4, 326, 352, 381
 Realm of, 6, 18, 24, 164, 168, 172, 182, 184, 185, 258, 260, 264n16, 265–267, 269, 270, 273, 273n1, 277, 278, 281, 283, 286n18, 295, 300–306, 305n17
Meaning, 18, 43–45, 80–82, 97, 98, 105, 111, 118, 119, 136, 137, 143, 145, 150–152, 156, 157, 160n17, 181–183, 182n3, 194, 197, 198, 225, 230, 235, 238, 257, 263, 268, 278, 279, 294, 296n5, 303n14, 315, 316, 318, 321, 328, 329, 333, 334n10, 342, 343n3, 346, 347, 349, 353, 354, 356–363, 366, 383, 384
Meditations on First Philosophy (Descartes, 1641), 96
Memory, 41–43, 42n8, 60, 87, 96, 100, 102, 114, 118, 135–137, 164, 178, 185, 187–189, 198, 245, 250, 274, 274n4, 282, 285n17, 301, 332, 335, 344, 348, 349, 355, 358
Metanoia, 14, 178, 179, 346, 347, 357, 359, 370

Metaphysics, 2, 17, 37–38, 49, 117, 118, 120, 134, 150, 150n2, 172, 196, 229, 245, 275, 275n6, 294, 317, 318, 332
The Middle Span (Santayana, 1945), 12
Mind, 5, 6, 19, 20, 22, 25, 28, 34–39, 41, 43, 44, 44n11, 46–49, 51n26, 54, 60, 63n12, 64, 65, 67, 69, 69n24, 74, 75, 86, 87, 89, 91, 98, 99, 101, 104, 106, 116, 117, 132, 134, 136, 152, 153, 155, 156, 156n11, 165, 171–173, 181–187, 183n3, 189, 190, 193, 195n4, 199, 206–208, 206n26, 213, 214, 214n37, 216, 221–226, 224n7, 224n8, 227n15, 230–235, 234n23, 242, 244, 245, 247–251, 265, 269, 274–277, 280, 281, 282n12, 284, 287, 294, 298, 307, 310–312, 314, 314n12, 316, 327, 328, 331, 331n9, 333–337, 337n11, 343, 345, 349, 350, 354, 357, 358n25, 360, 363, 364, 366, 366n34, 368n36, 369, 370, 376–381, 385
Monadology (Leibniz, 1714), 58
Moore, G. E. (1873–1958), 5, 73, 78–80, 82, 91, 92
Moral(s), 6, 18, 20, 23, 27, 29, 40, 41, 50, 69, 69n23, 74, 92, 118, 150, 186, 190, 191, 210, 219, 220, 224n8, 226, 227, 228n16, 231, 233, 235, 237, 243, 257, 268, 270, 275, 284, 287, 300n7, 309, 317n14, 318, 319, 332, 345, 351, 353, 365, 368n37, 369, 375, 376, 380, 385
My Host the World (Santayana, 1953), 12, 177

N

Nagel, Thomas (1937–), 74, 79, 81
Naturalism
 epistemological, 5, 150–156, 151n4, 158, 159
 ontological, 5, 150, 155

Nature, 4, 17, 20–28, 30, 36–38, 40, 42, 43, 45–47, 46n16, 49–53, 61, 63, 65, 66, 68, 69, 74, 75, 90, 92, 96, 97, 103–107, 113, 115–121, 125, 127, 128, 130–134, 139–145, 149n1, 150, 150n2, 152, 156, 156n11, 158, 159, 163, 165, 171, 173, 181, 182, 186, 188–190, 189n6, 194, 195n4, 196, 201–204, 207, 209, 212, 226, 228–231, 233–235, 238, 241, 244, 245, 247, 251–253, 259, 260, 262, 264, 265, 267, 268, 270, 274, 275, 277, 279, 279n9, 281, 282n12, 285, 287, 294, 296, 296n5, 299, 301, 306n18, 307n19, 309, 311–313, 315–318, 327, 328, 343, 344, 350n12, 352, 356, 358, 359, 362n29, 364–366, 366n34, 368, 368n36, 369, 374, 375, 377, 378, 382, 383

"The Need for a Recovery of Philosophy" (Dewey, 1917), 111

"A Neglected Argument for the Reality of God" (Peirce, 1908), 110

Nietzsche, Friedrich (1844–1900), 25, 203, 311, 321, 322, 345

"Normal Madness" (Santayana, 1925), 25, 235

O

Oakeshott, Michael (1901–1990), 374, 375, 386

On Certainty (Wittgenstein, 1969), 79

Oneirism, non-, 77, 78, 78n3, 82, 83

Ontology, 5, 6, 57, 62, 65, 98, 104, 109, 126, 128, 129, 149–160, 184, 197, 205, 228n16, 232, 234, 242, 243, 259, 265, 270, 273–288, 331, 342, 382

Order of evidence, 24, 135, 141, 164

Order of genesis, 140, 280

Overheard in Seville: The Bulletin of the Santayana Society, 29

P

Palmer, George Herbert (1843–1933), 75, 155n9

Pantheism, 318n15, 320

Parmenides (c. 500 BC), 6, 295, 296n5, 297–303, 302n12, 306, 307

Past, 41, 42, 44, 85, 95, 102, 110, 113, 115, 135, 155, 156, 181, 181n2, 187, 188, 198, 220, 246, 278, 281, 282, 285, 288, 298, 314, 315, 332, 333, 346, 348, 349, 351, 355, 359n27, 375–377, 381, 386

Peirce, Charles Sanders (1839–1914), 11, 50, 50n24, 63n13, 65n18, 109, 110, 112, 113, 116, 118, 164, 284, 285, 287, 287n22

Perception(s), 22, 23, 26, 34, 35, 37–43, 45, 46, 48, 49, 61, 68, 82, 83, 85, 97, 99, 102–104, 121, 165, 177, 180, 181, 185, 187–189, 194n3, 198, 200, 208n32, 210, 220, 236, 252, 285n17, 297, 301n8, 306, 307n20, 317, 333, 334, 343n2, 353, 353n16, 354, 356, 358, 364, 368n37, 369, 369n39, 380, 382

Persons and Places (Santayana, 1944), 111

Persons and Places (Santayana, critical edition, 1986), 11

Pessimism, 74, 321, 383

Phenomenalism, 48, 227n15, 228

Phenomenalist, 45–49

Philosopher, 2, 4, 5, 11–30, 45–47, 52, 54, 59, 64–66, 64n16, 74, 80, 82, 83, 85, 91, 96, 98, 101, 104–107, 109, 114, 119, 126, 132, 140, 145, 149, 151n3, 153, 153n8, 155, 159, 159n15, 160, 168, 170, 172, 173, 190, 198, 202, 219, 223–225, 224n7, 227, 228, 230, 231, 243, 247, 252, 253, 257, 273n1, 276, 278, 281, 284, 288, 294, 297, 306, 308–312, 314, 315, 317–321, 317n14, 325, 327, 329–331, 330n6, 333, 336, 338, 343, 348, 353, 359, 368, 369, 373–375, 378, 382, 383, 386

Philosophy, 28, 46n16, 74, 105, 107, 125, 131, 132, 145, 149n1, 190, 196, 270, 311, 315
  German, 228, 320, 326, 337, 352n15
  Greek, 294–298, 294n3, 313
  idealism, 17, 183n3, 378
  Indian, 294, 313, 313n7
  materialism, 17
  modern, 25, 47n17, 86, 96, 168, 194, 225, 227, 310, 311, 319–322, 326, 329, 375, 380
  monism, 312
  naturalism (*see* Naturalism)
  ordinary language (*see* Language, ordinary)
  stoicism, 212
  transcendental, 125, 126, 134, 141, 146, 170
  Western, 243, 309–322
Platonism and the Spiritual Life (Santayana, 1927), 186, 313
Platonov, Andrey (1899–1951), 5, 219–238
Postulates, 40, 40n5, 43, 51, 51n25, 131, 135, 137, 244, 287, 288, 362
Pragmatism, 12, 13, 18, 63n13, 67n21, 81, 118–120, 212, 264, 270, 271, 282, 284, 285, 329, 342, 361, 373
Pragmatists, 17–19, 58, 63n12, 65n18, 66, 67n21, 89, 95, 119, 173, 212, 212n35, 264, 281, 283–285, 285n16, 325, 329
Present moment, 38, 42–43, 62, 87, 88, 92, 95, 98–102, 105, 114, 135, 139, 140, 164, 181, 195, 199, 246, 274, 314, 332, 355n18
Primary qualities, 37
A priori, 5, 38, 51, 126–131, 134, 136, 141, 142, 165–169, 276, 336, 337
"A Proof of an External World" (Moore, 1939), 78
Protestantism, 376
Psyche, 19, 24, 27, 28, 132, 152, 165, 186, 206–212, 216, 217, 223, 223n5, 224n8, 228, 230–235, 237, 238, 267, 301, 327, 343n4, 348, 353, 364n31, 368n37, 369n39, 378, 380–383
Psychologism, 96, 337

Psychology, 126–129, 155, 158, 187, 234n23, 250, 309, 316, 327, 337, 369
  empirical, 126–128
  literary, 96, 105, 158, 186–188, 234n23, 326, 338, 367–370, 368n36, 368n37, 369n38
  scientific, 186–188, 368n37, 369
Pyrrho of Elis (c. 360–c. 270 BCE), 243
Pythagorean Theorem, 136, 167, 380

Q
Quine, Willard Van Orman (1908–2000), 45n13

R
Ramsey, Frank (1903–1930), 278
Realism, 20, 45–49, 48n20, 49n21, 62, 85, 91, 326
Reality, 18, 25, 28, 29, 37, 40, 42–49, 50n24, 60, 81, 82, 96, 99, 103–105, 111, 116, 120, 121, 125, 126, 128–131, 134, 137, 141, 142, 146, 151, 152, 155, 178, 179, 185, 185n5, 190, 195n4, 199, 200, 221, 227, 228n16, 229–231, 233–235, 234n23, 237, 243, 245–247, 249, 250, 265, 273–280, 274n4, 283n14, 284–287, 294–296, 298–300, 305, 307, 312, 328, 328n4, 331–333, 336, 344, 345, 348–357, 350n11, 350n12, 359, 362, 363, 365–367, 377, 378, 380, 381, 386
The Realm of Essence (Santayana, 1927), 1, 16, 44, 62n10, 327
The Realm of Matter (Santayana, 1930), 1, 62n10, 190, 266
The Realm of Spirit (Santayana, 1940), 1, 62n10, 225, 313
The Realm of Truth (Santayana, 1938), 1, 62n10, 190, 264
Realms of being (RB), 2–4, 6, 11, 14, 18, 25, 96n1, 118, 120, 152, 153n7, 159, 190, 228n16, 235, 242, 257, 275, 276

Realms of Being (Santayana, 1942), 1–4, 25, 26, 57, 62, 64, 96, 165, 177, 180, 190, 191, 195, 213, 216, 226, 232, 235, 263, 273, 293, 313, 327, 330
Redemption, 1, 309–322
Reductio ad absurdum, 2, 182
Reid, Thomas (1710–1796), 50, 51
Romanticism, 38, 332, 345, 350, 352n15, 354, 355, 367n35, 373, 376, 378, 381, 382
Rome, 3n2, 12, 15, 98, 375
Rorty, Richard (1931–2007), 28, 278, 284
Royce, Josiah (1855–1916), 11, 13, 23, 40, 40n5, 43, 43n9, 43n10, 45n14, 110n1, 326, 330n6
Russell, Bertrand (1872–1970), 14, 20, 127, 194, 195, 195n4, 251, 252, 319, 326
Russell, Frank (1865–1931), 379

S

Salvation, 111, 201, 226, 238, 313, 314, 320, 320n21, 321, 322n27, 378, 383
Santayana, Josefina (Borrás) (1826–1912), 14
Satipatthana Sutta, 213
Scepticism, 2, 2n1, 4–6, 12, 16–19, 25, 34, 36–39, 44–52, 45n13, 47n17, 47n18, 50n22, 50n23, 54, 57–69, 60n6, 73–93, 95–98, 101, 105–107, 111–116, 119, 137–140, 139n6, 146, 156, 157, 159, 159n14, 181, 183, 185, 193–204, 204n19, 209, 211, 229, 242–251, 258, 259, 259n3, 274, 275, 284, 294, 300, 306, 311, 314–316, 331, 332, 335, 342–345, 342n1, 347–350, 354–356, 359, 360, 362, 363, 365, 367, 382
    anti-, 73–93
    methodological, 76, 88, 331
    radical, 4, 6, 57, 73, 82, 86, 88, 93, 155–157, 158n13, 274, 288, 326, 347, 349, 354, 355, 360
    ultimate, 19, 44, 52, 60, 63, 115, 163–173, 181, 199, 202, 245, 332, 333, 342
    wayward, 19, 199, 246
Scepticism and Animal Faith (Santayana, 1923), 2–4, 11, 17, 18, 29, 34, 34n1, 47n18, 57, 60, 75, 85, 96, 97, 101, 104, 112–115, 118, 121, 125–146, 149–153, 155, 157, 158, 158n13, 160, 163, 178, 181, 181n2, 183, 190, 191, 193, 196, 227, 228, 235, 241, 258, 259, 263, 265, 269, 270, 273, 293–296, 309, 325–338, 373, 375
Schopenhauer, Arthur (1788–1860), 13, 40, 189, 189n6, 215n39, 311, 320–322, 345
Science, 5, 18, 21, 23, 27, 38, 45, 45n13, 48, 58, 59, 65, 65n18, 89, 97, 104–106, 114, 116, 120, 125, 127–129, 131, 132, 135, 138, 139, 141, 142, 145, 146, 149, 151, 154, 155, 166, 186, 188, 195, 195n4, 198, 208, 234n23, 251, 260, 266, 268, 277, 278, 285n17, 299, 307, 327, 329–332, 331n9, 335, 337, 337n11, 365, 366n34, 368, 369, 377, 383, 384
    behavioural, 127–131, 141, 368n37
Self, 5, 22, 25, 36, 38–40, 43, 43n10, 52, 96, 99, 102, 104, 118, 153n8, 154, 165, 170–172, 193, 196, 206, 207, 210, 211, 245, 246, 248–250, 263, 285, 296, 301n9, 312, 318, 327, 332, 333, 335, 336, 344–349, 344n5, 351, 352n15, 356, 358n24, 359, 361, 362, 362n28, 369n39, 370, 378, 383–385
Self-knowledge, 107, 207, 208, 280, 382
Sense-data, 39–41, 48, 81, 227n15
Sense of Beauty (Santayana, 1896), 12
Senses, 1, 2, 4, 11, 17, 18, 20, 22, 23, 25–27, 29, 34–36, 38, 40, 40n4, 41, 44–46, 48, 50, 51, 54, 59, 61, 62, 64n15, 65, 65n17, 68n22, 69, 74, 76, 77, 79–81, 83, 85, 86, 89, 90, 92, 93, 98, 98n3, 100–104, 111, 113, 116, 118, 126, 135, 140,

145, 150, 151, 154, 155n9, 157,
  159, 160, 165, 166, 169–173,
  181n2, 185–187, 185n5, 196, 197,
  199, 200, 204, 204n19, 206–208,
  213, 221, 223, 224, 227, 227n14,
  227n15, 229, 231–233, 237, 245,
  250, 251, 257, 261, 264, 266–268,
  270, 271, 275–277, 275n5, 285,
  286, 294, 296–299, 296n5, 300n7,
  301, 304, 313, 317, 320n21, 327,
  329, 331, 333, 336, 337, 342,
  343n3, 344–346, 348, 351,
  353–365, 356n20, 359n27,
  364n31, 369, 369n38, 370,
  381, 385
"The Sentiment of Rationality" (James, 1882), 110
Sextus Empiricus (c. 2nd century), 243
The Significance of Philosophical Scepticism (Stroud, 1984), 73
Sign(s), 1, 22, 23, 35, 39–41, 44, 48,
  51, 68, 103, 107, 116, 117, 136,
  141, 143, 154, 170, 171, 181, 182,
  189, 206, 252, 284, 286, 287, 296,
  315, 316, 349n10, 360, 368n36,
  379, 380
Singer, Beth J. (1927–2020), 59, 62–64
Singer, Irving (1925–2015), 277, 278, 306n18, 319
Skepticism and Naturalism (Strawson, 1985), 74, 242
Socrates (470–399 BCE), 44n11
Solipsism, 39, 62, 88, 98, 100, 101, 114,
  140, 164, 198, 245, 248, 375
  of the present moment, 87, 88, 92,
    98–102, 105, 106, 135, 139, 140,
    163, 164, 194, 195, 198, 199,
    246, 274, 314, 332, 342, 349,
    355n18, 362
  romantic, 38, 332, 354
Solipsist, 87, 88, 199, 246, 355
"Some Consequences of Four Incapacities" (Peirce, 1868), 112
Spinoza, Baruch (1632–1677), 6, 225, 278, 279, 294, 309–322
Spirit, 1, 2, 4, 5, 11, 15, 18, 19, 21, 23,
  26, 27, 40, 65, 83, 86, 92, 98, 106,
  111, 118, 130, 143, 150, 152–154,
  153n7, 156, 159, 165, 170, 178,
  180, 182, 184, 186–188, 190, 191,
  193n1, 197, 199, 201–204,
  206–212, 214–216, 219–238,
  260–262, 264, 267, 270, 273, 274,
  274n2, 277–279, 287, 294, 294n1,
  304, 306, 307, 307n20, 312, 313,
  317, 318, 320, 327, 335, 343n2,
  351–353, 360, 362, 363, 365, 373,
  378, 385
  realm of, 180, 182, 262, 301n9, 360
Spiritual discipline(s), 58, 69, 196, 317, 320n21
Spiritual exercise(s), 5, 193–217
Spiritual life, 5, 23, 198, 232, 238, 259, 260, 282, 319, 320, 330
Spiritual practice (s), 211–216
Sprigge, T. L. S. (1932–2007), 44n12,
  50n22, 88, 91, 195, 196, 202n15,
  203, 245, 246, 273n1, 283n14,
  286, 319
Stoic Pragmatism (Lachs, 2012), 212
Strawson, Peter (1919–2006), 5, 74, 77,
  79, 80, 83, 85, 89, 90, 90n8,
  151n3, 155n9, 242
Stroud, Barry (1935–2019), 73, 74, 77, 79, 81
Sturgis, George (1891–1944)
  (Santayana's nephew, son of Robert), 14, 15, 306n18
Sturgis, Robert (1854–1921)
  (Santayana's half-brother), 14
Sturgis, Rosamond (Thomas Bennet)
  (1895–1976) (Married George Sturgis), 15, 16
Subjectivity, 38, 45, 46, 231, 337, 378–381, 385
Substance, 4, 19, 20, 23, 25, 43, 44,
  46–49, 58–64, 68n22, 90, 91, 96,
  99, 102, 105, 116, 118, 119, 121,
  122, 144, 164–166, 170, 186, 195,
  200, 203, 203n17, 224n8,
  226–228, 228n16, 245, 247, 258,
  260, 265–268, 273n1, 276, 283,
  283n14, 294, 297, 300, 301n9,
  304n15, 305, 307, 309, 312,
  314–318, 327, 334, 335, 344,
  344n6, 349, 356n21, 362, 381–384
Sufficient reason, principle of, 37, 38, 193, 268, 282

T

Things-in-themselves, 47
Time, 1, 3, 11, 13, 15, 16, 19–22, 24, 26, 34, 41–43, 45, 49, 60, 67, 73, 76, 77, 83, 90, 97, 99–101, 106, 107, 112, 113, 118–121, 125–128, 132, 135, 136, 139–141, 143, 145, 149, 149n1, 151, 153, 157, 172, 181, 184, 185, 187, 195, 214, 215, 220, 221, 228, 232, 237, 246–248, 260, 263n14, 267, 268n20, 269, 277, 279, 281, 282, 285, 294, 294n2, 295, 296n5, 297, 298, 301, 303–307, 307n20, 309–311, 313, 315, 316, 321, 329, 332, 333, 337, 337n11, 342, 344–346, 348, 349, 350n12, 351, 352, 352n14, 356, 356n20, 359, 362–364, 362n28, 366n34, 368n37, 369n38, 376, 378, 379, 381, 382, 384–386
"To a Pacifist Friend" (Santayana, 1916), 14
Transcendental, 99, 104, 120, 121, 125, 126, 128, 130, 133–146, 170, 326–328, 331, 331n8, 333–338, 355
Transcendental criticism, 5, 125–146, 244
Transcendental logic, 126–128, 134, 135, 145
Treatise on the Emendation of the Intellect (Spinoza, 1677), 311
Truth, 6, 11, 17, 18, 22, 24–27, 34–38, 40, 48, 50–53, 51n26, 57–69, 74, 75, 78, 80–85, 87, 93, 97–99, 102, 105, 107, 110, 113, 116, 118, 119, 126–134, 136, 138, 142, 145, 151, 152n6, 153, 153n7, 154, 156, 163, 164, 166–169, 171–173, 182, 190, 191, 194, 194n2, 197, 198, 201, 204n19, 205, 206n25, 211, 221, 228n16, 230, 235, 237, 242, 246, 247, 250, 257, 259n4, 261, 263, 264, 270, 271, 273–288, 294, 297, 310, 313, 317, 318, 320, 327, 330, 334, 336, 350, 357, 359, 363, 365, 378, 379, 381, 382, 384
   conventional, 287

correspondence theory, 25
dramatic, 190
eternality, 281, 282, 282n12, 283n14, 286
literal, 169n2, 171–173, 287
mathematical, 167, 286
moral, 190
realm of, 2, 6, 159, 186, 261, 263, 264, 267, 270, 274, 277–287, 279n9, 280n11, 283n14, 314

U

"Ultimate Religion" (Santayana, 1936), 309, 322n27
"The Undergraduate Killed in Battle," (Santayana, 1916), 14
Unnatural Doubts (Williams, 1996), 74

V

Verificationism (including "verificationist," "verification criterion of meaning"), 81
Voltaire (François-Marie Arouet) (1694–1778), 58

W

Whitman, Walt (1819–1892), 178, 386
Williams, D. C. (1919–2006), 262, 265, 269
"The Will to Believe" (James, 1896), 110, 271
Wissenschaft, 252, 310
Wittgenstein, Ludwig (1889–1951), 5, 73, 75, 79, 80, 82, 85, 88–93, 89n6, 89n7, 90n8, 151n3, 155–157, 156n10, 156n12, 159n14, 268n21, 270n23, 342, 343, 343n3
World War I, 2
World War II, 15

Z

Zeno of Elea (c. 495–c. 430 BC), 306
Zeno's paradoxes, 6, 295, 302–305